COMPETITION LAW OF THE EU AND UK

Seventh Edition

SANDRA MARCO COLINO

Research Assistant Professor at the Chinese University of Hong Kong

OXFORD
UNIVERSITY PRESS

OXFORD
UNIVERSITY PRESS

Great Clarendon Street, Oxford OX2 6DP

Oxford University Press is a department of the University of Oxford.
It furthers the University's objective of excellence in research, scholarship,
and education by publishing worldwide in

Oxford New York

Auckland Cape Town Dar es Salaam Hong Kong Karachi
Kuala Lumpur Madrid Melbourne Mexico City Nairobi
New Delhi Shanghai Taipei Toronto

With offices in

Argentina Austria Brazil Chile Czech Republic France Greece
Guatemala Hungary Italy Japan Poland Portugal Singapore
South Korea Switzerland Thailand Turkey Ukraine Vietnam

Oxford is a registered trade mark of Oxford University Press
in the UK and in certain other countries

Published in the United States
by Oxford University Press Inc., New York

© Sandra Marco Colino, 2011

Fourth edition 2004
Fifth edition 2006
Sixth edition 2008

British Library Cataloguing in Publication Data
Data available

Library of Congress Cataloging in Publication Data
Data available

Typeset by Newgen Imaging Systems (P) Ltd, Chennai, India

Printed in Great Britain
on acid-free paper by
Ashford Colour Press Ltd, Gosport, Hampshire

ISBN 978–0–19–958732–2

1 3 5 7 9 10 8 6 4 2

Outline contents

Detailed contents

Preface to the Seventh Edition

It has often been said that everybody loves progress but nobody likes change. This statement somewhat unnerves me as the new author of an established textbook. When my colleague and friend Mark Furse asked me to take on this edition, I was honoured. Like many readers, I was surprised to learn in the preface to the last edition that it would be his last. Over six editions, Mark managed to put together a text that made the complex subject of competition law accessible even to novices in the field. I was delighted that the book would be kept going.

My initial enthusiasm soon turned into a daunting feeling of responsibility. It now fell to me to carry forward this project, and I was effectively stepping into the shoes of a competition law heavyweight. The year leading up to the completion of this edition I was very much a 'bookworm', trying my utmost to keep up to date with the new developments and deciding how best to incorporate them into the book.

Readers familiar with previous editions will be happy to know that it is not my intention to replace Mark, nor to give the book a change of direction. The aim of the seventh edition is precisely to build on the many strengths of its predecessors, while enhancing the learning features and keeping the material up to date. The increased accessibility is particularly intended for new readers: the summary maps covering the application of the main competition provisions have been simplified, further key cases have been introduced and reading recommendations have been increased. Students may also now download multiple-choice questions from the Online Resource Centre to test their understanding of each chapter. As for the updating process, the revisions have focused on competition law in the context of the current economic crisis. Maintaining the authority of competition law while at the same time finding ways out of the credit crunch is arguably the principal challenge at this time. This is reflected, *inter alia*, in the brand new chapter on State aid (Chapter 21), and in the commentary on the Lloyds/HBOS merger (Chapter 20). The book has also been 'Lisbonized' to include not only the terminology and numbering of the most recent reform of the Treaty, but also an overview of those amendments that affect the field (throughout the textbook, mainly at Chapter 2). Legislative changes and future proposals are also considered. At the EU level, there are new rules for vertical agreements and horizontal cooperation (Chapters 9 and 10); reviews of Art. 102, the 'modernized' procedural rules and the Merger Regulation were recently completed (Chapters 5–7, 14, and 19); record-breaking fines have been imposed for cartels and dominance (including the all-time high €1.06 billion on Intel, analysed in Chapter 14). The UK arena has seen new rules for director disqualification orders (Chapter 6); the first investigations—and convictions—under the cartel offence have been completed (Chapter 12); new procedural rules and guidelines for mergers were recently introduced (Chapter 20). Furthermore, there are talks of a major institutional overhaul that would imply merging the Office of Fair Trading and the Competition Commission and creating a new economic crime agency (Chapter 12).

I owe thanks to all those competition law enthusiasts that have helped me learn by sharing their energetic convictions; this includes colleagues in Hong Kong and Glasgow, academics, practitioners, and students. Friends and family continue in their unconditional support, and Martin's patience has proved limitless. Most of all, I am grateful to Mark for allowing me to leave an imprint on a project that he started more than 12 years ago with the publication of the first edition. For five years, he and Rosa Greaves have made me feel like part of a competition law team at Glasgow in which the passion for the subject always came hand in hand with collegiality of the best kind.

The law is updated as of 15 September 2010. All errors or omissions are mine alone.

Sandra Marco Colino
Hong Kong
September 2010

New to this edition

- A new chapter on state aid
- Revised, extended chapters on procedure/enforcement of competition law
- Fully updated to include the changes introduced by the Treaty of Lisbon and reference to the current economic crisis
- Analysis of the new Merger Guidelines and the review of art. 102, as well as the rules for vertical agreements and horizontal cooperation
- New detailed flow charts to aid understanding of the application of the principal EU and UK legal provisions

Note to the reader: The impact of the Treaty of Lisbon on the terminology used in this edition

On 1 December 2009, the Treaty of Lisbon entered into force. The impact of the new amendments on the competition law provisions of the Treaty is fully discussed in Chapter 2 (see, in particular, 2.3). However, some important modifications have been introduced in the general EU jargon which ought to be taken into consideration. The European Community is now the European Union, and the EC Treaty is known as the Treaty on the Functioning of the European Union (TFEU). In addition, the Court of First Instance (CFI) has been renamed the General Court (GC), while the European Court of Justice (ECJ) is now simply referred to as the Court of Justice. The term common market has also been replaced by internal market. A further change introduced by the Lisbon reform is that Treaty provisions have been renumbered. The full table of equivalences, as published in the Official Journal, ([2008] OJ C 115/361), can be downloaded from the Online Resource Centre. The reader is advised to keep a copy at hand.

In order to avoid unnecessary confusion, unless otherwise indicated this edition uses the new terms and numbering throughout. In addition, citations of scholarship, cases and legislation published prior to 1 December 2009 have also been amended where appropriate, and the new terms and Treaty provisions have been inserted in square brackets replacing any outdated references. The titles of all materials referenced will of course remain unchanged.

Table of cases

UK cases

European cases

Australian case

International Court of Justice case

Swedish case

US cases

Table of decisions and reports

UK decisions

European decisions

Reports

European Commission

Office of Fair Trading

Table of legislation

EU primary and secondary legislation (treaties and regulations)

Page references in bold indicate that the article is reproduced in full or in part

Treaties

List of abbreviations

AAC	average avoidable cost
ATC	average total cost
AVC	average variable cost
CA 98	Competition Act 1998
CAT	Competition Appeals Tribunal
CBI	Confederation of British Industry
CC	Competition Commission
CCAT	Competition Commission Appeals Tribunal (now the Competition Appeals Tribunal)
CDDA	Company Directors Disqualification Act 1986
CDO	competition disqualification order
CDU	competition disqualification undertaking
CFI	Court of First Instance (now the General Court)
DG Comp	Directorate General of Competition
DGFT	Director General of Fair Trading
DOJ	Department of Justice (USA)
DTI	Department of Trade and Industry
EA 02	Enterprise Act 2002
EAEC	European Atomic Energy Community (Euratom)
EC	European Community (now the EU)
ECHR	European Convention on Human Rights 1950
ECJ	European Court of Justice (now the Court of Justice)
ECMR	European Community Merger Regulation/European Community merger regime (now the EUMR)
ECN	European Competition Network
ECSC	European Coal and Steel Community
ECU	European Currency Unit (now replaced by the Euro, €)
EEA	European Economic Area
EEC	European Economic Community (now the EU)
EFTA	European Free Trade Area
EU	European Union
EUCAR	European Council for Automotive Research and Development
EUMR	European Union Merger Regulation
FTA	Fair Trading Act 1973
FTC	Federal Trade Commission (USA)
GATT	General Agreement on Tariffs and Trade
GC	General Court
GCI	Global Competition Initiative
GISC	General Insurance Standards Council

HHI	Herfindahl–Hirschman Index
ICN	International Competition Network
ICPAC	International Competition Policy Advisory Committee
IIB	Institute of Insurance Brokers
IPR	intellectual property right
JV	joint venture
MMC	Monopolies and Mergers Commission
NAFTA	North American Free Trade Agreement
NCA	Network of Competition Authorities
NCC	National Consumer Council
PCIJ	Permanent Court of International Justice
OECD	Organization for Economic Cooperation and Development
Ofcom	Office of Communications
Ofgem	Office of the Gas and Electricity Markets
OFT	Office of Fair Trading
OPEC	Organization of Petroleum Exporting Countries
RPC	Restrictive Practices Court
RPM	resale price maintenance
RTPA	Restrictive Trade Practices Act 1976
SCP	Structure–Conduct–Performance model
SFO	Serious Fraud Office
SIEC	Significantly impeding effective competition
SLC	Substantial lessening of competition/Substantially lessen competition
SO	Statement of Objection
SSNIP	Small but Significant Non-transitory Increase in Price
TEU	Treaty on the European Union
TFEU	Treaty on the Functioning of the European Union
UNCTAD	United Nations Conference on Trade and Development
USTR	United States Trade Representative
WTO	World Trade Organization

1

Introduction to competition law

KEY POINTS

- Competition law aims at protecting competition, not consumers, individual competitors or trading standards.
- US 'antitrust' is the starting point of modern competition law.
- Competition law is inextricably linked to economics, and economic analysis plays a key role.
- The Chicago and Harvard schools remain influential even today, and lay down the coordinates of the policy debate.

1.1 Introduction

The primary purpose of competition law is to remedy some of the situations in which the free market system breaks down. The point was well made in the House of Lords debate during the passage of the Competition Act 1998 that 'competition law provides the framework for competitive activity. It protects the process of competition. As such it is of vital importance' (Hansard (HL) 30 October 1997, col. 1156).

The 'invisible hand' that Adam Smith identified in 1776 ensures in most situations that free market economies left to their own devices will produce results more beneficial than can be realized by intervening in the markets. This conclusion has been supported by evidence put forward by economists over the last 200 years, and, since the collapse of East European planned economies, forms the basis for most of the world's economic systems. The process of competition is seen as being of value and meriting protection. In its White Paper *Productivity and Enterprise* (Cm. 5233, July 2001), the UK Government argued that

The importance of competition in an increasingly innovative and globalised economy is clear. Vigorous competition between firms is the lifeblood of strong and effective markets. Competition helps consumers get a good deal. It encourages firms to innovate by reducing slack, putting downward pressure on costs and providing incentives for the efficient organisation of production. As such, competition is a central driver for productivity growth in the economy, and hence the UK's international competitiveness.   (para. 1.1)

It is often said, however, that 'competition sows the seeds of its own destruction'; successful entrepreneurs may achieve positions where they are able to prevent others from competing and thereby damage the process as a whole. A variant on this problem is that there may be some situations in which there is only room for a single firm in a market, and, unless steps are taken to regulate the conduct of this firm, it too may act to the detriment of the economy. The fact that in both the EU and the UK a competitor harmed by another's unlawful anti-competitive conduct may go to court to seek damages or another suitable remedy also serves to place stress on the right of business people to conduct their affairs in a fair and reasonable commercial environment. Competition law is not, directly, about consumer protection or trading standards, although both may benefit from the application of competition law (see, however, Averitt, N. W., and Lande, R. H., 'Consumer Sovereignty: A Unified Theory of Antitrust and Consumer Protection Law', (1997) *Antitrust Law Journal* 713).

In the United Kingdom there are two systems of competition law: domestic law and the law of the European Union (EU). The relationship between these two regimes is examined in Chapter 3. With the passage of the Competition Act 1998, the domestic regime was strengthened and, following the demands of both the business community and consumer groups, brought into much closer alignment with EU law. An examination of these two regimes forms the basis of this book. Most of the law dealt with here is based on statutes or other public enactments. In both systems lawyers and regulators are likely to look for guidance to the operation of the antitrust law of the United States, which is briefly introduced in this chapter, and subsequently considered in relation to specific cases throughout the book. The common law of England and Wales remains applicable in a small class of cases, which are considered further in Chapter 23.

To the frustration of many lawyers, competition law is heavily reliant on economics. In practice lawyers handling the more complex cases are likely to rely on expert witnesses and documentation provided either by companies themselves or by firms of economic consultants. However, without some understanding of what questions should be raised, and what significance the answers then have, such communication becomes difficult and inefficient. It is for this reason that the reader of this book is faced with economics both later in this introduction, and in Chapters 8 and 18. It might be possible to pass these by, but the case law that is discussed elsewhere will be clearer if they are read, and then returned to as necessary. A useful text for the interested reader is Bishop, S., and Walker, S., *The Economics of EC Competition Law: Concepts, Application and Measurement*, London, Sweet & Maxwell (3rd edn, 2010).

1.2 The development of competition law

The United States' Sherman Act 1890 is taken as the starting point of modern competition (or in the US, 'antitrust') law, but the roots of competition law lie much deeper. Senator Sherman himself told the Senate that his bill did 'not announce a new principle of law, but applies old and well-recognized principles of the common law to the complicated jurisdiction of our State and Federal Government'. It has even been suggested, unconvincingly, that the Act is based in part on the Constitution of Zeno, Emperor of the East from 474 to 491, promulgated in 483. Roman legislation dealing with some aspects of competition pre-dates the Constitution by over 500 years.

In England, competition law has developed in fits and starts since before legal memory, and only in the last half of the twentieth century was it subjected to rigorous economic analysis. At present there is no satisfactory single history of the early competition laws, and much of the best work has been done by those researching the circumstances surrounding the creation of the Sherman Act in 1890 (see, e.g., Thorelli, H. B., *The Federal Antitrust Policy*, Stockholm (1954); see also Lord Wilberforce, Campbell, A., and Elles, N., *The Law of Restrictive Trade Practices and Monopolies*, London, Sweet & Maxwell (2nd edn, 1966)). Various Saxon kings had taken action against a range of trading practices, including, for example, the purchase of commodities before they reached their designated market place in order to enhance the price, and make a profit on a later sale—the crime of foresteel or forestalling, referred to in the Domesday Book (1086). Other laws set out punishments for ingrossers, regrators and travelling salesmen ('badgers'), who similarly purchased products in one market place to resell them in either the same or a neighbouring market at a higher price. At the time of the Magna Carta (1215) legislation provided that all monopolies were to be contrary to the law because of their pernicious effect on individual freedom.

The great plagues that swept across Europe in the late medieval period resulted in shortages of both labour and commodities. The various statutes which aimed to fix both prices and wages at pre-plague levels in order to prevent labourers moving to seek better-paid employment, thereby damaging the interests of landowners, were a response in part to problems created by these shortages. The 1349 Statute of Labourers is notable by virtue of its introduction of the requirement that merchants overcharging should pay multiple damages to injured parties, which is followed today in the US treble-damages suit (see Chapter 6).

It has also been suggested that the common law doctrine of 'restraint of trade' (which is defined in Chapter 23) emerged in response to the pressures caused by labour shortages. *John Dyer's* case (1414) YB 2 Hen 5 (of. 5, pl. 26) appears to be the first recorded case of restraint of trade. John, the Dyer, had sought to enforce a writ against a colleague who had covenanted not to practise the craft of dyeing in the same town for half a year. Fortunately for Dyer he was not in court when the case was heard, for the judge held that the provision was against the common law 'and by God, if the plaintiff were here, he should go to prison'. The rule that covenants in restraint of trade were not enforceable remained in place until the beginning of the seventeenth century, at which time added flexibility was introduced to accommodate changing circumstances (see, e.g., *Rogers* v *Parrey* (1613) 80 ER 1012).

By the middle of the nineteenth century the courts had introduced, and had begun to expand on, the relationship of the public interest to the operation of the doctrine. In *Horner* v *Graves* (1831) 131 ER 284, the judge brought the doctrine close to the modern day when he held that 'we do not see how a better test can be applied to the question whether reasonable or not, than by considering whether the restraint is not so large as to interfere with the interests of the public'. The extent to which restraint of trade was concerned with the issue of monopoly *per se* is a question that has not been fully resolved. It appears that judges were at least as swayed by arguments as to individual liberty, and as to the cost to the public purse of the support, however rudimentary, that might be available to the worker who was not able to secure employment because of the restraint's operation. More recent developments, discussed at 23.2.3, appear to bring the doctrine into the mainstream of competition law, and to link it directly with EU competition law.

There was little the common law could do to combat arrangements between businesses, and this area was left largely to various statutes. However, the doctrine of conspiracy crept into the area of trade regulation from the seventeenth century onwards, particularly in relation to the attempts of working people to organize themselves. The doctrine was applied to business situations in the eighteenth century, but then fell into disuse. It was confirmed in *Mogul SS Co. Ltd* v *McGregor Gow & Co.* [1892] AC 25, that it would be applied only where the objective of the conspiracy was illegal, and that it was not illegal to seek to improve a business position.

1.2.1 **Monopolies and the Crown**

The word 'monopoly' was probably first used in England by Thomas More in *Utopia* (1516). It carried a specific meaning:

A Monopoly is an Institution, or allowance by the King, by His Grant, Commission, or otherwise, to any person or persons, bodies politic or corporate, of or for the sole buying, selling, making, working or using of any thing, whereby any person or persons, bodies politic or corporate are sought to be restrained of any freedom, or liberty that they had before or hindered in their lawful trade.   (The US Supreme Court in *Standard Oil Co. of New Jersey* v *US* 221 US 1 (1911), citing Sir Edward Coke, *Institutes*)

Such monopolies were increasingly granted from the mid-1300s. In Elizabethan England (1558–1603) the system of Industrial Monopoly Licences was heavily abused as a mechanism for raising funds for the monarch without the inconvenience of consulting Parliament. Although Parliament protested, the Queen was able to persuade it to drop a Bill that would have curbed the practice. It was therefore left to the courts in 1602 to rule that a grant of a monopoly for the making of playing cards to one Darcy was illegal and void (*Darcy* v *Allin* (1602) 11 Co Rep 84b—also known as the *Case of the Monopolies*). Even at this time, the arguments against monopoly practices were becoming well rehearsed, and the court found that there were inevitable and unwelcome consequences of all monopolies: an increase in price, a reduction in quality and a reduction in the incentive to work. The position in the early 1600s was such that Ben Jonson, in *The Devil is an Ass* (1616), was able to satirize for his audiences the practice of granting monopolies and those who negotiated them: the character of Merecraft, 'The Great Projector', promoted and sold increasingly fantastical monopoly schemes, including an inventive scheme to monopolize the market in toothpicks.

The conflict between Crown and Parliament was resolved in 1623 with the passing of the Statute of Monopolies, which declared that 'All Monopolies...are altogether contrary to the Laws of this Realm, and so are and shall be utterly void and of none effect and in no wise to be put into use or execution'. In making an exception for patents for a period not exceeding 21 years save where these operated to raise prices or to damage trade, the statute also formed the basis for the modern law of patents. Monopolies could still be granted to trading corporations and guilds, a practice much used by Charles I. In the 'Great Case against Monopolies', *East India Company* v *Sandys* (1685) 10 St Tr 371, it was held that a distinction could be drawn between monopolies operating *within* the realm, and those established in order to compete *outside* the realm. In the latter situation it was accepted that only a firm in a strong position could trade successfully in the difficult conditions prevailing. This argument finds a modern counterpart in the debate on the relationship between competition and national industrial policy, in particular the promotion of 'national champions': 'Competition can be enormously beneficial in many cases, but where it involves the destruction of strong interests in a wider context, it could be weakening from UK PLC's point of view' (Graeme Odgers, MMC Chairman, *Evening Standard*, 5 May 1993).

In 1772, following a House of Commons committee report, most of the old laws were repealed. By 1844 all earlier Acts were revoked, since it was considered that the prohibitions had effects contrary to that intended and were partly responsible for inhibiting trade and raising prices. From that time until now, monopolies have not been prevented in the UK, and the modern law of competition deals with issues of the *abuse* of monopoly power, not with its existence *per se*. With a belief in the benefits of economic laissez-faire, the country did not return to competition law until after the Second World War. In 1948, legislation was introduced that established a domestic structure for the examination and control of anti-competitive conduct. The current domestic regime is found primarily in two statutes, the Competition Act 1998 (CA 98) and the Enterprise Act 2002 (EA 02).

1.2.2 Competition law and the EU

According to the Court of Justice of the European Union the provisions of EU law dealing with competition constitute 'a fundamental provision...essential for the accomplishment of the tasks entrusted to the [Union] and, in particular, for the functioning of the internal market' (*Eco Swiss China Time Ltd* v *Benetton International NV* case C–126/97 [2000] 5 CMLR 816, para. 36).

Provisions relating to competition law were included in the foundational Treaty of the European Economic Community (seed of the EU), the Treaty of Rome of 1957. Articles 85 and 86 of the Treaty (now arts 101 and 101 TFEU) related to the control of anti-competitive agreements and dominant firm abuses. Similar provisions had been placed in the earlier European Coal and Steel Community Treaty of 1951. There has been a substantial and interesting debate as to the policy pressures that underlay the inclusion of these provisions. David Gerber's seminal work *Law and Competition*

Policy in Twentieth Century Europe—Protecting Prometheus, Oxford, Clarendon Press (1998) deals in part with this question; the argument is made persuasively that, rather than slavishly adopting a US-style model based on ss. 1 and 2 of the Sherman Act (see below), the relevant Treaty provisions reflected a distinctly European approach to anti-competitive conduct. The German ordo-liberals are cited as a key influence in the determination of the European policy. Some commentators have attacked Gerber's thesis, and it may be argued that whatever the roots of the policy, its operation in practice remains heavily influenced by North American practices.

1.3 The experience of the United States

It is generally presumed that the Sherman Act, which ushered in the 'modern' era of competition law, was a response to irresistible pressures exerted from the agricultural heartland of the United States. Prices and wages were rising, yet farmers, faced with disproportionately higher freight costs set by the railway companies which combined to set standard rates, were not benefiting from the trend.

Section 1 of the Sherman Act prohibits 'every contract, combination . . . or conspiracy in restraint of trade' at a federal level (that is where inter-state trade would be affected). Decisions of the US Supreme Court have restricted these words, which would, if taken at face value, condemn nearly all business conduct to apply only to 'unreasonable' restraint of trade (*Standard Oil Co. of New Jersey* v *United States* 221 US 1 (1911)). This 'rule of reason' is at the heart of US law, and there is intense debate as to the place of such a rule in EU law (see further at 9.7 below). Section 2 of the Act is in the following terms: 'Every person who shall monopolize, or attempt to monopolize . . . any part of the trade or commerce among the several States . . . shall be guilty of a misdemeanor'. It is possible to argue that it is the legitimate goal of any businessman to 'monopolize' his industry, and in *United States* v *Grinnel Corp.* (1966) 384 US 563, a distinction was drawn between the 'wilful' acquisition of monopoly power, which fell to be condemned, and monopoly arising from better commercial practices which would escape the Act's application. Although it has been supplemented by other legislation over the last century, discussed in this book as appropriate, the Sherman Act remains central to antitrust policy in the United States (see generally Sullivan, E. T. (ed.), *The Political Economy of the Sherman Act: The First One Hundred Years*, New York, OUP (1991)). Given that economic principles do not, unlike law, vary from country to country, there are often good reasons to look to the large body of US case law to illuminate competition cases brought elsewhere.

There are, however, significant divergences in the underpinning philosophies of the US and European regimes, and principles from one regime should not be slavishly applied to the other without good justification:

Many valuable ideas for the interpretation of [Union] law can be derived from the discussions going on on the other side of the Atlantic and from the solutions found by the American courts. However, prudence must be counseled in transferring concepts and theories from one legal system to the other. There are substantial differences between the various elements going to make up US law and those going to make up [Union] law, with the result that not every problem confronting one of the two systems finds a counterpart in the other legal system.   (Advocate General Kirschner in *Tetra Pak Rausing SA* v *Commission* case T–51/89 [1991] 4 CMLR 334 at 343–4)

1.4 **Economics and competition law**

Economics can be employed in two main ways in relation to competition law. First, because competition law is aimed in part at remedying market failure, a general macro-economic argument can be made as to the existence of such market failure and the costs imposed by it. Secondly, micro-economic arguments are likely to be relied upon in each individual case to justify intervention or to defend a company's position. Attempts to avoid the 'problem' of economics are likely to result in bad law—as was the case with the Restrictive Trade Practices Act 1976, which adopted an overly legalistic approach in an attempt to disregard economic issues. In Chapters 8 and 13 specific issues relating to collusion between firms and to actions by individual firms are considered in detail, and in Chapter 18 the economics of mergers is discussed. This section introduces the general argument advanced to support intervention and some standard economic terms.

For readers who are interested in developing their economic expertise further a good accessible text that deals with competition strategy is Besanko, D., Dranove, D., and Shanley, M., *Economics of Strategy*, New York, John Wiley & Sons (4th edn, 2007). Specific references later in this text are given to Bishop and Walker, *The Economics of EC Competition Law*, because of its direct connection to the subject matter of this book. A US text, Hylton, K. M., *Antitrust Law: Economic Theory and Common Law Evolution*, Cambridge, CUP (2003) superbly links the substantive application of US law to economic theory.

1.4.1 **The problem of standards**

It is the presumed goal of entrepreneurs to maximize their profits, and to be as successful as possible. While Bill Gates probably did not envisage that Microsoft would become one of the largest and most profitable corporations in the world, if asked, he would probably have said that he would like it to. Now that it has assumed such a strong position, Microsoft's commercial practices have been scrutinized by competition authorities around the world, and practices that might be pursued legitimately by smaller firms may be condemned if followed by this giant (see for example, Key case 22.2). The managers of a business may determine a strategy for all the 'right' reasons as far as that business is concerned, and yet, on the basis of a test related to society's welfare, be attacked. To what standards then are businesses to conform? Competition law is often contrasted with environmental regulation. For any given standard in environmental law (e.g., 'mercury content to be no more than three parts per million') it is a relatively easy matter to test for any given sample whether the standard is indeed being broken. It is much harder to set similar tests in the area of competition law. This point was stressed by the UK Competition Appeals Tribunal when it stated that 'competition law is not an area of law in which there is much scope for absolute concepts or sharp edges' (*The Racecourse Association and others* v *Office of Fair Trading* [2005] CAT 29, para. 167).

In the United States 'monopolization' is condemned (see 1.3 above); in the European Union the standard of conduct for a monopolist is that it should not 'abuse' its 'dominant position' (see Chapter 14). It will be impossible to determine whether this standard is being breached without recourse to economic analysis. Among other things the regulator or complainant must consider: what is the relevant market? (e.g., is the market for bananas discrete, or is it part of the market for soft fruit, or all fruit?—*United Brands Co.* v *Commission* case 27/76 [1978] 1 CMLR 429). Is the firm a monopolist? Is the alleged 'abuse' in fact a legitimate business tactic? What effect is the alleged abuse having?

In the law relating to agreements (defined more precisely in Chapter 9), the standard is equally complex, with the core requirement being that agreements should not prevent, restrict, or distort competition, or be intended to do so. The question whether any particular agreement fulfils the relevant criteria may in some cases be obvious—for example, a cartel between all five producers of an essential product with the intention of raising prices clearly meets the criteria. At the other end of the scale, a distribution agreement which contains restrictions necessary to ensure the efficient channelling of the contract goods may both promote and hinder competition. In such cases it may be necessary to conduct sophisticated analyses of relevant markets and competitive structures to determine the actual effects.

1.4.2 **Industrial economics and markets**

The area of economics that is most important for competition law is industrial economics, which is the branch of the science that applies micro-economic tools—an individual's preferences for apples over pears, or the costs of making a chair instead of a table—to wider market situations. Markets are where producers and consumers interact, and in a theoretical world of 'perfect' competition a market will produce an efficient result. Efficiency has a particular meaning in economics. An efficient position is one in which the only way to make anyone better off is to make someone else worse off. This is to say it refers to a situation in which no more mutually advantageous bargains or contracts can be made. In any situation in which A can be made better off, with B being no worse off, it will be efficient for that transaction to take place. Such a situation is referred to as one of *Pareto optimum*. This theoretical ideal permits an examination of the extent to which observed market structures diverge from 'perfect competition' and the resulting harm. The requirements of perfect competition are that there must be very large, tending to infinite, numbers of producers and of consumers. The product is homogenous so that there are no significant differences between one producer's product and the next. Both producers and consumers are perfectly informed about the market and are motivated by the desire to maximize profits and satisfaction. When added to various assumptions made about the costs of production, the result is that no consumer or producer is able to influence the price of the product, and that the price at which the item is sold exactly matches the cost of making it. In observed markets these assumptions break down: consumers and producers will be able to influence the price of products, which are not homogenous, and neither group is likely to have perfect information about the market place. The antithesis of perfect competition is monopoly, with 'monopolistic', or imperfect, competition lying somewhere between the two.

When an economist uses the term 'monopoly' it has a specific meaning, different from that put forward by Coke's *Institutes* (above). A monopoly market is one in which there is only one producer. It is frequently pointed out by those questioning the basis of much of competition regulation that the most common situation in which monopoly arises is where it is the product of government action (e.g., by legal controls limiting entry into an industry, in particular where the state regulates an industry). Empirical observation suggests, in particular, that monopolies, even where they do exist, are unable to remain monopolies in the long run unless they are protected by legislative barriers to entry. A monopolist, unlike a firm in a perfectly competitive market, has the power to determine the price at which the product is sold. Adam Smith, whose *The Wealth of Nations* (1776) serves as the basis of modern economics, suggested that 'the price of monopoly is upon every occasion the highest which can be got'. The monopolist can achieve this by choosing how much of the product to supply.

1.4.2.1 The adverse consequences of monopolies

Ceteris paribus ('all other things being equal') prices are higher, and output less, in markets which are monopolistic than in markets which are perfectly competitive. A consequence of the steps taken to achieve this is that it results in a non-optimal allocation of resources, by sending the 'wrong' signals as to the value/cost of products. The monopolist, by raising prices above the production cost of an item, denies consumers who are in fact prepared to pay that cost the opportunity of doing so. The monopolist has, by raising the price of the product, sent the consumer a false signal about the true value of the product in relation to other products and less consumer demand is therefore satisfied under these conditions. Further, the money that would have been spent on the monopoly product is instead spent on other products thereby raising *their* prices and the market becomes distorted.

Another issue is that of 'consumer surplus'. If a monopolist can set only one price for a product, as is the usual case in competitive market conditions, a given number of consumers will buy the product. For one of these consumers the decision has been a marginal one, and had the price been any higher the purchase would not be made. Some of the other consumers might have been prepared to pay far more, and have, in effect, achieved savings on the purchase. Consider, for example, an item in a sale—one consumer might buy it only because it has been reduced in price, while another might have been quite happy to pay the full price and feel that they have got a bargain. The total amount of this 'saving' is known as the consumer surplus. If the monopolist could force each consumer to pay their maximum price the total revenue to the monopolist rises and the consumer surplus vanishes, which represents a transfer of income from the consumers to the monopolist. This issue is often dealt with in competition law under the heading of 'price discrimination' (see Chapter 16). It is not directly a matter that impinges upon the efficiency of the situation, but it is nevertheless of legitimate interest to a regulator concerned with the distribution of income.

In 1954, in an article which has assumed seminal importance but has led to a somewhat difficult and convoluted debate, Arnold Harberger attempted to quantify the total loss to US society from the monopolistic industries in the United States (Harberger, A. C., 'Monopoly and Resource Allocation', (1954) 44 *American Economic Review* 77). Harberger estimated the difference between the total consumer demand satisfied under competitive conditions, and the reduced demand satisfied under monopoly conditions (the 'welfare triangle', or 'Harberger triangle'). In fact Harberger's estimate was only 0.1 per cent of the national income. More recent studies, however, point to figures of between 4 per cent and 20 per cent, suggesting that Harberger's estimate is an understatement and may be seen as a lower boundary.

The strategic activity undertaken to achieve, or reinforce, a monopoly position ('rent seeking') may also represent a cost of monopolies. This might include excessive advertising that has no benefit in terms of increased sales, and aggressive competition that does not increase either consumer or producer welfare. The intense British Airways–Virgin Atlantic competition of the mid- to late 1990s is sometimes cited as an example of such conduct.

1.4.3 The policy debate—Harvard v Chicago, and the new industrial economics

Until the mid-1980s competition economists, regulators, and to a certain extent lawyers, could be placed into two broad camps: the Harvard school and the Chicago school. The crude divisions these labels suggest have largely broken down under the influence of more modern economic analysis. Nonetheless, there remains some value in the distinction, and it is still common to find these labels applied either to personalities or to approaches. The debate is not an abstract one as the policy implications of the ideas advanced by each school are very different.

The first major school of thought to develop emerged at Harvard University when, in the 1930s, researchers conducted analyses of specific industries. Their conclusions led to the Structure–Conduct–Performance model (SCP): performance is determined by firms' conduct, which is in turn determined by the market structure. Kaysen and Turner, for example, argued that the limitation of market power should be the central focus of competition policy and that market power should be reduced wherever this could be done without a corresponding cost in the performance of the industry (Kaysen, C., and Turner, D. F., *Antitrust Policy: An Economic and Legal Analysis*,

Cambridge, MA, Harvard UP (1959)). This is consistent with the general distrust of large businesses and corporations that was widely shared at the time.

One of the first practices that the Chicago school (and notably Stigler) examined was that of the welfare implications of the structure of an industry, and of barriers to entry into that industry. Where the Harvard economists had argued that higher barriers enabled incumbents to increase prices, the Chicagoans are concerned to examine the nature of the barrier, tolerating those which are the result of efficiency considerations. The SCP Harvard model is replaced by one in which performance dictates market structure—the 'reverse causation' argument. In other words, monopolistic industries are the result of efficiency and superior performance, and should not then be attacked precisely because the firms in them have succeeded. Thus Bork has argued that the real question for competition policy is whether 'artificial' barriers, not being the result of more efficient production or economies of scale, prevent the effective operation of the market (Bork, R. H., *The Antitrust Paradox*, New York, The Free Press (1993)). More generally, it is the tendency of the Chicago school to accept that, in the real world, the model of perfect competition can be used to explain most business behaviour, which is to say that all companies are constrained by competition. Alongside this sits the general assumption of the school that the only concern of competition policy should be the attainment of efficiency, and that ancillary 'non-economic' goals such as the equitable distribution of income, or the socio-political problems of a concentration of economic power should not be a part of any competition policy. For a recent text following a Chicagoan line see Gordon, R. L., *Antitrust Abuse in the New Economy*, Cheltenham, Edward Elgar (2002).

The Chicagoan assumption that real-world behaviour will tend to match that forecast by the perfect competition model is now being subject to increasingly rigorous challenges with the emergence of the new (or 'modern') industrial economics, which is informed in part by the empirical evidence provided in various antitrust actions. It appears to be now well established that the competitive assumptions made by some of the more extreme Chicagoans are incorrect, and are not supported by evidence. The standard-bearers of the Chicagoan viewpoint in the US over more recent years have been R. H. Bork and R. A. Posner, both of whom were appointed to the bench under the Republican presidencies, and who remain in a position to exercise some considerable influence over the debate in the States. Bork's *The Antitrust Paradox* (above) is a highly entertaining polemic, and provokes much debate, although it now lags behind contemporary economic argument. Posner's record in adjudicating antitrust actions in his time on the bench has been examined by North American commentators and found lacking. It has been noted that he has disregarded strong evidence, characterized by some economists as incontrovertible, to the effect that concentration in any industry is almost inevitably damaging to consumer welfare.

The more pragmatic line taken by the new industrial economics is that in a monopolistic market, where the expected benefits outweigh the likely costs, a profit-maximizing firm will engage in strategic behaviour. For adherents to the new industrial economics one of the roles of competition policy is to make the expected costs of such strategic behaviour sufficiently great to outweigh the expected benefits, thereby deterring such conduct. Broadly, the aims of competition policy are in line with the new industrial economics, although generalizations as to the aims of the various regimes are danger-ous (see further Chapter 2). As was noted above, the aim of competition policy is not to achieve perfect competition as an alternative to monopoly. The definition of com-petition more usually accepted by regulatory authorities is that of the 'workable com-petition' first discussed by J. M. Clark in 1940 (30 *American Economic Review* 241). Workable competition accepts that there are elements of monopoly in virtually all markets, and has, as its goal, making such structures compatible with strong competi-tion. It therefore contains an element of pragmatism that courts find more attractive than more rigorous economic models (see, e.g., *Metro-SB-Grossmärkte GmbH & Co. KG* v *Commission* case 26/76 [1978] 2 CMLR 1).

It should be noted, too, that an increasing emphasis on the impact of technology on industrial development is leading to some new approaches to markets and industry being developed (see, e.g., Sutton, J., *Technology and Market Structure*, Boston, MIT Press (1999)).

1.4.4 Basic tools of economic analysis

There is less controversy surrounding the basic tools of economics than there is about the policy implications of different market structures. The Harvard and Chicago schools alike are in agreement as to these components. Markets represent the aggre-gation of individual elements; there will be situations in competition law where these individual elements become important in determining the existence of anti-com-petitive behaviour, and in resolving other economic issues—such as the ability of a monopolist to raise prices or the existence of other products that restrict the monopo-list's power.

1.4.4.1 Demand, supply, and price

In a free market economy the price of any product is set by the relationship between the demand for the product and the supply of the product. *Ceteris paribus*, the greater the supply, and the less the demand, the less the price of the product will be. The demand for a product is the sum of the demand of individual consumers. In all save a few cases a consumer's individual demand for a product will be inversely related to its price, and can be represented diagrammatically as a 'curve' that slopes downwards from left to right (see Figure 1.1). The 'elasticity of demand', references to which are often encountered in competition cases, is the extent to which demand is sensitive to price. An inelastic demand curve denotes that consumers are unresponsive to changes in price: if price rises by 10 per cent demand falls by *less* than 10 per cent. The more inelastic demand is, therefore, the more a monopolist will be able to raise prices and still increase their income. It may be presumed that petrol has an inelastic demand. If the demand for petrol was in fact elastic the government would not be able to raise significant revenue by taxation on petrol, for any increase in tax would be more than matched by a drop in sales.

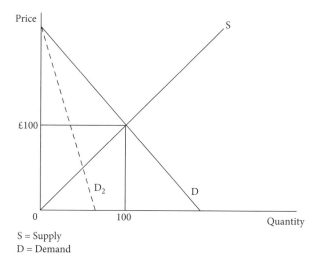

S = Supply
D = Demand

Figure 1.1 Demand and supply curves

Note: The price at which the product is sold, and the quantity sold, will be that where the demand and supply curves intersect. Demand curve D_2 is less elastic than D; if these two curves are looked at in isolation it will be seen that a change in price (from, e.g., £100 to £150) will have a bigger effect on D than on D_2.

An elastic demand curve denotes that consumers are very responsive to changes in price: if price rises by 10 per cent demand falls by *more* than 10 per cent, and in such a situation a monopolist raising prices will find that income will fall. Any product that has many substitutes is likely to have an elastic demand. The demand for compact discs is probably inelastic, but the demand for any individual disc will be more elastic. Thus if the price of all discs were to rise by 10 per cent, sales would probably not fall by as much as 10 per cent, but if The Killers' new CD was priced at 20 per cent more than any other disc, consumers might prefer to purchase an alternative from the wide range stocked by any music store. Supply curves slope upwards left to right, showing that the relationship between supply and price is that, *ceteris paribus*, the higher the price the greater the level of supply. The price of the product, the quantity supplied, and the quantity bought will be that set where demand and supply curves intersect.

As suggested above, the demand for a product will also be affected by the prices of *other* products, which is termed 'cross-elasticity of demand' or 'substitutability'. An examination of substitutability is almost essential in determining the boundaries of any given product market; this is emphasized further in 14.3.1. If demand for one product is highly sensitive to the price of another (e.g., clementines and mandarins) it is probably unwise to treat the market for clementines as being a separate one distinct from the market for mandarins. Producers and retailers of clementines will have to be always considering what is happening in the market for mandarins. Analysis of sub-stitutability accordingly features prominently in many competition cases. This is just one area in which the language of business may differ from the language of competition law. The sales or marketing director of any business may have a very clear view of the market that is being targeted by that business, but, if subject to a competition investigation, a very different definition of the market (often but not always a wider one) may be adopted.

1.4.4.2 Costs

Certain competition law issues cannot properly be resolved without an analysis of the costs faced by the company concerned. This is true of allegations of predation, where the charge is that the business is making losses or acting primarily with the intention of driving a competitor out of the market, or of preventing entry into the market, and of allegations of 'profiteering' where the company is accused of making too much profit (see Chapters 13 and 16).

Costs of production can be separated out in various ways. The primary divisions made by economists are between fixed and variable costs; marginal, average, and total costs; and short-run and long-run costs. Consider the example of a mass-produced motor car. In the short run fixed costs are those that stay constant whatever the level of production (e.g., the rent on the factories and perhaps research and development); variable costs alter according to the level of production (e.g., the cost of steel, plastics, and labour). Marginal costs are those of the additional unit of production (the cost of making one extra car). Generally marginal costs fall as production rises through the operation of 'economies of scale'. Economies of scale are the benefits that arise from producing more of any item. It is, for example, cheaper to produce the tenth motor car in a mass-production plant than it is to produce the first, and the 10,000th will be considerably cheaper still. Where there are economies of scale, the average cost, which is the total cost divided by the quantity produced, will fall as output rises. In the long run, there may be significant differences and the concept of fixed costs in particular becomes less definite, for even factories can be disposed of. The various cost curves are shown in Figure 1.2. Supply of a product will be determined by the costs of production and the demand for the product.

1.4.4.3 Markets

The definition of a 'relevant market' is essential to several aspects of competition law. Markets are where consumers and suppliers of a product or service interact. As was mentioned above (at 1.4.4.1) it may, for the purposes of rigorous analysis, be necessary to determine whether product A competes with product B. This is particularly important in the case of investigations into abuses of a dominant position, as we need to know in respect of what the undertaking is believed to be dominant. For example, is there a market for bus services? If there is it might be possible to apply the laws of dominance to a bus company that has a strong market position in a given area. On the other hand, if bus services compete strongly with rail and taxi services, with walking, and with the use of private cars, then it would probably not be possible to apply the law. As indicated above the most important factor here is that of the extent to which products are interchangeable one for the other.

The test favoured by competition authorities is the SSNIP test (which is discussed further at 14.3.4). This asks what the effect would be on product A of a Small but

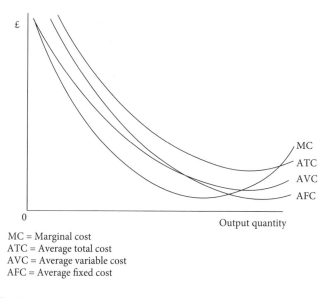

MC = Marginal cost
ATC = Average total cost
AVC = Average variable cost
AFC = Average fixed cost

Figure 1.2 Cost curves

Note: This figure assumes that there are economies of scale, so marginal and variable cost fall first. Once these economies are exhausted costs will begin to rise again.

Significant Non-transitory Increase in Price of product A by a hypothetical monopolist. To put this another way: if all of A were to be produced by one supplier, and the price of A were to rise by 5–10 per cent, and the price of all other products stayed constant, what would happen to the demand for A? In all save the most extreme circumstances *some* customers at least will switch to another product as they would be at the margin of the demand for product A. Other customers would accept a substantial price rise, while still remaining loyal to A. The question is whether the income lost from those customers who defect is more than compensated for by an increase in income from those remaining. Or to put it more simply still, would the price rise be profitable? If so, it is assumed that there is a market for A. If not, it would be necessary to determine to which products customers are switching most readily, and include those in the SSNIP test (i.e., run the same hypothetical exercise on the assumption that products A and B are controlled by the same supplier).

This exercise can be more than merely hypothetical as sales data may provide many answers. For example, if there is an unexpected heat wave in October, and sales of ice cream rise, it might be possible to determine whether sales of cold canned drinks have fallen—which might imply a degree of substitutability between the two products. In other circumstances this exercise can be more difficult, and the SSNIP test may fail to produce an accurate result. This is most clearly the case where there is an existing monopolist who has behaved intelligently. A monopolist is expected to raise the price of their product to the highest profitable level. Were the price to rise any further in such a case it would lead to losses, and might suggest to the unwary that the market was wider than for the monopolist's product. If there was a single supplier of bicycles and the price was raised to the maximum profitable level it might be that a further price rise would push some customers towards purchasing motorcycles, although it is highly unlikely that these are in the same relevant market.

Such a mistake was made by the US Supreme Court in the case of *United States* v *EI DuPont* 351 US 377 (1956). Here the court found that there was not a market for cellophane, as were the price to rise profits would fall. It is widely accepted that the court was wrong, as it started from a position where prices had *already* risen above the competitive level to the monopoly level. This danger is now known as the 'cellophane fallacy', or 'cellophane trap'. The *DG Competition discussion paper on the application of Article 82 of the Treaty to exclusionary abuses* (December 2005) also recognizes that this problem exists, indicating that the assumption that prevailing prices are competitive prices 'often does not hold in Article [102] cases' (para. 15). However, the discussion paper does not suggest a solution to this problem other than that of falling back on other types of evidence.

Further factors in defining relevant markets, and the importance of doing so in the areas of agreements, single firm conduct, and mergers, are dealt with as appropriate throughout this text.

1.4.5 **Barriers to entry**

The implications of barriers to entry are that their existence reinforces monopolistic tendencies in a market. Theoretical models of market structure focus only on *actual* competition facing producers, and make no reference to *potential* competition. It has long been recognized that the latter serves as a restraint on the conduct of incumbents (those already in the market) in the same way as the former. The higher the barriers that exist, the greater the ability of the incumbent to ignore the potential competition.

While the existence of barriers to entry in any given situation may be a matter of some concern to those investigating the market, there is intense debate between the Harvard and Chicago schools as to the policy implications of barriers to entry, and even as to what a barrier to entry is. The issue is of such importance that it should be dealt with at this early stage. At its very broadest, a barrier to entry is any factor that operates as a cost of a new entrant into a market. By this definition it might include such factors as lack of knowledge about the market; any premium rate paid for capital to compensate for the risk this lack of knowledge results in; the cost of acquiring the necessary physical capacity (plant and raw materials); the cost of establishing brand recognition with consumers, and a distribution system, etc.

Whether all barriers to entry should be a matter of concern to competition regulation is contested. Some barriers are the result of the success of the incumbent (e.g., the need to develop brand loyalty) and it may be argued that if the incumbent has had to overcome this hurdle it is, or has been over time, in no better a position than any potential entrant. Although such barriers reinforce the power of the incumbent, some (notably Chicagoans) argue that they are merely evidence of its efficiency, and thus should be of no concern to regulators. Adherents of the Harvard school would permit competition policy to examine *any* barrier, and in some circumstances to impose positive obligations on incumbents to reduce these. In an extreme case this could, for example, take the form of restricting their product lines so as to allow a niche for the entrant, or to allow entrants access to the incumbent's established distribution network. Such policies are likely to face severe resistance from businesses that have led the way into a market and succeeded, and whose officers are often perplexed at the demands made on them by the law.

All commentators would accept that barriers that result from governmental action are a source of legitimate concern; they will often be justified on the grounds of health and safety, or may be accompanied by ongoing industry regulation that will ameliorate the consequence of the market power granted to the incumbent.

1.4.6 Conclusion

Unfortunately the analysis conducted by the various regulatory authorities is often somewhat lacking in formal rigour, and the EU Commission decisions have in particular been criticized for squandering in-depth economic analysis. In its *Green Paper on Vertical Restraints* (see Chapter 9) the EU Commission argued that 'economic theory is just one of the sources of policy. In practice, the application of economic theory must take place in the context of the existing legal texts and jurisprudence.' Further, it went on to say that 'economic theories are necessarily based on simplifying assumptions often obtained in the context of stylised theoretical models that cannot take into account all the complexities of real life cases' (para. 86). It might plausibly be argued that, if an economic theory based on 'simplifying assumptions' has been tested and refined against empirical data, that theory could serve as a legal test and is at least as likely to produce reliable results as is a pragmatic individual analysis of each case.

Care should be taken over the way in which economic 'evidence' is used in competition cases. While economic consultants will regularly be employed to advance arguments in competition cases, and in many cases their evidence will be determinative of the issues, there are some dangers with constructing elaborate economic 'stories' to explain observed conduct. An illustration of the problems may be found in the UK case of *Napp Pharmaceutical Holdings Ltd* v *The Director General of Fair Trading* [2002] CompAR 13. Napp was condemned for discriminatory predatory pricing (the case is discussed in full in Chapter 16). Its economic consultants produced an argument to the effect that the undertaking was rationally pricing low in one sector as this ensured follow-through sales in another sector, and that this 'portfolio' pricing was a legitimate and profitable strategy that was available to all its competitors. The Competition Commission Appeals Tribunal (CCAT, now replaced by the Competition Appeals Tribunal), which heard the case, found no suggestion in the documents produced by Napp that it had in fact been consciously following such a strategy. The Tribunal noted that 'Napp does not strike us as a naïve or badly managed company', and argued that 'if its pricing policy had in fact been seen by Napp in the way that its economic consultants suggest, we would have expected the company's internal documents to demonstrate that' (para. 252).

1.5 **Resources**

There are a wide range of competition law resources, both in printed and electronic format. As well as the references throughout the text of this book, most chapters have at the end a list of suggested further reading. What follows here is a more general introduction to the materials available. An up-to-date list of the key official websites is found in the Online Resource Centre to this book.

1.5.1 **Official materials**

In addition to the necessary legislation and cases, most of which are available both online and in easily-accessible hard-copy formats, the various bodies responsible for the application of competition laws in the EU and UK publish a large amount of less formal material, including guidance, discussion documents, reports, and general information relating to their activities. The EU Commission also publishes a very useful quarterly newsletter, which contains often insightful analysis of recent developments and cases, as well as an annual report on its activities in relation to competition law. All this material is usually available on the various websites, and the more formal material is also published in books bringing together a range of competition law materials.

1.5.2 **Journals**

There are several journals dedicated to competition law. The most widely cited of these in Europe is the *European Competition Law Review*, published 10 times a year by Sweet & Maxwell. *Competition Law Journal*, published four times a year by Jordan Publishing, deals primarily with UK and EU developments, as does the online *Competition Law Review*. Internationally, a number of journals are of note: *Journal of Competition Law and Economics, European Competition Journal, World Competition Law & Economics Review, The Antitrust Bulletin*, and *Antitrust Law Journal*. Although much of the work in the international journals tends to relate to the law and practice as it develops in the USA, the discussions are often highly relevant to other jurisdictions.

1.5.3 **Commentaries**

A large number of books relating to competition law generally, or more specialized aspects of it, are available. In particular the practitioner market is served by substantial reference works, which are priced above the budget of students, and, unfortunately, often outside the budget even of university libraries. At various places in this book, and in reading recommendations at the end of chapters, some reference is made to these works. The gap between the academic study of competition law and the practical application of the law is a narrow one, and many practitioners contribute regularly to the literature of the subject.

There are three excellent books in print which set out the stories of cartel cases in a journalistic but accurate style. These are: Mason, C., *The Art of the Steal: Inside the Sotheby's–Christie's Auction House Scandal*, New York, GB Putnam's Sons (2004); Lieber, J. B., *Rats in the Grain: The Dirty Tricks and Trials of Archer Daniels Midland The Supermarket to the World*, New York, Four Walls Eight Windows (2000); and Eichenwald, K., *The Informant*, New York, Broadway Books (2000). A movie directed by Steven Soderbergh starring Matt Damon was recently made based on the latter (*The Informant!*, 2009).

FURTHER READING

Books

AMATO, G., *Antitrust and the Bounds of Power: The Dilemma of Liberal Democracy in the History of the Market* (1997) Hart Publishing, Oxford

BORK, R. H., *The Antitrust Paradox: A Policy at War with Itself* (1993) The Free Press, New York

EHLERMANN, C. F., and LAUDATI, L. L. (eds), *European Competition Law Annual 1997: Objectives of Competition Policy* (1998) Hart Publishing, Oxford

GERBER, D. J., *Law and Competition in Twentieth Century Europe: Protecting Prometheus* (1998) Clarendon Press, Oxford

MOTTA, M., *Competition Policy: Theory and Practice* (2004) Cambridge University Press, Cambridge

PORTER, M. E., *Competitive Strategy* (1980) The Free Press, New York

Articles

BAKER, J. B., 'Market Definition: An Analytical Overview', (2007) 74 *Antitrust Law Journal* 129

FOX, E. M., 'What is Harm to Competition? Exclusionary Practices and Anti-competitive Effect', (2002) 70 *Antitrust Law Journal* 371

HILDEBRAND, D., 'The European School in EC Competition Law', (2002) 25 *World Competition* 3

MAHER, I., 'Juridification, Codification and Sanction in UK Competition Law', (2000) 63 *Modern Law Review* 544

OECD, *Competition Law and Policy in the European Union* (2005) OECD (OECD and DG Comp websites)

ROSS, M., 'Promoting Solidarity: From Public Services to a European Model of Competition?', (2007) 44 *Common Market Law Review* 1057

WILLIMSKY, S., 'The Concept(s) of Competition', (1997) *European Competition Law Review* 54

WOOD, D. P., 'The Role of Economics and Economists in Competition Cases', (1999) *OECD Journal of Competition Law & Policy* 82

2

The European Union and United Kingdom competition regimes

KEY POINTS

- The subjects of EU and UK competition law are undertakings; however, the UK cartel offence is directed at individuals.

- The objective of EU competition law provisions has been disputed; efficiency considerations are crucial, but they must be balanced alongside other EU objectives.

- The integration of markets has been highly influential in the shaping of EU competition policy. UK competition laws are not governed by similar concerns.

- The role of the EU Commission in competition law is fundamental, and the European Courts have contributed to clarifying the interpretation of competition law provisions.

- In the UK, the OFT (and the sectoral regulators), the Competition Commission, and the Competition Appeals Tribunal are the principal regulatory organs.

2.1 Introduction

The enactment of the Sherman Act in the United States of America in 1890 was a major development in competition law. The US regime has had a pervasive influence on the development of the law elsewhere. In part this is because the success of the economy was attributed, among other factors, to the efficacy of the US antitrust law. The UK and EU regimes arose independently, although since the UK's accession to the EU on 1 January 1973 the UK's system has been largely aligned to that of the EU. The impetus for change came largely from industry in the UK whose interests would be likely to be served by a harmonized regime with a common set of standards. On 1 May 2004 a 'modernization' process which made substantial changes to the EU regime further refined the relationship between the two systems. This chapter serves as an introduction to the two regimes.

2.2 Undertakings—the subjects of competition law

'Undertakings' are the sole subjects of the substantive law relating to agreements and the abuse of dominant positions. This is the word used in the TFEU and in EU secondary legislation, and has been adopted in the UK Competition Act 1998 (CA 98). For the EU undertakings are the sole subjects of competition law, although in certain narrowly defined circumstances individual persons may be involved in investigation procedures. In the UK, the cartel offence extends only to individuals. In the early years of the application of competition law the word 'undertaking' caused some difficulties, and attempts to provide a precise definition were largely unsuccessful.

A broad understanding of the concept may be clear from the famous words used by the Court of Justice in *Höfner and Elser* v *Macrotron GmbH* case C–41/90 [1993] 4 CMLR 306. It was held that 'the concept of an undertaking encompasses every entity engaged in economic activity, regardless of the legal status of the entity and the way in which it is financed' (para. 21). This broad definition is widely used and accepted as the basic notion of undertaking for the purposes of the application of competition law. It does however leave some unanswered questions as to the basic elements of the concept: are there any limits to the term 'every entity'? What is understood to be an 'economic activity'? Subsequent decisions and cases have shed some light on these issues and have clarified the limits of the concept.

One of the first questions that the Commission had to address was whether or not an individual could be considered an undertaking. In defining the undertaking in any particular circumstance, it is necessary to look to the economic and factual reality of the situation, and not to legal structure. Therefore, a single individual may be an undertaking in circumstances where they have an impact on the market in a capacity other than that of a consumer. In *Reuter/BASF* 76/743/EEC (1976) OJ L254/40, an inventor was held to be an undertaking and therefore subject to art. 101. In *UNITEL* 78/516/EEC (1978) OJ L157/39 opera singers were brought within the scope of the law.

Parent and subsidiary companies may be held to be part of the same undertaking, and not to be their separate legal constituents. This can have the benefit of removing arrangements between them from the provisions of art. 101 and the Chapter I Prohibition, which require that 'two or more undertakings' be implicated in the practice (see, e.g., *Re Christiani & Nielsen* 69/165/EEC [1969] CMLR D36 and more recently, *Viho Europe BV* v *Commission* case T–102/92 [1995] 4 CMLR 299; and see further 9.2.5). Although parent companies may be liable for the acts of their subsidiaries, the General Court (GC) has made it clear that it is not sufficient for the Commission merely to assert that one undertaking *was able to* exert a decisive influence over the other. Rather the Commission must demonstrate, in order to find the parent liable for a subsidiary's acts, that 'such decisive influence [exists] on the basis of factual evidence, including, in particular, any management power one of the undertakings may have over the other' (*Cooperatieve Verkoop-en Productievereniging van Aardappelmeel en Derivaten Avebe BA* v *Commission* case T–314/01 [2007] 4 CMLR 1, at para. 136). The question of whether the mere fact that a company holds 100 per cent of the shares of a subsidiary is enough to create a presumption that the parent exerted decisive control over it was recently clarified by the Court of Justice in the *Akzo Nobel* case (*Akzo Nobel NV and others* v *Commission* case C–97/08 [2009] ECR I-8237). The 2002 *Stora* judgment had raised doubts in this respect, since the Court referred to additional factors such as the fact the parent supervised the commercial policy of the subsidiary, or that they were jointly represented in the administrative procedure (*Stora Koparbergs*

Bergslags v *Commission* case T–354/94 [2002] 4 CMLR 34 at paras 28–9). In *Akzo Nobel*, the court confirmed that

> in the specific case where a parent company has a 100% shareholding in a subsidiary which has infringed the [Union] competition rules, first, the parent company can exercise a decisive influence over the conduct of the subsidiary and, second, there is a rebuttable presumption that the parent company does in fact exercise a decisive influence over the conduct of its subsidiary. (para. 4)

Undertakings do not have to be making profits nor even be engaged in profit-making activity: in the course of a proceeding relating to the 1990 football World Cup, the EU Commission expressly stated that organizations did not have to be profit making as long as they were engaged in economic activity (*Distribution of Package Tours During the 1990 World Cup* 92/521/EEC (1992) OJ L326/31). In restricted circumstances, commercial activities carried out by arms of the state may not fall within the definition of 'undertaking', although this cannot serve as a broad exemption. For example, in the case of *Coapi* 95/188 (1995) OJ L122/37, the Commission condemned a decision of an association of industrial property agents in Spain. Coapi argued that as it was responsible for the discharge of functions assigned to it by virtue of Spanish law (Law No. 2/1974), and was governed by public law, it could not be regarded as an undertaking for the purposes of EU competition law. The Commission, relying on the definition given by the Court in *Höfner* (above), held that these facts did not prevent Coapi from being regarded as an undertaking subject to the provisions of art. 101. This was confirmed by the Court of Justice in *MOTOE*, as explained below.

State undertakings that are *purchasing* goods on the market for use in the provision of services are *not* undertakings for the purposes of competition law. In the case of *Federación Nacional de Empresas de Instrumentación Científica, Médica, Técnica y Dental (FENIN)* v *Commission* case T–319/99 [2003] 5 CMLR 1 the GC upheld a Commission decision finding that the national health service of Spain was not acting as an undertaking when it purchased services from the market place, even though it was a monopsony (monopolistic purchaser). The Court held, at para. 37 that

> an organisation which purchases goods—even in great quantity—not for the purpose of offering goods and services as part of an economic activity, but in order to use them in the context of a different activity, such as one of a purely social nature, does not act as an undertaking simply because it is a purchaser in a given market.

In *Cisal* (*Cisal di Battistello Venanzio & Co. Sas* v *Istituto Nazionale Per L'Assicurazione Contro Gli Infortuni Sul Lavoro (INAIL)* case C–218/00 [2002] 4 CMLR 24) the Court of Justice considered the position of INAIL, a body 'entrusted by law with the management of a scheme providing insurance against accidents at work and occupational diseases' (para. 21). It has been accepted in a number of cases that *any* activity consisting in offering goods or services on a market is an economic activity (see, e.g., joined cases C–180–184/98 *Pavlov and others* v *Stichting Pensioenfunds Medische Specialisten* [2000] ECR I–6451, at para. 75). In the present case it was argued that services provided by the alleged undertaking were fully comparable to those provided by a private insurer. The

Court found, however, that the insurance scheme operated with a clear social, rather than commercial, purpose. The effect of the scheme was to subsidize poorer-paid workers by contributions from better-paid workers, and INAIL's activity was subject to close supervision by the State. In this instance, therefore, the Court of Justice held that INAIL was not, for the purposes of EU competition law, an undertaking.

The Court of Justice recently had to decide whether the Automobile and Touring Club of Greece (ELPA), a non-profit organization entrusted by national law to give consent to the organization of motorcycling events, would be subject to EU competition law (*Motosykletistiki Omospondia Ellados (MOTOE)* v *Elliniko Dimosio* case C–49/07 [2008] 5 CMLR 11). In paras 25 to 29 of the judgment, the Court explained that neither the fact that it did not intend to make profits nor the fact that it took part in the decision-making process of public authorities could prevent ELPA from being considered an undertaking. The organization and commercial exploitation of motor-cycling events is an economic activity, and insofar as ELPA carries out these tasks arts 101 and 102 may be applicable to its conduct.

The question of the extent to which professional associations—for example the Bar, or the British Medical Association (BMA)—are undertakings whose conduct and decisions may be subject to the constraints of competition law has been a matter of some discussion. In February 2002 the Court of Justice shed some light on this issue in a case relating to the Dutch Bar (*Wouters, Savelbergh and Price Waterhouse Belastingadviseurs BV* v *Algemene Raad Van de Nederlandse Orde Van Advocaten* case C–309/99 [2002] 4 CMLR 27). First, the Court held that individual members of the Bar carried out economic activities in that they offered their services for a fee and 'bear the financial risks attaching to the performance of those activities' (para. 48). Secondly, the association of *individual* members in the Bar would constitute an '*association of undertakings* within the meaning of art. [101(1)]' (para. 64), although the Bar *itself* would not be classed as an undertaking for the purposes of art. 102. Rather, the Bar 'acts as the regulatory body of a profession, the practice of which constitutes an economic activity' (para. 58). This does not automatically mean that the conduct of such professional associations will be condemned; rather, because the conduct attaches to an 'undertaking' or 'association of undertakings', its (anti-) competitive impact can be examined in the light of the appropriate legislation and standards. Note that in *Arduino* v *Compagnia Assicuratrice RAS SpA* case C–35/99 [2002] 4 CMLR 25 the Court of Justice held that the adoption by the state of a national rule approving fees set by the Italian Bar Council was not caught by art. 101.

Sporting bodies may also constitute undertakings. Decisions taken by sporting bodies that do not relate to economic activity, as would be the case in an amendment by FIFA to the offside rule, would not fall within the scope of competition law. However, where decisions have to do with economic activity then challenges based on competition law may be launched. This was the case, for example, in *Adidas-Salomon AG* v *Roger Draper and Derek Paul Howorth* [2006] EWHC 1318 (Ch), where Adidas mounted a challenge to dress codes introduced by the owners, organizers, and promoters of the four international tennis 'grand slam' tournaments.

An attempt to strike out the action on the grounds that the defendants were not undertakings failed.

Apart from providing a test as to the application of art. 101(1), the limits of the term undertaking for the purposes of competition law can be relevant to the fact-finding procedure of Regulation 1/2003 (see Chapter 5), and to the penalties imposed under that regulation.

For the purposes of United Kingdom law, the same approach is taken under the terms of the CA 98 as is taken under EU law. In the case of *The Institute of Independent Insurance Brokers* v *The Director General of Fair Trading* [2001] CompAR 62 the CCAT held that the Office of Fair Trading (OFT) had been incorrect to dismiss a complaint on the grounds that the entity, the activity of which formed the basis of the complaint, was not an undertaking. The Director was called upon to look at various rules relating to insurance set by the General Insurance Standards Council (GISC). This described itself as 'an independent, non-profit making organisation, funded entirely by membership fees, whose main purpose is to make sure that general insurance customers are treated fairly'. However considering all the facts, including that GISC was set up as a private company, existing solely by contract, and was run by a board of directors, the Tribunal found that it could see 'no compelling reason why GISC should not be regarded itself as an undertaking' (para. 258).

The OFT has held that a health care trust purchasing social care services is not acting as an undertaking (*The North & West Belfast Health and Social Services Trust* CA/98/11/2002). On appeal the Competition Appeals Tribunal (CAT) found that the Trust *was* acting as an undertaking when it purchased services, and remitted the case to the OFT (*BetterCare Group Limited* v *Director General of Fair Trading* [2002] CompAR 226) which made a new decision on other grounds. Following the ruling of the GC in *FENIN* the OFT issued *Policy note 1/2004: The Competition Act 1998 and public bodies* (OFT 443, January 2004). In essence this summarizes the EU case law, and seeks to depart from the ruling of the CAT—which in the light of *FENIN* does appear to be incorrect in law. The conclusion of the OFT is set out at para. 27 of the policy note:

generally where a public body is only a purchaser of goods or services in a particular market and is not involved in the direct provision of any goods or services in that market or a related market, that body will not be an undertaking for the purposes of the CA98.

2.3 The European Union

2.3.1 The legal order

The European Union legal order is governed by the primary legislation of the relevant treaties, to which all 27 Member States have acceded. For the purposes of competition law the most important treaty is the Treaty on the Functioning of the European Union (TFEU). This treaty, which was originally the European Economic Community (EEC)

Treaty, and subsequently renamed the European Community (EC) Treaty, has been amended on a number of occasions, both in response to the accession of new Member States and to pressures for institutional reform. One of the most significant developments in the life of the EU in recent years has been the accession of 10 new Member States on 1 May 2004, which was shortly followed by the accession of another two countries—Romania and Bulgaria—on 1 January 2010. The sheer scale of this enlargement created a pressure on the application of competition law that led to a major reform, or modernization programme, designed to make the system more manageable. At the same time as the accession arrangements were being implemented discussions were under way on how to reform the texts of the European treaties. These discussions eventually culminated in the emergence of the Treaty Establishing a Constitution for Europe (the Constitutional Treaty) in 2004. Following its rejection by popular referenda in France and the Netherlands in 2005 the ratification process was abandoned, and the Treaty became legally defunct. Some of its provisions have been incorporated into the Lisbon Treaty, the latest reform of the fundamental legal documents of the EU. It came into force on 1 December 2009, proving that the 'constitution' label of the Treaties had been discarded for once and for all.

For a better understanding of the literature, it is worth noting that the Lisbon Treaty made some important changes to fundamental terminology and to the numbering of Treaty provisions. The first fundamental change in Union jargon is that the 'European Community' is now the 'European Union', and the legal personality of the former has been transferred to the latter (see below for details on the creation of the EU). As a result, the EC Treaty was renamed Treaty on the Functioning of the European Union, which is part of the broader Treaty on the European Union (TEU) also referred to in this book. Other relevant terminology changes are that the 'common market' is now the 'internal market', the European Court of Justice (ECJ) has been renamed the Court of Justice of the European Union, and the Court of First Instance (CFI) has become the General Court (GC). With regard to the numbering, virtually all the provisions have been renumbered, including arts 101 and 102 TFEU (which were previously 81 and 82 EC); this book uses the current numbering; however care should be taken when reading pre-Lisbon documentation to avoid confusion. A table of equivalences has been published in the Official Journal ([2008] OJ C115/361). It is advisable to keep a copy at hand.

As with other Union policy areas, EU competition law is established and developed via a variety of legal sources. At the top of the legal hierarchy is the TFEU. By itself the Treaty does not provide sufficient detail to permit the existence of a fully and completely functioning legal order, and a considerable quantity of secondary legislation has been made. Article 288 TFEU lists the types of secondary legislation that may be adopted by the EU: regulations, decisions, and directives. In the field of competition law regulations and decisions have been the instruments of choice. Regulations have been adopted to give effect to the broad principles set out in arts 101 and 102 TFEU, and to establish EU rules and procedures relating to merger control. Decisions are issued by the EU Commission which has a unique power of enforcement in this field of EU law. European Union competition law may be enforced by way of decisions made by the EU Commission, and art. 288 provides that: 'A decision shall be binding in its entirety. A decision which specifies those to whom it is addressed shall be binding only on them.' These Commission decisions, together with all primary and secondary legislation are subject to the review of the Court of Justice and the General Court. Their judgments can, therefore, be said to form a third relevant legal source of competition law. In the arena of competition law, so-called 'soft-law' is also important. This takes the form of notices and guidance published by the EU Commission, which explain and clarify the law, and which although not formally legally binding may in certain circumstances create legitimate expectations in those subject to the application of the relevant law.

Competition law featured as part of the EU regime from its inception as provisions in this respect were made in the European Coal and Steel Community (ECSC) Treaty, signed by the original six members in 1951. The ECSC Treaty has now expired (see *Expiry of the ECSC Treaty (Antitrust) (Merger Control) Communication 2002* (2002) OJ C152/03). The inclusion of these provisions arose in part from the 'absence of, or at least the major imperfections of, competition readily visible in the [relevant] markets' (Goyder, D. G., *EC Competition Law*, Oxford, OUP (1993), p. 19) and in part from the example of the USA whose economic success was perceived to be based partly on its free competition policies (for a challenging and distinctive view of the impact of US law on the development of EU competition policy, see Gerber, D. J., *Law and Competition in Twentieth Century Europe: Protecting Prometheus*, Oxford, Clarendon Press (1998)).

The Treaty of Rome 1957, which created the EEC, provided the blueprint for a much greater economic integration than that envisaged in the ECSC Treaty, and the various amendments to the Treaty since then have left its competition regime virtually intact. One of the effects of the Treaty on European Union (Maastricht; TEU) 1992 (entry into force 1 November 1994) was to amend the EEC Treaty to become the European Community Treaty. The European Community was to be the first of the three pillars of the newly created European Union, the other two pillars being the Common Foreign and Security Policy and Justice and Home Affairs (subsequently renamed Police and Judicial Co-operation in Criminal Matters in 2003). This three-pillared EU was maintained until 1 December 2009, when the Lisbon Treaty (initially named the Reform Treaty) gave the European Union a single legal personality and abolished the term 'European Community'. Those seeking a fuller discussion of the nature of EU law and of the 'new legal order' that is the Union (*NV Algemene Transport-en Expeditie Onderneming Van Gend en Loos* v *Nederlandse Belastingadministratie* case 26/62 [1963] 1 CMLR 105) should refer to a current edition of a specialist Union law textbook.

2.3.2 Key Treaty provisions

2.3.2.1 The tasks of the Union

Former art. 2 of the EC Treaty set a very broad set of objectives of the then European Community. This included 'a high degree of competitiveness and converging economic performance'. While this was primarily an expression of industrial policy, competition law is one of the means by which this object may be achieved. Former art. 3 EC laid down more specific tasks or activities which are to be undertaken for the purposes of achieving the objectives set out in art. 2. Article 3(1)(g) provided that one of these activities was the development of 'a system ensuring that competition in the internal market is not distorted'. This provision has frequently been referred to by the European Courts when setting out the functions of competition law in response to particular challenges, and it has often been held that arts 101 and 102 TFEU should be interpreted in the light of arts 2 and 3(1)(g) EC.

These provisions no longer appear as such in the Treaty after the Lisbon reform. Although some provisions of the TFEU and the TEU substantially provide similar principles, the references to competition have been removed from the primary objectives of the EU, since art. 3(1)(g) has been repealed. This was a matter of some surprise; it was reported that the removal was at the insistence of the French President, Nicolas Sarkozy, and reflected a dissatisfaction in France with an emphasis in the EU on free competition. The practical impact of the elimination of this provision on the enforcement of competition law in the EU is questionable. Neelie Kroes, the former head of DG Comp, argued that there would be no effect, while others have been less sanguine (see, e.g., 'Removal of Competition Clause Causes Dismay', *Financial Times* 24 June 2007). Although the jurisprudence of the European Courts has made frequent reference to this fundamental provision in the past it might be the case that there is a lesser need to resort to basic principles as the law develops and becomes clearer and more entrenched. Moreover, references to competition appear in other parts of the Treaty: art. 3(1)(b) TFEU acknowledges the exclusive competence of the EU to establish the competition rules necessary for the functioning of the internal market, while art. 120 TFEU forces the Union and the Member States to respect the 'principle of an open market economy with free competition' when pursuing their economic policies. In addition, Protocol (No. 27) on the Internal Market and Competition has been attached to the Lisbon Treaty, further diminishing the legal implications of the disappearance of art. 3(1)(g).

2.3.2.2 Articles 101 and 102—the key substantive provisions

Article 101 introduces a prohibition against 'agreements between undertakings, decisions by associations of undertakings and concerted practices which may affect trade between Member States and which have as their object or effect the prevention, restriction or distortion of competition within the internal market' (and see Chapter 9). Article 102 prohibits the 'abuse by one or more undertakings of a dominant position within the common market or a substantial part of it … in so far as it may affect trade between Member States' (and see Chapter 14). Conduct falling within the scope of these articles is prohibited without the need for further investigation.

2.3.2.3 Articles 103 and 105—implementation of arts 101 and 102

Article 103 makes provision for the enactment of any 'appropriate regulations or directives to give effect to the principles set out in Articles 101 and 102 […]'. The key regulation adopted under this authority is Regulation 1 of 2003, which is discussed in detail in Chapter 5. Various other procedural regulations and, in particular, block exemption regulations have been enacted: the former are largely dealt with in Chapter 5, the latter in Chapter 10. Although not expressly provided for in the Treaty, the Union has also introduced a regime to control large merger situations in the EU. This now finds expression in Regulation 139/2004, which is discussed in Chapter 19.

Article 105 places the Commission at the heart of the EU competition law regime, as it 'shall ensure the application of the principles laid down in arts 101 and 102'. The Commission is required to investigate infringements of the law, and if it finds that the law has been breached it 'shall propose appropriate measures to bring it to an end'. The arm of the Commission with responsibility for the development, application, and supervision of EU competition law is the Directorate General Competition, which will be referred to as DG Comp throughout this text. The current Director General for Competition is Alexander Italianer, while Mr Joaquín Almunia took over from Neelie Kroes as Competition Commissioner in January 2010. Mr Almunia is also the Vice-President of the Commission. Although much of the day-to-day enforcement of competition law has now been delegated to the national competition authorities of the Member States, and to national courts in the case of private actions, the Commission still retains a key role. The relationship between the powers of the Commission and of national authorities is examined later in this chapter, and in Chapter 3.

2.3.2.4 Articles 106–109—public undertakings and state aids

Outside of arts 101 and 102, other aspects of Union policy have an impact upon competition regulation. Most obviously art. 106 applies to public undertakings and undertakings 'to which Member States grant special or exclusive rights'. The requirement of the article is that 'Member States shall neither enact nor maintain in force any measure contrary to the rules contained in the Treaties', which is to say that state-owned or state-established or regulated undertakings are in no better position in relation to EU competition law than their private sector, market-regulated counterparts. However, undertakings falling within art. 106(2) may be placed in a more favourable position, being given the leeway to operate outside of the usual rules where these rules would 'obstruct the performance, in law or in fact, of the particular tasks assigned to them'.

Articles 106–109 TFEU relate to the control of state aids. DG Comp has as one of its central tasks the review and control of such aid. This is an area that brings its staff into frequent conflict with the Member States. State aids are dealt with in detail in Chapter 21.

2.3.3 The function of EU competition law

There is no clear statement in the TFEU as to the function of competition law. Limited guidance was provided in former arts 2 and 3(1)(g) of the EC Treaty (see 2.3.2.1). Article 101 emphasizes that consumers' interests are to be taken into account in deciding whether the legal exception of art. 101(3) applies and that consumers must be allowed 'a fair share of the resulting benefit'; and art. 102 is silent, save in its pejorative reference to 'abuse'. Korah has written that, in the EU, 'there is no agreement as to what objectives should be pursued by competition policy' ('EEC Competition Policy—Legal Form or Economic Efficiency', (1986) *Current Legal Problems* 85). The Court of Justice and the Commission have indicated what the primary goals of EU competition policy *might* be. In *Metro-SB-Grossmärkte GmbH & Co. KG* v *Commission* case 26/76 [1978] 2 CMLR 1 at 2, the Court held that

The requirement…that competition shall not be distorted implies the existence on the market of workable competition, i.e., the degree of competition necessary to ensure the observance of the basic requirements and attainment of the objectives of the Treaty, in particular the creation of a single market achieving conditions similar to those of a domestic market.

Thus the position appears to be that competition policy is just one area that will be balanced alongside other objectives of EU policy as the need requires, and is not, exclusively, a tool to achieve efficiency maximization. It is the case therefore that, as other policy requirements change over time, so too might the application of competition law. However, there is increasing evidence that efficiency considerations are coming to the fore.

 The Commission has made various claims for the operation of the law in its annual reports. The widest are those made in the 1972 Report which places stress on the general benefits of the policy:

Competition is the best stimulant of economic activity since it guarantees the widest possible freedom of action to all. An active competition policy…makes it easier for the supply and demand structures continually to adjust to technological development…Through the interplay of decentralised decision-making machinery, competition enables enterprises continuously to improve their efficiency…competition is an essential means for satisfying…the individual and collective needs of our society.   (p. 11)

In the same report the Commission also emphasized the importance of consumer interests (p. 12) and the effects of anti-competitive actions on individual undertakings. In its ninth report the Commission set out its goals at the time with some clarity:

The first fundamental objective is to keep the common market open and unified…There is…a continuing need—and this is the primary task of the [Union]'s competition policy—to forestall and suppress restrictive or abusive practices of firms attempting to divide up the market again so as to apply artificial price differences or impose unfair terms on their consumers…

 It is an established fact that competition carries within it the seeds of its own destruction. An excessive concentration of economic, financial and commercial power can produce such far-reaching structural changes that free competition is no longer able to fulfil its role as an effective regulator of economic activity. Consequently, the second fundamental objective of the [Union]'s competition policy must be to ensure that at all stages of the [internal] market's development there exists the right amount of competition in order for the Treaty's requirements to be met and its aims attained. The desire to maintain a competitive structure dictates the Commission's constant vigilance over abuses by dominant firms…

Thirdly, the competition system instituted by the Treaty requires that the conditions under which competition takes place remain subject to the principle of fairness in the market place. [These principles are]...

First, equality of opportunity must be preserved for all commercial operators in the [internal] market.

A second aspect of the principle of fairness in the market place is the need to have regard to the great variety of situations in which firms carry on business...this factor makes it necessary to adapt the [Union] competition rules so as to pay special regard in particular to small and medium [size] firms that lack strength.

Finally, equity demands that the Commission's competition policy takes account of the legitimate interests of workers, users and consumers. (*Ninth Report on Competition Policy* (1980), pp. 9–11)

For many years it was clear that a fundamental aim of the Union was to integrate the economies of the Member States, and this had an impact on the application of competition law. This dominant concern has been continually restated in decisions and cases, and is evidenced in the continuing rule that territorial protection in distribution agreements is not permitted where parallel imports are excluded. The Court of Justice has held, in *Établissements Consten Sarl and Grundig-Verkaufs-GmbH* v *Commission* cases 56 and 58/64 [1966] 1 CMLR 418 at 471, that

an agreement between a producer and a distributor which might tend to restore the national divisions in trade between member-states might be such as to thwart the most basic objects of the [Union]. The Treaty, whose preamble and text aim at suppressing the barriers between States...could not allow undertakings to restore such barriers.

The expansion of the EU that took place in May 2004 and January 2007 has also undoubtedly had an impact on the way competition law is applied. Thus, in its *White Paper on Modernisation of the Rules Implementing Articles [101] and [102]* (1999) OJ C132/1, the Commission recognized that

Economic and monetary union is certain to have major consequences for competition policy. It will first entail further economic integration and, in the long term, will strengthen the effects of the internal market by helping to remove the last economic barriers between Member States. It also will help to cut the overall costs of intra-[Union] trade by reducing transaction costs. Such factors will encourage undertakings to develop trade and thus increase competition throughout the Union. A single currency will also increase price transparency and thus highlight price differences still existing between Member States. Economic operators may, when faced with stronger competition, be tempted to take a protectionist attitude to avoid the constraints of adapting to the new conditions, thereby compensating for their lack of competitiveness in a new environment. Lastly, the fact that some member states are...not part of the monetary union may encourage undertakings to partition markets. (para. 6)

As part of the modernization programme the EU Commission has emphasized repeatedly its move to a system of competition law which is clearly related to economic criteria and analysis. This policy is reflected in the block exemption regulations, which were adapted so as to reduce the reliance on legal formalism which had attracted so much criticism, and in guidelines relating to horizontal and vertical agreements (see Chapter 9 generally). In its *Guidelines on the application of Article 81(3) of the Treaty* (2004) OJ C101/97 at para. 13 the Commission states that

The objective of Article [101] is to protect competition on the market as a means of enhancing consumer welfare and of ensuring an efficient allocation of resources. Competition and market integration serve these ends since the creation and preservation of an open single market promotes an efficient allocation of resources throughout the [Union] for the benefit of consumers.

This is a more focused statement of a 'pure' economic approach, with the efficient allocation of resources at centre stage, than had previously been found in official material. Similarly, in the *DG Competition Discussion Paper on the Application of Article 82 of the Treaty to Exclusionary Abuses* (December 2005), DG Comp makes frequent references to an 'efficiency defence' for conduct. One of the key elements of modernization is that the application of competition law has been substantially devolved. It will certainly be easier for the 27 national competition authorities to produce consistent results in applying the law if the focus is economic efficiency, rather than the 'workable competition' referred to in *Metro*.

2.3.4 The regulatory organs

2.3.4.1 The EU Commission

Article 105 TFEU confers upon the EU Commission the primary role in the enforcement of Union competition law. This is consistent with the broad function of the Commission as 'guardian of the Treaty', or 'watchdog of the Union'. Rules relating to the Commission are set out in the Treaty at arts 244–49. In addition, art. 17(1) TFEU provides that the Commission should promote the general interest of the Union, ensure compliance with EU law, and exercise specific powers given to it by the Treaties. The Commission consists of 27 Commissioners, nominated by the Member States, and accepted en masse by the European Parliament. Administratively the Commission is divided into Directorates General, with one Directorate General having responsibility for competition policy, which includes the contentious areas of state aids, and merger policy as well as 'antitrust'. A list of the Directorate's personnel and their areas of responsibility is set out at the Commission's website (the address of which is given below at the end of this section).

Following modernization of the enforcement and application of EU competition law the relationship between the Commission and other actors involved in its application underwent a significant change. The Commission's role is now to supervise the operation of competition policy—it occupies a central role in the European Competition Network (see 2.3.4.3 below)—and to play the lead role in the formulation of that policy as change is needed. Some of the secondary legislation gives it exclusive powers—this is particularly the case in respect of the Merger Regulation discussed in Chapter 19. Under Regulation 1/2003 (Chapter 5), the Commission has the power to investigate infringements of the law, and to take appropriate action, on its own initiative, or in response to complaints. However, each Member State is also required to apply the law in specific cases with the use of appropriate national procedures applied by the relevant national competition authority.

The Commission produces an annual report for the European Parliament detailing its activities in competition law over the year. DG Comp also publishes a multilingual quarterly newsletter (*Competition Policy Newsletter*). Press releases, current decisions, and developments may be found on the Commission's website at: **http://ec.europa.eu/ competition/index_en.html.**

2.3.4.2 The Advisory Committee

Article 14 of Regulation 1/2003 makes provision for an Advisory Committee on Restrictive Practices and Dominant Positions. It must be consulted before the Commission takes various decisions, in particular when they have an adverse effect on those to whom they are addressed. The Committee shall be composed of 'representatives of the competition authorities of the Member States' (art. 14(2)), making it an important link between the Commission and the members of the EU. The Commission is required to 'take the utmost account of the opinion delivered by the Advisory Committee' (art. 14(5)). The Committee can also discuss cases under consideration by National Competition Authorities, but cannot deliver a formal opinion in respect of these (art. 14(7) and part 4 of the Commission *Notice on cooperation within the Network of Competition Authorities* (2004) OJ C101/43).

2.3.4.3 National competition authorities, the European Competition Network and national courts

The relationship between EU and national competition law is explored in the following chapter, but it is necessary at this point to introduce the roles of the relevant national competition authorities (NCAs), and the European Competition Network (ECN) in relation to the enforcement of EU competition law. In Regulation 1/2003 the basic role of the national competition authorities is set out at art. 5:

The competition authorities of the Member States shall have the power to apply arts [101] and [102] of the Treaty in individual cases. For this purpose, acting on their own initiative or on a complaint, they may take the following decisions:

— requiring that an infringement be brought to an end,
— ordering interim measures,
— accepting commitments,
— imposing fines, periodic penalty payments or any other penalty provided for in their national law.

They may also decide that there are no grounds for action (see Chapter 5). Prior to May 2004 most NCAs did not have the power to apply arts 101 and 102 TFEU, and because of the legal structure of the EU regime were precluded from applying the legal exception of art. 101(3). Every Member State is now required to designate a relevant authority as an NCA. In the UK the OFT, and sector regulators with concurrent powers (see 2.4.4.1) have been designated.

While this new system has led to a faster resolution of competition cases, it also raises the prospect of inconsistent enforcement of the law. The ECN was established to address these problems. Thus art. 11(1) of Regulation 1/2003 provides that 'the Commission and the competition authorities of the Member States shall apply the [Union] competition rules in close cooperation'. Article 11 imposes the following conditions: The Commission is required to send NCAs copies of important documents in its possession, and NCAs must tell the Commission whenever they commence formal investigative measures. Likewise, when NCAs intend to take any infringement decision, or to accept commitments, or to withdraw the benefit of a block exemption regulation (see Chapter 10), they shall inform the Commission, and provide it with a summary of the case and a copy of the proposed decision. This information may also be made available to the other members of the ECN. The use to which information can be put is restricted by virtue of art. 12 of Regulation 1/2003 (see Chapter 5).

The Commission has produced a *Notice on cooperation within the Network of Competition Authorities* (2004) OJ C101/43, and the OFT—the UK's NCA—published a competition law guideline, *Modernisation: The OFT's application of EC Regulation 1/2003 and the United Kingdom legal exception regime* in December 2004 (OFT 442).

The role of national courts in the application of the law is considered where appropriate throughout this book, and in particular in Chapter 7. Generally the position is that both arts 101 and 102 TFEU may be invoked before national courts because both articles are said to be 'directly effective'. Both obligations and rights flow from them, and although the majority of the case law up to 2004 had been based around defensive measures, an increasing tendency to use the law as a sword (i.e., to seek damages, an injunction, or some form of specific performance) is becoming evident. The principle of 'direct effect' is considered below at 2.3.5.3. Both the Commission and the NCAs are entitled in some cases to reject complaints made to them on the grounds that an investigation of the complaint would not accord with their administrative and enforcement priorities, and that a national court may be a better forum for the dispute to be resolved in.

National courts ruling on directly effective EU law may also have recourse to the procedure set out in art. 267 TFEU. This provides a formal link between any court or tribunal in a Member State and the Court of Justice, giving the latter the ability to 'give preliminary rulings concerning', *inter alia*, '(a) the interpretation of the Treaties'; and '(b) the validity and interpretation of acts of the institutions, bodies, offices or agencies of the Union'. The purpose of the article is to restrict the scope for divergence in the application of EU law by national courts. To that end, national courts or tribunals 'against whose decision there is no judicial remedy' are obliged to 'bring the matter before the Court' (art. 267(3)). Lower courts or tribunals have discretion to refer (art. 267(2)). The article does not serve as an appeal process—questions must be asked in the abstract and the answers provided are unlikely to be such as to determine the outcome of the case on the facts. However, they may often be conclusive on the point of law in question. The jurisdiction of the GC only extends to art. 267 references in those specific areas laid down by the Statute for the Court of Justice (art. 256). Although national courts may be reluctant to involve themselves in areas of law in which they have little expertise, such as is the case with competition issues and the UK courts, the reference procedure should assist them with such matters. The relationship between national courts and the EU Commission was explored in *Masterfoods Ltd* v *HB Ice Cream Ltd*; *HB Ice Cream Ltd* v *Masterfoods Ltd* case C–344/98 [2001] 4 CMLR 14 (see 3.2).

The UK Competition Appeals Tribunal (CAT) is classed as a Tribunal and is competent to refer matters to the Court of Justice. It is probably the case that the OFT is not. In 2005 the Court of Justice ruled that the Greek Competition Commission (*Epitropi Antagonismou*) was *not* competent to make references under art. 267. The Court held that although the body enjoyed operational independence from Government, its members were ministerial appointments, and were subject to dismissal by the minister. Further, the ability of the EU Commission to relieve the authority of any particular case suggested that proceedings initiated before the authority were not of a judicial nature (*Synetairismos Farmakopoion Aitolias & Akarnanias (Syfait)* v *GlaxoSmithKline plc* case C–53/03 [2005] 5 CMLR 1).

2.3.4.4 The Court of Justice, the General Court, and specialized courts

Article 19 TEU provides that the Court of Justice of the European Union—comprising the Court of Justice, the GC and the specialized courts—'shall ensure that in the interpretation and application of the Treaties the law is observed'. Recognizing that the Court of Justice was overstretched, with cases frequently taking two years or more to be heard, the Court of First Instance (known as the General Court since the Lisbon Treaty reform) was created by Council Decision 88/591, and began work in 1989. The GC is now governed by art. 256 TFEU, which provides that it has 'jurisdiction to hear and determine at first instance actions or proceedings' enumerated in the Treaty, 'with the exception of those assigned to a specialised court [...] and those reserved [...] for the Court of Justice'. Furthermore, its decisions may be 'subject to a right of appeal to the Court of Justice on points of law only'. Cases brought under art. 263 TFEU by individuals and undertakings (see 2.3.4.4.1) are included in the GC's jurisdiction, and it is consequently heavily involved in determining matters of competition law. In particular the GC has been determined to ensure that the Commission respect the rights of undertakings against which proceedings are brought. The Lisbon Treaty further provides the possibility to establish specialized courts following the procedure laid down in art. 257 TFEU to alleviate the burden of the Court of Justice and the GC. These courts would 'hear and determine at first instance certain classes of action or proceedings brought in specific areas'. It is likely that in the near future a court that specializes in EU competition law will be created.

The numbers of judges to be appointed to each of the courts, and the qualifications they are required to possess, are set out in the EU Treaty and the TFEU. Both the GC and the Court of Justice function by way of chambers which must contain at least three judges, thus giving the courts the ability to hear several cases simultaneously. The role of the Advocate General, who has no direct equivalent in domestic law, is to assist the Court of Justice (art. 19(2) TEU). This function is fulfilled by way of the opinions delivered to the court at the penultimate stage of the proceedings. The opinion is not binding on the court, which delivers only a single unanimous judgment, but is very often followed. It may be of interest as it is likely to be both more wide ranging and more speculative than the final judgment, which is often terse and focused directly to the point at issue.

As well as its specific roles in relation to arts 263, 265, and 340 TFEU (see 2.4.4.4.1) the Court of Justice may have, in accordance with art. 261 TFEU, unlimited jurisdiction to review the penalties imposed by the Commission on the basis of Regulations adopted by the Council or jointly by the EP and the Council. This includes fines imposed by virtue of Regulation 1/2003. The court 'may cancel, reduce or increase the fine or periodic penalty payment imposed' (Regulation 1/2003, art. 31). At the time of writing there have been no cases in which the Court of Justice has increased the fine imposed by the Commission, but many in which it has reduced it (see Chapter 6).

Appeals from the GC to the Court of Justice can only be made on points of law, within two months of the GC notifying the parties of its decision. Three specific grounds are set out in the Protocol on the Statute of the Court of Justice of the European Union (art. 58):

(a) lack of competence of the GC;

(b) breach of procedure before the GC; and

(c) breach of Union law by the GC.

The Court of Justice will not, therefore, review the GC's own judgments on the facts of the case (*Hilti AG v Commission* case C–53/92P [1994] 4 CMLR 614, and *Deutsche Bahn AG v Commission* case C–436/97P [1999] 5 CMLR 775). Thus, for example, in the case of *Aalborg Portland* the Court of Justice held that appeals to it were to 'be based only on grounds relating to the infringement of rules of law, to the exclusion of any appraisal of the facts' (para. 48). The only occasion on which the Court might be involved in reviewing facts would be where there was 'clear evidence' that the evidence produced before the GC was 'distorted' (para. 49) (*Aalborg Portland A/S v Commission* cases C–204/00 etc. [2005] 4 CMLR 4). Neither will it interfere in the GC's assessment of fines where the latter has in turn considered the penalties imposed by the Commission (*BPB Industries plc and British Gypsum Ltd v Commission* case C–310/93P [1997] 4 CMLR 238). Were such a further review permitted, the benefit of a quicker process offered by the creation of the GC would be lost, merely adding yet another judicial stage to an already drawn-out process.

The operation of the appeals procedures has been subject to criticism from the legal community and business on the grounds that, notwithstanding the introduction of the GC (and a fast-track procedure available in cases where time is of the essence, including mergers), cases progress too slowly. In April 2007, following an initiative of the CBI, the House of Lords published a significant report reviewing the position, and discussing the arguments for the creation of a specialist EU Competition Court

(House of Lords, European Union Committee: 15th Report of Session 2006–07, *An EU Competition Court: Report with Evidence,* HL Paper 75). It took evidence from a number of parties, including officials at DG Comp, and the President of the GC. The EU Committee did not, in the end, support the creation of a new court, arguing that this would be unlikely in itself to lead to great time savings, as it would be faced with the same amount of complex litigation as the GC, and instead recommended changes to current procedures. In particular it was suggested that case management be improved, that the work load of the GC be reduced in other areas, and that changes in the way DG Comp handled cartel cases (e.g., by moving towards settlement—see 5.6) could reduce the amount of litigation following the making of infringement decisions.

The GC and Court of Justice have jurisdiction to review acts taken by the EU Commission or its failures to act, as well as to rule on claims based on non-contractual liability.

2.3.4.4.1 Challenges to the Commission—arts 263, 265, and 340 TFEU

Acts of the EU institutions, including decisions of the Commission, are subject to review by the Court of Justice and GC on various grounds. Articles 263 and 265 provide a procedure akin to judicial review: under the former, acts of the institutions which produce legal effects may be challenged; under the latter, the failure to act may be challenged. Article 340 sets out rules relating to a quasi-tortious liability of the Union for the acts of its servants.

Article 263 provides in part that

The Court of Justice of the European Union shall review the legality of legislative acts...of the Commission...other than recommendations and opinions...

It shall for this purpose have jurisdiction...on grounds of lack of competence, infringement of an essential procedural requirement, infringement of the Treaties or of any rule of law relating to its application, or misuse of powers.

...

Any natural or legal person may...institute proceedings against a decision addressed to that person or against an act addressed to that person or which is of direct and individual concern to them, and against a regulatory act which is of direct concern to them and does not entail implementing measures.

...

The proceedings provided for in this article shall be instituted within two months of the publication of the measure, or of its notification to the plaintiff...

While the protection of the article obviously extends to the decisions with which the Commission imposes penalty payments, which also fall within art. 261, and otherwise enforces the law under Regulation 1/2003 (see Chapter 5), the Court of Justice has held that the article will also apply to a range of other actions relating to competition policy, and can be invoked in circumstances other than where a formal decision has been made. Thus the Court of Justice, in *IBM v Commission* case 60/81 [1981] 3 CMLR 635, held that an act is open to review where 'it is a measure definitively laying down the position of the Commission...and not a provisional measure intended to pave the way for a final decision'. Therefore, the rejection of a complaint may be reviewed (*CICCE v Commission* case 298/83 [1986] 1 CMLR 486), as may a decision to allow a party to proceedings to examine documents obtained by the Commission (*AKZO Chemie BV v Commission* case 53/85 [1987] 1 CMLR 231).

While it might be difficult for parties other than those to whom the decisions are addressed to establish the necessary *locus standi* to mount a challenge under the article, it would appear that any complainant under art. 7(1) of Regulation 1/2003 whose complaint leads to a decision will be able to mount a challenge. This is so because they may be presumed to have 'direct and individual concern'. Such an expansive approach to *locus standi* follows from the analogous anti-dumping case of *Timex Corporation* v *EC Council and Commission* case 264/82 [1985] 3 CMLR 550, where the applicant had been the source of the initial complaint to which the Commission responded. However, the Court has held that the Commission is not required to respond to all complaints by launching a full investigation, and is allowed to determine its own priorities (*Automec srl* v *Commission* case T–24/90 [1992] 5 CMLR 431—see 7.2.1).

The most fruitful grounds for challenge under art. 263 TFEU tend to be that an essential *procedural* requirement has been breached, and both the Court of Justice and the GC would appear now to require scrupulous observance of the procedures on the part of the Commission. Thus in *BASF AG v Commission* cases T–80/89, etc. [1995] ECR II–729, the GC struck down a decision which had not been correctly transposed into all official languages.

The Court of Justice will not inquire into the matters of economic fact on which the Commission has based its decision, but will

limit its review…to verifying whether the relevant procedural rules have been complied with, whether the statement of the reasons for the decision is adequate, whether the facts have been accurately stated and whether there has been any manifest error of appraisal or a misuse of powers. (*Remia BV* v *Commission* case 42/84 [1987] 1 CMLR 1, at para. 34)

However, this formula leaves significant room for the Court to go over the factual grounds relied on by the Commission, and in practice the distinction between a review of the application of the law, and of the factual evidence, can become blurred. In the 'wood pulp' cases (*A. Ahlström oy* v *Commission* cases C–89/85, etc. [1993] 4 CMLR 407) the GC, for example, relied heavily upon economic evidence in rejecting a Commission decision (see further Chapter 9). It does appear to be the case that the GC is more prepared to consider the detail of the facts of the case than is the Court of Justice, which is required to take a somewhat more formal legal approach.

The effect of a successful challenge under art. 263 is, according to art. 264, to render the decision, or the affected parts of it, void. The Commission is not prevented in these circumstances from re-examining the matter.

Article 265 provides that

Should the…Commission…in infringement of the Treaties, fail to act, the Member States and the other institutions of the Union may bring an action before the Court of Justice of the European Union to have the infringement established…

The action shall be admissible only if the institution...concerned has first been called upon to act. If, within two months of being so called upon, the institution...concerned has not defined its position, the action may be brought within a further period of two months.

Any natural or legal person may, under the conditions laid down in the preceding paragraphs, complain to the Court that an institution...of the Union has failed to address to that person any act other than a recommendation or an opinion.

Article 265 is less likely to form the basis of successful applications to the Court of Justice. In part this is because there are fewer situations in which it is likely to be invoked in practice, and in part because the obligation on the Commission is only to define its position. It may fulfil this obligation by an action that falls some way short of a decision reviewable under art. 263 (see, e.g., *Spijker Kwasten v Commission* case 231/82 [1984] 2 CMLR 284), as it does not owe a complainant the duty to take a final decision (*GEMA v Commission* case 125/78 [1980] 2 CMLR 177). The effect of a successful action is to require the Commission to take the necessary steps to merely define its position (see further Chapter 7).

Article 340 provides in part that

In the case of non-contractual liability, the Union shall, in accordance with the general principles common to the laws of the Member States, make good any damage caused by its institutions or by its servants in the performance of their duties.

Although this provision is rarely invoked it would cover, for example, the situation in which Commission officials exceeded their powers in the process of carrying out any investigations authorized by Regulation 1/2003 and caused damage in the process. Article 268 provides that any disputes founded on art. 340(2) shall be heard by the Court of Justice. One case in which the applicant was successful was that of *Adams v Commission* case 145/83 [1986] 1 CMLR 506. This arose from a notorious incident in which Stanley Adams, an Englishman working in Switzerland, had provided to the Commission evidence of infringements of competition law by his employer. When the Commission returned documents to the undertaking they were so labelled as to reveal the identity of the informant, who subsequently faced prosecution under Swiss domestic law. The Court held that the Commission was liable to Mr Adams for its negligence in revealing the source of the complaint. The case became famous following the broadcast of a TV film, *A Song For Europe*, starring David Suchet as Stanley Adams.

More significantly art. 340 may also be invoked where the Commission has wrongfully blocked a merger, and may form the basis of an action for damages brought by the wronged undertakings. This was the case in *Schneider Electric SA v Commission* case T–351/03, judgment of 11 July 2007 (see 19.2.5).

2.3.5 Subsidiarity, the duties of the Member States, and conflicts between domestic and Union law

The relationship between EU law and the national legal regimes is governed by various constitutional principles. Some of these are set out in the TFEU, and others have been developed by the Court of Justice in its jurisprudence.

2.3.5.1 Article 5 TEU—subsidiarity

Article 5(3) of the TEU provides that

Under the principle of subsidiarity, in areas which do not fall within its exclusive competence, the Union shall act only if and in so far as the objectives of the proposed action cannot be sufficiently achieved by the Member States, either at central level or at regional and local level, but can rather, by reason of the scale or effects of the proposed action, be better achieved at Union level.

When the concept of subsidiarity was introduced in 1993, many commentators pointed out that, at least with respect to competition law, the principle had been in operation from the inception of the Treaty. EU jurisdiction is established only where trade between Member States is likely to be affected by the conduct in question, and, although this test has been interpreted expansively (see, e.g., *La Technique Minière* v *Maschinenbau Ulm GmbH* case 56/65 [1966] 1 CMLR 357), it serves to curtail greatly the circumstances in which EU competition rules apply. This, in turn, leaves a large measure of discretion to national governments in the structure and operation of their domestic competition law regimes. The concept of 'trade between Member States' is explored more fully in the following chapter, as is the refined relationship between the EU Commission and the Member States in the application of EU competition law. Perhaps the clearest expression of the principle of subsidiarity may be found in Regulation 139/2004 relating to the control of mergers under EU law. Here the powers of the EU Commission and of the Member States are exclusive save in tightly defined circumstances. In essence, where mergers may have substantial cross-border impacts it is probable that they will be subject to the jurisdiction of the Commission. Where they seem to affect primarily a single state they are likely to fall within the jurisdiction of that state.

2.3.5.2 The principle of supremacy of EU law

Article 4(3) TEU provides that Member States shall

take any appropriate measure, general or particular, to ensure fulfilment of the obligations arising out of the Treaties or resulting from the acts of the institutions of the Union.

The Member States shall facilitate the achievement of the Union's tasks and refrain from any measure which could jeopardise the attainment of the Union's objectives.

This duty of sincere cooperation applies equally to the measures relating to competition law as to any other obligation, although in this context art. 105 TFEU (see 2.3.2.3) is also relevant in defining the roles of the Commission and the Member States, as is Regulation 1/2003.

Where Union law exists it is supreme in relation to national law (*Costa* v *ENEL* case 6/64 [1964] CMLR 425), and will prevail in the event of there being any conflict. This principle of the supremacy, developed by the Court of Justice, extends even to provisions of national constitutions (*Internationale Handelsgesellschaft mbH* case 11/70 [1972] 1 CMLR 255, and in relation to Acts of Parliament—see *R* v *Secretary of State for Transport, ex parte Factortame Ltd* case C–213/89 [1990] 3 CMLR 1). The Court of Justice ruled on the matter specifically in relation to competition law in *Wilhelm v Bundeskartellamt* case 14/68 [1969] CMLR 100, holding that where German cartel laws conflicted with EU law the latter must take precedence.

The relationship between EU and national competition law has been clearly spelled out in Regulation 1/2003, art. 3 (see Chapter 3).

2.3.5.3 Direct effect

In the landmark case of *NV Algemene Transport-en Expeditie Onderneming Van Gend en Loos* v *Nederlandse Belastingadministratie* case 26/62 [1963] 1 CMLR 105, the Court of Justice established that where articles of the Treaty are clear, precise, and unconditional they are capable of creating rights vested in individuals which can be enforced against Member States ('vertical direct effect') in national courts. In *Defrenne* v *Sabena (No. 2)* case 43/75 [1976] 2 CMLR 98, the principle was extended to allow such rights to be enforced against other persons not being part of the state ('horizontal direct effect'). The principle applies equally to regulations, which are, by the wording of art. 288 'binding in [their] entirety and directly applicable in all Member States'. Articles 101 and 102 both have direct effect.

The first competition case in the UK in which this principle was clearly recognized was that of *Garden Cottage Foods Ltd* v *Milk Marketing Board* [1983] 2 All ER 770, HL, where Lord Diplock suggested that a breach of EU law may give rise to a remedy for damages for breach of a statutory duty. It has been suggested that the judgment of the Court of Justice in the case of *Francovich* v *Italian Republic* cases C–6 and 9/90 [1993] 2 CMLR 66, in which it was established that a Member State becomes liable for its breaches of Union law to those who can show harm as a result of the breach where an identifiable right has been infringed, further increases the pressure for national courts to find remedies for those injured by breaches of directly effective competition provisions. There is now no doubt as to the role that the direct effect of EU competition law plays in the Union legal order, and cases are regularly brought on the basis of the application of this principle. The House of Lords confirmed the position in the UK in the now leading case of *Inntrepreneur Pub Company (CPC) and others* v *Crehan* [2006] UKHL 38 (see also 9.4). Private actions generally are discussed in Chapter 7.

2.4 **The United Kingdom**

2.4.1 **Introduction**

Although the UK has a rich history of competition law (see Chapter 1), there is a clean break between earlier laws, and the post-war system of competition control. This post-war system has itself been almost completely replaced by the two key statutes, the Competition Act 1998 (CA 98) and the Enterprise Act 2002 (EA 02). These apply competition law to most sectors of the economy, and even where some sectors—such as utilities—operate under special regimes, the competition rules of these Acts are generally applicable to them, although the body applying the law may vary. For discussion of the earlier law—including the Restrictive Trade Practices Acts 1976 and 1977 which may still be invoked in rare circumstances—refer to older competition law texts.

2.4.2 The Competition Act 1998

The CA 98 relates primarily to the control of agreements between two or more undertakings, for which provision is made in the 'Chapter I Prohibition', and to abuses committed by dominant firms, the 'Chapter II Prohibition'. The Act also provides the necessary investigative and enforcement powers, although these are supplemented by statutory instruments. The Act repealed much of the then existing competition law legislation. The prohibitions of the Act came into force on 1 March 2000, subject to certain transitional provisions. At the time of the Act's enactment the Government made clear that its overriding objective was to reduce the burdens on industry by aligning domestic law with Union law:

To ensure smooth interaction between the [EU] legal and business environment and the UK prohibitions, we intend that the UK prohibitions would be interpreted in a manner consistent with the equivalent provisions under [EU] law. Clause 58 of the Bill [s. 60] has this effect. Such consistency would be of great benefit to so many of our businesses that currently have to worry about two different approaches to competition policy. It delivers a level playing field for our business community in the UK as firms become more and more engaged in European home markets.   (Lord Simon, Hansard (HL) 30 October 1997, col. 1145)

The substantive provisions of the Act are intended to operate in much the same way as is the case in the application of EU competition law, and to this end s. 60 of the Act requires those enforcing it to follow EU law unless there is a 'relevant difference'. This provision is discussed fully in the following chapter. The Chapter I and II Prohibitions are discussed in detail in Chapters 11, 15, and 16, and procedure is dealt with in Chapters 5–8. The Office of Fair Trading has published a number of guides to the operation of the Act, which are available on its website, **www.oft.gov.uk**.

Amendments to the CA 98 were made by the EA 02 (see below), and further amendments were made in 2004 to accommodate the EU modernization process by way of the CA 98 and Other Enactments (Amendment) Regulations 2004, SI 2004/1261.

2.4.3 The Enterprise Act 2002

The EA 02 reformed those areas of law which had been largely untouched by the CA 98: merger control is dealt with in Chapter 20, and market investigation references which replaced the monopoly investigations of the Fair Trading Act 1973 are discussed in Chapter 17. The Act also introduced a new cartel offence, as well as competition disqualification orders (CDOs). These stand apart from the rest of competition law in that they are directed to individuals. The offence permits the imposition of gaol sentences and very high fines. This is discussed in Chapter 12. CDOs are analysed in Chapter 6.

2.4.4 **The regulatory organs**

In the UK, the key organs in the application of competition law are the OFT, the CC, and the CAT. These are explained below. Currently, there are talks of a major institutional overhaul, as the Coalition government has suggested merging the OFT and the CC (see Preston, R., 'OFT and Competition Commission Likely to Merge' (16 September 2010) *BBC News*), as well as creating a new unit to fight economic crime that would be in charge of applying the cartel offence (see 'Conservatives Confirm Plans for a Single Economic Crime Agency' (26 April 2010) *Times Online*).

2.4.4.1 The Office of Fair Trading

The Office of Fair Trading existed prior to the introduction of the CA 98, but it was put on to a new footing by the EA 02. The provisions relating to the OFT are ss. 1–8 and Sch. 1. Section 1 of the Act puts the OFT on a firm statutory footing. Thus the OFT becomes a Non-ministerial Government Department, and is a Crown body. Section 2 abolished the office of the Director General of Fair Trading (the Director), and earlier case law and decisions will still refer to the Director rather than to the OFT, which was a body supporting the Director.

The general functions of the OFT, set out in ss. 5–8, are the acquisition of information, the provision of information to the public (for example the OFT is required to publish an annual plan and an annual report) and the provision of information and advice to ministers. More detailed rules relating to the constitution of the new OFT are set out in Sch. 1, of which para. 1 provides that the OFT itself 'shall consist of a chairman, and no fewer than four other members appointed by the Secretary of State'. The terms of appointment are to be determined by the Minister, but shall not exceed five years, although this may be renewable. Once the Chairman and other members are appointed, they may be removed by the Minister only on grounds of 'incapacity or misbehaviour'. Internal rules of procedure are published by the OFT on its website (**www.oft.gov.uk**).

The primary roles of the OFT in the sphere of competition law are: to act as the lead NCA in the UK, applying arts 101 and 102 or assisting the EU Commission as appropriate; to enforce the Chapter I and II Prohibitions of the CA 98; to review mergers and possibly to refer them to the Competition Commission (CC—see 2.4.4.2); to conduct reviews of markets and possibly to make market investigation references to the CC; and to act as the body with primary responsibility for investigating breaches of the cartel offence, although in the investigation and prosecution of such offences it will act in partnership with the Serious Fraud Office in England and Wales, and with the Procurator Fiscal in Scotland (see Chapter 12). The OFT has struggled somewhat with its workload under the CA 98 and the EA 02, and has gone through substantial changes in the years since the Competition Act came into force. It has been criticized in a significant number of cases by the CAT (see 2.4.4.3), and both the National Audit Office and the Parliamentary Public Accounts Committee have attacked it for being too slow and insufficiently targeted in the cases and work it takes on. The OFT has responded to these criticisms, and has adopted internal procedures designed to ensure that its case load is manageable and directed to those areas in which it will make the most significant impact (see OFT, *Competition prioritisation framework,* October 2006).

In relation to a number of industries—water, gas and electricity, rail transport, communications, civil aviation, and the postal service—the special sector regulators appointed to manage competition in those industries have the power to apply the Competition Act and other provisions, including arts 101 and 102 TFEU as appropriate. These are referred to as the 'concurrent regulators'. A concurrency working group exists to coordinate the work of these bodies with that of the OFT.

Following the modernization of EU competition law, and the change in the relationship between EU and national law, the OFT prepared a number of guidelines, which are a useful and free resource that attempt to explain clearly the relevant law. As appropriate they are referred to throughout this text.

2.4.4.2 The Competition Commission

It is vitally important that the UK Competition Commission (CC—among competition professionals the CC is often referred to as 'CoCo') *not* be confused with the EU Commission. The CC was a creation of the CA 98, and replaced the earlier Monopolies and Mergers Commission (MMC). The CC is the body charged, under the general competition legislation, with investigating and enforcing mergers and market investigation references when these are referred to it by the OFT. It does not have the power to initiate its own actions. The CC also has a role in relation to certain specific sector regulations, but this is not dealt with in this text. For a broad discussion of the role of the CC, see the CC's publication, *General Advice and Information Guidance.* The CC has also published its rules of procedure. All CC documents are available on the CC website, **www.competition-commission.org.uk**.

The CC rules of procedure set out the rules applicable to references under the EA 02. In each case reference groups are established (i.e., merger reference groups, and market reference groups). Each group must consist of at least three persons, one of whom may, but need not necessarily, be the Chairman of the CC. The Chairman of the CC or, in his or her absence, a Deputy Chairman, may attend meetings of any group and offer advice, which the group is bound to have regard to. However, the Chairman or the Deputy may not vote unless they are serving on the relevant group. Currently, the Chairman of the CC is Peter Freeman. The role of the CC in relation to the specific areas of competition law is set out in each of the relevant chapters.

2.4.4.3 The Competition Appeals Tribunal

The Competition Appeals Tribunal (CAT) took over the functions of the Competition Commission Appeals Tribunal (CCAT) established under the CA 98. For the sake of simplicity, in this text the name CAT is used, even where this may be historically inaccurate. The CAT is an independent tribunal, and hears appeals in relation to the Chapter I and II Prohibitions, and decisions taken by both the OFT and CC in relation to market investigation references and mergers, as well as in relation to the application of EU competition law by the OFT. It may also hear claims brought under provisions set out in the Enterprise Act for damages where there has been an infringement decision made by the OFT, or other appropriate body (see 7.3.1.2). The CAT has no role in relation to the cartel offence. In the case of *Napp Pharmaceutical Holdings Ltd v The Director General of Fair Trading* [2002] EWCA Civ 796, [2002] UKCLR 726 the Court of Appeal recognized that the CAT was 'an expert and specialist tribunal, specifically constituted by Parliament to make judgments in an area in which judges have no expertise' (*per* Buxton LJ at para. 34). As such it fell into the category identified in *Cooke* v *Secretary of State for Social Security* [2002] All ER 279 as being a body whose judgments the Court of Appeal would be reluctant to interfere with. This is not to say, however, that an appeal from a judgment of the CAT would always be fruitless. In a case relating to merger control in 2005 the Court of Appeal substantially overturned a CAT judgment relating to the relevant standard to be applied by the OFT (*OFT* v *IBA Health Ltd* [2004] EWCA Civ 142, [2004] UKCLR 683—see further Chapter 20).

The provisions relating to the CAT, and the Competition Service which supports it (see below), are to be found in ss. 12–16 of and in Schs 2–5 to the EA 02. It was created by s. 12, and consists of a President appointed by the Lord Chancellor, and further members. The current President is Sir Gerald Barling, QC, and the first President was Sir Christopher Bellamy, a former judge at the GC and an expert competition lawyer. Members may be either appointed as ordinary members or to form a panel of Chairmen for a term of no more than eight years. The Lord Chancellor is responsible for the appointment of the President and the panel of Chairmen, while the Secretary of State bears a similar responsibility for ordinary members. Appointments are made on a part-time basis, and ordinary members will be able to continue with their 'day jobs' (see Sch. 2 for details).

In any proceeding before the Tribunal, it shall consist of a Chairman, who must be either the President or a member of the panel of Chairmen, and two other members. Decisions are to be made by majority vote, in any case where there is not unanimous agreement (s. 14). They may be enforced by the High Court in England and Wales (Sch. 4, para. 2), or may be recorded for execution in the Books of Council and Session in Scotland (Sch. 4, para. 3). In Northern Ireland, decisions may be enforced with the leave of the High Court in Northern Ireland (Sch. 4, para. 5). Part 2 of Sch. 4 makes provision for the Tribunal Rules which may be adopted by the CAT. The matters covered include the institution of proceedings, the possibility of holding pre-hearing reviews, the conduct of the hearing, quorum of the Tribunal, fees to be chargeable 'in respect of specified costs of proceedings', and interim orders.

The CAT is supported by the Competition Service, whose role is 'to fund, and provide support services to' the CAT (s. 13). Schedule 3 puts more detail on the bare bones of s. 13. The Competition Service consists of the President and the Registrar of the CAT, and at least one member appointed by the Secretary of State in consultation with the President of the CAT.

2.4.4.4 The Secretary of State for Business, Innovation and Skills

One of the most significant aspects of the reform of domestic competition law was to greatly reduce the powers of the Secretary of State for Business, Innovation and Skills (previously the Secretary of State for Trade and Industry), who had previously played an important function in the application of the regime. Following the changes to the system made by the EA 02 the role of the Secretary of State is largely limited to making special interventions in merger and market reference investigations on public interest grounds. These are tightly defined in the legislation, as explained in the relevant chapters.

2.4.4.5 The national courts

As well as having a role in applying arts 101 and 102 in disputes brought before them the relevant national courts may also apply the Chapter I and II Prohibitions, and may hear certain claims based on damage following breaches of orders made or undertakings given in relation to merger and market investigation references. These are dealt with primarily in Chapter 7, but also as appropriate in the text.

FURTHER READING

Books

CRAIG, P., and DE BÚRCA, G., *EU Law: Text, Cases and Materials* (2007) 4th edn, Oxford University Press, Oxford

Articles

DEMETRIOU, M., 'Preliminary References and Competition Law', [2002] *Competition Law Journal* 345

LOURI, V., ' "Undertaking" as a Jurisdictional Element in EC Competition Rules', (2002) *Legal Issues in European Integration* 143

WILS, W. P. J., 'The Undertaking as Subject of EC Competition Law and the Imputation of Infringements to Natural or Legal Persons', (2000) 25 *European Law Review* 99

3

The relationship between European Union and United Kingdom competition law

KEY POINTS

- EU law takes precedence over Member State law in the event of any conflict.

- Where a national competition authority applies its own competition law to a situation in which art. 101 TFEU might be applied, it *must* also apply art. 101 TFEU, and it ought not reach a result inconsistent with this.

- In the application of national laws relating to monopoly abuse, art. 102 TFEU must also be applied, but a stricter standard can be set under national law.

- EU competition law can only be applied where there is an effect on trade between Member States.

- The UK has largely aligned its competition law to that of the EU. In some areas differences remain, but these differences should not give rise to conflicts with EU law.

3.1 Introduction

The relationship between EU competition law and national competition law is a complex one. It has been clarified by legislation (Regulation 1/2003 on the implementation of the rules of competition laid down in arts 101 and 102 of the Treaty (2003) OJ L1/1) but the position is not simple despite the straightforwardness of the basic principles. Articles 101 and 102 TFEU (which are discussed respectively in Chapters 9 and 14) apply only in situations in which trade between Member States may be affected, as discussed in this chapter. In such scenarios national competition law may also be applied, but may not reach a result which frustrates the application of EU law. When anti-competitive agreements are made, or when there is an abuse of a dominant position and trade is not affected, the matter is exclusively one for national law. In practice Member States have aligned their competition laws with the laws of the EU so as to clarify and simplify the position for companies subject to the legislation. This tendency has been particularly pronounced in the UK where the Competition Act 1998 was introduced expressly to bring the domestic system into line with that of the EU. In the case of merger control (dealt with in Chapters 19 and 20) the EU and domestic systems are stark alternatives—a merger may be evaluated under either, but not both, of the regimes, and if the EU asserts jurisdiction this is exclusive save in specified limited circumstances.

3.2 General principles governing the relationship between EU and national competition law

In any case where there is a conflict between Union and national law, Union law takes precedence. This duty on Member States is not specifically set out in the Treaty, but has been clarified by the Court of Justice in a number of cases, starting with *Costa* v *ENEL* case 6/64 [1964] CMLR 425. It is also implicit in the concept of direct effect, which recognizes that duties are owed by Member States to their citizens on the basis of EU law. In the UK the matter was resolved beyond all doubt in *R* v *Secretary of State for Transport, ex parte Factortame Ltd (Factortame II)* [1990] 3 CMLR 1, in which the Court of Justice confirmed, as in the light of its own previous case law it was bound to do, that the operation of even Acts of Parliament should be set aside where they would conflict with Union obligations. The judiciary have accepted that this means that 'the Treaty of Rome is the supreme law of this country, taking precedence over acts of parliament' (*Stoke-on-Trent City Council* v *B&Q plc* [1990] 3 CMLR 31, *per* Hoffmann LJ). This principle is applied particularly in the light of art. 4(3) TEU (former art. 10 EC). This provision has been widely interpreted by the Court and been used as the foundation for a range of duties imposed on the Member States and authorities which are emanations of the state. Article 4(3) provides that

The Member States shall take any appropriate measure, general or particular, to ensure fulfilment of the obligations arising out of the Treaties or resulting from the acts of the institutions of the Union.

The Member States shall facilitate the achievement of the Union's tasks and refrain from any measure which could jeopardise the attainment of the Union's objectives.

In relation to competition law, in the landmark case of *Wilhelm* v *Bundeskartellamt* case 14/68 [1969] CMLR 100, the Court of Justice accepted the possibility of divergence between Union and national law, but held that 'parallel application of the national system should only be allowed in so far as it does not impinge upon the uniform application, throughout the [Internal] Market, of the [Union] rules' (para. 6). This conclusion followed inevitably from the imperative force of Union law over national law, and from the application of art. 4(3) TEU: it would be incompatible with the Treaty to allow national laws to obstruct the aims of the Treaty. However, national authorities would be acting within their powers where they intervene against an agreement, in application of their internal law, even when the examination of the position of that agreement with regard to the [Union] rules is pending before the Commission, subject, however, to the proviso that such application of the national law may not prejudice the full and uniform application of the [Union] law. (para. 7)

A similar position was reached in *GB-INNO-BM NV* v *Vereniging van de Kleinhandelaars in Tabak* case 13/77 [1978] 1 CMLR 283, concerning the relationship of a provision of Belgian law with aspects of EU competition and trade rules. Here the Court held, *inter alia*, that the

Treaty imposes a duty on member-states not to adopt or maintain in force any measure which could deprive [art. 102] of its effectiveness…[and] Member States may not enact measures enabling private undertakings to escape from the constraints imposed by art. [101]. (paras 31 and 33)

Where a practice has been condemned at Union level it cannot be allowed to continue on the grounds that it is not condemned under national law. By way of example, in *Vereniging van Samenwerkende Prijsregelende Organisaties in de Bouwnijverheid (SPO)* v *Commission* case I–29/92 [1995] ECR–II 289, a cartel operating in the Dutch building industry was condemned by the Commission despite having been expressly approved by the Dutch Minister of Economic Affairs.

In the case of *Masterfoods Ltd* v *HB Ice Cream Ltd*; *HB Ice Cream Ltd* v *Masterfoods Ltd* case C–344/98 [2001] 4 CMLR 14, which demonstrates clearly problems that could arise in relation to the application of two legal situations to the same conduct, the administrative relationship between the application of EU competition law by the Commission and by the national courts was explored in some detail. In this case, which arose out of challenges to ice cream freezer cabinet exclusivity in Ireland, the Irish courts and the Commission were, independently, considering the same agreements in the light of the application of art. 101. The Irish High Court had found that the freezer exclusivity agreements were not restrictive of competition, and had injuncted another undertaking from placing its products in HB's freezers. The Commission, on the other hand, found that HB's agreements were in breach of art. 101(1) (in *Van den Bergh Foods Ltd* 98/531 (1998) OJ L246/1), although at the time at which the case was heard the operation of the Commission decision had been suspended by the GC (*Van den Bergh Foods* v *Commission* case T–65/98R [1998] 5 CMLR 475). The fact that the Commission decision was contested before the GC was clearly a factor that made the waters even more muddy than they were to begin with.

The question of how to avoid inconsistent application of competition law between national courts and the EU institutions was 'the central issue' in the case, as Advocate General Cosmas recognized (para. A14). He first noted that the facts examined by the Commission and the national court were not the same, as they related to different time periods, and it was theoretically possible (although on a reading of the case unlikely) that the agreements could have not been restrictive of competition at one time, but been restrictive at another. In *Stergios Delimitis* v *Henninger Bräu* case C–234/89 [1992] 5 CMLR 210 the Court had held that the handing down of conflicting decisions was contrary to the principle of legal certainty, and 'must therefore be avoided when national courts give decisions on agreements or practices which may subsequently be the subject of a decision by the Commission' (at para. 47). In the present case however, the *Delimitis* principles had already been breached as there was 'not merely a potential, but a clear and imminent, conflict between the decision of the first instance Irish court and a decision of the Commission that has already been adopted' (para. A25). The risk was that the Irish Supreme Court, from which the reference was taken, might also produce a decision that was in conflict with that of the Commission.

The Court held that

where a national court is ruling on an agreement or practice the compatibility of which with articles [101](1) and [102] of the Treaty is already the subject of a Commission decision, it cannot take a decision running counter to that of the Commission, even if the latter's decision conflicts with a decision given by a national court of first instance.   (para. 60)

Regulation 1/2003 has now made express provision for the relationship between national courts and the Commission in the application of arts 101 and 102 TFEU. In particular, art. 16(1) of the regulation provides that

When national courts rule on agreements, decisions or practices under art. [101] or art. [102] of the Treaty which are already the subject of a Commission decision they cannot take decisions running counter to the decision adopted by the Commission. They must also avoid giving decisions which would conflict with a decision contemplated by the Commission in proceedings it has initiated.

Article 15 of the regulation provides for a cooperative approach between the courts and the Commission: courts may ask the Commission for information in its possession, or for opinions; copies of judgments made by national courts are to be forwarded to the Commission by the NCAs; and NCAs may make observations to the courts in writing, and, with the permission of the court, orally. The Commission also may, 'where the coherent application of art. [101] or art. [102] of the Treaty so requires…acting on its own initiative, submit written observations to courts of the member states' (art. 15(3), and see generally *Commission Notice on the cooperation between the Commission and the courts of the EU Member States in the application of articles 81 and 82 EC* (2004) OJ C101/65). However, there is no mechanism by which the Commission will be automatically informed of procedures before the national courts prior to the making of any judgment. While its opinions are only that, the requirements of art. 16 (added to the inexperience of most national courts with the application of competition law) are likely to ensure that they are highly persuasive.

That tensions can still arise in the application of the principles of EU competition law by national courts is evident in the judgment of the House of Lords in *Inntrepreneur Pub Company (CPC) and others v Crehan* [2006] UKHL 38 (see also 9.4). The case had a long and complex history, flowing from the application by pub owners of 'beer ties' on licensees. Following an action by Mr Crehan seeking damages against Inntrepreneur on the grounds of a breach of art. 101 TFEU the judge at first instance found that no infringement had taken place. This was overturned at the Court of Appeal and an award of damages was made in the sum of £130,000. The Court of Appeal referred aspects of the case to the Court of Justice, which ruled that national courts were obliged to give effect to art. 101. For the House of Lords the question was that of whether the judge at first instance had been correct to make his own decision which was not at first blush entirely consistent with the approach of the Commission in similar cases. Lord Hoffmann held that it fell to the English court to determine the application of art. 101 TFEI, and that it did so exercising concurrent jurisdiction with the EU Commission. As a matter of law, however, it was not possible, Lord Hoffmann argued, 'to see how the exercise of this power can be combined with "deference" to someone else' (para. 69). The fact that the Commission had made decisions in similar cases was 'only part of the evidence' which the court would take into account, and if 'upon an assessment of all the evidence, the judge comes to the conclusion that the view of the Commission was wrong [it would not be consistent] with his judicial oath [to] nevertheless follow the Commission' (ibid.). The House of Lords held, in effect, that the Court of Appeal had shown undue deference to Commission decisions and that in the present case there was no issue—as there had been in *Masterfoods*—of outright conflict in the application of the law. The response of the Lords was criticized by a number of leading competition lawyers, who argued that the result would be to deter private actions (see, e.g., *Financial Times*, 20 July 2006, 'Ruling Seen as Blow to Anti-Competitive Cases').

3.3 Changes introduced by the 'modernization package' and Regulation 1/2003

Regulation 1/2003 made a number of significant changes to the application of competition law in the EU. The two most important of these are to some extent interlinked: conferring direct effect upon all of art. 101, and setting out clear rules on the relationship between national and Union law. Recitals (8) and (9), and art. 3 are the key provisions in this latter respect. Article 3 is set out here in its entirety given its importance:

(1)   Where the competition authorities of the member states or national courts apply competition law to agreements, decisions by associations of undertakings or concerted practices within the meaning of art. [101](1) of the Treaty which may affect trade between member states within the meaning of that provision, they shall also apply art. [101] of the Treaty to such agreements, decisions or concerted practices. Where the competition authorities of the member states or national courts apply national competition law to any abuse prohibited by art. [102] of the Treaty, they shall also apply art. [102] of the Treaty.

(2)   The application of national competition law may not lead to the prohibition of agreements, decisions by associations of undertakings or concerted practices which may affect trade between member states but which do not restrict competition within the meaning of art. [101](1) of the Treaty or fulfil the conditions for the application of art. [101](3) of the Treaty or which are covered by a Regulation for the application of art.

[101](3) of the Treaty. Member states shall not under this Regulation be precluded from adopting and applying on their territory stricter national laws which prohibit or sanction unilateral conduct engaged in by undertakings.

(3)   Without prejudice to general principles and other provisions of [Union] law, paras (1) and (2) do not apply when the competition authorities and the courts of member states apply national merger control laws nor do they preclude the application of provisions of national law that predominantly pursue an objective different from that pursued by arts [101] and [102] of the Treaty.

The core elements of this article are, therefore, as follows: (1) in any situation in which art. 101 is relevant it shall be enforced, even if national law is also being applied; (2) national law cannot reach a different result, and in particular it *may not* prohibit an agreement that is permitted under art. 101; (3) art. 101 shall be applied even if national law is also being enforced, but national law may be stricter than art. 102; (4) where objectives which are not competition objectives are present, such as for example the social objectives that accompany a universal provision requirement, it is not necessary to apply arts 101 or 102. There is uncertainty within the UK as to what legislation specifically would be considered to predominantly pursue an objective different from that pursued by arts 101 and 102 TFEU. There is also an implication that the goals of arts 101 and 102 are primarily 'competition' based, although as explained in the previous chapter there has in the past been a recognition from both the EU Commission and the European courts that competition law serves wider Union objectives than would be suggested by a 'pure competition' test. The sector-specific regulators in the UK are to publish guidance which deals, *inter alia*, with this aspect.

The full ramifications of art. 3 can be seen in a case brought in England in 2004 in which the complainant relied in part on the operation of the restraint of trade doctrine (see Chapter 23). This is an ancient part of the common law of England and Wales, and has traditionally been seen as being less about competition than about the liberty of the subject. In that case, however, the court held that its ability to apply the doctrine was restricted—or would have been restricted had the case been heard later in the year—by the requirements of art. 101 that the court felt obliged to apply by virtue of art. 3 of Regulation 1/2003 (*Days Medical Aids Ltd* v *Pihsiang Machinery Manufacturing Co. Ltd* [2004] EWHC 44 (Comm) at paras 265–6).

It will be noted that although a stricter approach can be applied by a national authority under national law to conduct which is an abuse of a dominant position falling within art. 102 EU, it cannot take a tougher stance on agreements falling within art. 101. The logic underpinning this is that the application of art. 101 implies an assessment of both the advantages and disadvantages of an agreement, and that if there are no disadvantages then the agreement may be presumed to be beneficial. This is very strongly the case in respect of the third paragraph of art. 101—the 'legal exception'—as here there is an express authorization, on the grounds that benefits will flow, of a practice that would otherwise be illegal. Therefore, it might be argued that to condemn an agreement that passes these hurdles would be equivalent to frustrating one of the aims of EU competition policy. In the case of art. 102, however, there is no such reasoning. The article deals exclusively with 'abuse', a loaded term, pejorative in nature, and the fact that something is not an abuse says little about its value. Above all, there is no express permissive part of the article. It is also the case, less logically but equally importantly, that some Member States lobbied to retain the power to control further dominant firm conduct at the time the regulation was being drafted.

The OFT has set out its response to the requirements of art. 3 in its *Modernisation Guideline* (December 2004). The thrust of the UK's response is set out at para. 4.28 which is in the following terms:

Where the Regulators apply the Chapter I and/or Chapter II prohibitions, and there may be an effect on trade between Member States, they are also obliged, by Article 3 of the Modernisation Regulation, to apply Articles [101] and/or [102].

Wherever the OFT is applying a penalty in respect of breaches of arts [101] or [102] it will take into account any penalties imposed in relation to breaches of the Chapter I Prohibition and the Chapter II Prohibition (the issue of penalties is dealt with in Chapter 6).

3.4 'Trade between Member States' as a jurisdictional limit to the application of EU competition law

3.4.1 The interpretation given by the case law

The boundary line between EU and domestic law is determined according to whether the practice in question may affect trade between Member States. Thus, art. 101(1) TFEU prohibits anti-competitive agreements 'which may affect trade between member states', and art. 102 TFEU prohibits any abuse of a dominant position 'in so far as it may affect trade between Member States'. The purpose of the provision is

to define, in the context of the law governing competition, the boundary between the areas respectively covered by [Union] law and the law of the Member States. Thus [Union] law covers any agreement or any practice which is capable of constituting a threat to freedom of trade between Member States in a manner which might harm the attainment of the objectives of a single market between the Member States, in particular by partitioning the national markets or by affecting the structure of competition within the [Internal] Market. On the other hand conduct the effects of which are confined to the territory of a single Member State is governed by the national legal order.   (*Hugin Kassaregister AB and Hugin Cash Registers Ltd* v *Commission* case 22/78 [1979] 3 CMLR 345, at 373)

In practice it will not be difficult to show that most transactions of any real size are capable of affecting trade between Member States, and the Court's definitive statement of the meaning of the requirement in *Société Technique Minière* v *Maschinenbau Ulm* case 56/65 [1966] ECR 235 does not provide a very satisfactory clarification: 'it must be possible to foresee with a sufficient degree of probability on the basis of a set of objective factors of law or of fact that the agreement in question may have an influence, direct or indirect, actual or potential, on the pattern of trade between the Member States' (at 249; the problems with translation of cases become apparent if the alternative report, [1966] CMLR 357, at 375, is referred to, as the wording is substantially different, although the sense is not altered).

An extreme reading of this report ('possible to foresee an indirect potential influence on the pattern of trade') would permit the application of EU law to almost any situation.

3.4.2 **Appreciability—the Commission Notice on the effect of trade**

As part of the modernization package the EU Commission published its *Guidelines on the effect of trade concept contained in articles 81 and 82 of the Treaty* (2004) OJ C101/97. For EU jurisdiction to apply there must be an effect on trade, and that effect must be appreciable. It is made clear that the requirement 'is an autonomous [Union] law criterion, which must be assessed separately in each case' (para. 12). The concept of trade does not refer only to the flow of goods, but covers 'all cross-border economic activity including establishment' (para. 19). Thus, for example, an abuse which prevented a new undertaking entering a market held by the abuser might fall within the rubric, even though the entrant was not actually providing goods at the time. Any practice which affects the competitive structure of the market will, according to the existing case law, affect trade between Member States. It is also the case that a practice extending to the entire territory of only one state may by its very nature affect trade between Member States by compartmentalizing the market (see, e.g., *Dutch Acceptance Giro System* 1999/687 (1999) OJ L271/28, paras 61–3).

Although the wording of the test in *Société Technique Minière* implied a very broad interpretation of the principle, the Commission accepts in the notice that any effect must be sufficiently probable for EU jurisdiction to be invoked. However, 'there is no obligation or need to calculate the actual volume of trade between member states affected by the agreement or practice' (para. 27). This means, for example, that where an agreement restricts parallel trade it is not necessary to establish what trade levels would have taken place in the absence of the agreement. The test exists not to quantify harm, but merely to delimit jurisdiction. It was already clear from cases such as *Consten and Grundig* that an increase in the pattern of trade as a result of an agreement would fall within the rubric, and this is made clear in the notice where the Commission indicates that the term 'pattern of trade is neutral' (para. 34).

For an effect on trade to be appreciable, which is a requirement, it is again necessary to evaluate each situation. The broad position, set out in para. 45 of the notice, is that

When by its very nature the agreement or practice is capable of affecting trade between member states, the appreciability threshold is lower than in the case of agreements and practices that are not by their very nature capable of affecting trade between member states. The stronger the market position of the undertakings concerned, the more likely it is that an agreement or practice capable of affecting trade between member states can be held to do so appreciably.

While market share is important, and the Commission makes reference to the roughly consistent 5 per cent applied by the Court, it 'has not always been a decisive factor' (para. 46). In particular, it is important to take into account the turnover of the under-takings in the products concerned. In support of this proposition the Commission cites the Court of Justice ruling in *Musique Diffusion Française* v *Commission* cases 100–103/80 [1983] 3 CMLR 221 in which the Court held that although the products in question accounted for just 3 per cent of the sales in national markets, the agreements were capable of appreciably affecting trade due to the high turnover of the relevant parties. A further clarification of this principle is made in the Commission notice on agreements of minor importance (2001) OJ C368/13, at para. 3. It specifies that agreements between small and medium-sized undertakings, as defined in the notice, would not be likely to be found to have an impact on trade between Member States. Similarly, at para. 52 of the trade notice the Commission sets out some quantitative criteria which it suggests 'in principle' show that agreements do not affect trade. These are that (a) the aggregate market share of the parties does not exceed 5 per cent; (b) in the case of horizontal agreements, that the aggregate turnover of the parties does not exceed €40 million, and for vertical agreements that the turnover of the supplier of the products is below this threshold. A short-term safe harbour exists under which these figures may be exceeded by 10 per cent in the case of turnover and 2 per cent in the case of market share for two years. For agreements which may by their very nature be thought to bear an effect on trade, there is a rebuttable presumption that this is indeed the case where these turnover figures are surpassed. The same principle will apply to those agreements which affect more than a part of one state where the market share of the parties is in excess of 5 per cent. Part 3 of the notice applies these criteria to com-mon forms of agreements and abuses.

3.5 The response in the UK to EU competition law

3.5.1 The Competition Act 1998

When the CA 98 was brought forward the government made it very clear that one of its key reasons in doing so was to align domestic law with that of the EU. Thus:

I cannot over-emphasise that the purpose of the Bill is to ensure as far as possible a consist-ency with [EU] approach and thereby to ease burdens for business. (Lord Haskel, Hansard (HL) 17 November 1997, col. 417)

It should be stressed that the CA 98 was introduced at a time when there was no posi-tive obligation on any Member State to align its law to that of the EU. Only the general principles of EU law, and the *Walt Wilhelm* judgment were required to be followed. However, it was abundantly clear that EU competition law was in many respects more effective than was domestic competition law, and that for undertakings to operate within two legal regimes which were, prior to the enactment of the CA 98, very different, was expensive. The fact that Union law was taken as a given meant that the pressure to reform was placed on the national system. This insistence, coming from a range of sources, was made very clear in the Trade and Industry Committee Fifth Report, *UK Policy on Monopolies* (HC 249, 1995). This alignment was substantially achieved by the introduction of two prohibitions that mirrored those of art. 101 TFEU and art. 102 TFEU. At the same time procedures were also brought closer. Under Regulation 1/2003 it is national procedures that will be used—as will be discussed in Chapters 5, 6, and 7—to enforce the law in the vast majority of cases. Following modernization, some differences in the substance of the law that did remain have been removed. In the case of the law of mergers and market investigation references, and the cartel offence (see 3.5.2 below) differences remain.

The clearest indication of the move to consistency underlying the enactment of the CA 98 is found in s. 60 of that Act. This remarkable provision is set out here in its entirety:

60.—(1) The purpose of this section is to ensure that so far as is possible (having regard to any relevant differences between the provisions concerned), questions arising under this Part in relation to competition within the United Kingdom are dealt with in a manner which is consistent with the treatment of corresponding questions arising in [Union] law in relation to competition within the [Union].

(2) At any time when the court determines a question arising under this Part, it must act (so far as is compatible with the provisions of this Part and whether or not it would otherwise be required to do so) with a view to securing that there is no inconsistency between—

   (a) the principles applied, and decision reached, by the court in determining that question; and

   (b) the principles laid down by the Treaty and the European Court, and any relevant decision of that Court, as applicable at that time in determining any corresponding question arising in [Union] law.

(3) The court must, in addition, have regard to any relevant decision or statement of the Commission.

(4) Subsections (2) and (3) also apply to—

   (a) the Director; and

   (b) any person acting on behalf of the Director, in connection with any matter arising under this Part.

(5) In subsections (2) and (3), 'court' means any court or tribunal.

(6) In subsections (2)(b) and (3), 'decision' includes a decision as to—

   (a) the interpretation of any provision of [Union] law,

   (b) the civil liability of an undertaking for harm caused by its infringement of [Union] Law.

In the view of the Director General, 'relevant decision or statement of the Commission' (s. 60(3)) means decisions or statements which have the authority of the European Commission as a whole, such as, for example, decisions on individual cases under art. [101] and art. [102] of the Treaty. It would also include any clear statements which the European Commission has published about its policy approach in the *Annual Report on Competition Policy*. (See, e.g., *The Chapter I Prohibition Guidelines*, para. 2.1.)

It is clear from the application of the CA 98 in the first four years since its prohibitions began to bite that the OFT and the Competition Appeals Tribunal (CAT) have taken great efforts to refer to Union law, and to ensure consistency with it. Although s. 60 was referred to at the time of the Act's passage by certain lawyers as 'the Klondike clause', or 'the El Dorado clause', in anticipation of a large amount of litigation as to the meaning of the term 'relevant difference', there has in fact been little such substantive debate.

3.5.2 The Enterprise Act 2002

The EA 02 applies to both competition and insolvency law. In relation to the former three main substantive areas were addressed: merger control (Chapter 20), market investigation references (Chapter 17), and the introduction of the cartel offence (Chapter 12). It was noted early on in this chapter that the merger control regimes of the EU and UK are largely exclusive, although there is some small overlap between them in certain respects.

Market investigation references are distinct to the UK, and allow an examination of an entire market which appears not to be functioning competitively, with the possibility of a range of remedies being imposed. The OFT accepts that art. 3 of Regulation 1/2003 *might* apply to such investigations but that 'the obligation to apply arts [101] and [102] in parallel with national competition law will arise only at the stage where remedies are imposed by the CC following a reference' (*Market Investigation References Guideline* (March 2006), para. 2.12). The OFT does not believe that merely making such a reference, or holding an investigation, would invoke this obligation.

In the case of the cartel offence, under which individuals may be imprisoned if they have dishonestly engaged in activity condemned in s. 188 of the Enterprise Act, Recital (8) of Regulation 1/2003 provides that the Regulation 'does not apply to national laws which impose criminal sanctions on natural persons except to the extent that such sanctions are the means whereby competition rules applying to undertakings are enforced'. As the OFT points out in its draft *Modernisation Guideline*, the 'offence is aimed at dishonest activity by *individuals*' (emphasis added) and 'the cartel offence is not a means whereby competition rules applying to undertakings are enforced' (para. 4.21).

3.6 Conclusion

As far as the application of arts 101 and 102 is concerned the modernization process has clarified some important principles. There was, prior to the enactment of the regulation, genuine debate, for example, as to whether a Member State could condemn, under its national law, a practice that appeared to fall within the legal exception of art. 101(3). It is now clear that this cannot happen. The importance of the test of whether trade between Member States may be affected by an agreement or by an abuse is now enhanced, for in relation to art. 101 where trade is affected national competition law cannot go further than the application of that article, and in some respects undertakings may benefit from this. It is therefore possible that some may paradoxically be encouraged to structure conduct *so as* to affect trade. As long as the effect is not hypothetical, and is appreciable, EU competition law may be invoked.

However, some new problems have been created. There will be some discussion inevitably over what constitutes law that is not considered to be 'national competition law', such that it may be applied to the conduct of undertakings without the need to consider the application of arts 101 and 102 if there is also an effect on trade. The absolute obligation to apply EU law will also impact on national courts considering disputes where national competition law, but not EU competition law, is being argued. As was noted above at 3.3 this may have far-reaching, and perhaps unintended, consequences.

FURTHER READING

Articles

FAULL, J., 'Effect on Trade Between Member States', (1991) *Fordham Corporate Law Institute* 485

VENIT, J., 'Brave New World: The Modernization and Decentralization of Enforcement under Articles 81 and 82 of the EC Treaty', (2003) *Common Market Law Review* 545

4

International issues and the globalization of competition law

KEY POINTS

- The coexistence of competition law regimes around the world inevitably implies that companies that trade internationally may find themselves subject to the law of a 'foreign' state.
- While in the US the effects doctrine is relied on to assert jurisdiction, in the EU there has been no explicit adoption of the effects doctrine. Instead, the EU relies upon an 'implementation' doctrine.
- Under principles of comity a state may recognize the interests of another state when applying its competition law.
- Multilateral initiatives have been taken to try to resolve difficulties, but there is at present no single global agreement on competition law.

4.1 Introduction

In a world where commerce is increasingly globalized, competition law inevitably raises issues that cut across national and regional boundaries. Both those enforcing the law, and those subject to its enforcement, are affected by issues relating to territoriality and jurisdiction. This can be better understood using some examples. For instance, large mergers are likely to involve firms from two or more different states (such as the recent acquisition of the US mobile network system manufacturer Motorola by its Dutch competitor Nokia Siemens Networks). Even when the merging parties are in the same country, if the merger is large enough it could threaten competition beyond national borders. The same goes for large monopoly cases—the case against Microsoft being an excellent example of conduct that may be punishable in more than one jurisdiction, with decisions against it both in the EU (see Chapter 22) and the US. In the case of agreements, when these are entered into between undertakings based in more than one state there is bound to be consequences in the countries where those firms are located, if not beyond. Freyer made the point elegantly when he wrote that 'the enforcement of antitrust laws bears directly upon the conduct and competitiveness of business firms experiencing the technological, political, and cultural challenges of converging local, national, and global markets' (Freyer, T. A., 'Antitrust and Bilateralism: The US, Japanese and EU Comparative and Historical Relationships', in Jones, C. A., and Matsushita, M. (eds), *Competition Policy in the Global Trading System*, The Hague, Kluwer Law International (2002), p. 3).

There are several reasons why disparities in national laws are a cause of concern. First, they represent a cost to companies that increasingly operate in more than one state. These costs can relate both to learning the newly encountered law and to adapting a method of operation acceptable in one state to another state which may insist upon different commercial arrangements. Disparate laws may also lead to the erection of secondary import barriers by states that are, prima facie, committed to free market access and to the principles of the World Trade Organization (WTO) which has assumed responsibility for the operation of the trade agreements concluded under the auspices of the General Agreement on Tariffs and Trade (the GATT). There is also a problem with the territorial effects of commercial decisions, which may impact upon more than one state with differing legal consequences in each state. This can lead to conflicts between national authorities competing for jurisdiction and, in the worst cases, either to multiple, conflicting actions taken against companies, or to companies avoiding actions altogether. Such a situation could lead also to the raising of the difficult problems posed by private international law, 'conflicts of laws'. If private litigants are involved this scenario is quite likely to arise, and it may also arise where a public authority proceeds on the basis of the 'effects' doctrine (see 4.2.1 below).

The EU Commission has responded to some of the concerns raised by these issues mainly by engaging in bilateral agreements and by engaging in multilateral discussions via the WTO, the Organization for Economic Cooperation and Development (OECD), and the United Nations Conference on Trade and Development (UNCTAD). In this chapter a distinction will be drawn between public, institutional enforcement of competition law, which may raise issues of public international law, and private actions before national courts.

4.2 **Public enforcement**

Public enforcement of competition law will take place, typically, where a company based in a territory carries out acts which fall to be condemned under that territory's law. Such a situation will usually raise no issues that need addressing at the international level. Two other possible scenarios are more likely to lead to problems, however. The first arises where a company is based in several states and is carrying out activities that are illegal in some states but not in others. If the company is attacked in those states where it is infringing but its headquarters lie elsewhere, how will the state in which it is primarily based respond? The second situation arises where a company or companies based entirely in one state engage in behaviour that is condemned in another. This was the situation in the GE/Honeywell merger, where an act that was entirely legal in the United States was condemned in the EU (see 4.2.4 below). Not all states recognize the validity of such actions, which are generally based on the 'effects' doctrine, and the United Kingdom in particular has been hostile to moves to base jurisdiction on 'effects'. The United States readily claims such jurisdiction, and the EU achieves very similar ends by slightly different terminology.

4.2.1 The formulation of the effects doctrine and its application in the US

The effects doctrine is a controversial part of international law, the position of which is not yet universally recognized. Under the doctrine a state may assume jurisdiction where an act that is committed in another state, by citizens or companies of other states, has effects in the former. This was accepted by the Permanent Court of International Justice in the *Lotus* case (*The SS Lotus* (*France* v *Turkey*) (1927) PCIJ ser. A, no. 10), although there continues to be strong debate among commentators about the exact scope of that judgment. By way of example, this doctrine implies that if a group of Japanese and Korean businesses agreed to cooperate in raising prices for televisions in the EU, but were not based in the EU and sold into the EU only through agents who were themselves unconnected with the concerted action, the application of the effects doctrine might allow the EU Commission to take action against the companies, and the Court of Justice to uphold any fines imposed.

The US has long applied the effects doctrine in the enforcement of antitrust law, the primary authority deriving from the case of *United States* v *Aluminum Co. of America* (*ALCOA*) 148 F2d 416 (2d Cir. 1945). Both private claims, including those seeking treble damages, and public cases brought by the Department of Justice may be based on actions implemented in other countries that have a significant impact in the United States. This situation is explained clearly in the Antitrust Enforcement Guidelines for International Operations, issued by the US Department of Justice in April 1995:

SITUATION: A, B, C, and D are foreign companies that produce a product in various foreign countries. None has any US production, nor any US subsidiaries. They organize a cartel for the purpose of raising the price for the product in question. Collectively, the cartel members make substantial sales into the United States, both in absolute terms and relative to total US consumption.

DISCUSSION: These facts present the straightforward case of cartel participants selling products directly into the United States. In this situation, the transaction is unambiguously an import into the US market, and the sale is not complete until the goods reach the United States. Thus, US subject matter jurisdiction is clear under the general principles of antitrust law expressed most recently in *Hartford Fire*. The facts presented here demonstrate actual and intended participation in US commerce.

There are restrictions on the operation of these principles. The 'act of state doctrine', the doctrine of 'foreign governmental compulsion', and the principle of comity all serve to limit the extraterritorial application of the law. The first of these is a general principle of public international law that provides that national courts cannot review the actions of sovereign states where that act takes place within the state. Thus a state body would not be found to be in breach of the Sherman Act were it to engage in activity that, if undertaken by a private party, would constitute a breach. Where a private party is *required* as a matter of national law to engage in activity that breaches United States antitrust law that law will also not be enforced (see, e.g., *American Banana Co.* v *United Fruit Co.* 213 US 347 (1909)). The act of state doctrine has no place within intra-European Union relationships, where the Member States may themselves be liable if they encourage, or tacitly support, breaches of the law. This position flows from art. 4(3) TEU (see 2.3.5.2 above). The application of the principle of comity is discussed below at 4.2.4.

4.2.2 The EU—implementation

In the Union legal order, the most important case relating to the extraterritorial application of arts 1011 and 1022 is *Re Wood Pulp Cartel: A. Ahlström Oy* v *Commission* (joined cases C–89, 104, 114, 116, 117, and 125–129/85 [1988] 4 CMLR 901). In this complex case the Commission had found that 41 producers of wood pulp, used in paper manufacture, and two trade associations had breached art. 101(1) (*Wood Pulp* 85/202 (1985) OJ L85/1). Thirty-six of these undertakings were based outside the EU. *Inter alia* the Commission held that the members of a trade association in the US had concerted on price announcements, had monitored any deviations from those prices, and had concerted on transaction prices. An argument from these companies to the effect that they were unaware that their conduct breached the Treaty was accepted. However, the argument of the companies to the effect that the Act provided a total defence was rejected by the Commission and by Advocate General Marco Darmon, on the grounds that it did not actively *compel* the companies to organize their activity in this way, but merely exempted them from the application of US antitrust law.

The Commission argued that art. 101 applies even if the parties to the agreement are outside the EU and other markets are affected (para. 79). In its submission to the Court it further stated that the Union's jurisdiction 'is not in breach of any prohibitive rule of international law … in so far as its jurisdiction is based on the effects within the [Union] of conduct which occurred elsewhere' ([1988] 4 CMLR 901, at 915). Recognizing that 'the "effects doctrine" is still contested under international law' the Commission argued that 'the objections come primarily from the United Kingdom and not from the OECD or other countries' (pp. 915–16). Intervening in the case the United Kingdom asked the Court of Justice to resolve the issue by the application of territorial jurisdiction, that is, to find that the agreement had to the necessary extent been operated within the EU, rather than by any application of the effects doctrine. The Advocate General's view was that the Union should be able to assert extraterritorial jurisdiction where the 'effects of the conduct alleged … were substantial, direct and foreseeable' (p. 938). The key paragraphs of the judgment of the Court of Justice are 16–18. The Court said that the decisive factor was the place where the agreement was implemented (in this case the internal market). 'Accordingly the Union's jurisdiction to apply its competition rules to such conduct is covered by the territoriality principle as universally recognised in public international law' (para. 18).

In choosing to refer to the 'implementation' of the agreement instead of the 'effect' of the agreement, the court may have been doing little more than applying an 'effects' doctrine in language that would be acceptable to the UK. The application of the US-style 'effects' doctrine and *Wood Pulp*'s 'implementation' may in practice produce equivalent results. However, this has left some uncertainty. What, for example, would be the position where there existed an anti-competitive agreement between Japanese producers with no direct selling arms in the EU? Would the agreement be said to be 'implemented' where EU customers placed orders for the products directly in Japan, under contracts governed by Japanese law? If there is a genuine distinction between 'implementation' and 'effect' it might be that in this hypothetical case there would be no jurisdiction under Union law, and that such jurisdiction might be assumed only where the Japanese companies were actively soliciting sales from the EU instead of passively responding to orders.

The question of territorial jurisdiction was returned to in the case and decision in relation to the *Gencor/Lonhro* merger (97/26 (1997) OJ L11/30), on appeal *Gencor Ltd v Commission* case T–102/96 [1999] 4 CMLR 971. In this case, which is discussed at 19.2.2.4.1 in relation to merger control, the Commission blocked a merger between the South African interests of the two companies. The GC was called upon to consider both the territorial scope of the EU Merger Regulation (EUMR) (at paras 78–88), and the compatibility of the decision with public international law (at paras 89–111). In determining the territorial scope of the EUMR, the GC confirmed the position as being that jurisdiction does not exclude concentrations which, while relating to 'activities outside the [Union], have the effect of creating or strengthening a dominant position as a result of which competition in the [Internal] Market is significantly impeded' (para. 82). When the undertakings attempted to rely on *Wood Pulp* in order to restrict the territorial application of the regulation the GC held that

According to *Wood Pulp*, the criterion as to the implementation of an agreement is satisfied by mere sale within the [Union], irrespective of the location of the sources of supply and the production plant. It is not disputed that Gencor and Lonhro carried out sales in the [Union] before the concentration and would have continued to do so thereafter.   (para. 87)

The approach of the GC was to introduce into the extraterritorial operation of the EUMR a two-stage process. The first stage, to be answered by reference to *Wood Pulp*, is that of whether there is territorial jurisdiction. The second stage is to determine whether, having exercised jurisdiction, the substantive tests set out in the EUMR should be applied so as to block a merger. The Court concludes by holding that 'the arguments by which the applicant denies that the concentration would have a substantial *effect* in the [Union] must therefore be rejected' (para. 99, emphasis added).

4.2.3 The evolution of the position of the UK

In 1969—before its accession to the EU—the United Kingdom vigorously protested at the application of EU competition law to a UK-based company in *Dyestuffs* (OJ (1969) L 195/11). Under this decision the EU Commission had found that a number of undertakings in the dyestuffs industry had operated a cartel contrary to art. 101. Fines were imposed on, *inter alia*, ICI, which had its headquarters in the UK but had subsidiaries in the EU. Before the Court of Justice the issue was dealt with very simply, with the Court merely relying on the fact that, via its subsidiary, ICI *was* based in the EU (*ICI* v *Commission* case 48/69 [1972] CMLR 557). This has been termed the 'economic entity doctrine', which had been explicitly rejected by the UK courts in *Re Schweppes Ltd's Agreement* [1965] 1 All ER 195.

The position taken by the UK in this respect has now changed. Intervening in the *Wood Pulp* case the United Kingdom took a more relaxed stance. The Competition Act 1998 limited the application of domestic competition law to situations in which the practice condemned 'is, or is intended to be, *implemented* in the United Kingdom' (s. 2(3), emphasis added). The jurisdiction asserted over anti-competitive practices that have an impact in the UK under the CA 98 is intended to be an explicit and inflexible implementation of the *Wood Pulp* case law. In the passage of the Act Lord Simon explained that by 'copying out the test in *Wood Pulp* on the face of the Bill, we are also ensuring that in the event that [EU] jurisprudence develops and creates a pure effects-based doctrine, the application of the UK prohibitions will not follow suit' (Hansard (HL) 13 November 1997, col. 261). Following the modernization of EU competition law it is conceivable that, should the Court of Justice embrace the effects doctrine, the OFT would in the future be obliged to apply it in the context of enforcing either art. 101 or art. 102 TFEU.

4.2.4 Comity and 'positive comity'

Standard international law texts are likely to draw a clear distinction between international law and international comity: the law is binding and comity is not. Thus comity has been defined as 'rules of goodwill and civility, founded on the moral right of each state to receive courtesy from others' (Shearer, I. A., *Starke's International Law*, London, Butterworths (1994), p. 18). This then is a principle of reciprocal courtesy, that may be of limited application in practice. In competition law comity has taken on a slightly different meaning.

4.2.4.1 The US approach

The courts of the United States have, since the mid-1970s, turned to the doctrine of comity as a restraining factor in cases in which US antitrust law is applied to situations and parties outside the country's borders. For example, in *Laker Airways* v *Sabena, Belgian World Airlines* 731 F.2d 909 (1984) the court held that 'when possible, the decisions of foreign tribunals should be given effect in domestic courts, since recognition fosters international cooperation and encourages reciprocity, thereby promoting predictability and stability'. The approach of the courts has been to balance the interests arising out of the application of US antitrust law against the harm to comity that such an application may lead to, as the case law reflects (see, *inter alia*, *Timberlane Lumber Co.* v *Bank of America (Timberlane I)* 549 F.2d 597 (9th Cir. 1976); *Mannington Mills, Inc.* v *Congoleum Corp.* 595 F.2d 1287 (3d Cir. 1979); *Hartford Fire Ins. Co.* v *California* 113 S. Ct. 2891 (1993); and *United States* v *Nippon Paper Indus. Co.* 109 F.3d (1st Cir. 1997)).

4.2.4.2 The EU approach

The European Commission has shown that it is ready to embrace the principle of comity where it has the discretion to do so (see, e.g., *Boeing/McDonnell Douglas* 97/816 (1997) OJ L336/16, below). The application of the EUMR (see Chapter 19) raises particular problems in this respect. The EU Commission does not appear to have discretion as to whether or not at least to consider any merger, wheresoever it is concluded, that falls within the threshold criteria set out in the Regulation. In some instances even such an examination is likely to be a matter of concern to other states. However, as seen above (4.2.1), the GC has limited the circumstances in which a merger can be blocked, although in *Honeywell International Inc.* v *Commission* case T–209/01, 14 December 2005, the GC upheld a Commission decision blocking a merger between two US-based companies.

There have been three important decisions which have related to mergers that would be carried out by companies whose production was entirely outside the EU. In *Gencor/Lonhro* 97/26 (1997) OJ L11/30, on appeal *Gencor Ltd* v *Commission* case T–102/96 [1999] 4 CMLR 971, the market in question was primarily that of platinum mined in South Africa. Although the decision itself does not deal expressly with issues of jurisdiction, it is clear that there was consideration of the South African position (see, e.g., paras 168–71). In its comment on the case in the *26th Annual Report on Competition Policy 1996*, the Commission found it 'worth underlining that, from the outset of the procedure, the South African authorities have been kept informed . . . of developments in this case and have attended the hearings organised in Brussels' (p. 184).

The *Boeing* case (97/816 (1997) OJ L336/16) was particularly susceptible to charges of political interference in the regulatory process, although this was denied on both sides of the Atlantic. The merger between Boeing and McDonnell Douglas reduced the number of manufacturers of large commercial aircraft from three to two. As a result of this Airbus Industrie, based in Europe and part-owned by four European governments, was left facing a single dominant competitor. The Federal Trade Commission (FTC) publicly acknowledged that this level of structural restriction in the market was a problem, but then cleared the merger, holding that there was no effective competition between the merging firms to be snuffed out. The EU Commission cleared the merger only after being given various assurances by Boeing relating to future commercial conduct. US commentators, and Boeing's attorneys in particular, have argued that the concessions had little to do with the merger itself, but that the Commission was exploiting the situation to secure advantages for Airbus. Prior to the eleventh-hour settlement there had been speculation that if the merger proceeded contrary to Union law the severest of fines would be imposed and that Boeing planes landing in Europe might be seized. The case is a perfect illustration of the problems that may arise in respect of such transactions and, notwithstanding the level of cooperation between the EU and the United States, 'diverging approaches of the competition authorities in Brussels and Washington made it impossible to reach commonly accepted solutions' (Schaub, A., 'International Cooperation in Antitrust Matters: Making the Point in the Wake of the Boeing/MDD Proceedings', (1998) 1 *Competition Policy Newsletter*, p. 4).

Even more controversially, in July 2001 the EU Commission blocked the proposed merger between General Electric Inc. (GE) and Honeywell Inc. (*General Electric/Honeywell* No. COMP/M.220 of 3 July 2001, unpublished). In doing so, the Commission took a stance which was in direct opposition to that adopted by the US authorities, which had cleared the merger. The Commission was particularly disappointed in this case that offers of divestment and conduct remedies put forward to the merging parties were not accepted. Three articles in the Fall 2001 issue of *Antitrust* deal with this case with interesting perspectives. In December 2005 the GC upheld the Commission decision (*Honeywell International Inc.* v *Commission* case T–209/01, judgment of 14 December 2005).

It should be recognized that although the approach of the EU Commission in the Boeing and GE cases attracted considerable criticism within the United States, the latter's authorities have similarly examined mergers in situations where production has been outside the United States. This was the case, for example, with the Guinness/Grand Metropolitan merger leading to the creation of Diageo in 1998.

4.2.4.3 Positive comity

Where comity requires a country to respect another's interests in the application of its national law, 'positive comity' has greater force and might suggest, *inter alia*, that a country should enforce its own competition law in order to assist another country where it might not otherwise do so were it to consider purely national interests. This principle is prominent in the EU–US cooperation agreements, and has led to situations in which the EU investigated anti-competitive conduct being pursued in its territory on behalf of the US, and it is of concern to the US authorities. One such complaint, for example, has been made about the European-wide airline reservation system, 'Amadeus', which the United States authorities believe has an adverse impact on United States' commercial interests (see below).

4.2.5 **Bilateral agreements**

The EU, the UK, and the United States have all concluded bilateral agreements relating to competition enforcement with a range of parties, and in some cases with each other. As well as its agreement with the EU the United States has also concluded agreements with, among others, Germany (which remain in force notwithstanding the links with the EU), Canada, and Australia.

In 1991 the Commission and the US authorities had reached a formal agreement on cooperation in the application of competition laws, but, following a challenge to the legal basis of the agreement by the French government, this was struck down by the Court of Justice on the basis of fundamental breaches in procedure (*France* v *Commission* case C–327/91 [1994] 5 CMLR 517). The Agreement, the purpose of which 'is to promote cooperation and coordination and lessen the possibility or impact of differences between the Parties in the application of their competition laws' (art. 1(1)) has now been readopted in its correct form on the basis of arts 103 and 352 TFEU, as well as former 300(3) EC (now replaced by 218 TFEU) (95/145/EC, ECSC, (1995) OJ

L95/45). The two parties concluded a further Agreement, on positive comity alone, which was signed on 4 June 1998, the EU–USA Positive Comity Agreement 1998, 98/386 (1998) OJ L173/28. This agreement, from which mergers are excluded, creates a presumption that in some cases a Party will either suspend or defer its usual enforcement measures.

The *Competition Laws Cooperation Agreement 1999 (EC/ECSC/Canada)* 1999/445 (1999) OJ L175 entered into force on 29 April 1999. It makes provision for consultation, coordination, and cooperation in the enforcement of competition law. It is, in essence, similar in approach to the agreement concluded with the US. The EU has also concluded bilateral agreements with Canada (*Competition Laws Co-operation Agreement 1999 (EC/ECSC/Canada)* 1999/45 (1999) OJ L175/1), which makes provision for consultation, coordination, and cooperation in the enforcement of competition law, and with Japan (*Decision Concluding the Agreement between the European Community and Japan concerning co-operation on anti-competitive activities* 2003/520 (2003) OJ L183). In May 2004 the Commission also entered into an agreement with China relating to the development of a structured dialogue on competition. A similar agreement was entered into with Korea in October 2004 (IP (04) 1325, 28 October 2004).

For its part, in October 2003, the UK entered into agreements with Canada, and with Australia and New Zealand. In both cases the agreements, which are in very similar terms, relate to the 'coordination of enforcement activities' ([2004] UKCLR 972, [2004] UKCLR 979). They do not extend to the criminal enforcement of the cartel offence (see Chapter 12).

4.2.6 Multilateral cooperation and globalization

4.2.6.1 The European Economic Area

There are several instances of multilateral cooperation in respect of competition policy. The most notable is that between the EU and the other members of the European Economic Area (EEA). The relevance of the EEA—concluded between the EU and the EFTA states with the exception of Switzerland—is declining as its members assume full membership of the European Union. It entered into force on 1 January 1994 ((1994) OJ L1/3), and Liechtenstein acceded on 1 May 1995. As Austria, Finland, and Sweden have since joined the Union the non-EU contracting states are therefore Iceland, Norway, and Liechtenstein. Broadly the relevant law of the EEA mirrors that of the EC, arts 53 and 54 EEA reflecting arts 101 and 102 TFEU. Article 57 EEA essentially incorporates the ECMR into the EEA.

4.2.6.2 The North American Free Trade Area

In North America, Chapter 15 of the North American Free Trade Agreement (NAFTA, 32 ILM 605 (1993)) concluded between the US, Canada, and Mexico, commits the parties to cooperation on antitrust matters. Among other provisions, each of the Parties is required, by virtue of the Agreement, to 'adopt or maintain measures to proscribe anti-competitive business conduct and take appropriate action with respect thereto' (art. 1501(1)). Primarily the provisions relate to the conduct and maintenance of state 'designated' monopolies, and they do not set new standards for the regulation of private anti-competitive conduct.

4.2.6.3 The OECD

In the preamble of its *Revised Recommendation of the OECD Council Concerning Cooperation Between Member Countries on Restrictive Business Practices Affecting International Trade*, OECD Doc. No. C(95)130 (Final), 28 July 1995), the OECD suggests that 'if Member countries find it appropriate to enter into bilateral arrangements for cooperation in the enforcement of national competition laws, they should take [the Recommendation] into account'. It would appear that the EC/USA Cooperation Agreement has been so influenced. Although the OECD has expressed an interest in competition law matters which is commensurate with its membership of industrialized nations, it has not taken formal steps towards harmonization. In 1998 a working group on international antitrust cooperation published a Recommendation on the prosecution of hard-core cartels, which was approved by the General Council. This group is also examining ways of resolving jurisdictional problems in relation to mergers having an international dimension.

4.2.6.4 The WTO

The WTO is primarily concerned with the free flow of trade, and with the elimination of trade barriers wherever possible. Its membership is nearly universal. A Draft International Antitrust Code was submitted to the members of the GATT in July 1993, although no substantial progress was made. More important was the failure of earlier efforts leading to the Havana Charter, which the United States refused to ratify. However, because of the increasingly close relationship between trade and competition policy, the WTO established a working party following the 1996 Singapore conference, under the chairmanship of the French Vice President of the *Conseil de la Concurrence* (competition council), to report on whether negotiations were advisable in this area. This followed an initiative from the EU Commission suggesting that it might be possible to reach international agreement in some key areas, such as the response to cartels (see Commission Press Release (1995) IP/95/752, 12 July). The prospects for success are uncertain. Neither the EU nor the USA envisages a globally binding agreement. Announcing the formation of an International Competition Policy Advisory Committee, Joel Klein of the Department of Justice, Antitrust Division set out the US position in words that do not suggest that the WTO group will succeed in creating a harmonized regime:

this working group can play an important educational role in demonstrating the important contributions of antitrust to efficient national markets and open international trade, and in fostering international cooperation. We are less persuaded that the time is ripe for the negotiation of global antitrust rules.   (24 November 1997)

The future of the possibilities for international competition cooperation in the context of the WTO was discussed at the Doha Ministerial Conference, and parties signing up to the Doha declaration accepted that there was a valid case for the WTO to negotiate and conclude a multilateral Agreement on Trade and Competition. This proposal has yet to materialize.

4.2.6.5 ICPAC, the Global Competition Forum, and the International Competition Network

On 28 February 2000 the International Competition Policy Advisory Committee (ICPAC), founded in 1997 by the US antitrust authorities, submitted its final report (this is available at **http://www.justice.gov/atr/icpac/finalreport.htm**). Although the report was commissioned by the US authorities and prepared by US experts, it was well received internationally. The report made recommendations in relation to multi-jurisdictional merger review, cooperation in cartel enforcement, and the intersection of trade and competition policy. The ICPAC group suggested that the WTO was not the natural home for competition policy initiatives, and recommended instead the establishment of a new Global Competition Initiative for addressing the international concerns relating to competition enforcement.

In November 2001 the US Department of Justice (DOJ) and FTC, and the EU Commission, became the founding members of the 'International Competition Network' (ICN). This is a 'virtual' network, and has no permanent resources or institutions. Its role is to enhance cooperation between its members, which number over 50 and which include the leading developed nations (including the EU) as well as countries ranging from Armenia to Zambia. The web address of the ICN is **www.internationalcompetitionnetwork.org**.

4.3 **Private parties and the enforcement of judgments**

4.3.1 **Conflicts of laws**

There are three issues that face any private party in a dispute which involves jurisdictional matters beyond the bounds of that party's state: where should the action be brought? Under which law should the action be brought? How will any judgment be enforced? It would be possible to envisage a situation in which the courts of one state would hear the action and apply the law of another state, with the judgment being enforced in the courts of yet another country. These are complex matters that lie beyond the scope of this book. The interested reader should refer to one of the specialist texts dealing with private international law or conflicts of laws.

4.3.2 **Private actions**

There have been a number of cases in which private parties have sought remedies, or damages, in their own courts against companies based in another jurisdiction, or where claimants have sued outside their jurisdiction in the jurisdiction of the defendant. A number of claims have arisen out of the international prosecution of the vitamins cartel, which resulted in a plea bargain in the US (see US DOJ press release, 6 April 2000), and in an infringement decision in the EU (Commission Decision 2003/2 *Vitamins* (2003) OJ L6/1).

A South African company, Empagran SA, sought to recover damages from Hoffmann-La Roche, one of the cartel participants, in the US. Hoffmann-La Roche itself is a company based in Switzerland. The transactions between the claimant and defendant had no connection with the US, the only relationship being that Hoffmann-La Roche had pleaded to a violation of s. 1 of the Sherman Act. In spring 2004 the case came before the Supreme Court of the United States as *F. Hoffmann-La Roche Ltd* v *Empagran SA* 524 US S. Ct. (2004). The judgment was not an easy one. Justice Breyer summed up the issue facing the Court:

> The issue before us concerns (1) significant foreign anti-competitive conduct with (2) an adverse domestic effect and (3) an independent foreign effect giving rise to the claim. In more concrete terms, this case involves vitamin sellers around the world that agreed to fix prices in the United States and independently leading to higher vitamin prices in other countries such as Ecuador. We conclude that, in this scenario, a purchaser in the United States could bring a Sherman Act claim under the [Foreign Trade Antitrust Improvements Act 1982] based on domestic injury, but a purchaser in Ecuador could not bring a Sherman Act claim based on foreign harm.

The question presented to the Court recognized that the transactions in question occurred wholly outside the US. In reaching its conclusion it was clearly swayed by a recognition of the interests of other states, for it argued that in interpreting ambiguous legislative language it would do so 'to avoid unreasonable interference with the sovereign authority of other nations'. In so far as the antitrust rules of the US reflected a wish to address *domestic* injury caused by foreign anti-competitive conduct the Court held that it was reasonable to apply those laws to the foreign conduct, but not when the injury was not a domestic one, as was the case here. In reaching this conclusion the Court accepted that there was little consensus in the world of competition law, and that 'even where nations agree about primary conduct, say price-fixing, they disagree dramatically about appropriate remedies'.

It has been claimed that this judgment serves to greatly limit the possibility of private actions based on foreign injury being brought in the US courts, and that as such it should be welcomed. Others are less optimistic, and point to the fact that the Court places great emphasis on the fact that the antitrust injury complained of here is 'independently caused' foreign injury. It is not the case, therefore, that *Empagran* shuts the door on claims based on foreign harm completely; rather it leaves it swinging in the wind, and whether claims can be successfully pursued may rest on the ingenuity of the lawyer presenting the case to link the foreign injury to domestic action.

In the UK a similar action was brought in the case of *Provimi Ltd* v *Aventis Animal Nutrition SA and others and other actions* [2003] EWHC 961 (Comm), [2003] All ER (D) 59 (May). Seven defendant companies were sued by three claimants in the UK courts on the basis of a breach of art. 101 TFEU. Some of the claimants and some of the defendants had no connection with the UK, and the claimants were relying in part upon Council Regulation 44/2001 (*on Jurisdiction and the Enforcement of Judgments in Civil and Commercial Matters* (2001) OJ L12/1) and the Lugano Convention (*Lugano Convention on Jurisdiction and Judgments in Civil and Commercial Matters 1988*, Lugano, 16 September 1988, Decision 88/592/EEC (1988) OJ L319). The cases were further complicated by the presence of jurisdictional clauses inserted into some of the contracts under which the sales were made. The court rejected the defendants' arguments to the effect that it had no jurisdiction to hear the case, and the matter proceeded to be dealt with on the substance of the claim (see further, Furse, M., '*Provimi* v *Aventis*: Damages and Jurisdiction', [2003] Comp Law 119).

4.3.3 **The World Trade Organization**

The WTO agreement of 1994 is intended to be directed to the restrictive acts of governments. It appears, however, to have a limited potential for private antitrust litigants. In 1995 Eastman-Kodak filed a petition with the US authorities, based on s. 301 of the 1974 Trade Act (19 USC 2411), alleging that Fuji was hindering the distribution of Kodak film in Japan by operating an exclusionary distribution system that was blocked to Kodak, and that the Japanese Government was participating in limiting access to the Japanese markets. In May 1995, Kodak filed a petition with the US Trade Representative (USTR) inviting it to investigate the matter. The USTR agreed to pursue the issue, and in the summer of 1996 the USTR found that acts which restricted the sale of photographic materials by US exporters to Japan could be attributed to the Japanese Government. Section 301 of the 1974 Trade Act gives the USTR the discretion to take action when it finds that the actions of a foreign government are 'unreasonable or discriminatory'. The choice of approach is a wide one: at one extreme the US government can take unilateral counter-measures. Such a step is, however, contentious and carries with it the risk of retaliation by the country against whose interests the steps are being taken.

The US authorities thus decided to turn to the binding dispute resolution procedure established in the WTO at the Uruguay Round. This procedure gives members access to a dispute mechanism in the event of a conflict based on the trade laws of the GATT. A panel of three to five members is appointed to hear any dispute. The final complaint did not rely on the basis of the specific allegations made by Kodak, but was brought on the basis that 'Japan's laws, regulations and requirements affecting the distribution' of film treated importers 'less favourably', in breach of trade obligations. Only governments have access to this procedure; the hearings are closed to the public; private parties and counsel are, by custom, excluded; and governments are the only subjects of the proceedings.

By seeking a ruling to the effect that the Japanese Government was impeding imports in its tacit support of anti-competitive industrial practices maintained in Japan the dispute moved to a new level, in which Kodak and Fuji ceased to act directly as litigants. The EU Commission also joined the panel as a third party due to its economic interest in the matter (see Press Release IP/98/122). Early in 1998 the WTO disputes settlement body rejected the United States' case on the merits, although it accepted that a similar route would remain open in the future (Panel Report, *Japan—Measures Affecting Consumer Photographic Film and Paper*, WT/DS44/R, 31 March 1998; note that this has not been appealed). The panel also concluded that, in the appropriate circumstances, an action taken by a private party that has the effect of hindering trade may also be deemed to be governmental (para. 10.56).

Such a procedure has clear advantages to the respective parties: although they are likely to be pressing their respective claims behind the scenes, they are not being required to invest heavily in the proceedings. The main drawback is that this procedure can be invoked only when it can be established that a government's action, or inaction, is involved as part of the original antitrust claim, and where the complainant can persuade its own government to bring the matter before the WTO. Although this is a somewhat tortuous route that will be beyond the reach of most companies and will require great patience, the position remains that lawyers

involved in international competition matters should keep in mind the possibility that the relevant trade agency might be convinced to bring a competition-related matter to the WTO for a resolution that might otherwise be unavailable in the antitrust system. (First, H., 'The Intersection of Trade and Antitrust Remedies' (1997) *Antitrust*, Fall, p. 21)

4.4 Conclusion

It is too early—and perhaps too optimistic—to envisage the creation of a global competition regime, with an international competition authority. The pattern at present is one of developing countries being encouraged to adopt competition laws, and for expertise gained by states with developed competition regimes to be shared with the rest of the world. The ICN and the WTO appear to be the fora most engaged in this process. One result of this process is that at the present time over 100 countries are believed to have in place some form of competition law, and China adopted a competition law regime in 2007.

FURTHER READING

Books

DABBAH, M. M., *The Internationalisation of Antitrust Policy* (2003) CUP, Cambridge

EPSTEIN, R. A., and GREVE, M. S. (eds), *Competition Laws in Conflict: Antitrust Jurisdiction in the Global Economy* (2004) The AEI Press, Washington, DC

ZACH, R. (ed.), *Towards WTO Competition Rules: Key Issues and Comments on the WTO Report (1998) on Trade and Competition* (1999) Kluwer Law International, The Hague

ZANNETTIN, B., *Cooperation Between Antitrust Agencies at the International Level* (2002) Hart Publishing, Oxford

Articles

Cocuzza, C., and Montini, M., 'International Antitrust Co-operation in a Global Economy', (1998) *European Competition Law Review* 156

Fox, E. M., 'Towards World Antitrust and Market Access', (1997) 91 *American Journal of International Law* 1

Fox, E. M., 'The WTO's First Antitrust Case—*Mexican Telecoms*: Modest World Antitrust', (2006) *Antitrust* 21(1), 74

Jenny, F., 'Competition Law and Policy: Global Governance Issues', (2003) 26 *World Competition* 609

Maher, I., 'Competition Law in the International Domain: Networks as a New Form of Governance', (2002) *Journal of Law and Society* 111

Torremans, P., 'Extraterritorial Application of EC and US Competition Law', (1996) 21 *European Law Review* 280

Van Gerven, Y., and Hoet, L., 'Gencor: Some Notes on Transnational Competition Law Issues', (2001) 28 *Legal Issues of European Integration* 195

5

Procedure—Investigation

KEY POINTS

- As established in Regulation 1/2003, the EU Commission has its own powers to investigate infringements of EU competition law. It may cooperate with national competition authorities (NCAs), who also have their own powers.

- NCAs and the EU Commission cooperate through the European Competition Network (ECN).

- The EU Commission may obtain information, or may investigate on-site, but does not have criminal jurisdiction.

- Undertakings subject to investigation have rights that must be observed.

5.1 Introduction

Over the next three crucial chapters, the rules that govern the enforcement of competition law in the EU and the UK will be explored. This chapter deals with the way in which infringements of arts 101 and 102 TFEU and the Chapter I and II Prohibitions are investigated and attacked. The penalties that may be imposed following the finding of infringements are dealt with in the following chapter, while third-party rights, including the role of the civil courts, are discussed in Chapter 7. This should provide the reader with a solid overview of the procedural rules. Other parts of the book assess the provisions that apply to specific areas of competition law. Investigative powers and procedural provisions in relation to the merger control regimes are considered in Chapters 19 and 20, and market investigation references in the UK are dealt with in Chapter 17. The criminal procedures that may be applied to prosecute the cartel offence in the UK fall within Chapter 12.

5.2 General background to competition law enforcement

5.2.1 Enforcement in the EU

Procedural law is frequently referred to as the 'nuts and bolts' of the law, as it regulates the way substantive law is applied and enforced. The 'nuts and bolts' of EU competition law underwent a thorough reform in 2004. On 1 May that year, coinciding with the accession of ten new Member States to the European Union, the so-called 'Modernization Package' entered into force, a set of binding and non-binding legislation at the frontispiece of which sits Regulation 1/2003 on the implementation of the rules of competition laid down in arts 81 and 82 of the Treaty (2003) OJ L1/1.

The 'Modernization Package' put an end to four decades of the application of Regulation 17/62 ((1962) OJ 13, 204), the first ever legislation to regulate the way in which EU competition law provisions were to be applied. In particular, it was argued that the older regulation was ineffective in balancing the two key objectives of simplified administration and effective supervision (Regulation 1/2003, recital (2)). While the older law is not specifically discussed here, principles established under it remain valid under the new regime, as do a number of cases, particularly those relating to the rights of the defence. These are dealt with throughout this chapter as necessary.

A basic understanding of the main changes made by Regulation 1/2003 is important to grasp fully the policy underpinning the regulation. To sum up, there are four principal strands of reform in the modernization of EU competition law. First of all, it establishes a decentralized system of enforcement, enhancing the role of national competition authorities and courts. Article 101(3), which until then could only be applied by the Commission, is since 2004 directly applicable by authorities and courts of the Member States (see 5.4.1 and Chapter 9). Secondly (and allied to the idea of decentralized enforcement), it lays down enhanced cooperation mechanisms between enforcers; this is mainly achieved through the European Competition Network (ECN), analysed below at 5.4.3. Thirdly, the former *ex ante* control of agreements has given way to *ex post* supervision. As a result, agreements are now pursued once they have entered into force. This implies a system focused on anticompetitive *effects* rather than potential threats. Fourthly, in order to grant effective control of those practices that are harming the competitive process, the Commission now has enhanced investigatory powers (see 5.4).

5.2.2 Enforcement in the UK

As Figure 5.1 below reflects, following the modernization of EU competition law the role of national authorities in its application is greatly enhanced. While the EU Commission possesses autonomous powers to act, the national competition authorities are also required to apply arts 101 and 102, and to do so under their relevant national procedures. In the UK these powers are set out in the Competition Act 1998 (CA 98), such that in most circumstances, it will make little difference whether the OFT is investigating a breach of the Chapter I Prohibition, or a breach of art. 101. Because national procedures are used by the members of the European Competition Network (ECN) there will, inevitably, be differences in the procedures used, and some of these will be substantial. The treatment here relates exclusively to the Commission's autonomous powers, and the powers available to the UK authorities.

Entity	Responsibilities
Commission	– Enforces Articles 101 and 102 TFEU – Broad investigatory powers – 'Law-maker, policeman, investigator, prosecutor, judge and jury' – *Ex post* control of infringements – Coordination through ECN
NCA	– Apply Articles 101 and 102 TFEU in their entirety in individual cases – Enforce national competition law provisions – May require that an infringement be brought to an end, order interim measures, accept commitments or impose fines
Private parties	– May complain to a public enforcer or commence proceedings before a national court to enforce national competition law and Articles 101 and 102 TFEU – Entitled to a Union right to damages, regardless of the national law

Figure 5.1 Current responsibilities of the enforcers of competition law at a glance

5.3 **The burden and standard of proof**

It is generally accepted that the law of arts 101 and 102 TFEU, and the equivalent provisions of the CA 98 (the Chapter I and II Prohibitions) are part of civil or administrative law. However, the application of the law may give rise to substantial penalties (see Chapter 6). By way of example, Intel was fined a record €1.06 billion in a Commission decision (COMP/C-3/37.990 [2009] OJ C227/13) and was also required to take immediate steps to cease the infringements conduct on the market. There may well, therefore, be disputes as to whether the powers possessed by the authorities have been exercised correctly. It has been accepted that, for the purposes of the human rights guarantees enshrined in the European Convention of Human Rights 1950 (ECHR), the law should be treated *as if* it were criminal. As a result, the standards of art. 6 of that Convention are relevant to the proceedings; this means that those subject to the law are entitled to the presumption of innocence guaranteed by art. 6(2) of the Convention. This is expressly provided for in art. 2 of Regulation 1/2003:

In any national or [Union] proceedings for the application of arts [101] and [102] of the Treaty, the burden of proving an infringement of art. [101](1) or of art. [102] of the Treaty shall rest on the party or the authority alleging the infringement.

However, where it has been established that an infringement of art. 101(1) TFEU, or s. 2 of the CA 98, has occurred, an undertaking may, in certain circumstances (see 9.6.1 and 11.2) seek to obtain the benefit of a 'legal exception'. The onus is on the undertaking or association of undertakings claiming the benefit of these provisions to bear the burden of proving that the conditions are fulfilled (see *The Racecourse Association and others* v *OFT* and *The British Horseracing Board* v *OFT* [2005] CAT 29, at paras 130–4). Similarly it is for an undertaking which is alleged to have committed an abuse of a dominant position to provide evidence that its conduct is objectively justified if it seeks to rely on that defence (see 14.5.1.1 below).

This, however, does not explain the *standard* of proof that is required to establish the existence of an infringement. The European Courts have not spelled out what exactly that burden is, referring only to 'the requisite legal standard' (or in the French, *suffisance de droit*). This 'legal standard' is poorly defined. In the early case of *Europemballage and Continental Can* v *EC Commission* case 6/72 [1973] CMLR 199, the Court of Justice rejected a Decision which had found the existence of an infringement, holding that the Commission 'had not, as a matter of law, sufficiently shown the facts and the assessments on which it is based'. In the case of *Remia* the Court held that it would limit its review of any decision challenged

to verifying whether the statement of reasons for the decision is adequate, whether the facts have been accurately stated and whether there has been any manifest error of appraisal or a misuse of powers.   (*Remia BV* v *EC Commission* case 42/84 [1987] 1 CMLR 1, para. 34)

In the UK, the powers set out in the CA 98, as amended by the Enterprise Act 2002 (EA 02) and by the Competition Act 1998 and Other Enactments (Amendment) Regulations 2004, SI 2004/1261, are similar to those of Regulation 1/2003, and the same protections apply. The CAT appeared in *Napp Pharmaceutical Holdings Ltd* v *The Director General of Fair Trading* [2002] CompAR 13 to require a very high standard of proof from a relevant competition authority seeking to sustain an infringement decision. It argued that the undertaking was 'entitled to the presumption of innocence and to any reasonable doubt there may be' (para. 109). In the case of *JJB Sports plc* v *OFT* [2004] CAT 17 [2005] CompAR 29, it sought to clarify the standard. It held, therefore that

the reference by the Tribunal to 'strong and compelling' evidence at [para. 109] of *Napp* should not be interpreted as meaning that something akin to the criminal standard is applicable to these proceedings. The standard remains the civil standard. The evidence must however be sufficient to convince the Tribunal in the circumstances of the particular case, and to overcome the presumption of innocence to which the undertaking concerned is entitled.   (para. 204)

For a comment on the position in the UK under the terms of the CA 98 see Louveaux, B., and Gilbert, P., 'The Standard of Proof under the Competition Act', (2005) *ECLR* 173.

5.4 Enforcement of EU competition law by the Commission

The body responsible for ensuring the observance of EU competition law is the EU Commission. Where its acts produce legal effects it may in turn be overseen by the GC, under the review powers conferred by way of art. 263 TFEU, with the possibility of further appeal to the Court of Justice. Articles 101 and 102 do not, in their own words, establish the necessary mechanism for enforcement of the proscriptions contained therein; the Commission's powers are set out in Regulation 1/2003, which replaced Regulation 17 of 1962 in May 2004. This regulation sets out the procedures to be adopted by the Commission when pursuing possible breaches of arts 101 and 102 TFEU, and the penalties that may be imposed where undertakings are found to have breached the law. The Commission may, in this respect, be characterized as 'law-maker, policeman, investigator, prosecutor judge and jury' (see Jones, A., and Sufrin, B., *EC Competition Law: Text, Cases and Materials* (2008) OUP, Oxford). For the remainder of this section the structure of the regulation will be followed.

5.4.1 Regulation 1/2003

As seen above at 5.2, Regulation 1/2003 made key changes in the application of EU competition law. Importantly, it fundamentally altered the way in which art. 101 (discussed in Chapter 9) is enforced. This was effected by granting direct applicability to art. 101(3), the exception provided for in the Treaty for those agreements that, although contrary to 101 TFEU, may have beneficial effects that save them from the nullity rule contained in art. 101(2). Up until 2004, national authorities could apply arts 101(1) and 101(2) TFEU, but lacked the power to apply the exemption contained in the third paragraph of the provision. The consequences of granting direct applicability are addressed fully in Chapter 9, and are also considered in Chapter 7. The regulation, in a related move, profoundly adjusted the relationship between the EU Commission and the Member States in the enforcement of EU competition law. This change is explained in part in Chapter 3. It also made changes to the specific powers of investigation and enforcement available to the Commission in the prosecution of alleged infringements. These latter changes are the core of this chapter.

5.4.1.1 The subjects of investigation

Although it has been stressed earlier that the subjects of competition law are 'undertakings' (see 2.2), there are increasing instances where this is not strictly the case. In the UK the cartel offence is targeted not at undertakings, but at individuals (discussed in Chapter 12). In the EU one of the changes effected by Regulation 1/2003 was, in limited circumstances, to extend the power of the Commission to allow it to 'interview any persons who may be in possession of useful information' (para. 25—this finds formal expression in art. 19 of the regulation), and in certain cases to enter private homes if business records are kept there (para. 26, and art. 21 of the regulation). However, individuals—unless they are simultaneously undertakings—may not be found to be in breach of the substantive provisions of arts 101 and 102. The scope of the Commission's power is purely procedural, and is designed to make easier the uncovering of infringements by undertakings.

5.4.2 **Broad investigatory powers conferred by Regulation 1/2003**

The regulation gives the Commission and the national authorities powers to make certain decisions necessary for the application of arts 101 and 102, and to take the steps necessary to lead to these decisions. It has broader competences than the national authorities, and under the terms of the regulation still sits at the apex of EU competition law.

Article 2 of the regulation sets out the relevant burden of proof when an attempt is made to establish an infringement, or when an undertaking is seeking to rely on the legal exception provided for in art. 101(3). It

shall rest on the party or the authority alleging the infringement. The undertaking or association of undertakings claiming the benefit of art. [101](3) of the Treaty shall bear the burden of proving that the conditions of that paragraph are fulfilled.

In respect of the application of art. 101(3) TFEU (the exemption) it is appropriate that the party seeking to rely on it has to establish its validity. This provision applies only to situations in which art. 101(1) also applies—this is to say, to situations in which prima facie an illegal, prohibited agreement is operating (Article 1(1)). The onus is then on the party seeking to operate in this manner to justify the derogation from the general rule.

5.4.2.1 Articles 4–10 of the regulation

EU competition law may be applied at the first instance by three sets of institutions: DG Comp, national authorities and the national courts. National authorities are empowered expressly by art. 5 to take the following decisions:

- requiring that an infringement be brought to an end;
- ordering interim measures;
- accepting commitments;
- imposing fines, periodic penalty payments, or any other penalty provided for in their national law.

The reference to penalties 'provided for in their national law' in the last element opens up the possibility of some divergence, although in practice harmonization has already largely occurred in this area. The UK amended its provisions in relation to penalties to bring them into line with the Commission's powers set out in Regulation 1/2003. Article 6 simply provides that '[n]ational courts shall have the power to apply arts [101] and [102] of the Treaty'. The powers of national courts are considered further in Chapter 7.

5.4.2.1.1 Termination of infringements

The key power available to the Commission in respect of individual cases is set out in art. 7. This provides that where it finds an infringement the Commission 'may by decision require the undertakings and associations of undertakings concerned to bring such infringements to an end'. The coercive powers in this respect are very strong indeed. Thus

it may impose on them any behavioural or structural remedies which are proportionate to the infringement committed and necessary to bring the infringement effectively to an end.

The Commission has in the past imposed a wide range of behavioural remedies. These include, for example, requiring an undertaking to resume supplies to a customer (*BBI/Boosey & Hawkes: interim measures* 87/500 (1987) OJ L286/36); requiring Microsoft to offer an amended version of one of its operating systems (*Microsoft* 2007/53/EC (2007) OJ L32/23); or forcing an ice cream manufacturer to alter its distribution system by removing exclusivity from freezer cabinets (*Van den Bergh Foods Ltd* 98/351 (1998) OJ L246/1).

The reference to structural remedies was not found in Regulation 17. These powers, however, are to be used proportionately, and not in circumstances in which less drastic remedies will resolve the problem. According to recital (12) of Regulation 1/2003, remedies are proportionate 'where there is a substantial risk of a lasting or repeated infringement that derives from the very structure of the undertaking'.

Member States' authorities do *not* have the power to impose structural remedies in relation to breaches of arts 101 and 102 TFEU. This is to be presumed from the fact that there is only express reference to the power of the Commission in this regard. Nonetheless, they may impose structural remedies in relation to breaches of national law if the appropriate powers are available. Indeed, there would be jurisdictional issues arising from the attempt of one authority to impose a structural solution in relation to an undertaking located in the territory of another authority. The Commission may also make decisions to the effect that there has been a breach of arts 101 or 102, but that no such breach is continuing. While the efficacy of this might be questioned, art. 7(1) provides that such decisions may be taken only where there is a 'legitimate interest in doing so'. Limitation periods set out in the regulation impose some further restriction on the ability of the Commission to act in such a fashion. It is most likely to do so where such a decision would act as a precedent to discourage others from participating in similar illegal conduct in the future.

5.4.2.1.2 Interim measures

Regulation 17 did not make explicit the power of the EU Commission to order interim measures. It took the Court of Justice to confirm this power

when the practice of certain undertakings in competition matters has the effect of injuring the interests of some Member States, causing damage to other undertakings, or of unacceptably jeopardising the [Union]'s competition policy. (*Camera Care Ltd* v *Commission* case 792/79R [1980] 1 CMLR 334, at para. 14)

In Regulation 1/2003 this power is set out on the face of the regulation, art. 8 of which provides that 'in cases of urgency due to the risk of serious and irreparable damage to competition' the Commission may order interim measures.

5.4.2.1.3 Commitment decisions

In addition to taking formal decisions under art. 7, the Commission may, under art. 9, accept commitments from undertakings 'to meet the concerns expressed to them by the Commission in its preliminary assessment'. The Commission may take a decision to formalize these commitments and to make them binding. This may prove to be a useful power. In the US, the practice of entering into consent decrees whereby the public authorities forsake the risks of litigation for the certainty of a binding negotiated settlement is common, and has advantages for both the authorities and the undertaking in question. If nothing else this provision removes the linguistic confusion caused by the fact that the Commission in the past has accepted 'undertakings' from undertakings relating to future conduct (see, for example, *IBM* (Bull EC 10–1984) and *Digital* (IP/97/868)). These did not have binding force. The new 'commitment decisions' do not amount to either a finding, or an admission, of an infringement. They are stated in the preamble to the regulation to be 'without prejudice to the powers of competition authorities and courts of the member states to make such a finding and decide upon the case' (para. 13). The same paragraph also makes it clear that such resolutions will not be appropriate in the more serious cases where the Commission was considering the imposition of a penalty. The power to accept commitments, and make decisions in this respect, is also made available to the national authorities under art. 5.

Once a commitment decision is made the Commission may reopen the procedure in only one of three situations. The first arises where there has been a material change in the circumstances since the decision was made (art. 9(2)(a)). The second and third may occur either where the undertaking acts contrary to its commitment (art. 9(2)(b)), or where the decision was based on incomplete, incorrect, or misleading information provided by one of the parties (art. 9(2)(c)). For a good discussion of this new power see Temple Lang, J., 'Commitment Decisions under Regulation 1/2003: Legal Aspects of a New Kind of Competition Decision', [2003] *ECLR* 347.

The first commitment decision was made in the case of the Bundesliga's selling of media rights (Commission press release IP (04) 1110, 17 September 2004). The Commission had been concerned that exclusive selling of commercial broadcasts under the 'Ligaverband' might have been in violation of art. 101. Under the commitment the joint selling arrangement stayed in place, but the Bundesliga undertook to offer unbundled packages of rights for a duration not exceeding three years. On 22 June 2005 DG Comp published its decision relating to a commitment entered into by the Coca-Cola Company (reported at [2006] 4 CMLR 27). The Commission had first investigated various practices relating to a joint dominant position held by Coca-Cola Company and its bottlers on the market for carbonated soft drinks. The company was protected by barriers to entry in the form of sunk advertising costs. DG Comp was particularly concerned that its practices led to foreclosure of third-party competition, reducing pressure on prices. The commitments offered were found by the Commission to be adequate to address its concern, and remained in place until 31 December 2010. Similarly, commitments were also accepted in *De Beers/Alrosa* in relation to the long-term practice of the maintenance of exclusive purchasing agreements between the world's largest and second largest producers of diamonds (decision of 22 February

2006, [2006] 5 CMLR 26). There was then a legal challenge mounted before the GC by Alrosa (*Alrosa Company Ltd* v *Commission* case T–170/06, [2007] 5 CMLR 7), and the decision was annulled on the grounds that Alrosa had not had the opportunity properly to comment on the individual commitments offered by De Beers.

In March 2006 DG Comp accepted commitments from the FA Premier League (FAPL) relating to the selling of broadcasting rights to Premiership games. The commitments, which expire on 30 June 2013, oblige the FAPL to sell six packages of live games to at least two UK broadcasters. The concern raised by DG Comp was that the way in which the FAPL administered the joint selling arrangement on behalf of the FAPL clubs reduced choice and innovation in broadcasting and raised prices. A penalty could be imposed on the FAPL if the commitments are broken, without the Commission 'having to prove any violation of the [EU] Treaty's competition rules' (IP/06/356, 22 March 2006),

5.4.2.1.4 Inapplicability

In addition to decisions finding a breach of arts 101 or 102 TFEU, or to those imposing interim measures, or accepting a commitment, the Commission may, where 'the [Union] public interest…so requires' find that the provisions of arts 101 or 102 are inapplicable to the activities of an undertaking or association of undertakings (similar to negative clearance granted under Regulation 17). It is likely to be used only exceptionally, where a precedent is required, and probably in respect of 'new types of agreements or practices that have not been settled in the existing case law and administrative practice' (para. 14).

5.4.2.2 Cooperation between DG Comp and the Member States: the European Competition Network (arts 11–16)

Although the modernization process has simplified the enforcement of competition law in many respects, it has also created a more complex relationship between DG Comp and the national competition authorities and between the national competition authorities themselves. Chapter IV of the regulation, which deals with 'Cooperation', remains somewhat unclear. The broadest of statements in respect of this chapter of the regulation is found in art. 11(1) which provides simply that 'The Commission and the [NCAs] shall apply the [Union] competition rules in close cooperation'. To this end information shall be shared between the Commission and the NCAs (art. 11(2)), and the latter are obliged to inform the former whenever they intend to act in relation to the application of arts 101 or 102.

NCAs must notify the Commission thirty days before requiring that an infringement be brought to an end, accepting commitments or withdrawing the benefit of a block exemption regulation (see Chapter 10). The Commission shall be provided with a summary of the case, and, at its request, any other relevant documents. This information may then be made available to the competition authorities of the other Member States (art. 11(4)). If the Commission itself decides to open proceedings against the undertakings the authorities of the Member States shall be relieved of their competence to apply arts 101 or 102 to that situation. However, where a NCA is already examining the practice in question the Commission shall not act without first consulting it (art. 11(6)).

Matters relating to the exchange of information are highly sensitive, and undertakings are greatly concerned at the increased flow of information among the members of the ECN. Article 12, which should be read alongside art. 28 ('professional secrecy'), governs the way in which information may be exchanged among members of the network. Confidential information is expressly excluded (art. 12(1)), although all information may 'only be used in evidence for the purpose of applying arts 101 or 102 of the Treaty and in respect of the subject matter for which it was collected by the transmitting authority' (art. 7(2)). This means that information supplied to the OFT by other NCAs or DG Comp may not, for example, be used in relation to the prosecution of the cartel offence under domestic law. Article 12(3) imposes further limits on the way in which exchanged information can be used to support the imposition of sanctions on *natural persons*, which would again extend to the cartel offence. Article 28 requires that information collected by the Commission in the application of its powers (see below) 'shall be used only for the purpose for which it was acquired', and that this or information collected and exchanged by the members of the ECN, shall not be disclosed where it is 'of the kind covered by the obligation of professional secrecy' (art. 28(2)).

Article 13 sets out the conditions under which an investigating authority shall terminate or suspend proceedings. Although the article does not preclude two or more authorities from acting against an agreement or practice, it does provide that wherever one authority is doing so this 'shall be sufficient grounds for the others to suspend the proceedings before them or to reject the complaint' (art. 13(1)). A concern that has been widely discussed relating to the operation of the ECN is that it may lead to a number of actions being taken against the same practice. Article 13 is designed in part to alleviate this.

The role of the Advisory Committee, discussed in Chapter 2 at 2.3.4.2, is set out in art. 14. Cooperation between the Commission and the national courts, and the requirements of arts 15 and 16, have been considered in Chapter 3.

5.4.2.3 Informal guidance on novel questions

Regulation 1/2003 does not contain within it procedures under which matters may be notified to the Commission for consideration or guidance. However, DG Comp has recognized the possibility that new matters may still arise, in relation to which there is a lack of assistance in the existing case law. Recital (38) of the regulation acknowledges this. In such circumstances the parties may ask DG Comp for guidance. Such requests will be dealt with only where the relevant goods or services are economically important, and/or the practice is widespread, and/or there are substantial investments linked to the operation concerned. Further, the Commission will act only on the basis that it does not itself need to seek further information. Neither will the Commission consider hypothetical situations (see generally *Commission Notice on informal guidance relating to novel questions concerning articles 81 and 82 of the EC Treaty that arise in individual cases (guidance letters)* (2004) OJ C101/78).

5.4.2.4 Articles 17–22: fact finding

The specific investigative functions provided for by Regulation 1/2003 are set out in Chapter V of the regulation, arts 17–22. These are backed up by powers in arts 23 and 24 to impose financial penalties on those who fail to cooperate with investigations. In the UK the CA 98, ss. 61–65I legislates for the OFT's powers in relation to inspections under arts 20, 21, and 22(2) of Regulation 1/2003.

5.4.2.4.1 *Investigations into sectors of the economy, or types of agreements*

Article 17 gives the Commission a general power to conduct wide-ranging investigations either into particular types of agreements, or across sectors of the economy. In January 2004 the institution announced that it was launching just such an investigation into the sale of sports rights to Internet and 3G service providers (see Commission press release IP (04) 134, 30 January 2004). The article gives the Commission the power to publish a report, but in the absence of specific breaches of arts 101 or 102 by specific undertakings it has no general competence to deal with market failure in the way that is available to the UK authorities under the market investigation reference provisions of the EA 02 (see Chapter 17). The Commission noted that such inquiries were particularly appropriate 'for enquiring into sectors where business practices are not yet established and competition is shaped through one shot big size agreements as in the New Media/3G content sector'. The Commission has hinted that such inquiries might become more common, as they provide a suitable instrument 'for investigating cross-border market concerns and examining sector-wide practices that do not normally fall within the scope of an individual case'. In June 2005 further sector inquiries were launched in financial services and in gas and electricity markets (Commission press releases IP/05/719, 13 June 2005, and IP/05/716, 13 June 2005). On 16 February 2006 DG Comp published its preliminary report in which it identified a number of problems with their operation. It announced that some competition concerns would be pursued, including one into the prevalence of long-term supply contracts in the wholesale gas sector. It is argued by a number of commentators that this latter practice has the effect of restricting wholesale supplies into the UK, thereby raising UK prices for gas significantly above a competitive level.

5.3.2.4.2 *Requests for information*

Article 18 of the regulation gives the Commission the power to obtain information from undertakings and associations of undertakings. This power may be exercised either by request, or by decision. There are few limitations in the wording of this article, although there is a requirement that the information sought be 'necessary'. It has been held by the GC that 'necessary information' is anything which has a relationship with possible infringements of arts 101 and 102 (see *SEP* v *Commission* case T–39/90 [1992] 5 CMLR 33). At the same time as making any request or decision the Commission must forward a copy to the competent authority of the relevant Member State (art. 18(5)).

The Commission has the choice of issuing either a request or a decision when it is gathering information. Where it sends a simple request it is required to state the legal basis and purpose, to specify the information required, to fix a time limit for its production, and to indicate the penalties that are available under art. 23 for supplying incorrect or misleading information (art. 18(2)). Similar obligations are imposed by virtue of art. 18(3) which relates to decisions requiring that information be supplied. However, in this case the Commission must also indicate the penalties that are available under art. 24 for non-compliance, and the right of review of that decision before the Court of Justice under art. 263 TFEU.

The obligations of art. 18 may be imposed only on undertakings, and it is their owners, or their representatives, which shall supply the information. Duly authorized lawyers may act for their clients, but in the event that incomplete, incorrect, or misleading information is supplied it is the undertaking itself which remains responsible for the breach.

5.4.2.4.3 The taking of statements

The Commission has the power to take statements from any natural or legal person 'who consents to be interviewed' (art. 19(1)). However, it does not have the power to compel a natural person to submit themselves to an interview, although it may ask questions in the course of an investigation following art. 20. It is likely that this power will be used most often in non-contentious cases, as would be the case where the Commission was gathering information from a customer or competitor of an undertaking whose activity was subject to scrutiny. The Commission must inform the relevant authority of the Member State in whose territory the interview is taking place if this is at the premises of an undertaking, although there is no obligation to do so in other circumstances. At the request of the relevant authority, its officials may assist and accompany those of the EU Commission.

5.4.2.4.4 Inspections

The most intrusive power of the EU Commission is its right to conduct investigations at the premises of an undertaking. Thus art. 20(1) provides that the Commission 'may conduct all necessary inspections of undertakings and associations of undertakings'. Article 21 further provides that where 'serious' breaches of arts 101 or 102 are being investigated, the Commission may conduct inspections at private premises. In both cases they may require the cooperation of the relevant national authorities, including the courts and the police, to effect such inspections. There is no requirement on the Commission to first avail itself of the powers given in art. 18 before making use of art. 20. Indeed the first time that an undertaking may become aware of an art. 20 inspection is when the relevant officials arrive at its premises with their notification and demand access (so-called 'dawn raids'—terminology which is not used by the EU Commission, but which has entered the language of competition law).

Article 20(2) provides that the Commission officials, and other accompanying persons (likely to be representatives of the relevant NCA), have the power:

(a) to enter any premises, land and means of transport of undertakings and associations of undertakings;

(b) to examine the books and other records related to the business, irrespective of the medium on which they are stored;

(c)   to take or obtain in any form copies of or extracts from such books and records;

(d)   to seal any business premises and books or records for the period and to the extent necessary for the inspection;

(f)   to ask any representative or member of staff of the undertaking or association of undertakings for explanations on facts or documents relating to the subject-matter and purpose of the inspection and to record the answers.

There are requirements in the article for close liaison between the Commission and the relevant authorities of the Member State on whose territory the inspection is taking place. National authorities must afford the Commission 'necessary assistance, requesting where appropriate the assistance of the police or of an equivalent enforcement authority so as to enable them to conduct their inspection' (art. 20(6)). Article 20(6)–(7) deals with the situation in which national judicial approval is necessary for any such inspection. The judicial authority may ask for detailed information, but is not permitted to 'call into question the necessity for the inspection nor demand that it be provided with the information in the Commission's file'. This follows the judgment of the Court of Justice in the case of *Roquette Frères SA* v *Directeur Général de la Concurrence de la Consommation et de la Répression des Fraudes* case C–94/00 [2003] 4 CMLR 1. Here the Court responded to a reference for a preliminary ruling from a French court concerned as to the limits on its powers to review requests for judicial approval for an investigation. It held, that

In accordance with the general principle of [Union] law affording protection against arbitrary or disproportionate intervention by public authorities in the sphere of the private activities of any person…a national court having jurisdiction under domestic law to authorise entry upon and seizures at the premises of undertakings suspected of having infringed the competition rules is required to verify that the coercive measures sought…by the Commission…are not arbitrary or disproportionate to the subject-matter of the investigation ordered. Without prejudice to any rules of domestic law governing the implementation of coercive measures, [Union] law precludes review by the national court of the justification of those measures beyond what is required by the foregoing general principle. (para. R1)

Once an investigation is under way the undertaking is under a duty to cooperate fully. It is not sufficient to give the officials unfettered access to all files and records. Employees must actively help find the material sought (see, e.g., *Fabbrica Pisana* 80/334 (1980) OJ L75/30, in which the undertaking had made all its files available but had not assisted the Commission's officials in finding the relevant documents). The Commission appears to be determined to demonstrate the importance of cooperation, which includes not intruding in its investigations. In January 2008, a fine of €38 million was imposed on E.ON Energie AG for breaching a Commission seal on documents (art. 20(2)(d)) during an inspection. Such conduct, it was established, clearly jeopardizes the effectiveness of the investigation, as it gives a company the opportunity to destroy incriminating evidence. Article 23 of Regulation 1/2003 lists those situations in which fines can be imposed, and refers to when 'seals affixed in accordance with Article 20(2)(d) by officials or other accompanying persons authorised by the Commission have been broken' (art. 23(1)(e)). An undertaking is not entitled to have a lawyer present while the investigation is in progress, although the Commission has indicated in its 12th Report on Competition Policy that it may be prepared to wait for one to arrive as long as this does not unduly delay matters.

A contentious area has been that of legal professional privilege. This was first dealt with in *AM&S Europe* v *Commission* case 155/79 [1982] 2 CMLR 264, in which the undertaking had applied to the Court of Justice to strike down the Commission action after it had seized material held by the undertaking's in-house lawyers. The Advocate General conducted a thorough review of the law relating to legal privilege in the Member States, and the Court held that only in recognizing the privilege attaching to documents emanating from independent lawyers relating to the client's right of defence did the laws of the Member States converge to the extent necessary for a common protection to be recognized. Thus the Court affirmed that Regulation 17 was to be interpreted so as to protect such communications only. It indicated in *Hilti AG* v *Commission* case T–30/89A [1990] 4 CMLR 602 that, in certain highly restricted circumstances, the protection might apply to communications with in-house lawyers (see also *VW* 98/273 (1998) OJ L124/61, paras 198–9), although this proposition was largely rejected in the most recent case to deal with the issue of legal privilege in detail, *AKZO Nobel Chemicals Ltd* v *Commission* case T–112/05 [2008] 4 CMLR 12, confirmed by the Court of Justice (case 550/07 P, judgment of 14 September 2010. See also cases T–125/03R and T–253/03R [2004] CMLR 15). During the course of its investigation at the premises, the applicants claimed that some of the documents sought by the Commission might be covered by legal professional privilege. The documents were in two sets. Set A consisted of a memorandum that had been prepared for the purpose of obtaining external legal advice in connection with a competition law compliance programme maintained by the undertaking. Set B were handwritten notes by the General Manager of one of the undertakings relating to the preparation of the memorandum, and emails between him and a Dutch lawyer who was also employed within the undertaking's legal department. The applicants brought an action before the GC. Although preliminary stages in a proceeding that will lead to a final decision are not usually capable of being challenged under art. 263 TFEU, the GC held that in the case of a decision by the Commission to refuse to recognize certain documents as being subject to legal professional privilege 'constitutes an act capable of being challenged by an action for annulment' (para. 48). An applicant would also be entitled to apply for a suspension of the effect of the Commission decision until such time as the court made a ruling in the case.

The Court found that the documents in Set A were not covered by legal professional privilege as they were not communications with an independent lawyer or internal notes commenting on such communications. The GC did hold, however, that such documents might be covered 'provided that they were drawn up exclusively for the purpose of seeking legal advice from a lawyer in exercise of the rights of the defence' (para. 123). Given, however, that legal professional privilege constituted an exception to the powers of the Commission as set out in the relevant regulations a strict approach would be taken to such documents, with the undertaking being obliged to have *proved* that the documents were prepared *exclusively* for that purpose. The GC agreed with the Commission in that the privilege did not apply to Set B either. With regard to in-house lawyers the Court pointed to the judgment of the Court of Justice in *AM&S* as stipulating that where privilege was asserted the lawyer should not be bound to the client by a contract of employment (para. 166 of *AM&S*). In September 2010, the Court upheld the decision of the GC, announcing that 'the current legal situation in the member states does not justify consideration of a change in the case law towards granting in-house lawyers the benefit of legal professional privilege'.

There is debate as to the extent to which the Commission is able to exploit its power to ask for oral explanations (art. 20(2)(e)). While the regulation does not restrict the article so as to apply it only to specific officers of the undertaking, or to specific subject matter, it would appear that the Commission is not able to ask any employee of the undertaking any question. In *National Panasonic (UK) Ltd* v *Commission* case 136/79 [1980] 3 CMLR 169, Advocate General Warner suggested that the power related to 'specific questions arising from the books and business records which [the Commission officials] examine' in the course of the investigation. If this is a comprehensive statement of the Commission's power, which has been doubted, it would rule out 'fishing trips' by its officials. The Commission has stated elsewhere that it is for the undertaking to nominate the appropriate persons to answer questions, as it is not in the position to judge the competence or knowledge of individual employees (*Fabbrica Pisana* 80/334 (1980) OJ L75/30).

There have been many occasions on which undertakings have challenged the way in which the Commission has conducted its investigation. *National Panasonic* is one of the most significant cases. Commission officials arrived at the sales offices of Panasonic in Slough at about 10 a.m. on 27 June 1979. The officials notified the undertaking's directors of a decision taken on 22 June authorizing an on-the-spot investigation. The directors asked if the investigation could be delayed while the undertaking's solicitor travelled to the scene from Norwich and the officials stated that their authorization entitled them to act immediately. The inspection, which lasted until 5.30 p.m., began at 10.45 a.m. and the undertaking's solicitor did not arrive until 1.45 p.m. Panasonic subsequently appealed against the decision and, *inter alia*, asked the Court of Justice to order that all documents seized be returned or destroyed. It argued that this was the first time that the Commission had proceeded to a formal investigation by way of decision without first affording the undertaking the opportunity to submit of its own volition to an informal investigation. In fact since 1973 there had been 24 other cases in which the Commission had so acted, and it was contended that there was too great a risk that, if both stages of the procedure were followed, evidence would be destroyed or removed. The Commission claimed that, even if only the one-stage procedure were followed, there were sufficient safeguards for the undertaking concerned. In doing so it pointed to eight factors:

(a) the need for written authorization;

(b) the need for a formal decision taken by the Commission;

(c) the fact that only 'necessary' investigations could be carried out;

(d) the requirement that the decision be adequately reasoned;

(e) the requirement that the Commission consult the competent authority of the Member State concerned;

(f) the fact that the decision must state within it the right to challenge under art. 263 TFEU;

(g) the fact that a successful challenge would deprive the Commission of the right to use any materials obtained; and

(h) the availability of a remedy under art. 340 TFEU were the Commission officials to exceed their authority.

The Court rejected the general arguments made by Panasonic, and in doing so affirmed that the procedures applied did not infringe the rights invoked, unsuccessfully, by the applicant.

The Commission officials may not use force in carrying out their investigation (*Hoechst AG v Commission* cases 46/87 and 227/88 [1991] 4 CMLR 410, para. 31), although they may be able to fall back on the assistance of national authorities where this is necessary to compel an undertaking to comply with an investigation.

The power to inspect 'other premises' given in art. 21 of Regulation 1/2003 is more controversial. The evidence however is clear that documents which may shed light on the operation of cartels in particular are being stored in private premises so as to put them out of the reach of the Commission. In order to inspect 'other premises', which include 'the homes of directors, managers and other members of staff of the undertaking' (art. 21(1)) the Commission *must* seek the prior authorization of the judicial authority of the Member State concerned. Officials have the powers set out in art. 20(2)(a)–(c).

5.4.2.5 Penalties

Penalties levied in the case of substantive infringements of arts 101 and 102 TFEU are discussed in the following chapter. Penalties may also be imposed in the event of an undertaking subject to investigation committing procedural breaches (such as the fine imposed on E.ON for breaching an inspection seal—see 5.4.2.4.4). Provision is made for these in art. 23(1) of Regulation 1/2003. Where undertakings supply false or misleading information, or fail to comply with a decision requiring them to submit information, or to an inspection, or give misleading answers, they may be fined up to 1 per cent of their total turnover in the preceding business year. In addition, periodic penalty payments may be imposed of up to 5 per cent of the average daily turnover in the preceding business year per day to compel undertakings to terminate an infringement or to supply information demanded, or to submit to an inspection (art. 24). Articles 25 and 26 set out limitation periods in relation to the imposition of penalties.

5.4.2.6 Hearings and access to file

Once the Commission has conducted its inquiries it must, before making any decision, give the undertaking(s) concerned the chance to be heard (art. 27, Regulation 1/2003). It may also hear applications from other natural or legal persons who can 'show a sufficient interest' (para. 3). The general procedure for these hearings is set out in Commission Regulation 773/2004 (2004) OJ L123/18. This regulation, which entered into force on 1 May 2004, makes provision for the hearing of those to whom objections are addressed (arts 11–12), applicants and complainants, and other third parties (art. 13).

Hearings are conducted by 'the Hearing Officer', appointed by the Commission (art. 14, whose terms of reference are set out in Decision 2001/462 (2001) OJ L162/21). The role of the Hearing Officer has changed substantially since the post was intro- duced in 1982. This reflects the difficult role the Commission has had to play both as the guarantor of the rights of undertakings involved in competition proceedings, and as the agency charged with pursuing those in breach of the law. The essence of the role of the Hearing Officer is set out in Commission press release IP/01/736 (23 May 2001), which states that

This new Mandate of the Hearing Officer will substantially improve the overall account- ability of the Commission's decision-making process in merger and antitrust proceedings, ensuring that all fundamental rights of parties and economic operators involved in its pro- cedures are respected.

The key function which ensures that this aim is met is set out in Commission Decision 2001/462, art. 1, which provides that the 'Commission shall appoint one or more hearing officers . . . who shall ensure that the effective exercise of the right to be heard is respected in competition proceedings before the Commission'. The most significant change from the earlier practice introduced in the 2001 Decision is that the Hearing Officer is no longer part of the mainstream of the Competition Division of the Commission, a practice which had been previously criticized. It is now attached directly to the office of 'the member of the Commission with special responsibility for competition' (art. 2(2)). During the hearings which take place the Hearing Officer 'shall ensure that the hearing is properly conducted and contributes to the objectivity of the hearing itself and of any decision taken subsequently' (art. 5). Currently, there are two Hearing Officers: Michael Albers and Wouter Wils.

Article 14 of Regulation 773/2004 sets out further details relating to hearings. Parties invited to attend may do so in person, or may be represented by a lawyer. The oral hearings are not public, and persons may be heard separately so as to protect busi- ness secrets. A difficult and contentious issue is the extent to which an undertaking should have access to documents held by the Commission relevant to the case, some of which may well have been obtained from the undertaking's commercial rivals. Article 27(2) of Regulation 1/2003 deals with the question in the following terms:

[Parties] shall have access to the Commission's file, subject to the legitimate interest of undertakings in the protection of their business secrets. The right of access to the file shall not extend to confidential information and internal documents of the Commission or the competition authorities of the Member States. In particular, the right of access shall not extend to correspondence between the Commission and the competition authorities of the Member States, or between the latter.

The Commission recognized in its *23rd Annual Report* that 'the disclosure to the parties of any relevant information is an essential part of the procedure' (citing *Hoffmann-La Roche & Co. AG* v *Commission* case 85/76 [1979] 3 CMLR 211, (1993) *Annual Report*, point 199). In *Hoffmann* the Court of Justice held that any undertaking must be able to have its views heard and, in particular, must be able to comment 'on the documents used by the Commission to support its claim that there has been an infringement' (at para. 11). The matter is complicated, as was recognized in *Hoffmann-La Roche*, by the obligation of secrecy imposed on the Commission by way of art. 28 of Regulation 1/2003.

Decision 2001/462 in effect enshrines what became known as the '*AKZO* procedure' (*AKZO Chemie BV* v *Commission* case 53/85 [1987] 1 CMLR 231). Under it, the Commission will notify the undertaking from which the document has been taken that it intends to allow a third party to inspect the document. The first undertaking will then have the opportunity to contest the decision before the court prior to the release of the information. In the *Soda Ash* series of cases (cases T 30–32/91 and T 36–37/91 [1996] 5 CMLR 57 ff.) the GC annulled decisions of the Commission in part because they had violated rights of the appellants in denying them access to various files. The Court held that 'it is not for the Commission alone to decide which documents are useful to the defence and the advisors of the company must have the opportunity to examine documents which may be relevant'.

The Court in *Soda Ash* suggested that the Commission should either allow the undertaking's lawyers unfettered access to the documents held by it prior to the hearing, or make available a list of *all* documents in its possession. This judgment will make life difficult for the Commission, and has been criticized as imposing impractical demands in operation (see, Ehlermann, C. D., and Drijber, B. J., 'Legal Protection of Enterprises: Administrative Procedure, in particular Access to Files and Confidentiality', [1996] *ECLR* 375).

In 2005 the Commission issued a revised version of a *Notice on the rules for access to the Commission file* (2005) OJ C325/7. It relates to proceedings under both Regulations 1/2003 and 139/2004 (the EU Merger Regulation—see further Chapter 19). Under the terms of the notice, access to file will be granted to those to whom the Commission addresses its statements of objections (SO), which is to say those who need to defend themselves against the allegations made in the SO. Access will be given to all documents 'which have been obtained, produced and/or assembled by [DG Comp] during the investigation' (para. 8). However, internal documents, business secrets and other confidential information are excluded. Where confidential information is contained in the Commission file it will attempt, where possible, to provide non-confidential versions of the same documents, although it may be necessary for this to be simply in the form of a summary of the document. Access to the file will normally only be granted to each applicant once during the proceedings after the notification of the Commission's SO to the parties, however where evidence is received after such access has been given, further access to this new evidence will be possible. The procedure by which the Notice may be relied upon is clearly set out in the document itself, as are more details relating to the designation and treatment of confidential information.

5.4.2.7 Secrecy

Any information obtained by the Commission in the course of its investigations must be treated carefully by the Commission and can 'be used only for the purpose for which it was acquired' (art. 28). The concern of undertakings is that the power to examine business records is sufficiently wide as to extend to all information held by the company, with the exception of independent legal advice. The Commission has held that 'business secrecy cannot be invoked against Commission officials ... since ... the same Regulation provides that they shall not disclose information' (*Fides* 79/253 (1979) OJ L57/33). Thus undertakings may be required to surrender highly sensitive information relating both to industrial processes and to marketing. The Commission has repeatedly relied on its obligation under art. 28 to deny the undertaking concerned the opportunity to withhold information. The point was made forcefully in *FNIC* (*Fédération nationale de l'industrie de la chaussure de France* 82/756 (1982) OJ L319/12) where the company refused to hand to the Commission certain 'confidential documents' which, the company argued, went 'far beyond the investigators' terms of reference'. The Commission reiterated its long-held view that undertakings 'may invoke the confidentiality of such documents only within the framework of [art. 20]'.

The requirement of art. 28 is that the Commission and competent authorities shall not disclose any information gained under the regulation and 'of the kind covered by the obligation of professional secrecy'. This article is itself based on arts 17(3) and (7) TEU, which provide a more general guarantee that Union institutions and officials shall not disclose information of the kind covered by the obligation of professional secrecy, in particular information about undertakings, their business relations or their cost components. The Court of Justice has held that this requisite is crucial as regards the rights of the undertakings in the process (*Dow Benelux NV* v *Commission* case 85/87 [1991] 4 CMLR 410), and in *AKZO* (case 53/85 [1987] 1 CMLR 231) it argued that '[b]usiness secrets are thus afforded a *very special* protection' (para. 28, emphasis added). However, as the Commission notes in its notice on access to the file (see above), this remains a problem as no case has fully discussed the criteria for determining that any particular piece of information is a business secret. In the event that any information is shared between the Commission and the NCA, the obligation in Regulation 1/2003 is binding on all bodies (art. 28(2)).

Article 30(2) of Regulation 1/2003 provides a further guarantee in that when the Commission publishes any formal decision that it takes in relation to a particular proceeding 'the publication ... shall have regard to the legitimate interest of undertakings in the protection of their business secrets'.

The tension between the requirement of secrecy and confidentiality on the one hand and the right of undertakings to have access to pertinent information in order to ensure that their rights are observed on the other is a very clear one. The very strict position taken by the Court in *AKZO* was largely determined by the fact that the undertaking seeking access to the confidential information was the complainant, and a competitor of AKZO.

5.4.2.8 Rights of the parties and fundamental protections

At face value the powers accorded to the Commission under Regulation 1/2003 are substantial, and the only significant recognition of the rights of the defence appears in art. 27. At art. 27(2) it is stated that 'the rights of defence of the parties concerned shall be fully respected in the proceedings'. The regulation itself is largely silent on what these rights are, and in order to clarify this area it is necessary to turn to the case law of the European Courts.

The extent to which legal persons, as distinct from natural persons, should be accorded fundamental rights is a matter of intense debate: the question is whether it is 'appropriate to extend a privilege, which began as a protection for individuals, to an artificial entity such as a corporation' (*Environment Protection Authority* v *Caltex Refining Co. Pty Ltd* (1993) 118 ALR 392, at 553 *per* McHugh J). More pithily Lord Denning has said that a company has 'no body to be kicked or soul to be damned' (*BSC* v *Granada TV* [1981] AC 1096).

In the EU there is a further complication in that there is no clear standard of 'fundamental rights' set out in the founding treaties. Instead the Court of Justice has developed, at first slowly and then with greater force, a jurisprudence of general principles of law, drawing in part on international instruments in which the Member States have participated. The Court confirmed in *Firma J. Nold KG* v *Commission* case 4/73 [1974] 2 CMLR 338, that the European Convention on Human Rights 1950 (ECHR) is of particular importance in this regard, and all Member States of the EU are bound equally by its provisions, although the two regimes are legally and politically distinct. This judicial activity received belated support by the Member States in art. 6(3) TEU, which provides that '(f)undamental rights, as guaranteed by the European Convention ... and as they result from the constitutional traditions common to the Member States, shall constitute general principles of the Union's law'. The application of fundamental rights jurisprudence in relation to the competition procedures has caused problems for the Court, which remains bound by the words of the legislation.

In *National Panasonic (UK) Ltd* v *Commission* case 136/79 [1980] 3 CMLR 169, the applicant's contention that its fundamental rights had been infringed was rejected, but the Court of Justice left open the possibility that such rights could be relied upon where the Commission's actions could be shown to be disproportionate. In *AM&S Europe* v *Commission* case 155/79 [1982] 2 CMLR 264, at 322, the Court concluded that EU law 'must take into account the principles and concepts common to the laws of [the Member States]'. A similar position was reached in *Hoechst AG* v *Commission* cases 46/87 and 227/88 [1991] 4 CMLR 410, in which the Court held that 'regard must be had in particular to the rights of the defence' (at 465); and in *Soda Ash* cases T 30–32/91 and T 36–37/91 [1996] 5 CMLR 57 ff., the GC referred to the need to achieve the general requirement of 'equality of arms'.

The most substantial arguments relating to fundamental rights made to date are those in *Orkem SA* v *Commission* case 374/87 [1991] 4 CMLR 502. The Commission had made a decision demanding information in respect of which an earlier request had been largely ignored. The undertaking's argument was that the documents requested were potentially self-incriminating. Advocate General Darmon recognized that 'exploitation to the full of any latitude allowed by the legal rules and efforts to ensure [that the] broadest interpretation of that latitude is acknowledged to constitute a positive right are the very essence of defence' (art. 513). He focused on the distinction between the *investigative* stage of the Commission's proceedings, the purpose of which is to check the existence of 'a given factual and legal situation', and the *statement of objections* wherein 'there is a much greater protection' afforded to the undertaking. As regards the alleged right not to incriminate itself, the Advocate General argued that, on an inspection of the text of the regulation, it was clear that it 'did not intend to give undertakings to which a request for information was addressed the right not to incriminate themselves'. More strongly, he stated that the machinery of the regulation appeared to him 'to be intellectually incompatible with the right to silence'. In giving judgment the Court allowed greater protection to the individual than the Advocate General had suggested. It drew a somewhat uneasy distinction between documentary evidence and oral explanations, and held that the Commission could compel an undertaking to provide documents in its possession, but that it not 'to provide it with answers which might involve an admission on its part of the existence of an infringement which it is incumbent upon the Commission to prove'. Only purely factual answers may be required (*Mannesmannrohren-Werke AG v Commission* case T–112/98 [2001] 5 CMLR 1).

The case of *Orkem* was further discussed in *Otto v Postbank* case C–60/92 [1993] ECR I–5683, which came before the Court of Justice as an art. 267 reference from the Dutch courts. The defendant in domestic proceedings had argued that national law was incompatible with EU law because it was obliged to produce incriminatory evidence. One of the arguments made by the defendant was that this evidence could, and probably would, come to the attention of the Commission which might use it as part of its own enforcement procedure. The Court held that the Commission would not be able to use any such evidence in order to establish an infringement of the relevant parts of the Treaty, but that in the case in question it would not interfere as the matter was strictly one between private parties and did not involve the possibility of a penalty imposed by a public authority.

In the *Modernisation White Paper* an amendment was suggested to Regulation 17, 'to make it quite clear that in the course of an investigation the authorised Commission officials are empowered to ask the undertakings representatives or staff any questions that are justified by and related to the purpose of the investigation, and to demand a full and precise answer' (para. 113). The relevant provision, which is now set out at art. 20(2)(e) of Regulation 1/2003, does somewhat clarify the position (see 5.3.2.4.4). It will be noted that the wording focuses on questions relating to explanations of facts or documents.

The relationship in particular between the law of the Human Rights Convention and the treatment of these rights under Union law remains a complex and not altogether satisfactory one. In *Funke v France* (1993) 16 EHRR 297, the European Court of Human Rights emphasized that the Convention's provisions apply to commercial matters as well as to personal rights, and that special provisions of law could not justify the restriction of such rights. This is in conflict with the view of the Advocate General in *Orkem* and suggests that the Court may need to reconsider this area if it intends to stay in line with Convention law. In *Stichting Certificatie Kraanverhuurbedrijf (SCK) and Federatie van Nederlandse Kraanver-huurbedrijven (FNK)* v *Commission* joined cases T–213/95 and T–18/96 [1998] 4 CMLR 259, the GC avoided any substantive discussion relating to the application of Convention law directly to competition proceedings (in response to an argument based largely on the application of art. 6 of the ECHR). It did this by noting instead that 'it is a general principle *of [Union] law* that the Commission must act within a reasonable time in adopting decisions following administrative proceedings relating to competition policy' (emphasis added). Since it was held that the matter fell directly within EU law, which would ensure adequate safeguards, any discussion of the Convention became unnecessary.

The GC itself was found by the Court of Justice to have acted too slowly in delivering judgment in *Baustahlgewebe GmbH* v *Commission* case T–145/89 [1995] ECR II–987, on appeal C–185/95P [1999] 4 CMLR 1203. The appellant relied on art. 6(1) of the Convention in seeking an annulment of the GC ruling, and of the earlier Commission Decision in *Welded Steel Mesh* 89/515 (1989) OJ L260/1. The appeal against the decision was lodged in October 1989, and it was five years and six months before judgment was delivered (22 months after the close of the hearing). The Court of Justice held, notwithstanding the fact that 'the procedure called for a detailed examination of relatively voluminous documents and points of fact and law of some complexity' (para. 36), that 'the proceedings before the [GC] did not satisfy the requirements concerning completion within a reasonable time' (para. 47). The Court found, however, that this breach was insufficient to annul the proceedings in their entirety, and in the alternative the applicant was awarded €50,000 (the appellant, having lost on some of the heads of its appeal, was also obliged to pay its own costs and three-quarters of those of the Commission). Following the judgment the applicant asked the Commission to consider a reduction in the penalty and the interest accrued. This overture was rejected, and the principal amount of the fine was paid on 11 September 1997. On 2 February 2004, the applicant received a letter stating the amount of money that it still considered to be owed, at which point the applicant argued that the Commission was time-barred from seeking to recover these further funds. It relied on the fact that the limitation period set under Regulation 2988/74, art. 4, of five years, had expired on 18 September 2002. The applicant brought a further case before the GC to annul the Commission's attempt to enforce further payment, and was successful in this regard (*Ferriere Nord SpA* v *Commission* case T–153/04 [2006] 5 CMLR 24).

5.4.3 The European Competition Network

The ways in which cooperation between members of the European Competition Network (ECN) functions is dealt with at some length in the *Commission Notice on cooperation within the of Competition Authorities* (2004) OJ C101/43. It explains that the Network

is a forum for discussion and cooperation in the application and enforcement of [EU] competition policy. It provides a framework for the cooperation of European competition authorities in cases where arts [101] and [102] of the Treaty are applied and is the basis for the creation and maintenance of a common competition culture in Europe.   (para. 1)

One of the key issues for the ECN to manage is case allocation. Part 2 of the notice deals with the division of work. It is recognized that cases may be dealt with by a single NCA (possibly with the assistance of other NCAs or the Commission), several NCAs acting in parallel, or the Commission. In most instances it will be the authority that receives the complaint, or initiates proceedings, that will be in charge, and it will use its own procedures during the investigation. In some cases it will be necessary to reallocate the case 'for an effective protection of competition and of the [Union] interest' (para. 7). Indeed, there is an obligation on network members to 'endeavour to reallocate cases to a single well-placed competition authority as often as possible' (para. 7). Three factors are set out as being important in determining which authority is the best placed:

(1) the agreement or practice has substantial direct actual or foreseeable effects on competition within its territory, is implemented within or originates from its territory;

(2) the authority is able to effectively bring to an end the entire infringement i.e. it can adopt a cease and desist order the effect of which will be sufficient to bring an end to the infringement and it can, where appropriate, sanction the infringement adequately;

(3) it can gather, possibly with the assistance of other authorities, the evidence required to prove the infringement.   (para. 8)

Article 11 of Regulation 1/2003 creates a mechanism for members of the ECN to inform each other about investigations at an early stage by way of the Commission (art. 11(3)), which also has an obligation to inform the Member States (art. 11(2)) about its own investigations. Where the same practice comes before a number of members of the ECN they may suspend proceedings or reject complaints on the grounds that another authority is dealing with the matter (art. 13), although there is no obligation on the NCA to do so. Article 11(4) and (5) is intended to provide for a mechanism to ensure consistent application of the law.

Some concerns have been expressed about the divergent expertise and resources of the 27 Member State NCAs. The Commission does not have a formal power to oversee their functioning, but in response to a parliamentary question about this issue it referred to the operation of a regular peer-review process undertaken within the context of the OECD. It also pointed out that an obligation on the NCAs to inform the Commission before they intend to apply EU competition law will 'contribute to the coherent application of [Union] competition law' ((2004) OJ C51E/248, 26 February 2004 [2004] 4 CMLR 921).

5.5 Enforcing competition law in the United Kingdom

5.5.1 The Competition Act 1998

5.5.1.1 Investigation

The powers given to the Office of Fair Trading (OFT) to investigate, remedy and punish breaches of the CA 98 are set out in Chapter III of that Act. These are also the powers that are to be used when the OFT is investigating breaches of arts 101 and 102 TFEU. The most important guidelines in this respect published by the OFT are: *Powers of Investigation; Enforcement: Incorporating the Office of Fair Trading's guidance as to the circumstances in which it might be appropriate to accept commitments* and *OFT's guidance as to the appropriate amount of a penalty.* There have been only a few cases relating to this area as of September 2010.

The powers of investigation the Act confers are bestowed exclusively on the OFT. In the *IIB* case the CAT noted that the Act has endowed 'the [OFT], in the public interest, with wide ranging and draconian powers, exercised on behalf of the State, which may substantially affect the civil rights and obligations of those concerned' (*Institute of Independent Insurance Brokers* v *The Director General of Fair Trading* [2002] CompAR 141, para. 57). The OFT has the power to conduct any investigation where it has 'reasonable grounds for suspecting' that either of the two prohibitions or arts 101 and 102 TFEU are being infringed (s. 25). To this end, s. 26 relates to the general power to gather information. Sections 27 and 28 refer to entering business premises without and with a warrant respectively, while s. 28A allows entering domestic premises under a warrant.

Upon the presentation of a written notice to that effect the OFT may require 'any person to produce to it a specified document, or to provide it with specified information which it considers relates to any matter relevant to the investigation' (s. 26(1)). This is the provision that, according to the guideline *Powers of Investigation*, will be most frequently used. The OFT is able to take copies of the document or of extracts from it, and to require 'any person who is a present or past officer of [the person], or is or was at any time employed by him, to provide an explanation of the document' (s. 27(6)(a)(i)–(ii)). This latter ability to require an explanation from 'any person' who has been an employee or officer of the undertaking is a substantial one, and may conflict with obligations arising under the ECHR (see above in relation to EU law). It is inevitable that there will be disputes over the meaning of 'explanation', with undertakings insisting that they are not required to incriminate themselves when giving an 'explanation' of any particular document. Concern was expressed in the House of Lords that this provision would allow for the possibility of 'an investigating officer shimmying up to the cleaning lady and extracting from her the skeleton key' (Hansard (HL) 17 November 1997, col. 388), and the Confederation of British Industry (CBI) pressed very strongly for changes to these provisions. The Government's view, however, was that 'the statutory investigatory powers must be able to cater for the very worst case of unscrupulous concealment of evidence of a cartel or other anti-competitive behaviour', although generally 'full use of the powers provided in the [Act] should…be unnecessary' (col. 391). There was specific recognition that it might often be the case that secretaries and younger assistants have a great deal of knowledge about practices referred to in documents or under investigation, whereas a more senior manager might lack the 'hands-on' involvement. The question of the extent to which there is a right to silence is to be resolved by reference to EU case law.

Investigations of undertakings' premises may be conducted either with or without prior notice. Section 27 of the Act gives the OFT, or an 'investigating officer', power to 'enter any business premises'. Following an amendment made in 2004 (Competition Act 1998 and other Enactments (Amendment) Regulations 2004, SI 2004/1261), private homes are expressly excluded from this provision. Section 27(6) provides that '"business premises" means premises…not used as a dwelling'. Entry to homes is now covered by s. 28A.

In relation to many of the investigations which will be carried out under this section, the investigating officer is required to give two working days' notice before the power of entry is enforced (s. 27(2)). Section 27(3), however, provides that in situations where there is a 'reasonable suspicion' that the premises are being occupied by a party to an agreement or conduct under investigation, the two-day notice may be waived. The period may also be inapplicable when 'the investigating officer has taken all such steps as are reasonably practicable to give notice but has not been able to do so' (s. 27(3)(b)). The powers that relate to such an investigation are similar to those found in Regulation 1/2003. Thus the investigating officer may take any necessary equipment with them, which might include, for example, portable photocopiers and computer disks (s. 27(5)(a)). Any person on the premises may be required 'to produce any document which [the officer] considers relates to any matter relevant to the investigation' and 'to provide an explanation of it' (s. 27(5)(b)). They may further be required to 'state to the best of his knowledge and belief, where any such document is to be found' (s. 27(5)(c)).

As well as permitting the officer to take copies of, or extracts from, any document (s. 27(5)(d)), a special provision relates to material held in computer systems. Where this is 'accessible from the premises' and is relevant to the investigation, this must be produced in a form 'in which it can be taken away' and in which it is 'visible and legible', which presumably means that a print-out must be provided (s. 27(5)(e)). The reference to material which is 'accessible from the premises' is an interesting one, and it appears to extend to material held on computer systems outside of the premises under investigation, but which can be accessed over a network from the site. This would mean that where the internal information system of the company under investigation was so set up, international records from a multinational company could all be accessed through a single site investigation in the UK, thus avoiding the complexities of establishing jurisdiction and enforcing warrants elsewhere. This conclusion follows if the company is using the information itself as part of its management system. Data held in hard copy at the premises and relied upon on that basis would not be protected and the undertaking should not be able to deny the investigating officers access to the information simply on the basis of which part of their computer system the material is stored on.

While investigations conducted under s. 27 of the Act require that two days' written notice be given, the OFT may use powers under s. 28 of the Act to conduct an investigation without warning following the issuing of a warrant to that effect by a judge. A warrant may be sought either where documents required to be produced under s. 26 or s. 27 have not been produced, or where there is a reasonable ground for believing that if the notice required by s. 27 was given the documents would be destroyed, removed, or concealed (s. 28(2)(b)). It may also be requested where an investigating officer acting under the powers in s. 27 has been unable to gain access to the site. Once the warrant has been issued the powers are the same as for s. 27, with two notable exceptions: first, the officer may enter the premises 'using such force as is reasonably necessary for the purpose' (s. 28(2)(a)); secondly, whereas under s. 27 an officer without a warrant may only request specific documents, according to s. 28(2)(b) the officer may also search business premises without a warrant for any relevant documentation.

Although the introduction of the right to enter by force was criticized by the Concervatives, the Government clung to it, with Lord Simon being 'thoroughly of the view that the right to entry using reasonable force is a necessary part of ensuring that the process of investigation goes forward. It is a key element of our strategy' (Hansard (HL) 17 November 1997, col. 406). These powers are to be exercised only at 'the very limits of investigation' in 'exceptional cases in which we know that the rogues have thus far repelled all boarders', ibid., col. 409). Later the Government confirmed that force would not be used against persons, but that, if the circumstances were to arise, force could be used inside premises to gain entry to specific parts: 'every subsequent door, if closed, could be broken down to enter the premises' (Hansard (HL) 19 February 1998, col. 339).

Section 28 powers were used for the first time, although the use of force does not appear to have been necessary, in the course of the OFT investigation leading to the decision *Market Sharing by Arriva plc and FirstGroup plc* CA 98/9/2002, 30 January 2002. Here the OFT

applied to the High Court and the Court of Session for warrants to enter premises of the two undertakings in England and Scotland, and exercise powers under s. 28 of the Act. Warrants were issued on 4 and 6 October 2000. Unannounced visits to the premises took place on 10 and 11 October 2000 and copies of documents were taken.   (para. 7)

For an example of the approach taken by a court in response to an application for a warrant by the OFT see *Application for a warrant under the Competition Act 1998* [2003] EWHC 1042 (Comm), [2003] UKCLR 765. Here the OFT applied for a warrant without notice, following a suspicion that the unnamed defendants had been engaged in price fixing. Morrison J was 'satisfied that what is summarised in...skeleton argument, justifies me in concluding that there are presently reasonable grounds for suspecting that the defendants have been engaged in unlawful conduct' (at para. 3). The practical dynamics underlying such investigations are clearly explained by the judge at para. 5:

On the basis of...the first affidavit of Edward Francis Lennon, a principal investigation officer in the Cartel Investigations Branch of the Competition Enforcement Division of the

OFT, I am satisfied that there are reasonable grounds for suspecting that there are, on the premises named in the warrants, documents which the OFT are entitled to see in the course of their investigation. As to the second requirement, the evidence shows that a 'warning shot across the defendants' bows' has already been fired by the Director General of Fair Trading. The target companies, if they have been doing what the OFT suspect, are likely to have taken steps to make detection difficult and to be continuing so to act. The stakes are high, since the penalties if guilt is established are likely to be high. The entities being investigated include one of a substantial size, and whose reputation, apart from its financial position, may be damaged if incriminating material is found. There is, therefore, a strong inducement or motive for hiding the truth. The material which the OFT are most interested to see is relatively easy to conceal, given advance notice. For these reasons, I am satisfied that there are reasonable grounds for suspecting that the written material would be concealed or destroyed. It is in the public interest that if there has been wrongdoing it is uncovered and revealed.

The *Powers of Investigation* guideline follows the approach of the EU Commission in relation to the legal advice to which an undertaking may have access during the course of an investigation (paras 4.10–4.11). Thus it is made clear that an undertaking may contact its legal advisers, and that 'the authorised officer will grant a request to wait a short time for legal advisers to arrive at the premises before the inspection continues if he considers that it is reasonable to do so in the circumstances'. This provision is also set out in the Competition Act 1998 (Office of Fair Trading's Rules) Order 2004, SI 2004/2751, para. 3). There is no definition of what constitutes 'a reasonable time' and the Order simply provides that this means 'such period of time as the officer considers is reasonable in the circumstances'.

Section 28A relates specifically to the power to enter domestic premises. In such cases entry is possible only when acting under a warrant. Once it has been issued the powers are substantially the same as for s. 28. Domestic premises in this context means any premises used as a dwelling, which are also used in connection with the affairs of an undertaking, or where documents relating to the affairs of an undertaking are stored (s. 28A(9)).

Any person who does not comply with a requirement imposed under s. 26, 27, 28, or 28A is guilty of an offence, and may be liable to a fine. Where the offence has been the obstruction of an officer acting under a warrant issued under s. 28 or 28A the person may, on conviction, be fined, or imprisoned for a maximum of two years (s. 42). Fines and/or imprisonment may similarly be imposed where any person destroys or disposes of a document that they have been required to produce under s. 26, 27, 28, or 28A (s. 43), or where any person gives information to the Director which is materially false or misleading when that person knows it to be so, or is reckless as to its status (s. 44).

It is perhaps in recognition of the problems caused by the *AM&S* judgment (*AM&S Europe* v *Commission* case 155/79 (1982) 2 CMLR 264), and reiterated in the recent *AKZO Nobel* case (*AKZO Nobel Chemicals Ltd* v *Commission* case 550/07 P, judgment of 14 September 2010) that specific provisions in s. 30 of the Act relate to privileged communications. 'Privileged communication' is defined in s. 30 as being a communication 'between a professional legal advisor and his client' or 'made in connection with, or in contemplation of, legal proceedings and for the purposes of those proceedings'. No person shall be required to produce any material under any provision in the Act that falls within this definition. This is one area in which the Act explicitly is out of step with Union law, and where UK practice will not be affected by future developments in EU case law. As was clearly stated in the debates

it is the government's intention that the [OFT] should *not* be able to require, under his investigative powers, the production of legal advice and other material enjoying legal professional privilege, whether the lawyer concerned is an external lawyer or an 'in-house' lawyer. (Hansard (HL) 17 November 1997, col. 416)

This is consistent with the approach adopted by the House of Lords in *Alfred Compton Amusement Machines Ltd* v *Customs and Excise Comrs (No. 2)* [1974] AC 405, where the court held that no distinction could be made between the two groups.

The position in the UK now is a somewhat unfortunate one. Where the OFT is investigating a breach of the Chapter I and II Prohibitions, or is itself investigating a breach of arts 101 or 102 it is s. 30 which applies. However, where the OFT is assisting the EU Commission conducting an investigation on UK soil under the powers conferred by Regulation 1/2003 it is the less restrictive approach taken by the EU which will prevail (see *Powers of Investigation* part 6, para. 6.2).

It will be clear that these powers are very substantial, and at least match those held by the Commission. In fact, given that the Court of Justice has made moves towards increasing the protections afforded to undertakings with reference to 'general principles of law' and the European Convention on Human Rights, the powers given to the Director may be greater than those arising under Regulation 1/2003. Some mention should be made here of the fact that the Human Rights Act 1998 was progressing through Parliament at the same time as the CA 98, and that the former requires courts and tribunals, where possible, to interpret domestic legislation so as to conform to the international obligations set out in the Human Rights Convention. It is likely that, as has been the case in the EU, cases will be brought challenging the application of the investigation powers, particularly where investigations are followed by the imposition of substantial penalties. Section 60 of the CA 98 does not apply to the investigative process, as there are relevant differences between the provisions of the Act and those of Regulation 1/2003 (see, e.g., Pertetz, G., 'Detection and Deterrence of Secret Cartels Under the UK Competition Bill', [1998] ECLR 145). However, the effect of s. 60 is to import into UK law the so-called high-level principles of EU law, such as fairness or due legal process. In these respects jurisprudence in the UK should take into account the development of these principles in the EU.

It is recognized in the *Powers of Investigation* guideline, for example, that the approach to be taken to self-incrimination is the same as under Union jurisprudence. Thus 'the OFT may compel an undertaking to provide specified documents or specified information but cannot compel the provision of answers which might involve an admission on its part of the existence of an infringement' (para. 6.6).

5.5.1.2 Interim measures

Under s. 35 the Director has the power to impose interim measures on those suspected of infringing either of the prohibitions where a reasonable suspicion to that effect exists. These powers may (and are likely to) be exercised notwithstanding that an investigation is in progress. Such interim measures may be taken in order to prevent serious and irreparable harm to any person, or general damage to the public interest. The OFT may also accept 'informal interim assurances' where it is satisfied that these will prevent any harm. The procedures relating to interim measures are dealt with in the *Enforcement Guideline* at part 3.

Interim directions were granted against the London Metal Exchange (LME) in February 2006 (*Directions given pursuant to s. 35 of the Competition Act 1998: London Metal Exchange,* 27 February 2006 [2006] UKCLR 523). In this case the OFT found that it had reasonable grounds to suspect that the LME had abused a dominant position in the provision of trading platforms in the metals markets and was engaged in predatory pricing and exclusionary price discrimination. The LME had announced that it was going to extend its trading hours, and the OFT held the preliminary view that this action would force the complainant from the market, and would damage the competitive process. However, on 5 May 2006 the OFT lifted the interim directions, stating only that it had received 'substantial and material new evidence' and no longer considered it necessary to act urgently (OFT Press Release, 15 May 2006 [2006] UKCLR 549). This was subsequently criticized by the CAT which held that the OFT should be satisfied that the information it was relying on was of an appropriate quality, should be wary of simply relying on information submitted by a complainant, and 'that it should learn from its mistakes' (*London Metal Exchange Ltd* v *OFT* [2006] CAT 19, [2006] CompAR 781, para. 166).

5.5.1.3 Commitment decisions

In line with the new powers available to the EU Commission to accept commitments from undertakings and to formalize these, the OFT also has the power to accept commitments. This power is set out at ss. 31A–31E of the CA 98, and is dealt with in the *Enforcement Guideline* at part 4. The OFT has accepted commitments on only a few occasions. An example arose on 1 March 2006 when it accepted commitments from Associated Newspapers Limited (ANL) relating to exclusive contracts entered into with London Underground Ltd and a number of rail operators. The contracts provided that ANL would have exclusive access to trains and underground stations to distribute the free *Metro* newspaper. The case was closed following the offer of acceptable commitments reducing the level of exclusivity (*London-Wide Newspaper Distribution* CA98/02/2006 [2006] UKCLR 491).

5.5.1.4 Infringement decisions

The OFT has taken a number of infringement decisions in relation to the Chapter I and II Prohibitions, which are dealt with at the relevant parts of this text. Sections 32–34 of the CA 98 set out the power to require the termination of infringements. Wherever the

OFT makes an infringement decision any appeal is to be to the Competition Appeals Tribunal. This procedure applies in relation also to decisions made in respect of arts 101 and 102 TFEU.

The first decision to be published relating to the acceptance of commitments in the UK was in the context of agreements entered into between the British Horseracing Board and the Jockey Club ([2004] UKCLR 1621). The CAT commented on the commitment procedure in *Wanadoo* and noted that it was indeed desirable to be able to settle cases at an appropriate stage. At the same time it was careful not to stifle the flow of formal decisions and cases which would increase the understanding of the Act and its prohibitions, and remarked on when it might be appropriate to proceed to a final decision instead of accepting commitments:

> Much will depend on the nature and seriousness of the infringement alleged, and the likely effectiveness and practicability of any undertakings offered. The fact that the case raises important issues or affects an important sector of the economy may point to the desirability of proceeding to a decision. Cases in which smaller companies are suspected of having infringed the competition rules may equally warrant decisions, for reasons of deterrence, visibility or educational effect. It is for the OFT or other regulator to balance all these various considerations, also taking into account available resources. (*Wanadoo (UK) plc (formerly Freeserve.Com plc)* v *Ofcom* [2004] CAT 20 [2005] CompAR 430, at para. 126)

5.5.1.5 The right to be heard before a decision is taken

Wherever the OFT intends, following any investigation permitted under s. 25, to make a decision to the effect that either the Chapter I or Chapter II Prohibitions or arts 101 or 102 TFEU have been infringed, it must give written notice of that to the appropriate person, and give that person an opportunity to make representations (s. 31).

5.5.2 Judicial review

In principle the acts of domestic competition authorities are subject, in accordance with the Supreme Court Act 1981 and Part 54 of the Civil Procedure Rules, to judicial review. This is an area of law in which there has been rapid growth in recent years, and for a detailed analysis a specialist text should be referred to (for an interesting discussion of some of the aspects, see Black, J., *et al.*, *Commercial Regulation and Judicial Review*, Oxford, Hart Publishing (1998)). Generally, the greater the discretion available to any authority to act the less likely is a judicial review application to be successful. This is certainly the case where the competition authorities are concerned. Both the OFT and the CC have very wide discretion in the exercise of their powers, and there is little prospect of *Wednesbury* unreasonableness (*Associated Provincial Picture Houses Ltd* v *Wednesbury Corpn* [1948] 1 KB 223) applying to a formal decision made by either body. This is particularly so when the final views of these bodies are conditioned by detailed analyses of economic principles which the courts are unlikely to review (see Sir Gordon Borrie, QC, 'The Regulation of Public and Private Power' [1989] *PL* 552).

The majority of the very few reported cases in this area arise out of challenges to decisions taken in relation to merger control. However, it has been established that the law of judicial review relates to the operation of the bodies responsible for competition law at the investigative stage. In *Secretary of State for Trade and Industry* v *Hoffmann-La Roche & Co. AG* [1975] AC 295, at 368, Lord Diplock held that

it is the duty of the Commissioners to observe the rules of natural justice in the course of their investigation—which means no more than that they must act fairly by giving to the person whose activities are being investigated a reasonable opportunity to put forward facts and arguments in justification of its conduct.

In *R* v *MMC, ex parte Matthew Brown plc* [1987] 1 WLR 1235, Macpherson J held that 'provided each party has its mind brought to bear on the relevant issues it is not in my judgment for the court to lay down rules as to how each group should act in a particular enquiry'. As has been noted above, the CC's reports tend to be very detailed and densely argued. While one might take issue with the conclusions drawn, there is only a remote possibility that an action could be founded on the basis that the CC did not bring its mind to bear on the relevant issues. A partially successful judicial review was mounted on behalf of Thomson Holidays against the Foreign Package Holidays (Tour Operators and Travel Agents) Order 1998, SI 1998/1945, which followed the MMC report into the supply of foreign package holidays (Cm. 3813, 1998) (*R* v *Secretary of State for Trade and Industry, ex parte Thomson Holidays* [2000] UKCLR 189). In part the Order was struck down because it prohibited restrictions that were not found by the MMC to operate against the public interest.

A further partial success arose in *Interbrew SA and Interbrew UK Holdings Ltd* v *The Competition Commission and the Secretary of State for Trade and Industry* [2001] UKCLR 954 in which it was found that a remedy required following a merger report was unreasonable in the light of the lack of opportunity the undertaking concerned had had to comment on the proposed remedy in the course of the inquiry. However, the CC's substantive findings regarding the public interest were left largely intact (see CC press release 20/01, 23 May 2001, [2001] UKCLR 734). The fact that so many of the decisions taken by the OFT or the CC in the exercise of their specific powers under the relevant Acts are subject to an appeal process clearly set out in the relevant competition legislation is likely to reduce the grounds on which judicial review may be sought. See, for example, 20.2.6.

5.6 Settlements

The workload that DG Comp and the OFT face in tackling illegal anti-competitive conduct is substantial, and particularly so in relation to cartel conduct. This reflects the success of leniency policies (see 6.3.1.1 and 6.4.1.2). Given that those fined are often likely to mount legal challenges to the infringement decisions, cases can last ten years or more. In order to address this problem, in 2008 the Commission adopted Regulation 662/2008 (2008) OJ L171/3, which amends Regulation (EC) 773/2004 (2004) OJ L123/18 as regards the conduct of settlement procedures in cartel cases.

The regulation introduced a simplified procedure to settle such cases, enabling the parties to obtain a 10 per cent reduction of the fines imposed provided they admit their involvement in the cartel and their liability after examining the evidence against them. It further makes the process more flexible, as the parties are able to take some of the steps before the adoption of the Statement of Objections. The first settlement decision came in July 2010, when all but one of the producers of animal feed phosphates involved in a cartel for more than three decades opted to follow the procedure established in Regulation 662/2008. Their fines were reduced by 10 per cent (Commission press release IP/10/985 (20 July 2010)).

Officials at the OFT have also made public reference to moves to introduce settlements, and in the UK the Office of the Rail Regulator (ORR) agreed a settlement in *English Welsh and Scottish Railway Limited* (the decision was regrettably both unnumbered and undated). Although the OFT decision in *Exchange of information on future fees by certain independent fee-paying schools* CA98/05/2006 [2007] UKCLR 361 (see 11.4.1, and Key case 11.1) was formally an infringement decision it too was the result in part of an agreement between the schools accused of infringing the law and the OFT to speed up proceedings and reduce costs. In a similar move the OFT in March 2007 offered reduced penalties to construction companies involved in cartels in an effort to fast-track a substantial and long-running investigation into the construction industry. While it is too early to be emphatic as to the characteristics of 'settlements' the term would be applied to a situation in which the authorities move to a formal investigation, and then agree with the undertakings subject to that investigation to take a decision on certain terms, with agreed penalties or remedial conduct, with the addressees of the decision accepting not to appeal. There is some doubt as to whether at law the final part of this rubric could be enforced. It is unlikely that the courts would wish to see their legitimate jurisdiction ousted in this way.

5.7 Future outlook: review of Regulation 1/2003

The EU Commission recently embarked upon an evaluation of the first five years of the life of the new enforcement rules. A public consultation was launched in 2008, and the conclusions materialized into the Report on the Functioning of Regulation 1/2003 (April 2009). The enactment of this report follows an obligation contained in Regulation 1/2003 itself. After analysing different aspects of the new regime, the conclusions are overwhelmingly positive. The Commission believes that

Regulation 1/2003 has brought about a landmark change in the way the European competition law is enforced. The Regulation has significantly improved the Commission's enforcement of Articles [101] and [102 TFEU]. The Commission has been able to become more proactive, tackling weaknesses in the competitiveness of key sectors of the economy in a focused way.

The [EU] competition rules have to a large extent become the 'law of the land' for the whole of the EU. Cooperation in the ECN has contributed towards ensuring their coherent application. The network is an innovative model of governance for the implementation of [Union] law by the Commission and Member State authorities. (paras. 46 and 47)

There are areas in which the report argues that further improvement is necessary. Among the problems highlighted are the lack of harmonization of the national procedures, which may affect the uniformity of the sanctions imposed for breach or EU competition law rules, as well as some issues relating to national divergences in relation to unilateral conduct. In addition, there are suggestions in order to ensure effective enforcement, such as the imposition of periodic penalty payments to ensure compliance with decisions. It leaves open the possibility to introduce further legislative reforms in the future to address these issues.

FURTHER READING

Books

EHLERMANN, C. D., and ATANASIU, I. (eds), *European Competition Law Annual 2002: Constructing the EU Network of Competition Authorities* (2004) Hart Publishing, Oxford

KERSE, C. S., and KHAN, N., *EC Antitrust Procedure* (2005) Sweet & Maxwell, London

NAZZINI, R., *Concurrent Proceedings in Competition Law: Procedure, Evidence and Remedies* (2005) OUP, Oxford

Articles

AMEYE, E., 'The Interplay Between Human Rights and Competition Law in the EU', (2004) *European Law Review* 332

NORDSJO, A., 'Regulation 1/2003: Power of the Commission to Adopt Interim Measures', (2006) *ECLR* 299

REICHELT, D., 'To What Extent Does the Co-operation within the European Competition Network Protect the Rights of Undertakings?', (2005) 42 *Common Market Law Review* 745

RILEY, A., 'EC Antitrust Modernisation: The Commission Does Very Nicely—Thank You! Part One: Regulation 1 and the Notification Burden', (2003) *European Competition Law Review* 604

RILEY, A., 'EC Antitrust Modernisation: The Commission Does Very Nicely—Thank You! Part Two: Between the Idea and the Reality: Decentralisation under Regulation 1', (2003) *European Competition Law Review* 657

WARD, T., and GARDNER, P., 'The Privilege against Self-Incrimination under the ECHR', (2003) *Competition Law Journal* 200

WILS, W. P. J., 'The Combination of the Investigative and Prosecutorial Function and the Adjudicative Function in EC Antitrust Enforcement: A Legal and Economic Analysis', (2004) 27 *World Competition Law & Economics Review* 201

6

Procedure—penalties and leniency arrangements

KEY POINTS

- The EU Commission may fine undertakings that infringe EU competition law. Fines may be up to 10 per cent of the turnover of the undertaking.
- Leniency may be granted to parties who notify the EU Commission of illegal activity, or who assist its investigations; it may also impose structural and conduct remedies.
- The OFT has fining powers modelled on those of the EU Commission, and also operates a leniency programme; it has further announced policy of providing financial incentives of up to £100,000 to whistle-blowers.
- Under UK legislation company directors may be disqualified in certain circumstances.

6.1 Introduction

The issue of how best to compel businesses and individuals to comply with the law within a system designed to modify corporate conduct is a difficult one. Whereas individual unlawful acts may be presumed to be committed for the immediate gain of the perpetrator, the decision-making process within complex organizations, such as the modern company, is less focused and harder to direct externally. In industrial economics, a general presumption is that companies have as their main goal profit maximization. If this was strictly true, the issue for competition law would be relatively straightforward: the task of the law would be to create a structure of penalties where the *likely cost* of unlawful anti-competitive conduct more than outweighed the *likely benefit* to the company of engaging in that conduct.

In practice, it is not apparent that all companies act with a view to increasing profits at all times. Even were they to do so, there may be a difference between the goals of the organization as a whole and those of its individual officers. Competition within a company might have the effect of encouraging managers to take risks that are disproportionate to the potential rewards where those risks are not borne directly by that manager: if an unlawful informal agreement between managers in two companies works well, the revenue flow to that manager's division may be greatly improved; if the agreement is discovered, the punishment will be spread across the company as a whole. There have been occasions where individual officers have demonstrated a blatant disregard for the strictures of competition law. For example, in *Pioneer* 80/256 (1980) OJ L60/21 a letter written by one of the officers involved in a restrictive practice read: 'I am well aware of EEC rules regarding parallel exports but quite frankly at times I am more concerned with justice than with the law itself'. An interesting survey of compliance and deterrence in relation to UK and EU competition law was carried out by Frazer in 1994 and is reported on at (1995) 58 *MLR* 847. Frazer found that respondents in UK-registered companies with a turnover of at least £200 million were 'motivated more by questions of legitimacy than by the desire to avoid penalties' (p. 855).

One of the issues for competition law is that of whether penalties should be imposed on only the company as a whole, or on individual managers too, where they can be shown to be responsible for the infringement. At the EU level the fines permitted under Regulation 1/2003 may be levied only against the undertaking which is the subject of Union law. Under domestic law fines may be imposed against the company in breach of the Chapter I and Chapter II Prohibitions of the Competition Act 1998 (CA 98), and individual officers may be fined or imprisoned where they have obstructed an investigation or provided misleading information (see Chapter 5). This chapter explores the *financial* penalties imposed for breaches of competition law in the EU and the UK. Importantly, both jurisdictions have leniency regimes in force to encourage companies to come forward with information on illegal cartels, and provide for the imposition of remedies to correct anti-competitive situations. These are also analysed in the present chapter. The *criminal* penalties of the UK cartel offence and the relevant leniency arrangements are the subject of Chapter 12, while UK market investigation references (that may lead to the imposition of a wide range of remedies) are examined in Chapter 17.

6.2 General overview of the types of penalty and their adequacy

Broadly speaking, the 'weapons' in the enforcers' arsenal to use against those who attack competition are of three kinds: remedies, imprisonment, and fines. The first of these weapons may be the most powerful, and includes conduct, structural, and third-party remedies. The power to order the modification of corporate conduct includes, for example, determining the price at which a product may be sold; however, structural remedies may go so far as the complete break-up of a company. There are two significant objections to such modifying orders. The first is that they may often require a continued supervision to ensure compliance, which is burdensome on the relevant enforcer. The second is that they do not always sit well within a framework of free-market economics which competition law is often intended to support. Third-party remedies—injunctions and damages—also play a significant role. These are considered in the following chapter.

Incarceration—the second weapon—is a well-publicized feature of the US system, and has been an option in the UK in relation to hard-core cartel conduct since the entry into force of the Enterprise Act 2002 (EA 02). Even in the US, the fact is that imprisonment for antitrust offences is not widely used; nonetheless, some writers have suggested that it should act as a potent deterrent. It has been pointed out that company officers are, as a group, 'exquisitely sensitive to status deprivation' (Geiss, G., 'Deterring Corporate Crime', in Ermann, M. D., and Lundmann, R. J. (eds), *Corporate and Governmental Deviance* (1978) OUP, Oxford, p. 278). There have been several high-profile US cases in recent years, including convictions against executives of Hoffmann-La Roche and the owner of Sotheby's. The first imprisonments for breach of UK competition law fell on three officials of Dunlop Oil in 2008. This is covered in more detail in Chapter 12.

The argument in favour of the efficacy of fines, the third weapon, is a persuasive one: companies take part in anti-competitive conduct in order to boost profits; remove those profits and the incentive for illegal conduct vanishes. Voices in favour of the imposition of massive fines highlight that they are more efficient and less expensive than the other options, including incarceration (Elzinga, K., and Breit, W., in *The Antitrust Penalties*, New Haven, Yale UP (1976)). Within the EU and the various national jurisdictions there is now a consensus in favour of the imposition of fines based on turnover. Turnover figures have the advantage of being available through the requirements to maintain accounts, and are not readily open to manipulation. However, they are not always an accurate indicator of an ability to pay. A company fined 5 per cent of turnover in a high-turnover, low-profit-margin business will be harder hit than a company fined 5 per cent of turnover in a low-turnover, high-profit-margin business.

Despite these shortcomings, the alternative advanced by Viscount Trenchard of establishing 'a maximum penalty which would have an equal effect in its application to all companies' (Hansard (HL) 30 October 1997, col. 1176), is clearly flawed. A single-figure maximum does *not* have an equal effect on all companies. If the top fine were, say, £10 million, this would have less deterrent effect on a company with a turnover of £1 billion than it would on a company with a turnover of £50 million. Further, a set figure allows companies to conduct cost–benefit analyses as to whether to break the law or not. Such strategic behaviour can be redressed only by a variable level of penalty, such that the wrongdoer cannot, before the event, calculate its risk. The UK adopted in the CA 98 the same measure as the EU, which is to say that fines may be levied at up to 10 per cent of turnover (see below). Even this measure was described in the debate on the Bill as being 'grossly excessive' (Lord Fraser of Carmyllie, Hansard (HL) 30 October 1997, col. 1152).

6.3 Penalties in the European Union

6.3.1 Fines

Article 23 of Regulation 1/2003 gives the Commission the power to impose on undertakings fines where breaches of procedural law, or where substantive breaches of arts 101 and 102, have occurred. Article 23(1) sets the tariff in respect of procedural breaches. These include a refusal to supply information following a Decision ordering it, or the supply of incorrect or incomplete information. The first time any company was fined by virtue of this provision was July 2006, when Microsoft was forced to pay €280.5 million for its failure to comply with obligations imposed on it by the EU Commission in its decision of 2004 (see 22.3). Under the terms of this decision, the company was compelled to produce technical documentation; however the Commission argued that the information supplied was incomplete and inaccurate. In such cases, the penalties can be up to a maximum of 1 per cent of turnover in the preceding business year. This is a significant change from the position set out in Regulation 17, where there was a limit of €5,000. However, the more important provision is that of art. 23(2) in which it is provided that

The Commission may by decision impose fines on undertakings and associations of undertakings where, either intentionally or negligently:

(a) they infringe art. [101] or art. [102] of the Treaty; or

(b) they contravene a decision ordering interim measures under art. 8; or

(c) they fail to comply with a commitment made binding by a decision pursuant to art. 9.

For each undertaking and association of undertakings participating in the infringement, the fine shall not exceed 10 per cent of its total turnover in the preceding business year.

Article 23(5) provides that decisions taken under arts 1 and 2 'shall not be of a criminal law nature'. Lastly, by virtue of art. 24 the Commission may impose periodic penalty payments up to 5 per cent of the daily turnover of the undertaking in order to compel it to: (a) terminate an infringement; (b) comply with an interim measures decision; (c) comply with a binding commitment; (d) supply complete and correct information ordered by way of a decision; and (e) submit to an inspection ordered by a decision.

6.3.1.1 General rules for setting the amount of fines

That the Commission has a wide discretion both as to whether a fine should be imposed at all, and as to the level of any such fine, flows from the wording of art. 23 itself. Article 23(3) provides in addition that 'in fixing the amount of the fine, regard shall be had both to the gravity and the duration of the infringement'. This discretion is fettered by the general principles of law developed in the context of art. 263 TFEU. However, when challenges against the level of fines have been upheld this has generally been on the grounds that the factual findings of the Commission have been incorrect, not that it has acted beyond its powers in imposing the fine at all. In *Miller International Schallplatten GmbH* v *Commission* case 19/77 [1978] 2 CMLR 334, Advocate General Warner argued that

a fine of 10 per cent of turnover may be taken to be appropriate to an intentional infringement of the gravest kind and of considerable duration. At the other end of the scale, a fine of less than 1 per cent is appropriate for a merely negligent infringement, of the most trivial kind and continuing only for a short time, in a case where, nonetheless, the circumstances warrant the imposition of some fine.   (p. 346)

Pressure on the Commission to clarify its fining policy resulted in the first guidance relating to penalty levels being issued in 1997 ((1997) OJ C9/3). The institution eventually bowed following the insistence of undertakings, the legal community, and even the human rights field, with cases such as *Société Stenuit* v *France* (1992) 14 EHRR 509). The institution had been concerned that clarification might result in undertakings determining whether it would be profitable to commit infringements, and had also argued that the calculation of a penalty was 'a question of appraisal rather than simple calculation' (*Musique Diffusion Française* v *Commission* cases 100–103/80 [1983] 3 CMLR 21 at para. 263).

In September 2006 the Commission published a revised version of its *Guidelines on the method of setting fines pursuant to art 23(2)(a) of Regulation 1/2003* ((2006) OJ C217/02). The guidelines in some respect mark a significant departure from the earlier guidance, which, *inter alia*, set out three levels of the gravity of infringements. This approach has now been abandoned, and the new guidelines are based on the legislative requirement that the penalty imposed cannot exceed 10 per cent of the turnover of the undertaking from the preceding year. It should also take into account the duration and the gravity of the infringement. Deterrence features prominently in the preamble, as the Commission notes that

Fines should have a sufficiently deterrent effect, not only in order to sanction the undertakings concerned (specific deterrence) but also in order to deter other undertakings from engaging in, or continuing, behaviour that is contrary to arts [101] and [102 TFEU] (general deterrence). (para. 4)

A two-stage process is to be used in calculating the amount of the penalty. First the Commission will determine a 'basic amount'. Secondly, in light of factors set out in the guidance, the quantity may be adjusted either upwards or downwards. The basic amount 'will be set by reference to the value of sales . . .' in accordance with the methodology established in the guidelines. The Commission will first 'take the value of the undertaking's sales of goods or services to which the infringement directly or indirectly relates in the relevant geographic area within the EEA' (para. 13). Normally this figure will relate to the sales made during the last full business year of the participation of the undertaking in the relevant infringement. In the case of worldwide conduct the Commission notes that it may not be sufficient to consider only the sales in the EEA, in which case the Commission

may assess the total value of the sales of goods or services to which the infringement relates in the relevant geographic area (wider than the EEA), may determine the share of the sales of each undertaking party to the infringement on that market and may apply this share to the aggregate sales within the EEA of the undertakings concerned. (para. 18)

It is further indicated that 'as a general rule, the proportion of the value of sales taken into account will be set at a level of up to 30 per cent of the value of sales' (para. 21). Having determined the sales, the basic amount of the fine will be 'related to a proportion of the value of sales, depending on the degree of gravity of the infringement, multiplied by the number of years of infringement' (para. 19). A number of factors will be crucial to establish whether the proportion of sales value figure should be at the higher or lower end of the 30 per cent normal boundary. These include the nature of the infringement, its geographic scope, and whether it has been implemented (para. 22). A high tariff will be applied in the case of '[h]orizontal price-fixing, market sharing and output limitations' (para. 24). The basic scale value will then be multiplied by the number of years to take into account the duration of the infringement. In relation to the three categories referred to above, a basic sum will be applied of 15–20 per cent of the value of sales, irrespective of the duration of the infringement, as a deterrence mechanism (para. 25).

Limitation periods for the imposition of penalties are provided for in Regulation 2988/74 *concerning limitation periods in proceedings and the enforcement of sanctions under the rules of the European Economic Community relating to transport and competition* (1974) OJ L319/1. For substantive breaches of arts 101 and 102 the period is five years (art. 1(b)), and in respect of breaches of the investigatory procedure it is three years (art. 1(a)). The Court of Justice and the GC have annulled penalties on the basis that this time limit was exceeded (see, e.g., *Commission v CMA CGM* case C–236/03 [2005] 4 CMLR 7).

6.3.1.2 Aggravating and mitigating factors

A number of aggravating and mitigating circumstances are set out. Their presence in a particular case may determine what further adjustments are made to the level of the penalty imposed. The three aggravating circumstances listed are repeat infringements, obstruction or non-cooperation during the course of an investigation, and acting as the leader or instigator of an infringement. Mitigating circumstances include prompt termination of infringements (although this will not apply in the case of secret agreements or practices, including cartels), evidence of the infringement having been committed as a result of negligence, limited involvement in the infringement, cooperation with the Commission outside the scope of the leniency notice going beyond the legal obligation to cooperate, and situations in which the anti-competitive conduct has been authorized or encouraged by public authorities or legislation. At para. 31 of the guidelines the Commission further indicates that it will 'take into account the need to increase the fine in order to exceed the amount of gains improperly made as a result of the infringement where it is possible to estimate that amount'.

Some final points include an acceptance by the Commission that in limited circumstances it may consider the ability of the undertaking to pay the fine imposed, with the possibility of a reduction being granted 'solely on the basis of objective evidence that imposition of the fine…would irretrievably jeopardise the economic viability of the undertaking concerned and cause its assets to lose all their value' (para. 35). Finally the Commission notes that it may in some cases impose a fine which is purely symbolic, although no indication is given as to when this rubric may be applied. This may serve to send out a warning that novel infringements of dubious legality are in fact breaches of competition law (see deBroca, H., 'The Commission revises its Guidelines for setting fines in antitrust cases', (2006) *Competition Policy Newsletter*, No. 3, p. 1). An example of a symbolic fine was that imposed on AC-Treuhand for its accessory role in facilitating a cartel (*AC-Treuhand AG* v *Commission* case T-99/04 [2008] ECR II-1501—see 9.2.4). Before Regulation 1/2003, token fines were already imposed, for instance, where infringements were committed as a result of genuine negligence. In *1998 Football World Cup* 2000/12 (2000) OJ L5/55 the Commission concluded that the French ticketing authorities adopted arrangements similar to those taken in earlier competitions, and that the area was so specific that clear guidance could not be drawn from earlier decisions. As a result, having found the relevant undertaking to have abused its dominant position, the fine was only €1,000.

In *Showa Denko KK* v *Commission* case C–289/04 P [2006] 5 CMLR 14 (see also, e.g., *SGL Carbon* v *Commission* case C–308/04 P [2006] 5 CMLR 16) the Court of Justice commented on the relationship between penalties applied in the EU, and those established in other jurisdictions. The appellant had argued that a number of principles obliged the Commission to take into account penalties imposed outside the Union in respect of a cartel with global reach. The Court held that *non bis in idem* did not apply, holding that there was no 'principle of law obliging the Commission to take account of proceedings and penalties to which the appellant has been subject in non-Member States' (para. 57) (see also Eilmansberger, T., and Thyri, P., 'Third Country Antitrust Sanctions and EC Law—Comments on the Advocate General's Opinion in C–308/04 P *SGL Carbon* v *Commission*', (2006) *ECLR* 397).

The high level of fines often imposed by the Commission has been challenged before the European Courts. For instance, the GC was asked to establish whether the penalties set out in the decision in the *Vitamins* case (2003/2 (2003) OJ L6/1) were excessive. The judgments in *BASF AG* v *Commission* (case T–15/02 [2006] 5 CMLR 2) and *Daiichi Pharmaceutical Co. Ltd* v *Commission* (case T–26/02 [2006] 5 CMLR 3) set out clearly the approach to the imposition of penalties in several key respects. In *BASF* the GC held that the Commission was *not* required in the statement of objections (SO) to be precise in the way in which each relevant factor would be used to calculate the final penalty. Moreover, it would be inappropriate for it to do so given that this would pre-empt the final decision, which would only be taken after giving the parties an opportunity to present their case. BASF had argued that the Commission took the opportunity of the *Vitamins* case to change its fining policy. The GC held that it was entitled to do this, and was 'not under an obligation to put undertakings on notice by warning them of its intention to increase the general level of fines' (para. 59). The Commission was, however, bound by its own guidance, and could not depart from it save to the extent that might be required by 'higher-ranking law' (para. 119). It had increased the starting amount of the penalty by 100 per cent 'in order to ensure that the fine has a sufficient deterrent effect' (Decision 2003/2, at para. 697). BASF was unsuccessful in challenging this uplift, with the Court establishing that 'the Guidelines cannot give rise to a legitimate expectation as to the level of the starting amount, of amounts added to it for reasons other than the duration of the infringement and, thus, of the final figure for fines to be imposed in respect of very serious infringements' (para. 252). BASF did however succeed on a number of points in relation to errors made in the application of the leniency notice. In *Daiichi*—the second case—the appellant argued that the Commission had erred in taking into account the worldwide turnover of the Japanese undertaking in setting its penalty. The GC found that it was quite legitimate to do this, 'given, first, the worldwide scale of the relevant geographic market... and, second, the worldwide scale of the cartel itself' (para. 78). A similar conclusion was reached in a different case by the Court of Justice (*Showa Denko KK* v *Commission* case C–289/04 P [2006] 5 CMLR 14 at para. 16).

The Commission has been particularly harsh on recidivism. In *Flat glass* 84/388 (1984) OJ L212/13, it emphasized the fact that two of the parties were guilty of previous infringements. They had negotiated an agreement with the Commission and then observed the letter, but not the spirit, of the undertaking. This led to the imposition of a higher fine than would otherwise have been the case. The financial penalties in *LdPE* 89/191 (1989) OJ L74/21 were also influenced by the fact that several of the parties had already been the subject of Commission action in *Dyestuffs* (*ICI* v *Commission*) case 48/69 [1972] CMLR 557). In 2008, a 60 per cent increase was applied when fining a repeat offender for participating in a market-sharing cartel in the car glass industry (*Car Glass* COMP/39.125 (2008) OJ C173/13), raising the total to a whopping €896 million. In *Tetra Pak II* 92/163 (1992) OJ L72/1, the Commission also stressed that it would try to recover illicit profits where these could be identified. This point was subsequently reiterated in the *21st Report on Competition Policy* (point 139). While the profit level will not be the starting point for the assessment of the fine, the fact that the Commission will attempt at the absolute minimum to recover any gain made remains a guiding principle.

Fines have been reduced in the past where participants in cartels have played a limited role in relation to the hard-core members. This was the case in *LdPE* (above) where Shell and BP were fined relatively small amounts, reflecting the restricted level of their involvement in the cartel meetings. Undertakings may see their fines shrink if they are merely responding to another's illegal activity (*Welded steel mesh* 89/515 (1989) OJ L260/1). Cooperation during the course of the investigation was also rewarded in *IPTC Belgium* (above). The 'reasonable doubt' attenuation provision of the guidelines reflects the fact that undertakings have been subjected to lesser penalties where the behaviour has not previously penalized. For example, in *BDTA* 88/477 (1988) OJ L233/15 the Commission dealt with the actions of a trade association which organized trade exhibitions, and reduced the fine because this was the first such case. In *Wood Pulp* 85/202 (1985) OJ L85/1 the Commission moderated or removed altogether the fines for undertakings that were based in the United States and were operating within US antitrust law (see further Chapter 4).

Over time, the average amount of the fines imposed by the Commission has greatly increased. From 1970 to 1974 the average level was €411,604; twenty years later, the average level for a similar period—1990 to 1994—was €4,135,220. The Commission is taking a greater proportion of its proceedings against larger undertakings and cartels, where both the impact of the infringement and the ability to pay are greater. In addition, it has quite deliberately increased the tariff from time to time to strengthen the enforcement of competition policy. In *Pioneer* 80/256 (1980) OJ L60/21, the fines imposed amounted to between 2.4 and 4 per cent of turnover, whereas previous fines had been 2 per cent of turnover at the most. The Commission argued that this was necessary in view of the increasing maturity of the Union regime, and that in deciding to increase levels they had not exceeded their discretion. On appeal (*Musique Diffusion Française SA* v *Commission* cases 100–103/80 [1983] 3 CMLR 221) the Court agreed, holding that 'the proper application of the [Union] competition rules requires that the Commission may at any time adjust the level of fines to the needs of that policy' (para. 109).

The Commission has consistently demonstrated a strong stance against any practice which results in the re-creation of the trade barriers it has sought so hard to dismantle, and any conduct that may pose a threat to market integration. Importantly, in January 1998 the Commission imposed a fine of €102 million on Volkswagen following a finding that the company had, in breach of art. 101(1), prevented Italian dealers in its cars from reselling these to customers from other parts of the Union (*VW* 98/273 (1998) OJ L124/61, on appeal *Volkswagen AG* v *Commission* case T–62/98 [2000] 5 CMLR 853—as a result of which the fine was reduced (to €90 million). A total of €1.3 billion was imposed on the companies involved in the car glass market-sharing cartel (*Car Glass* COMP/39.125 (2008) OJ C173/13). This was shortly followed by fines totalling €1.1 billion—E.ON and GdF Suez being fined €553 million each—for a similar cartel in the gas sector in 2009 (*E.ON and GdF* COMP/39.401 (2009) OJ C248, 16.10.2009, pp. 5–6).

With regard to abuses committed by powerful undertakings, the amounts of the fines have also risen considerably. As will be seen in Chapter 22, Microsoft was fined €497,196,304 in 2004 (*Microsoft* 2007/53/EC (2007) OJ L32/23). In May 2009 the Commission imposed a fine of €1.06 billion on Intel, the world's largest microprocessor manufacturer. The sum represents 4.15 per cent of the firm's turnover in 2008, and is the biggest fine ever imposed on a single company for abuse of dominance. The decision is analysed in detail in Chapter 14.

6.3.1.3 Leniency for 'whistle-blowers'

In December 2006 the Commission published a new version of its *Notice on Immunity from Fines and Reduction of Fines in Cartel Cases* (2006) OJ C298/17. It is aimed at participants in 'secret cartels', which 'are often difficult to detect and investigate without the co-operation of undertakings or individuals implicated in them' (para. 3). The broad principle is that those engaged in such cartel conduct may, if they cooperate to the required extent, benefit from a partial or total reduction in the penalty imposed if an infringement decision is made. While it may appear at first blush to be inequitable for 'guilty' parties to avoid a penalty, the Commission argues that 'the interests of consumers and citizens in ensuring that secret cartels are detected and punished outweigh the interest in fining those undertakings that enable the Commission to detect and prohibit such practices'. Similar policies are applied in other leading jurisdictions, notably the US, and have been proven to be successful. A glance at the numbers of leniency applications lodged in the EU shows that the policy has some success: between February 2002 and December 2006 some 167 leniency applications were received, of which 87 were for full immunity, and 80 for a reduction in a penalty.

Full immunity will be provided to any undertaking which is the first to disclose the existence of an illegal cartel, and its participation in it (para. 8). The evidence must be sufficient to enable the Commission to either 'carry out a targeted inspection' (para. 8(a)), or 'find an infringement' (para. 8(b)). To this end the undertaking must provide a 'corporate statement' which, *inter alia*, provides a 'detailed description of the alleged cartel arrangement, including for instance its aims, activities and functioning' (para. 9(a)).

As a result of confidentiality, the applicant may be uncertain as to whether it is indeed the first to offer information to the Commission. This may make potential whistle-blowers hesitant to come forward, since immunity will not be granted if the Commission already has sufficient evidence to justify an inspection (para. 8(a)), or to establish an infringement (para. 8(b), which further requires that no undertaking has been granted conditional immunity under para. 8(a)). Evidence suggests that certainty is an important factor in encouraging leniency applications. This justifies the attempt to set clearer thresholds in the 2006 notice, in which further qualifications as to when an undertaking may be able to benefit from full immunity are laid down. First, the undertaking must 'cooperate genuinely, fully, on a continuous basis and expeditiously' with the procedure (para. 12). This includes providing evidence, answering questions and requests promptly, not destroying or concealing proof, and not disclosing its application before a statement of objections has been issued. The undertaking must also immediately end its involvement in the cartel, unless the Commission requires it to continue in order 'to preserve the integrity of the inspections'. Any company which has coerced another to join or stay in the cartel is not eligible for full immunity.

Where an undertaking does not meet the criteria for the award immunity it may still qualify for a reduction in its penalty. To this end, it must supply the Commission with evidence with 'added value with respect to the evidence already in the Commission's possession' (para. 24). It is also obliged to cooperate and cease its participation in the cartel in the exact same way as with full immunity. The concept of 'added value' is explained at para. 25, and 'refers to the extent to which the evidence provided strengthens, by its very nature and/or its level of detail, the Commission's ability to prove the alleged cartel'. Undertakings may be eligible for discounts on a sliding scale: 30–50 per cent reduction to the first undertaking providing significant added value; 20–30 per cent to the second; and up to 20 per cent for any remaining undertakings meeting the criteria (para. 26).

The relevant procedures to be followed are set out in the Notice, as are further requirements in relation to 'corporate statements'. Finally it should be noted that while leniency may be granted in full or in part to applicants under the Commission programme, this leniency has no impact on follow-on civil actions, under which those granted immunity may still be required to pay damages as determined in national courts.

Some concern has been raised in relation to the operation of the leniency programme within the context of decentralized enforcement, modernization, and the European Competition Network (ECN). The notorious lack of harmonization in this area is dealt with in the *Commission Notice on cooperation within the Network of*

Competition Authorities (2004) OJ C101/43. To minimize risks, leniency applicants are advised to simultaneously apply 'for leniency to all competition authorities which have competence to apply article [101] of the Treaty in the territory which is affected by the infringement and which may be considered well placed to act against the infringement in question' (para. 38). In September 2006 the ECN further attempted to address the problem introducing a Model Leniency Programme (MLP). It takes the approach of offering 'soft harmonization', setting out the procedural and substantive requirements that all leniency programmes should offer. However, it falls short of a full harmonization of procedures, and does not permit a single application to be made which will simultaneously take effect in all Member States and at the Commission. In one respect the programme does offer applicants a clear benefit: where a full application has been made to the EU Commission in a case that will involve three or more Member States, a temporary summary application may be made to the national authorities. If any of them intend to act, more time will be given in order to put together a full application.

In 2009, three years after the endorsement of the MLP, the ECN published a Report on the Assessment of the State of Convergence (October 2009). It acknowledged that the attempts to align national leniency programmes following the recommendations made in the MLP have been successful. In the UK, this attempt is reflected in the revised *Guidance on Leniency and No Action* (December 2008), analysed below. However, full convergence has not yet occurred, and the ECN calls for a reflection on whether the successes to date ought to encourage further alignment. Both the MLP and the report are available from the ECN website (**http://ec.europa.eu/competition/ecn/**).

It is worth noting that the Leniency Notice is not the only means of obtaining a reduction in the fines imposed. As seen in the previous chapter (5.5), a new settlement procedure for cartels was introduced in June 2008 in the shape of Regulation 662/2008 (2008) OJ L171/3, which allows undertakings in a cartel to obtain a 10 per cent reduction of the fine imposed if they admit their involvement and liability. There may be cases in which both this reduction and the leniency policy may be applicable; in such scenarios, the Commission has clarified that they will be cumulatively applied.

6.3.2 **Other orders**

Articles 7–9 of Regulation 1/2003 deal with the decisions that the Commission may make in respect of conduct which infringes arts 101 and 102, and were already discussed in Chapter 5. While it is not strictly correct to characterize these as 'penalties', to the undertaking subject to any such decision it may well feel as if a punishment is being imposed. The central power here is that held by the Commission to 'require the undertakings and associations of undertakings concerned to bring such infringement to an end'. In order to achieve this termination it 'may impose on them any behavioural or structural remedies which are proportionate to the infringement committed and necessary to bring the infringement effectively to an end' (art. 7(1)). The wording of this provision allows the Commission to make any order that it considers to be appropriate, although all such orders may be challenged by way of art. 263 TFEU before the GC.

The power to order structural remedies (typically divestiture, or the break-up of a company) is relatively new, and will be employed only in exceptional circumstances where a conduct remedy will not be readily available. It is not the case that all infringement decisions will be accompanied by behavioural orders. In many cases the Commission merely requires that the infringement be terminated but does not prescribe behaviour, leaving it to the undertaking to determine what is required so as to bring its conduct within the bounds of legal acceptability. A typical behavioural remedy might be to resume supplies to a customer where these have been illegally stopped (as was the case in *BBI/Boosey & Hawkes: Interim measure* 87/500 (1987) OJ L286/36)), or to withdraw a threatened predatory price cut—see *ECS/AKZO: Interim measure* 83/462 (1983) OJ L252/13).

6.4 The United Kingdom: financial penalties, imprisonment, and directors' disqualification

6.4.1 The Competition Act 1998

6.4.1.1 Fines

The CA 98 incorporates a penalty system that is similar to that of EU law. By virtue of s. 36, the OFT may impose a penalty where either the Chapter I or the Chapter II Prohibitions are infringed. It is also responsible, where appropriate, for imposing penalties in respect of breaches of arts 101 and 102 TFEU where it takes action against these. Section 36(8) provides that 'no penalty fixed by the OFT under this section may exceed 10 per cent of the turnover of the undertaking (determined in accordance with such provisions as may be specified in an order made by the Secretary of State)'. Turnover is to be calculated in accordance with the Competition Act 1998 (Determination of Turnover for Penalties) Order 2000, SI 2000/309 as amended by the Competition Act 1998 (Determination of Turnover for Penalties) (Amendment) Order 2004, SI 2004/1259. 'Section 36(8)' turnover is not restricted to the turnover in the relevant product and geographic market.

The threshold may be amended by order of the Secretary of State, but it is unlikely that this figure would ever be revised upwards. Companies may appeal against any fines levied, which become recoverable by the OFT as if they were a civil debt (s. 37). Turnover is to be that of the UK, not worldwide or EU. Appeals may be made against decisions of the OFT to the Competition Appeals Tribunal (CAT) and then to the Court of Appeal (s. 49(1)(b)). Unlike the General Court, the CAT reviews the decision taken by the OFT from scratch in relation both to penalties and to any required conduct changes. It is required to consider the case 'on the merits' (Sch. 8, para. 3(1)), and if it is necessary and appropriate to 'make any other decision which the OFT could itself have made' (Sch. 8, para. 3(2)(e)). The CAT may raise, lower, or revoke altogether any penalty (Sch. 8, para. 3(2)(b)), and is not bound by any guidance issued by the OFT in this respect. As the CAT recognized in *Napp Pharmaceuticals Holdings Ltd* v *The Director General of Fair Trading* [2002] CompAR 13, 'the [CA98] contains no provision which requires the Tribunal to even have regard to that Guidance' (para. 497). It has further held that the *Guidance* 'cannot be treated as if the OFT is merely making a mechanical calculation according to a predetermined mathematical formula' (*Argos Ltd and Littlewoods Ltd* v *OFT* [2005] CAT 13 [2005] CompAR 834, para. 171).

The CAT has described its own role in the process by explaining that it is to 'focus primarily on whether the overall penalty imposed [by the OFT] is appropriate for the infringements in question' (*Argos Ltd and Littlewoods Ltd* v *OFT* [2005] CAT 13 [2005] CompAR 834, para. 172). On a number of occasions, it has adjusted the fines. Curiously in 2005 it *increased* a penalty imposed on one party to the replica football kit price-fixing agreement (see 11.4.2.1) on the grounds that the undertaking in question had not cooperated during the proceedings (*Umbro Holdings Ltd and others* v *OFT* [2005] CAT 22 [2005] CompAR 1060). It is generally accepted that the penalties imposed are 'criminal' within the meaning of the European Convention of Human Rights, and in particular in the context of the application of art. 6, the right to a fair trial. However, as the CAT recognized in *Napp*, they are characterized in English law as a 'civil debt'. In this case, the Tribunal held that the general approach whereby the CAT would start from first principles, although in doing so it would clearly have in mind any penalty imposed by the OFT, is consistent with the requirements of art. 6. An appeal may be made from the CAT to the Court of Appeal in relation to the level of any penalty imposed (s. 49(1)(b)).

Given the emphasis in the CA 98 on conformity with EU law, it is likely that fines will be assessed in a way similar to that employed by the EU Commission. In *Napp* the CAT confirmed that EU law should be followed in determining the broad policy relating to fines (see para. 455). However, in relation to the calculation of the exact fine within the broad parameters set out in the Act, the CAT took the view that, given the differences between the approach taken by the OFT and that of the EU Commission's guideline, it did not feel obliged to take the latter into account in making its own decisions. In situations where the condemned conduct has also been subject to the imposition of a penalty under EU law, the OFT is to have regard to that penalty in assessing the level of the fine under domestic law.

'Small agreements', as defined by secondary legislation (and see s. 39), and 'conduct of minor significance' otherwise falling within the Chapter II Prohibition (s. 40) have some (albeit limited) immunity from the imposition of fines. This immunity may, in certain circumstances, be withdrawn by the OFT. The relevant thresholds are set out in the Competition Act 1998 (Small Agreements and Conduct of Minor Significance) Regulations 2000, SI 2000/262. These provide that small agreements (s. 39(1)) are those where the combined applicable turnover in the year preceding the infringement did not exceed £20 million (para. 3). The threshold in respect of s. 40(1) is £50 million (para. 4).

The approach that will be taken to the setting of penalties is laid down in the OFT's *Guidance as to the Appropriate Amount of a Penalty* [2006] UKCLR 113, produced by the OFT to comply with its statutory duty under s. 38(1) of the Act. The tone of the guidance is established at the very outset, where the OFT explains the policy objectives underlying the approach. These are 'to impose penalties on infringing undertakings which reflect the seriousness of the infringement and to ensure that the threat of penalties will deter undertakings from engaging in anti-competitive practices'. Accordingly, it intends 'to impose financial penalties which are severe' (para. 1.4).

The broad five-step approach is similar to that adopted by the EU Commission:

1. calculation of the starting point by applying a percentage determined by the nature of the infringement to the 'relevant turnover' of the undertaking;
2. adjustment for duration;
3. adjustment for other factors;
4. adjustment for further aggravating or mitigating factors;
5. adjustment if the maximum penalty of 10 per cent of the turnover would be exceeded, and to avoid double jeopardy. (para. 2.1)

These factors are discussed further in the guidelines.

The first penalty imposed by the OFT under the Act was a fine of £3.21 million levied against Napp Pharmaceuticals (*Napp Pharmaceutical Holdings Ltd* CA98/2/2001 [2001] UKCLR 597, on appeal *Napp Pharmaceuticals Holdings Ltd* v *The Director General of Fair Trading* [2002] CompAR 13). The undertaking had been condemned for discriminatory predatory pricing to one customer base, and for excessive pricing to another. When the case reached the CAT, the Tribunal was concerned about the OFT's attempt to recover any profits made as a result of the illegal conduct. Such an adjustment is dealt with as part of the third step in the calculation of the penalty, the amount of profit made being 'another factor'. The CAT noted the difficulty of calculating what the gain actually was. In the case in question, the parties were unable to agree within a million pounds. Any figure would most likely underestimate the gain, as it would not be able to take into account the long-term benefit to the undertaking of an enhanced reputation for toughness and competitiveness. The CAT expressed the view that 'this method of calculation, so it seems to us, is more suited to the process for assessing the damages in civil litigation, rather than the fixing of a deterrent penalty' (para. 508).

It is also worth noting that the operating of a compliance programme is expressly recognized as a mitigating factor (penalty guidance, part 3). In order for this to apply the parties must show that the programme is active, visibly supported by senior management, backed up by appropriate procedures and appropriate training, and properly audited and reported.

6.4.1.2 Leniency for 'whistle-blowers' and other financial incentives for cooperation

The OFT approach to 'whistle-blowers' was, in its early days, more influenced by the similar US programme than by the one operated by the EU Commission. Recent reforms however have brought it closer to the EU scheme. Leniency was invoked for the first time in the decision *Market Sharing by Arriva plc and First Group plc* (CA98/9/2002, 30 January 2002), in which both companies benefited from the operation of the scheme as they provided the OFT with evidence of cartel activity. Arriva's fine was reduced by 36 per cent, and FirstGroup avoided penalty altogether. Although the latter did not approach the OFT until after the investigation had begun, it was the first of the two parties to do so. It was offered 100 per cent reduction in November 2000, on the condition that it would provide evidence of the cartel, cooperate with the OFT throughout the investigation, and comply with all the conditions set out in the *Guidance on Penalties* (paras 70–1).

On 1 June 2005, the Director of Competition Enforcement at the OFT was reported in the *Financial Times* as saying that 'there are concerns that the leniency arrangements have not been persuading people to come forward as much as we would like'. Indeed, there is little public evidence of cases being brought to the attention of the OFT prior to the commencement of at least an informal inquiry. Published decisions reflect many situations in which an undertaking notifies its participation in anti-competitive conduct only once it has been attacked for operating one illegal arrangement (see further Chapter 11).

Under the UK revised *Guidance on Leniency and No Action* (December 2008), the OFT will offer of total immunity (civil and/or criminal) for the first to come forward, as well as a reduction in fines for those who cooperate at a later stage. Total immunity can be of two types: Type A, which is automatically granted when the company approaches the OFT before an investigation has been launched; and Type B, provided if the company is the first to come forward but an investigation is ongoing, in which case it will be discretionary. In the latter scenario, when total immunity is denied, leniency (type B) is likely to be applicable. There is another kind of leniency, type C, granted to those companies who are not the first to blow the whistle. This will entail a reduction of up to 50 per cent in the fines imposed.

In the 2008 guidance it is established that, before contacting the OFT, the company seeking leniency must have a 'genuine intention to confess' and be willing to offer 'continuous and complete cooperation'. The OFT will, so far as is possible, attempt to maintain confidentiality as to the identity of any undertaking coming forward (para. 8.43). The revised guidance also introduced additional advice for companies as to how to conduct their internal investigations both before and after approaching the OFT. They must be conducted 'with integrity and with an eye to future criminal proceedings'. It suggests the parties seek specialist criminal legal advice.

In February 2008, the OFT announced a new policy of offering financial incentives of up to £100,000 to those willing to provide 'accurate, verifiable and useful' information to tackle illegal cartels (see Press Release 'OFT offers financial incentives for information regarding cartel activity' (2008) OFT 31/08). The specific amounts to be awarded in each case are to be determined according to a set formula, ruling out negotiation. Cartel participants may not benefit from the incentive, following the principle that one is not to be rewarded for its own illegal activity. They can apply for leniency instead.

6.4.2 **The Enterprise Act 2002**

6.4.2.1 The cartel offence

The cartel offence, set out in Part 6 of the EA 02, is the only substantive area of competition law operating in the UK to be criminal in nature. Any person in breach of s. 188 may, on conviction, face a term of imprisonment of up to five years. The offence is dealt with in more detail in Chapter 12.

6.4.2.2 Directors' disqualification

Although the cartel offence has received the lion's share of attention, the threat of directors' disqualification following breaches of competition law is likely to have at least as much impact on ensuring compliance with the law. Shortly before the introduction of the EA 02, the Government indicated that it would be 'in the public interest that directors who have engaged in serious breaches of competition law should be exposed to the possibility of disqualification on that ground alone' (White Paper, *A World Class Competition Regime* (Cm. 5233, July 2001) para. 8.24).

Section 204 of the Enterprise Act amends the Company Directors Disqualification Act 1986 (CDDA) inserting new ss. 9A–9E. Section 9A of the CDDA provides that the appropriate court must make a competition disqualification order (CDO) against a person following an application by the OFT or other concurrent regulator, where two conditions are met. The first requirement is that an undertaking of which that person is a director commits a breach of competition law. This applies in relation to the Chapter I and II Prohibitions, and to arts 101 and 102 TFEU. The second condition is that 'the court considers that his conduct as a director makes him unfit to be concerned in the management of a company'. In making this assessment the court is required to consider the matters set out in s. 9A(6). These are that the person's conduct contributed to the breach, that (if it did not contribute) the person had reasonable grounds to suspect the breach and took no steps to prevent it, or that they did not know of the breach but should have known of it. The court may also consider the involvement of the director in any other infringements of competition law. It is irrelevant 'whether the person knew that the conduct of the undertaking constituted the breach' (s. 9A(7)). The OFT may also, instead of proceeding with the formal steps, accept a competition disqualification undertaking (CDU) from a person, which, once made, operates in a very similar way to a formal CDO.

In the event that a director is disqualified the maximum period of disqualification is 15 years (s. 9A(9)). During the term of the disqualification it is a criminal offence for the person to: be a director of a company; act as a receiver of a company's property; in any way, whether directly or indirectly, be concerned to take part in the promotion, formation, or management of a company; or to act as an insolvency practitioner (s. 1(1)).

On 29 June 2010, the OFT published *Director disqualification orders in competition cases*, with modifications to the 2003 *guidance on competition disqualification orders.*

In general, the changes broaden the possibilities of applying for a competition qualification order (CDO). There is an attempt to increase the responsibility of directors for the actions of an undertaking, as well as to encourage them to 'blow the whistle'. the OFT indicates that it will follow a five-step process in considering whether to apply for a CDO (s. 4(2)). It will:

1. consider whether a company of which the person is a director has committed a breach of competition law; in some exceptional cases it may be possible to apply for a CDO even where the breach of competition law has not been established by a decision or judgment (s. 4(7));

2. consider the nature of the breach. Before 2010, it was necessary that a financial penalty had been imposed. The new rules only mention that applications for a CDO might have more chance of succeeding 'in cases involving more serious breaches, such as those in which a financial penalty has been imposed' (s. 4(11)). Therefore, it is no longer imperative that the company has been fined, but financial penalties make a CDO more likely;

3. consider whether the company in question benefited from leniency; section 4(13) explains that, save in a few exceptions (s. 4(14), the OFT or Regulator 'will not apply for a CDO against any current director [...] whose company benefited from leniency in respect of the activities to which the grant of leniency relates';

4. consider the extent of the director's responsibility for the breach. This is the primary factor when considering applying for a CDO. It is possible to apply if the director's conduct 'contributed to the breach of competition law', if it did not 'but he had reasonable grounds to suspect that the undertaking's conduct constituted the breach and took no steps to prevent it', or if 'the director did not know but ought to have known that the undertaking's conduct constituted the breach. (s. 4(17). This is to say, ignorance may not be an excuse; and

5. have regard to any aggravating and mitigating factors, which respectively increase and decrease the likelihood of applying for a CDO. These factors are listed in sections 4(25) and 4(26).

In the event that any director is convicted of a cartel offence the convicting court has the power to make a disqualification against that person, and in these cases the OFT will not make use of its powers under the CDDA.

6.4.2.3 Market investigation references and merger investigations

The orders that may be made, and remedies that may be imposed in relation to market investigation references and merger investigations are dealt with in Chapters 17 and 20 respectively.

FURTHER READING

Books

Dannecker, G., and Jansen, O. (eds), *Competition Law Sanctioning in the European Union* (2004) Kluwer Law International, The Hague

Kerse, C. S., and Khan, N., *EC Antitrust Procedure* (2005) Sweet & Maxwell, London, Part 7

Wils, W. P. J., *The Optimal Enforcement of EC Antitrust Law: Essays in Law and Economics* (2002) Kluwer Law International, The Hague

Articles

Levy, N., and O'Donoghue, R., 'The EU Leniency Programme Comes of Age', (2004) 27 *World Competition* 75

Richardson, R., 'Guidance Without Guidance—A European Revolution in Fining Policy? The Commission's New Guidelines on Fines', (1999) *European Competition Law Review* 360

Sandhu, A. S., 'The European Commission's Leniency Policy: A Success?', (2007) *ECLR* 148

Wils, W. P. J., 'Is Criminalization of EU Competition Law the Answer?', in Cseres, K. J., Schinkel, M. P., Vogelaar, F. O. W. (eds), *Criminalization of Competition Law Enforcement: Economic and Legal Implications for the EU Member States* (2006) Edward Elgar, Cheltenham

7

Procedure—complaints and third-party rights

KEY POINTS

- Complaints may be made to the EU Commission or to the OFT and other national competition authorities. Complainants have limited rights during proceedings.
- Articles 101 and 102 TFEU have direct effect, and may be relied on in litigation before the courts in the EU.
- Claimants may seek damages or other remedies.
- In the UK damages may be sought before the Competition Appeals Tribunal.
- The number of private actions is increasing, and efforts are being taken to encourage more private litigation.

7.1 Introduction

This chapter focuses on competition law enforcement in private claims before the courts. Private enforcement of competition law is a very obvious and prominent feature of the US antitrust system, where individual enforcement is a vital part of the regime and is encouraged by the availability of treble damages under s. 4 of the Clayton Act:

[A]ny person who shall be injured in his business or property by reason of anything forbidden in the antitrust laws may sue therefor . . . and shall recover threefold the damages by him sustained, and the cost of suit, including a reasonable attorney's fee. (15 USC s. 15)

The effect on the infringing party of paying damages is little different than if a fine were being levied. The effect upon the legal system, however, is more noticeable: the burden of enforcement will pass from the relevant public authorities to wronged individuals, who may often have greater motivation to bring actions as they are more directly linked to the harm. The nature of the regimes in the European Union and the United Kingdom is that public regulation is to the fore, and individual rights often appear ancillary to this. This is also a consequence of the legal culture of Europe, where there is a certain reluctance to involve the courts in commercial matters, in high contrast to that of the US, where parties bring actions much more readily. This factor has clearly been a matter of some exasperation to the EU Commission, which for many years has tried to encourage an increase in private actions brought directly by injured parties in the Member States. In the UK, during debates on the passage of the CA 98 suggestions were made by MPs on the Conservative benches that the penalties for breaches of the new UK law should be reduced as enforcement would flow from third parties. However, the Labour Government of the time argued that

ordinary consumers and small companies, who will commonly be the victims of anti-competitive agreements and abuses by small and medium sized enterprises, are less likely and less able to pursue their rights through courts than would a big business.   (Hansard (HL) 17 November 1997, col. 436)

Both the EU Commission and the OFT have in recent years sought to shift the burden of competition law enforcement, focusing their own efforts on the more significant cartel cases, and encouraging complainants to bring private actions as an alternative to relying on overstretched public agencies. They have published discussion documents relating to private rights, and there are now concerted efforts underway to enhance the position of private litigants in the competition law arena. These developments are dealt with below. For an excellent, although slightly dated, general discussion of this area see Jones, C. A., *Private Enforcement of Antitrust Law in the EU, UK and USA*, Oxford, OUP (1999).

7.2 **Private enforcement and European Union law**

As part of the modernization process, the EU Commission has published guidelines designed to assist both private actions before the courts (*Guidelines on co-operation between the Commission and the National Courts* (2004) OJ C101/54) and complainants bringing matters to the attention of the relevant national competition authority (*Commission notice on the handling of complaints by the Commission under arts 81 and 82 EC* (2004) OJ C101/65). In the latter guideline the Commission makes clear that it 'wishes to encourage citizens and undertakings to address themselves to the public enforcers to inform them about suspected infringements of the competition rules' (para. 3). Under the enforcement regime of Regulation 1/2003 a complainant has a choice as to whether to bring a matter to the attention of the Commission, to a relevant national competition authority, or before a national court in the form of a private action. Paragraph 8 of the notice suggests that a private action before a court may be a more fruitful avenue than a complaint to one of the authorities:

While national courts are called upon to safeguard the rights of individuals and are thus bound to rule on cases brought before them, public enforcers cannot investigate all complaints, but must set priorities in their treatment of cases. The Court of Justice has held that the Commission, entrusted by art. [105](1) [TFEU] with the task of ensuring application of the principles laid down in arts [101] and [102] of the Treaty, is responsible for defining and implementing the orientation of [Union] competition policy and that, in order to perform that task effectively, it is entitled to give differing degrees of priority to the complaints brought before it. [See further the case of *Automec Srl* v *Commission* below at 7.2.1.1]

7.2.1 Involvement in proceedings

7.2.1.1 Filing complaints

Historically the Commission has received many complaints from third parties about anti-competitive activity. This, coupled with the high level of notifications of agreements under former Regulation 17, meant that it was significantly overburdened and not able to take effective action in all appropriate cases. In 2002, shortly before the 2004 procedural overhaul, 321 cases were registered, of which 101 were based on complaints made by third parties; 363 cases were closed; and 805 were left outstanding. These figures were not encouraging for third parties seeking redress through an administrative route, although the Commission focused its activity on the most serious breaches.

Regulation 1/2003, art. 7(2) provides that '[t]hose entitled to lodge a complaint for the purposes of paragraph 1 are natural or legal persons who can show a legitimate interest and member states'. There is little law on what constitutes a 'legitimate interest', and the practice of the Commission has been generally to assume that it is held by every party making a complaint. In essence the view is that where undertakings operating in the market are affected by the alleged anti-competitive conduct, or where conduct is likely to have a direct and foreseeable effect on that undertaking, a legitimate interest will arise. This follows the approach taken by the GC in cases such as *Bureau Européen des Medias et de l'Industrie Musicale (BENIM)* v *Commission* case T–114/92 [1996] 4 CMLR 305.

In *Automec srl* v *Commission* case T–24/90 [1992] 5 CMLR 431, in an attempt to compel the Commission to act in response to a complaint, the applicant relied on art. 265 TFEU (former 232 EC):

Should the European Parliament, the European Council, the Council, the Commission or the European Central Bank in infringement of the Treaties, fail to act, the Member States and the other institutions of the Union may bring an action before the Court of Justice of the European Union to have the infringement established...

The action shall be admissible only if the institution, body, office or agency concerned has first been called upon to act. If, within two months of being so called upon, the institution, body, office or agency concerned has not defined its position, the action may be brought within a further period of two months.

Any natural or legal person may, under the conditions laid down in the preceding paragraphs, complain to the Court that an institution, body, office or agency of the Union has failed to address to that person any act other than a recommendation or an opinion.

The Court held that the Commission was entitled to prioritize its workload, with the emphasis in enforcement policy inevitably shifting from time to time in response to the wide range of factors that the Commission was expected to consider. It also argued that the Commission was not obliged necessarily to follow every case presented to it, and was entitled to select the cases it could focus on. This judgment has been often cited to persuade courts and authorities in the Member States to assume more of the burden of enforcement, and has also been relied on by the OFT in the UK.

Where the Commission has taken action in response to a complaint, the complainant will have the necessary *locus standi* to bring an action challenging any subsequent decision on the basis of art. 263 TFEU, former 230 EC (see, e.g., *Timex Corp* v *EC Council and Commission* case 264/82 [1985] 3 CMLR 431). The relevant part of this article is:

Any natural or legal person may, under the conditions laid down in [this provision], institute proceedings against an act addressed to that person or which is of direct and individual concern to them, and against a regulatory act which is of direct concern to them and does not entail implementing measures.

The link between arts 263 and 265 was emphasized in *Guerin Automobiles* v *Commission* case C–282/95P [1997] 5 CMLR 447. The Court of Justice held that the Commission was obliged to take a decision in a reasonable period of time where it had received a complaint. However, this requirement is met with a formal statement that it does not intend to pursue the matter. If a decision is not taken, the complainant may rely on art. 265 to enforce the obligation to act, and may use art. 263 to challenge a decision when it is eventually made. *Guerin* appears to strengthen the position of a complainant beyond that established in *Automec* in that it emphasizes that the Commission must act definitively. Nonetheless, the number of procedural hurdles to be subsequently overcome, and the time and cost that this can entail, are likely to be beyond the reach of many applicants. In *UPS Europe SA* v *Commission* case T–127/98 [2000] 4 CMLR 94, the plaintiff was successful in its art. 265 action.

A fruitful challenge to a rejection of a complaint was also mounted in *Micro Leader Business* v *Commission* case T–198/98 [2000] 4 CMLR 886. The applicant contacted the Commission about various practices engaged in by Microsoft that restricted its ability to obtain Microsoft products in Canada for resale in the EU. When the complaint was rejected, the Court held that the evidence was sufficient at least to indicate that there might be an abusive practice, and that the Commission should have examined the complaint more carefully. The rejection was therefore annulled, and the Commission was obliged to reconsider the complaint and to pay the costs of the court action. Similarly, in *Union Française de l'Express (UFEX)* v *Commission* case T–77/95 [2001] 4 CMLR 35 the GC held that the Commission had failed to adequately assess the seriousness and duration of the infringements and had not therefore been in a position to determine whether the Union interest would best be served by pursuing the complaint.

7.2.1.2 Development of proceedings

Regulation 773/2004 (OJ L101/18) *relating to the conduct of proceedings by the Commission pursuant to Articles 81 and 82 of the EC Treaty* lays down the basic rules relating to proceedings. In art. 6, complainants are given a role to play once the Commission has issued a statement of objections:

(1) Where the Commission issues a statement of objections relating to a matter in respect of which it has received a complaint, it shall provide the complainant with a copy of the non-confidential version of the statement of objections and set a time-limit within which the complainant may make its views known in writing.

(2) The Commission may, where appropriate, afford complainants the opportunity of expressing their views at the oral hearing of the parties to which a statement of objections has been issued, if the complainants so request in their written comments.

As art. 6(2) makes clear, a complainant does not have the *absolute* right to be heard during the oral proceedings (see also *Kish Glass & Co Ltd* v *Commission* case T–65/96 [2000] 5 CMLR 229, paras 32–3). For further consideration of the Commission's approach to complaints, see the *Notice on the handling of complaints*.

Third parties and complainants may also have the right to appear before the GC and Court of Justice in the event that there are actions relating to Commission activity (or lack of it). Thus, for example, in the case of *Microsoft Corp* v *Commission* case T–201/04 R (III) [2005] 4 CMLR 18 the GC heard applications from a number of trade associations and individual bodies that wished to intervene in the proceedings when Microsoft appealed against the infringement decision (2007/53/EC (2007) OJ L32/23). Not all these applicants were in support of the Commission. The essential requirement is that the person in question must have established a direct and existing interest in the result of the case.

7.2.2 **Direct effect and damages**

7.2.2.1 Direct effect and *Garden Cottage Foods*

Given that there is only limited access to the Court of Justice, individual complainants seeking to rely on EU law must do so through the national courts under the principle of direct effect. When the Treaty of Rome originally entered into force in 1958 it remained unclear whether it was intended to give rise to such actions on the part of individuals. However, in the landmark case of *NV Algemene Transport-en Expeditie Onderneming Van Gend en Loos* v *Nederlandse Belastingadministratie* case 26/62 [1963] 1 CMLR 105, it was established that where Treaty provisions are clear, precise, and unconditional they are capable of creating rights vested in individuals which can be enforced against Member States ('vertical direct effect').

Soon afterwards, in *Defrenne* v *Sabena (No. 2)* case 43/75 [1976] 2 CMLR 98, the principle was extended to allow such rights to be enforced against other persons not being part of the state ('horizontal direct effect'). The principle applies equally to regulations, which are, by the wording of art. 288 'binding in [their] entirety and directly applicable in all Member States'. Both art. 101 and art. 102 meet the criteria for direct effect set out in *Van Gend*. The effect of this is that an undertaking engaging in conduct that falls within the prohibitions may face actions before national courts brought by those harmed by that conduct (see, e.g., *Belgische Radio en Télévisie (BRT)* v *Société*

Belge des Auteurs, Compositeurs et Éditeurs (SABAM) case 127/73 [1974] 2 CMLR 238). The case of *Francovich* v *Italian Republic* cases C–6 and 9/90 [1993] 2 CMLR 66 made further emphasis on the place of remedies in the Union legal order. It established that a Member State becomes liable for its breaches of EU law to those who can show harm where an identifiable right has been infringed, and should then compensate accordingly.

It should be noted that, as explained in Chapter 5, art. 101(3) has only had direct effect since 1 May 2004 by virtue of the entry into force of Regulation 1/2003. This reflects a fundamental shift in enforcement of the article. Prior to this date only the first two paragraphs of art. 101 had direct effect, and the Commission had exclusive competence to apply the exemption contained in the third paragraph. The effect of this was that neither national courts nor national competition authorities could rule on the application of the article in its entirety. Where a complainant or a defendant relied on art. 101(1), say, to avoid a contractual obligation, the national court would be able to rule only on this part of the article. If the court entered into a discussion of the competition law aspects of the case, it would subsequently have to ask the party relying on the contract to refer it to the Commission for a decision, which could take a considerable period of time. One of the thrusts of the modernization programme was to facilitate the application of EU competition law by the national courts by removing this practical obstacle to the effective administration of justice.

The most important early case in the UK dealing with these issues is that of *Garden Cottage Foods Ltd* v *Milk Marketing Board* [1983] 2 All ER 770, HL. The plaintiff was a distributor of butter sold in bulk that obtained its supplies from the defendant, and then made a profit by distributing the butter to purchasers elsewhere in the Union. The plaintiff, over the relevant period, made 90 per cent of its purchases from the defendant, and sold 95 per cent of its goods to a single Dutch company. In March 1982, the defendant, a statutory body undeniably in possession of a dominant position in the market in England and Wales, announced a new sales policy. The effect of this was that it would in the future sell bulk butter to only four companies, which did not include the plaintiff. The result was that the plaintiff would be required to pay more for its butter. The substance of the case revolved around the issue of whether an injunction would be granted to restrain the defendant from altering its selling practices. At the Court of Appeal an injunction had been granted ([1982] 3 All ER 292, CA) and this decision was reversed by the House of Lords. What was important in this case was not the approach of the Court to the granting of an injunction in competition cases, although that is a matter of note, but the *obiter dictum* of Lord Diplock relating to the duty imposed by art. 102. His Lordship, first referring to the judgment of the Court of Justice in *BRT* v *SABAM* (above), suggested at pp. 775–6 that

The rights which the article confers on citizens in the United Kingdom accordingly fall within section 2(1) of the [European Communities Act 1972]. They are without further enactment to be given legal effect in the United Kingdom and enforced accordingly.

A breach of the duty imposed by article [102] not to abuse a dominant position in the [Internal] Market or in a substantial part of it can thus be categorised in English law as a breach of statutory duty that is imposed not only for the purpose of promoting the general economic prosperity of the [Internal] Market but also for the benefit of private individuals in whom loss or damage is caused by a breach of that duty.

If this categorisation be correct, and I can see none other that would be capable of giving rise to a civil cause of action in English private law on the part of a private individual who sustained loss or damage by reason of a breach of a directly applicable provision of the [TFEU], the nature of the cause of action cannot, in my view, be affected by the fact that the legislative provision by which the duty is imposed takes the negative form of a prohibition of particular kinds of conduct rather than the positive form of an obligation to do particular acts.

This is generally accepted as the correct position, although there has been inevitable debate about the characterization of the right of action as being one for breach of statutory duty. In practice this pigeon-holing of the action, a consequence of the dualist approach taken by the UK to international law, is of little significance. The legal technicalities of the route taken to obtain a Union-derived remedy is less important than the fact that the remedy is available.

7.2.2.2 Damages for breach of EU competition law

There have been few cases in the EU in which damages have been awarded to a complainant alleging harm as a result of a breach of EU competition law. The most significant success in the UK has been that of a Mr Crehan, a pub landlord awarded damages following a breach of art. 101(1) in the terms and conditions of his tenancy. Following a long legal battle, he was awarded the sum of just over £130,000 by the Court of Appeal (*Bernard Crehan* v *Inntrepreneur Pub Company CPC* [2004] EWCA Civ 637, [2004] UKCLR 1500—see further 9.4 below). This award was overturned by the House of Lords, which held that the Court of Appeal had erred in requiring the judge at first instance to show undue deference to decisions of the EU Commission (*Inntrepreneur Pub Company (CPC) and others* v *Crehan* [2006] UKHL 38).

The Court followed *Crehan* in a case referred to it from the Italian courts. It stated that, in the absence of EU rules governing third-party rights in relation to the application of art. 101(1) and 101(2), it was for each domestic legal system to flesh out the details, as long as it was fully recognized that 'any individual can claim compensation for...harm suffered where there is a causal relationship between that harm and an agreement or practice prohibited under art. [101 TFEU]' (*Manfredi* v *Lloyd Adriatico Assicurazioni SpA* cases C–295/04 etc. [2006] 5 CMLR 17). The Court stressed that while it was for the national systems to determine matters such as the operation of limitation periods, and the availability of punitive damages, such rights must accord with the principle of equivalence (i.e., they must be at least equal to rights based on national law in similar cases).

The Court made clear, however, its strong support for the development of such rights, reminding the referring court that 'actions for damages before the national courts can make a significant contribution to the maintenance of effective competition in the [Union]' (at para. 91, citing *Crehan*, para. 27; see also Hanley, C., 'The abandonment of deference' (2007) 44 *CMLRev* 817). The most substantial of these cases was determined before the Swedish Court of Appeal in *Scandinavian Airlines System* v *Swedish Board of Civil Aviation* (unreported), also known as the Arlanda Terminal 2 case. In this case SAS was obliged to pay for an expansion of the main Stockholm airport's new terminal 2, although after using the terminal SAS found that it was not appropriate for its needs and pulled out. Following a general change to the operation of the airport system in Sweden SAS had been charged a landing tariff at the terminal, in addition to its contribution to the building costs. The essence of SAS's case was that the dual charges, which it uniquely faced, amounted to price discrimination in breach of art. 102(c). On appeal the claim was upheld and SAS was awarded very substantial damages, in the sum of nearly €100 million. For a thorough review of this case, see Pettersson, T., and Alwall, J., 'Discriminatory Pricing: Comments on a Swedish Case', [2003] ECLR 295, and Bernitz, U., 'The Arlanda Terminal 2 Case: Substantial Damages for Breach of Article 82', [2003–04] *Comp Law* 195.

In 2003, what could have been an important case was launched in the UK following an infringement decision by the EU Commission in relation to an illegal cartel operating in the vitamins market (*Vitamins* 2003/2 (2003) OJ L6/1). The claimant alleged that it had suffered loss as a result of the operation of the cartel, and sought damages on that basis. An early attempt to have the case rejected was unsuccessful (*Provimi Ltd v Aventis Animal Nutrition SA and others* [2003] All ER (D) 59 (May). See further Furse, M., '*Provimi v Aventis*: Damages and Jurisdiction', [2003] *Comp Law* 119). Unfortunately, in 2008 the CAT ruled that the claim was not brought in on time, and in 2009 a request for a time extension was denied (see 7.3.1.2). Therefore, the award of damages was not clarified.

7.2.2.3 Advantages and disadvantages of private enforcement of EU competition provisions

There are difficulties in pursuing cases in national courts. For instance, the courts in the UK tend to be generally reluctant to deal with the economic issues that competition law raises and have little expertise in this area (see Chapter 23 for the approach taken under common law). Another problem is that they are understandably reluctant to contribute to a multiplicity of actions. In *MTV Europe v BMG Records (UK) Ltd* ((1995) 17 July, CA (unreported)) the plaintiff was seeking damages for an alleged breach of arts 101 and 102 and was simultaneously pressing a complaint before the EU Commission. The defendant succeeded in persuading the Court of Appeal to confirm the decision of the judge at first instance delaying proceedings at least until the Commission had considered the matter.

One of the delicate issues to be resolved relates to the defence of 'passing on'. Suppose, for example, a cartel results in the raising of prices of a raw material used to manufacture a product which is sold on at a profit to others. The question arises as to whether the purchasers of the material from the cartel, who may be presumed to have paid a higher price than would otherwise be the case, have been harmed. If they have passed on the cost increase to their customers it may be argued that they have suffered no harm. Attractive though this argument may be, one easy objection is that if they were in any event able to pass on higher prices to their customers they should have done so, as profit maximizing firms. Under the cartel situation, however, they would have lost profit equal to the price increase imposed. In the case of *BCL Old Co. Ltd and others* v *Aventis SA* [2005] CAT 2 [2005] CompAR 470 this 'virgin territory' was recognized as raising difficulties. At a preliminary stage of the proceedings the CAT noted only that 'the questions of whether defendants are entitled to raise the "passing on defence"…what is the effect of any such defence, and who bears the burden of proof are novel and important issues'.

The advantages of bringing private actions directly before the national courts are set out in the *Guidelines on co-operation between the Commission and the National Courts*. At para. 10 the Commission notes that national courts must work in a way which is compatible with EU law. Furthermore, the case law of the Court of Justice in this regard establishes that:

  (a) where there is an infringement of [Union] law, national law must provide for sanctions which are effective, proportionate and dissuasive;

  (b) where the infringement of [Union] law causes harm to an individual, the latter should under certain conditions be able to ask the national court for damages;

  (c) the rules on procedures and sanctions which national courts apply to enforce [Union] law
  • must not make such enforcement excessively difficult or practically impossible (the principle of effectiveness) and they
  • must not be less favourable than the rules applicable to the enforcement of equivalent national law (the principle of equivalence).

National courts faced with a dispute relating to the application of arts 101 or 102 may turn to the Commission for assistance in accordance with art. 15 of Regulation 1/2003. Article 15(1) provides that in relevant proceedings national courts may 'ask the Commission to transmit to them information in its possession or its opinion on questions concerning the application of [Union] competition rules'. Further, national competition authorities may, on their own initiative, submit written observations to courts dealing with such disputes, and may make oral representations with the permission of the court (art. 15(3)). The Commission is also allowed to send written observations 'where the coherent application of art. [101] or art. [102] of the Treaty so requires'. Sometimes, national courts ruling on directly effective Union law may also have recourse to the art. 267 TFEU procedure. This provides a formal link between any court or tribunal in a Member State and the Court of Justice:

The Court of Justice of the European Union shall have jurisdiction to give preliminary rulings concerning:

  (a) the interpretation of the Treaties;
  (b) the validity and interpretation of acts of the institutions, bodies, offices or agencies of the Union.

Where such a question is raised before any court or tribunal of a Member State, that court or tribunal may, if it considers that a decision on the question is necessary to enable it to give judgment, request the Court to give a ruling thereon.

Where any such question is raised in a case pending before a court or tribunal of a Member State against whose decisions there is no judicial remedy under national law, that court or tribunal shall bring the matter before the Court.

The purpose of this provision is to restrict the scope for divergence in the application of EU law by national courts and to facilitate the availability of EU law rights. It does not serve as an appeal process—questions must be asked in the abstract and the answers provided by the Court of Justice may not necessarily determine the outcome of the case on the facts. The jurisdiction of the GC does not extend to art. 267 references (art. 256(1)). Domestic courts have shown themselves willing to make references in competition cases. The principle of supremacy currently contained in article 4(3) TEU would be applicable were they reluctant to do so; the courts, being emanations of the state to which the duties of art. 4(3) are addressed, are equally bound to cooperate in the application of Union law.

A problem that is particularly noticeable in UK law is that established case law makes it difficult to obtain injunctions in relation to competition law matters. The criteria for the granting of injunctions set out in *American Cyanimid Co.* v *Ethicon Ltd* [1975] AC 396, HL, mean, *inter alia*, that injunctions will not be granted where damages are an adequate remedy. This proved to be an insurmountable problem for the plaintiff in *Garden Cottage Foods*.

The general principle is that it is national procedures which apply throughout proceedings in national courts, and remedies and sanctions are generally matters for national law. Although there have been calls to introduce a directive on remedies to ensure some consistency across the EU and a reduction in 'forum shopping', this has been resisted. However, national courts are, in some circumstances, under an obligation to adapt national procedures to fulfil EU obligations. In particular, national rules which prevent a complainant obtaining a remedy in appropriate circumstances might have to be set aside as a result of the requirement to effectively apply Union law.

7.3 United Kingdom law relating to complaints before national courts

7.3.1 The Competition Act 1998

Third-party rights under the CA 98 are intended to mirror those available under arts 101 and 102 TFEU. The EA 02 further reinforced these rights, and introduced some new procedures designed to facilitate the bringing of private claims. The OFT has published its own guidance: *Involving Third Parties In Competition Law Investigations: Incorporating Guidance on the Submission of Complaints* [2006] UKCLR 1107.

7.3.1.1 Third-party involvement in public enforcement

Generally, the involvement of third parties in the procedures will be limited to making representations to the OFT complaining about anti-competitive conduct, and will only be allowed in special circumstances. Some provisions in the Act do allow for specific consideration of third-party interests. Importantly, s. 35 provides that the OFT may impose interim measures if 'it is necessary for it to act under this section as a matter of urgency for the purpose:—(a) of preventing serious, irreparable damage to a particular person' (see Chapter 5). Section 47, amended by s. 17 of the EA 02, provides the main procedure under which third parties may appeal against decisions of the OFT. Currently appeals are made directly to the CAT. The operative requirement is that the Tribunal must consider that the potential appellant 'has a sufficient interest in the decision with respect to which the appeal is made' (s. 47(2)). There is no definition provided of what constitutes 'a sufficient interest', and this remains to be worked out through case law. However, it appears to be the case that *locus standi* is likely to be wider than in respect of the operation of art. 263 TFEU.

The decisions that may be challenged by third parties are those falling within s. 47. They include those as to whether the Chapter I or II Prohibitions or arts 101 and 102 TFEU have been infringed, and decisions to make, or not make, directions. With regard to who can appeal, the CAT must be able to establish that they have 'a sufficient interest in the decision with respect to which the appeal is made' (s. 47(2)). Individuals not subject to an enforcement action in the UK may seek leave to intervene in cases before the CAT, as with EU law. A number of such applications have been granted by the Tribunal.

There have been cases in which the OFT has objected to appeals on the grounds that it had not, in fact, made a decision capable of being appealed. The matter first arose for consideration in the case of *Bettercare*. Correspondence had passed between Bettercare and the OFT relating to a complaint made by the undertaking. The OFT closed the file and refused to reopen the matter when requested to do so. On appeal it argued that it had not made a decision within the meaning of the CA 98. The CAT found, however, that in the absence of any definition of 'decision' in the Act itself it had to look at the 'question of substance, not form' (*Bettercare Group Ltd v The Director General of Fair Trading* [2002] CompAR 226). The Tribunal found that the OFT had, in reaching the view that the entity complained of was not an undertaking, made a decision to the effect that the Chapter II Prohibition had not been infringed. Similarly in *Freeserve. com plc v Director General of Telecommunications* [2003] CompAR 1 the CAT held that correspondence between Oftel and the complainant constituted a decision that could be appealed. The relevant law was summed up in the case of *Claymore Dairies Ltd and Express Dairies plc v Director General of Fair Trading* [2004] CompAR 1, at para. 122. A distinction between a situation in which the OFT had merely exercised administrative discretion, and one in which it had made a decision as to the existence of an infringement. The test, the CAT said, is that of whether the OFT has genuinely abstained from expressing a view, one way or the other, even by implication, on the question whether there has been an infringement. In the case of *Aquavitae (UK) Ltd v The Director General of Water Services* [2004] CompAR 117 the CAT exceptionally found that a closure of a file by Ofwat did not constitute an appealable decision. The applicant had expressly stated at the time the action was initiated that it was not making a complaint under the CA 98.

When the OFT takes a decision in response to a complaint, it is obliged to give the complainant such information as is necessary in order to allow him or her to comment on the proceedings. The leading case in this respect is *Pernod-Ricard SA and Campbell Distillers Ltd* v *OFT* [2004] CAT 10, [2004] CompAR 707, relating to a complaint about the conduct of Bacardi-Martini Ltd in relation to the supply of white rum. The OFT proceeded as far as issuing a Rule 14 notice stating that it intended to find the company in breach of the Chapter II Prohibition, but after the company offered certain assurances to the OFT it was decided to resolve the case by accepting these. The complainant argued that it had been denied the right to participate in the proceedings, and that as it had not seen a copy of the Rule 14 notice it was not able to effectively argue against the stance adopted by the OFT. The CAT established that a non-confidential version of such a notice should be made available to complainants, and expressed concerns about the need 'to introduce an important element of transparency and balance into the administrative proceedings which are conducted behind closed doors' (para. 237). Similarly in *Wanadoo*, Ofcom was criticized for communicating a decision to a party, but not telling other affected parties what the content of the decision was (*Wanadoo (UK) plc (formerly Freeserve.Com plc)* v *Ofcom* [2004] CAT 15, [2005] CompAR 286).

Where the OFT or other regulator exercising concurrent jurisdiction makes a decision to close proceedings, it must set out the relevant facts and legal considerations relied on in considerable detail 'so as to enable all interested parties to understand the analysis' on which the basis of the decision to close the file was made (*Claymore Dairies Ltd and Arla Foods UK plc* v *Office of Fair Trading supported by Robert Wiseman Dairies plc* [2005] CAT 30, [2006] CompAR 1, at paras 171–2). This is particularly the case if these proceedings have resulted in a lengthy and formal investigation.

The CAT has shown itself to be supportive of complainants in a number of cases; some would even argue that it has gone too far. It has drawn a wide approach to the question of which 'decisions' may be appealed (see above). It has also allowed some discretion in permitting appellants to register appeals after the deadline has passed, and in awarding costs. Perhaps the clearest expression of this trend is found in the case of *Terry Brannigan* v *OFT* [2006] CAT 28, [2007] CompAR 420. A publisher of two free local newspapers had complained to the effect that a dominant competitor was excluding him from the market. The OFT had declined to act due to 'insufficient resources' and suggested that Mr Brannigan might wish to consider a private action. On 12 March 2006 the registry of the CAT received a letter from the complainant asking it to act. A private hearing then took place, at which the OFT's Director of Competition Enforcement gave an undertaking to have the complaint revisited. The OFT sent a further letter to Mr Brannigan stating that it considered the grounds for suspecting an infringement to be weak. Mr Brannigan then formally appealed to the CAT, but his notice was not in order at first. The Tribunal decided that it would allow him further time to put together the appeal, given that it had taken him three years to get any meaningful response from the OFT, and that it would not be impossible for him to advance a case. He was unsuccessful (*Terry*

Brannigan v *Office of Fair Trading* [2007] CAT 23). Since the OFT had chosen not to conduct a full investigation, the CAT was very likely to reject the appeal, holding that in all respects the decision was not erroneous in law, fact, or appraisal. There was, however, a sting in the tail when the CAT noted in its final paragraph that it could 'understand [Mr Brannigan's] frustration that he is no further forward now than he was when his newspapers first went out of business' (para. 134). It drew attention to the appellant's point that 'having regard to the money that the OFT has spent "basically just defending their right not to look into it" he wonders whether some of that money would have been better spent investigating his claims'.

7.3.1.2 Claims for damages before the CAT

Claims for damages for injury suffered by anti-competitive conduct may be brought generally before the courts by those injured; these will be analysed later (see 7.3.1.3). However, there is also an alternative procedure under s. 47A of the CA 98 (inserted by s. 18 of the EA 02). It applies to 'any claim for damages' or 'any other claim for a sum of money' brought by a person 'who has suffered loss or damage as a result of the infringement of a relevant prohibition' (s. 47A(1)). Claims may be made directly before the CAT, with the claimant relying upon the fact that a breach of art. 101 or 102 TFEU, or the Chapter I or II Prohibitions of the CA 98, has been established by a relevant authority. It is also required that either an appeal has been unsuccessful, or there has been no appeal within the time limit set for this. In such a case, the sole task of the CAT will be to establish that harm has occurred, that it is caused by the breach identified in the infringement decision, and the amount of the harm.

The first such case to come before the CAT was that of *BCL Old Co. Ltd and others* v *Aventis SA* [2005] CAT 2, [2005] CompAR 470. This action followed the EU Commission infringement decision 2003/2 *Vitamins* (2003) OJ L6/1 (see 9.3.2.1 below). However, in September 2008 the CAT ruled that the claim had not been submitted on time, and in November of the following year it rejected an application for a time extension (*Grampian Country Food and others* v *Sanofi-Aventis and others* [2009] CAT 29). As a result, the first time the CAT actually considered the substance of a follow-on claim for damages after the finding of an infringement related to the *Genzyme* case (see 15.2.5 and 16.2.4). Healthcare at Home Ltd (HHL) sought damages from Genzyme Ltd (*Healthcare at Home Ltd* v *Genzyme Ltd* [2006] CAT 29, [2007] CompAR 474). The CAT dealt only with the question of interim relief, and awarded £2 million. The fact that some of the claims of Genzyme were described as 'nonsense' (para. 69) gave weight to the claimant's conviction that it would obtain judgment for a substantial sum. The powerful message sent by the Tribunal to the defendant as to its probable lack of success led to the case being settled in early 2007.

Although unclear from the guidelines, the general principles of EU law suggest that decisions made by other national authorities in other Member States in relation to arts 101 and 102 TFEU may also be invoked and relied upon, in the appropriate circumstances, before the CAT.

In the White Paper, *A World Class Competition Regime* (Cm. 5233, July 2001), which presaged the EA 02, the Government set out a proposal to facilitate claims where a number of consumers had been harmed by the effect of anti-competitive action:

The Government wishes to take specific steps to facilitate damages actions on behalf of consumers. Often such cases will involve a large number of harmed parties—each of whom may only have suffered relatively small loss. In such cases, it is much more sensible that claims are brought on behalf of those that suffer by representative consumer bodies.

Section 47B of the CA 98 makes provision for representative claims to be brought before the CAT on behalf of a number of consumers by designated bodies. This option is only available in respect of goods or services received 'otherwise than in the course of a business' (s. 47B(7)) and hence excludes intermediate businesses harmed by upstream conduct. The consumers must be specified in the claim, although it is possible for claims already initiated to be consolidated into a representative claim. In the event that damages are awarded these will be to 'the individual concerned' (s. 47B(6)), although the CAT may, 'with the consent of the specified body and the individual, order that the sum awarded must be paid to the specified body'.

As at September 2010, the only action that has been brought using this procedure was settled in January 2008. The Consumers' Association initiated proceedings against JJB Sports plc after the House of Lords refused to grant leave to challenge a decision of the Court of Appeal confirming a fine of £6.7 million on JJB for engaging in price fixing (*JJB Sports plc v OFT* [2006] EWCA Civ 1318). In the run-up to the 2000 UEFA European Championship, JJB and its competitor Sports Soccer plc fixed the prices of replica England football shirts, and a similar arrangement was renewed the following year for Manchester United shirts. Under the settlement, consumers who purchased said shirts in those years and joined the action received a payment of £20. Consumers who did not join the action but retained proof of purchase were entitled to £5 or £10. The case is analysed in detail at 11.4.1.

7.3.1.3 Private actions in the courts

Originally the CA 98 did not make specific references to third-party actions in the civil courts. However, during the debate on the passage of the Act Lord Simon confirmed that 'it is true that third parties have rights to seek damages in the courts as a result of actions there' (Hansard (HL) 17 November 1997, col. 456). Section 58 of the Act makes oblique reference to third-party actions, in providing that the OFT's factual findings are, in most situations, binding in proceedings brought otherwise than by the OFT. Section 60 requires domestic law to be interpreted and applied consistently with EU law, and includes a specific reference to 'civil liability of an undertaking for harm caused by its infringement of [Union] law'.

The EA 02 inserted a new s. 58A into the CA 98, clarifying the link between public enforcement and private rights. It is now expressly recognized that there may be proceedings before the courts in which damages may be claimed. Any court is bound by decisions of the OFT or the CAT to the effect that relevant provisions of the CA 98 have been infringed. There is no reference to claims other than those brought for damages or monetary relief, and therefore one might wonder whether it applies to claims for other forms of relief, such as injunctions or specific performance. As s. 58 applies to all claims, it may be that s. 58A will likewise do so, or that in the alternative it does little more than explain the effect of s. 58.

A number of private actions have already been reported under the Act, and the pace of activity is on the increase. Some actions are fairly quickly dismissed on summary judgment (see, e.g., *Unipart Group Ltd* v *O₂ (UK) Ltd* [2004] EWCA Civ 1034, [2004] UKCLR 1453). Thus, for example, in *The Wireless Group plc* v *Radio Joint Audio Research Ltd* [2004] EWHC 2925, [2005] UKCLR 203 the High Court struck out a claim as having no reasonable prospect of success. Radio Joint Audio Research Ltd (RAJAR) was sued by a radio broadcaster. The claimant had argued that RAJAR's research understated the broadcaster's audience figures, and thereby weakened its ability to sell advertising. It was alleged that in failing to adopt an alternative method of assessing audience figures RAJAR was abusing a dominant position. Lloyd J was robust in holding that it was 'impossible to see how that decision could be said to be an abuse of a dominant position' as it was clearly capable of being objectively justified (para. 76).

It is perhaps to be expected that in the early years of a legal regime cases are brought which are not well founded. However, as the principles to be applied become better established the ratio of successful cases might be anticipated to increase. The first reported case was brought on the basis of an alleged breach of the Chapter II Prohibition (*Claritas (UK) Ltd* v *The Post Office and Postal Preference Service Ltd* [2001] UKCLR 2). The Court found that the alleged abuse had not taken place on a 'relevant market for the purposes of s. 18' and dismissed the application. However, the OFT later found that there was a relevant market, and stressed that 'in order to establish an infringement of the Chapter II Prohibition it is not necessary to show an abuse on the market which an undertaking dominates' (*Consignia plc and Postal Preference Service Limited* CA98/4/2001 [2001] UKCLR 846—following *Tetra Pak International SA* v *EC Commission* case C–333/94P [1997] 4 CMLR 662).

In *Synstar Computer Services (UK) Ltd* v *ICL (Sorbus) Ltd and International Computers Ltd* [2001] UKCLR 585 there was an allegation that a software maintenance contract system maintained by the defendant was in breach of both the Chapter I and the Chapter II Prohibitions. A complaint had also been filed with the OFT, and the Court stayed the proceedings pending the outcome of this investigation. All parties in the case recognized that the CAT was better equipped to deal with the sensitive issues, and in particular market definition, which this case appeared to revolve around. The OFT subsequently made a finding that there had been no breach of the Act, and no appeal was made to the CAT (*ICL/Synstar* CA98/6/2001 [2001] UKCLR 902).

More substantial arguments were developed in *Hendry and others* v *The World Professional Billiards and Snooker Association Ltd* [2002] UKCLR 5. Here the claimants were snooker players and a company incorporated for the purpose of exploiting the Internet in relation to snooker. They argued that World Professional Billiards and Snooker Association (WPBSA) rules were in breach of both the Act's prohibitions. The court found that Rule A5 of the WPBSA rules was in breach and was void. This

rule provided in part that 'members shall not enter or play in any snooker tournament, event or match without the prior written consent of the Board'. It was believed
that this may not have been intended to restrict competition, but that its effect was to
do so by limiting the sources of income to which players could have access. Damages
sought by the claimants were not awarded, however, as the bulk of the claim was
dismissed.

In *Attheraces Ltd* v *The British Horseracing Board* [2005] EWHC 3015 (Ch), [2006]
UKCLR 167 the court held that the British Horse Racing Board Ltd (BHB) had abused a
dominant position in the market for pre-race data which was supplied under licence to
broadcasters. The claimant argued, successfully, that BHB had supplied the data only
at prices which were excessive, unfair, and discriminatory. It was also being required
to give undertakings in relation to intellectual property rights asserted by the BHB
which were not relevant to the transactions. The court found that there was no doubt
that BHB was dominant, and that the terms it imposed were indeed unreasonable
and unfair. In a long judgment the court appears to have dealt carefully with complex
issues of economic analysis, including an assessment of whether prices charged were
excessive (see 16.2.2 below). The court did not reach a decision as to what remedies
might be granted. The Court of Appeal, however, was unconvinced by the reasoning
applied at first instance and an appeal was successful. It held that the judge at first
instance incorrectly applied the law relating to excessive pricing, and did not take
into account the true purpose of art. 102, which was to protect competition, and not
business competitors (*Attheraces Ltd* v *The British Horseracing Board Ltd and BHB
Enterprises plc* [2007] EWCA Civ 38).

Injunctions have sometimes been sought, although there have been no reported
cases in which final injunctions have been granted. The first case in which an interim
injunction was granted was *Network Multimedia Television Ltd (t/a Silicon.Com)* v
Jobserve Ltd [2001] UKCLR 814. The claimant successfully argued that the defendant
had acted in breach of the Chapter II Prohibition when it refused to accept job advertisements from clients who had also advertised with the claimant. It was held 'without
hesitation, that there is a serious issue to be tried in relation to the alleged abuse' (at
para. 88). An appeal was dismissed (*Jobserve Ltd* v *Network Multimedia Television*
[2001] UKCLR 184) on the grounds that there was a complex and serious matter to be
tried.

Not all claims have been as successful as this. In *Getmapping plc* v *Ordnance Survey*
[2002] UKCLR 410, an application for interlocutory relief was rejected by Laddie J on
the grounds that the claimant had no credible case. It had been argued that Ordnance
Survey had abused its dominant position when setting specifications for certain map-
ping services, which resulted in the exclusion of the claimant. In *Suretrack Rail Services
Ltd* v *Infraco JNP Ltd* [2002] EWHC 1316 Laddie J held that

applications for interlocutory relief, whether mandatory or prohibitory, should not be seen
as means by which a court can be persuaded to grant relief on the basis of a claim to rights
which it is fairly confident would not be upheld at the trial. The more confident it is that
the claimant will fail at the trial, the less likely it is that an interlocutory injunction will be
appropriate.   (para. 14)

7.3.2 **Super-complaints**

Sections 11 and 205 of the EA 02 make provision for 'super-complaints'. Section 11 applies in situations where 'a designated consumer body makes a complaint to the OFT that any feature, or combination of features, of a market in the United Kingdom for goods or services is or appears to be significantly harming the interests of consumers'. It is for the Secretary of State to designate a body as a super-complainant, and the DTI has issued guidance for those who aspire to this status. They give the OFT, or other appropriate concurrent regulator, the chance to evaluate a situation and determine what action, if any, is appropriate. This process was explained in para. 2.4 of OFT guidance published in 2003:

The super-complaint process is intended to be a fast-track system for designated consumer bodies to bring to the attention of the OFT and the Regulators, market features that appear to be significantly harming the interests of consumers. When deciding whether or not to make a super-complaint, careful thought should be given as to whether the super-complaint process is the most effective route. It may be that specific competition or consumer legislation would provide a more immediate and/or effective means of satisfying and addressing the issue. For example when the feature of a market that is, or appears to be, significantly harming the interests of consumers relates to single firm conduct.   (*Super-complaints: Guidance for designated consumer bodies*)

Super-complaints are required to be dealt with within a strict timetable, and the OFT or regulator will keep the super-complainant informed of the proceedings. As of September 2010 the following super-complainants had been designated: the Consumers' Association ('Which?'), the National Consumer Council ('Consumer Focus'), the Consumer Council for Water, the National Association of Citizens Advice Bureaux (NACAB), the Scottish Association of Citizens Advice Bureaux ('Citizens Advice Scotland'), the Campaign for Real Ale (CAMRA) and the General Consumer Council of Northern Ireland (GCCNI). The OFT has launched a considerable number of investigations following complaints made by super-complainants. These range from the markets for banking in Northern Ireland to care homes, doorstep selling, the supply of beer in pubs and cash ISAs.

7.3.3 **The Enterprise Act 2002 and third-party rights**

Certain third-party rights are also available in relation to concluded market investigation references which have resulted in the imposition of orders, or the acceptance of undertakings, or in relation to the merger control process in the UK. These are considered further in the relevant chapters below.

7.4 **Reform of the law relating to private actions**

Following the *Courage* case, there has been an attempt on the part of the Commission to harmonize the law relating to private actions in Europe. The *Green Paper on damages* saw the light in December 2005 (*Damages actions for breach of the EC anti-trust rules*, COM(2005)672, 19 December 2005), and in April 2007 the OFT published *Private actions in competition law: effective redress for consumers and business* (OFT 916). The OFT notes at para. 2.12 that problems still exist in relation to private actions:

It is difficult to assess the extent of demand that exists for greater redress of harm caused by cartels and other anti-competitive practices. Businesses and consumers are often unaware that they are being, or have been, harmed by such behaviour. Cartels are covert, and other anti-competitive practices (for example, predatory pricing) are often difficult to identify. Even if a consumer becomes aware of anti-competitive behaviour, it may be that the individual's loss is so small that it is not in his interest to pursue an individual claim to recover it, although the aggregate loss to consumers at large may be very significant. Legal costs and uncertainty as to the outcome of the proceedings may also act as a disincentive to the bringing of well-founded claims by both consumers and businesses. It is notable that, so far, consumers appear to have obtained virtually no redress in private competition law actions. It is unclear how extensively businesses have obtained redress to date, given that few successful cases have been reported and that the details of any private settlements that have been reached are often confidential.

The OFT discussion paper takes as its starting point the observation that 'most of the main structural and legal elements for effective private actions in competition law are already in place in the UK' (para. 1.2) but then notes, as set out above, that difficulties remain. In a similar way, the Green Paper clearly voiced the Commission's opinion that there is insufficient private enforcement of EU competition law, and that damages to those injured are too rarely paid. In an attempt to address these issues, in 2008 the Commission published its White Paper on Damages (*Damages actions for breach of the EC antitrust rules*, COM (2008) 165, 3 April 2008), at the heart of which lies the right to compensation for breach of EU competition rules. The Commission's primary objectives are, on the one hand, to establish effective minimum judicial protection and, on the other, to guarantee uniformity and coherence in the award of damages across the EU. As regards the first objective, the Commission sees the need for full compensation for damages caused by breach of the Treaty's antitrust provisions. This includes 'not only the actual loss due to an anti competitive price increase, but also to the loss of profit as a result of any reduction in sales and encompasses a right to interest' (s. 2.5).

Promoting uniformity and coherence—the second objective—is crucial, as the White Paper proposes granting binding effect to all final decisions of NCAs (s. 2.7). To this end, the Commission emphasizes the need for both Community and national measures, and points to both substantive and procedural obstacles at national level that hamper actions for antitrust damages in national courts. These obstacles, the White Paper states, must be removed through harmonized rules on damage actions. In promoting the goal of harmonization, the Commission proposes a set of measures. These include promoting disclosure of evidence to speed up claims (s. 2.2), and increasing access to justice for those with smaller claims (particularly for consumers and SMEs) by allowing collective redress and bringing actions through approved representatives (s. 2.1).

In March 2009, the European Parliament showed its support by approving a *Resolution on the Commission's White Paper on damages actions for breach of the EC antitrust rules*. However, to date no legislation has been adopted implementing the changes called for in the White Paper.

FURTHER READING

Books

EHLERMANN, C. D., and ATANASIU, I. (eds), *European Competition Law Annual 2001: Effective Private Enforcement of EC Antitrust Law* (2003) Hart Publishing, Oxford

JONES, C. A., *Private Enforcement of Antitrust Law in the EU, UK and USA* (1999) OUP, Oxford

KERSE, C. S., and KHAN, N., *EC Antitrust Procedure* (2005) Sweet & Maxwell, London, Part 2.II

Articles

BREALEY, M., 'Adopt *Perma Life* but Follow *Hanover Shoe* to Illinois? Who Can Sue for Damages for Breach of EC Competition Law?', [2002] *Competition Law Journal* 127

EILMANSBERGER, T., 'The Green Paper on Damages Actions for Breach of the EC Antitrust Rules and Beyond: Reflections on the Utility and Feasibility of Stimulating Private Enforcement through Legislative Action', (2007) 44 *Common Market Law Review* 431

JONES, C. A., 'Private Antitrust Enforcement in Europe: A Policy Analysis and Reality Check', (2004) *World Competition Law & Economics Review* 13

KENNELLY, B., 'Damages Actions before the CAT and the Passing On Defence', [2004] *Competition Law Journal* 238

KOMNINOS, A., 'The EU White Paper for Damages Actions: A First Appraisal', (2008) *Concurrences Review* 2-2008, 84-92

MONTI, G., 'Anti-competitive Agreements: The Innocent Party's Right to Damages', (2002) *European Law Review* 282

PHEASANT, J., 'Damages Actions for Breach of the EC Antitrust Rules: The European Commission's Green Paper', (2006) *European Competition Law Review* 535

REICH, N., 'The "Courage" Doctrine: Encouraging or Discouraging Compensation for Antitrust Injuries?', (2005) 42 *Common Market Law Review* 35

RODGERS, B., 'The Interface between Competition Law and Private Law: Article 81, Illegality and Unjustified Enrichment', (2002) *Edinburgh Law Review* 217

SEGAL, I., and WHINSTON, M., 'Public vs. Private Enforcement of Antitrust Law: Survey', (2007) *European Competition Law Review* 306

WILS, W. P. J., 'Should Private Antitrust Enforcement Be Encouraged?', (2003) 26 *World Competition* 472

8

An introduction to the economics of agreements, collusion, and parallel conduct

KEY POINTS

- Horizontal agreements may raise concerns that competition is being harmed, but may be difficult to detect.
- The problems of policing horizontal conduct may be exacerbated in oligopoly markets where there are few competitors.
- Cartel arrangements may be difficult to put in place, but may have long-term success.
- Vertical agreements are less likely to raise competitive concern, unless they are linked to the exercise of market power, or contribute to the exclusion of competitors from a market.

8.1 Introduction

Multi-firm conduct is often a more difficult phenomenon to analyse and to identify than is single firm or monopoly behaviour. At the most general level the point is simply made: if a single firm can damage the market and produce unwelcome welfare effects, then so too can a group of firms which act together *as if* they were one. This is known as the 'cartel', or 'cartelization'. The difficulty inherent in the economic analysis of multilateral conduct has meant that the legal response in the EU and the UK is to attack such situations either where observed market conduct is indicative of anti-competitive behaviour, or where physical evidence, such as documents and communications, shows that firms have attempted, even if unsuccessfully, to coordinate conduct. Legislation in this area usually makes reference to 'agreements, decisions, or concerted practices' between firms (see 9.2.1–9.2.3). In practice the distinction is often not made since the legal consequences are identical, and in this chapter the word 'agreement' is frequently taken to apply to all three situations. An explanation of what each of these terms implies is given in Chapter 9. The economic analysis here would apply equally to the cartel offence of the Enterprise Act 2002, although the way the offence is structured removes the need to engage in sensitive economic analysis.

8.2 Horizontal restraints and competition law

Horizontal agreements are those between firms at the same level of production or distribution, and who are therefore competitors (see Figure 8.1). These agreements may contain restrictions of competition known as horizontal restraints, and will in most cases be of concern to authorities: the inevitable tendency of such contracts is to approximate the circumstances of monopolistic competition. As a result, horizontal agreements will be often proscribed. Thus in the US one of the long-standing rules of antitrust is that price fixing is to be condemned *per se*, and is not brought within the 'rule of reason' (*United States* v *Trans-Missouri Freight Association* 166 US 290 (1897)). Even where the ostensible purpose of such agreements is apparently benign, such as to agree standards or to harmonize technology, the underlying purpose may in fact be anti-competitive. The attainment of monopoly pricing by a cartel is likely to be accompanied by more deleterious effects than in the case of a true monopoly; a group of smaller firms is unlikely to have attained the efficiencies of production that flow from a monopolist's economies of scale. Cartels and collusion are discussed in Bishop, S., and Walker, M., *The Economics of EC Competition Law: The Concepts, Application and Measurement*, London, Sweet & Maxwell (3rd edn, 2010) (hereinafter *The Economics of EC Competition Law*).

8.2.1 The problem of oligopoly

In atomistic markets where there are a great number of competitors, agreements between firms operating at the same level of production are unlikely to be of concern to competition authorities (although note that in *Vereniging van Samenwerkende Prijsregelende Organisaties in de Bouwnijverheid (SPO)* v *Commission* case T–29/92 [1995] ECR II–289 an investigation into the Dutch building industry involved thousands of undertakings). Much effort would be required to put an agreement in place, and in the absence of a mechanism to punish firms that broke the agreement—which would be illegal under almost all regimes—cheating would be inevitable. The more concentrated the market is, the more likely it is that the firms will be able successfully to agree to dampen or restrict competition. An oligopolistic market is one in which only a few firms compete, or in which a few firms hold the bulk of the market power, albeit with numbers of smaller competitors at the periphery (banking, petrol, etc.). It is in these markets where business managers may be unable to resist 'a bit of corporate nookie' (Lord Lucas, Hansard (HL) 30 October 1997, col. 1161), that competition concerns arise most readily.

A problem for any authority or complainant becomes that of distinguishing between conduct which is based on agreements, whether formal or informal, and conduct which is the result of each firm responding rationally to the actions of the others. For

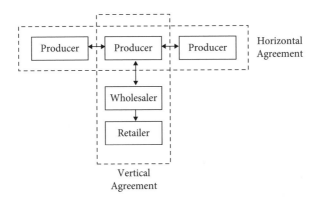

Figure 8.1 Horizontal and vertical agreements

example, if petrol prices generally rise by the same margin within a short time, is that because the companies have agreed to raise their prices together, or because once one company does so it makes sense for the others to follow suit? The MMC has consistently held that the petrol market in the UK is competitive, in spite of public concerns to the contrary (see, e.g., Cm. 972, *The Supply of Petrol* (1990)).

In 1838 the economist Cournot suggested that, even assuming *independent decisions* made by oligopolists, prices in such markets would be higher than in perfectly competitive markets, and such markets can achieve what is now referred to as a 'Nash–Cournot equilibrium'. Distinguishing between the anticipated higher price of oligopolistic industry and 'artificially' maintained higher prices is one of the central problems facing competition authorities.

8.2.2 Cartels

A cartel may be defined as 'an explicit arrangement designed to eliminate competition' (Kaserman, D. L., and Mayo, J. H., *Government and Business: The Economics of Antitrust and Regulation*, Fort Worth, The Dryden Press (1995), p. 152). Cartels are attractive to participants: if the cartel succeeds, total profits to the participants will be higher than would be the sum of individual profits in what would otherwise be a competitive market. As Terry Wilson puts in the movie *The Informant!* (2009). '[i]t's better to have the elephants inside the tent pissin' out, than outside the tent pissing in'. A perfect cartel would be one in which the group as a whole set production where marginal cost for the group equalled marginal revenue, which is to say that the cartel would collectively behave exactly like a single-firm monopoly. In practice such perfection will be unobtainable.

For the EU Commission the danger of cartels is that they

generate situation rents for the most powerful companies since they need not make an effort either to improve the quality of their products or to improve productivity. At the same time, however, cartels artificially keep the least efficient companies in the market, weaken the productive apparatus, and thus inflict considerable damage on the economy in general and eventually also on EU jobs.   (IP (98) 1068, 3 December 1998 [1999] 4 CMLR 13)

The example of a cartel that is most often used in economics texts is that of the Organization of Petroleum Exporting Countries (OPEC), which continues to have a strong influence on the world market in oil. Even here, in a situation in which the participants, being sovereign nations, are not subject to the rigours of national antitrust laws, the cartel is unable to raise prices to the level that would have been obtained under a monopoly situation. The challenge for antitrust enforcement with respect to cartels is to exacerbate the inherent weaknesses in order either to make membership so unattractive as to force the abandonment of the cartel, or to minimize the effects of the anti-competitive arrangements.

There are two major problems that economists have identified as facing any cartel: these may be characterized as the problems of 'agreement' and 'adherence'. In the mid-1950s emphasis was placed on the difficulties cartel members would have in agreeing on matters of fundamental policy, such as the correct response to make to a new entrant, or the trade-off between short- and long-term profits. One researcher identified a cartel where prices had not changed for 10 years, in spite of rising costs, because the two largest members which were able to block any changes preferred to maintain low prices to keep new entrants out of the market (Fog, B., 'How Are Cartel Prices Determined?', (1956) 5 *Journal of Industrial Economics* 16). There are several factors that make it difficult for cartels to reach agreement. For example, product differentiation will require cartel members to agree on what may be a very complex price schedule, rather than a single price. This is a problem for OPEC, as oil is not a homogeneous product but is produced at different grades with different sulphur contents. Differences in the costs facing firms in the industry will also make agreement harder: larger firms in the cartel, which are more likely to benefit from economies of scale, may want lower prices than the smaller firms, and it may become difficult to put into place arrangements acceptable to all to limit production.

Once the agreement problem is overcome, the second, more significant, problem relates to adherence. The problem facing cartels is as follows:

If a cartel is successful in restricting its joint output and raising price, it creates an incentive for individual member firms to cheat, expand their outputs, and undermine the cartel. A *single* firm will always profit by cheating on the cartel. But *all* firms have this same incentive, and if all firms expand their output, the cartel breaks down. On this reasoning, cartels are inherently unstable.   (Martin, S., *Industrial Economics: Economic Analysis and Public Policy*, London, Macmillan (2nd edn, 1994), p. 162)

The position may be explained by reference to game theory, on which most cartel/oligopoly models are now based. Game theory, developed by John von Neumann and Oskar Morgenstern (*Theory of Games and Economic Behaviour*, Princeton, Princeton UP (1944)) is, at its most elaborate, incredibly complex, but a simple demonstration will show how the problem may be addressed. A branch of game theory deals with the 'Prisoner's Dilemma' which can be related to the behaviour of two competing oligopolists (technically the prisoner's dilemma game is one in which the dominant strategy leads to a sub-optimal outcome). Consider the following situation: Penelope and Javier rob the university payroll; they are arrested by Pedro, who is convinced of their guilt but does not have the evidence to obtain a conviction unless he can get a confession. Pedro can prove a lesser charge of dangerous driving, and if convicted of this offence both Penelope and Javier will go to prison for one year. If either one of the prisoners confesses and is prepared to testify against the other, that prisoner will receive no gaol term at all and the other will go to prison for 10 years. If both prisoners confess each will go to prison for five years. The prisoners are held separately in the police station and do not have the opportunity to coordinate their conduct. The resulting strategic position therefore looks like this:

		Penelope's strategies	
		Don't confess	Confess
Javier's strategies	Don't confess	$-1, -1$	$-10, 0$
	Confess	$0, -10$	$-5, -5$

(For example, if Javier does not confess, and Penelope does, Javier faces 10 years in prison, and Penelope none.)

In this position the combined welfare of the parties dictates that neither should confess, and both will go to prison for one year. The incentive for each of the parties to break the fraternal criminal bond and grass on the other is strong, but of course if both do this then each faces a longer prison sentence than if each had remained silent. Only if the two prisoners can exchange information during the process, and are prepared to forgo some short-term benefit in order to improve their collective position, can it be assured that the outcome will be optimal to the two. If two companies are substituted for Penelope and Javier, and profit figures for the prison sentences, the game becomes applicable to a two-firm cartel situation. The position is further complicated in the real world of cartels in that 'the game' may be repeated many times, giving the players an opportunity to learn the consequences of their strategic behaviour, and to adapt to a strategy that is optimal. For example, if the game is played only once there is no punishment that can be meted out by one player on the other (in our fictional world Penelope may order a hit on Javier, but in a cartel situation what can the 'loser' do?). If the game is played over many rounds, with no clear end in sight it may become apparent to all players that the rewards of cheating first time round are offset by a failure to reap long term profits, as cheating by one member should result in retaliation in the form of lower prices by others, and that cooperation is preferable to competition. Economic theory predicts this outcome in games in which cheating can be detected, parties can respond effectively to cheating (by increasing their competitiveness), and the game does not have a clearly determined end.

Finding physical, documentary evidence of the existence of cartels is a difficult matter. Baroness O'Caithan drew attention in the Lords to a case resolved by the Restrictive Practices Court (RPC) under the old UK regime:

The paint-makers' price fixing cartel, which was ended by an undertaking to the [RPC] in early June [1997] had been going on for years. It was quite obvious that the companies involved knew exactly what they were doing and knew it was illegal. Why else would they have used assumed names to book hotel conference facilities?   (Hansard (HL) October 30 1997, col. 1167)

Given the difficulties of establishing the existence of cartels, a tactic employed by most authorities is to implement measures designed to destabilize cartels, which find their expression in leniency programmes.

Analysis of the instability of cartels is based largely on pioneering work done by George J. Stigler ('A Theory of Oligopoly', (1964) 72 *Journal of Political Economy* 44). Stigler focused on the fact that much of the conduct in a cartel will be furtive, and that a poor flow of information will mean that strategic activity is carried out largely on the basis of conjecture and guesswork. A price-cutting firm is unlikely to announce the fact, and published prices may reflect no change at all. Instead any price cuts are likely to be agreed discreetly with customers. In a cartel situation firms will in any case be facing a reduced demand as price rises with the implementation of the cartel, and it will be difficult for firms to determine if demand reductions are the result of this inevitable process or the cheating of other members. Firms will also be used to a variation in sales, and only if the reduction is below their expectations may they suspect cheating. Stigler's results show that the greater the number of firms in the cartel, the greater is the likelihood of cheating being able to go undetected. Nonetheless, if firms are able to pool their information the probability of detection of any cheating rises dramatically. It is then clear that one of the tasks of competition policy is to make such information exchange risky, and in most regimes the availability of hard physical evidence of cartelization is likely to bring swift condemnation.

The prediction that there is an inverse relationship between numbers in cartels and the likely success of cartels is a logical one. In a cartel with 15 members there is a total of 105 paired relationships between members. This rises to 190 relationships in a cartel of 20 members, and 1,225 in a cartel with 50 members (formally the number of paired relationships is given by $N(N-1)/2$). Only if a central control mechanism can be established are larger cartels ever likely to be successful. This is normally done through a trade association or perhaps via the appointment of a specific cartel management team (as was the case in *Pre-Insulated Pipe Cartel* 1999/60 (1999) OJ L24/1). The activities of trade associations tend to be closely scrutinized by competition authorities. A survey of antitrust actions against cartels taken in the United States found that where only a few firms were involved, and the market conditions were relatively uncomplicated, there were few instances of formally structured collusion. In 606 cases studied the average number of participants was just under 17, and as the number of participants in each case increased, so too did the complexity of the arrangements that were put in place to facilitate the success of the cartel (Fraas, A. G., and Greer, D. F., 'Market Structure and Price Collusion: An Empirical Analysis', (1977) 26 *Journal of Industrial Economics* 21).

For some time it was argued that even where cartels existed they were limited in their harm. It is undeniably hard to determine the extent to which any given cartel may lead to an inflation of prices against those which would arise in a competitive market. However, recent work suggests that the overcharges may be very significant. In 2006 it was estimated that an average overcharge might be as high as 40 per cent, with international cartels having a higher average overcharge than domestic cartels (see Connor, J. M., and Bolotova, Y., 'Cartel Overcharges: Survey and Meta-analysis', *International Journal of Industrial Organisation*, (2006) vol. 24, p. 1109; see also *OECD Report on the Nature and Effect of Cartels*, 2002).

8.2.3 Price leadership

It can be difficult to distinguish between cartels in which prices are maintained across a range of producers or suppliers, and other situations in which price leadership is present. Markham distinguished three categories of price leadership, none of which is likely to be condemned by competition authorities without further evidence of actual collusion (Markham, J. W., 'The Nature and Significance of Price Leadership', (1951) 41 *American Economic Review* 891).

Dominant firm leadership occurs where in any market one firm is sufficiently large in relation to other producers to be the only one capable of significantly affecting the market. In such a case the dominant firm is likely to set prices as if it were a monopolist, and the smaller firms will have little to gain from diverging much from this price. Competition law will accept such situations, and does not require firms to price at what would be irrational levels in order to maintain a fiction of vigorous price competition.

Barometric price leadership is more complex. It is a characteristic of markets in which the price leader changes frequently, and in which the response to any change in price tends to be less swift than in the situation where there is a single dominant firm. Whether a price will be followed will depend not on the identity of the company setting the price, but on whether the change, even if set by a small company, reflects a generally perceived need in the market for a price adjustment. This was considered to be the case by the EU Commission in *Zinc producer group* 84/405 (1984) OJ L220/27.

The third situation, which poses the greatest problem for competition law, arises in markets where the product is homogenous, and where there are few producers facing similar costs. Here any one firm would accurately reflect the situation facing each firm, and it is likely that any one firm choosing to adopt a price leadership role would be followed. Conditions similar to these may be found in the United Kingdom in the banking and petrol industries, although the position in the petrol market is changing following the entrance into the market of supermarket chains.

In *Industrial Market Structure and Economic Performance*, Frederic Scherer and David Ross set out some interesting case studies of price leadership (Boston, Houghton Mifflin (3rd edn, 1990), pp. 250–60).

8.3 Vertical agreements and vertical restraints

In the case of most goods, and some services, there is a chain of production before the product reaches the consumer. Typically this will extend from the gathering of the raw material, and its first processing, to the retailer with whom the customer deals. Thus, for example, in the case of the motor industry the vertical chain begins with steel and plastics manufacturers, through the various stages of production of components and the cars themselves, to distributors and individual retailers. A vertical agreement is one between firms at different stages of the chain of production, and it will be immediately apparent that this is an essential and pervasive feature of commercial life. Figure 8.1 above illustrates how vertical agreements operate.

In the absence of vertical agreements the raw material would not arrive at the manufacturer's plant, and the finished car would not end up on a garage forecourt. A vertical agreement is to some extent a substitute for vertical integration. It was a matter of some surprise, therefore, when the Commission attacked an agreement between a manufacturer and a distributor as being anti-competitive in a very early competition decision (*Re Grundig* 64/556/EEC [1964] 1 CMLR 489; on appeal *Établissements Consten Sarl and Grundig-Verkaufs-GmbH* v *Commission* cases 56 and 58/64 [1966] CMLR 418; see 9.3.1.1). However, these agreements may contain vertical restraints, or potential restrictions of competition. Hughes, Foss, and Ross categorize vertical restraints into three kinds: First, a seller may agree not to supply goods to no one other than the buyer within a territory. Secondly, the purchaser often commits to buy goods only from that supplier and no other providers. Thirdly, in some cases, a vertical agreement may set some of the conditions (price, location, consumers) under which the products can be resold (Hughes, M., Foss, C., and Ross, K., 'The Economic Assessment of Vertical Restraints Under UK and EC Competition Law', (2001) *European Competition Law Review* 424).

Concerns as to the effects of vertical restraints have also underpinned several inquiries in the UK, including that into *Foreign Package Holidays*, completed in 1997. The question whether vertical restraints are anti-competitive remains a matter of debate, with the Chicago school in the 1980s arguing broadly that any and all vertical restraints should be legal, although the authors of the Commission Green Paper (below) note that a consensus is emerging, with economists being reluctant to generalize in what is a difficult area. In 1996 the OFT published its 12th Research Paper 'Vertical Restraints in Competition Policy' (Dobson, P. W., and Waterson, M.; and see also Bond, C., 'Vertical Restraints', (1997) *Fair Trading*, summer, p. 7), and in early 1997 the EU Commission published its *Green Paper on Vertical Restraints in EC Competition Policy* (COM(96) 721 final).

Broadly, the argument made in favour of examining vertical restraints is that while they may encourage inter-brand competition, for example competition between Nissan and Toyota cars, they may restrict intra-brand competition, for example competition between two sellers of Nissan cars, which may not be a significant problem if the customer has a wide choice of makes of cars to choose from. If vertical restraints or agreements are to be considered a problem, the analysis must take into account situations in which firms at the lower level of the chain, nearer consumers, exercise power over firms higher up the chain. Thus the OFT report recognizes that retailers hold increasing power in setting the contract terms on which they will deal with suppliers, and suggests that competition concerns may be raised where either party in the chain is in possession of market power. The threefold consideration put forward in the report is as follows:

(a) Is there horizontal market power at either the level of manufacturer or the level of retailer?

(b) Is the consumer likely to be significantly affected by the restriction?

(c) Is the result of the restriction to generate efficiency gains?

If the answer to (a) is in the affirmative, then consideration of (b) and (c) may allow a determination of whether the restriction is against the public interest. Even if the answer to (b) and (c) would be in the affirmative, the authors conclude that in the absence of horizontal market power there is unlikely to be any benefit from conducting further examination of the practice for anti-competitive effects.

It is a common assumption that vertical restraints are necessarily imposed to benefit the party higher up the chain of production, but this is not always the case. One of the strongest forms of vertical restraint is resale price maintenance (RPM), under which resellers are restricted in their ability to set prices. Usually the manufacturer or supplier specifies a minimum price below which the reseller may not sell the product. It is not easy to create scenarios in which this operates to the benefit of the supplier, and the immediate beneficiary tends to be the retailer. These sorts of restraints therefore may be requested by retailers, and may be an effective way to ensure that cheating is minimized in price-fixing cartels. It is perhaps in response to this possibility that, until the CA 98, the taking of any steps to enforce RPM was the only activity condemned *per se* in the UK regime. Chicagoan economists have argued that this supposition cannot be correct as there will be too much competition at the retail level to allow the retailers to impose conditions on those supplying to them. This conclusion is probably wrong, and it has been pointed out by Porter that retailers tend to operate in oligopolistic markets because they are dependent in turn on the ability of local customers to travel to them (Porter, M. E., *Interbrand Choice, Strategy, and Bilateral Market Power*, Cambridge, MA, Harvard UP (1976)).

FURTHER READING

Books

CARLTON, D. W., and PERLOFF, J. M., *Modern Industrial Organisation* (2005) 4th edn, Addison-Wesley, Boston, MA, Chapters 5 and 6

NEVEN, D., PANANDROPOULOS, P., and SEABRIGHT, P., *Trawling for Minnows: European Competition Policy and Agreements between Firms* (1998) Centre for Economic Policy Research, London

Articles

CONNOR, J. M., and LANDE, R. H., 'The Size of Cartel Overcharges: Implications for US and EC Fining Policies', (2006) 51 *Antitrust Bulletin*, p. 983

GYSELEN, L., 'Vertical Restraints in the Distribution Process: Strengths and Weaknesses of the Free Rider Rationale under EEC Competition Law', (1984) 21 *Common Market Law Review* 647

HAY, G. A., 'Horizontal Agreements: Concept and Proof', (2006) 51 *Antitrust Bulletin*, p. 877

9

Agreements in the EU: the elements of article 101 TFEU

KEY POINTS

- Article 101 TFEU applies to coordinated conduct.
- The most important question is that of whether there is in the conduct a prevention, restriction, or distortion of competition within the meaning of art. 101(1) TFEU.
- Some forms of conduct, such as horizontal price fixing, are deemed to be *per se* prohibited; others, such as vertical distribution agreements, must be analysed in order to determine the competitive effects of the conduct.
- For the prohibition to apply there must be an effect on trade between Member States.
- Article 101 has direct effect, and conduct prohibited is illegal without any decision to that effect being necessary. However, art. 101(3) permits an exception to be made where the restrictive conduct leads to certain benefits.
- A breach of art. 101 TFEU may incur penalties, damages, and a requirement of conduct modification, and also renders void any offending agreement.

9.1 Introduction

Article 101 TFEU reads as follows:

1. The following shall be prohibited as incompatible with the internal market: all agreements between undertakings, decisions by associations of undertakings and concerted practices which may affect trade between Member States and which have as their object or effect the prevention, restriction or distortion of competition within the common market, and in particular those which:

   (a) directly or indirectly fix purchase or selling prices or any other trading conditions;

   (b) limit or control production, markets, technical development, or investment;

   (c) share markets or sources of supply;

   (d) apply dissimilar conditions to equivalent transactions with other trading parties, thereby placing them at a competitive disadvantage;

(e)   make the conclusion of contracts subject to acceptance by the other parties of supplementary obligations which, by their nature or according to commercial usage, have no connection with the subject of such contracts.

2. Any agreements or decisions prohibited pursuant to this Article shall be automatically void.

3. The provisions of paragraph 1 may, however, be declared inapplicable in the case of:

— any agreement or category of agreements between undertakings;

— any decision or category of decisions by associations of undertakings;

— any concerted practice or category of concerted practices;

which contributes to improving the production or distribution of goods or to promoting technical or economic progress, while allowing consumers a fair share of the resulting benefit, and which does not:

(a)   impose on the undertakings concerned restrictions which are not indispensable to the attainment of these objectives;

(b)   afford such undertakings the possibility of eliminating competition in respect of a substantial part of the products in question.

This provision is intended to apply to any agreed coordinated conduct, howsoever structured, between two or more undertakings, and is more concerned with the economic impact of a practice than with its legal form. In this chapter the general principles covering art. 101 will be considered. It is easiest to approach the article by analysing each of its parts, and then by considering its operation as a whole. At the end of the chapter is a flow chart intended to aid in structuring the step-by-step analysis to determine whether a conduct falls within the scope of this provision. For the meaning of 'undertaking', see 2.2 above.

9.2 Article 101(1): the prohibition

It is immediately apparent that the effect of art. 101 is to make conduct falling within its ambit illegal, and the article may be relied upon by injured competitors and consumers. Undertakings in breach are liable to be fined by the Commission, and many of the largest fines handed out have been to those engaged in illicit cartels (see Chapter 6 and 9.3.2.1). The article is drafted so as to apply to any form of multilateral anti-competitive conduct, and 'has been interpreted so broadly and formalistically that any restriction on the freedom to act has been deemed to fall under the prohibition, irrespective of its impact on competition' (Amato, G., in *Robert Schuman Centre Annual on European Competition Law 1996*, p. 126).

The Commission does not always distinguish between the various forms of potential breach, and indeed in some cases has expressly refused to do so. In *Cartonboard* 94/601 (1994) OJ L74/21, for example, the Commission said that it did not consider it 'necessary, particularly in the case of a complex infringement of long duration, for the Commission to characterise it as exclusively an agreement or concerted practice. Indeed, it may not even be feasible or realistic to make any such distinction' (para. 128) (decision upheld on appeal in *Cascades SA* v *Commission* case T–308/94 [2002] 4 CMLR 33 and *Stora Kopparbergs Bergslags AB* v *Commission* case T–354/94 [2002] 4 CMLR 34, although some penalties were reduced). However, the approach taken to evidence of the breach, and perhaps to the penalty, may depend on the form that the proscribed conduct takes.

9.2.1 Agreements between undertakings

That any contract between two undertakings may be held to fall within art. 101 is clear, and many distribution, franchise, and service agreements have been examined, modified, and at times condemned. However, 'agreement' does not require that a formal contract be in place, or indeed that any more than one party behaves in a certain manner. The primary requirement of this part of art. 101(1) is that at least two parties must be involved. The article cannot in any circumstance be applied to entirely unilateral conduct. A detailed analysis of how the Commission and the European Courts have drawn the limits between unilateral and multilateral conduct can be found in section 9.2.5 below.

In *Polypropylene* 86/398 (1986) OJ L230/1, for example, the Commission found that the producers of polypropylene had been party 'to a whole complex of schemes, arrangements and measures decided in the framework of a system of regular meetings and continuous contact' (para. 80). Although the parties contended that no agreement was in place, the Commission held that it was not necessary for it to establish the presence of an agreement 'intended as legally binding upon the parties'. In its view an agreement exists wherever there is the necessary consensus between the parties 'determining the lines of their mutual action or abstention from action in the market', and it was certainly not necessary for the agreement to be made in writing. This point was emphasized in *National Panasonic* 82/853 (1982) OJ L354/28, where National Panasonic UK somehow managed to operate a dealership system throughout the UK without the benefit of written agreements. The company did not dispute that an agreement existed, and in fact had provided the Commission with evidence of the terms and conditions that it expected dealers to comply with.

9.2.2 Decisions by associations of undertakings

It is standard practice in many industries to belong to an association that acts on behalf of its member companies. Such actions might include industry-wide promotional campaigns, public education, market research, standards setting, and perhaps even charitable functions on behalf of workers. These associations may also act as a front for collusive activity: a unilateral statement from the association as to, for example, the desirability of price stability might be followed by action by all its members, each of them denying that they have in any way colluded with the others.

A classic example of such a situation arose in *Roofing felt* 86/399 (1986) OJ L232/15, where the action taken related primarily to the Cooperative Association of Belgian Asphalters (Belasco) which represented seven members in the industry. The members had drawn up an agreement, which provided for, *inter alia,* the adoption of a price list and minimum prices for all roofing felt supplied in Belgium, the allocation of quotas between members and penalties for breaches of decisions made under the agreement. The Commission pointed to the role played by Belasco, which it found 'was involved in a number of ways in the operation of the agreement'. It was Belasco which had managed the quota system, unilaterally employing an accountant for the purpose and administering the compliance mechanism.

The steps that an association takes do not have to be binding on its members to fall within art. 101(1). If this were to be a requirement, avoidance would be all too easy. In *Fire insurance* 85/75 (1985) OJ L35/20 (on appeal *Verband der Sachversicherer eV* v *Commission* case 45/85 [1988] 4 CMLR 264), an association protecting the business interests of industrial fire insurers in Germany argued in that the 'recommendation' it had made to lay down a collective flat rate and an across-the-board rise in premiums was expressly described as 'non-binding'. The Commission was not persuaded to this view, and held that a decision by an association of undertakings in breach of 101(1) exists if the recommendation 'was brought to the notice of members as a statement of the association's policy' (para. 23).

This case was followed by the EU Commission in *Fenex* 96/438 (1996) OJ L181/28, in which action was taken against an association of undertakings in the freight market in the Netherlands. The association had, for nearly 100 years, issued 'recommendations' to its members relating to various scales of charges. In its defence the association argued that the recommendations were non-binding. The Commission noted that the system had been in existence for a long time. The recommendation was drawn up and updated annually by a specialist body within the association, and subsequently the recommendation would be adopted by the board of directors. It would be then published accompanied by a circular drafted in strong terms. For example, one such circular read 'in view of the result arrived at members are *urgently recommended* to pass on the above mentioned tariff increase [5 per cent] in full' (para. 38, emphasis added). In the light of these facts the Commission held that 'the recommendation must be interpreted as being the faithful reflection of the association's resolve to coordinate the conduct of its members on the relevant market' (para. 41).

Consistently the Court has expressed concern that the rules governing trade associations should not be more than is necessary to achieve the *legitimate* objectives of that association. The fact that this was not the case was important in *Gottrup-Klim Grovvareforeninger* v *Dansk Landbrugs Grovvarelskab* case C–250/92 [1996] 4 CMLR 191. Here an association existed that had as its task facilitating cooperative purchasing of supplies, and the Court held that 'in order to escape the prohibition laid down in Article [101(1)] of the Treaty, the restrictions imposed on members by the statutes [of the association] must be limited to what is necessary [to ensure the legitimate aims of the association]'. There will even be situations in which the very creation of the association, or membership of it, will constitute a breach of art. 101(1) without the need to consider its actual operation. This appears to have been the case in *National Sulphuric Acid Association* 80/917 (1980) OJ L260/24, where the Commission indicated that the terms of the association in question were automatically such as to breach art. 101(1) (paras 29–36).

9.2.3 **Concerted practices**

Concerted practice is the most nebulous of the three categories caught by art. 101. It covers conduct ranging from a scenario in which an agreement appears to exist but is difficult to prove, to the difficult situations in which the conduct observable in the market diverges from that which would be expected (suggesting that firms are in some degree colluding). In a US case it was pointed out that 'the picture of conspiracy as a meeting by twilight of a trio of sinister persons with pointed hats close together belongs to a darker age' (*William Goldman Theatres Inc.* v *Loew's Inc.* 150 F.2d 738, 743n. 15 (3rd Cir. 1945)). Modern-day enforcers of competition policy are confronted with companies using a full range of practices by which to coordinate their behaviour, whether by way of conventions held in luxury hotels, unrecorded telephone calls and e-mails, or apparently innocent market announcements in the press.

The first significant case in which the Court of Justice dealt with concerted practices was *Dyestuffs* (*ICI* v *Commission* case 48/69 [1972] CMLR 557). It upheld a Commission decision where the undertakings were condemned on the basis of evidence of collusion in the setting of prices. The definition of concerted practice applied in that case was approved and expanded on in the next important case, *Suiker Unie* (*Coöperatieve Vereniging 'Suiker Unie' UA* v *Commission* cases 40–48/73, 50/73, 54–56/73, 111/73, 113–114/73 [1976] 1 CMLR 295), when the Court held that it was

a form of coordination between undertakings which, without having been taken to the stage where an agreement properly so-called has been concluded, knowingly substitutes for the risks of competition cooperation in practice between them which leads to conditions of competition which do not correspond to the normal conditions of the market, having regard to the nature of the products, the importance and number of the undertakings as well as the size and nature of the said market. Such cooperation in practice amounts to a concerted practice *inter alia* when it enables the persons concerned to consolidate established positions to the detriment of effective freedom of movement of the products in the [Internal] Market and of the freedom of consumers to choose their suppliers.   (paras 26–7 of the judgment)

The difficulties of establishing the existence of such a situation are compounded in particular where the market is an oligopolistic one, in which case a degree of similarity of conduct is to be expected: if it is appropriate for one producer to raise its prices it is quite probably appropriate for all to do so. In such a case it is not the fact that prices have risen at the same time, by possibly the same level, that will induce condemnation under art. 101(1). The task of the Commission is to show that this has been achieved by other than the operation of normal market forces—it is the method, and not the result, that is being condemned. This is made clear by the Court in the *Dyestuffs* case:

while it is permissible for each manufacturer to change his prices freely and to take into account for this purpose the behaviour, present and foreseeable, of his competitors, it is, on the other hand, contrary to the competition rules of the Treaty for a manufacturer to cooperate with his competitors, in whatever manner, to determine a coordinated course of action relating to an increase in prices. (para. 118)

It is exceptionally difficult to distinguish between situations in which an undertaking acts *intelligently* in response to another's conduct—which is quite lawful—, and acts *with knowledge* of another's conduct—which may be in breach of art. 101(1). In *Cimenteries CBR SA* v *Commission* joined cases T 25–26/95, etc. [2000] 5 CMLR 204 (in summary only) the GC explained that

The concept of concerted practice implies the existence of reciprocal contacts. That condition is met where one competitor discloses its future intentions or conduct on the market to another when the latter requests it or, at the very least, accepts it. Thus, failure by an applicant to object to or express reservations where a competitor reveals its position regarding the relevant market will deny the former the defence of being a purely passive recipient of information unilaterally passed on without any request on the part of the applicant.   (para. 1849)

A similar stance was taken in *Tate & Lyle plc, British Sugar plc and Napier Brown plc* v *Commission* joined cases T–202/98, etc. [2001] 5 CMLR 22 where the Court held that an undertaking would be implicated in the existence of a concerted practice where it attended a meeting whose purpose was limited 'to the mere receipt of information concerning the future conduct of their market competitors' (para. 58). This would apply even where that information could be obtained through legitimate channels by the undertakings.

In *Zinc producer group* 84/405 (1984) OJ L220/27, the Commission investigated coordination in the market for zinc under an agreement that extended from 1964 to 1977. When the agreement ended in 1977 the market structure meant that there was no one firm that could break ranks and set its own prices independently of the rest of the market. In such a situation, known as 'barometric price leadership' (see Chapter 8), undertakings do not have true economic independence but, in law, are not acting in a concerted fashion where all companies set the same prices. The Commission was careful to isolate this position from that which existed between 1964 and 1977, and did not condemn the undertakings in relation to subsequent conduct, notwithstanding the similarity in behaviour (paras 75–6).

There are, in essence, two ways in which the Commission may attempt to establish the existence of collusive conduct. The first, and most satisfactory, is to collect the physical evidence that supports such a conclusion. Records of meetings, copies of letters, statements by company personnel, and evidence presented by customers may all provide the necessary evidence. Although such evidence may often lead to the conclusion that an agreement is in place, it may fall short of the required formality but still be indicative of collusion. An alternative—and more difficult—route is for the Commission to base a case on the analysis of the market in question. It would argue that there is a divergence between the conduct that would be predicted under competitive conditions and the conduct observed and that the only explanation for such a divergence is that the relevant undertakings are colluding. This was the way in which the Commission proceeded in its decision in relation to *Wood Pulp* 85/202 (1985) OJ L85/1 (on appeal *Re Wood Pulp Cartel: A. Ahlström Oy* v *Commission* cases C–89, 104, 114, 116, 117, and 125–129/85 [1993] 4 CMLR 407; note that at [1988] 4 CMLR 901 the issue of territorial jurisdiction was dealt with—see Chapter 4). This important judgment deserves detailed scrutiny, and is the first key case of the chapter.

Key case 9.1 *A. Ahlström Oy* v *Commission* cases C–89, 104, 114, 116, 117, and 125–9/85 [1993] 4 CMLR 407—Court of Justice judgment (art. 101)

Facts

The Commission took action against 43 undertakings producing bleached sulphate pulp, used in the manufacture of fine-quality paper, based in both the Union and other producing states including the US and Canada. A large number of customers were based in the Union, and one firm alone supplied about 290 different paper manufacturers. Producers announced prices in advance for the following quarter-year. Such announcements were highly visible and were reported in the specialist trade press, and were likely to be followed quickly by similar announcements from competitors. Over a number of years prices in the EU rose steadily, irrespective of the fact that over some of this period the stocks of pulp held by producers were increasing, and that production costs varied. Prices were also constant irrespective of the source of the product, when it might have been expected that imports from Canada and the US would be more expensive than those from Scandinavia.

Decision of the Commission

The Commission referred to several telexes and other communications in its decision. Prices rose uniformly, rather than by 'the testing of the market by trial and error which can lead to higher or lower prices and can force the undertaking which was the first to announce a higher price to recall the higher price' (Decision: para. 87). In effect the increases were in response to changes in market conditions, among all suppliers, when it might be expected that prices would respond to a shock, but would take time to achieve a new equilibrium.

The core of the Commission's argument was that the parallel conduct of the firms 'cannot be explained as independently chosen parallel conduct in a narrow oligopolistic situation' (para. 82). It went on to say that the uniform market behaviour could only be accounted for 'by a concerted practice on the part of the addressees of this Decision' (para. 83).

Following the imposition of fines, several of the companies appealed to the Court of Justice. The appeal was dealt with in two parts: first, the issues of extra-territorial jurisdiction were addressed; and second the substantive issues were considered.

Findings

On the question of the territorial scope of EU competition law, the Court held that there was nothing in the wording of art. 101 that precluded the application of EU competition law to undertakings having their location outside the EU, and to situations where unlawful conduct might have been initiated outside the EU. The Court held that the case could be resolved in this respect by reference to traditional international law principles, and stated that on the facts the concerted practice—if there was found to be one—had been implemented in the EU.

The question whether the mere system of price announcements denounced by the Commission could itself constitute an infringement of art. 101(1) was vehemently rejected. The stance taken by the Court was that each individual price announcement was made by a producer to a consumer, and not to other producers. This being so, no one announcement would 'lessen each undertaking's uncertainty as to the future attitude of its competitors' (para. 64 of the judgment). There was, the Court suggested, no guarantee that any one price announcement would be followed by that undertaking's competitors. In fact, the announcement could result in a competitor taking the opportunity to announce a more competitive price. Moreover, according to the Court of Justice 'the Commission [had] no documents which directly establish[ed] the existence of concertation between the producers concerned'.

In such a scenario, 'parallel conduct cannot be regarded as furnishing proof of concertation unless concertation constitutes the only plausible explanation for such conduct' (para. 71). Article 101 TFEU should be interpreted in a way that 'does not deprive economic operators of the right to adapt themselves intelligently to the existing and anticipated conduct of their competitors' (para. 71). Following the analyses of the Court's own experts into the characteristics of the market, the Court accepted that 'in this case, concertation is not the only plausible explanation for the parallel conduct' (para. 126). The experts suggested that there were valid historical reasons for the price announcement system, and also explained that the pricing may be related to the oligopolistic nature of the market (para. 103). Therefore, as long as parties accused of parallel conduct (in the absence of hard evidence of coordination) can point to plausible explanations for the parallelism it will not be possible to sustain a finding of a breach of art. 101 TFEU.

Comment

Wood Pulp is an important case for two reasons. First it demonstrated the jurisdictional reach of EU competition law. Following the case it is clear that firms based outside the EU can be attacked for conduct taking place outside the EU, as long as this conduct is to some extent 'implemented' in its territory. Secondly, this case demonstrates with great clarity the problems that can arise in applying competition law in oligopolistic markets. Distinguishing between coordination arising through intelligent adaptation to the conduct of others, and coordination arising through illicit communication may be very difficult, and, in the absence of hard evidence, or informers, virtually impossible. Since *Wood Pulp*, the Commission has not brought a case based exclusively on market behaviour. It has instead sought to gain evidence of contact between parties, and has targeted its efforts towards unravelling cartels (and there is doubt as to whether there was a cartel at play in *Wood Pulp*) by increasing penalties and making clearer the rewards available through the operation of leniency programmes. The issue of whether public price announcements and offers (for example, a supermarket stating that it will never knowingly be undersold) are anti-competitive is a complex one for competition law. Consumers may value these, but the case can be made that such announcements support a dampening of competition. For example, what is the benefit of a supermarket in cutting its prices if a competitor has made it publicly clear that it will immediately respond?

FURTHER READING

Articles

Jones, A., 'Wood Pulp: Concerted Practice and/or Conscious Parallelism', (1993) *European Competition Law Review 273*

Van Gerven, G., and Navarro Varona, E., 'The *Wood Pulp* Case and the Future of Concerted Practices', (1994) *Common Market Law Review 575Books*

Stroux, S., *US and EC Oligopoly Control* (2004) Kluwer Law International, The Hague, pp. 77–80

The more recent action in the *Ferry operators—currency surcharge* decision (97/84 (1997) OJ L26/23) hints at the range of approaches that the Commission may now take. Here various operators of ferry services between the UK and continental Europe imposed surcharges on customers who had paid in sterling following the 17 per cent fall in the value of the pound in September 1992. The additional charges, which were designed to protect the operators from the full impact of the devaluation of the currency, were levied at the same amount, and their imposition took effect at the same time and was announced in identical terms. The Commission both indicated that this was not a plausible result in light of the fact that the operators faced very different cost structures dependent upon their size and management systems, and also relied on evidence and admissions of collusion collected in the course of an investigation.

Concerted practices may be distinguished from naked cartels (or 'hard-core' cartels), where there is an explicit agreement between undertakings. In practice however, the link is blurred as evidence of the agreement may be difficult to obtain. Cartels are discussed below at 9.3.2.1.

9.2.4 **Peripheral involvement in restrictive conduct**

The fact that an undertaking has only a peripheral role in any breach of art. 101, and is not a driving force in the illegal conduct, is not a defence to any action brought under the article. Nevertheless, fines may be lower for those that have played a less significant part. Thus, for example, in the *Polypropylene* decision (86/398 (1986) OJ L230/1) the Commission drew a distinction between the four largest producers which between them 'formed the nucleus of the arrangements and constituted an unofficial directorate' and other members with a less prominent role. However, the fact that Shell 'did not attend the plenary sessions', or that Hercules 'did not communicate its own detailed sales figures to other producers' was in neither case considered to be a mitigating factor in assessing the existence of a breach.

The strictness of this approach was even more evident in *LdPE* 89/191 (1989) OJ L74/21, which again related to a cartel operating in the plastics market. Three of the undertakings involved—BP, Shell, and Monsanto—required 'special examination'. None of them took a central role in the cartel, and it was acknowledged that their participation could be considered 'only a partial one'. As the Commission recognized, 'mere knowledge of the existence of a cartel does not constitute involvement in the infringement'. Neither would it constitute a breach to base one's own conduct on the basis of that knowledge, as BP and Shell contested. However, it was established that the undertakings had attended at least some of the meetings of the cartel. 'In the absence of any evidence of attendance at meetings or other contacts the Commission might well have given these three undertakings the benefit of the doubt' (para. 33), but even the minimal contact that could be shown was considered to be sufficient to establish the applicability of art. 101(1) to those undertakings. The fines that the undertakings were required to pay, however, were far less than those meted out to the other participants: BP, for example, was fined €750,000, compared to Bayer AG's fine of €2.5 million.

In July 2008, the GC had the first chance to confirm the position of the Commission in *Treuhand* (*AC-Treuhand AG v Commission of the European Communities* case T–99/04 [2008] ECR II–1501). In 2003, the Commission had fined 24 firms for operating a cartel in the market for organic peroxide. The Swiss consultancy company AC-Treuhand was also nominally fined for facilitating the cartel, as it had provided the premises and organized the meetings between the members of the cartel. On appeal, the GC insisted that passive co-perpetrators of an infringement and undertakings that have played an accessory role in the breach should also face responsibility. Indeed, art. 101 does not rule out the possibility that an undertaking that is not active on the market on which the restriction of competition occurs may be held liable for breach of the provision.

The Commission's rigorous policy against cartel facilitators has recently come under question following the decision in the marine hose cartel (COMP/39.406—*Marine Hoses* [2009] OJ C168/6). In 2009, PW Consulting escaped being fined after having organized meetings and generally helped to coordinate a cartel in the marine hose industry. The reason given by the Commission for this apparent inconsistency with its previous decisions was that it wished to avoid any risk of double jeopardy with the UK, where criminal proceedings against PW Consulting's former executive Peter Whittle were pending (see Chapter 12). It has been argued that a symbolic fine would have been more in line with established Commission policy towards cartel facilitators. See Kallaugher, J., and Weitbrecht, A., 'Developments under the Treaty on the Functioning of the European Union, Articles 101 and 102, in 2008/2009', (2010) 31 *European Competition Law Review* 307, at 317.

For a recent study on cartel facilitation, see Harding, C., 'Capturing the Cartel's Friends: Cartel Facilitation and the Idea of Joint Criminal Enterprise', (2009) 34 *European Law Review* 298.

9.2.5 Unilateral conduct

For the prohibition of art. 101(1) to be invoked there must be multilateral conduct. Unilateral conduct will be condemned under EU competition law only where it falls within art. 102. However, there are situations in which it may appear at first sight that art. 101 has been applied to unilateral conduct. Such a situation arose in *AEG-Telefunken* v *Commission* case 107/82 [1984] 3 CMLR 325, in which the undertaking contested a Commission decision (82/267 (1982) OJ L117/15) on the grounds that there had been no other undertakings involved. AEG had maintained a selective distribution system and refused to supply certain distributors which met the criteria laid down by AEG but which had a reputation for price cutting—AEG itself described its strategy as a 'high price policy'. It appeared from the wording of the decision that AEG was indeed the only offending party, and the decision was addressed only to it. However, when the undertaking appealed, the conclusion reached by the Court of Justice was that the refusals to supply, which had been endemic, were an integral part of the operation of the distribution system, and involved all the members of that system, who stood to benefit from the refusals. In effect, the Court found that the nexus of interest between AEG and its distributors was such that it was implicit in the agreements between AEG and each of the distributors that AEG would refuse to supply price-cutters. There have been other cases since where the Commission has pursued a similar line, notably *Sandoz* 87/409 (1987) OJ L222/28 and *Vichy* 91/153 (1991) OJ L75/57.

In *Johnson & Johnson* 80/1283 (1980) OJ L377/16, the Commission's decision to invoke art. 101 is more questionable. The institution investigated a situation in which the undertaking and its subsidiaries, including Ortho UK, acted to prevent the export from the UK to Germany of pregnancy-testing kits. In January 1977 Ortho had changed the contracts of sale that applied between it and its dealers so as ostensibly to permit the export of the testing kits within the EU. However, on investigation the Commission found that the company had acted unilaterally in making threats to dealers to withhold supplies, or to delay supplies, if the dealers in fact made exports even within the Union. While it is possible that this conduct could have been attacked under art. 102, the Commission chose to proceed under art. 101 and found that although the action was apparently unilateral the dealers all knew what the position was and that in effect the contracts of sale 'were still, therefore, subject to prohibitions of exports, which prohibitions formed an integral part of agreements within the meaning of art. [101(1)]' (para. 28).

In two more recent cases the Commission failed to persuade the GC that it had correctly found multilateral conduct in situations in which a producer either reduced quantities available for parallel trade, or issued a circular asking retailers to adhere to certain prices (*Bayer AG* v *Commission* case T–41/96 [2001] 4 CMLR 4 and *Volkswagen AG* v *Commission* case T–208/01 [2004] 4 CMLR 14). In these, and other similar cases, the GC has found that where an undertaking simply imposes conditions upon distributors, the necessary 'agreement' for the purposes of the application of art. 101(1) does not exist. This may be the case in particular where the wholesalers resist the terms being imposed (e.g., by ordering more than they are supplied by the producer). This matter is discussed further at 9.3.1.3.

In the case of *Unipart Group Ltd* v *O₂ (UK) Ltd* [2004] EWCA Civ 1034, [2004] UKCLR 1453, based on the application of art. 101, the Court of Appeal dealt with a claim from Unipart that the price it had paid for wholesale airtime from BT Cellnet, which later became O₂ was an illegal one, and sought damages. The Court held that 'a supplier may adopt whatever policy he regards as necessary to protect his commercial interests, provided only that in so doing he does not abuse a dominant position and that there is no relevant ' "concurrence of wills" between the supplier and his whole-saler' (para. 91). In setting high prices as part of an alleged margin squeeze (see 16.2.4) the Court found that Cellnet had been acting unilaterally, and that art. 101 could not therefore be applied.

9.2.6 'Object or effect'

It should be apparent from the wording of the article that an agreement may be condemned if it has *either* the object *or* the effect of preventing, restricting, or distorting competition. It would be an unusual position were undertakings to be allowed to conspire, ineffectually, to breach the law and be condemned only were they successful. In *La Technique Minière* v *Maschinenbau Ulm GmbH* case 56/65 [1966] 1 CMLR 357, the Court examined a distribution contract between a German producer of industrial earth-levellers and a French distributor. Following a disagreement between the parties La Technique Minière had asked the Cour d'Appel in Paris to declare the contract void on the grounds that it breached art. 101(1). Maschinenbau Ulm argued that the agreement did not partition the market and did not therefore fall within the prohibition. As this case arose under art. 267 TFEU the Court was not being asked to resolve the issue, but in its answers to the Cour d'Appel the Court indicated that

these [criteria] are not cumulative but alternative conditions, indicated by the conjunction 'or', suggest[ing] first the need to consider the very object of the agreement, in the light of the economic context in which it is to be applied...Where, however, an analysis of the said clauses does not reveal a sufficient degree of harmfulness with regard to competition, examination should then be made of the effects of the agreement.   (p. 375)

That the Commission is willing to bring actions against cartels even where they are not entirely successful is demonstrated by, *inter alia, Polypropylene* 86/398 (1986) OJ L230/1. During the course of investigations into the market for bulk thermoplastic polypropylene throughout the Union, the Commission uncovered substantial documentary evidence of 'an institutionalised system of meetings between representatives of the producers at both senior and technical managerial levels' (para. 1). At these meetings, 'the producers developed a system of annual volume control to share out the available market between themselves according to agreed percentage or tonnage targets, and regularly set target prices' (para. 1). Such conduct is a classic example of cartelization, where producers seek collectively to limit supplies, raise prices, and monitor observance of the agreement to alleviate the risk of its collapsing through strategic cheating on the part of the cartel members.

In fact the agreement was not as successful as the participants had hoped. The price level achieved in the market generally lagged some way behind the targets set at the meetings, and the price initiatives often ran out of steam, occasionally resulting in a sharp drop in prices. Over the period in question the industry was characterized by substantial over-capacity, and in such circumstances the temptation on the part of the cartel members to cheat would have been hard to resist. Faced with the evidence garnered by the Commission some of the producers in fact appeared to rely on their own cheating as a defence, pointing to sometimes substantial discrepancies between the delivery targets they had been set and the actual deliveries they had made. The alleged participants pointed also to the fact that market shares had changed substantially over the relevant period, a fact that they said was evidence of 'unrestricted' competition. The Commission rebutted most of these arguments. It argued that while there had been price instability, this was usually arrested by a revision of the targets and agreements, and that further falls which would have benefited consumers were thus prevented. That market shares had changed had been envisaged under the targets which had taken into account the ambitions of some of the newer entrants into the market. However, as the Commission also made clear, art. 101(1) would have been applicable notwithstanding failures in the cartelization of the market:

The fact that in practice the cartelisation of the market was incomplete and did not entirely exclude the operation of competitive forces does not preclude application of article [101]. Given the large number of producers, their divergent commercial interests and the absence of any enforceable measures of constraint in the event of non-compliance by a producer with agreed arrangements, no cartel could control totally the activities of their participants. (para. 92)

The 15 identified participants in the cartel were fined a total of €5,785,000.

A similar position was reached in *Ferry operators—currency surcharge* 97/84 (1997) OJ L26/23 (discussed above) where the fact that the operators found it extremely difficult actually to impose the charge that they had agreed to levy did not serve to exonerate them from the fact that they had, in breach of art. 101, colluded to impose the charge. Even in the case of a concerted practice the Court of Justice has indicated that it would be possible for a breach of art. 101(1) to flow from the mere contact preliminary to a concerted practice (see for example *Huls v Commission* case C–199/92P [1999] 5 CMLR 1016 at para. 163). While this does not seem an intuitive position it must be remembered that even in the case of a concerted practice some form of coordination, other than mere intelligent reflection, is called for.

The Commission has insisted that the only difference between agreements which are anti-competitive by object and those considered anti-competitive by effect is that the former are *presumed* to have anti-competitive effects (see, e.g., the *Guidelines on the application of article 81(3) of the Treaty* (2004) OJ C101/81, para. 21), while the harmful consequences of the latter need to be demonstrated. Therefore the legal consequences are identical, but if an agreement is considered anti-competitive by object the burden of proof is shifted: 'rather than a complainant needing to show detrimental consequences, it is for those engaged in the practice to demonstrate the absence of detrimental consequences' (Odudu, O., 'Restrictions of Competition by Object— What's the Beef?' (2008) 9 *Competition Law Journal* 11–17).

It is worth noting that some types of agreements have been widely recognized to be anti-competitive; these are principally those which contain hard-core restraints. In the *Irish Beef* case (*Competition Authority v Beef Industry Development Society Ltd* case C–209/07 [2009] 4 CMLR 6), the Court held that an agreement is anti-competitive by object where, had the arrangement not been in place, competition and rivalry would have been increased (paras 35–40). This rather broad interpretation appears to imply that the majority of horizontal agreements are anti-competitive by object. In the case of vertical agreements, *Consten and Grundig* and *GlaxoSmithKline* (see 9.3.1 below) suggest that they will only be anti-competitive by object when there is an intention to restrict parallel trade (for reasons that appear to be more closely linked with the protection of integration than competition), or when a minimum resale price is imposed by a supplier.

9.3 **The prevention, restriction, or distortion of competition**

An agreement between two or more undertakings will not be caught within art. 101(1) where it does not prevent, restrict, or distort competition. There is a substantial and vibrant debate about the way in which the Commission has applied this part of art. 101(1). It is clear that not all clauses within contract have such object or effect, and that there are situations in which agreements, even at the horizontal level, are either incapable of being anti-competitive, or the only distortion of competition may be a beneficial one (see in particular the *Guidelines on the Applicability of Article 101 to Horizontal Cooperation Agreements* (2010), at para. 2). The debate is similar to that surrounding the application of the rule of reason in US antitrust law which is referred to at the end of this chapter.

In one of the leading cases in this respect, *Gottrup-Klim v Dansk Landbrugs Grovvareselskab* case C–250/92 [1994] ECR I–5641, the Court of Justice held that the extent to which clauses in contracts were compatible with EU competition law could not be assessed 'in the abstract', but depended on both their content, and the 'economic conditions prevailing on the markets concerned'. In this case the Court ruled that it was not necessarily anti-competitive for a cooperative association to include a rule which prohibited members from also joining other cooperatives. Likewise, in *La Technique Minière v Maschinenbau Ulm GmbH* case 56/65 [1966] 1 CMLR 357 the Court of Justice held that where an agreement was necessary for an undertaking to penetrate a new market 'it may be doubted whether there is an interference with competition'. In a similar vein the Commission *Guidelines on the Applicability of Article 101 to Horizontal Cooperation Agreements* (2010), insist that cooperation between competitors is not likely to restrict competition if it enables firms to enter a new market or to launch a new product.

In its *Guidelines on Vertical Restraints*, the Commission sets out the factors that are important in determining whether a vertical agreement falls within art. 101(1) (see para. 111, and the subsequent discussion in paras 112–21). These are:

(a) nature of the agreement;

(b) market position of the parties;

(c)   market position of competitors;

(d)   market position of buyers of the contract products;

(e)   entry barriers;

(f)   maturity of the market;

(g)   level of trade;

(h)   nature of the product;

(i)   other factors.

In *European Night Services* v *Commission* joined cases T–374/94, etc. [1998] ECR II–3141 the matter was expressed this way:

> in assessing an agreement under [art. 101] account should be taken of the actual conditions in which it functions, in particular the economic context in which the undertakings operate, the products or services covered by the agreement and the actual structure of the market concerned unless it is an agreement containing obvious restrictions of competition such as price-fixing, market-sharing or the control of outlets. In the latter case, such restrictions may be weighed against their claimed pro-competitive effects only in the context of [art. 101(3)] of the Treaty, with a view to granting an exemption ... (paras 136–7, references omitted)

Much earlier than this, the Court in *Remia* v *Commission* case 42/84 [1985] ECR 2545 had held that a clause in an agreement relating to the transfer of a business, under which the seller agreed not to compete with the new owner of the business, would not fall within art. 101. The EU Commission had found that such a clause was within the prohibition, and had offered only a limited concession in its application of art. 101(3) (*Nutricia/ Zuid—Hollandse Conservenfabriek* 83/670 (1983) OJ L376/22). The Court held on appeal that against the background in which the agreement operated 'non-competition clauses ... have the merit of ensuring that the transfer has the effect intended. By virtue of that very fact they contribute to the promotion of competition' (para. 19). *Remia* was cited with approval by the Commission in *Glaxo Wellcome* 2001/791 (2001) OJ L302/1, relating to a system designed to restrict the flow of parallel imports of cheap pharmaceutical products from Spain into the more expensive Member States. In response to an application for negative clearance, the Commission held, *inter alia*, that

> The Court of Justice (and [General Court]) have always qualified agreements containing export bans, dual-pricing systems or other limitations of parallel trade as restricting competition 'by object'. That is to say, prohibited by art. [101](1) without there being any need for an assessment of their actual effects. In principle they are not eligible for exemption pursuant to art. [101](3).

This reference to certain restrictions as being anti-competitive 'by object' (see also *Volkswagen AG* v *Commission* case T–62/98 [2000] 5 CMLR 853, paras 89 and 178) brings the approach under art. 101(1) close to the US 'rule of reason', although the EU Commission has stated that such a rule has no place to play in the art. 101 system (see 9.7).

The principles developed in these cases may also be seen at play in *Visa International* 2001/782 (2001) OJ L293/94 in which the Commission made a decision of negative clearance in respect of the agreement between some 20,000 financial institutions responsible for the operation of the Visa network system. It was held that the rules relating to the operation of the agreement were not restrictive of competition. In particular a requirement under which a member of the Visa network could not acquire the right to join without issuing cards exploiting the network was not restrictive of competition as it ensured a large card base, thereby making the system as a whole more attractive to merchants (paras 18 and 65). In a later Decision—*Visa International (Multilateral Exchange Fee)* 2002/914 (2002) OJ L318/17—the Commission granted an individual exemption under art. 101(3) in relation to the intra-regional interchange fee scheme of Visa for consumer cards as applied to cross-border point-of-sale Visa card transactions between Member States. Perhaps the clearest discussion of the state of the law relating to this difficult issue is that given by Advocate General Lenz, in *Union Royale Belge des Sociétés de Football Association ASBL* v *Jean-Marc Bosman* case C–415/93 [1995] ECR I–4921 (at paras 262–9).

Where undertakings operating in different markets, and which are not current competitors, enter into an agreement relating to a third market this *may* fall outside the remit of art. 101(1). This was the case, for example, in *Elopak/Metal Box—Odin* 90/410 (1990) OJ L209/15, where Elopak and Metal Box collaborated in a joint venture to produce a new form of packaging carton for foodstuffs. The Commission held that the joint venture agreement fell outside the terms of art. 101 as the parties were not competitors, and the joint venture company, Odin, would effectively operate as an independent entity. This decision, along with *Konsortium ECR 900* 90/446 (1990) OJ L228/31, is an example of the Commission applying some of the principles of a 1983 policy statement on a 'realistic' approach to competition.

A similar approach was taken in the late 1990s case of *Cegetel* (1999) OJ L218/14 in which the Commission found that a joint venture relating to the provision of a fixed-voice telephony service in France, the founding companies of which were large operators in France, Germany, and the USA, did not fall within art. 101(1). As the parent companies were each unable to enter this market by themselves, the existence of the joint venture did not restrict either actual or potential competition. Generally, however, the Commission will take a broad view of the potential danger of restrictive conduct, and is more likely to find that such situations are encompassed within art. 101(1) but may benefit from an exemption (see, e.g., *KSB/Goulds/Lowara/ITT* 91/38 (1991) OJ L19/25).

9.3.1 Vertical agreements and art. 101

In the previous chapter, it was established that vertical agreements may contain restrictions of competition that could fall within the scope of art. 101. This is particularly so with regard to supply and distribution agreements. Distribution restraints vary in nature. Some restrictions relate to the price at which the contract goods may be resold; as seen in the previous chapter (8.3), the buyer may have to respect a minimum price imposed by the manufacturer (minimum resale price maintenance), or be forced to observe a maximum price (maximum resale price maintenance). Other restraints are unrelated to price, but may impose restrictions with regard to the territory or customers to whom the products may be resold. Depending on the kind of restrictions of competition involved, various categories of distribution agreements have been identified. These categories 'should not be regarded as black-box concepts: each vertical accord is unique and will include various restrictions that will inevitably present characteristics of more than one class' (Marco Colino, S., *Vertical Agreements and Competition Law: A Comparative Study of the EU and US Regimes* (2010) Hart, Oxford). Before exploring the implications of these restrictions for competition, the principal kinds of distribution agreements require clarification:

- Exclusive distribution: these are agreements in which the supplier grants exclusivity of the sale of the contract goods within a specified territory or to a group of customers. In exchange, the buyer may agree to sell only the supplier's goods.

- Exclusive supply: here, a supplier aims to create a new version of a good using the know-how and experience of the buyer. The latter will be the only one allowed to purchase the new product, while the buyer agrees to buy the product only from the supplier for the duration of the contract.

- Selective distribution: these systems require dealers to meet certain criteria before entering into the network, and are frequent in the sale of luxury products or complex goods that require a certain expertise. Selected distributors may only sell to final consumers, and are precluded from selling to unauthorized resellers.

- Franchising: these agreements include a licence granting the franchisee the right to trade under the mark and name of the franchisor. The former must ensure that the image and reputation of the brand is protected, and some restrictions of competition are allowed to this end (see *Pronuptia de Paris GmbH* v *Pronuptia de Paris Irmgard Schillgallis* case C–161/84 [1986] 1 *CMLR* 41).

- Single branding: here, an obligation is imposed on the buyer to purchase all or a specific quantity of the good or service from one particular supplier. These are common between pub owners and their drink suppliers.

Article 101(1)(a)–(e) sets out a non-exhaustive list of the restrictions to which the article is intended to apply. The article applies to both inter-brand and intra-brand competition. Inter-brand competition is that *between different brands*, for example, competition between Mercedes and BMW motor cars. Intra-brand competition is that *between goods of the same brand*, for example, competition between different retailers of Mercedes motor cars. Typically this means that EU competition law is applicable to vertical restraints (see Chapter 8), which are often considered to have a pro-competitive effect, the aim being to improve methods of distribution and to make it easier to bring products to the market. This conclusion is one of the most contentious reached in the application of EU competition law, and came as a surprise to many when the position was first established. It was driven largely by the fact that one of the underlying imperatives of EU competition law is to facilitate the integration of the national markets. Where vertical restraints obstruct such an integration, by, for example, allocating particular national or regional markets and territories to particular distributors, they are likely to be condemned. The key decision was that in *Établissements Consten Sarl and Grundig-Verkaufs-GmbH* v *Commission* cases 56, 58/64 [1996] 1 CMLR 418, which remains the most important case to be considered under art. 101, and one that demonstrates the application of most aspects of that provision. It is therefore discussed here in some detail.

9.3.1.1 *Consten and Grundig*

Grundig-Verkaufs-GmbH was a German manufacturer of consumer electronic goods. In April 1957 it entered into an exclusive distribution contract with the French firm Établissements Consten. Under the terms of this contract Consten was to be Grundig's sole representative in France, the Saar, and Corsica. Consten was required, *inter alia*, to purchase a certain minimum percentage of Grundig's exports into France, to adequately promote Grundig's products, and to provide an adequate after-sales service and maintain supplies of spare parts. Along with these obligations, Consten undertook not to sell competing products, and not to make any deliveries, direct or indirect, of its supplies to territories outside its contract area. Similar terms were to be found in the contracts Grundig maintained with its distributors in other European territories, and with the main German wholesalers. Grundig itself was enjoined from supplying, other than through Consten, the relevant goods into Consten's allocated territory.

In order to reinforce Consten's exclusive rights, it was assigned in France the trade mark GINT (Grundig International), which was carried on all Grundig products. The effect of this was that Consten would be able to bring an action, based on the infringement of its intellectual property rights, against any importer of Grundig's goods into France. If Consten ceased being Grundig's sole distributor in the relevant territory it was to return the GINT trademark to Grundig. The firm UNEF obtained Grundig products from German distributors in spite of the fact that they were not meant to supply such customers, and sold them into France at prices below those charged by Consten. Consten brought two actions against UNEF in the French courts, one based on the French law of unfair competition, the other for infringement of the GINT trade mark. In 1962 the case was adjourned following an application made by UNEF to the Commission which sought a declaration to the effect that the agreement between Consten and Grundig was in breach of art. 101(1).

Grundig notified its distribution agreements to the Commission on 29 January 1963, and sought a decision to the effect that art. 101(1) did not apply to such an agreement, or that if it did the agreement should be exempt by virtue of the application of art. 101(3). By a decision of 23 September 1964 (*Re Grundig's Agreement* 64/566/EEC; the official text is not published in English, but see [1964] CMLR 489) the Commission held that the contracts in question, and the assignment of the trade mark, constituted an infringement of the provisions of art. 101. Both Consten and Grundig brought actions to have the decision annulled. When the cases came before the Court of Justice the Italian and German governments were admitted as intervening parties, both of them in support of the two firms.

After rehearsing the facts Advocate General Karl Roemer noted that the case had 'taken on unusual proportions because of the economic and legal importance of the problems dealt with and the number of parties involved'. It was of no doubt, the Advocate General said, that 'contracts involving exclusive supply and purchase undertakings can have the effect of limiting competition, especially when they are accompanied by an absolute territorial protection'. There were, however, points of the Commission decision that concerned the Advocate General. In particular, the approach of the institution was apparently to consider only the 'object' of the agreement and not its concrete 'effect'. 'Article [101(1)]', the Advocate General said, 'requires really the comparison of two market situations: that which arises after the conclusion of an agreement and that which would arise in the absence of the agreement'. Such a concrete examination, if undertaken, might lead to the conclusion that an agreement in a particular case 'only has effects which are likely to *promote* competition'. This might be the case, it was suggested, where it would not be possible for a manufacturer to gain a purchase on the market unless it were to do so by way of appointing an exclusive distributor. Thus, the Advocate General opined, 'such an examination might have led to a finding that in the Grundig–Consten case the *suppression* of the sole sales agency would have involved a noticeable reduction in the offer of Grundig products on the French market'.

A second argument was made by the German government which the Advocate General felt 'deserves complete approval'. This was that a consideration of the competition between various distributors of Grundig products missed the point, and that any consideration of the market should have as its starting point an analysis of the competition between *similar competing* products. This is the distinction between intra-brand and inter-brand competition that is still a matter of debate. The Advocate General was of the opinion that the Commission was simply 'wrong in taking *exclusive* account of that internal competition…and in neglecting completely in its consideration competition with similar products'. Competition, it was suggested, should be judged in this case at the level of the wholesaler, where the dealers were technically competent to distinguish between the different brands of equipment, and to pass on the relevant details to the retailers. In fact, the market share held by Grundig in France in tape recorders and dictating machines was only about 17 per cent. There must therefore have been vigorous competition from other brands of similar, although not identical, products. In the market for televisions and radios it appeared that the competition was intense, and there was evidence that the prices charged for Grundig products had been reduced in response to this on several occasions. Taking these factors into account the Advocate General felt that 'the conclusions reached by the Commission in examining the criterion of "interference with competition" should be considered as insufficiently based and consequently should be disregarded'.

The Commission, in considering the requirement that the practice 'may affect trade' (see 9.5), had found it sufficient to demonstrate that 'following an agreement restricting competition the trade between Member States develops in *other* ways than it would have done without the agreement'. It was contended that this requirement was merely a 'criterion of competence', but the Advocate General was 'convinced that the very text of 'article [101(1)] prevents justification of that opinion'. His view was that in some of the Treaty's official languages the requirement was that there be an *unfavourable* influence on trade and that it was insufficient merely to demonstrate an influence. In the Advocate General's view it was the suppression of such exclusive arrangements that could have a harmful effect on trade and obstruct the integration of the market, as such steps could in fact reduce the flow of goods between the Member States. These criticisms, he felt, were sufficient to annul the decision.

The Advocate General subsequently considered the refusal of the Commission to grant an exemption to the contested agreement under art. 101(3). The Commission had accepted that it might be possible to contend that the agreements contributed to improving production and distribution, but not that consumers received any share in the resulting benefit. This would be impossible as long as the agreement conferred absolute territorial protection. Noting that the German Law against Restraint on Competition took a lenient approach to exclusive distribution agreements, the Advocate General felt that the Commission should do likewise in the application of art. 101(3), because 'as a general rule competition between *similar* products of different producers constitutes a sufficient regulator of the market'. In its application to the Court the Commission had argued that because art. 101(1) provided the *rule*, and art. 101(3) only the *exception*, it fell to the undertakings in particular cases to justify the application of the exemption. This would allow the Commission to adopt a role that was, in the view of the Advocate General, unacceptably passive.

Whether the individual criteria for the grant of an exemption had been fulfilled was also a matter of some debate. The Commission had not, the Advocate General felt, adequately argued why requiring Consten to undertake promotion of Grundig's products was an unnecessary restraint, and had failed to show that the bearing of this cost by Consten had not resulted in any benefit to the market. For an exemption to be granted consumers are expected to reap some of the benefits of the restrictive agreement along with the undertakings themselves. As the Advocate General noted, this requirement is 'a particularly delicate and difficult criterion to grasp'. As the submission of the German government suggested, it should be sufficient to show that there was lively competition between manufacturers of different products, as 'that guarantees at the same time that the consumers have a fair share in the profit, because [they] should only pay the price which develops on the market under the influence of effective competition'. Pointing to the likelihood that such exclusive dealing arrangements would promote competition, the Advocate General suggested that consumers might then be sharing the rewards. In conclusion Herr Roemer, supporting the arguments of the applicants and the two interested Member States, argued that the contested decision should be annulled *in toto* and referred back to the Commission for reconsideration.

As is usual in Union case law the judgment is somewhat shorter than the Advocate General's submission (13 pages and 46 pages respectively). On the question of whether art. 101(1) could be applied to vertical restraints, the Court held that

Neither the wording of article [101] nor that of article [102] gives ground for holding that the two articles are limited in effect according to the positions of the contracting parties in the economic process. Article [101] refers in a general way to all agreements which distort competition within the [Internal] Market and does not establish any distinction between those agreements as to whether or not they were made between operators competing at the same stage or between non-competing operators placed at different stages. In principle no distinction should be made where the Treaty does not make any distinction.

The Court was equally dismissive of the arguments made to the effect that the conferment of absolute territorial protection in a case where there existed competition at the level of the producers need not necessarily be condemned. The basic objectives of the Treaty, 'whose preamble and text aim at suppressing the barriers between Member States and which in several provisions gives evidence of a stern attitude with regard to their reappearance, could not allow undertakings to restore such barriers'. The Court further agreed with the Commission that the primary purpose of the requirement that trade between Member States be affected was to allow for jurisdictional competence to be determined. It was not therefore necessary to show that trade would have been greater had the agreement not been in place. In holding that 'the fact that an agreement favours an increase, even a large one, in the volume of trade' brings the agreement within art. 101, the Court could not have made the position clearer, nor more roundly rejected the argument of the Advocate General.

On the questions of the benefits of inter-brand over intra-brand competition, the Court found that it was quite acceptable for the Commission's analysis to proceed solely with reference to the competition in the market for Grundig's products. The mere possibility of increasing competition between producers by restricting competition between distributors of the same brand is thus not considered sufficient to establish that such restrictions should escape the prohibition of 101(1).

Lastly, the Court was satisfied that the Commission had properly considered the points relating to the award of an art. 101(3) exemption. The decision was annulled only in so far as it related to the entire agreement concluded between the parties, the Court holding that those parts of the agreement which did not breach the art. 101(1) prohibition could not be condemned.

9.3.1.2 The position of the European Courts in subsequent case law

A more flexible approach to the nature of competition in so far as it applied to exclusive distribution agreements may be seen in *Metro-SB-Grossmärkte GmbH & Co. Kg* v *Commission* case 26/76 [1978] 2 CMLR 1. A selective distribution system operated by SABA, a German manufacturer of radios, television sets and tape recorders was approved by the Commission (*SABA* 76/159 (1976) OJ L28/19). This followed a complaint by a cash-and-carry wholesaler which, by reducing the level of service that it offered to consumers, was able to charge lower prices than would usually be charged by SABA's distributors. Metro had argued that it was denied access to the distribution system established by SABA, and that this distribution system was in breach of art. 101(1) and therefore unlawfully maintained. Referring to the flexibility afforded by the concept of 'workable competition', the Court held that the nature of the competition could vary depending on the products and services in question, and the structure of the market. The Commission had found selective distribution systems to be unobjectionable as long as the resellers were chosen on the basis of objective criteria which had a genuine relationship to the product in question and as long as such criteria were not applied in a discriminatory manner. The argument was raised by Metro that such systems could lead to higher prices for consumers, and that the application of art. 101(1) required that price competition be maintained effectively. The Court's response was that

It is true that in such systems of distribution price competition is not generally emphasised either as an exclusive or indeed as a principal factor... However, although price competition is so important that it can never be eliminated, it does not constitute the only effective form of competition or that to which absolute priority must in all circumstances be accorded. The powers conferred upon the Commission under article [101(3)] show that the requirements for the maintenance of workable competition may be reconciled with the safeguarding of objectives of a different nature and that to this end certain restrictions on competition are permissible... For specialist wholesalers and retailers the desire to maintain a certain price level, which corresponds to the desire to preserve, in the interests of consumers, the possibility of the continued existence of this channel of distribution in conjunction with new methods of distribution based on a different type of competition policy, forms one of the objectives which may be pursued without necessarily falling under the prohibition contained in article [101(1)].   (para. 21)

Thus, although recognizing the primacy of price competition, the Court and the Commission both recognized that there could be situations in which some restriction would be acceptable if it fostered other types of competition. Here the nature of the product was such that a number of large and medium-scale producers offered products that consumers would regard as being generally interchangeable. In such a circumstance any restrictions on prices maintained by one producer would be constrained by the existence on the market of acceptable substitutes, and could be justified if the effect of the constraint was to make available to the consumer a level of supply, service, and after-sales commitment that would not be available in the absence of the restraint.

A similarly more sophisticated approach to the assessment of vertical agreements was taken in the case of *Sergio Delimitis v Henninger Bräu AG* case C–234/89 [1992] 5 CMLR 210 (Key case 9.2 below).

Key case 9.2 *Sergio Delimitis* v *Henninger Bräu AG* case C–234/89 [1992] 5 CMLR 210—Court of Justice judgment (art. 101)

Facts

In May 1985 Mr Delimitis entered into an agreement with the Henninger Bräu brewery under which the brewery was to let to Mr Delimitis a café in Frankfurt am Main, Germany. This was a tied arrangement under which Mr Delimitis was to purchase all his supplies of beer from the brewery, and soft drinks from subsidiaries of the brewery. The contract was terminated in 1986 and the brewery sought the sum of DM 6,032 that it believed was owed to it. Mr Delimitis believed that he owed nothing, and before the German regional court argued that the contract was unenforceable as it was illegal under art. 101(1). His claim was refused on the basis that the contract did not affect trade between states. The court held that individual contracts each related to individual situations and could not be regarded as a whole as having the purpose of restricting competition. Mr Delimitis appealed to the Higher Regional Court, which in turn made an art. 267 reference to the Court of Justice. *Inter alia* the Court was asked if individual agreements should be assessed in the context of a wider bundle of agreements to which they belonged, and if so what proportion of the market would need to be covered by the bundle of agreements. If the bundle approach was rejected the Court asked whether it was to assess the cumulative effects of the agreements 'by a comprehensive analysis of the respective circumstances'.

Findings

The Court noted the reasons for the existence of the tied arrangements in the beer market: the reseller (or tenant) would receive advantages in terms of favourable letting conditions, assistance with technical services, etc., and the supplier would have a guaranteed outlet for their product. The effect of the exclusive obligation on the tenant would be to encourage them to make their best efforts to promote and sell the products of the supplier, to the advantage of both parties. Such agreements would not have the object of restricting competition, but it was necessary to ascertain whether they had that effect (para. 13). Citing its earlier judgment in *Brasserie de Haecht* (case 23/67 [1968] CMLR 26) the Court stated that 'the effects of such an agreement had to be assessed in the context in which they occur and where they might combine with others to have a cumulative effect on competition' (para. 14). In the present case it was 'necessary to analyse the effects of a beer supply agreement, taken together with other contracts of the same type, on the opportunities of national competitors or those from other member states, to gain access to the market' (para. 15). The relevant market had to be determined in both its product and geographic aspects, and it was necessary to examine the nature and extent of the agreements in their totality. The mere fact that a bundle of similar agreements existed would not invite automatic condemnation, and the key issue was that of whether the agreement, in the context of a set of similar agreements, had the effect of foreclosing entry to the market. A new competitor must have 'real concrete possibilities' for entry (para. 21). Account had to 'be taken of the conditions under which competitive forces operate on the relevant market' (para. 22). The market position of the contracting parties had to be taken into account (para. 25), as would the duration of agreements.

Comment

In *Delimitis* the Court of Justice took a more subtle approach to restrictions of competition than in *Consten and Grundig*. It held that the central question was that of whether a network of intra-brand restrictions precluded inter-brand competition. If the answer to this question was yes, then the agreements in question might fall foul of art. 101(1), but if they did not preclude 'real concrete possibilities' of entry then the agreement(s) might be found, given their rationale, to be lawful under art. 101(1).

Note that this core part of the judgment does not make reference to art. 101(3) or the block exemption, but to the more important conditions under which an agreement is found at first instance to be subject to the strictures of art. 101(1). The case makes it clear that where the mere object of an agreement is not anti-competitive, a sensitive analysis must take place before it can be ascertained whether art. 101(1) applies. This judgment is followed in, for example, the important judgment of *European Night Services* (see 9.3).

FURTHER READING

Articles

Korah, V., 'The Judgment in *Delimitis*: A Milestone Towards a Realistic Assessment of the Effects of an Agreement or a Damp Squib?', [1992] *EIPR* 167

Lasok, K.P.E., 'Assessing the Economic Consequences of Restrictive Agreements: A Comment on the *Delimitis* Case', (1991) *ECLR* 194

9.3.1.3 Agency agreements

The Commission's *Guidelines on Vertical Restraints* at paras 12–21 deals with agency agreements. Agents, according to the *Guidelines*, are

a legal or physical person is vested with the power to negotiate and/or conclude contracts on behalf of another person (the principal), either in the agent's own name or in the name of the principal, for the:

— purchase of goods or services by the principal, or

— sale of goods or services supplied by the principal.

Genuine agency agreements do not fall within art. 101(1). Non-genuine agency agreements are likely, subject to the market share provisos, to fall within block exemption 330/2010, discussed in Chapter 10. The determination of whether an agency agreement is genuine or not goes to the question of the allocation of risk. If the agent does not bear the risks for the contracts negotiated, or bears only a minimal risk, then it is a 'genuine' agency agreement. In these cases the agent is, in effect, not exercising any independent economic activity, and is subsumed within the principal undertaking. These principles have been discussed in a number of cases, including *Confederación Española de Empresarios de Estaciones de Servicio* v *Compañía Española de Petróleos SA* (case C–217/05 [2007] 4 CMLR 5 at paras 42–6).

9.3.1.4 Vertical restraints—the current position

There has been substantial debate about the approach to take to vertical restraints in EU competition law since the decision in *Consten*. The core of the problem lies in what is usually referred to as the 'double nature' of vertical restraints, that is, the fact that depending on the circumstances, vertical agreements can have pro- or anti-competitive effects. In 1997 some of these debates were rehearsed in the Commission *Green Paper on Vertical Restraints in Competition Policy* (COM(96) 721 final, 22 January 1997). The introductory paragraphs set out the essence of the double nature of these agreements:

(1) The single market represents an opportunity for EU firms to enter new markets that may have been previously closed to them because of government barriers. This penetration of new markets takes time and investment and is risky. The process is often facilitated by agreements between producers who want to break into a new market and local distributors. Efficient distribution with appropriate pre- and after-sales support is part of the competitive process that brings benefits to consumers.

(2) However, arrangements between producers and distributors can also be used to continue the partitioning of the market and exclude new entrants who would intensify competition and lead to downward pressure on prices. Agreements between producers and distributors (vertical restraints) can therefore be used pro-competitively to promote market integration and efficient distribution or anti-competitively to block integration and competition. The price differences between Member States that are still found provide the incentive for companies to enter new markets as well as to erect barriers against new competition.

(3) Because of their strong links to market integration that can be either positive or negative, vertical restraints have been of particular importance to the Union's competition policy. Whilst this policy has been successful in over 30 years of application a review is now necessary.

The Commission invited comments as to its next steps towards legislative reform. In 1998, in response to the consultation process, the Commission published a White Paper (COM(98) 546 final) in which it made clear that its aim was to develop a 'more economics based approach' in which 'vertical agreements should be analysed in their market context'. This policy found shape in the block exemption Regulation 2790/99 on the application of art. 81 of the Treaty to categories of vertical agreements and concerted practices (1999) OJ L336/21, recently substituted by Regulation 330/2010 on the application of art. 101(3) of the TFEU to categories of agreements and concerted practices (2010) OJ L102/1. The new block exemption is discussed in the following chapter.

There is a plethora of cases dealing with territorial restrictions in distribution agreements, and work carried out on behalf of the UK Government during the passage of the Competition Act 1998 demonstrated that single-market considerations played the leading role in many of the cases dealing with vertical restraints. More recent decisions include *Novalliance/Systemform* 97/123 (1997) OJ L47/11, in which the infringing company quickly amended the terms of its distribution agreements following their notification to the Commission; *ADALAT* 96/478 (1996) OJ L201/1, dealing with export bans imposed in relation to a range of medicinal products by Bayer AG (see Key case 9.3); and *BASF Lacke + Farben AG and Accinauto SA* 95/477 (1995) OJ L272/17, dealing with the market for car paints, upheld on appeal, *BASF Coating AG* v *Commission* case T–175/95 [2000] 4 CMLR 33. A similar approach to that taken in *Bayer* was taken by the GC in the case of *Volkswagen AG* v *Commission* case T–208/01

[2004] 4 CMLR 14. This followed the second infringement decision the Commission had made in respect of VW's conduct in a relatively short space of time (*VW (II)* 2001/711 (2001) OJ L262/14) finding that the company was in breach of art. 81(1) by virtue of a circular sent to dealers asking them not to sell the VW Passat below certain prices. As with *ADALAT* the CG found that the Commission was incorrect to impute an agreement where none existed.

Key case 9.3 *Adalat* 96/478 (1996) OJ L201/1; *Bayer AG* v *Commission* case T–41/96 [2001] 4 CMLR 4; *Bundesverband der Arzneimittel-Importeure EC and Commission* v *Bayer AG* cases C–2/01 P and C–3/01 P [2004] 4 CMLR 13—Commission decision; GC judgment; Court of Justice judgment (art. 101)

Facts

Bayer AG was the parent company of one of the main European chemical and pharmaceutical groups. Through national subsidiaries it had a presence in all Member States. It manufactured and marketed drugs under the name of Adalat, or Adalate, which were designed to treat cardio-vascular diseases. The prices of drugs in Member States are often fixed by national authorities rather than by the free market, such that there can be significant price differences from one state to another. From 1989 Spanish wholesalers exploited these price differences by exporting quantities of the drug to the UK, where the price was higher than in Spain. From 1993 French wholesalers followed suit. As a result of these parallel imports into the UK, sales made by Bayer's UK subsidiary fell dramatically, resulting in a loss of turnover. Bayer responded by limiting the quantities of drugs it supplied to Spanish and French wholesalers, attempting, in effect, to supply the needs of those local markets, but not to give the wholesalers quantities sufficient to permit them to sell to other markets in the EU. Complaints were made to the Commission, which opened proceedings on the basis of art. 101 TFEU. The application of art. 102 TFEU would have depended on Bayer holding a dominant position, which might not have been the case if there were alternatives to the Adalat range of drugs. The Commission made an infringement decision, in which it held in part that 'the prohibition on the exportation to other member states of the products...*as has been agreed* as part of their ongoing business relations, between Bayer France and its wholesalers since 1991, and between Bayer Spain and its wholesalers since at least 1989' constitutes an infringement (art. 1, emphasis added). Bayer appealed to the GC which annulled the decision. A further appeal was made by third parties admitted to participate in the case and the Commission to the Court of Justice.

Findings

Advocate General Tizzano agreed with the GC that 'there [was] nothing in the documents before the Court to show that [Bayer] required any particular form of conduct on the part of the wholesalers concerning the final destination of the packets of Adalat supplied or compliance with a certain manner of placing orders' (GC, para. 120, AG's opinion para. 58). The Court of Justice was not in a position to review the factual findings of the GC, and rejected parts of the appeal relating to such findings. The Court was asked to find that in the absence of proof of an attempt by Bayer to obtain wholesalers' agreement to, or acquiescence in, its new commercial policy, the actual conduct of the wholesalers could lead to the conclusion that they did acquiesce in the policy, and that an agreement for the purposes of art. 101 TFEU existed. The Court was not prepared to overturn the GC's finding that the documents to which the Commission had referred did not demonstrate that the wholesalers were willingly compliant in restricting sales. The fact that the wholesalers had entered into discussions with Bayer in an attempt to persuade Bayer that their needs had grown did not establish that they acquiesced to a reduction in parallel trade. The Court was emphatic in stating at para. 70 that

The attempt to use [art. 101(1)] of the Treaty to penalise an undertaking not in a dominant position which decides to refuse deliveries to wholesalers, in order to prevent them from making deliveries to wholesalers, in order to prevent them from making parallel exports, clearly disregards the necessary conditions for applying [art. 101] and the general system of the Treaty…unilateral measures taken by private undertakings are subject to restrictions, by virtue of the principles of that Treaty, only if the undertaking in question occupies a dominant position on the market, within the meaning of [art. 102] which is not the case here.

The Court of Justice upheld the GC judgment, and the decision remained annulled.

Comment

It is worth noting the length of time the proceedings in this case took. The Commission decision was taken on 10 January 1996, and it was not until 4 January 2004—almost exactly eight years later, that the final judgment of the Court of Justice was handed down. This is not untypical of a case in which appeals have been made to the GC and then on to the Court of Justice, and is one reason why the Commission has explored alternatives to such confrontational procedures. The substance of the case flowed from single market considerations. In effect Bayer was seeking to partition the markets to reap the maximum reward for its own marketing of the products, depriving parallel traders of the chance to exploit these differences for *their* benefit. The question for the Commission was that of whether such a practice could be targeted through the application of arts 101 or 102 TFEU. The 'distortions' in the market flowed from national regulatory and purchasing policies, and were not attributable to Bayer. Bayer may not have been dominant (although it is often possible to draw very narrow market definitions in pharmaceutical cases), and therefore the only avenue open to the Commission was to establish the presence of, at least, a concerted practice, and in this case more likely an agreement, to which at least two parties were implicated. An agreement could not be found between Bayer and its subsidiaries, as these would most likely be held for the purposes of the application of art. 101 TFEU to be one and the same undertaking, so the Commission had no choice, if it was to condemn this conduct, to find that agreements limiting sales existed between Bayer and the third-party wholesalers. As the Court has made clear, however, there was no such agreement. There was rather a unilateral practice by Bayer, *imposed* on its wholesalers, of limiting the amounts of the products that would be supplied. Such unilateral practices cannot be attacked through the application of art. 101 TFEU. In this respect the position reached is similar to that in the important US case of *US* v *Colgate* 250 US 300, 39 S. Ct 465 (1919) in which the Supreme Court held that '[i]n the absence of any purpose to create or maintain a monopoly' a seller may freely 'exercise his own independent discretion as to parties with whom he will deal'. More broadly the *Colgate* 'safe harbour' in the US extends to situations where a customer does not 'agree' to a term in a contract, but simply has it imposed upon them. *Bayer* is important in demonstrating the limits to which art. 101 TFEU may be applied, and it is likely that these will be clarified in future cases.

FURTHER READING

Articles

BROWN, C., 'Bayer v Commission: The ECJ agrees', (2004) *ECLR* 386

JEPHCOTT, M., 'Commentary on Case T41/96 Bayer AG v Commission', (2001) *ECLR* 469

LIDGARD, H. H. L., 'Unilateral Refusal to Supply: An Agreement in Disguise?', (1997) *ECLR* 352

The €102 million fine imposed by the Commission on Volkswagen in January 1998 (*VW* 98/273 (1998) OJ L124/61)—on appeal (*Volkswagen AG* v *Commission* case T–62/98 [2000] 5 CMLR 853)—reduced by the Court to €90 million—is in itself proof of the Commission's abhorrence of distribution agreements which prevent parallel imports. In that case Italian distributors were effectively prevented from reselling to Austrian and German consumers. On a further appeal to the Court of Justice the judgment of the GC was confirmed (*Volkswagen AG* v *Commission* case C–338/00P [2004] 4 CMLR 7). A similar approach was taken by the Commission in *Mercedes-Benz* 2002/758 (2002) OJ L257/1 in which restraints were imposed on distributors preventing parallel trade between Member States. Correspondence obtained by the Commission included a letter in which Mercedes-Benz states that it was convinced that 'by adhering strictly to this policy, we can effectively combat internal competition...we therefore count on your unconditional support' (para. 78). DaimlerChysler AG, which had become the parent company, was fined €71.825 million.

In *JCB* 2002/190 (2002) OJ L69/1 the Commission took strong action against conditions in JCB's distribution agreements for its construction and earth-moving equipment and spare parts. This followed a complaint by a French company which sought to import this equipment into France from the UK, where prices were appreciably lower. As early as 1975, following an approach made by JCB, the Commission had informed the company that export bans in their agreements were illegal and should be deleted. Evidence showed that JCB continued to prevent parallel imports. For example, in a fax sent from a UK to a French distributor relating to a machine purchased in the UK, but found in France, the UK distributor wrote: 'we cannot be held responsible for this customer's actions, but as a result from this sale we will not be trading with this customer again' (para. 82). The Commission emphasized again the censure placed upon territorially restrictive agreements under art. 101 in no uncertain terms when it argued that such restrictions 'jeopardise the proper functioning of the single market, frustrate one of the principal aims of the [Union] and have been held for decades as infringements of [art. 101]' (para. 248). JCB was fined €39,614,000, although on appeal this was reduced to €30 million by the GC which partially annulled the decision (*JCB Service* v *Commission* case T–67/01 [2004] 4 CMLR 24). However, the Commission was successful in a cross-appeal, and the Court of Justice found that the GC had acted incorrectly in reducing the penalty (*JCB Service* v *Commission* case C–167/04 [2006] 5 CMLR 23).

In 2004 the Commission took a decision relating to distribution restrictions imposed by the Topps Group (*Pokémon Cards: Topps Group*, Decision of 26 May 2004, reported at [2006] 4 CMLR 28). It produced and marketed collectables, including Pokémon cards. These were distributed throughout the EU where a parallel import trade existed, and Topps sought to bring this to an end. The Commission argued for a narrow market definition, but did not close the issue: 'the definition of the relevant market can be left open since this case concerns a restriction of competition by object' (para. 48; see also para. 130). The steps taken by Topps included putting pressure on distributors not to supply known parallel traders. For example, on 11 September 2000, an e-mail was sent by Topps' International Sales and Marketing Manager to its Spanish distributor stating that

You are buying stickers at half price of France and your wholesalers can obviously sell into France cheaper than our distributor [...] Can you please try and find out who could be selling this in France. Can you please investigate for me.

A further e-mail was sent two days later:

Further to my recent email…a response is still awaited. I would be obliged if you could provide a response/explanation immediately. I regret to inform you that until an explanation has been received, Topps will be unable to provide any further stock to Este.

Clearly the threat of cessation of supplies had an effect. The same day Este responded to Topps in the following terms:

Here enclosed you find a copy of the letter we are going to send to our wholesalers. As you can see we are going to stop the distribution of Spanish stickers in France…(at paras 68–70).

The Commission found that the infringement was a serious one, but in view of the cooperative conduct of Topps and its prompt cessation of the infringement, imposed a penalty of €1,590,000 (significantly below the starting point of €2,650,000).

At 9.7 the relationship between the application of art. 101(1) and art. 101(3) is discussed in further detail, employing the US terminology of 'the rule of reason'—a concept that some have sought to import into EU law. Section 9.3 of this chapter demonstrates that the key issue in the application of art. 101(1) is that of whether the particular practice which is the subject of scrutiny falls within this central rubric. We have seen that Court of Justice jurisprudence reacts strongly to vertical restrictions which run counter to the single market project, but that in other areas a more flexible approach may be taken. One of the most recent cases to deal with this issue in the context of vertical restraints is that of *GlaxoSmithKline Services Unlimited* v *Commission* case T–168/01 [2006] 5 CMLR 29, subsequently appealed before the Court (*GlaxoSmithKline Services Unlimited* v *Commission* case C–501, 513, 515, and 519/06 [2010] 4 CMLR 2). After the ruling of the GC, Professor Korah noted very quickly that it 'will have to be included in every cases and materials book on [EU] competition, so many important points were made' (Korah, V., 'Judgment of the Court of First Instance in *GlaxoSmithKline*', [2007] Comp Law 101, at 109). However, the judgment was overturned by the Court of Justice in 2009.

GlaxoSmithKline (GSK) had, through its Spanish subsidiary, notified a selling arrangement to the EU Commission under which different prices for its pharmaceuticals would be charged in Spain depending upon the nature of the purchaser. The aim was to reduce parallel trade into Member States with higher prices. The Commission took a decision finding that the agreement was in breach of art. 101(1) TFEU, and was not capable of benefiting from an exemption under art. 101(3) (*Glaxo Wellcome* 2001/791 (2001) OJ L302/1). GSK did not dispute that the purpose of the agreement was to restrict parallel trade but appealed to the GC, arguing in part that it was not correct to hold that every restriction of trade should automatically be found to lie within the illegality of art. 101(1).

The GC agreed, holding that the EU Commission had failed to consider fully the impact of the agreement in its proper legal and economic context. At paras 120–2 the GC commented on the meaning of the judgment in *Consten*, holding that, contrary to the assertion by the EU Commission, the Court did not

hold that an agreement intended to limit parallel trade must be considered by its nature, that is to say, independently of any competitive analysis, to have as its object the restriction of competition. On the contrary, the [Court of Justice] merely held, first, that an agreement between a producer and a distributor which might tend to restore the national divisions in trade between member states might be of such a kind as to frustrate the most fundamental objectives of the [Union], a consideration which led it to reject the plea alleging that art [101](1) was not applicable to vertical agreements . . . while it is accepted that an agreement intended to limit parallel trade must in principle be considered to have as its object the restriction of competition, that applies in so far as the agreement may be presumed to deprive final consumers of those advantages. However, if account is taken of the legal and economic context in which GSK's General Sales conditions are applied, it cannot be presumed that those conditions deprive the final consumers of medicines of such advantages.

In the context of the pharmaceuticals markets, the GC found that the system of national price controls had an important impact, and that the Commission had failed to consider this in its decision. It could not be presumed that the system of parallel trade actually affected the welfare of final consumers; in fact it was possible that parallel trade merely advantaged traders, and otherwise caused inefficiencies to arise in the market. Korah has noted that this decision 'amounts to a radical change of view' (at p. 104). Had the judgment been upheld, it would have meant that agreements designed to restrict parallel imports would no longer automatically fall foul of art. 101(1). Unfortunately, in October 2009 the Court of Justice overturned the GC's ruling following an appeal. It considered that the GC had committed an error of law in saying that agreements may only be restrictive by object if they bear clear negative effects for consumers; the Court reminded the GC that the aim of EU competition law is 'to protect not only the interests of competitors or of consumers, but also the structure of the market and, in so doing, competition as such' (para. 63). The Court further confirmed the general principle that agreements that reduce parallel trade constitute a restriction by object, and the pharmaceutical sector is no exception. Therefore, the agreement would indeed fall within the prohibition in 101(1), and the weight of the economic analysis thus shifts to 101(3). In this regard, the Court of Justice agreed with the GC in that the Commission had failed to adequately examine GSK's arguments in favour of exempting its agreement. It rejected the argument that art. 101(3) requires showing that economic benefits are 'probable'; instead, as the GC had contested in its decision, it is only necessary to prove that advantages are 'likely'.

A new set of *Guidelines on Vertical Restraints* (2010) OJ C130/1 was published in 2010, coinciding with the adoption of new Regulation 330/2010 (analysed in Chapter 10). At paras 23–73 these set out general rules for the assessment of vertical restraints and for the application of the block exemption. The starting point is the recognition of the fact that 'for most vertical restraints competition concerns can only arise if there is insufficient competition at one or more levels of trade', and that if there is no market power, it will be assumed that non-hardcore vertical restraints will not have appreciable effects. Additionally, vertical restraints which have the effect of reducing inter-brand competition will be analysed with greater concern. Some analysis of specific categories of vertical restraint is provided in paras 128–229 of the *Guidelines*. The practices dealt with there are: single branding, exclusive distribution, exclusive customer allocation, selective distribution, franchising, exclusive supply, upfront access payments, category management agreements, tying, and recommended and maximum resale prices. In each case, the *Guidelines* should be read through carefully.

9.3.2 **Horizontal agreements**

The treatment in this section is broken into two parts: anti-competitive agreements and potentially benign agreements (also referred to as 'cooperation agreements'). For the present purposes the first category refers to those agreements, typically in the forms of cartels, that are unlikely to have redeeming features. The second refers to categories of agreements which may, on the face of it, be entered into for pro-competitive reasons, but where it may be possible for harm to flow depending on the exact way in which the agreement operates.

9.3.2.1 Anti-competitive agreements

Cartels are considered one of the most important threats to competition. As seen in Chapter 8, when potential competitors agree to cooperate rather than compete the effects on the market can be similar to those of monopolies. Some of the most common types of cartels include agreements that imply:

- price fixing: the competitors agree to sell their products at an agreed price, below which none of them will offer the goods;
- restrictions of production or supply: by limiting output, competitors may also charge a higher price for the products;
- market sharing: firms agree not to enter each other's territory, effectively eliminating competition in those markets; and
- bid rigging: the competing undertakings responding to a call for tenders or bids have prearranged the bids they are submitting.

In recent years, partly as a result of a particular drive by DG Comp, there has been a relatively large number of actions brought against cartels. Although it must by now be general knowledge in the business community that cartel conduct is illegal, and can attract severe penalties, some of the evidence uncovered in the course of competition investigations is astonishing. In a decision taken late in 2003 for instance, the Commission produced evidence of no less than 149 separate meetings over an 18-year period. A favourite location for such assignations would appear to be hotels near airports (*Electrical and Mechanical Carbon and Graphite Products* C (2003) 4457 final, [2005] 5 CMLR 20, Annex I to the Decision). One of the best examples of cartel decisions is *Pre-Insulated Pipe Cartel* 1999/60 (1999) OJ L24/1, an infringement that began with a national cartel in Denmark in 1990, and by 1994 had been extended to cover the entire Union. The list of restrictions of competition set out in para. 147 of the decision is an impressive one, and, even allowing for some reductions in the level of fines imposed in accordance with its notice on the non-imposition of fines in cartel cases (see Chapter 6), the total fines amounted to €92,920,000. The decision was upheld by the GC on appeal (*LR AF 1998 A/s* v *Commission* case T–23/99 [2002] 5 CMLR 10). A very good description of the operation of this cartel, and the steps taken to counteract it, may be found in *Competition Policy Newsletter* (1999) February, p. 27.

Although in a number of cases the Commission has uncovered evidence of sophisticated managerial arrangements and structures created to facilitate the operation of cartels it is not necessary that such structures be in place for art. 101 to apply (see, e.g., *Cimenteries CBR SA v Commission* cases T–25–26/95 etc. [2000] 5 CMLR 204, at paras 4126–7), and the lack of such a structure may not lead to a reduction in penalties. Thus for example, in *Carbonless Paper Cartel* 2004/337/EC (2004) OJ L115/1 the Commission was asked by one of the parties to take into account the fact that the cartel was limited in scope because of the lack of clear institutional structure when imposing the fine. The Commission rejected these arguments, pointing out that the mechanisms that *were* in place were quite adequate to achieve the aims of the cartel, and that this was all that was required (at paras 379–81).

One of the most high-profile cases of recent years attracted the attention of competition authorities around the world when the cartel was exposed to the FBI. In the EU the investigation culminated in the EU Commission decision *Amino Acids Cartel—Archer Daniels Midland Co. and others* 2001/418 (2001) OJ L152/24. A number of leading companies in the production of amino acids, led by the US company Archer Daniels Midland (ADM), put in place elaborate arrangements to market-share and fix prices. The story of uncovering the cartel is told in Eichenwald, K., *The Informant*, New York, Broadway Books (2000), which was turned into a movie in 2009. In *Archer Daniels Midland* v *Commission* case T–224/00 [2003] 5 CMLR 12 the GC upheld the Commission decision, although it reduced the amount of the penalty imposed. A further reduction was imposed by the Court in *Archer Daniels Midland Co.* v *Commission* case C–511/06 P [2009] 5 CMLR 15, which partly annulled the GC's earlier judgment.

The uncovering of this cartel led to investigations in a number of related industries involving many of the same undertakings. In *Citric Acid* 2002/742 (2002) OJ L239/18 the Commission took action against a cartel which allocated sales quotas to its members, fixed target and 'floor' prices, eliminated price discounts and established the exchange of specific customer information. Substantial penalties were imposed, and the Commission did not feel constrained by the fact that some of the cartel members had already paid criminal fines in the USA and Canada in respect of the same conduct. An interesting feature of this case was the reliance the Commission placed on an FBI report given to it by one of the cartel participants. Despite ADM's claims to the contrary, the GC held that the Commission acted properly in relying on this document, which it had obtained legally. It also noted that ADM had been informed of the impact of the FBI report in the statement of objections, therefore its procedural rights had not been infringed (*Archer Daniels Midland Co* v *Commission* case T–59/02 [2006] 5 CMLR 28 at paras 264–70).

The year 2001 was particularly outstanding as far as fines are concerned. The Commission took 10 cartel decisions, and imposed fines totalling €1,836 million. When compared to the mere €113 million of the previous year (see Figure 9.1 below), it would appear that the Commission was taking a tougher stance in the fight against cartels following the new 'economics-based' approach introduced by the reforms of the time. In the complex *Vitamins* case alone (2003/2 (2003) OJ L6/1) a fine of €855.23 million was imposed on the various parties. The cartel was notified to the Commission by one of the participants, Rhône-Poulenc, seeking to benefit from the leniency programme. This application was facilitated by the fact that the company 'played only a passive role in the vitamin D3 infringement. It did not attend any of the cartel meetings and was

Million Euro

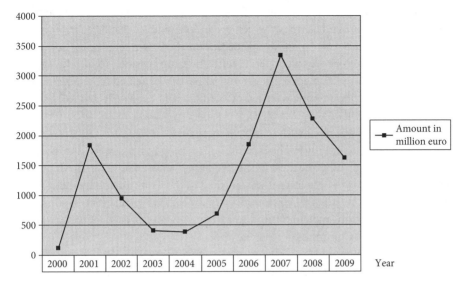

Figure 9.1 Total amount of fines imposed by the Commission on Cartels, 2000–09

not allocated an individual market share' (para. 725). Eleven different cartels were identified in the decision by the Commission, relating to different vitamins, folic acid, beta-carotene, and carotinoids. The cartels generally flowed from a period of intense price competition during which prices fell dramatically. In the summer of 1989 at least two top-level meetings were held in Zurich between executives of Hoffmann-La Roche AG and BASF AG. The discussions that took place at the second meeting were described in some detail by BASF:

On the first day senior executives responsible for vitamin marketing in each company, together with some product managers,…agreed the allocation between the four producers of the world and regional markets on the basis of their respective achieved sales in 1988.

…

On the second day, the chairmen of the fine chemicals division or the equivalent and the heads of vitamins marketing of each company joined the meeting to approve the agreed quotas and to establish 'confidence' between the participants that the arrangements would be respected. The maxim 'price before volume' was accepted as the underlying principle of the cartel. Specific pricing levels were also discussed.   (paras 163–5)

The cartel expanded, both in terms of products and markets covered, and the participants. It was eventually attacked in a number of jurisdictions, including the USA where prosecutions were brought on the basis of s. 1 of the Sherman Act.

A price-fixing cartel was also tackled in *Graphite Electrodes* 2002/271 (2002) OJ L100/1. ('Graphite electrodes are ceramic-moulded columns of graphite used primarily in the production of steel in electric arc furnaces' (para. 4).) Eight undertakings were found to have been party to an agreement (or concerted practice) covering the entire EU under which they fixed prices, put into place a mechanism to facilitate the price fixing, allocated markets, restricted output, agreed to retain certain technologies only to the participants (so as to limit the growth in potential competition) and set up procedures to monitor the agreement. The Commission decision followed dawn raids carried out in France and Germany which produced evidence that fitted in with material also found by US and Japanese authorities on their own territories. Some of the cartel members then chose to cooperate with the Commission. Total fines of €218.8 million were imposed. On appeal seven of the parties benefited from a reduction in their penalties, although none were exonerated (*Tokai Carbon Co. Ltd v Commission* cases T–236/01 etc. [2004] 5 CMLR 28).

A smaller cartel was dealt with in *Luxembourg Brewers* 2002/759 (2002) OJ L253/21 in which the five main brewers in Luxembourg reached an agreement to ensure the mutual observance and protection of the tied agreements entered into with outlets in the country. It came to light after it was notified to the Commission by Interbrew SA, which had taken control of a Luxembourg brewer and instructed its two subsidiaries in the market to stop implementing the agreement. Interbrew benefited from total leniency under the Commission's leniency policy.

In 2007, fines amounted to an all-time record high total of €3,334 million. That year, for instance, the Commission took action against lift manufacturers imposing a fine of €992 million on manufacturers. The media took delight in pointing out that the lifts installed in the Commission's Brussels' headquarters were affected by the cartel. More recently, in 2008 a record fine of €896 million was imposed on Saint Gobain in the context of a market-sharing cartel in the car glass industry (its fine was increased by 60 per cent for being a repeat offender—see *Car Glass* COMP/39.125 (2008) OJ C173/13). In 2009, fines of €553 million were imposed on both E.ON and GdF Suez for a cartel in the gas sector in 2009 (*E.ON and GdF* COMP/39.401 (2009) OJ C248/5). Despite a drop in the overall total of the fines imposed in 2008 and 2009, it is clear that the firm fining policy continues.

9.3.2.2 Potentially benign horizontal agreements

The range of material about which undertakings at a horizontal level may agree is vast, and includes not only prices and market sharing, but also practices which are wholly pro-competitive, or whose pro-competitive effects may outweigh the anti-competitive effects. In *European Night Services* v *Commission* joined cases T–374/94 etc. [1998] ECR II–3141 the Court drew a distinction between different types of horizontal agreements. The first task, the Court said, was to assess carefully the competitive conditions in which such agreements operated. It might be the case that a horizontal agreement would not even fall within art. 101(1) if it had no deleterious effect on competition. However, where certain restrictions are present, set out in the case as being price fixing, market sharing, or the control of outlets (para. 136), it must be presumed automatically that art. 101(1) applies. It would then become necessary to analyse carefully the competitive conditions in order to see if the requirements for the application of art. 101(3) were met.

Guidelines on the Applicability of Article 81 EC to Horizontal Cooperation Agreements were published in January 2001, substituting earlier guidelines and notices, including the 1968 *Notice on Agreements, Decisions and Concerted Practices in the Field of Cooperation between Enterprises* ((1968) OJ C75/3). The 2001 Guidelines recently underwent a review process, and were replaced by the Guidelines on the Applicability of Article 101 of the Treaty on the Functioning of the European Union to Horizontal Cooperation Agreements in January 2011.

The difficulty in dealing with benign horizontal cooperation is that there is always a risk that parties will coordinate in an anti-competitive fashion. Such coordination can have serious consequences both for economic welfare and for the integration of the single market. Thus it is recognized in the introduction to the *Guidelines* that:

2. Horizontal co-operation agreements can lead to substantial economic benefits, in particular if they combine complementary activities, skills or assets. Horizontal cooperation can be a means to share risk, save costs, increase investments, pool know-how, enhance product quality and variety, and launch innovation faster.

3. On the other hand, horizontal co-operation agreements may lead to competition problems. This is, for example, the case if the parties agree to fix prices or output or to share markets, or if the co-operation enables the parties to maintain, gain or increase market power and thereby is likely to give rise to negative market effects with respect to prices, output, product quality, product variety or innovation.

The *Guidelines*, which should be read carefully, focus on cooperation between competitors, (which includes both 'actual' and 'potential' competitors), as well as cooperation between non-competitors (for instance, 'between two companies active in the same product markets but active in different geographic markets', para. 1). They focus on cooperation which may generate efficiency gains, mainly 'research and development agreements, production agreements including subcontracting and specialisation agreements, purchasing agreements, commercialisation agreements, standardisation agreements including standard contracts, and information exchange' (para. 5). Since research and development agreements and production agreements—which include specialization agreements—are subject to block exemptions, they are considered in the following chapter.

The *Guidelines* deal first with the situations in which such agreements may fall within art. 101(1) (paras 23–47). Some are unlikely to be within the scope of the prohibition, particularly where there will be no coordination of competitive conduct. This will be the case where (as in *Elopak/Metal Box—Odin* 90/410 (1990) OJ L209/15, discussed above at 9.3) the parties could not independently carry out the activity covered by the cooperation. In such scenarios, it will be in an entirely new activity which would not exist without that level of collaboration. Therefore pre-existing competition is not being undermined.

In one of its last decisions taken under Regulation 17/62 the Commission considered a series of agreements entered into between two of the UK mobile telephone network operators, O_2 and T-Mobile. Parts of the agreement relating to the sharing of sites for infrastructure were found not to fall within art. 101(1), resulting in the grant of negative clearance declaration to that effect. Provisions relating to reciprocal roaming were granted exemptions of varying lengths depending on whether they related to urban or rural areas on the grounds that the agreement facilitated the development of 3G mobile communications coverage in the UK, but would not be entrenched in the future (O_2 *UK Ltd and T-Mobile UK Ltd (UK Network Sharing Agreement)* 2003/570/EC (2003)

OJ L200/50; similar treatment was accorded to an arrangement along the same lines in Germany in *T-Mobile Deutschland/O$_2$ Germany (Network Sharing Rahmenvertrag)* 2004/207/EC (2004) OJ L75/32). The approach of the Commission was later criticized by the GC, which held that the Commission had failed to demonstrate properly that the agreement could prevent, restrict, or distort competition (see 9.7).

Agreements will almost always fall within art. 101(1), and will almost always be prohibited, where they are considered anti-competitive by object. This is the case when they serve to engage in 'price fixing, output limitation or market allocation' (paras 128 and 205 inter alia). Agreements that do not fall within these categories have to be analysed more fully to determine whether they fall under art. 101(1). To this end, the central consideration will be the 'legal and economic context in which competition would occur in the absence of the agreement with all of its alleged restrictions', which requires taking 'into account competition between the parties and competition from third parties, in particular actual or potential competition that would have existed in the absence of the agreement' (para. 29). The position of the parties in the markets affected by the cooperation is also crucial, because it is the undertakings' market power which is likely to be determinative of whether harmful effects flow from the agreement (paras 39–47). The base line of the Commission is that such agreements cannot be tolerated where they have the effect of 'eliminating' competition (see art. 101(3)).

One of the indices typically used is the Herfindahl–Hirshman Index, or HHI, a tool employed by the US authorities in merger control. It provides a useful first indicator of market concentration. Formally the HHI is the sum of the squared market shares of the companies on the relevant market, or $8s1^2 \ldots sn^2$ (where sn is the market share of firm n). Thus, in a market with four firms, each of which has a 25 per cent market share, the HHI would be $25^2 + 25^2 + 25^2 + 25^2 = 2,500$. In a total monopoly market the HHI would be 10,000 (100^2), and in a market of 100 firms, each with only 1 per cent market share, it would be 100. Where the HHI is less than 1,000, the concentration will be characterized as low, between 1,000 and 1,800 it will be moderate, and over 1,800 high. Although the current *Guidelines* do not refer to HHI, they stress the importance of 'the market position of the parties and the concentration in the market' (para. 45). The 2000 *Guidelines* explained how a post-cooperation HHI may in some cases 'be decisive for the assessment of the possible market effects of a cooperation'.

As well as conducting such analysis, it must be demonstrated that the requirements of art. 101(3) are met (discussed below). For a detailed consideration of the approach to be taken in relation to each of the categories of agreement, reference should be made to the relevant section in the *Guidelines*.

9.3.2.3 Information exchange

Whereas the 2000 *Guidelines* did not deal with information-sharing agreements, the current Guidelines include a chapter on these (section 2, paras 55–110). The introduction of this chapter follows the recent trend set by competition authorities to take a tougher stand on potentially anti-competitive information exchanges. Fines have been imposed, *inter alia*, for publicizing statistics, gathering market information, and industry benchmarking.

The pro-competitive effects of information exchange are recognized in para. 57, but sharing certain types of information may facilitate coordination, particularly in markets which are concentrated, transparent, stable, or symmetric (para. 58). More specifically, the concerns identified relate to the potential collusive outcome of information exchange, inter alia, when it may lead the undertakings involved to reach a common understanding to coordinate their behaviour, or when the exchange may serve to monitor whether or not the companies involved in collusion are actually adhering to what they had agreed (paras. 66–68). Another worry is that, competitors may become aware of new or potential entrants to the market and target them in order to prevent them from doing so (paras 69–71). If such information exchange takes place in the context of an existing cartel, it will be anti-competitive by object, as the Court of Justice clarified in *T-Mobile Netherlands BV v Raad van bestuur van de Nederlandse Mededingingsautoriteit* case C–8/08 [2009] 5 CMLR 11. Here, the Court had to decide whether a concerted practice existed where GSM operators individually reduced the commissions they paid to resellers of their services following a meeting where they had discussed how high these commissions were. The Court said that 'an exchange of information which is capable of removing uncertainties between participants...must be regarded as pursuing an anticompetitive object...' (para. 41).

When the exchanges are not considered anti-competitive by object (paras 72–74), the Commission stresses that the legality of such exchanges needs to be determined on a case-by-case basis (para. 75). In such scenarios, the Commission will be highly swayed by the extent to which the information is individualized. Already in its *7th Annual Report on Competition Policy* it explained that the 'provision of collated statistical material is not in itself objectionable' but that 'the organised exchange of individual data from individual firms...will normally be regarded by the Commission as practices...which are therefore prohibited'. The leading cases in this respect are *UK Tractors Information Agreement* 92/157 [1992] OJ L68/19 and *Fatty Acids* 87/1 (1987) OJ L3/17.

In the latter case an agreement was entered into by the four major chemical producers in the EU. Under the agreement the parties, having first established their respective average market shares over the previous three years, set out to exchange information regarding their total sales in Europe for each quarter, with the intention of allowing each party to monitor the behaviour of each other, and to adjust its own conduct accordingly. As the Commission noted the information exchanged was 'of a kind normally regarded as business secrets' (para. 1). At para. 45 of the decision the Commission held that an agreement

based on an exchange of confidential information on the one hand about traditional market positions and on the other hand providing a means of monitoring their future performance, has inherent restrictive effects upon competition...through the exchange of information they artificially increased transparency between them by obtaining knowledge of each other's activities which they would not have had in the absence of the agreement... [T]his will inevitably have led them to temper their competitive behaviour towards each other.

9.3.2.4 Standards-setting agreements

Agreements relating to standards setting are dealt with in Part 7 of the *Guidelines*. They are defined as those which 'have as their primary objective the definition of technical or quality requirements with which current or future products, production processes, services or methods may comply' (para. 257). In high-tech industries, such as computing, where equipment needs to be able to interface with other equipment, standards setting is increasingly important. Standards may be set by public or private bodies. In the case of public bodies it is unlikely that competition law will involve itself, and the only requirement is that any such standards do not distort competition, and are not used to raise barriers to trade.

In relation to private standards setting the general principles set out in the *Guidelines* follow previous decisions taken by the Commission. Where standards are 'open' (that is, open to all, and not discriminatory or exclusionary) they are unlikely to fall within art. 101(1) (paras. 280–283). For example, in *TUV/Cenelec* (*28th Annual Report on Competition Policy* (1998), p. 159) the Commission negotiated a settlement whereby a standard developed by Cenelec was 'opened' up to all qualified certifiers, a procedure which the Commission hoped would 'serve as a model for application procedures in related fields'. Standards may, however, be used to restrict competition by setting criteria which are unattainable by some parties. The question then becomes one of whether art. 101(3) may be applied. If that is to be the case the standard must serve a valid end and meet the general criteria for exemption discussed below.

The leading decision dealing with the application of art. 101(3) to a standards-setting agreement is that of *X/Open Group* 87/69 (1987) OJ L35/36. A number of significant undertakings in the computing industry notified the Commission of an agreement to standardize various matters relating to the use of the computer operating system UNIX. The objective was to increase the number of applications that could be written to work with UNIX. The group intended to limit its membership, with a requirement that applicants be 'major manufacturers in the European information technology industry, with their own established expertise concerning UNIX'. The revenue of any applicant to the group would be expected to be about US$500 million from information technology activity. The Commission found that the agreement would fall within art. 101(1), but that it would be exempt under art. 101(3). A crucial factor was that the standards created by the group would be well publicized and relevant technical information would be made widely available.

9.3.2.5 Professional rules

Rules regulating professions—lawyers, doctors, architects—may fall within art. 101(1), although whether this is the case will depend on an analysis of the rule in question. The fact that a professional rule contains an element of restriction will not necessarily bring it within the prohibition. Thus in *Wouters, Savelbergh and Price Waterhouse Belastingadviseurs BV* v *Algemene Raad Van de Nederlandse Orde Van Advocaten* case C–309/99 [2002] 4 CMLR 27 the Court of Justice dealt with the question, *inter alia*, of whether it was a breach of art. 101(1) for the Dutch Bar Council to impose a rule preventing its members from entering into certain multidisciplinary partnerships. The first two named claimants were therefore prevented from entering into a partnership with accountants. The Court found that it was reasonable for the Dutch Bar 'to consider that members of the Bar might no longer be in a position to advise and represent their clients independently' (para. 105) if they belonged to such a partnership. The restrictions inherent in the professional rules in this case did not, the Court held, 'go beyond what is necessary in order to ensure the proper practice of the legal profession' (para. 109), and in conclusion the rules did not infringe art. 101(1).

There have, however, been instances in which professional associations have been punished for, *inter alia*, price fixing. In 2004 the Commission condemned a 'guideline' relating to fee scales applying to architects in Belgium as being in breach of art. 101(1) and imposed a penalty (*The Belgian Architects' Association* 2005/8/EC, 24 June 2004).

In February 2004 the Commission published a *Report on Competition in Professional Services* (see press release IP (04) 185, 9 February 2004) which examined the state of competition among lawyers, notaries, accountants, architects, engineers, and pharmacists. The report found that anti-competitive restrictions among the professions were still common, and often lacked any objective justification. A difficulty with tackling this area is that there are a number of sound economic arguments in favour of some restrictions, particularly the fact that there is an imbalance between the knowledge of the professional and the consumer of the service offered. However, such theories do not usually support horizontal price fixing, and in its press release the Commission noted that 'price controls are not an essential instrument for ensuring high-quality standards'.

9.3.3 Mergers and joint ventures

The application of art. 101 to mergers and joint ventures is considered in Chapter 19.

9.4 Article 101(2): void agreements

An important consequence of the application of art. 101(1) is that an agreement, or relevant parts of it, will be void. Because of the nature of the prohibition there need not be any formal decision to the effect that art. 101(1) applies for it to be null. This position is made clear in *Beguelin Import Co. v GL Import Export SA* (case 22/71 [1972] CMLR 81) where the Court held that 'since the nullity imposed by Article [101(2)] is absolute in character, an agreement which is void because of that provision has no effect between the contracting parties and cannot be pleaded against third parties' (para. 29). Thus any national court dealing with the issue may find that a contract or parts of that contract are void where one of the parties to an action can demonstrate that art. 101(1) applies to the situation.

The effect of art. 101(2) runs either from the date at which art. 101(1) became effective, or the date of the conclusion of the agreement, whichever is the later. The nullity sanction does not necessarily apply to an agreement in its entirety. Where the offending clauses can be separated from the agreement without stripping its essence, this will be permitted. However it is primarily a matter of national, not Union, law. Whether this is possible is to be determined in the light of all the relevant circumstances objectively and not necessarily by reference to the views of the parties. Thus in *La Technique Minière* v *Maschinenbau Ulm GmbH* case 56/65 [1966] 1 CMLR 357, the Court held (at 376) that

The automatic nullity in question applies only to those elements of the agreement which are subject to the prohibition or to the agreement as a whole if those elements do not appear severable from the agreement itself. Consequently, all other contractual provisions which are not affected by the prohibition, since they do not involve the application of the Treaty, fall outside the [Union] law.

The Court has also argued that where the matter falls to be decided before a national court the test of severability is to be that which would normally be applied in equivalent national law (*Société de Vente de Ciments et Bétons de L'Est SA* v *Kerpen and Kerpen GmbH* case 319/82 [1985] 1 CMLR 511). There is therefore the potential for a different result to be arrived at depending on the country in which an action is brought, although it is unlikely that this will be a matter of great difficulty in practice.

As has been discussed in Chapter 7, competition law is not used as a sword as often as it could be. One of the most common ways for EU competition law to be introduced before the national courts is for a party contesting a contractual obligation to raise what has become known as the 'Euro-defence' (or 'competition defence'). In such a case the defendant pleads that there is no obligation because the clause or contract in question is in breach of art. 101(1) (see, e.g., *Chemidus Wavin Ltd* v *Société pour la Transformation et l'Exploitation des Resines Industrielles SA* [1978] 3 CMLR 514). English courts have tended to be wary of these 'defences', recognizing the potential of such a defence to serve as an effective obfuscating tactic: if an art. 267 reference is made in such a case the matter may take up to 18 months to be resolved. Nevertheless when the argument is made it will have to be addressed properly at trial. Such 'defences' may also be raised on the basis of art. 102 although this is less likely. Again the courts may be sceptical of the claims (see, e.g., *Hoover plc* v *George Hulme (Stockport) Ltd* [1982] FSR 565).

It is for national courts to rule on the validity of contracts falling within art. 101 in actions relying on the direct effect of EU law. There has been uncertainty as to the approach that would be adopted by courts in the UK. The issue has been discussed particularly in cases arising out of challenges to leases between pub tenants and breweries. The key question was whether either party could, to any extent, rely on a contract falling within art. 101(1), as such a contract was presumed to be 'illegal'. The issue was referred to the Court of Justice by way of an art. 267 reference from the Court of Appeal in the cases of *Crehan* v *Courage Ltd and others* [1999] UKCLR 110 and 407. Late in 2001 the Court gave its response (*Courage Ltd* v *Crehan* case C–453/99 [2002] UKCLR 171) and held in particular that, while it was for the national court to determine the appropriate procedures by which the rights given under art. 101 should be invoked, national courts should take into account 'the economic and legal context in which the parties find themselves and ... the respective bargaining power and conduct of the two parties to the contract' (para. 32). The Court stressed that in cases where a small agreement was concluded within a network of similar agreements 'the party contracting with the person controlling the network cannot bear significant responsibility for the breach of art. [101], particularly where in practice the terms of the contract were imposed on him by the party controlling the network' (para. 34).

When the case returned for further consideration to the national court, Park J held that the contractual ties in question did not have the effect of preventing, restricting, or distorting competition, so did not find it necessary to rule on the question of damages, although he made it clear that had the contracts fallen within art. 101(1) they would have been available (*Crehan* v *Inntrepreneur Pub Company and Brewman Group Ltd* [2003] EWHC 1510 (Ch), [2003] UKCLR 834). In May 2004 the Court of Appeal ruled that Park J had been in error, as he had failed to show due deference to relevant Commission decisions, and awarded damages to Mr Crehan in the sum of just over £130,000 (*Bernard Crehan* v *Inntrepreneur Pub Company CPC* [2004] EWCA Civ 637, [2004] UKCLR 1500). There was then a further appeal to the House of Lords, which reversed the judgment of the Court of Appeal holding that the Court of Appeal was in error when it reversed the decision on the ground that the judge at first instance should have followed the EU Commission (*Inntrepreneur Pub Company (CPC) and others* v *Crehan* [2006] UKHL 38).

9.5 Trade between Member States

The importance of the phrase 'trade between Member States', and its application has been considered at 3.4.1 above. It is the agreement which must affect trade.

It is worth noting that in the 2001 notice on agreements of minor importance (2001) OJ C368/13 the Commission recognizes that 'agreements between small and medium-sized undertakings...are rarely capable of appreciably affecting trade between member states' (para. 3). For these purposes small and medium-sized undertakings are defined as those with fewer than 250 employees and having an annual turnover not greater than €40 million, or an annual balance sheet total not exceeding €27 million. In *The Dutch Acceptance Giro System* 1999/687 (1999) OJ L271/28 the Commission found that an agreement between undertakings in the Netherlands relating to inter-bank commission payments, with only a negligible involvement by banks from other Member States, would not meet this requirement.

9.6 Limits on the application of article 101(1) and (2)

From the above it becomes apparent that the prohibition of art. 101(1) is broad and indiscriminate. Multilateral anti-competitive conduct may be caught irrespective of the form that the conduct takes. It applies to a wide range of practices, and the jurisdictional test of an effect on Union trade is not a demanding one. At the same time the limits on the application of the prohibition have become more clearly defined. Most obviously the article is ameliorated in the application of art. 101(3). The Court of Justice has also developed *de minimis* criteria which are not themselves set out in the article.

9.6.1 Exceptions under Article 101(3)

Article 101(3) TFEU

sets out an exception rule, which provides a defence to undertakings against a finding of an infringement of Article 101(1) of the Treaty. Agreements, decisions of associations of undertakings and concerted practices caught by Article 101(1) which satisfy the conditions of Article 101(3) are valid and enforceable, no prior decision to that effect being required. (*Guidelines on the application of article 81(3) of the Treaty* (2004) OJ C101/81, para. 1)

Article 101(3) has direct effect. While this may seem unexceptional, this position has existed only since 1 May 2004, and is a result of the modernization process encapsulated in Regulation 1/2003. As seen in Chapter 5, previously art. 101(3) did not have direct effect, and the EU Commission had *exclusive* power to rule on its application. There were, in essence, two ways in which art. 101(3) could be invoked: either by making an individual application to the Commission or by structuring an agreement so as to fall within a block exemption regulation (see Chapter 10). The Commission was overstretched, receiving hundreds of notifications per year. It resorted to administratively convenient but legally uncertain measures to resolve cases. In particular, it developed the use of the 'comfort letter' under which it bound itself, but not others, as to the result. Crucially, whenever the application of art. 101(1) was pleaded before a national court, the party seeking to rely on the contract or agreement could not plead the application of art. 101(3), and their only recourse was to persuade the national court to stay the proceedings while an application for individual exemption was made to the Commission. This led to some considerable dissatisfaction with the process. For example, in the case of *Crehan* (discussed above), the judge accepted that 'I can understand that Mr Crehan and his professional advisers feel disenchanted by the way in which Inntrepreneur caused their counterclaim to be held up for years while Inntrepreneur pursued a European route to get rid of it' (*Crehan v Inntrepreneur Pub Company and Brewman Group Ltd* [2003] EWHC 1510 (Ch), [2003] UKCLR 834, at para. 146).

As a result of these problems, the modernized enforcement rules establish a

directly applicable exception system in which the competition authorities and courts of the Member States have the power to apply not only art. [101](1) and art. [102] of the Treaty...but also art. [101](3) of the Treaty. (Regulation 1/2003, recital (4))

Where any party seeks to rely on what is now referred to as the 'legal exception' (although it is likely that the term 'exemption' is so entrenched it will be used for some time) it is for that party to establish its application. Article 2 of Regulation 1/2003 provides that

The undertaking or association of undertakings claiming the benefit of art. [101](3) of the Treaty shall bear the burden of proving that the conditions of that paragraph are fulfilled.

In essence, the appropriate procedure for the application of art. 101(3) now is for the parties seeking to rely on the legal exception—if it is accepted that the agreement might fall within the scope of art. 101(1)—to make their own evaluation of the exception's application, and to be prepared to defend this before a national court or national competition authority. A key document to be considered in any such case is the Commission *Guidelines on the application of article 81(3) of the Treaty* (2004) OJC 101/97.

In some circumstances undertakings may make applications to the relevant member of the network of competition authorities to seek clarification that their assessment of the application of art. 101(3) is correct, and the Commission has retained the power to rule in novel cases. Article 10 of Regulation 1/2003 therefore provides that the Commission may, 'where the [Union] public interest relating to the application of arts [101] and [102] of the Treaty, so requires', make a finding that the conditions of art. 101(3) are satisfied. The Commission has published a *Notice on informal guidance relating to novel questions concerning arts. 81 and 82 of the EC Treaty that arise in individual cases (guidance letters)* (2004) OJ C101/78 in which it recognizes that the way in which art. 101(3) functions may create legal uncertainty, and permits undertakings to approach it where cases 'give rise to genuine uncertainty because they present novel or unresolved questions' (para. 5).

The Commission believes that its vertical and horizontal guidelines, along with the *Notice on the application of art. 81(3)* and previous case law, provide undertakings with most of the information that they need to make their own assessment of the situation, and assist the courts and members of the network of competition authorities to rule as appropriate. In key areas, and in particular in relation to vertical agreements and certain categories of cooperation agreements, block exemption regulations are also in place that will automatically exempt a large number of agreements from the application of art. 101(1) (see Chapter 10).

9.6.2 Article 101(3)—the conditions

The wording of art. 101(3) provides that the legal exception will be available where the agreement or concerted practice in question

contributes to improving the production or distribution of goods or to promoting technical or economic progress, while allowing consumers a fair share of the resulting benefit, and which does not:

  (a) impose on the undertakings concerned restrictions which are not indispensable to the attainment of these objectives;
  (b) afford such undertakings the possibility of eliminating competition in respect of a substantial part of the products in question.

It was confirmed in *Atlantic Container Line AB* v *Commission* case T–395/94 [2002] 4 CMLR 28, following earlier case law, that the four conditions set out in art. 101(3) are cumulative, such that 'non-fulfilment of only one of those conditions' would make it impossible for an undertaking to benefit from the application of the provision. According to the notice 'the four conditions of art. 101(3) are also exhaustive. When they are met the exception is applicable and may not be refused' (para. 38).

The notice deals with the substantive application of the criteria in some detail, and should be relied on to provide useful guidance in this respect. The first condition for the application of art. 101(3) is that there is an efficiency gain as a result of the restriction. Any such gain must be clearly substantiated, so that it is possible to evaluate: (a) the nature of the claimed efficiencies; (b) the link between the agreement and these efficiencies; and (c) the likelihood and magnitude of each of the efficiencies claimed of the agreement. Efficiencies either may be of cost, or may take the form of new or improved products. Under the third condition of the article it must also be demonstrated that the restrictions in the agreement are necessary to the attainment of these efficiencies.

Consumers must benefit from the gain, but the general expectation is that in markets which are competitive these will be passed on as part of the inevitable process of competition. For example, in the *Metro* case the Court first considered the fact that the agreement assured 'a more regular distribution' of the goods in question to the benefit of both producer and retailer (para. 43). Then the Court held that

In the circumstances of the present case regular supplies represent a sufficient advantage to consumers for them to be considered to constitute a fair share of the benefit resulting from the improvement brought about by the restriction on competition permitted by the Commission...the grant of exemption may...be considered as sufficiently justified by the advantage which consumers obtain from an improvement in supplies.   (para. 48)

This is not always the case, however. In condemning the operation of an association of building contractors in the Netherlands market the Commission, supported by the GC, found that although the contractors undeniably benefited from the operation of the rules determined by the association this benefit was not passed on to the customer. Even accepting that some of the benefits claimed did exist, because, for example, the customer would have to consider fewer bids, 'that benefit is limited by comparison with the disadvantages which he must bear and the benefits obtained from that system by contractors' (*Vereniging van Samenwerkende Prijsregelende Organisaties in de Bouwnijverheid (SPO)* v *Commission* case T–29/92 [1995] ECR II–289, para. 295).

The meaning of 'consumer' is not necessarily limited to the end-users purchasing through retail outlets. The industrial user of a product, or a manufacturer purchasing a component to be used in its production process, may also be a consumer for the purposes of art. 101(3). In *Kabel-metal-Luchaire* 75/494 (1975) OJ L222/34, an agreement between two industrial companies was exempted when 'electrical-equipment and motor-vehicle manufacturers and their customers, obtain[ed] a fair share of the benefits...for as a result of this agreement they have at their disposal in the common market goods tailored to their needs' (para. 11).

Some concern has been expressed that, in giving pre-eminence to the role of price competition, the Commission has not permitted the consumer to benefit from other types of competition. For example, in *VBBB/VBVB* 82/123 (1982) OJ L54/36 (on appeal *Vereniging ter Bevordering van het Vlaamse Boekwezen (VBVB) and Vereeniging ter Bevordering van de Belangen des Boekhandels (VBBB)* v *Commission* cases 43/82 and 63/82 [1985] 1 CMLR 27) the Commission considered an agreement operated by the main Dutch and Belgian book publishers and sellers under which resale price maintenance was applied. This position had its counterpart in the Net Book Agreement operated in the United Kingdom. Under the terms of the agreement booksellers would be prevented from increasing their individual market share by competing with other booksellers on price. In seeking an exemption, the parties claimed that it produced benefits that were shared by the consumers, as it increased both the range of books published and the number of outlets in which they could be purchased.

Similar arguments were made before the Court of Justice following the Commission's finding that the agreement was in breach of art. 101(1) and that no exemption would be granted. The applicants also relied, unsuccessfully, on art. 10 of the European Convention on Human Rights which guarantees the right to freedom of expression. As was the case in *Metro*, the applicants claimed that while the effect of the agreement was to restrict price competition, (here by resellers in relation to each individual book), it left unimpaired competition between the various publishers. The applicants felt that by taking the view that price competition was the essential ingredient the Commission had ignored the particular characteristics of the book market. The institution did not share the applicants' view that for the consumer the consideration put on the price of a book was secondary to that relating to the diversity of stocks. The Court, noting the Commission's argument that 'the resale price maintenance system totally eliminates price competition at retail level' (para. 43 of the judgment), rejected the applicants' claims. Accepting that there might be situations in which art. 101(1) would not be breached by a restriction on price competition that was more than balanced by other factors, the Court nevertheless held that in this case the agreement's effects were too marked to be removed from the scope of the prohibition by the granting of an art. 101(3) exemption.

On the other hand, in *REIMS II* 1999/687 (1999) OJ L275/17 the EU Commission exempted an agreement between 16 European postal operators which fixed the fees for the costs of delivering cross-border mail (so-called terminal dues). At para. 65 it noted that 'it has to be acknowledged that the REIMS II Agreement is a price-fixing agreement with unusual characteristics'. Some sort of arrangement was clearly necessary in order for the postal system to work, and in the absence of a general agreement there would need to be bilateral accords, with the costs entailed by this. Further, the agreement would clearly produce the substantial advantage of increasing the quality of cross-border mail services (paras 69–76).

A difficulty facing the courts is that the language of the notice is very much about 'efficiency', whereas the Commission has, in the past, taken into account wider considerations. In September 1998, for example, an art. 101(3) comfort letter was issued to members of the European Council for Automotive Research and Development

(EUCAR) relating to an agreement between major manufacturers to collaborate in research aimed, *inter alia*, at reducing car emissions. In doing so, the Commission noted that 'research must be at the pre-competitive stage' (Press Release IP/98/832, 25 September 1998). Environmental concerns also led to the Commission granting an art. 101(3) exemption in respect of an agreement between manufacturers and importers of washing machines to reduce sales of the least efficient products (*CECED Agreement* 2000/475 [2000] OJ L187/47). In *Metro* the Commission took into consideration the fact that several Member States had enacted legislation that differentiated between resale and wholesale outlets. The aim was to afford a limited protection to retailers from competition from wholesalers, in order to increase the range of outlets. The Court's view was that it was acceptable for the Commission to apply a similar policy when deciding whether to grant an exemption under art. 101(3) to the selective distribution system maintained by SABA (at para. 29 of the judgment). This is of concern to some commentators who would prefer that the scope of the review be limited strictly to competitive matters. However, the fact that the Court has held repeatedly that EU competition policy is to be considered in the light of the other objectives of the Treaty would suggest that such a wider application is appropriate—another objective of the Treaty should not be obstructed by a rigid interpretation of art. 101(3) (see also *Remia BV* v *Commission* case 42/84 [1987] 1 CMLR 1, at para. 42).

9.6.3 **Article 101(3) and art. 102**

The fact that an undertaking has the benefit of an exception will not necessarily serve as a defence to an action brought on the basis of art. 102. The exception relates specifically to the application of art. 101(1) and not to EU competition law in general. This point was clarified by the GC in *Tetra Pak Rausing SA* v *Commission* case T–51/89 [1991] 4 CMLR 334, where the Court rejected Tetra Pak's argument to the effect that the principle of legal certainty would be undermined if an art. 101(3) decision could not be relied on in all circumstances. A similar view was taken by the Commission in *Cewal* 93/82 (1993) OJ L34/20 (at para. 20) where it held that the fact that the parties benefited from one of the block exemptions did not prevent the application of art. 102.

9.6.4 *De minimis* **rules and the notice on agreements of minor importance**

On its face, art. 101(1) prohibits all anti-competitive agreements where trade is affected irrespective of the size of the parties in question or the impact they may have. Were this in fact the case the article would paralyse business activity. The initial approach of the Commission and the Court was to remove from the application of the article those agreements where the market share of the parties concerned was only minimal. For example, in the case of *Franz Völk* v *Ets Vervaecke Sprl* case 5/69 [1969] CMLR 273, an agreement was not condemned under art. 101(1) even where it contained clauses that, in other contexts, would have been clearly in breach. It was an exclusive distribution agreement providing absolute territorial protection between a German producer of washing machines and a distributor based in Belgium. The manufacturer's market share was, at 0.6 per cent, considered to be insignificant, and the agreement related to only 600 units. The Court held that 'an agreement escapes the prohibition of Article [101] when it only affects the market insignificantly, account being taken of the weak position held by the parties on the market in the products in question' (para. 3). It should be noted, however, that art. 101 will still apply at market shares greatly below those necessary to establish dominance under art. 102.

These *de minimis* decisions have been 'codified' in a Commission *Notice on agreements of minor importance*, which has been regularly overhauled since the first notice was introduced. While such notices cannot have the force of law, and do not bind the Commission, they are considered to be of the status of at least 'soft law' by those seeking guidance from them. In the most recent version of the notice the Commission makes it clear that where undertakings rely on the notice in good faith and assume that an agreement is covered it will not impose fines if it subsequently finds them to be in breach. In cases where the notice does apply 'the Commission will not institute proceedings either upon application or its own initiative' (para. 4). The most recent version of the *de minimis* notice was published in 2001 ((2001) OJ C368/13) and, according to the accompanying press release (IP/02/13, 7 January 2002), 'reflects an economic approach'. Under the 2001 notice the relevant thresholds for the application of art. 101(1) are different depending on whether agreements are made between competing or non-competing undertakings. In the case of competitors, or potential competitors, the threshold is 10 per cent of any of the relevant markets affected by the agreement(s) (para. 7(a)). Where the undertakings are not competitors or potential competitors the threshold is 15 per cent (para. 7(b)). In situations in which it is not readily easy to determine whether the relevant undertakings are competitors or not, the lower threshold is to be applied.

For the first time the notice sets out a threshold to apply to situations in which there exists a network of small agreements which have a cumulative effect. In this respect the formula is a little more complex. Both the thresholds set out in para. 7 are reduced to 5 per cent in respect of individual agreements, and a cumulative foreclosure effect is considered to be unlikely to exist if less than 30 per cent of the relevant market is affected by a network of parallel agreements. This is to say that, for example, where there is a network of parallel agreements which covers 20 per cent of the market, and a new one is entered into between parties which have less than 5 per cent of the overall market, both the individual agreement and the network of similar agreements will be found not to be appreciable.

Certain 'hard-core' restrictions are considered sufficiently onerous as to invite condemnation even where they are entered into by parties whose market shares would be such as to fall within the application of the notice. In relation to competitors these are agreements which have as their object the fixing of prices when selling the products to third parties, the limitation of output or sales, and the allocation of markets or customers. In the case of agreements between non-competitors, the restrictions prohibited are those which restrict the ability of a buyer to determine its minimum sale price, the maintenance of absolute territorial protection, various restrictions relating to the operation of selective distribution systems, and restrictions on the ability of a supplier of components to a manufacturer that would limit the ability of the supplier to make those components available as spare parts. These hard-core restraints largely coincide with those contained in the relevant block exemptions (analysed in Chapter 10).

The fact that an agreement or conduct falls above the thresholds set out in the notice does not mean that such agreements necessarily appreciably restrict competition. It is noted in para. 2 of the notice that such agreements 'may still have only a negligible effect on competition and may therefore not be prohibited by Article [101](1)'. However, such agreements would not benefit from the shortcut to safety provided by the *de minimis* notice.

9.7 Article 101 and the rule of reason

Similarities between the approach of arts 101 and 102 TFEU, and that of the Sherman Act, ss. 1 and 2, have encouraged speculation as to the place of doctrines developed in the US context in Union law. There has been much discussion as to the place of the 'rule of reason' in the EU. Section 1 of the Sherman Act is, in part, in the following terms:

Every contract, combination in the form of trust or otherwise, or conspiracy, in restraint of trade or commerce among the several States, or with foreign nations, is declared to be illegal. Every person who shall make any contract or engage in any combination or conspiracy hereby declared to be illegal shall be deemed guilty of a felony.

As was noted in Chapter 1, on its face this provision would condemn a wide range of competitive activity, much of it beneficial. US courts responded to this legislative straitjacket by developing an approach, itself based on the common law, in which the question is asked whether the restraint under attack 'is one that promotes competition or one that suppresses competition' (*National Society of Professional Engineers* v *United States* 435 US 679 (1978), at 691). The test was first introduced in *Standard Oil Co. of New Jersey* v *United States* 221 US 1 (1911), and was given some shape in 1918. Thus the

true test of legality is whether the restraint imposed is such as merely regulates and perhaps thereby promotes competition or whether it is such as may suppress or even destroy competition. To determine that question the court must ordinarily consider the facts peculiar to the business to which the restraint is applied; its condition before and after the restraint was imposed; the nature of the restraint and its effect, actual or probable. The history of the restraint, the evil believed to exist, the reason for adopting the particular remedy, the purpose or end sought to be attained, are all relevant facts.   (*per* Brandeis J in *Chicago Board of Trade* v *United States* 246 US 231 at 238 (1918))

Under the rule of reason a plaintiff must generally show first that the practice in question is likely to damage competition. It is then for the defendant to establish that there are clear benefits that flow from the restraint, and that it is necessary for those benefits to be achieved. *Inter alia* vertical restraints fall to be considered under the rule of reason and it is unlikely that they will be condemned except in situations where inter-brand competition is very weak (see, e.g., *Tunis Bros Co.* v *Ford Motor Co.* 952 F.2d 715 (1991)).

In the case of *Métropole* the GC expressly ruled that there was no rule of reason applied in relation to art. 101 (*Métropole Television (M6) and others* v *Commission* case T–112/99, 18 September 2001). Here the applicants relied in part upon earlier judgments, including *European Night Services*, to establish the existence of a 'rule of reason'. The approach of the court was to say that those judgments could not

> be interpreted as establishing the existence of a rule of reason in [Union] competition law. They are, rather, part of a broader trend in the case-law according to which it is not necessary to hold, wholly abstractly and without drawing any distinction, that any agreement restricting the freedom of one or more of the parties is necessarily caught by the prohibition laid down in [art. 101(1)] of the Treaty.   (para. 76)

The approach of the court is somewhat disingenuous. Earlier on in the judgment the GC was even more emphatic holding that 'contrary to the applicants' assertions the existence of such a rule has not, as such, been confirmed by the [Union] courts' (para. 72). At para. 74, the GC notes that it is only in the framework of art. 101(3) that 'the pro and anti-competitive competition aspects of a restriction may be weighed'. As seen above in relation to the application of art. 101(1) there are a number of cases in which there clearly are restrictions on the parties within the ordinary understanding of the term, but where the Commission and the courts have held that there is not a restriction for the purposes of art. 101(1). The language of *Métropole* appears to be applicable *only* to those circumstances in which a restriction already exists, and in that case the GC was stating only the obvious. It is also possible to read the judgment as supporting the proposition that art. 101(1) encompasses only economic efficiency based analysis, and that any other considerations are to be dealt with via the application of art. 101(3). Even the UK CAT has had 'some difficulty in reconciling the approach of the [Court of Justice] . . . with that of the [GC] in *Métropole*' (*The Racecourse Association and others* v *The Office of Fair Trading* [2005] CAT 29, 2 August 2005, at para. 167). The fact remains that there appear to be tensions in the approach.

The interrelationship between art. 101(1) and (3) was considered again by the GC in the case of *O₂ (Germany) GmbH & Co. OHG* v *Commission* (case T–328/03 [2006] 5 CMLR 5), in the context of an appeal against a Commission decision relating to an agreement between O_2 and another mobile communications operator which provided for the sharing of infrastructure and 'roaming' of services (*T-Mobile Deutschland/ O₂ Germany* 2004/207, (2004) OJ L75/32). In 2001 the parties had applied for either negative clearance or for an exemption under art. 101(3). Although the Commission had found that the roaming provisions infringed art. 101(1) an exemption was granted under art. 101(3) for a limited period of time. The GC held that the obligation of the Commission (and hence of anyone carrying out analysis under art. 101(1)) was to consider the impact of the agreement on existing and potential competition. In this case the Court pointed to the importance of considering what the position would be *in the absence of* an agreement in the case of markets subject to liberalization or which were rapidly developing or emerging (paras 71–2). The Commission had made several unsupported assumptions about the ease with which O_2 could enter the 3G market, and had not fully explained why roaming restricted competition. The applicant was successful in persuading the GC to partially annul the decision (see also Robertson, B., 'What is a Restriction of Competition? The Implications of the CFI's Judgment in O_2 Germany and the Rule of Reason', (2007) *ECLR* 252). This case bears several strong similarities to *European Night Services* (see 9.3). Note too the treatment of similar issues in *GlaxoSmithKline Services Unlimited* v *Commission* case T–168/01 [2006] 5 CMLR 29 and *GlaxoSmithKline Services Unlimited* v *Commission* case C–501/06 and others [2010] 4 CMLR 2 discussed at 9.3.1.4).

While many have been unable to resist the temptation of comparing the operation of the rule of reason with the process under art. 101, the argument is a complex one and of doubtful value. The availability of art. 101(3) has meant that major problems have not been created for undertakings when their arrangements fall within the scope of art. 101(1). The analysis followed under art. 101(3) is akin to, but not the same as, that carried out in applying the rule of reason. Arguments based on an application of the rule of reason in relation to art. 101 tend to be designed to remove from the scope of the article altogether many of the agreements considered to fall under art. 101(3), and would thus deprive the operation of art. 101 of much of its current flexibility. In its *Modernisation White Paper* the Commission accepted that it was, in effect, advocating an approach similar to the rule of reason, and noted that it had

already adopted this approach to a limited extent and has carried out an assessment of the pro- and anti-competitive aspects of some restrictive practices under art. [101(1)] ... However, the structure of [art. 101] is such as to prevent greater use being made of this approach.   (para. 57)

Summary map

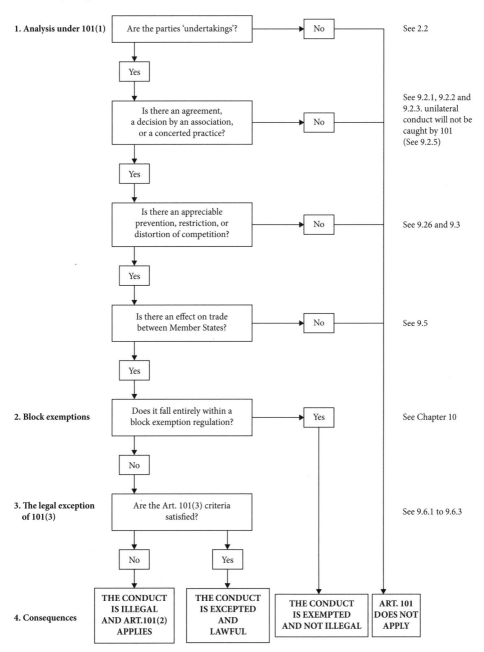

FURTHER READING

Books

FAULL, J., and NIKPAY, A. (eds), *The EC Law of Competition* (2007) 2nd edn, OUP, Oxford, Chapter 2

KONKURRENSVERKET, *Fighting Cartels— Why and How?* (2001) Swedish Competition Authority, Stockholm

STROUX, S., *US and EC Oligopoly Control* (2004) Kluwer Law International, The Hague, Chapters 4 and 7

Articles

BAILEY, 'Scope of Judicial Review under Article 81 EC', (2004) 41 *Common Market Law Review* 1327

BISCOLLO, E. F., 'Trade Associations and Information Exchange under US and EC Competition Law', (2000) 23(1) *World Competition* 29

BLACK, O., 'Concerted Practices, Joint Action and Reliance', (2003) *European Competition Law Review* 219

CAPOBIANCO, A., 'Information Exchange under EC Competition Law', (2004) 41 *Common Market Law Review* 1247

HARDING, C., 'Capturing the Cartel's Friends: Cartel Facilitation and the Idea of Joint Criminal Enterprise', (2009) 34 *European Law Review* 298

KALLAUGHER, J., AND WEITBRECHT, A., 'Developments under the Treaty on the Functioning of the European Union, Articles 101 and 102, in 2008/2009',

(2010) 31 *European Competition Law Review* 307

KORAH, V., and SUFRIN, B., 'Oligopolistic Markets and EC Competition Law', (1992) *Yearbook of European Law* 59

MEYRING, B., 'T-Mobile: Further Confusion on Information Exchanges between Competitors', (2010) 1 *Journal of European Competition Law and Practice* 30-32

MONTI, G., 'Article 81 and Public Policy', (2002) *Common Market Law Review* 1057

NAZZINI, R., 'Article 81 EC Between Time Present and Time Past: A Normative Critique of "Restriction of Competition" in EU Law', (2006) 43 *Common Market Law Review* 497

ODUDU, O., 'Interpreting Article 81(1): Demonstrating Restrictive Effect', (2001) 26 *European Law Review* 261

ODUDU, O., 'The Meaning of Undertaking within Art 81 EC', (2004–05) 7 *Cambridge Yearbook of European Legal Studies* 211

SUFRIN, B., 'The Evolution of Article 81(3) of the EC Treaty', (2006) 51 *Antitrust Bulletin* 915

VAN GERVEN, G., and NAVARRO VARONA, E., 'The *Wood Pulp* Case and the Future of Concerted Practices', (1994) *Common Market Law Review* 575

VEROUDEN, V., 'Vertical Agreements and Article 81(1) EC: The Evolving Role of Economic Analysis', (2003) 71 *Antitrust Law Journal* 525

10

Block exemption regulations under article 101 TFEU

KEY POINTS

- Block exemption regulations automatically bring certain categories of conduct within the terms of art. 101(3) TFEU, preventing the need to conduct case-by-case analysis of the most prevalent commercial agreements.

- In all block exemptions, market share thresholds are set out which, if exceeded, will preclude the application of the regulation.

- The presence of specified 'blacklist' clauses will exclude the application of the regulation; other 'grey list' clauses may individually fall outside the regulation, but will not remove the entire agreement from its scope.

- Any clause or agreement not falling within a block exemption regulation may still be assessed within the terms of art. 101(3) on an individual basis.

- In practice many firms will take the block exemption regulations as a starting point for their relevant commercial contracts.

10.1 Introduction

Block exemption regulations have become crucial in the application of the exception contained in Article 101(3) TFEU to agreements whose pro-competitive effects may outweigh any potential threats to competition. They were originally introduced with the aim of alleviating an overburdened Commission when it alone had the power of granting exemptions. When an agreement is tailored to meet the conditions of a block exemption, legality is automatic and no further examination is required to establish that it satisfies the conditions of art. 101(3).

The following are the main block exemptions as of September 2010:

- Regulation (EU) 330/2010 on the application of art. 101(3) of the Treaty to categories of vertical agreements and concerted practices (2010) OJ L102/1;

- Regulation (EU) 1218/2010 on the application of art. 101(3) of the Treaty to categories of specialization agreements (2011) OJ L335/43;

- Regulation (EU) 1217/2010 on the application of art. 101(3) of the Treaty to categories of research and development agreements (2011) OJ L335/36;
- Regulation (EU) 461/2010 on the application of art. 101(3) of the Treaty to categories of vertical agreements and concerted practices in the motor vehicle sector (2010) OJ L129/52;
- Regulation (EC) 772/2004 on the application of art. 81(3) of the Treaty to categories of technology transfer agreements (2004) OJ L123/11 (this is dealt with at 22.2.2).

The Commission has also published a number of guidelines and explanatory notes which further clarify the rules set out within the regulations. Of particular importance are the *Guidelines on Vertical Restraints* (2010) OJ C130/1, *Guidelines on the applicability of Article 101 to Horizontal Agreements* (2010) OJ C11/1, *Guidelines on the application of Article 81 of the EC Treaty to technology transfer agreements* (2004) OJ C101/2, and the *Supplementary Guidelines on Vertical Restraints in Agreements for the Sale and Repair of Motor Vehicles and for the Distribution of Spare Parts for Motor Vehicles* (2010) OJ C138/16. All these documents are available on the DG Comp website **http://ec.europa.eu/competition/antitrust/legislation/legislation.html**).

The current block exemptions are in part an attempt to reflect economic considerations and the needs of business. They are therefore less prescriptive than earlier versions, and tend to set a benchmark share of the relevant market within which they are applicable. This chapter fleshes out the details of the principal block exemptions currently in force, and provides a step-by-step guide to their application in the shape of a general flow chart (see summary map at the end).

10.2 Common aspects to all block exemptions: legal basis and withdrawal

Article 103 TFEU provides that the secondary legislation necessary to give effect to the principles set out in arts 101 and 102 'shall be laid down by the Council, on a proposal from the Commission and after consulting the European Parliament'. Such legislation may be designed, *inter alia*:

    (b) to lay down detailed rules for the application of Article 101(3), taking into account the need to ensure effective supervision on the one hand, and to simplify administration to the greatest possible extent on the other.

The authority for adopting block exemptions stems from this provision. They are made on the basis of the experience gained by the EU Commission in the application of art. 101(3), and are designed to clarify the enforcement of the provision in specific categories of agreements.

Two Council regulations establish the general framework within which block exemption regulations may be made. These are Regulation 19/65 ((1965) OJ 533) and

Regulation 2821/71 ((1971) OJ L285/46). The latter gave the Commission the authority to issue regulations relating to bilateral exclusive dealing arrangements, while the former provided an equivalent power applicable to categories of agreements relating to intellectual property. It was amended in 1999 by Regulation 1215/99 (1999) OJ L148/1, which was part of the follow-up to the *Green Paper on Vertical Restraints* discussed in the previous chapter. Recital (9) of Regulation 1215/99 made clear the thrust of the changes that were to be effected, stating that 'the Commission should be empowered to replace the existing legislation with legislation which is simpler, more flexible and better targeted, and which may cover all types of vertical agreements'.

Importantly, in relation to the balance of power between the Member States and the Commission, a new para. 7(2) was added to Regulation 19/65, which gives the Member States the power to withdraw the benefit of a block exemption regulation in cases where an agreement falling within its terms has 'certain effects which are incompatible with the conditions laid down in art. [101](3)…in the territory of a Member State, or in part thereof, which has all the characteristics of a distinct market'. The block exemptions considered in this chapter are those that were enacted under these instruments. Further authorization has been given in specific areas, such as transport and insurance.

Provision is further made in art. 29 of Regulation 1/2003 (Chapter IX) for the withdrawal of the benefit of a block exemption in individual cases. Article 29(2) is in similar terms to art. 7(2) of Regulation 19/65, but art. 29(1) additionally provides that the Commission may,

acting on its own initiative or on a complaint, withdraw the benefit of such an exemption Regulation when it finds that in any particular case an agreement, decision or concerted practice to which the exemption Regulation applies has certain effects which are incompatible with art. [101](3) of the Treaty.

10.3 Block exemptions for vertical agreements

10.3.1 Regulation 330/2010: the umbrella block exemption

The case *Établissements Consten Sarl and Grundig-Verkaufs-GmbH* v *Commission* cases 56, 58/64 [1966] CMLR 418 confirmed that art. 101 could be applicable to vertical agreements, including those designed to facilitate the marketing and distribution of goods. As was discussed in Chapter 8, the approach taken by the vast majority of economists to vertical agreements is that, in the absence of significant market power, they are likely to be more beneficial than harmful, and allow producers to offer incentives to retailers to invest in the distribution and promotion of their goods or services.

In practice, most such agreements would have benefited from an individual exemption under art. 101(3) under the pre-modernization system, and would now benefit from the legal exception (see Chapter 9). However, when notifications were required, and when the Commission had exclusive competence in this area, the burden falling on the institution nearly led to the collapse of the system. The amount of notifications was particularly the high in the early days, and therefore the first ever block exemption was adopted already in 1967. Since then, many reforms have taken place. The present block exemption applicable to general vertical agreements, Regulation 330/2010, introduced some relatively minor changes to its predecessor, Regulation 2790/99—the first 'new-style' block exemption. The latter replaced a number of specific block exemptions for different kinds of vertical agreements (exclusive distribution, exclusive purchasing and franchising), placing them under a single 'umbrella' block exemption.

10.3.1.1 General aspects

Regulation 330/2010 should be read alongside the Commission Notice, *Guidelines on Vertical Restraints*, published in May 2010. Recital (3) of the regulation identifies a range of vertical agreements which can normally be regarded as satisfying the conditions laid down in art. 101(3). This category

includes vertical agreements for the purchase or sale of goods or services where those agreements are concluded between non-competing undertakings, between certain competitors or by certain associations of retailers of goods. It also includes vertical agreements containing ancillary provisions on the assignment or use of intellectual property rights.

It comprises not only standard distribution agreements, but also franchising agreements, and the *Guidelines*, at paras 43–6, deal with the assignment of know-how that is central to franchising.

The recitals to the regulation iterate the arguments made in favour of such agreements in the case law and previous decisions. It is recognized that

(6) Certain types of vertical agreements can improve economic efficiency within a chain of production or distribution by facilitating better coordination between the participating undertakings. In particular, they can lead to a reduction in the transaction and distribution costs of the parties and to an optimisation of their sales and investment levels.

(7) The likelihood that such efficiency-enhancing effects will outweigh any anti-competitive effects due to restrictions contained in vertical agreements depends on the degree of market power of the parties...

This focus on market power was already introduced by Regulation 2790/99, and is precisely what marked the most significant difference between the operation of the 'new-style' regulations and their predecessors. Where the earlier regulations set out detailed lists of acceptable, 'white' clauses, and unacceptable, 'black' clauses, the current regulation provides that, with some limited exceptions, all vertical restraints are acceptable unless they are coupled to significant market power. Recognizing that there may still be some situations in which the effect of agreements may be harmful, and in particular those in which there are parallel networks of vertical agreements which have a foreclosure effect, there is mention in some of the recitals of the power of the Commission and the Member States to withdraw the benefit of the exemption based on art. 29 of Regulation 1/2003.

Article 1 of the regulation defines basic terms relevant to its application. The core provision is that of art. 2(1), which provides that:

Pursuant to Article 101(3) of the Treaty and subject to the provisions of this Regulation, it is hereby declared that Article 101(1) of the Treaty shall not apply to vertical agreements.

It then goes on to clarify that the exemption is only applicable to those agreements that contain vertical restraints, as those which do not will naturally not be caught by art. 101(1). Subsequently, the remainder of art. 2 further defines the scope of the exemption. Article 2(2) states that it applies also to agreements between associations of undertakings and their members as long as all members are retailers of goods, and if no individual member has a turnover in excess of €50 million (without prejudice of the possible application of art. 101(1) to horizontal agreements between members of the association). Article 2(3) includes provisions relating to vertical agreements that, having as their main object the purchase or distribution of goods or services, also contain an assignment of intellectual property rights. The conditions for exemption are set out in the *Guidelines* (para. 31). The main purpose for exempting these is to ensure that the benefit of the regulation applies to 'vertical agreements where the use, sale or resale of goods or services can be performed more effectively because IPRs are assigned to or licensed for use by the buyer' (*Guidelines*, para. 32).

Following art. 2(4), agreements between competitors will not normally benefit from the exemption. However, under the limited circumstances laid down in this provision, non-reciprocal vertical agreements between competing undertakings may be exempted. Non-reciprocal vertical agreements are those in which 'while one manufacturer becomes the distributor of the products of another manufacturer, the latter does not become the distributor of the products of the first manufacturer' (Dhabba, M., *EC and UK Competition Law: Text, Cases and Materials* (2004) CUP, Cambridge, p. 145).

10.3.1.2 Market share thresholds and hard-core restrictions

The limiting principle is set out in art. 3, para. 1, which provides that

The exemption provided for in Article 2 shall apply on condition that the market share held by the supplier does not exceed 30 % of the relevant market on which it sells the contract goods or services and the market share held by the buyer does not exceed 30 % of the relevant market on which it purchases the contract goods or services.

A novelty of Regulation 330/2010 is that the market share threshold applies in relation to both the supplier and the buyer. This, according to the Commission, is its response to the increasing power of dealers.

Article 7 relates to the issue of the calculation and assessment of market share. Although this economic analysis resolves many of the problems that flowed from the overly formalistic approach adopted under the earlier block exemptions, it does not provide a solution to every problem that is always simple. To some extent it has replaced formalistic legal analysis with sophisticated economic analysis, and although for a great many small and medium-sized undertakings this does not present any problem, there is a class of firms for which there may be genuine doubt whether they are operating at the 30 per cent threshold. Recital 7 refers to the by now standard definition of goods or services 'regarded...as interchangeable or substitutable by the buyer, by reason of the products' characteristics, their prices and their intended use'. In order to calculate the market shares, art. 7 of the regulation provides an analytical framework. Market shares are to be calculated on the previous year's data where these are available, and they may, for a two-year period, exceed 30 per cent as long as they do not rise above 35 per cent. If they are initially below 30 per cent, but then rise to above 35 per cent, the period of grace shall be limited to one year.

The threshold is not, however, the only limitation to the scope of the block exemption. Agreements as a whole will not be covered by the exemption in situations in which, either by themselves or in combination with other factors, they have one of a number of objectives. The blacklist of hard-core restrictions of art. 4 includes:

(a) setting fixed or minimum sale prices (maximum prices and price recommendations may be acceptable in some circumstances);
(b) setting territorial restrictions except in certain defined, limited circumstances;
(c) restricting cross-supplies in a selective distribution system;
(d) restrictions accepted by a buyer of components which prevent the supplier of those components from selling them as spare parts to end-users or repairers not approved of by the buyer.

EU competition law has maintained a strict antipathy towards minimum price setting in vertical agreements. This position is followed in the UK in the application of the CA 98. Until very recently the position in the US was also that minimum price setting was a *per se* offence under s. 1 of the Sherman Act. However, in 2007 the Supreme Court ruled that minimum price setting arrangements would in future be analysed under the rule of reason, holding that such agreements might benefit competition, and could 'give consumers more options to choose among low-price, low-service brands; high-price, high-service brands; and brands falling in between' (*Leegin Creative Leather Products, Inc. v PSKS, Inc.*, 127 S. Ct. 2705 (2007), *per* Justice Kennedy).

The maintenance of the blacklist of the new block exemption reflects that the EU regime is still far from adopting the increasingly tolerant US stance. Nonetheless, the new Guidelines on Vertical Restraints have introduced some flexibility in the interpretation of these hard-core restrictions, somehow taking them out of the *per se* illegality box. In Section 4, there are some examples of situations in which hard-core restrictions may be necessary. The list is not exhaustive. Some relevant examples are allowing vertical price-fixing for short promotions in 'a franchise system or similar distribution system applying a uniform distribution format or a coordinated short term low price campaign' (para. 225), or enabling restrictions of passive sales outside the allotted territory for up to two years to allow distributors of new products to recover their investments (paras 60–2). This may bring about a drastic change in the treatment of minimum resale price maintenance and absolute territorial protection.

The approach to territorial restrictions follows that long established by the Commission, in that the protection of exclusively assigned territories must permit passive sales, although active sales may be prevented. The *Guidelines* provide wider clarification of 'active' and 'passive' sales, and also refer to the implications of marketing over the Internet. The definitions of para. 51, in full, are as follows:

- "Active" sales mean actively approaching individual customers by for instance direct mail, including the sending of unsolicited e-mails, or visits; or actively approaching a specific customer group or customers in a specific territory through advertisement in media, on the internet or other promotions specifically targeted at that customer group or targeted at customers in that territory. Advertisement or promotion that is only attractive for the buyer if it (also) reaches a specific group of customers or customers in a specific territory, is considered active selling to that customer group or customers in that territory.
- "Passive" sales mean responding to unsolicited requests from individual customers including delivery of goods or services to such customers. General advertising or promotion that reaches customers in other distributors' (exclusive) territories or customer groups but which is a reasonable way to reach customers outside those territories or customer groups, for instance to reach customers in one's own territory, are considered passive selling. General advertising or promotion is considered a reasonable way to reach such customers if it would be attractive for the buyer to undertake these investments also if they would not reach customers in other distributors' (exclusive) territories or customer groups.

The question of Internet sales is an important one. It is generally recognized that the development of e-commerce threatens to radically change concepts of 'exclusivity' and assigned territories. At para. 52, the Commission deals with the issue at some length, taking as the starting point the basic principle that '[e]very distributor must be free to use the internet to sell products'.

In the Guidelines, the situation where a customer contacts a distributor through the distributor's website and places an order is considered to be one of passive selling. Further, the language used on the website will be irrelevant. There follows a list of hard-core restrictions of passive selling which will prevent agreements from benefiting from the exemption. The position here is likely to have been influenced by the experience gained in the US, where the issue of Internet selling has already led to some difficulties. It was reported in 1998, for example, that Tupperware had prohibited its more than 7,000 'sales consultants' from selling its products through the consultants' own websites. Tupperware had argued that the product needed live demonstrations in order to be most effectively sold.

Article 5 provides that certain obligations within an agreement will not be covered, although the actual agreement will still benefit from the exemption to the extent to which they can be separated out from the agreement as a whole. The first two of these relate to non-compete obligations, while the third relates to any provision under which members of a selective distribution system are prevented from selling competing brands.

As of September 2010, there are no cases yet on the application of Regulation 330/2010. The application of its predecessor, Regulation 2790/99, was considered in Commission decision *JCB* 2002/190 (2002) OJ L69/1. Following a notification some 27 years earlier, a distribution agreement between the JCB Group and various appointed distributors in respect of construction and earth-moving equipment and spare parts was condemned. In 1996 a complaint was lodged by a French undertaking alleging that JCB had taken active steps to prevent it sourcing supplies from the UK, where they were cheaper than in France. The Commission found, *inter alia*, that Regulation 2790/99 was not applicable to the agreements in question, as the market share of JCB for backhoe loaders was 40 per cent by value and 45 per cent by volume. Even if a wider market definition were adopted, bringing the market share within the 30 per cent threshold, the agreements incorporated hard-core restrictions. On appeal (*JCB Service* v *Commission* case T–67/01 [2004] 4 CMLR 24) the GC substantially upheld the decision in so far as it related to territorial restrictions, although it did find that the Commission had failed to establish adequately some of the other alleged breaches and reduced the fine. The Court of Justice however subsequently declared that the GC had erred, and increased the fine again (*JCB Service* v *Commission* case T–67/01 case C–167/04 [2006] 5 CMLR 23).

10.3.2 Motor vehicle sector agreements—Regulation 461/2010

Back in 2002, Regulation 461/2010, replaced the heavily criticized Regulation 1475/95 on the application of art. [101(3)] of the Treaty to certain categories of motor vehicle distribution and servicing agreements (1995) OJ L145/25. The very broad approach underpinning the regulation was that stricter rules than those set out in the general block exemption for vertical agreements are necessary in the case of vertical agreements in the motor sector, and there was too a recognition of the fact that 'motor vehicles are expensive and technically complex mobile goods which require repair and maintenance at regular and irregular intervals' (recital (21)). In its explanatory brochure the Commission cited research showing that the cost of purchasing a car and the cost of maintaining it both account for about 40 per cent each of the full cost of ownership (para. 3.2).

Regulation 1400/2002 was due to expire on 31 May 2010. In the run-up to the reform, the Commission acknowledged that the specific rules were at times 'clearly overly complicated and restrictive and have had the indirect effect of driving up distribution costs' (Press Release 27 May 2010, IP/10/619). It also noted that the primary car market for the sale of new vehicles did not present problems that needed to be tackled in specific legislation. As a consequence, the new block exemption, Regulation 461/2010, establishes that agreements in this sector will be governed by Regulation 330/2010 from 1 June 2013. Until then, the provisions of Regulation 1400/2002 that refer to this market will remain in force. Some problems do persist in the car aftermarket (repair and maintenance, spare parts). To address these issues, Regulation 461/2010 includes a new list of specific hard-core restrictions, which entered into force on 1 June 2010. They aim primarily at affording additional protection to independent repairers and spare parts suppliers vis-à-vis manufacturers.

A full analysis of the specific rules for the car sector is beyond the scope of this text. Those seeking further details on the reform may read Marco Colino, S., 'Recent Changes in the Regulation of Motor Vehicle Distribution in Europe—Questioning the Logic of Sector-Specific Rules for the Car Industry', (2010) 6 *Competition Law Review* 203. A critical analysis of Regulation 1400/2002 written by members of an automotive sector group may also be found at [2003] ECLR 254 (Automotive Sector Groups of Houthoff Buruma and Liedekerke Wolters Waelbroeck Kirkpartick, 'Flawed Reform of the Competition Rules for the European Motor Vehicle Distribution Sector').

10.3.3 Technology transfer agreements—Regulation 772/2004

The application of Regulation 772/2004 is discussed at 22.2.2.

10.4 The horizontal block exemptions

Not all cooperation between undertakings that are competitors, or potential competitors, is necessarily bad, and two special cases are dealt with by way of block exemption regulations.

10.4.1 Research and development

There is a general commitment on the part of the EU to the fostering of research and development (R&D) which is emphasized in the Treaty itself. Article 179, introduced by the Single European Act, is, in part, in the following terms:

1. The Union shall have the objective of strengthening the scientific and technological bases by achieving a European research area in which researchers, scientific knowledge and technology circulate freely, and encouraging it to become more competitive, including its industry, while promoting all the research activities deemed necessary by virtue of other chapters of the Treaties.

2. For this purpose the Union shall, throughout the Union, encourage undertakings, including small and medium-sized undertakings, research centres and universities in their research and technological development activities of high quality; it shall support their efforts to cooperate with one another, aiming, notably, at permitting researchers to cooperate freely across borders and at enabling undertakings to exploit the internal market potential to the full, in particular through the opening up of national public contracts, the definition of common standards and the removal of legal and fiscal obstacles to that cooperation.

Generally, they are among the small class of horizontal agreements that are actively encouraged by the competition authorities. The Commission has made it clear that in many cases it does not consider that they are in any way restrictive of competition, and are not therefore caught by art. 101(1). In its *14th Annual Report on Competition Policy* (1984) it recognized the importance of R&D to the development of the economy:

Competition...relies increasingly on innovation...The introduction of new processes and products on the market stimulates competition within the [internal] market, and helps to strengthen the ability of European industry to compete internationally...R&D plays an essential role. In fact R&D promotes and maintains dynamic competition, characterised by initiation and imitation and in doing so assures economic growth.

...in many cases the synergy arising out of a cooperation is necessary because it enables the partners to share the financial risks involved and in particular to bring together a wider range of intellectual and mental resources and experience, thus promoting the transfer of technology. In the absence of such cooperation, the innovation may not take place at all, or otherwise not as successfully or efficiently. Also the present situation in the [Union] demands more rapid and effective transformation of new ideas into marketable products and processes, which may be facilitated by joint efforts by several undertakings.

The Commission has always shown a favourable attitude towards R&D cooperation provided that competition is maintained by the existence of different independent poles of research.

While statements such as these demonstrate a flexible attitude, it is a general requirement, consistent with the wording of art. 101(3), that such agreements should not contain restrictions which go beyond those necessary to undertake the project successfully and to exploit its fruits. Particular attention will be paid to terms which limit the conduct of the participants after the conclusion of the project. Greater concerns will be raised in markets which are highly concentrated.

10.4.1.1 General scope of Regulation 1217/2010

The above factors have informed the current block exemption, in which R&D is defined as

the acquisition of know-how relating to products, technologies or processes and the carrying out of theoretical analysis, systematic study or experimentation, including experimental production, technical testing of products or processes, the establishment of the necessary facilities and the obtaining of intellectual property rights for the results.   (art. 1(1)(c))

The regulation exempts from the application of art. 101(1) all R&D agreements under which undertakings pursue a wide range of activities including joint research and development with or without joint exploitation of the results and, as a novelty, joint 'paid-for research' agreements, in which one of the parties pays for the R&D carried out by another party. With regard to the latter, the parties are also free to decide whether they will exploit the results jointly or separately.

Ancillary restrictions which are not directly about R&D but the presence of which is a necessary component of the agreement may also be covered by the operation of the regulation. Article 3(2) to (5) sets out the conditions for the granting of an exemption:

(2)   The research and development agreement must stipulate that all the parties have full access to the final results of the joint research and development or paid-for research and development, including any resulting intellectual property rights and know-how, for the purposes of further research and development and exploitation, as soon as they become available. Where the parties limit their rights of exploitation in accordance with this Regulation, in particular where they specialise in the context of exploitation, access to the results for the purposes of exploitation may be limited accordingly. Moreover, research institutes, academic bodies, or undertakings which supply research and development as a commercial service without normally being active in the exploitation of results may agree to confine their use of the results for the purposes of further research. The research and development agreement may foresee that the parties compensate each other for giving access to the results for the purposes of further research or exploitation, but the compensation must not be so high as to effectively impede such access.

(3)   Without prejudice to paragraph 2, where the research and development agreement provides only for joint research and development or paid-for research and development, the research and development agreement must stipulate that each party must be granted access to any pre-existing know-how of the other parties,

if this know-how is indispensable for the purposes of its exploitation of the results. The research and development agreement may foresee that the parties compensate each other for giving access to their pre-existing know-how, but the compensation must not be so high as to effectively impede such access.

(4)   Any joint exploitation may only pertain to results which are protected by intellectual property rights or constitute know-how and which are indispensable for the manufacture of the contract products or the application of the contract technologies.

(5)   Parties charged with the manufacture of the contract products by way of specialisation in the context of exploitation must be required to fulfil orders for supplies of the contract products from the other parties, except where the research and development agreement also provides for joint distribution within the meaning of point (m)(i) or (ii) of Article 1(1) or where the parties have agreed that only the party manufacturing the contract products may distribute them.

The recitals set out the power of the Commission and the Member States to withdraw the benefit of the block exemption from individual agreements by virtue of art. 29 of Regulation 1/2003.

10.4.1.2 Market share thresholds and hard-core restrictions

Consistent with the new economics-based approach, art. 4 provides the market share test that is similar to that of Regulation 330/2010. The aim is to ensure that the exemption does not cover agreements which may give the 'undertakings the possibility of eliminating competition' (recital 13). Where the parties are not competing at the time of the agreement the exemption will last for the duration of the R&D. When the agreement provides for the joint exploitation of results the exemption will last for seven years from the date at which the contract products are first put on the market (art. 4(1)). At the end of this period the exemption will continue to apply for as long as the market share of the parties does not exceed 25 per cent (art. 4(3)). This balances the fact that it is likely to be the case that R&D agreements may lead to the development of a market in which the parties are the only players, and will have a 100 per cent market share, against the fact that without the joint R&D such a market might not exist at all. It is thus possible to have a seven-year exemption in respect of a very high market share where the parties do not start off as competitors. Where two or more of the parties are competing in the market for products which can be improved or replaced by the contract products, the exemption shall last for the same period as set out in art. 4(1), but only for as long as the parties do not have a combined market share of more than 25 per cent of the relevant market (art. 4(2)(a)). For 'paid-for research' agreements, the same threshold will apply to the combined 'market share of the financing party and all the parties with which [it] has entered into research and development agreements' for those contract products or technologies (art. 4(2)(b)). Provisions in art. 7 relating to the calculation of market shares are similar to those set out in Regulation 330/2010.

Article 5 of the regulation removes from its scope entire agreements that have one of seven objectives. These include: (a) the elimination of independent poles of research; (b) limiting output or sales; (c) price fixing; and (d)–(g) a number of territorial restrictions, having their origins in various practices. Some exceptions are considered with regard to these hard-core restrictions in the article itself.

10.4.2 **Specialization agreements—Regulation 1218/2010**

In the *Guidelines on the Applicability of Article 101 to Horizontal Cooperation Agreements* (2011) OJ C11/1 published at the same time as the horizontal block exemption regulations, specialization agreements are dealt with as part of the wider set of 'production agreements'. This recognizes the fact that there are a number of forms in which production agreements can manifest themselves, and that specialization agreements, in which the parties agree unilaterally or reciprocally to 'cease production of certain products or to refrain from producing those products and to purchase them from the other party' (*Guidelines*, para. 152), are merely one such form. The benefits of specialization agreements are referred to in recital (6) of the regulation, which recognizes that

Agreements on specialisation in production are most likely to contribute to improving the production or distribution of goods if the parties have complementary skills, assets or activities, because they can concentrate on the manufacture of certain products and thus operate more efficiently and supply the products more cheaply. The same can generally be said about agreements on specialisation in the preparation of services. Given effective competition, it is likely that consumers will receive a fair share of the resulting benefits.

10.4.2.1 Scope of the block exemption

The agreements covered by the block exemption are set out in arts 1(a) to (c), and include three main types:

- Unilateral specialization agreements: these involve, for instance, ceasing production of a good, and agreeing to buy it from a competitor. Unilateral specialization was not covered by the block exemptions until 2000, when former Regulation 2658/00 included it in its scope.
- Reciprocal specialization agreements: the parties may agree to either start producing different end products (for instance, one may concentrate on the production of electric wall and alarm clocks while the other produces only mechanical alarm clocks; see *Jaz-Peter* 78/194 (1978) OJ L61/17) or focus on manufacturing different components for the same final product (such as that between a producer of electric transmissions for buses and the manufacturer of the buses they are for—see Commission decision *ACEC/Berliet* [1968] OJ L201/7).
- Joint production agreements: these would include agreements in which the parties agree to jointly produce certain goods.

Ancillary IP provisions are also covered (art. 2(2)). Paragraph (3) of art. 2 further extends the exemption to related purchasing and marketing agreements, and to specialization agreements that include exclusive supply or exclusive purchasing obligations, as well as joint distribution.

10.4.2.2 Market share thresholds and agreements not covered by the block exemption

The market share limit set out in art. 3 is a combined market share of 20 per cent, a level lower than that set out in the R&D block exemption. This reflects the fact that the restrictions on competition in the case of specialization agreements can be more severe than that in R&D. Where the market shares are initially less than 20 per cent they may rise to a maximum of 25 per cent for two consecutive years, or may exceed 25 per cent for one year, without the benefit of the exemption being lost (art. 5(d) and (e)).

Article 4 sets out the categories of agreements which cannot benefit from the block exemption, which are those that: (a) fix prices; (b) limit output or sales; and (c) allocate markets or customers. However, to the extent that it is necessary to set prices or produce agreed amounts in the context of a production joint venture, this will be permitted as part of the integration of functions within the joint venture.

In situations in which the market shares set out in the Regulation are exceeded it is almost certain that the requirements of art. 101(1) will be met, and an individual analysis under art. 101(3) will be necessary. The Commission, however, is still inclined to take a favourable view of such agreements (see, e.g., *Bayer/Gist-Brocades* 76/172 (1976) OJ L30/13, and *Jaz-Peter* 78/194 (1978) OJ L61/17).

Summary map

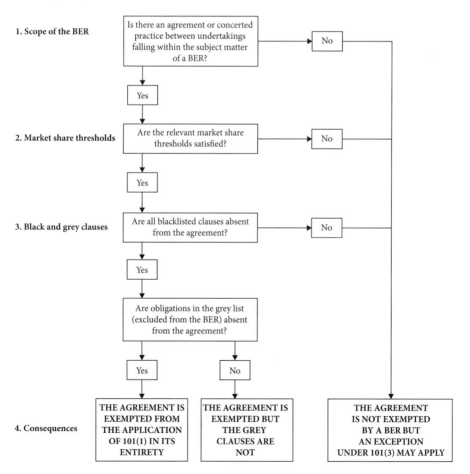

1. Scope of the BER	Is there an agreement or concerted practice between undertakings falling within the subject matter of a BER? → No
	Yes
2. Market share thresholds	Are the relevant market share thresholds satisfied? → No
	Yes
3. Black and grey clauses	Are all blacklisted clauses absent from the agreement? → No
	Yes
	Are obligations in the grey list (excluded from the BER) absent from the agreement?
	Yes No
4. Consequences	THE AGREEMENT IS EXEMPTED FROM THE APPLICATION OF 101(1) IN ITS ENTIRETY	THE AGREEMENT IS EXEMPTED BUT THE GREY CLAUSES ARE NOT	THE AGREEMENT IS NOT EXEMPTED BY A BER BUT AN EXCEPTION UNDER 101(3) MAY APPLY

FURTHER READING

Books

FAULL, J., and NIKPAY, A. (eds), *The EC Law of Competition* (2006) 2nd edn, OUP, Oxford, Chapters 6 and 7

MARCO COLINO, S., *Vertical Agreements and Competition Law: A Comparative Study of the EU and US Regimes* (2010) Hart, Oxford

Articles

MARCO COLINO, S., 'Recent Changes in the Regulation of Motor Vehicle Distribution in Europe – Questioning the Logic of Sector-Specific Rules for the Car Industry', (2010) 6 *Competition Law Review* 203

VOGELAAR, F., 'Modernization of EC Competition Law, Economy and Horizontal Cooperation between Undertakings', (2002) 37 *Intereconomics* 19–27

WHISH, R., 'Regulation 2790/99: The Commission's "New Style" Block Exemption for Vertical Agreements', (2000) 37 *Common Market Law Review* 887

11

The Chapter I Prohibition

KEY POINTS

- The Chapter I Prohibition is the domestic equivalent of art. 101 TFEU.

- It is to be applied and interpreted in a way that is consistent with the application of art. 101 TFEU, unless there is a 'relevant difference'.

- There is no requirement for an effect on trade between Member States, and the prohibition has been applied to localized agreements.

- If art. 101 TFEU is applicable to any practice being examined under the Chapter I Prohibition, it must be applied. The Chapter I Prohibition may also be applied in conjunction with this, but the result must not be inconsistent.

- A breach of the Chapter I Prohibition may incur penalties, damages, and a requirement of conduct modification, and also renders void any offending agreement.

11.1 Introduction

Section 2 of the Competition Act 1998 (CA 98) puts into place a prohibition on anti-competitive agreements that is similar to that of art. 101 TFEU:

2.—(1) Subject to section 3, agreements between undertakings, decisions by associations of undertakings or concerted practices which—

    (a) may affect trade within the United Kingdom, and

    (b) have as their object or effect the prevention, restriction or distortion of competition within the United Kingdom,

are prohibited unless they are exempt in accordance with the provisions of this Part.

(2) Subsection (1) applies, in particular, to agreements, decisions or practices which—

    (a) directly or indirectly fix purchase or selling prices or any other trading conditions;

    (b) limit or control production, markets, technical development or investment;

    (c) share markets or sources of supply;

    (d) apply dissimilar conditions to equivalent transactions with other trading parties, thereby placing them at a competitive disadvantage;

    (e) make the conclusion of contracts subject to acceptance by the other parties of supplementary obligations which, by their nature or according to commercial usage, have no connection with the subject of such contracts.

(3) Subsection (1) applies only if the agreement, decision or practice is, or is intended to be, implemented in the United Kingdom.

(4) Any agreement or decision which is prohibited by subsection (1) is void.

(5) A provision of this Part, which is expressed to apply to, or in relation to, an agreement is to be read as applying equally to, or in relation to, a decision by an association of undertakings or a concerted practice (but with any necessary modifications).

(6) Subsection (5) does not apply where the context otherwise requires.

(7) In this section 'the United Kingdom' means, in relation to an agreement which operates or is intended to operate only in a part of the United Kingdom, that part.

(8) The prohibition imposed by subsection (1) is referred to in this Act as 'the Chapter I prohibition'.

Because of the overriding nature of s. 60 (see 3.5.1), requiring this provision to be interpreted consistently with EU law, it should be applied in much the same way as art. 101 TFEU. However, the extent to which single market issues have been determinant in some of the EU case law may lead to divergence and to some difficulty. The relevant guidelines in respect of the Chapter I Prohibition are *Article 81 and the Chapter I Prohibition*, *Vertical agreements*, *Assessment of conduct*, and *Trade associations, professions and self-regulating bodies*.

11.2 Exceptions and exemptions

Section 3 of the CA 98 sets out generalized exclusions which include mergers and concentrations—dealt with under the relevant provisions of the Enterprise Act 2002 (EA 02) (see Chapter 20)—and agreements examined under other Acts, which may include activities that are supervised directly by one of the industry regulators (Sch. 2). The Secretary of State has been given the power to modify these excluded classes, by either adding to or removing from the list. Further, the prohibition will apply only where an agreement has an appreciable effect on trade and competition. Section 6 makes provision for block exemption regulations, and s. 10 introduces 'parallel exemptions' which are relevant where a practice benefits from the legal exception of art. 101 (or would benefit were art. 101 applicable). The legal exception regime is the same as for the application of art. 101, with the criteria in s. 9 of the Act mirroring those of art. 101(3). In the UK legislation the term 'exemption' is still used.

    Under the 'old' regime, only a small number of agreements were notified to the OFT for consideration for either a negative clearance or exemption. For example, following consultation leading to some adaptation of the agreement a decision of negative clearance was made in respect of the standard conditions for licensing the commercial exhibition of films (*Film Distributors' Association Ltd* CA98/10/2002 [2002] UKCLR 243). Exemptions were granted to *Link Interchange Network Limited* CA98/7/2001 [2002] UKCLR 59, and in respect of the *Memorandum of Understanding on the Supply of Fuel Oils in an Emergency* CA98/8/2001 [2002] UKCLR 74.

In April 2004 the OFT found that a notified agreement relating to the sale of certain media rights held by racecourses in Great Britain infringed the Chapter I Prohibition, and was not capable of benefiting from an exemption in its entirety (*Notification by Arena Leisure plc/Attheraces Holdings Limited/British Sky Broadcasting Group plc/Channel Four Television Corporation/The Racecourse Association Limited* CA98/2/2004 [2004] UKCLR 995). In essence the agreement related to the collective sale by virtually all racecourses in Great Britain to broadcast races over the Internet for the purposes of facilitating betting in off-course betting shops. The OFT found that the collective sale was restrictive of competition, and that although the agreement did contribute to the production or distribution of goods and services, the restrictions were not indispensable to the achievement of this objective. On appeal the CAT disagreed with the OFT, and was robustly critical of its approach (*The Racecourse Association and others* v *OFT* [2005] CAT 29). It held that the approach taken to what would have happened had the rights been sold individually was not realistic, and concluded that such a process would not have been successful in leading to the development of the new service. At para. 202 of its judgment, the CAT referred to the 'imprecise and somewhat shifting hypothetical counterfactual situation which formed the basis of the OFT's case', and remitted the case for reconsideration.

11.2.1 Block exemptions

Block exemptions may be made to cover categories of agreements which fall within the terms of s. 9. Any such exemption must be proposed and published by the OFT (ss. 6 and 8), and may be made by the Secretary of State as an Order in Parliament. Only one block exemption had been created thus far—the Competition Act 1998 (Public Transport Ticketing Schemes Block Exemption) Order 2001, SI 2001/319, as amended by the Competition Act 1998 (Public Transport Ticketing Schemes Block Exemption) (Amendment) Order 2005, SI 2005/3347. A revised guideline relating to the application of this block exemption was published in November 2006 (OFT 439).

11.2.2 Parallel exemptions

In s. 10 it is provided that '[a]n agreement is exempt from the Chapter I prohibition if it is exempt from the Union prohibition', i.e., from art. 101(1). While in effect this merely recognizes the requirement imposed by Regulation 1/2003, art. 3(2), the provision in fact goes further than this. It applies not only to agreements which are excepted from art. 101(1), but also to those which would be, by virtue of the operation of a block exemption, where the agreement in question is not actually subject to EU law because it has no impact on trade between the Member States (s. 10(2)). One effect of this section then is to import wholesale into the UK domestic arena all Union block exemptions. The OFT is granted the power to cancel the benefit of the parallel exemption (s. 10(5)).

11.3 *De minimis* thresholds and appreciability

During the passage of the CA 98 the Government indicated that, subject to later consultation, classes of agreements would be exempt from the imposition of financial penalties, but not from any other adverse consequences of breach in accordance with s. 39 ('small agreements') where the turnover of the parties in question was between £20 million and £50 million (Hansard (HL) 17 November 1997, col. 434). The relevant thresholds are set out in the Competition Act 1998 (Small Agreements and Conduct of Minor Significance) Regulations 2000, SI 2000/262. These provide that small agreements (s. 39(1)) are those where the combined applicable turnover in the year preceding the infringement did not exceed £20 million (para. 3). The threshold in respect of s. 40(1) is £50 million (para. 4). This 'safe harbour' does not affect the application of art. 101 TFEU by the OFT.

The appreciability test is the same as for the EU—see 9.6.4.

11.4 Horizontal and vertical agreements

Section 2(2) of the CA 98 includes the list of examples of anti-competitive agreements which mirrors that of art. 101. As with art. 101 this 'is a non-exhaustive, illustrative list and does not set a limit on the investigation and enforcement activities of the OFT. The guideline *Article 81 and the Chapter I Prohibition* does not deal in detail with various types of unlawfully coordinated conduct. However, the EU guidelines on horizontal and vertical agreements discussed in Chapter 10 will be applied in the UK.

11.4.1 Horizontal agreements—infringement decisions

The first cartel to be penalized by the Director under the new regime demonstrated sharply the improvements that the CA 98 has made to the system of competition enforcement in the UK. While anti-competitive conduct in the bus industry had bedevilled the operation of the Competition Act 1980, in *Market Sharing by Arriva plc and FirstGroup plc* CA98/9/2002 [2002] UKCLR 322, the Director was able to deal decisively with this market. In the case in question the Director concluded that the two undertakings had breached the Chapter II Prohibition by entering into a market-sharing agreement in respect of bus routes within Leeds. The OFT investigation followed the receipt of an anonymous complaint which alleged that Arriva Yorkshire had entered into an agreement with First Leeds to swap bus routes.

The market affected was small, and the initial complaint referred only to two local routes.

On-site investigations were carried out in October 2000, and both companies benefited from the operation of the leniency scheme in relation to the operation of cartels (see Chapter 6). One of the board members of Arriva Yorkshire, Mr Peter Harvey, had arranged a meeting in a private room at a Yorkshire hotel where the participants were senior staff of both Arriva and FirstGroup. These meetings were not declared by the FirstGroup participants on a form linked to training in compliance procedures with the Competition Act, which asked the participants to note all contacts with competing companies. The Director found that the object of the agreement was 'clearly to share markets geographically by mutual withdrawal from the relevant bus routes' (para. 42). Penalties were imposed, although FirstGroup's was reduced to nil following the application of the leniency scheme.

One of the more unusual horizontal cases considered by the OFT related to an agreement between cattle auctioneers in Northern Ireland which fixed commission rates. This was announced to farmers by way of a press release sent to the *Irish News* and *Farmers Life*. The OFT condemned the arrangement, but did not issue a penalty given the dire straits in which the industry found itself at the time the arrangement was entered into, as a result of both the BSE and foot and mouth disease epidemics (CA98/1/2003 [2003] UKCLR 433).

Some of the actions examined below at 11.4.2.1, such as *Agreements between Hasbro UK Ltd, Argos Ltd and Littlewoods Ltd fixing the price of Hasbro toys and games* CA98/8/2003 [2004] UKCLR 717 contain an element of horizontal agreement alongside the more central vertical arrangement. This was also the case in *Price-fixing of replica football kit* CA98/06/2003 [2004] UKCLR 6. On appeal the CAT dealt at some length with defences raised by the parties, and there was a substantial discussion of the elements that needed to be in place for the finding of a concerted practice (*JJB Sports plc v OFT* [2004] CAT 17 [2005] CompAR 29—see further 7.3.1.2). *Inter alia*, the OFT had found that Umbro Holdings Ltd, the manufacturer of replica football kits, had entered into a number of arrangements with retailers relating to the prices at which the kits would be sold. One of the retailers, JJB Sports Ltd, argued that there was not the necessary communication between the parties to establish a concerted practice. Umbro could easily have inferred the price at which JJB would sell the kit in question as it was JJB's invariable policy to sell replica shirts at £39.99 during the launch period. However, the CAT noted that JJB's witnesses themselves accepted that the market was not a certain one, and that the standard price did not reflect in-store promotions or discounting campaigns which varied in some cases on a day-by-day basis.

The CAT held that an agreement could 'be constituted by an "understanding" even if there is nothing to prevent either party from going back on, or disregarding, the understanding in question' (para. 637). There then follows a very clear discussion of the meaning of 'concerted practice', drawing on the relevant EU case law (paras 638–43). For the CAT the evidence showed that 'JJB at the very least indicated to Umbro that it would not discount the England shirt below £39.99 immediately before and during Euro 2000, on the understanding, express or implied, that Sports Soccer and other retailers would not discount either' (para. 645). Both cases subsequently reached the Court of Appeal, which supported the CAT in its findings (*Argos Ltd and Littlewoods Ltd* v *OFT; JJB Sports plc* v *OFT* [2006] EWCA 1318, [2006] UKCLR 1135). In a long judgment the Court paid particular attention to the test set out in *Bayer AG* v *Commission* (see 9.3.1.3) for the existence of collusion:

> The proposition … can be stated in more restricted terms: if (i) retailer A discloses to supplier B its future pricing intentions in circumstances where A may be taken to intend that B will make use of that information to influence market conditions by passing that information to other retailers (of whom C is or may be one); (ii) B does, in fact, pass that information to C in circumstances where C may be taken to know the circumstances in which the information was disclosed by A to B; and (iii) C does, in fact, use the information in determining its own future pricing intentions, then A, B and C are all to be regarded as parties to a concerted practice … (at para. 141)

The findings of fact made by the CAT were such as to bring the case within this proposition, whichever of Argos or Littlewoods was cast in the role of retailer A.

UK competition enforcers have also examined a number of 'pure' horizontal agreements. Most prominent among these is a chain of cases relating to bid-rigging in the construction industry. Bid-rigging (which may be a criminal act—see 12.2.1.4) occurs when parties responding to tenders agree among themselves who will respond, or the prices at which bids will be entered. The first action in which this practice was condemned related to contracts for flat-roofing services in the West Midlands (*Collusive Tendering in Relation to Contracts for Flat-Roofing Services in the West Midlands* CA98/1/2004 [2004] UKCLR 1119). Nine companies were implicated in a cartel which involved price fixing. Most, but not all, of the contracts were public sector works, of which the most prominent category related to school roofs. The OFT brought forward a substantial amount of evidence, including faxes between the parties, among which were a number from one 'competitor' to another setting out the price at which the recipient of the fax was to bid for the contract in question. The decision was upheld on appeal (*Apex Asphalt and Paving Co Ltd* v *OFT* [2005] CAT 4 [2005] CompAR 507). Similar decisions were made in relation to bid-rigging in the north east of England (*Collusive Tendering for Felt and Single Ply Flat-roofing Contracts in the North East of England* CA98/02/2005 [2005] UKCLR 541) and in Scotland (*Collusive Tendering for Mastic Asphalt Flat-roofing Contracts in Scotland* CA98/01/2005 [2005] UKCLR 638). The OFT has also found that suppliers of a material used in the double-glazing industry were engaged in an illegal horizontal arrangement to fix prices (*Agreement between UOP Ltd, UKAE Ltd, Thermoseal Supplies Ltd, Double Quick Supplyline Ltd and Double Glazing Supplies Ltd to Fix and/or Maintain Prices for Desiccant* CA98/08/2004 [2005] UKCLR 227) ; and that an agreement to fix prices existed in the market for stock check pads used to take orders in restaurants (*Price fixing and market sharing in stock check pads* CA98/03/2006 [2007] UKCLR 211).

In September 2005 the OFT found that certain aspects of the MasterCard system breached the Chapter I Prohibition (*Investigation of the Multilateral Interchange Fees provided for in the UK Domestic Rules of MasterCard UK Members Forum Ltd*

CA98/05/05 [2006] UKCLR 236). The case was a complex one (the decision is in excess of 250 pages), but in essence concerned the fee arrangements operating within the system. It was argued that as the EU Commission had exempted similar arrangements operated by Visa (see 9.3) the OFT was obliged to take the same approach in the present case. The OFT found, however, that there were factual differences between the two systems, and that the MasterCard method could be characterized as a price-fixing agreement, which had as its object the restriction of competition. No penalties were imposed as the agreements had both been notified to the OFT, and modified by the time the final decision was made. Unfortunately the case did not end there. Appeals were lodged with the CAT, and when the OFT submitted its defence Visa (which had become involved in the case) claimed that there were substantial differences between the decision, and the defence submitted to the appeal. The OFT, in a surprising move, argued that the decision was 'indicative' rather than 'dispositive', and that parts of it were '*obiter dicta*'. The CAT pointed out in no uncertain terms the formal nature of an infringement decision, and the OFT was ordered to file within a fortnight a schedule containing, in summary form, paragraph by paragraph, what parts of the decision were being relied upon and what were not (*Mastercard UK Members Forum Ltd v OFT* [2006] CAT 10, [2006] CompAR 585). The OFT then indicated that approximately 250 paragraphs of the decision would be affected by the changes made in its defence, and reached the conclusion that it would withdraw the decision, an approach described by the CAT, rather kindly, as 'highly regrettable' (*Mastercard UK Members Forum Ltd v OFT* [2006] CAT 14, [2006] CompAR 595, para. 28). To clarify matters the Tribunal itself took the decision to set the original infringement decision aside.

By far the most controversial case to be decided by the OFT to date is that relating to the practice of a number of fee-paying schools to exchange information relating to their fee-setting through a mechanism known as the 'Sevenoaks Survey'. The decision, which was the result of a difficult settlement between the parties and the OFT, is insanely long, running to 548 pages in the version published in the UKCLR (*Exchange of information on future fees by certain independent fee-paying schools* CA98/05/2006 [2007] UKCLR 361—see also OFT press release 88/06, 'Independent Schools Agree Settlement, 19 May 2006). This case is dealt with further as Key case 11.1.

Key case 11.1 *Exchange of information on future fees by certain independent fee-paying schools* (CA98/05/2006, 20 November 2006, [2007] UKCLR 361)—Competition Act investigation and decision (Chapter I Prohibition)

Facts

On 27 April 2003 the *Sunday Times* published an article in which reference was made to an arrangement between certain fee-paying schools in the UK under which information would be exchanged between them relating to future fees. Each year, from 1997 until June 2003 the bursar of Sevenoaks School received fee information from up to 49 other schools. It consisted of fees charged for the previous year, for the coming year, and prospective fees for the following school year. This was then put into spreadsheet form, and circulated to all respondents at least twice a year. It became clear during the course of the investigation that the purpose of the exercise was to allow each of the 50 schools to take into account the fee levels of the others when setting their own fees. The system was known as the 'Sevenoaks Survey'.

By June 2003 two schools, Eton College and Winchester College, had approached the OFT to request leniency, and were granted conditional reductions in penalties. The first on-site investigations under s. 27 of the Competition Act took place in June 2003. More interviews took place, more leniency applications were made, and computers were forensically examined. A large number of s. 26 notices were sent to schools requiring that information be given. Some schools approached the OFT with a view to offering commitments under s. 31A of the Act. On 3 November 2005 a statement of objections was issued. The OFT was then approached by the Independent Schools Council (ISC) which raised the prospect of exploring an agreed resolution. It was emphasized that all targets of the investigation were charitable or not-for-profit organizations. The terms of the resolution reached are discussed below.

Findings

The Decision is exceptionally long, running to 1,438 paragraphs and containing a number of annexes. In cases brought under the Chapter I Prohibition the OFT takes the view that it is not necessary to define the relevant market unless it is impossible to determine without doing so whether the practice in question was liable to affect trade in the UK and was anti-competitive. In this case the practice involved an agreement and/or concerted practice that had *as its object* the prevention, restriction, or distortion of competition. Defining the market would normally be relevant in determining the penalty to be applied, but was not necessary in this case as an agreement had been reached with the schools as to the penalty to be paid. Perhaps because of the novelty of the case the OFT did undertake some market analysis, and concluded that in the case of boarding places the relevant product market was that for the provision of educational services to boarding pupils at independent fee-paying schools (para. 283). Article 101 did not apply in this case as there was unlikely to have been any appreciable effect on trade between Member States (para 1295). The fact that the schools operated as charities, or did not make a profit, did not mean that they were not undertakings, and the schools were carrying on some form of commercial activity (paras 1314–20). By participating in the survey the schools knowingly substituted practical cooperation between them for the risks of competition, and at the least had engaged in a concerted practice. It was implicit that there was a gentlemen's agreement that fee increase figures submitted to the survey would accurately reflect future fee levels (para. 1367). As regards the exchange of information generally the OFT held that 'the unilateral disclosure or exchange of future pricing information between competitors...has as its obvious object the prevention, restriction or distortion of competition' (para. 1357). In such a case it would not be necessary to demonstrate that there had been an *effect* on competition.

Comment

This case involved a significant number of parties acting in an organized manner for some six years. It is relevant that it began at a time when the Competition Act was not in force, although it is likely that this practice would have invited condemnation under the earlier domestic competition law regime had it been disclosed. The authority in this case was aware that the case was sensitive. Much comment centred around the fact that if substantial penalties were imposed, or legal fees incurred, an impact would be felt on education. The time between the opening of the investigation and the taking of the decision was around 40 months, and there was a possibility of this being significantly extended if most of the parties were to contest the decision point by point, and were to appeal (it is likely that some, if not all, of the schools would have had access to high quality legal representation). The settlement reached, the full terms of which are spelt out at para. 36 of the decision, is somewhat peculiar. The schools agreed each to pay a nominal penalty of £10,000, and to make an ex gratia payment into an educational charitable trust in the combined amount of £3 million (an average of £60,000 per school) to benefit the pupils who had attended the participant schools during the relevant years. The settlement in this case does not benefit those who may have been damaged by the action—the parents who paid. The decision was not challenged, but it would have been possible for the parents to bring a follow-on action in the CAT. They would have been hampered by having to establish that the illegal conduct led to fees being charged that were higher than they would otherwise have been, as the decision does not establish this.

The case which has attracted the most attention in the UK to date, and which also throws into relief the link between civil enforcement of the CA 98 and the criminal provisions of the Cartel Offence (see Chapter 12) is that of British Airways. Virgin Atlantic gave information to the OFT that disclosed the existence of an agreement between it and British Airways to coordinate the imposition of fuel-price surcharges on transatlantic routes. The notification to the OFT sparked both civil and criminal investigations—the former directed at the undertakings, the latter at certain key personnel. It was subject to investigation in both the UK and the US, and British Airways set aside a considerable amount of money to fund the penalties it anticipated. The subsequent findings of infringement resulted, *inter alia*, in the OFT imposing a penalty of £121.5 million for its breach of the Chapter I Prohibition, and the US DOJ a penalty of $300 million. Class action suits were also filed in the US courts. In the UK, criminal proceedings were withdrawn in May 2010 due to a lack of evidence—for which the OFT has been highly criticized. Another well-known cartel investigation of recent years is that into the marine hose cartel, which involved cooperation between the EU and US authorities and ended with the imprisonment of three executives. The criminal aspects of both the British Airways and the marine hose cases are further discussed in Chapter 12.

Fines totalling £129.5 million were imposed in September 2009 on 103 construction firms in the UK for bid-rigging (*Bid Rigging in the Construction Industry in England* case CE/4327–04, OFT Decision CA98/02/2009). The illegal practices are said to have affected building projects such as schools, universities, hospitals, as well as private housing projects. In September 2010 the most recent investigation conducted by the

OFT was launched. It will examine a potential cartel between lorry manufacturers ('OFT Price-Fix Probe into Leading Vehicle Makers', 16 September 2010, BBC News).

11.4.2 Vertical agreements

Early on in its preparation for the CA 98, the DTI indicated that it was intended to remove most vertical agreements from the scope of the Chapter I Prohibition. Research carried out on behalf of the DTI indicated that in the majority of formal decisions and cases decided in relation to vertical agreements under EU law, single-market considerations were to the fore. Such considerations would clearly be largely irrelevant in the UK, and Lord Simon, in the House of Lords, suggested that

There remains a case therefore for special treatment of vertical agreements under the Bill to avoid the burden of unnecessary notification and to ease the so-called 'straitjacket' which existing European block exemptions impose. (Hansard (HL) 9 February 1998, col. 901)

In February 2000 the Government introduced the Competition Act 1998 (Land and Vertical Agreements Exclusion) Order 2000, SI 2000/310 to give effect to this policy. Even before the modernization programme was put into place the Government had announced its intention to withdraw the exclusion order following concerns that it dampened private litigation in cases where genuine harm was being caused. There was also a recognition that in fact much of the OFT's work was, nevertheless, taken up with vertical agreements. Modernization provided a further spur to this intention, and SI 2000/310 was repealed by the Competition Act 1998 (Land Agreements Exclusion and Revocation) Order 2004, SI 2004/1260. The law relating to vertical agreements in the UK is dealt with in the guideline *Vertical agreements* [2006] UKCLR 141, and is also discussed briefly in Part 7 of *Assessment of conduct*.

11.4.2.1 Infringement decisions

Vertical price fixing has been attacked by the OFT on a number of occasions. In *John Bruce* a UK distributor of 'automatic slack-adjusters', used primarily in commercial vehicles, agreed minimum prices with its dealers, including Unipart. John Bruce argued that without the price maintenance the supplies would simply not be viable. The OFT appears to have partly accepted this, noting that there were 'special circumstances' and 'pro-competitive effects arising from John Bruce's actions' (para. 97). Still, a penalty *was* imposed, as the view was that resale price maintenance 'is a very serious infringement of the Chapter I Prohibition' (*Price fixing agreements involving John Bruce (UK) Limited, Fleet Parts Limited and Truck and Trailer Components* CA98/12/2002 [2002] UKCLR 435). Vertical price fixing was also condemned in *Lladró*, in which the manufacturer of luxury figurines operated a selective distribution system, and strongly discouraged retailers from offering promotional discounts or sales (*Agreements between Lladró Comercial SA and UK retailers fixing the price of porcelain and stoneware figurines* CA98/04/2003 [2003] UKCLR 652). Lladró was concerned that such actions might damage the perceived value of the brand. Somewhat controversially the OFT recognized that legitimate steps could be taken to protect the value of the Lladró trade mark. However, it also held that restrictions amounting to resale price maintenance (whether directly or indirectly imposed), including those which restrict a retailer's ability to advertise resale prices, cannot be objectively justified on the grounds that they are necessary to protect the reputation or image of a trademark. In the [OFT's] view, any such reputation or image derives not from the supplier's ability to control the resale price of the products or services bearing the trademark, but from other factors, including (in particular) the actual quality of those products or services and the environment in which they are sold.   (para. 76)

While many economists would agree with this, it is nevertheless the case that many consumers do equate price to quality, particularly in respect of 'luxury' branded goods.

Two more significant cases have resulted in a great deal of litigation, in part because they have involved a number of parties and different sets of arrangements. The first of these related to price fixing in the market for toys (*Agreements between Hasbro UK Ltd and distributors fixing the price of Hasbro toys and games* CA98/18/2002 [2003] UKCLR 150), and the second in relation to replica football kits.

Hasbro was the leading manufacturer of toys in the UK, and in February 2001 the OFT launched an investigation into suspected agreements between it and 10 distributors. This followed the receipt by the OFT of a circular originating in one of the Hasbro distributors, in the following terms:

All distributors, that is the Club Group and Youngsters, have had to sign new distributor contracts that forbid any discounting off Hasbro list prices. This means that no-one, Youngsters included, can offer any settlements, retrospective rebates or ordinary discount off Hasbro list prices.   (cited at para. 10 of the decision)

Information requests and on-site inspection visits were made. Hasbro agreed to cooperate, thereby benefiting from the leniency programme. When asked, David Bottomley, one of the directors, admitted that 'Yes, I was the instigator of it'. Hasbro was subsequently fined £4.95 million, having been given a 45 per cent reduction for its cooperation with the investigation. The company lodged an appeal with the CAT, but subsequently withdrew this.

Following this decision the OFT made a further one in February 2003 in relation to agreements entered into between Hasbro and Argos, and Hasbro and Littlewoods (*Agreements between Hasbro UK Ltd, Argos Ltd and Littlewoods Ltd fixing the price of Hasbro toys and games* CA98/2/2003 [2003] UKCLR 553). The OFT found in this respect that sometime in 1998–9 a pricing initiative undertaken by Hasbro led directly to an overall agreement and/or concerted practice between the three undertakings. By 1 March 2000, the date at which the CA 98 became effective in this respect, agreements were at least in place in relation to Action Man and core games. The importance to Hasbro of this arrangement was that these two catalogue stores were the price leaders for other high-street retailers. The market in toys and games is highly competitive. Were prices to be reduced, thereby restricting sellers' profit margins, retailers would be reluctant to stock a wide range of toys and games. By maintaining higher margins Hasbro was able to place more of its toys into retail outlets. One of Hasbro's executives told the OFT that

We put [a] plan together to put profit into [the] retail sector. Had discussions with Argos, but they were unwilling to take on the plan because they were concerned about other retailers undermining them. Initiative was discussed with other retailers. Other retailers were always going to follow prices of Argos and Index. So other retailer[s] felt whatever Argos and Index did was crucial to strategy.   (para. 42)

A joint e-mail was then sent to members of the Hasbro sales team by the account managers for the Argos and Littlewoods accounts. This began:

Neil and I have spoken to our respective contacts at Argos and Index and put together a proposal regarding the maintenance of certain retails within our portfolio. This is a step in the right direction and it is fair to say that both Accounts are keen to improve margins but at the same time are taking a cautious approach in case either party reneges on a price agreement…It goes without saying that Action Man and Games prices will be maintained as per earlier agreements…The proof of the pudding will be when both Catalogues are published, but Neil and I are confident that they will play ball.   (para. 49)

This drew a prompt response from a Sales Director:

Ian…This is a great initiative that you and Neil have instigated!!!!!!!!!! However, a word to the wise, never ever put anything in writing, its highly illegal and it could bite you right in the arse!!!! suggest you phone Lesley and tell her to trash? Talk to Dave. Mike.

The initiative worked, and was subsequently repeated in later catalogues.

The OFT found that there were two vertical agreements, and also a horizontal one between the two retailers, in which Hasbro played the role of facilitator. One problem was that not all evidence received during the course of the investigation was consistent, but the approach of the OFT was to place more reliance on statements that were consistent with written evidence, and particularly those which were supported by contemporaneous documentary evidence (paras 15 and 97). Hasbro received a 100 per cent reduction in penalty, Argos was fined £17.28 million, and Littlewoods £5.37 million. Argos and Littlewoods promptly appealed, leading the CAT to resolve a number of procedural points. In the appeal the OFT sought to rely in part upon three important witness statements that had not been put before the parties during the proceedings leading up to the making of the decision. The CAT decided to remit the matter back to the OFT (*Argos Ltd and Littlewoods Ltd v OFT* [2004] CompAR 80), which subsequently published an amended version of its decision, reaching the same conclusions on the substance of the abuse (*Agreements between Hasbro UK Ltd, Argos Ltd and Littlewoods Ltd fixing the price of Hasbro toys and games* CA98/8/2003 [2004] UKCLR 717). This was then subject to a further appeal with judgment being given in December 2004 (*Argos Ltd and Littlewoods Ltd v OFT* [2004] CAT 24, [2005] CompAR 588). The CAT sustained the OFT findings, and held that the 'evidence amply establishes that at least from the [autumn/winter] 1999 catalogue onwards until mid-2001 there was an "agreement" within the meaning of the Chapter I Prohibition' (para. 671). The case shows the extent to which an agreement need not be formally consecrated:

The 'agreement' that we find to exist was not a formal agreement, nor was it a legally binding agreement. The agreement was a verbal agreement. It was not reduced to writing. The agreement did not result in any guarantee that Argos would follow Hasbro's RRPs, and there were some exceptions.   (para. 672)

Argos was given assurances by Hasbro that if it held to the RRPs other retailers would follow, and the evidence suggested that although the relevant staff at Argos were not at first persuaded that this was the case, at some point they were. Later the CAT dealt with the issue of the penalties (*Argos Ltd and Littlewoods Ltd* v *OFT* [2005] CAT 13, [2005] CompAR 834) and reduced them on the grounds that the OFT might have defined the market too widely when making the calculation. In April 2005 the CAT refused leave to appeal to the Court of Appeal (*Argos Ltd and Littlewoods Ltd* v *OFT* [2005] CAT 16, [2005] CompAR 1000).

The second large case was decided by the OFT in August 2003 (*Price-fixing of replica football kit* CA98/06/2003 [2004] UKCLR 6). The investigation was launched following a complaint from Sports Soccer Ltd alleging that price fixing in this market was widespread. After making extensive inquiries the OFT identified the presence of a number of agreements: between Umbro (the manufacturer) and Sports Soccer in relation to the England home replica kit, and on all new licensed kit; between Umbro, Sports Soccer, and four leading retailers in relation to England replica shirts at the time of Euro 2000; between Umbro and Manchester United and at least two retailers; between at least JJB, Sports Soccer, and Umbro in relation to Manchester United and England replica shirts for the remainder of 2000 and 2001. Penalties were imposed on a number of parties including £158,000 on the Football Association, and £1,652,000 on Manchester United. Umbro was fined £6,641,000. On appeal the OFT findings were substantially upheld (*JJB Sports plc* v *OFT* [2004] CAT 17, [2005] CompAR 29—see also discussion above at 11.4.1 and 7.3.1.2).

11.4.3 Trade associations, the professions, and self-regulating bodies

A clear discussion of the relevant rules in relation to trade associations, the professions, and self-regulating bodies is set out in the relevant guideline. The original position under the Chapter I Prohibition was that professional rules could be subject to an exclusion from the Act following an application from the professional body to that effect. However, the OFT was concerned about the possible anti-competitive effects of such rules. In March 2001 a report prepared by the economic consultancy LECG into this subject was published (OFT 328 [2001] UKCLR 352). Following this the OFT gave a response, noting that

Restrictions on supply in the case of professional services, just as with other goods and services, will tend to drive up costs and prices, limit access and choice and cause customers to receive poorer value for money than they would under properly competitive conditions. Such restrictions will also tend to inhibit innovation in the supply of services, again to the ultimate detriment of the public.

The general exclusion has now been withdrawn, and the professions are subject to the same principles as all other providers of goods and services. Like the EU Commission, the OFT has continued to examine the impact of competition in the professions. In October 2003 it found that the system for awarding the title of QC to members of the Bar in England and Wales distorted competition and did not serve the best interests of consumers (*The Future of Queen's Counsel: Response from the Office of Fair Trading*, OFT 680, October 2003 [2004] UKCLR 332, and see OFT press release PN131/03, 17 October 2003). However, this report is not binding, and the OFT has not declared that an infringement of competition law exists.

Summary map

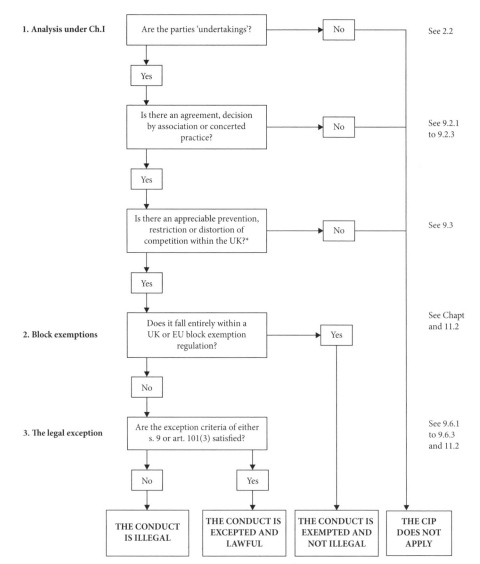

* By contrast to Art. 101, no effect on trade between Member States is required for the application of the CIP. If however there is such an effect, Art. 101 may also be applicable, and a conflicting result cannot be reached under the application of domestic law.

FURTHER READING

Articles

BAILEY, D., 'Contours of Collusion: Football Shirts and Toys and Games', (2006) *Competition Law* 225

FISSE, B., 'Recent OFT Cartel Decisions Illustrate Fundamental Flaws in UK Cartel Law', (2009) at http://www.brentfisse.com/images/Fisse_Recent_OFT_Cartel_Decisions_041009.pdf

WERDEN, G. J., 'Initial Thoughts on the American Needle Decision', (2010) *The Antitrust Source*

12

The cartel offence

> **KEY POINTS**
>
> - The cartel offence is a UK criminal law stand-alone offence directed to individuals.
> - It applies to horizontal price fixing, market sharing, bid rigging, and production limitation agreements when the conduct is 'dishonest'.
> - Individuals can be prosecuted and may face imprisonment and/or a fine.
> - It would be possible for conduct to fall both within art. 101 TFEU or the Chapter I Prohibition *and* the cartel offence.

12.1 Introduction

After a hiatus of 330 years, Part 6 of the Enterprise Act 2002 (EA 02) made it a criminal offence to engage in cartel activity implemented in the UK. The last legislation to impose criminal sanctions in respect of anti-competitive conduct in the UK, enacted in the reign of Edward VI, provided, *inter alia*, for an offender to 'sit in the pillory and lose one of his ears'. This Act was repealed in 1772, and the penalties provided for in the EA 02 are slightly less dramatic. Currently, the maximum penalty for a breach of s. 188 is a term of imprisonment of five years. During the extensive debates on this part of the Act, the Opposition of the time dismissed these provisions as 'great for a headline but not much else' (Mr Waterson, Hansard, 17 June 2002, col. 112). Elsewhere, however, it has been noted that this is 'possibly one of the most intriguing developments in English criminal law of recent years' (Harding, C., and Joshua, J., 'Breaking Up the Hard Core: The Prospects for the Proposed Cartel Offence', [2002] Crim LR 933 at 933).

The UK follows Member States such as Germany, France, the Slovak Republic, and Ireland, who have equivalent criminal sanctions. In 2001 the OFT published a substantial report commissioned to examine whether a new criminal offence should be introduced into domestic law (*The Proposed Criminalisation of Cartels in the UK—A report prepared for the Office of Fair Trading by Sir Anthony Hammond KCB QC and Roy Penrose OBE QPM* (November 2001) [2002] UKCLR 97 (hereinafter the Penrose Report)). This in turn followed a joint DTI/Treasury Department report which concluded that

[a]lthough the Competition Act 1998 strengthens the deterrent effect against anti-competitive behaviour, the project team is concerned that it may not go far enough. In particular, the penalties for engaging in cartels may not be enough to deter such action.   (quoted in the Penrose Report, at para. 1.3)

The project team concludes that US experience suggests that there is a strong case for introducing criminal penalties, including custodial sentences, for those who engage in cartels, alongside a new civil sanction of director's disqualification.

The essential features of the cartel offence are that it is: (1) a stand-alone offence, unconnected to the remainder of the competition law framework in the UK; and (2) directed towards individuals and not towards undertakings, which remain the exclusive subjects of the application of arts 101 and 102 TFEU and the Chapter I and II Prohibitions of the Competition Act 1998. The offence extends to the whole of the UK. It is purely a matter of domestic law, as there is no power within the TFEU itself to allow criminal liability to be imposed in respect of EU competition law. However, it is expressly acknowledged in Recital (8) of Regulation 1/2003 that

this Regulation does not apply to national laws which impose criminal sanctions on natural persons except to the extent that such sanctions are the means whereby competition rules applying to undertakings are enforced.

There are concerns to be raised about the way in which the operation of the offence may interact with the application of EU competition law, as the same body, the OFT, is primarily responsible for both aspects of the competition law regime within the UK. In particular, care needs to be taken to separate civil and criminal investigations to ensure that the rights of the defence in criminal cases, which are stronger than in civil cases, are adequately protected.

It is not possible in this book to provide a full analysis of all aspects of the offence. Detailed matters of criminal law, and particularly procedure, which are subject to frequent legislative change, are not dealt with here. Rather, this chapter focuses on the substance of the offence, and studies the first cases in which it has been applied. For a full (although somewhat outdated) analysis see Furse, M., and Nash, S., *The Cartel Offence*, Oxford, Hart (2004).

12.2 **Prosecution of cartels prior to the entry into force of the Enterprise Act 2002—conspiracy to defraud**

The EA 02 has no retroactive effects, and therefore the cartel offence may not be applied to cartels enforced before its adoption. Nonetheless, under English law there exists a common law offence of conspiracy to defraud, which was expressly preserved by the Criminal Law Act 1977. This had long been ignored by competition lawyers, but garnered some attention to crush down cartels prior to the entry into force of the offence. Two examples of this deserve particular scrutiny.

First, the Serious Fraud Office (SFO) carried out investigations, with a view to prosecution, in relation to cartels the pharmaceuticals sector engaged in before the EA 02. Secondly, in March 2007 the High Court refused to declare unlawful the extradition of Ian Norris to the US, where he was wanted in respect of an alleged breach of s. 1 of the Sherman Act (*Norris* v *United States* [2007] EWHC 71 (Admin)). The US argued that extradition should be granted on the grounds that Mr Norris' conduct would have been illegal had it been carried out in the UK on the basis of the operation of the conspiracy to defraud offence. Mr Norris vigorously contested his extradition for years, given that at the time the alleged violations were committed there was no equivalent cartel offence in the UK. Extradition requires 'dual criminality'—the offence must be recognized, although not necessarily in identical terms, in the state from which extradition is requested. Indeed, in March 2008 the House of Lords ruled against his extradition for this very reason. However, in September that year a US district judge ruled that Mr Norris should be extradited in relation to the subsidiary charge of obstruction of justice; the then Home Secretary backed the decision. Subsequent appeals were dismissed, including a last resort to the European Court of Human Rights. He was extradited on 23 March 2010 (see Whelan, P., 'Resisting the Long Arm of Criminal Antitrust Laws: *Norris* v *The United States*', (2009) 72 *Modern Law Review* 272–83).

12.3 **Basic elements of the offence**

The ingredients of the offence are set out at s. 188 of the EA 02. Section 188(1) provides:

An individual is guilty of an offence if he dishonestly agrees with one or more other persons to make or implement, or to cause to be made or implemented, arrangements of the following kind relating to at least two undertakings (A and B).

Section 188(2) sets out six categories of arrangement the implementation of which will be deemed to fall within the terms of the offence. Thus it is provided that:

The arrangements must be ones which, if operating as the parties to the agreement intend, would—

    (a) directly or indirectly fix a price for the supply by A in the United Kingdom (otherwise than to B) of a product or service,

    (b) limit or prevent supply by A in the United Kingdom of a product or service,

    (c) limit or prevent production by A in the United Kingdom of a product,

    (d) divide between A and B the supply in the United Kingdom of a product or service to a customer or customers,

    (e) divide between A and B customers for the supply in the United Kingdom of a product or service, or

    (f) be bid-rigging arrangements.

The offence entered into effect on 20 June 2003. Even before then, the SFO was using existing powers to investigate a cartel. On 9 November 2003 the *Sunday Times* reported that 'on the morning of April 10 last year, the senior executives of several British drug companies were awakened by the sound of police banging on their front doors' ('Strong Medicine', *Sunday Times*, 9 November 2003, Business Section, p. 5). It was reported that 'Operation Holbein', an investigation into allegations of fraud and price fixing in the supply of generic drugs to the NHS was the Serious Fraud Office's 'largest and possibly most expensive inquiry ever'. The link was inevitably made to the new offence, with the report's authors claiming that if the head of the SFO, Robert Wardle, was successful, he could 'pave the way for his office to become inquisitor general of Britain's commercial cartels'. See also *R (on the application of Kent Pharmaceuticals Ltd)* v *Director of the Serious Fraud Office* [2003] EWHC 3002 (Admin), [2003] All ER (D) 298, where the court dealt with the extent to which seizure of various documents in the course of the investigation was lawful.

The SFO has, following a memorandum entered into with the OFT, been given the lead role in prosecuting the cartel offence. Apart from the specific provisions relating to the offence in the EA 02 it will be substantially reliant on its powers provided by the Criminal Justice Act 1987. Section 2 of this Act enables the SFO to obtain search warrants, to compel persons to answer questions, and to provide information and produce documents for the purposes of the criminal investigation. In Scotland, the Criminal Law (Consolidation) (Scotland) Act 1995 provides that the Lord Advocate can nominate a person to exercise the same powers as the SFO, and the Head of the International and Financial Crime Unit has been so appointed. The OFT itself, via its Cartels Investigation Branch, plays a key role in investigating breaches of the offence, and works closely with the SFO in this respect.

12.3.1 Situations in which the offence may be applied

It was always going to be the case that the offence would extend only to hard-core cartel conduct. The Penrose Report argued that it should only be applied to horizontal agreements and not to vertical relationships (para. 1.12). Very much in this line, the White Paper explained that:

7.19 The new criminal offence will cover hard-core cartels only—widely recognised as the most serious form of competition breach. The most common form of hard-core cartel involves illegal price-fixing—where a number of firms agree what price should be charged for a particular product. In most cases, this will be above what the competitive market price would be.

7.20 However, cartels can also involve conduct which achieves the same economic result by different means. This includes agreeing not to compete for each other's customers—which leaves each firm free to set higher prices (market sharing). Or firms could agree to reduce levels of output—which also increases the price that they can charge.

7.21 In some cases, firms will agree to inflate the price charged in a tender-bidding process and enter bids which ensure that one company in the cartel will win, but on better terms than would otherwise be the case (collusive tendering). The OFT believes that public sector contracts are particularly vulnerable to these practices. As such, they could hit taxpayers hard—because Local Authorities or Government departments have to pay more for public services.

7.22 In all these cases, the effect is the same—prices rise and consumers pay more than they should. The Government intends that the new criminal offence will cover each of these different types of cartel.

Price fixing at the horizontal level, whether it be direct or indirect, is prohibited. While the most obvious form of price fixing would be that which set a single price, or set of prices, for a customer or customers, it is also possible to envisage situations in which there might be coordination on discounts, quantity rebates, and so on. Any such arrangement that would have the same effect as a direct agreement to set selling prices may fall foul of the provision.

For the offence to be operative arrangements must be made between two parties. Because the offence is defined as making such arrangements, it is not necessary that they be implemented, with the exception of those entered into outside the UK. The four categories of arrangement that are condemned are price fixing, limitation of production or supply, the sharing of markets, and bid-rigging (defined in Chapter 9). These are generally considered to be the most serious forms of anti-competitive activity. In addition, s. 188(3) provides that in the case of s. 188(2)(a), (b), and (c) (see above), both firms (A and B) must be engaged in the anti-competitive practice. This requirement is set out clearly in the *Explanatory notes to the Enterprise Act* published by the DTI at para. 408. Further conditions relating to the horizontal nature of the arrangements are laid down in s. 189. In each of the instances of s. 188, it is necessary, as an additional element of the offence, that the supply of the product or service by A would be 'at a level in the supply chain at which the product or service would at the same time be supplied by B in the United Kingdom' (s. 189(1)).

12.3.1.1 Section 188(2)(a)—price-fixing arrangements

Section 188(2)(a) relates to horizontal price-fixing arrangements—the most generally recognized form of cartel. For this section to apply, the relevant arrangements must be such as to constitute a direct, or indirect, reciprocal fixing of a price by both A and B for a product or service in the UK to a third party or parties. Although s. 188(2)(a) makes reference only to A, s. 188(3) provides that B must also be an active party to the arrangement. There is no requirement for the product or service to be identical, or indeed even substitutable but, by virtue of s. 189(1) it is necessary for the prosecution to demonstrate that 'A's supply of the product or service would be at a level in the supply chain at which the product or service would at the same time be supplied by B' in the UK. The arrangement as to price would not necessarily have to be one which led to an increase in prices by both parties. Even an arrangement which led to the parties lowering their prices—for example to provide a joint response to the threat of entry into the market affected—would be caught if it could be shown to have been entered into dishonestly. Equally, an arrangement under which B would maintain its price at a constant level while A increased its price would be caught.

12.3.1.2 Section 188(2)(b) and (2)(c)—limitations of supply or production

Section 188(2)(b) and (c) relates to the limiting of production or supply. For the arrangements to fall within the offence both A *and* B must limit the production or supply of goods or services which would be supplied at the same level in the supply chain. It would appear that an agreement between A and B to refuse to supply C could be caught by this subsection, as well as a more generic agreement to reduce supplies overall. There is no requirement that the goods or services being produced be supplied in the UK.

A difficulty could arise in respect of both of these elements of the offence (as well as with bid rigging) if parties were not to act simultaneously. Suppose, for example, A were to cut its production or supply of a product in 2011, and B were to do so in 2012. It might be somewhat difficult to demonstrate—in the absence of supporting evidence of communication between the parties—that an arrangement was in place. It would, it is suggested, be incumbent on the prosecuting authority to bring forward some documentary or testamentary proof to establish the existence of the ingredients of the offence.

12.3.1.3 Section 188(2)(d) and (2)(e)—market-sharing arrangements

For an arrangement to infringe either of subsections (2)(d) and (e) it must be one which would lead to a division of the market or customers, between A and B in the UK. Any such division need not necessarily be on the basis of a geographical allocation, but could be by any means whereby individual customers were denied the choice of supplier of the product or service in question.

12.3.1.4 Section 188(2)(f)—bid rigging

Bid-rigging arrangements are defined in s. 188(5) as being

arrangements under which, in response to a request for bids for the supply of a product or service in the United Kingdom, or for the production of a product in the United Kingdom—

(a)   A but not B may make a bid, or

(b)   A and B may each make a bid but, in one case or both, only a bid arrived at in accordance with the arrangements.

It is further provided in s. 188(6) that bid-rigging arrangements are excluded from the scope of this provision where the person requesting the bids was notified of the arrangements at or before the time of the making of the bid. It is interesting therefore that in the *Explanatory notes* the position is taken that '[b]id-rigging is the only one of the prohibited activities where for all practical purposes the carrying out of the activity described in this section will in itself invariably indicate a dishonest intention' (para. 409). It has been argued by a number of parties that bid-rigging arrangements are to be regarded as *per se* dishonest.

12.3.2 **Dishonesty as the standard of conduct**

There was some debate as to the standard of conduct that would be required for an offence to be committed. In the Penrose Report dishonesty was the preferred option:

The advantage of this approach is (a) it signals that the offence is serious and should attract a substantial penalty and (b) it would go a long way to preclude a defence argument that the activity being prosecuted is not reprehensible or that it might have economic benefits or is an activity which might have attracted exemption domestically or under [EU] law. The possible disadvantage is that some might argue that an offence which depends on an approach of 'dishonesty' may be difficult for juries to understand. However, given the context in which hard core cartels take place, we believe that, in most cases, the facts will demonstrate that the parties realised what they were doing was dishonest and was contrary to the law.   (para 2.5)

The test for dishonesty in England and Wales, which is a question of fact to be determined by the jury, was established in the case of *R* v *Ghosh* [1982] 2 All ER 689. It is the jury who ultimately determines whether the defendant has acted dishonestly, and it is a matter of fact. In *Ghosh* Lord Lane CJ observed that it was necessary to consider whether the dishonesty in question related to a course of conduct or described a state of mind. In a judgment which has stood the test of time, the Court of Appeal settled on a double test which involves both objective and subjective considerations. First of all, the jury is required to determine whether the act done would, according to the standards of reasonable people, be considered to be dishonest. Secondly, it must consider whether the defendant would have realized that this was the view of reasonable people. If the answer to both questions is in the affirmative, then dishonesty is established. The position is a little more complex in Scotland, where it remains unclear if dishonesty is a feature of certain aspects of criminal law.

Although the purpose of basing the offence on the standard of 'dishonest' conduct was to define it tightly—and to mark a move to acting against the object of agreements—it was suggested in the debates on the passage of the Act that the definition was anything but tight. Some have pointed out that the persons drafting this legislation failed to understand fully the role of dishonesty in the criminal law and used it to 'bridge a perceived weakness in the objective definition of the prohibited conduct' (See Harding, C., and Joshua, J., 'Breaking Up the Hard Core: the Prospects for the Proposed Cartel Offence', [2002] Crim LR 933–44 at 939). An opposition amendment to replace 'dishonestly' with 'knowingly or recklessly' was resisted by the Government on the grounds that that would have significantly *expanded* the scope of the offence. This implies also that there is a need for some positive act, and not merely a failure to act, for the offence to be established. Peretz and Lewis have recognized that the standard of 'dishonesty' is one that will be familiar to criminal lawyers, although not to the competition bar. They are probably correct when they write that in the context of the cartel offence

the question of whether individuals acted dishonestly is likely to be determined by the extent to which they were open about what they were doing. If, for example, the agreement operated by covert meetings held under a soubriquet, with all records being destroyed, it will probably not be hard to establish dishonesty, the badges of fraud being present.   (Peretz, G., and Lewis, J., 'Go Directly to Jail: Losing Badly in "Monopoly"', (2003) NLJ 99)

12.3.3 **The application of the cartel offence to date**

The success of the criminal offence depends on how adequately it is applied. In a speech delivered in May 2002, Margaret Bloom declared that the intention was therefore to have a 'relatively small number of prosecutions' with a 'significant deterrent effect', focusing only on the most serious cartels.   (Bloom, M., 'Key Challenges in Public Enforcement: A Speech to the British Institute of International and Comparative Law', 17 May 2002, OFT website (**www.oft.gov.uk**))

At the time of writing, more than seven years since the entry into force of the cartel offence, there has only been one conviction under s. 188. In 2007, three former executives of Dunlop were sentenced to imprisonment for their role in a worldwide cartel in the marine hose industry. The imprisonment terms were subsequently reduced by the Court of Appeals in 2009. This constitutes our key case of the chapter.

Key case 12.1 *R* v *Whittle & others* [2008] EWCA Crim 2560; [2009] UKCLR 247; judgment of the Southwark Crown Court; judgment of the Court of Appeal (criminal division) on appeal (s. 188 Enterprise Act 2002, s. 2 Company Directors Disqualification Act 1986)

Facts

For many years, the world's major manufacturers of marine hose—a rubber piping product that is used to transfer oil between tanker vessels and storage facilities—engaged in a market-sharing cartel involving price fixing and bid-rigging. They regularly communicated by telephone, fax, and e-mail to ensure that market shares and prices were maintained. Dunlop was one of the companies involved. In May 2007, arrests were made in the US following the secret recording of a meeting of the cartel members in Houston. Among those arrested were the applicants of this case, Whittle, Brammar, and Allison, who worked for Dunlop in different capacities. They confessed, provided the OFT with their confessions before an investigation began and agreed to plead guilty to a UK cartel offence.

Findings

After pleading guilty to a cartel offence under s. 188, Whittle and Allison were sentenced to three years' imprisonment, while Brammar was sentenced to 30 months. Furthermore, in application of s. 2 of the Company Directors Disqualification Act 1986, Whittle and Allison were each disqualified for seven years and Brammar for five years. They challenged the terms of imprisonment, which on appeal were reduced to two and a half years for Whittle, two years for Allison and 20 months for Brammar.

Comment

This case marked the first ever criminal conviction in the UK for establishing a cartel, and followed a major international investigation involving transnational cooperation between competition authorities. Cynics have highlighted that it is disappointing that the only conviction so far is the result of a confession. The effectiveness of the cartel offence is further questioned by the recent collapse of an investigation against British Airways for fixing passenger fuel surcharges, as explained below.

In January 2009, shortly after the conviction of the Crown Court, the EU Commission imposed a fine of €131 million on five of the six marine hose producers (all but the whistle-blower) involved in a worldwide cartel after conducting its own separate investigation under Article 101 TFEU (*Marine Hoses* (2009) COMP/39406 OJ C168/6–8).

FURTHER READING

Press releases

European Commission, 'Antitrust: Commission Fines Marine Hose Producers €131 Million for Market Sharing and Price-Fixing Cartel' (28 January 2009) IP/09/137, at **http:// europa.eu/rapid/pressReleasesAction.do?reference=IP/09/137&guiLanguage= de**

OFT, 'Three Imprisoned in First OFT Criminal Prosecution for Bid Rigging', (11 June 2008) 72/08, online at **http://www.oft.gov.uk/news/press/2008/72-08**

Other investigations under s. 188 have been launched, not always with success. Notably, the OFT recently investigated a cartel between British Airways (BA) and Virgin Atlantic fixing the fuel surcharges charged to passengers between 2004 and 2006. Virgin came forward and offered to cooperate, and in exchange it obtained corporate and individual immunity in the UK and the US (see 12.4). After imposing a fine of £121 million on BA in the civil proceedings, four BA executives faced charges under s. 188 of the EA 02. Unlike those involved in the marine hose cartel, they pleaded not guilty. During the investigation, and following the insistence of the defence, about 70,000 e-mails that Virgin claimed had been corrupted were recovered, which suggested that Virgin had decided to raise prices prior to being in contact with BA. As a consequence of the lack of evidence, the OFT withdrew criminal proceedings and the case against the BA executives was closed on 11 May 2010.

The possibility that Virgin may have withheld evidence has led to questioning the adequacy of immunity. In addition, the OFT has been criticized for its ingenuousness in accepting Virgin's claim that the requested e-mails had been corrupted and were not relevant without any further investigation. The defence counsel claimed the OFT had been 'guilty of incompetence at a monumental scale' in its handling of the case. Furthermore, it questioned the potential contradictions of the leniency regime in relation to the cartel offence:

So it is the world turned upside down. If you say you are honest in making an agreement, then you may go to prison. If you say you did nothing wrong, then you're at risk of being charged but if you say you were dishonest, then you and your company will not be punished, you will keep your job.

The OFT continues in its investigations to reveal the potential for criminal convictions. In September 2010, it announced a new criminal investigation into a possible cartel between lorry makers for potential price-fixing ('OFT Price-Fix Probe into Leading Vehicle Makers', 16 September 2010, BBC News, online at **http://www.bbc. co.uk/news/business-11330540**). An executive of Mercedes-Benz was arrested on suspicion of breaching the cartel offence.

12.4 The relationship of the offence with the Competition Act 1998 and EU competition law

Because the offence is a stand-alone provision, there is in theory no relationship between it and the civil provisions of the CA 98 and arts 101 and 102 TFEU. In practice, however, it is possible that the same conduct will be investigated and attacked under both the civil law, in an action against undertakings, and the criminal law in an action against persons. The OFT is generally precluded from using evidence obtained in the course of a civil investigation under the CA 98 to pursue a cartel prosecution, although it may use statements made in the course of interviews where these counteract evidence subsequently given in the criminal procedure.

During the criminal proceedings against British Airways (12.3.3), there was a preliminary appeal that questioned whether the cartel offence is part of what Regulation 1/2003 refers to as 'national competition law'. If so, the next doubt is whether the effect of art. 5 of the Regulation would be that only the OFT can impose sanctions for an offence following the procedure laid down in that provision (*IB* v *R* [2009] EWCA Crim 2575). The defendants questioned the jurisdiction of the Crown Court on this basis; the Court of Appeals confirmed that, as a stand-alone offence, s. 188 is not subject to the enforcement rules of Regulation 1/2003 which refer to the relationship between national competition authorities and the Commission in the application of Articles 101 and 102 TFEU.

One issue in which there is likely to be an overlap arises in relation to the leniency programmes operated in relation to the civil laws, and 'no-action letters' (see 12.4) operated in relation to the cartel offence. At the time the offence was introduced the OFT indicated that it had engaged in extensive discussions with the EU Commission relating to the new offence, and had considered in particular the impact of the offence on leniency policies:

An undertaking should apply for leniency to both the OFT and the Commission where the cartel involves more member states than the UK. The first undertaking to apply in a cartel should be eligible under the EU civil leniency policy and the UK civil leniency policy for full leniency unless they were the instigator of the cartel, compelled others to take part or played the leading role...In this way we have ensured the compatible working of the EU and UK regimes. The OFT will discuss with the Commission the handling of individual [EU] cartel cases where the UK may wish to mount a criminal prosecution. These will be considered case by case.   (Bloom, M., 'Key Challenges in Public Enforcement: A Speech to the British

Institute of International and Comparative Law', 17 May 2002, OFT website (**www.oft .gov.uk**))

It is clear that an offence may be committed by the instigators of a cartel operating in Europe where the arrangements are 'implemented' in the UK. However, there are limitations on the ability of the OFT to recycle the evidence obtained relating to any action taken by the EU Commission or by another national competition authority to sustain a prosecution in relation to the offence.

MacCulloch has expressed the concern that the operation of the offence may have an impact on the way in which the OFT fulfils its functions as a member of the NCA network (MacCulloch, A., 'The Cartel Offence and the Criminalisation of UK Competition Law', [2003] *JBL* 616). It is possible for example that the OFT will feel it is obliged to give primacy to the enforcement of art. 101 TFEU, or the Chapter I Prohibition, and may not prosecute the cartel offence where it is not envisaged that there is a very strong prospect of success.

12.5 'No-action letters'

As seen in Chapter 6, leniency programmes operated by the EU Commission and the OFT are an important plank in the detection of cartels in particular, and one of the concerns expressed vociferously about the introduction of the cartel offence was that the threat of criminal penalties would in fact undermine the approach to leniency. This concern was raised in the Penrose Report:

5.9 The difficulty faced by the OFT is how to provide sufficient comfort against criminal prosecution and the imposition of custodial sentences for potential whistleblowers who inform on other cartel participants. In particular, the OFT would need a policy which would:

- provide sufficient 'certainty' to whistleblowers that they would not personally face criminal prosecution, and
- be consistent with the existing leniency policies operated under civil procedures in both the UK *and* the [EU] in respect of undertakings whilst maintaining the integrity of the SFO as the prosecuting authority and the criminal justice system in the UK as a whole.

Express provision is made in the Act for the leniency programme at s. 190(4):

Where, for the purpose of the investigation or prosecution of offences under section 188, the OFT gives a person written notice under this subsection [a no-action letter], no proceedings for an offence under section 188 that falls within a description specified in the notice may be brought against that person in England and Wales or Northern Ireland except in the circumstances specified in the notice.

The problems of the interaction between the leniency programme and the cartel offence have been highlighted above in the analysis of the prosecution against the

British Airways executives allegedly involved in a cartel to fix fuel surcharges (see 12.3.3). The OFT has issued *The Cartel Offence: Guidance on the issue of no-action letters for individuals*, which sets out the terms of its approach to leniency. At the outset it should be noted that the position of no-action letters is a little different in Scotland than is the case in the remainder of the UK. The OFT cannot bind the Lord Advocate in Scotland, whose prosecutorial discretion is absolute. However, it was pointed out in committee that a similar procedure under which Customs and Excise employs a leniency programme has given rise to no substantial problems, and that concerns will be allayed by the good working relationship between the OFT, the SFO, and the Scottish authorities.

The leniency programme operated in relation to the cartel offence finds its expression in the instrument of 'no-action letters'. These are explained in the following terms:

In the context of the cartel offence, immunity from prosecution will be granted in the form of a 'no-action letter', issued by the OFT under section 190(4) of the Enterprise Act. A no-action letter will prevent a prosecution being brought against an individual in England and Wales or Northern Ireland for the cartel offence except in circumstances specified in the letter. Whilst guarantees of immunity from prosecution cannot be given in relation to Scotland, cooperation by an individual will be reported to the Lord Advocate who will take such cooperation into account.   (para. 3.2)

There are five main conditions that must be met in order for a no-action letter to be issued by the OFT. These are that the individual must: (1) admit participation in a criminal offence; (2) provide the OFT with all available information regarding the cartel; (3) cooperate completely and continuously throughout the investigation; (4) not have coerced another to participate in the cartel; and (5) cease participation in the cartel, unless instructed to continue by the OFT or other investigating authority. It is thus clear that the OFT contemplates that there may be occasions when it has an informant operating under supervision inside a cartel, passing back all relevant information to the OFT or SFO.

While satisfaction of these conditions is necessary for the issuance of a no-action letter, it is not sufficient. Where there is enough information to bring a successful prosecution against the applicant individual, or the OFT is in the process of gathering that information, it will not grant a no-action letter. The effect of this policy must be to encourage early applications where an investigation is under way. In addition, in order to benefit from a no-action letter the approach must come from the individual or a lawyer representing that person. It appears from the guidance that the OFT will not itself initiate the process. Any such approach by a lawyer may be made at the first instance on an anonymous basis. Approaches may also be made on behalf of a named individual, or a group of named individuals by an undertaking or by its lawyer in the course of an investigation into breaches of either the Chapter I Prohibition of the CA 98 or art. 101 TFEU in accordance with the terms of the relevant leniency notices. In the latter case the relevant notice applies to undertakings, but where one of them qualifies for full immunity from penalties it is anticipated that named individuals, ex-employees or directors of that undertaking will be granted the benefit of a no-action letter.

In the event that any such approach is made, the Director of Cartel Investigations will give 'an indication' as to whether the OFT might be prepared to issue a no-action letter. If it is, any individual who hopes to benefit from one will be interviewed, although the information given in the process will not subsequently be used against them in criminal proceedings unless either they 'knowingly or recklessly provided information that is false or misleading in a material particular' (para. 3.7) or the letter is subsequently revoked.

At the end of the interview process three results are possible. The first of these is that the OFT concludes that the applicant is not at risk of criminal prosecution. In this case it will not issue a no-action letter, but will confirm its conclusion in writing. While the exact legal status of such a communication is unclear, it will at the least raise a legitimate expectation on behalf of the recipient that no criminal action will follow. There does remain the possibility, however, that the OFT may later obtain further information which might influence it to reassess the position. In such a case it would be reasonable to believe that the OFT would reconsider the application, and would be minded to do so favourably.

The second possible result is that the OFT determines that without a no-action letter there would be a possibility of criminal prosecution, but that the applicant confirms that they will meet the criteria for the grant of such a letter, in which case it will be issued. Where the prosecution would be brought in Scotland the cooperation will be reported to the Lord Advocate with a request that an early decision be made as to whether the individual remains liable for prosecution. A third possibility is that the OFT establishes that a prosecution is possible, and that the individual does not meet the criteria to be issued a no-action letter. In this case, the interview may not be used against the individual. This would imply that there is little to be lost in making an application. In practice, however, there may be some concerns that while the OFT may not use the information given at the interview, it may be encouraged to pursue lines of inquiry as a result of the interview that it might otherwise have overlooked.

No-action letters may be revoked in two circumstances. The first of these is where the recipient of the letter ceases to satisfy the conditions for the grant of a letter discussed above. The second arises where the recipient has 'knowingly or recklessly provided information that is false or misleading in a material particular' (para. 3.11). If a no-action letter is revoked any immunity conferred by the letter will cease to exist as if it had never been granted. A particular consequence of this is that any information given at the initial interview may be used in the course of any subsequent prosecution. Before revoking a no-action letter the OFT will give the recipient notice of the decision in writing, and a reasonable opportunity to make representations. It may, but is not required to, give the applicant the possibility to remedy any breach of the compliance conditions within a reasonable time, after an explanation as to the breach of the conditions has been given.

12.6 **Conclusion and outlook**

It seems that the OFT is attempting to use the cartel offence to ensure that it purports the desired deterrent effect. The conviction of the executives involved in the marine hose cartel, as well as their disqualification, is an important step in this regard. What is clear is that those engaged in business cannot ignore the determination to vigorously tackle cartels. The OFT has long insisted that the provisions are a vital plank in acting against hard-core anti-competitive conduct; as such, it needs to ensure that criminal investigations are thoroughly conducted to avoid the problems encountered in the case against the BA executives (12.2.3).

The new Coalition Government announced in May 2010 its intention to create a new agency to tackle all economic crimes, with experts from the SFO, the FSA, and the OFT (O'Keane, M., 'Cartel Prosecution Failings Need to be Priority of New Economic Crime Agency', (24 May 2010) *Guardian*, online at **http://www.guardian.co.uk/law/2010/may/24/economic-crime-agency**). Some have argued against it because of the economic cost (Leigh, D., and Evans, R., 'Cost of New Economic Crime Agency Could Be Prohibitive', (2 June 2010) *Guardian*, online at **http://www.guardian.co.uk/business/2010/jun/02/economic-crime-agency-scheme-cost**). If created, this agency would have the power to apply the cartel offence. It could be a step towards invigorated criminal enforcement in the UK.

FURTHER READING

Books

CSERES, K. J., SCHINKEL, M. P., VOGELAAR, F. O. W. (eds), *Criminalization of Competition Law Enforcement: Economic and Legal Implications for the EU Member States* (2006) Edward Elgar, Cheltenham

FURSE, M., and NASH, S., *The Cartel Offence* (2004) Hart Publishing, Oxford

Articles

HARDING, C., AND JOSHUA, J., 'Breaking Up the Hard Core: the Prospects for the Proposed Cartel Offence', [2002] *Crim LR* 933–44

JOSHUA, J., 'Shooting the Messenger: Does the UK Criminal Cartel Offense Have a Future?', (2010) *Antitrust Source*

LEVER, J., and PIKE, J., 'Cartel Agreements, Criminal Conspiracy and the Statutory "Cartel Offence"', (2005) *European Competition Law Review* 90 and 164

MACCULLOCH, A., 'Honesty, Morality and the Cartel Offence', (2007) *European Competition Law Review* 355

STEPHAN, A., 'The UK Cartel Offence: Lame Duck or Black Mamba?', (2008) *CCP Working Paper* 08–19

13

An introduction to the economics of monopoly abuse

KEY POINTS

- A monopolist, strictly, is a firm which is the sole supplier in a relevant market.
- Monopolists are able to determine the market price, and this will be higher than the competitive price, with the quantity supplied being lower.
- This leads to a loss of welfare to society as a whole, and also a redistribution of income from some of the monopolist's customers to the monopolist.
- The monopolist may also engage in wasteful strategic behaviour to protect its privileged position.

13.1 Introduction

There are arguments that support the need for some intervention in the competitive structure, but do not necessarily justify action against individual monopolists. These were advanced in Chapter 1. The Harvard/Chicago debate is not a purely theoretical one, and nowhere is this more significant than in relation to the policy prescriptions relating to the control of monopoly conduct. If the extreme Chicago approach is correct, there would be little need to apply competition law to the conduct of privately maintained monopolies. Article 102 TFEU (see Chapter 14) could, along with the Chapter II Prohibition (see Chapter 15), be abandoned, leaving competition regulators to focus on the twin problems of distortions to the competitive structure resulting from state conduct and the maintenance of cartels. State aids and state-maintained, or created, barriers to entry have indeed received increasing attention from the EU Commission, and much time has been taken up in the UK with deregulation initiatives in the utilities sectors (see the discussion of natural monopolies at 13.2.5). If, on the other hand, the Harvard school adherents are correct, the anti-competitive conduct of a single firm in possession of a significant degree of market power may still raise genuine concerns that cannot be resolved by the operation of the market place in the absence of regulatory intervention. This is the assumption underpinning art. 102 and its domestic equivalents. The economics of monopoly control is considered in

Bishop, S., and Walker, M., *The Economics of EC Competition Law*, London, Sweet & Maxwell (3rd edn, 2010).

13.2 **Individual monopolies**

To the economist a monopoly is, quite simply, a market in which the industry is in the hands of one producer. Competition law, however, extends to situations which are monopolistic—which is to say a market in which there are a number of sellers, into which new firms may enter, but in which each firm has a degree of control over price by virtue of selling products that are not identical to those of its competitors. Generally, potentially anti-competitive actions undertaken by a single firm will be subject to legal proceedings only where that firm has a significant degree of market power. It is a source of some confusion that legislation and case law make reference to 'monopoly' to describe such market power, disregarding the stricter economic definition. Market shares are usually used as a proxy by which to establish, prima facie, the appropriate market power at which intervention may be triggered. In the EU shares of around 50 per cent generally require the undertaking to demonstrate that it is *not* in a dominant position (see further at 14.3.5.1); and in the USA a share of at least 50 per cent, and likely around 70 per cent, will establish the degree of monopoly power required under the Sherman Act (see, for a survey of the relevant authorities, *Domed Stadium Hotel, Inc.* v *Holiday Inns, Inc.* 732 F.2d 480 at 489–90 (5th Cir. 1984)).

The attractions to company directors of attaining monopoly have never been better expressed than in *The Godfather*:

Like any good businessman he came to understand the benefits of undercutting his rivals in price, barring them from distribution outlets by persuading store owners to stock less of their brands. Like any good businessman he aimed at holding a monopoly by forcing his rivals to abandon the field or by merging with his own company...Like many businessmen of genius he learned that free competition was wasteful, monopoly efficient. (Puzo, M., *The Godfather* (1969), Ch. 14)

Expressed this way the strategy may not be far removed from that adhered to in many boardrooms, although clearly Don Vito Corleone was prepared to resort to anti-competitive practices that would be better addressed by way of the criminal law than by way of competition law. The problems to be addressed by competition law are that, first, monopolies may not always be efficient and, secondly, the pursuit of predatory or exclusionary tactics may have harmful welfare effects as well as, less abstractly, damaging individual target firms, along with their investors and managers.

The allegations faced by monopolists most frequently are that:

(a) the monopoly price is higher than the price would be in a competitive market, which is the area that is usually of most concern to consumer advocates;

(b) output is lower and therefore potential demand that could be efficiently met is going unanswered, a corollary of which is that the income that would have been spent on the monopolist's product is being spent elsewhere, distorting other prices in the economy;

(c) predatory behaviour may directly damage the interests of other legitimate competitors and indirectly harm consumers; and

(d) the monopolist, in order to protect a profitable position, may erect barriers that prevent new entrants coming into the market to correct the behaviour referred to in (a) and (b).

Ancillary concerns are that monopolists, contrary to the Godfather's view, may be *less efficient* than firms in a more competitive market and may stifle innovation. Following Leibenstein this type of inefficiency is sometimes called 'X-inefficiency', and relates primarily to an inefficient use of existing resources. X-inefficiency arises if the same inputs might result in more outputs (Leibenstein, H., 'Allocative Efficiency v. X-Efficiency', (1966) 59 *American Economic Review* 392). Competition law is not well placed to deal directly with X-efficiency concerns, which would require a strongly interventionist approach, or with the problem of reduced monopoly output. Instead the focus of the law is on facilitating the emergence of stronger competition to the monopolist by tackling predation, exclusion, and barriers to entry. *Ceteris paribus* stronger competition should reduce the other identifiable harms. Depending on the emphasis given to individual rights and consumer welfare in the relevant regime, other issues such as high pricing or refusal to deal may be addressed where they are readily identifiable.

13.2.1 Higher prices/lower output

The formal proof by which higher pricing and lower output arises in monopoly markets is a standard feature of industrial economics and is not unduly technical. The aim of all firms is assumed to be profit maximization, and although this may not be the case in all situations, it is a reasonable working assumption. The consequence of this is that, when considering what quantity of any product to market, firms will set the level where the marginal cost (MC) of production is equal to the marginal revenue (MR) the firm makes from that unit of production: if the MC is £5 and the MR is £10 a profit-maximizing firm would produce the extra unit as it would make a £5 profit on the sale; if the MC is £10 and the MR is £5 the firm would not produce it as it would make a £5 loss.

Whereas in perfect competition the firm has no control whatsoever over the price at which the item is sold, and takes the price set by the market, a monopolist *makes* the price. Adam Smith famously suggested that 'the price of monopoly is upon every occasion the highest which can be got' (Smith, A., *An Inquiry Into the Nature and Causes of the Wealth of Nations* (1776), Book One, Ch. VII). It is the essence of monopoly that the monopolist has the power to set the price of its product, which is effected by altering the amount that is supplied. As with perfect competition, marginal cost will be set equal to marginal revenue, but the outcome is very different, as Figure 13.1 shows. In the case of perfect competition price = MC, with the outcome being PC, QC. In the

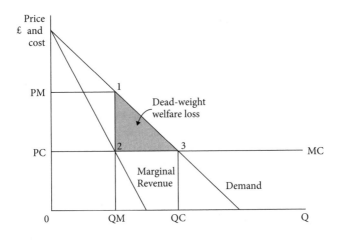

Figure 13.1 The monopoly effect

Notes: 1. The assumption of constant marginal cost is a simplifying one, and is unlikely to be matched in the real world. However, to relax this assumption does not change the analysis.

2. The rectangle PM, PC, 2, 1, represents a transfer of wealth from consumer to the monopolist. The triangle 1, 2, 3, shows 'dead-weight welfare loss', potential demand that could be supplied efficiently but, under single-price monopoly, is not (see Chapter 1).

case of monopoly MR = MC, with the outcome being PM, QM. The monopoly price, PM, is higher than the competitive price, PC, and the quantity produced, QM, is less than would be produced in a perfectly competitive market, QC.

13.2.2 **Monopoly profits**

Measuring the variables discussed above, and assessing the extent of the loss of wealth caused by any one monopoly, is exceptionally difficult. In the UK in particular, but not exclusively, assessments have been made in some cases of the profits made by individual monopolists to determine whether these are 'excessive' and indicative of abuse. A report prepared for the OFT's research paper series offers an interesting, although at times very technical, approach (Graham, M., and Steele, A., *The Assessment of Profitability by Competition Authorities*, London, OFT (1997)). A problem with assessing profits, recognized by the authors, is that 'high levels of profit are associated with both competition failure and successful competitive advantage...the competition authorities must...distinguish high profits due to successful advantage from those due to failures of competition' (para. 1.2). Even where very high profits are identified these may simply be the result of very efficient production and innovation, and not be evidence of market abuse. Similarly, the fact that a monopoly makes low profits does not necessarily mean that it is not abusing its position. It might rather be very inefficient, and be surviving only because it is engaged in perpetrating abuses. See also *The Economics of EC Competition Law*, paras 3.58–3.69, and da Silva, L. C., Neils, G., and Chua, S., 'Assessing Profitability in the Context of Competition Law', [2003/2004] Comp LJ 248.

13.2.3 **Predatory and exclusionary conduct**

Predation may be broadly defined as conduct intended primarily to harm competitors, which is likely to result in a short-term loss in order to allow a long-term gain. It is most generally, although not exclusively, associated with pricing policies, and predatory pricing is considered in some detail in Chapter 14. As Myers emphasizes, there are other categories of anti-competitive conduct involving low prices that are not, strictly, predatory and that may be better described as 'exclusionary' (Myers, G., *Predatory Behaviour in UK Competition Policy*, London, OFT (1994)). Whether predation or exclusionary conduct can be successful is a matter of sharp disagreement, and while economic modelling may be of assistance it is suggested that the issue cannot be resolved simply by reference to abstract analysis. Decisions as to whether to enter any given market are made by entrepreneurs who will to some extent be swayed by their individual assessment of risks. Thus one commentator has evocatively recognized that

A house with a high wall surrounding its property, iron bars on the windows and a moat will be hard to enter without the permission of the owner. It has 'structural' barriers to entry. A second house with a small 'No Trespassing' sign and a two-foot high white picket fence has low structural barriers to entry. It has been pointed out, however, that if the second house has, in addition to the sign and the fence, a lawn strewn with the lifeless corpses of failed entrants, the next entrant may be effectively deterred. (Rapp, R. T., 'Predatory Pricing Analysis: A Practical Synthesis', NERA, Working Paper No. 2 (1990), pp. 6–7)

It is clear from the case law that the competition authorities recognize reputation effects as playing a significant role in strengthening or maintaining a company's strong position (such an acknowledgement was made by the OFT in its decision *Predation by Aberdeen Journals Ltd* CA98/5/2001 [2001] UKCLR 856 (para. 56)). The EU Commission too has supported a claim of dominance against the largest producer of soda ash in the EU by referring to 'the perception of Solvay by other [Union] producers as the dominant producer and their reluctance to compete aggressively for Solvay's traditional customers' (*Soda Ash—Solvay* 91/299 (1991) OJ L152/21, para. 45).

13.2.4 **Barriers to entry**

'The concept of barriers to entry is', as Bork notes, 'crucial to the antitrust debate' (Bork, R. H., *The Antitrust Paradox*, New York, The Free Press (1993), p. 310). The question to be considered is whether economic theory suggests that a monopolist is able to so harm the market structure as to remove or reduce the threat of competition from other companies. It will be immediately apparent that the answer to this question lies at the heart of the Chicago/Harvard debate. A recognition of the role of barriers to entry supports the Structure–Conduct–Performance model advanced by the Harvard School, and discussed in Chapter 1.

Michael Porter, associated with the Harvard Business School, approaches competition issues from the perspective of a company that wishes to strengthen or protect its position, and is not therefore primarily concerned with competition law. The problem for an incumbent is that 'new entrants to an industry bring new capacity, the desire to gain market share, and often substantial resources. Prices can be bid down or incumbents' costs inflated as a result, reducing profitability'. The threat of entry, he argues, depends 'on the barriers to entry that are present, coupled with the reaction from existing competitors that the entrant can expect' (Porter, M. E., *Competitive Strategy*, New York, The Free Press (1980), p. 7). Porter lists five major barriers to entry: economies of scale; product differentiation; capital requirements; switching costs (i.e., the costs to a buyer of switching to a new supplier); and access to distribution channels. By exploiting and reinforcing these barriers it is suggested that incumbents can increase their power to act independently of competition. Whether competition law can be invoked to reduce these barriers will depend on the circumstances of the particular case: notably the law has tackled product differentiation (e.g., *Contraceptive Sheaths* (Cmnd. 8689, 1982 and Cm. 2529, 1994)) and access to distribution channels (e.g., *Films* (Cm. 2673, 1994)). The presence of economies of scale, which is a form of efficiency, or the requirement that entrants must meet the capital costs of entrance, are not matters that should, or can, be addressed by competition law.

The real question to be resolved in any case 'is whether there exist *artificial* entry barriers that are *not forms of superior efficiency*' (Bork, *The Antitrust Paradox*, above, p. 311, emphasis added). Many economists and antitrust commentators would not, in fact, accept that any of the 'barriers' on Porter's list should fall to be resolved by the application of competition law. It is also here that the theoretical debate is at its most intense, and it is not likely to be resolved in the foreseeable future. In practice the competition lawyer may not need to pursue this debate, as many of the cases may be resolved on the basis of observable conduct. Where, for instance, firms have entered and become established in an industry, that in itself will negate the need for discussion about barriers in most legal proceedings. This may also be the case where there is clear evidence of failed attempts at entry over time.

The issues of vertical integration and vertical restraints which may be associated with both monopolistic and competitive structures are considered in Chapter 8.

13.2.5 Natural monopolies

In one situation a monopoly *is* the efficient market solution. Whether this is the case is determined by the scope of economies of scale: if these are very large in relation to market demand, formally, such that there is no price at which two firms could cover their costs, costs of production are at their lowest level when only one firm is in the market. This will be the case where marginal costs are still falling when the final consumer's demand is satisfied, and will arise in particular where fixed costs are by far the greater component of production, with variable costs being of relatively minor importance. Traditionally such industries have been found to exist where a large and expensive infrastructure is an integral part of that industry (i.e., the utilities, rail transport, and telecommunications). Another type of natural monopoly may also exist under situations of 'network returns'. These arise in industries which are heavily reliant on standards and on product compatibility. A good example is the computing industry. If two operating systems for desktop computers exist, one of which is a superior product (it may even be cheaper) and one of which is already on most computers, it is likely that the requirement that one computer be able to communicate with another will mean that the more popular package will remain dominant, irrespective of other features. The role of such network economies played an important role in the debate about Microsoft's practices and its place in the market.

Developing successful strategies to control these industries has been difficult, and for many years the tendency in 'mixed' economies was to take them into public ownership and therefore direct state control. In the late 1970s and throughout the 1980s the UK led the way in replacing state ownership with private shareholder ownership, regulating conduct by way of licensing systems that restrict both price rises and the return on capital that can be retained by the company. In some cases this has been achieved by separating the various elements of the infrastructure of what were once highly vertically integrated industries. Typically the approach now is to create strict licence conditions for the elements of the infrastructure that remain natural monopolies, and to encourage competition among the remaining elements, whether downstream or upstream.

13.3 Social concerns

Senator Kefauver, author of the United States' Celler–Kefauver Act 1950, argued in support of the Act that 'the history of what has taken place in other nations where . . . economic control [is] in the hands of a very few people is too clear to pass over', thus suggesting that competition law may be employed in the pursuit of socio-political goals. The fact that monopolies redistribute income, generally from the poor to the wealthy (see, e.g., Powell, I., 'The Effect of Reductions in Concentration on Income Distribution', (1987) 69 *Review of Economics and Statistics* 75), may also be used in some quarters to support interventionist arguments. There is no reason why tools of competition law cannot be used in support of wider social objectives, such as income redistribution, but the efficiency of any such move must be doubted. It is unlikely that the application of a sophisticated, and therefore costly, competition law can be more effective in this area than the imposition of, say, a windfall tax on monopoly profits. Fears as to the concentration of power in the hands of the few are also probably better addressed other than by way of competition laws. A well-developed competition law that follows clear economic criteria should, in any event, play its part in raising welfare generally by supporting the competitive process.

13.4 Conclusion

The approach taken to monopolies under competition law is determined in part by the recognition accorded to individual rights in the competitive process. When the

Chicago economists posit efficiency tests as the only acceptable standard by which to frame legislation, they do so without regard to an individual businessman whose efforts have been stifled by the predatory conduct of a more powerful incumbent and without due recognition of 'reputation' effects. The fact that sooner or later the incumbent will be challenged successfully will be of little concern to the bankrupt entrepreneur who has made the first effort, but the position of the failed business is not, in the overall economy, significant. In both the EU and UK regimes competition enforcement is largely complaint driven. This forces the courts, and therefore economists as expert witnesses, to consider the (anti-)competitive impact of short-run activity that might be expected to have little long-run repercussions. Whereas in the 1960s and 1970s such analysis might have been considered to be of questionable value, more recent developments in economic modelling have shown that harmful welfare effects may, in fact, flow from such conduct, although the debate is by no means settled.

FURTHER READING

Books

BESANKO, D., *et al.*, *Economics of Strategy* (2009) 5th edn, John Wiley & Sons, Hoboken, Chapter 6

CARLTON, D. W., and PERLOFF, J. M., *Modern Industrial Organisation* (2005) 4th edn, Addison-Wesley, Boston, MA, Chapter 4

MATEUS, A. M., *Competition Law and Economics: Advances in Competition Policy Enforcement in the EU and North America* (2010) Edward Elgar, Cheltenham

Articles

KAVANAGH, J., 'Assessing Margin Squeeze under Competition Law', (2004) *Competition Law Journal* 187

14

The elements of Article 102 TFEU

KEY POINTS

- Article 102 TFEU applies to abusive conduct engaged in by undertakings in a dominant position.

- The question of whether an undertaking is in a dominant position can be answered only by determining the market in which it operates, and its power within that market.

- The dominant position must be in a 'substantial part' of the internal market.

- Abuses can take many forms, and include conduct which is designed to preserve or expand the power of the undertaking ('exclusionary abuses') or conduct aiming to exploit the power of the undertaking ('exploitative abuses').

- There must be an effect on trade between Member States.

- No exemptions are available, but the alleged abusive conduct may be defended on the grounds that it is 'objectively justifiable'.

- A breach of art. 102 TFEU may incur penalties, damages, and a requirement of conduct modification.

14.1 Introduction

Article 102 TFEU is enacted in the following terms:

Any abuse by one or more undertakings of a dominant position within the internal market or in a substantial part of it shall be prohibited as incompatible with the internal market in so far as it may affect trade between Member States.

   Such abuse may, in particular, consist in:

   (a) directly or indirectly imposing unfair purchase or selling prices or other unfair trading conditions;

   (b) limiting production, markets or technical development to the prejudice of consumers;

   (c) applying dissimilar conditions to equivalent transactions with other trading parties, thereby placing them at a competitive disadvantage;

(d) making the conclusion of contracts subject to acceptance by the other parties of supplementary obligations which, by their nature or according to commercial usage, have no connection with the subject of such contracts.

This provision condemns only the 'abuse' of a dominant position; the mere holding of such a position, or tactics employed by undertakings to attain it when they are not yet dominant, is not outlawed. In contrast, s. 2 of the US Sherman Act condemns 'monopolisation', and is designed to control the practices whereby firms *gain* market power (where the firm already has a sizeable market share). In *US* v *Grinnel Corp.* 384 US 563 (1966) the court sought to attack the 'wilful' acquisition of monopoly power as opposed to the attainment of monopoly through better commercial practices. In *Europemballage Corp. and Continental Can Co. Inc.* v *Commission* case 6/72 [1973] CMLR 199, the Court of Justice made clear the position that the *creation* of a dominant position could not be condemned under art. 102—only its subsequent abuse could be controlled (para. 26 of the judgment).

The result of the application of art. 102 is that a differential standard of conduct applies to undertakings in a dominant position than to others in the market place. This can be a source of some distress to the managers of a company who may not be able to respond to competitive situations as they would wish, and as perhaps they might have been lawfully able to do when the undertaking was still climbing towards its dominant position. The Court of Justice has explained that such an undertaking 'has a special responsibility not to allow its conduct to impair genuine undistorted competition on the [Internal] Market' (*Nederlandsche Banden-Industrie Michelin NV* v *Commission* case 322/81 [1985] 1 CMLR 282, para. 57). As it has greater capacity to distort the market through its actions, it may be reasonable to maintain such a differential standard and to impose this 'special responsibility'.

Broadly, the questions to be asked in relation to the application of art. 102 are:

(a) Is there an undertaking holding a dominant position?

(b) Does this dominant position extend to a substantial part of the internal market?

(c) Is the dominant position being abused?

(d) Is the nature of this abuse such as to affect trade between Member States?

These questions constitute the essence of the summary map included at the end of this chapter, and will be dealt with individually in the next pages.

14.2 Main differences in the application of arts 101 and 102 TFEU

Article 102 TFEU forms the basis of actions far less often than does art. 101. It unavoidably applies to fewer undertakings, and as the guidelines on penalties note (see 6.3.1), 'large undertakings usually have legal and economic knowledge and infrastructures which enable them more easily to recognise that their conduct constitutes an infringement and be aware of the consequences stemming from it under competition law'.

Unlike what happens under art. 101, once an undertaking is found to be in breach of art. 102 there is no opportunity for an exemption to be sought. As Advocate General Lenz stressed in *Ahmed Saeed*, this was a deliberate decision taken by the writers of the Treaty, implicit in the adoption of the term 'abuse': 'abuses cannot be approved, or at any rate not in a community which recognises the rule of law as its highest principle' (*Ahmed Saeed Flugreisen and Silver Line Reisebüro GmbH* v *Zentrale zur Bekämpfung Unlauteren Wettbewerbs eV* case 66/86 [1990] 4 CMLR 102 at 116). This is not to say, however, that there is no elasticity in the application of the article. The concept of 'abuse' is a flexible one and will usually be determined only after careful analysis of each situation.

Another significant difference between art. 102 and art. 101 is that whereas the latter condemns 'anti-competitive' conduct, the prohibition of art. 102 may be extended to situations in which an undertaking exploits its position purely for its own benefit, without reference to the effect that this behaviour may have on competitors. Indeed, in some situations exploitative conduct (14.5), such as charging 'excessive' prices, may serve as a spur to more effective competition by sending a signal to potential entrants as to the high level of profits that may be earned in the market. Yet, it may be condemned as an abuse.

The wording of art. 102 does not make reference to the 'object or effect' rubric found in art. 101. It appears, following recent case law, that it is *not* necessary to demonstrate that there is an anti-competitive effect in order to prove that an illegal abuse is taking place. This was recently confirmed by the GC in two cases relating to exclusionary practices, *Manufacture Française des Pneumatiques Michelin* v *Commission* case T–203/01 [2004] 4 CMLR 18 and *British Airways* v *Commission* case T–219/99 [2004] 4 CMLR 19 (an appeal against the latter was dismissed by the Court of Justice in *British Airways* v *Commission* case C–95/04 [2007] 4 CMLR 22). They are discussed elsewhere in relation to the abuses considered. At para. 293 of *British Airways* and para. 239 of *Michelin* the GC held that in effect it is not necessary for an infringement of 102 TFEU to exist; it is enough to prove that the abuse 'tends to restrict competition, or...that the conduct is capable of having, or likely to have, such an effect'. The approach of the court has attracted criticism for adopting a standard for the determination of 'abuse' which is too low. It has been argued that

the [GC] has set a threshold for exclusionary abuse that requires no actual harm, no likelihood of harm, but rather merely the *potential* for harm. This threshold focuses on the restriction on the customer, rather than the effect on the competitor...Aside from the rather conclusory language of object and effect in *Michelin II*, there is no attempt to explain the rationale for these rules in law or competition policy.   (Kallaugher, J., and Sher, B., 'Rebates Revisited: Anti-competitive Effects and Exclusionary Abuse under Article 82', [2004] *ECLR* 263)

14.3 **The meaning of 'dominant position'**

The Court of Justice has defined 'dominant position' as

a position of economic strength enjoyed by an undertaking which enables it to prevent effective competition being maintained on the relevant market by giving it the power to behave to an appreciable extent independently of its competitors, customers and ultimately of its consumers.   (*United Brands Co.* v *Commission* case 27/76 [1978] 1 CMLR 429, para. 65)

Dominance does not require that there be *no* competition. In *Hoffmann-La Roche & Co. AG* v *Commission* case 85/76 [1979] 3 CMLR 211, the Court held that a finding of dominance 'does not preclude some competition…but enables the undertaking which profits by it, if not to determine, at least to have an appreciable influence on the conditions under which that competition will develop, and in any case to act largely in disregard of it' (para. 39). There is no fixed formula by which the dominance referred to in art. 102 may be established. Rather, by analysis of each case the following matters must be resolved:

(a) the relevant product market within which dominance is alleged;

(b) the relevant geographical market over which the alleged dominance extends;

(c) the relevant time period; and

(d) the relative strength of the alleged dominant undertaking.

The last matter may itself call for an examination of several aspects, most important but not exclusive of which is the market share of the relevant product held by the undertaking. Some care must be taken in defining the 'relevant market', which has a different meaning from the word 'market' in general commerce. The 'relevant market' may not be limited to the undertaking's definition of its sales area or the traditional definition applied by the industry to its sector. Defining it is crucial for determining whether or not an undertaking holds a dominant position; this section will explore the elements that need to be considered.

14.3.1 **The relevant product market**

In order to define the relevant product market, it is necessary to think in terms of *substitutability* (1.4.4.1). An example helps to understand this. Imagine you are thinking of buying a car, and you particularly like sport utility vehicles (SUVs). You have seen an advert for Volkswagen's first hybrid, the new Touareg. You are drawn to it because it is big and yet its pollution levels are low. When you get to the local Volkswagen car dealership, it does not have the Touareg on sale yet, but there is a Volkswagen Polo on offer; it runs only on diesel. Would you consider buying it? If the answer is yes, then both cars may form part of the same relevant market. This is likely to be true if the car on sale has similar features to that which you were originally looking for. However, the Polo is not an SUV but a much smaller car, and you also were looking for an environmentally friendly vehicle. Therefore, it is highly unlikely that you will be tempted to purchase it, as it will not be fit for your needs. Of course, not every consumer will react in the same way in such a situation. When it comes to defining the relevant market, it is necessary to try to establish what most consumers would consider to be substitutes of a specific good or service; the question is thus how likely consumers are to buy the discounted Polo instead of the Touareg.

The above example reflects that there is an element of subjectivity in the definition of the relevant product market. Generally, it is in the interests of a defendant under-taking to describe the product market as broadly as possible, and for the Commission to define it narrowly. The more narrowly the market is defined, the greater the market share of any one undertaking will be, and the greater the likelihood of falling within the scope of the competition provisions. Thus the manufacturer of the Volkswagen Touareg motor car will have a 100 per cent share of the market, which is to say a total monopoly, if the product market is defined as being 'new Volkswagen Touaregs'. If the market is extended to that of hybrid SUVs, the market share will drop to a level that probably remains significant but falls well short of monopoly. If the relevant market is extended to include all motor cars, including perhaps second-hand vehicles, and certain forms of public transport which to some extent compete with new cars, the market share will be insignificant.

14.3.1.1 The implications of substitutability—the SSNIP test

As explained above, the most important factor in defining the relevant product mar-ket is that of substitutability (or 'cross-elasticity'). In *Hoffmann-La Roche*, the Court of Justice stated that '[t]he concept of the relevant market presupposes that there is a suf-ficient degree of interchangeability between all the products forming part of the same market'. Substitutability can be analysed from the perspective of both the consumer of the product ('demand substitutability') and the suppliers or potential suppliers of the product ('supply substitutability'). In its notice on market definition (see 14.3.4) the Commission points to the formal test of 'demand substitution arising from small, permanent changes in relative prices'. This implies asking the following question: to what extent would customers switch to readily available substitutes in response to a hypothetical, small (5–10 per cent) change in price of the product whose market is being assessed? In the United States this is referred to as the 'SSNIP' test, where SSNIP stands for a 'small but significant non-transitory increase in price' (see also 1.4.4.3, above). Supply substitution requires that suppliers of other products are able to switch production in the short term in response to small but permanent changes in price. Necessarily, as these postulated changes in price are small and as an effect of the switch in supply is likely to result in smaller market shares for all suppliers, the cost of switching production must be small and the risk not substantial.

One of the more important European cases arose in relation to the market for bananas (*United Brands Co.* v *Commission* case 27/76 [1978] 1 CMLR 429). In 1975 the Commission adopted a decision relating to certain conduct carried out by United Brands Continental, a subsidiary of a US firm accounting for 35 per cent of world banana exports (Key case 14.2). It held that the market in question was that specifi-cally for bananas, as against a more general market for soft fruit or for all fruit, and found the company had engaged in a range of abusive conduct. When the case reached the Court of Justice, the problem was defined as being one of whether bananas were 'reasonably interchangeable by consumers with other kinds of fresh fruit' (para. 12). United Brands argued that bananas 'compete with other fresh fruit in the same shops, on the same shelves, at prices which can be compared, satisfying the same needs: consumption as a dessert or between meals' (para. 13). The Commission however argued that it was right to treat bananas as being part of a discrete market, and pointed in particular to the fact that 'the banana is a very important part of the diet of certain sections of the community' (para. 19), namely, the very young, the elderly, and the sick. The fruit possessed unique characteristics: 'appearance, taste, softness, seedlessness [and] easy handling' (para. 31). Further, at that time, bananas were unusual in being available all the year round. The Court held that 'a very large number of consumers having a constant need for bananas are not noticeably or even appreciably enticed away' by other fruit and that 'consequently the banana market is a market which is sufficiently distinct from the other fresh fruit market' (para. 35).

It may often be possible to establish that, because of a set of preferences peculiar to that group, particular groups of consumers are insensitive to the price of a given product. However, care should be taken before concluding from this that a separate market exists over which dominance is more easily established. The question is not one of how much the monopolist could in theory charge that group for the product, but one of whether the remaining consumers' behaviour will act as a limit on pricing decisions. Unless a monopolist seller of bananas can isolate the sick and elderly, and force them to pay more, the price can be raised only across the entire supply. This might increase the revenue from that one group, but it is likely to be more than offset by a fall in profit from other consumers who are able to switch to different products. Market analysis should, if results are to be meaningful, focus on the group of consumers who can switch consumption at the margin, and not on the group who cannot—this is the essence of the SSNIP test.

Similar analysis to that of *United Brands* was conducted in *Nederlandsche Banden-Industrie Michelin NV* v *Commission* case 322/81 [1985] 1 CMLR 282. The Commission had condemned the well-known tyre manufacturer for, *inter alia*, its policies relating to dealer discounts and bonuses. Michelin argued that the Commission had incorrectly defined the relevant market and, in so doing, had inflated its market share. The market for tyres is a complex one. Tyres are supplied both with the original vehicle purchase and as replacements; they are available in different sizes, qualities, and treads, depending in part upon the vehicle to which they are to be attached; old tyres may be given new treads ('retreads') and these compete with new replacement tyres. In taking its decision the Commission defined the relevant market as that for new replacement tyres for lorries, buses, and similar vehicles.

Michelin claimed that the relevant market should also include car and van tyres. The Court made the point that 'there is no interchangeability between car and van tyres on the one hand and heavy-vehicle tyres on the other' (para. 39). Responding to the supply-side substitutability argument, it was noted that to switch production between tyres for heavy vehicles and those for cars and vans was no easy matter and would require the investment of considerable time and money by manufacturers. Neither did the Court accept that retreads competed directly with new replacement tyres, even though there might be an element of substitution—Michelin had itself conceded that a retread would not always be as safe or reliable as a new tyre. A similar conclusion on market definition was made in *Michelin (II)* 2002/405/EC (2002) OJ L58/25. It is interesting to note that in 1980 the courts in the United States found, basing their view in part on the existence of a $30 price differential, that separate markets existed in the case of radial and non-radial tyres in the case of *Donald B. Rice Tire Co.* v *Michelin Tire Corp.* 483 F. Supp. 750 (D. Md. 1980).

While the Commission has usually been successful in defending its market definitions, it lost the notable case of *Europemballage Corp. and Continental Can Co. Inc.* v *Commission* case 6/72 [1973] CMLR 199. Here the Court held that the Commission had failed adequately to justify its reasoning in defining the three relevant markets as being those for 'light containers for canned meat products', 'light containers for canned seafood', and 'metal closures for the food packing industry'. It is analysed further as Key case 14.1.

Key case 14.1 *Continental Can Co. Inc.* (1972) OJ L7/25; *Europemballage Corporation and Continental Can Co. Inc.* v *Commission* case 6/72 [1973] CMLR 199—Commission Decision, Court of Justice judgment (art. 102)

Facts

Continental Can Company Inc. was a New York based firm manufacturing metal packages, packaging materials of paper and plastic, and machines for manufacturing and using those packaging materials. Through a succession of share purchases in 1969 it acquired 85.8 per cent of the share capital of Schmalback-Lubeca-Werke AG (SLW), a German company active in the same market. In the same year it entered into discussions with the Metal Box Company Ltd relating to the creation of a European holding company for packaging in which certain of its licensees would participate. In 1970 an agreement was signed between Continental Can and TDV under which the Europemballage Corporation was set up in Delaware, and this latter corporation made an offer for the shares of TDV. Soon afterwards the Commission contacted the undertakings drawing their attention to the possible illegality of the arrangement, and Metal Box withdrew from its planned participation. Europemballage carried out the purchase of shares in TDV, and the Commission opened a procedure. It found that a breach of art. 102 had taken place, as Continental Can, through SLW, occupied a dominant position 'over a substantial part of the [internal] market for light packaging for preserved meat, fish and crustacea and on the market in metal caps for glass jars' (art. 1). It had subsequently abused this position by the purchase of shares in TDV. An appeal was made.

Findings

Continental Can disputed the power of the Commission to apply EU competition law to the activities of a US-based corporation. The Court held that it had acted through its subsidiary, Europemballage, and that its conduct could be attributed to the parent company. Thus the transaction was 'to be attributed not only to Europemballage, but also first and foremost to Continental' (para. 16). It was, the applicants said, contrary to the intentions of the authors of the Treaty to apply the principles set out in art. 102 TFEU to merger situations. None of the examples of conduct set out in the article included mergers, and there was nothing in the conduct undertaken by Continental Can which in any way flowed from its alleged dominant position. However, the Court pointed to the wording of art. 102 which made reference to '*any* abuse'. The list set out in the article was merely illustrative, and was aimed broadly at practices that would be detrimental to consumers either directly, but also through their impact on the competition structure. In light of this analysis 'the strengthening of the position of an undertaking may be an abuse . . . regardless of the means and procedure by which it is achieved' (para. 27).

However, it was first necessary to establish that Continental Can held a dominant position in a relevant market. The Commission had referred to three separate markets, but did not set out in any substantial detail how those three markets differed from each other, and why they should be considered separately. Similarly, 'nothing is said about how these three markets differ from the general market for light metal containers, namely the market for metal containers for fruit and vegetables, condensed milk, olive oil, fruit juices and chemico-technical products' (para. 33). The Court found that the Commission appeared to be uncertain as to its approach to market definition. It had drawn distinctions between different conditions under which packagers could themselves supply the products, but had not set out any proper criteria for differentiating among them, or for evaluating the power of this supply-side substitution. The decision was annulled on the grounds that it did not sufficiently show the facts and the assessments on which it was based.

Comment

Three factors are particularly significant about this case. The first is that the Commission failed because it did not define the relevant market properly. While it might now seem evident that market definition is fundamental and must be dealt with effectively, cases continue to fall on this ground. An example may be found in civil litigation in the UK in the case of *Chester City Council and Chester City Transport Limited* v *Arriva plc and Arriva Cymru Ltd and Arriva North West Ltd* [2007] EWHC 1373 (Ch). Rimer J dismissed a claim brought on the basis of the Chapter II Prohibition of the Competition Act 1998 on the ground that the relevant market had not been made out to the standard of proof required. The second element is the link between this case and the development of merger control in the EU (see Chapter 19). Although the Commission lost the argument on market definition, the Court of Justice agreed that an abuse could be found in an already dominant undertaking acquiring a weaker competitor. Third, the case demonstrated clearly, at an early stage of the development of EU competition law, that conduct which would normally be quite unobjectionable could be unlawful when carried out by a dominant undertaking. This is to say that it is not necessarily the *form* of conduct which falls to be condemned under art. 102, but rather the *effect* of that conduct—a principle consistent with the 'special responsibility' set out in *Michelin* (see 14.1).

FURTHER READING

Article

Vogelenzang, P., 'Abuse of a Dominant Position in Article 86', (1976) 13 *CMLRev* 61

Demand- and supply-side substitutability may be the most important factor in the determination of the relevant product market, but other factors may also be relevant. In some instances, such as in *AKZO Chemie BV v EC Commission* case C–62/86 [1993] 5 CMLR 215 (considered in detail in Chapter 16), the Court has accepted the Commission's view that the action of the allegedly dominant undertaking is itself evidence of the bounds of the product market. It is surely correct that if an undertaking apparently engages in an abusive practice, which would be commercially beneficial only if a dominant position was held, it may be presumed that it does indeed have a dominant position.

The failure to come to court with a carefully considered market analysis may have fatal consequences for the progress of the case. In *Sockel GmbH v The Body Shop International plc* [2000] UKCLR 262, an action was dismissed largely because the claimant had failed to adequately define the market. An abuse of a dominant position was alleged on the part of Body Shop, relying on the fact that its franchise system set out the bounds of the relevant market, without any consideration of competition from other brands and outlets.

14.3.1.2 Spare parts and ancillary products

The issue of spare parts and ancillary products was first dealt with by the EU authorities in the case of *Hugin* (*Hugin Kassaregister AB and Hugin Cash Registers Ltd v Commission* case 22/78 [1979] 3 CMLR 345). The Commission had taken a decision that the non-dominant supplier of cash machines held a dominant position in the market for spare parts for those machines (78/68 (1978) OJ L22/23). The Court agreed that, based on arguments relating to substitutability, the spare parts were not interchangeable with those for other machines. It was also unreasonable to suggest that a consumer purchase a new cash register from a different supplier as an alternative to fitting a spare part in an existing device.

The case has been followed since (see, e.g., *Volvo AB v Erik Veng (UK) Ltd* case 238/87 [1989] 4 CMLR 122) but it has raised concerns. It may be argued that a consumer choosing an initial purchase (in *Hugin* a cash register, and in *Volvo*, a motor car) must consider, as part of that decision, aspects such as the costs of maintenance and after-sales servicing, of which the availability of spare parts is just one element. In neither of the above cases did the undertaking hold a dominant position in the primary market; as the consumer is able to make a choice at this stage, it is very much to the disadvantage of the undertaking if it has thrust upon it unexpected and unwelcome responsibilities in the secondary market, for which it may not have budgeted, following a finding of dominance in that market. This claim is persuasive as long as the assumption of symmetry of knowledge between consumer and undertaking remains valid, but falls down where the consumer lacks access to information on which to base such calculations at the point of original purchase.

A similar assertion may be made in relation to ancillary products (or 'consumables'/'lock-ins') such as toner cartridges for printers, or semi-manufactured products to work with industrial machinery. It might be expected that the consumer, even more so than with spare parts, is in a position to factor in the ancillary items at the time of making the initial purchase. Two major cases are of particular importance: *Hilti AG v Commission* case T–30/89 [1992] 4 CMLR 16 and *Tetra Pak International SA v Commission* case T–83/91 [1992] 4 CMLR 76 (*Tetra Pak II*). In *Hilti* the Court held that a distinction could be made between three separate markets: a nail-gun used in the construction trade, the cartridge strip in which the nails were placed, and the nails themselves. As with *Hugin, Hilti* did not hold a dominant position in the market for fixing systems for use in the construction industry, but did hold such a position in relation to the two ancillary markets. In *Tetra Pak II* the Commission argued that the market for filling machines to package liquid foods into cartons was a different market from that for the cartons into which the foods were placed (92/163 (1992) OJ L72/1). The Court agreed. This would be an example of supply-side substitutability where manufacturers making cartons for their own machines could also, with minimal adjustment to production lines, produce cartons for other machines.

In its *25th Report on Competition Policy* (COM(96) 126 final) the Commission accepted that this is a difficult area in which complaints can be resolved only on a case-by-case basis. It implies taking into account 'all important factors such as the price and life-time of the primary product, transparency of prices of secondary products, prices of secondary products as a proportion of the primary product value, information costs and other issues' (point 86). Such an approach was taken in *Pelikan/Kyocera* (point 87) where the Commission dealt with a complaint relating to activity in the market for toner cartridges for printers. It was held that Kyocera was not dominant in a secondary market for cartridges to be used with its printers, as consumers 'were well informed about the price charged for consumables and appeared to take this into account in their decision to buy a printer'. Four factors were set out as being important when making the assessment whether a secondary market existed independently of the primary market:

(1) Would the consumer be in a position to make an informed choice at the point of initial purchase about the life cycle of the product, and the associated costs of any consumables? For example, in the case of a printer and toner cartridges would the consumer be able to 'punish' a company that appeared to abuse its power in the aftermarket by making a different choice in the primary market?

(2) Would the consumer actually make that choice?

(3) Would a sufficient number of consumers respond to apparent abuses in the aftermarket by adjusting their choices in the primary market?

(4) Would the response time of consumers be quick enough to protect those locked in to the aftermarket?

There has been much criticism of the approach taken by the EU Commission in this area, and of the *Hugin* decision in particular. Some support for such a course may be adduced from the US case of *Eastman Kodak Co.* v *Image Technical Services Inc.* 504 US 451 (1992), where a broadly similar stance was taken in relation to 'locked-in' customers for spare parts where the cost of switching would be high. This has been followed in similar cases in the US.

14.3.2 The relevant geographic market

Having considered what the relevant product market is, the geographic boundaries of that market must then be shown. This is an important consideration; while an undertaking may be dominant in a very small area—the classic example of which is the bus company that is dominant with respect to a single route—art. 102 requires that a dominant position extend to a 'substantial part' of the EU (see 14.4). The close link between these two considerations has been made clear by the Court of Justice, which has held that the application of art. 102 'presupposes the clear delimitation of the substantial part of the [EU] in which [an undertaking] may be able to engage in abuses which hinder effective competition and this is an area where the objective conditions of competition applying to the product in question must be the same for all traders' (*United Brands Co.* v *Commission* case 27/76 [1978] 1 CMLR 429, para. 44). An examination of the geographic market should also take into account that an undertaking may appear to be dominant in one territory, but may be restrained by competition or the threat of competition from outside that area.

In *United Brands* (Key case 14.2), the Commission considered that the geographic market constituted Germany, Denmark, Ireland, and the Benelux countries, but excluded the other three Member States of the time (UK, Italy, and France) on the grounds that the legacy of history was such that there existed special circumstances relating to the import of bananas in those countries. The undertaking contested further that each Member State constituted a separate market as the conditions of competition were different in each state, with different customs systems and different patterns of consumption. The Court argued that it is the conditions of competition, and not the result of that competition, that are important in determining the boundaries of the geographic market. In each of the six states the market was free, and the conditions of competition were the same for all undertakings. As a result, they 'form[ed] an area which [was] sufficiently homogenous to be considered in its entirety' (at para. 53). Thus the fact that there are price differences between areas is not in itself evidence of separate markets (see, e.g., *Soda Ash–Solvay* 91/299 (1991) OJ L152/21).

In some instances the identification of the relevant area will be relatively straight-forward. There may, for instance, be specific evidence pointing to a clear boundary to the market. In a series of cases relating to television guides and television list-ings the relevant areas were, in each case, those in which the television programmes themselves were primarily intended to be received (see, e.g., *RTÉ v Commission* case T–69/89 [1991] 4 CMLR 586 (Ireland) and *BBC v Commission* case T–70/89 [1991] 4 CMLR 669 (UK)). The action of a state monopoly, or of state regulation, may also define the market strictly. This was the situation in *British Leyland plc v Commission* case 226/84 [1987] 1 CMLR 185, which related to the system of a national approval cer-tificate for motor cars. The position may be more complicated where there is an appar-ently national market, as might be the case for any national newspaper, but where there is nevertheless some inter-state trade. If *The Times* is sold on news-stands in the major cities in Europe in small numbers, is the relevant geographic market that of the UK or wider, extending into the entire continent?

There has been some criticism of the approach taken by the Commission and the Court in defining the geographic market in the first *Michelin* case. Although it was rec-ognized that the main tyre companies competed at the global level, the Commission had argued that the actions of each subsidiary were tailored to the specific conditions of each national market and had treated the Netherlands as a separate market from the rest of the Union. The Court agreed, since 'in practice dealers established in The Netherlands obtain their supplies only from suppliers operating in The Netherlands' (*Nederlandsche Banden-Industrie Michelin NV v Commission* case 322/81 [1985] 1 CMLR 282, para. 26). The possibility of consumers going across the border for their tyres should have been discussed more fully. It is likely that the competitive conditions in the country were, at the least, moderately affected by the availability of supplies from elsewhere in the EU.

As a rule of thumb the size of the market is in inverse proportion to the product's transportation costs relative to the value of the product: a product with a high value and a low transportation cost will have a large geographic market, whereas a product with a low value and a high transportation cost will have a small geographic market. That transport costs may be highly influential in determining the boundaries to the market may be seen in *Napier Brown–British Sugar* 88/518 (1988) OJ L284/41. The Commission considered that the UK constituted a separate geographic market, *inter alia*, because imports into the UK over the period immediately preceding its action had amounted to only 5–10 per cent of consumption. It noted that this was partly the result of 'the natural barrier of the English Channel, which gives rise to additional transport costs'. Sugar represents a classic example of a product with high transport costs in relation to value: it is bulky and relatively cheap.

In situations where transport costs do not constitute a significant barrier to trade, the relevant geographic market may often be that of the entire Union (see, e.g., *ECS/ AKZO* 85/609 (1985) OJ L374/1, para. 66). In *Tetra Pak I (BTG Licence)*, which con-cerned the market for packaging machines and consumables for liquid foods, the Commission held that 'even if there exist the differing demand conditions between Member States, the [EU] is the relevant geographical market... transport costs for both machines and cartons are not significant. In fact carton packaging machinery supplied to dairies in the [EU] comes from producers all over the world' (88/501 (1988) OJ L272/27, para. 41).

14.3.3 **The relevant time period**

Time is a factor that must be considered in order to establish the relevant period over which the dominance is alleged, and over which the alleged abuse may have been perpetrated. It is extremely rare for the analysis of the temporal market to be a significant feature of a decision or case. The most notable example arises out of the 1973/74 oil crisis. A Commission decision held that the critical situation had led to the creation of a series of temporarily defined separate markets in favour of each supplier. Customers were unable to switch as supplies were being rationed, and suppliers were making them available only to their traditional customers (*ABG Oil companies operating in the Netherlands* 77/327 (1977) OJ L117/1). While the Commission lost the case on appeal on different grounds, the Court left intact the temporal arguments (*BP v Commission* case 77/77 [1978] 3 CMLR 174). The Commission's determination of the time constraints over which the relevant market is defined is not likely to be successfully challenged, but there may be arguments as to the duration of the alleged abuse as it is a factor for the level of any fines imposed (Chapter 6).

14.3.4 **The Commission notice on market definition**

In 1997 the Commission published a *Notice on the definition of the relevant market for the purpose of Community competition law* ((1997) OJ C372/5). The notice firmly places the SSNIP test at the heart of market definition. Indeed, in its subsequent decision relating to the *1998 Football World Cup* 2000/12 (2000) OJ L5/55 (paras 66–74), the Commission was explicit in its application of the notice's SSNIP test to define the relevant market (but see *Virgin/British Airways* 2000/74 (2000) OJ L30/1, where the Commission indicated that it was not required to perform the SSNIP test, and that the methodology set out in the notice was merely an illustration of the way in which markets operated).

The notice applies equally to analysis conducted for the purposes of applying arts 101 and 102 and the EU Merger Regulation (see Chapter 19), as well as the EEA Agreement. The Commission recognizes that, because the purpose for which competition law is being applied may be different under each legislative head, the methodology outlined above 'might lead to different results depending on the nature of the competition issue being examined', but that certain basic principles apply in all cases. These economic constants are the factors that serve as competitive restraints on the undertaking whose conduct or concentrative transaction is being analysed: demand substitution and supply substitution.

Supply-side substitution, which is a factor in market definition, is to be distinguished from potential competition, which is not. The notice makes clear the fact that the Commission does not consider it appropriate to take into account potential competition (see, e.g., *Europemballage Corp. and Continental Can Co. Inc. v Commission* case 6/72 [1973] CMLR 199) at the stage of market definition. This is not to say that this factor is disregarded, but that 'the conditions under which potential competition will actually represent an effective competitive constraint depend on the analysis of specific factors and circumstances related to the conditions of entry' and that, if required, such analysis will be carried out only *after* the relevant market has been defined. The key distinction between supply-side substitution and potential competition lies in the time period over which each may take place, with potential competition arising only over a longer time frame.

The notice sheds useful light on the practicalities of market analysis and the extent to which the Commission may be able to avoid the sort of analysis undertaken in the *United Brands* case. It is apparent that in the right circumstances cases will be fairly quickly dealt with where the issue is simply one of 'whether product A and product B belong or do not belong to the same product market', and where the determination that they do will at once eliminate any competition concerns. If more detailed analysis is called for the Commission may contact main customers, companies, relevant professional associations, the undertakings directly involved, and companies in upstream markets (defined as those closer to the original source of production or raw input). Factors that may serve as evidence to define product markets include an analysis of the product characteristics, evidence of substitution in the recent past, various econometric and statistical approaches, views of customers and competitors, consumer preferences as perhaps identified by consumer surveys commissioned within the industry in the past, barriers and costs of switching consumption and the possible existence of different groups of consumers and price discrimination.

A broadly similar approach is taken to the geographic market, the objective being, as indicated above, 'to identify which companies selling the products in the relevant market are actually competing with the parties and constraining their behaviour, with the focus placed on prices'. The evidence that the notice suggests may be used to define the geographic market includes: past evidence of diversion of orders to other areas; basic demand characteristics, including factors such as national preferences; views of customers and competitors; current geographic patterns of purchases; trade flows; and barriers and costs of switching sources.

The notice does not deal with the issue of the temporal definition of the market.

14.3.5 The relative strength of the alleged dominant undertaking

Having established the relevant market—product, geographic area, and time period— the next requirement for art. 102 to apply is that dominance in that market be established. Dominance may be attributed to an undertaking by virtue of a variety of factors, of which the most important is market share. However, market share may not be the sole determinant, and situations may arise in which an undertaking commands a large market share yet is not dominant. This might be the case, for example, where there is the serious threat of *potential* competition. Likewise there may be situations where an undertaking has a seemingly innocuous share but the relatively weak positions of its main competitors lead to dominance.

14.3.5.1 Market share

The role that market shares play in determining dominance is fundamental. In some circumstances, a particular share may, by itself, be relied upon in establishing the existence of a dominant position. The classic statement in this context is to be found in the case of *Hoffmann-La Roche*. The appellant undertaking manufactured various vitamins, each of which was treated as a separate product market. The Court of Justice held that

although the importance of the market shares may vary from one market to another the view may legitimately be taken that very large shares are in themselves, and save in exceptional circumstances, evidence of the existence of a dominant position. An undertaking which has a very large market share and holds it for some time, by means of the volume of production and the scale of the supply which it stands for—without those having much smaller market shares being able to meet rapidly the demand from those who would like to break away from the undertaking which has the largest market share—is by virtue of that share in a position of strength which makes it an unavoidable trading partner and which already because of this secures for it, at the very least during relatively long periods, that freedom of action which is the special feature of a dominant position.   (*Hoffmann-La Roche & Co. AG v Commission* case 85/76 [1979] 3 CMLR 211, para. 41)

The point made in this judgment that very large market shares may by themselves be conclusive of dominance was cited in *AKZO*, where the Court held that a share of 50 per cent would satisfy this test (*AKZO Chemie BV v Commission* case C–62/86 [1993] 5 CMLR 215). In *Michelin (II)* 2002/405 (2002) OJ L58/25 the Commission relied partly on the fact that 'all the analyses combine to show that Michelin's share of the two relevant markets has exceeded this [50 per cent] threshold consistently for more than 20 years' (para. 175).

The Commission appears on occasion to be more conservative than the Court in its use of market share. In *BBI/Boosey & Hawkes: interim measures* 87/500 (1987) OJ L286/36, Boosey & Hawkes, the leading manufacturer of musical instruments for brass bands, was found to have 'a market share of some 80 per cent to 90 per cent'. Nonetheless, noting that 'a high market share does however not on its own create a presumption of dominance', it pointed also to other evidence. However, there are clear instances where a finding of dominance is made by exclusive reference to market share. In *Decca* (*Decca Navigator System* 89/113 (1989) OJ L43/27) the undertaking had a legal monopoly in relation to the relevant market for the period during which it held patents in respect of the relevant technology, and thereafter held a market share such as to constitute a de facto monopoly. No other evidence was necessary to establish dominance.

Generally, the approach appears to be that a market share of 70 per cent and above will almost certainly constitute a dominant position; a share of 50–70 per cent will raise a presumption of dominance; a share of 40–50 per cent may support a conclusion of dominance; and a share of below 40 per cent is highly unlikely to permit the finding of dominance unless other evidence is overwhelming. In *Virgin/British Airways* 2000/74 (2000) OJ L30/1 dominance was found to exist at a point when BA's market share of the total airline sales in the UK in 1998 amounted to 39.7 per cent (para. 41). There were other factors strongly indicative of dominance, including the relatively low market shares of other parties. On appeal the GC upheld the findings of the Commission, arguing that

The economic strength which BA derives from its market share is further reinforced by the world rank it occupies in terms of international scheduled passenger-kilometres flown, the extent of the range of its transport services and its hub network.

According to BA's own statements, its network operations allow it, in comparison with its five competitors, to offer a wider choice of routes and more frequent flights.

It is further shown…that, in 1995, [BA] operated 92 of the 151 international routes from Heathrow Airport and 43 of the 92 routes in service at Gatwick, that is to say several times the number of routes served by each of its three or four nearest rivals…   (*British Airways plc* v *Commission* case T–219/99, 17 December 2003, paras 212–14)

Until 2008, 39.7 per cent was the lowest figure at which a finding of dominance had been sustained. In August that year, Ofcom held that British Telecom had been dominant in the market for NTS call termination/hosting between May 2004 and December 2005 with a market share below 31 per cent (*NCCN 500* (2008) CW/00823/03/05). However, it concluded that it had not abused its dominant position and there were no grounds for further investigation. In its *Guidance on the enforcement of Art. 82 in relation to exclusionary conduct* (December 2008), the Commission recognizes that when a company has a market share of less than 40 per cent, 'dominance is not likely'. Whether this non-binding threshold will be regarded in future decisions remains to be seen.

14.3.5.2 Competitors' positions

The relative size of the competitors' market shares were determining evidence as to the existence of a dominant position in relation to certain vitamins in *Hoffmann-La Roche* (above). In the market for vitamin C the Court, for instance, pointed to the fact that 'the gap between Roche's shares (64.8 per cent) and those of its next largest competitors (14.8 per cent and 6.3 per cent) was such as to confirm the conclusion' of dominance (para. 63). In the market for other vitamins, where Roche's market share was smaller, they were considered supporting evidence. For example, in vitamin A the market shares were 47 per cent to Roche, and 27 per cent, 18 per cent, 7 per cent, and 1 per cent to the other producers. The relevant market was found to be oligopolistic, and

Roche's share, which is equal to the aggregate of the shares of its two next largest competitors, proves that it is entirely free to decide what attitude to adopt when confronted by competition.   (para. 51)

In *Sabena* (*London European* v *Sabena* 88/589 (1988) OJ L317/47) the Commission found that the market share held by the undertaking in the market of computerized airline reservation systems in Belgium was between 40 and 50 per cent. As such a share would not, by itself, support a claim of dominance, it noted that 'the ratio of market shares held by the undertaking concerned to those held by its competitors is also a reliable indicator' (para. 24). In this case the five competing systems were each used by no more than 20 agencies, as compared to the 118 agencies using the Sabena system.

14.3.5.3 Barriers to entry

As noted in Chapter 13, the role played by barriers to entry in industrial economics and antitrust analysis is of vital importance. The establishment of the market share of the allegedly dominant undertaking cannot by itself determine the competitive restraints under which the company operates. It is possible, albeit unlikely, that an undertaking could have a 100 per cent market share and yet not be able to reap significant profits if it is constantly aware of the danger of potential competition. This might be triggered by higher prices signalling to entrepreneurs that profits can be made in the market. Barriers to entry are not, however, easily analysed and often require a more dynamic long-term view of market structure than does a straightforward static analysis of current market shares.

The situation is further complicated by disagreements between industrial economists as to the meaning of the term 'barrier to entry' and as to those factors that may legitimately be considered to be barriers. It is in the definition of this term that one of the most dramatic differences lies between the Harvard and Chicago schools. In its decisions the Commission has pointed to the existence of identifiable barriers to entry, but has not developed an entirely satisfactory framework. For example, in *Tetra Pak I* (88/501 (1988) OJ L272/27), as well as relying on the undertaking's 91.8 per cent market share in the relevant market—'machines capable of filling cartons by an aseptic process with UHT-treated liquids'—the Commission considered that the 'barriers to entry to produce aseptic packaging machines are particularly high, which severely limits the entry of new competitors' (para. 44.3). This may be true, but it is not adequately supported by detailed reasoning found within the decision itself.

In the absence of a sophisticated analysis, the Commission has turned instead to a range of evidence which it considers to be indicative of dominance. It has not always clarified whether these secondary factors are also considered proof of barriers to entry or of dominance *per se*.

14.3.5.4 The resources, size, and commercial superiority of the undertaking

In *British Plasterboard* (*BPB Industries plc* 89/22 (1989) OJ L10/50), once the Commission found that the undertaking's share of the plasterboard market in Great Britain was between 98 and 96 per cent for the relevant period, it may seem unnecessary to have referred to other factors to support the argument that the company enjoyed a dominant position. Nevertheless the 'substantial economies in producing on a large scale in integrated industrial complexes' (para. 116) enjoyed by BPB were also highlighted. Further, the extensive product range carried by BPB and the fact that architects were on occasion specific in requiring the use of BPB's products were additional points used as evidence. The failings of a static, snapshot analysis are perhaps demonstrated by this decision. While on these facts it appears the BPB's position would be unassailable, an MMC report in 1990 (*Plasterboard*, Cm. 1224) found that BPB's market share had fallen from 96 per cent to 65 per cent in two years following the entry of new competition into the market.

Undertakings which have succeeded in developing an efficient and strong distribution system may find that this is one factor that supports a finding of dominance. Thus, for instance, in *Eurofix-Bauco/Hilti* 88/138 (1988) OJ L65/19 the Commission emphasized Hilti's 'strong and well-organised distribution system—in the [EU] it has subsidiaries and independent dealers integrated into its selling network' (para. 69). In *Soda Ash* (*Soda Ash—Solvay* 91/299 (1991) OJ L152/21) dominance was established by reference to, *inter alia*, the company's manufacturing strength (with plants in six Member States), its upstream integration as the largest producer of salt in the EU, and Solvay's 'excellent market coverage as the exclusive or near-exclusive supplier to almost all the major customers in the [Union]'.

The Commission may turn not only to product ranges, but also to the services offered by the allegedly dominant company (both where these are the primary activity and where they are ancillary to the supply of the primary product). In a decision taken in respect of shipping services between Zaire and Angola and various North Sea ports (*Cewal* 93/82 (1993) OJ L34/20), the assertion of dominance was supported by reference to the 'network of routes, the capacities of [Cewal's] fleet and the frequency of the services it can provide' (para. 59). The level of technical support that could be provided by Michelin's large number of representatives (*BF BV/NV NBI Michelin* 81/969 (1981) OJ L353/33), which was greater than that of rival manufacturers, was also an important indicator.

14.3.5.5 Technical superiority and the possession of know-how and intellectual property

Technical superiority was considered relevant by the Court of Justice in *Hoffmann-La Roche & Co. AG* v *Commission* case 85/76 [1979] 3 CMLR 211 as a further indication that Roche held a dominant position (para. 51). Similar considerations were raised in *Eurofix-Bauco/Hilti* 88/138 (1988) OJ L65/19, where Hilti's DX 450 nail-gun was commended for its 'novel technically advantageous features' which were subject to patent protection. The Commission also drew attention to Hilti's 'extremely strong research and development position'. In *Tetra Pak I* 88/501 (1988) OJ L272/27, Tetra Pak's first-mover advantage was pointed out: 'it was the first to develop the technology and has vast experience . . . its technology and machines are partially protected by patents' (para. 44.2).

The possession of copyright in published material may also lead to a conclusion of dominance if the relevant market is drawn tightly. The Commission dealt with complaints relating to the practices of the IBA, BBC, and RTÉ television networks, in relation to programme listings. The undertakings' policy was to reserve to themselves the right to publish advance details of schedules, and they relied in part on their copyright in these listings to obstruct magazines that were attempting to compete with the authorized publications. The Commission held that 'the factual monopoly held by the broadcasting organisations in relation to their . . . listings is strengthened into a legal monopoly' by virtue of the application of copyright laws, and that the companies therefore held a dominant position (*Magill TV Guide/ITP/BBC and RTE* 89/205 (1989) OJ L78/43).

14.3.5.6 Super-dominance

Recent developments in the law of dominance suggest that there has been a refinement to the 'special responsibility' of *Michelin* in the case of undertakings which are 'super-dominant'. This follows from the comments of the Advocate General in the case of *Compagnie Maritime Belge SA* v *Commission* joined cases C-395 and 396/96P [2000] 4 CMLR 1076:

> To my mind, art. [102] cannot be interpreted as permitting monopolists or quasi-monopolists to exploit the very significant market power which their superdominance confers so as to preclude the emergence either of a new or additional competitor. Where an undertaking...enjoys a position of such overwhelming dominance verging on monopoly, comparable to that which existed in the present case...it would not be consonant with the particularly onerous special obligation affecting such a dominant undertaking not to impair further the structure of the feeble existing competition.   (para. 137)

The 'particularly onerous special obligation' referred to here may be witnessed at play in some of the 'essential facility' cases discussed in Chapter 16, where undertakings enjoyed total monopoly in some areas of the market and were able to exclude potential competition from other parts. The Court had already recognized in *Tetra Pak* v *Commission (No. 2)* case C–333/94P [1997] 4 CMLR 662 that the scope of the special responsibility provided for in *Michelin* must be considered in the light of the particular facts of each case. The comments of the Advocate General in *Compagnie Maritime Belge* seem to do little more than provide a convenient label for a situation in which the analysis of the particular facts shows that the existing competition to the monopolist is 'feeble' rather than just 'weakened'.

14.3.5.7 Joint dominance

The law relating to joint dominance (also known as 'collective dominance' and 'oligopolistic dominance') is dealt with here in relation to art. 102, and in Chapter 19 in relation to merger control. The development of the two threads has been inextricably connected. However, following amendments to the merger regulation, the link has been broken (see Chapter 19).

The leading case relating to joint dominance in the context of art. 102 is *Compagnie Maritime Belge SA* v *Commission* joined cases C-395 and 396/96P [2000] 4 CMLR 1076. The case arose by way of an appeal from *Cewal* 93/82 (1993) OJ L34/20 where the Commission had condemned members of a liner conference for attempting, collectively, to eliminate an independent competitor. One of the issues that fell to be dealt with was the extent to which a number of undertakings could *collectively* occupy a dominant position, and the factors conditioning this. Article 102 indeed makes reference to a dominant position held by 'one or more' undertakings, and the Court held that this expression implies that a dominant position may be held by two or more economic entities legally independent of each other, provided that from an economic point of view they present themselves or act together on a particular market as a collective entity. (para. 36)

To establish that such a position exists it is necessary to examine the economic links or factors which give rise to a connection between undertakings. It is not sufficient that the undertakings in question are linked by a practice which would fall within art. 101(1), but such an agreement can result in a position of joint dominance, depending on the way in which the agreement would be implemented. In this case the way in which the liner conference agreement operated presented the parties 'on that market as a collective entity *vis-à-vis* their competitors, their trading partners and consumers' (para. 44).

Joint dominance was also discussed in the context of art. 102 in *Irish Sugar* 97/624 (1997) OJ L258/1, on appeal *Irish Sugar plc* v *Commission* case T–228/97 [1999] 5 CMLR 1300, paras 38–68. It was accepted by all that 'there must be close links between the two entities, and that those links must be such as to be capable of leading to the adoption of the same conduct and policy on the market in question' (para. 45). Here the joint dominance related to a vertical arrangement between a dominant producer of sugar, and the sole bulk distributor of the product in the same Member State.

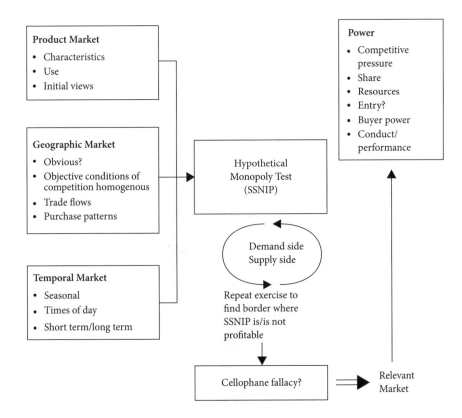

Figure 14.1 The assessment of market power

14.4 **The meaning of 'substantial part' of the internal market**

Article 102 applies where the dominant position identified is found to exist in 'the internal market or in a substantial part of it'. Clearly if dominance extends throughout the EU this jurisdictional hurdle is overcome. The meaning of 'substantial part' is, however, open to interpretation, and is likely to be an inconstant factor: what may have counted as substantial in a Community of six may not be in a Union that has expanded to 27 members. As a result, previous case law may not be a fail-safe guide to future determinations.

It has been traditionally argued that a market extending to a single Member State will meet the threshold, but this may no longer be the case. While there are obvious political difficulties in holding that a state is not 'substantial', the increasing strength of the internal market might allow the authorities to argue that a state-wide market will not automatically be so classed. However, in *Irish Sugar* 97/624 (1997) OJ L258/1 the Republic of Ireland was found to be a substantial part of the internal market although it accounted for only 1.2 per cent of the market for the sale of sugar in the EU. The concept also must be related to the specific market for the product in question, and not merely to an examination of the size of the absolute geographic area identified in defining the market boundary.

14.4.1 **The case law on 'substantial part'**

While a single Member State may not now automatically be substantial, there is no doubt that areas of Member States can be, and that the Union can support several substantial markets in the same product as long as in each the conditions of competition are different (see the discussion of *United Brands*, above). The case of *Suiker Unie* (*Cooperatieve Vereniging 'Suiker Unie' UA*) v *Commission* cases 40–48/73, 50/73, 54–56/73, 111/73, 113–114/73 [1976] 1 CMLR 295) remains one of the most important in determining the meaning of 'substantial'. One of the applicants (Raffinerie Tirlemontoise) was alleged to occupy a dominant position on the sugar market in Belgium and Luxembourg, which the Commission had held to be a substantial part of the internal (then 'common') market. It claimed that this was inconsistent with the small level of production of sugar in Belgium relative to the rest of the Union and with the low number of consumers in the two of the then six Member States. The view taken by the Court was that it would be necessary to take into account 'the pattern and volume of the production and consumption of the said product as well as the habits and economic opportunities of vendors and purchasers' (para. 371). Also relevant would be the fact that the organization of the sugar market by the Union had tended to reinforce national boundaries. In the year 1971–72 sugar production in the EU as a whole stood at 8,100,000 tonnes, and Belgian production at 770,000 tonnes (9.6 per cent of the total). Consumption in Belgium was 350,000 tonnes, compared to 6,500,000 tonnes in the Union (i.e., it was 5.4 per cent of the total). The Court held that these market shares, taken together with the other relevant factors, were such as to mean that the Belgo-Luxembourg market did constitute a substantial part of the Union.

In relation to another applicant, Sudzucker-Verkauf, the question was whether the 'southern part of Germany' constituted a substantial part. At the time, the population of the area in which the undertaking held its position was 22 million, and its production was about 800,000 tonnes. This was 'sufficiently large, so far as sugar is concerned, to be considered … as a substantial part' (para. 448).

14.4.2 Infrastructure and facilities

A straightforward comparison of the relative size of the geographic area of the market with that of the Union as a whole will not always be sufficient to establish the meaning of 'substantial part'. In a chain of decisions, very small geographic areas have been held to be 'substantial'. These include airports (Brussels Airport) and ports (Holyhead, Rødby, and Roscoff), all of which may be small in themselves but which may be the essential point of access to a market that is itself substantial (see further Chapter 16).

Key case 14.2 *Chiquita* (1976) OJ L95/1; *United Brands Company and United Brands Continentaal BV* v *Commission* case 27/76 [1978] 1 CMLR 429— Commission decision, Court of Justice judgment (art. 102)

Facts

United Brands Company (UBC) was a US-based undertaking. Its European subsidiary, United Brands Continentaal BV, was responsible for coordinating the sales of the company in the Member States, with the exception of the UK and Italy. UBC was the largest supplier of bananas on the world market. A complaint was made to the EU Commission by a Danish banana wholesaler, Th. Olesen, and by undertakings based in Ireland. The Commission notified UBC in April 1975 that it believed that the undertaking was abusing its dominant position by engaging in the following practices: (1) requiring its distributors not to sell bananas while they were still green; (2) charging its distributors in the Member States different prices without any objective justification; (3) charging some distributors prices up to 138 per cent of those charged to others, and thereby imposing excessive prices; and (4) refusing to supply bananas to Olesen on the ground that it had taken part in a promotional campaign for a rival. The Commission adopted an infringement decision finding that the abuses set out above had taken place, requiring changes to UBC's commercial arrangements, and imposing a penalty. UBC appealed.

Findings

The first question for the Court was that of whether UBC held a dominant position, and this in turn required a definition of the relevant product market to be reached. Advocate General Mayras discoursed at length on the question of whether bananas were to be seen as a product distinct from other fresh fruit, or possibly wider foodstuffs in general. His opinion starts with the statement that: 'there is no doubt that a mother who gives her young child a fruit yoghurt will not give him a banana as well. But no one would dream of asserting that for this reason milk products are a substitute for bananas'. The Court took a slightly more robust approach, holding at the outset that in order to distinguish bananas as a separate product market 'it must be possible for it to be singled out by such special features distinguishing it from other fruits that it is only to a limited extent interchangeable with them and is only exposed to their competition in a way that is hardly perceptible' (para. 22). There was a significant degree of statistical evidence which showed that banana prices were not sensitive to the changes in the availability of other fresh fruits. The Court then held that:

This small degree of substitutability is accounted for by the specific features of the banana and all the factors which influence consumer choice. The banana has certain characteristics, appearance, taste, softness, seedlessness, easy handling, a constant level of production which enable it to satisfy the constant needs of an important section of the population consisting of the very young, the old and the sick.   (paras 30–1)

The relevant geographic market was defined as being one where the objective conditions of competition were the same for all suppliers, and in the present case was largely divided along national lines. UBC's market share was judged as being some 45 per cent. In addition it had access to considerable resources, was vertically integrated, and the 'cumulative effect of all the advantages enjoyed by UBC thus ensure[d] that it [had] a dominant position on the relevant market' (para. 127).

The clause in the contracts of sale prohibiting distributors and ripeners from selling green bananas was designed to prevent arbitrage around the Union. The Court found that this practice 'tightened' UBC's economic hold on the market and was an abuse. The refusal to supply Olesen was a sanction taken against an existing customer to deter others from participating in marketing campaigns for rivals. It was not objectively justifiable, and such a course of conduct 'amounts...to a serious interference with the independence of small and medium sized firms in their commercial relations with the undertaking in a dominant position and this independence implies the right to give preference to competitors' goods' (para. 194). That UBC imposed discriminatory prices based on the point of origin of the purchasing distributor was clear, in breach of art. 102(c). The Court did not accept the argument that the differences responded to uneven patterns of demand.

The Court dealt with the question of whether UBC had charged 'unfair' prices (in breach of art. 102(a)), by charging a price which bore 'no reasonable relation to the economic value of the product supplied', and which was 'unfair' (paras 250–2). It did not find that the Commission had brought forward sufficient evidence relating to the costs incurred by UBC to make such a finding in the present case. On this point only the Commission was defeated, the rest of the decision surviving intact.

Comment

The *United Brands* case is usually cited as an example of how not to proceed with market definition exercises. The reference to the characteristics of the product is not inconsistent with the operation of the more sophisticated SSNIP test (see 14.3.4), but is not in itself sufficient to determine the bounds of a product market. While issues such as the texture and taste of a product may have an impact on demand curves, they are not in themselves determinative (it is hard to believe that the Court was suggesting that demand derived from the fact that a banana is yellow and bendy).

Certainly in discussing the special situation of the very young, the sick, and the old, the Court made a mistake. Such consumers are 'infra-marginal': they have a low elasticity of demand for the product, and are prepared to pay a price above the competitive level. However, the banana seller is unable to identify these customers at the point of sale and to impose different conditions on them. It must instead apply a single price at the point of sale, and infra-marginal consumers are 'protected' by marginal consumers who may well defect to alternative products. The proper economic question is that of whether a price rise targeted at infra-marginal consumers will be rendered unprofitable because of the loss of sales to marginal consumers.

The case is also instructive because of the range of conduct that fell to be considered: price discrimination, selling conditions, excessive pricing, and refusals to supply. The driving force behind the case may be presumed to be the extent to which United Brands sought to divide the internal market, supporting its price discrimination by a ban on the reselling of unripened bananas (and thereby preventing arbitrage). The treatment of discriminatory pricing remains a standard one, as does the approach to refusals to supply when used to discipline customers offering competing products (see the later case of *BBI/Boosey & Hawkes*). Any discussion of excessive pricing usually also begins with a discussion of this case, but the decision in *Port of Helsingborg* has clarified the *United Brands* test to a useful degree.

14.5 The concept of abuse

Article 102 contains a list of abusive practices deemed unlawful. It 'merely gives examples', and is thus 'not an exhaustive list of the kinds of abusive exploitation of a dominant position prohibited by the Treaty' (*Europemballage Corp. and Continental Can Co. Inc. v Commission* case 6/72 [1973] CMLR 199, para. 26). Accordingly, the Commission and Court have condemned practices not set out in the list. In *Continental Can*, for example, the acquisition of shares in a competing undertaking, which had the effect of increasing the power of an *already* dominant position, was considered an abuse (see Chapter 19).

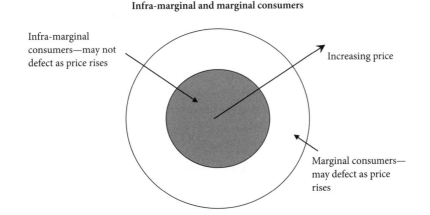

Infra-marginal and marginal consumers

Infra-marginal consumers—may not defect as price rises

Increasing price

Marginal consumers— may defect as price rises

The 'special responsibility' that dominant firms have not to impair or distort competition (*Nederlandsche Banden-Industries Michelin NV* v *Commission* case 322/81 [1985] 1 CMLR 282, at 327) suggests that standards of permissible conduct in the EU will be higher than, for example, in the US. The meaning of abuse might therefore be such as to go beyond the requirement not to act so as to impair the efficient operation of the market. In the EU, the Court of Justice has defined abuse holding that it is

an objective concept relating to the behaviour of an undertaking in a dominant position which is such as to influence the structure of a market where, as a result of the very presence of the undertaking in question, the degree of competition is weakened and which, through recourse to methods different from those which condition normal competition…has the effect of hindering the maintenance of the degree of competition still existing in the market. (*Hoffmann-La Roche & Co. AG* v *Commission* case 85/76 [1979] 3 CMLR 211, para. 91)

The reference to 'normal competition' in this context is questionable. Many practices that have been condemned under art. 102 are not abnormal, but their use by undertakings which are in a position of some strength has an impact that draws the attention of the Commission.

Abuses can take many forms, but are broadly divided into two categories: exclusionary and exploitative. On the one hand, exclusionary abuses, also known as anti-competitive abuses, are designed to preserve or expand the power of the undertaking by somehow harming competitors and thus affecting the structure of the market. On the other hand, exploitative abuses aim to exploit the power of the undertaking (by, *inter alia*, charging supra-competitive prices or limiting production). Both types may be caught by art. 102.

The cases *Manufacture Française des Pneumatiques Michelin* v *Commission* (case T–203/01 [2004] 4 CMLR 18) and *British Airways* v *Commission* (case T–219/99 [2004] 4 CMLR 19) confirmed that, for exclusionary abuses, it is not necessary to demonstrate specific effects for establishing an infringement of art. 102 TFEU. It is to be doubted that the same principle would apply in relation to exploitative abuses, in which the very concept of 'exploitation' is intimately interconnected with the concept of 'abuse'.

In its *Discussion paper on the application of Article 82 of the Treaty to exclusionary abuses* (December 2005), the Commission set out a framework within which the analysis of exclusionary abuses is to take place, arguing that

[t]he concern is to prevent exclusionary conduct of the dominant firm which is likely to limit the remaining competitive constraints on the dominant company, including entry of newcomers, so as to avoid that consumers are harmed. This means that it is competition, and not competitors as such, that is to be protected. (para. 54)

It is *not* the purpose of this area of law, the Commission stresses, 'to protect competitors from dominant firms' genuine competition based on factors such as higher quality, novel products, opportune innovation or otherwise better performance'. This position is confirmed in the *Guidance on the enforcement of Art. 82 in relation to exclusionary conduct* (December 2008), which stresses that

[t]he emphasis of the Commission's enforcement activity in relation to exclusionary conduct is on safeguarding the competitive process in the internal market and ensuring that undertakings which hold a dominant position do not exclude their competitors by other

means than competing on the merits of the products or services they provide. In doing so the Commission is mindful that what really matters is protecting an effective competitive process and not simply protecting competitors. This may well mean that competitors who deliver less to consumers in terms of price, choice, quality and innovation will leave the market.   (para. 6)

14.5.1 Examples of abusive conduct

Abuses arising out of predatory, discriminatory, and excessive prices, and refusals to supply are considered in some detail in Chapter 16. The examples given here are not a comprehensive listing, but will give some indication of the range of practices that have been condemned and the sort of evidence that is likely to attract the interest of the EU Commission.

14.5.1.1 Exclusive purchasing and tie-in sales

Purchasing requirements are sometimes used in order to extend a dominant undertaking's influence or to increase its profits. The most common of these practices are exclusive purchasing requirements, by virtue of which a purchaser agrees not to buy the same product from any other source, and tie-in sales, whereby the buyer will be supplied with one product only if another is also purchased. In its extreme position, where tie-in sales extend across the complete range of the dominant supplier, such a practice may be termed full-line forcing.

Exclusive purchasing requirements were first dealt with in detail in *Vitamins* 76/642 (1976) OJ L223/27 (on appeal, *Hoffmann-La Roche & Co. AG v Commission* case 85/76 [1979] 3 CMLR 211). Hoffmann's strategy in relation to its bulk sales of synthetic vitamins was to conclude fidelity (exclusive) agreements with customers wherever possible. In essence, Hoffmann would provide the major part of each customer's requirements at the most favourable price in the market. Moreover, at regular intervals, customers would be given a rebate if they had indeed obtained most of their supplies from Hoffmann. The company's ability to obtain information about, and to react to, its competitors' practices was enhanced by an 'English clause' in the contracts, which provided that Hoffmann would meet any price offered to a customer by any reputable supplier, or that if it failed to do so it would not remove the benefit of the rebates if the customer bought from the competing supplier. Generally these contracts were concluded for a period of five years, guaranteeing a stable outlet which would potentially exclude other competitors from developing strength.

The Commission found this conduct to be abusive as 'by its nature it hampers the freedom of choice and equality of treatment of purchasers and restricts competition between bulk vitamin manufacturers' (para. 22). It also took the view that the fidelity rebates fell expressly within art. 102(c), 'applying dissimilar conditions to equivalent transactions', because they were not related to objective cost factors. When the case came before the Court of Justice, it held in para. 89 that

An undertaking which is in a dominant position on a market and ties purchasers—even if it does so at their request—by an obligation or promise on their part to obtain all or most of their requirements exclusively from the said undertaking abuses its dominant position.

The Court further argued that in the absence of exceptional circumstances the granting of rebates designed to support exclusive purchase obligations would be caught by art. 102(c).

In *ICI* (*Soda Ash ICI* 91/300 (1991) OJ L152/40) the company offered its customers a 'top-slice rebate' with substantial financial incentives for purchasing more than the expected regular 'core' supplies from it. By tying its customers in this way ICI was able, in effect, to regulate the remainder of the market, and to control both the quantity and the price at which its competitor was able to sell.

Tying and full-line forcing imply 'making the conclusion of contracts subject to acceptance by the other parties of supplementary obligations which, by their nature or according to commercial usage, have no connection with the subject of such contracts'. They fall within art. 102(d) unless there are objective reasons to justify the tie. In the *Michelin* decision (*BF BV NV NBI Michelin* 81/969 (1981) OJ L353/33) one of the concerns of the Commission was that, for 1977, the bonus system operated by Michelin linked the purchases of light tyres to heavy tyres. This is to say that a customer who would ordinarily purchase its heavy tyres from Michelin and its light tyres from another supplier would be encouraged to purchase all its tyres from Michelin in order to earn the bonus. Some do not consider such a practice to have an anticompetitive effect, but it would appear that the parties themselves believe that it is possible to extend monopoly power from one market to another. If Michelin were the only manufacturer of heavy tyres and informed customers that they would not be supplied with such tyres unless also purchasing Michelin's light tyres, the customers would have little option but to refuse to deal with other suppliers.

The Commission examined Michelin's rebate policy again in *Michelin (II)* 2002/405 (2002) OJ L58/25. In essence the scheme was designed to encourage customers to buy more of the Michelin brand in the face of competition from other suppliers of new tyres. Between 1980 and 1998 Michelin operated a complex system of rebates. Several abusive aspects were identified. Because Michelin paid its rebates up to 13 months after the dealer bought and sold the tyres, dealers were often selling initially at a loss, and were uncertain as to the amount of the rebate that would be paid. This encouraged dealers to be loyal to Michelin when they might have had a preference for another manufacturer's product. As the decision explained,

[s]ince it was essential, for the dealer's very survival in certain cases to receive as large as possible an amount of quantity rebates (these being the only means of restoring the dealer's profit margin) and in view of the extremely long period over which Michelin recorded orders, a dealer could not take the risk at any given moment of diversifying his range to any significant extent at Michelin's expense since this could have jeopardised his ability to reach the rebate threshold and could thus have had a major effect on the overall cost price of the Michelin tyres purchased over the year.   (para. 229)

Other abuses included service and progress bonuses, which were also found to have such loyalty-inducing effects and to be unfair in the way in which they were applied and paid. A fine of €19.76 million was imposed on Michelin. This included a substantial uplift as the undertaking had already been punished in the earlier decision. The Commission decision was upheld in its entirety by the GC (*Manufacture Française des Pneumatiques Michelin* v *Commission* case T–203/01 [2004] 4 CMLR 18). The GC was particularly concerned by a rebate system that operated in relation to the entire quantity purchased by the customer, rather than in stepped increments; 'The longer the reference period, the more loyalty-inducing the quantity rebate system' (para. 88). The court was also quick to dismiss claims made by Michelin to the effect that the system was economically justified. It appears from the judgment that it is incumbent on the undertaking to demonstrate that there are genuine efficiencies which justify its operation. At paras 108–9 the GC held that

the applicant provides no specific information in that regard. It merely states that orders for large amounts involve economies and that the customer is entitled to have those economies passed on to him in the price that he pays... Far from establishing that the quantity rebates were based on actual cost savings the applicant merely states generally that the quantity rebates were justified by economies of scale in the areas of production costs and distribution. However, such a line of argument is too general and is insufficient to provide economic reasons to explain specifically the discount rates chosen for the various steps in the rebate system in question.

The position in *Hilti* was more obvious than in *Michelin*. In this case (*Eurofix-Bauco/Hilti* 88/138 (1988) OJ L65/19) the company, which held a dominant position in relation to the market for fastening systems for use in the professional building industry (nail-guns), tied the sales of the two accessories, nails and cartridges, used by them. While there is a clear connection between the three products, they may be legitimately viewed as separate markets. Many manufacturers are able to make the cartridges that are used to propel the nails, and are also able to make the nails themselves. In several cases Hilti either took or threatened legal action, based on its patents, to prevent the manufacture and marketing of cartridges that would be compatible with its nail-guns. The Commission found that Hilti had maintained a policy of only supplying the cartridge strips for use in its guns when the purchaser also took the necessary number of nails, and of reducing discounts on orders of cartridges if nails were not simultaneously purchased. This attempt to restrict competition was found to constitute an abuse, as the policies pursued left 'the consumer with no choice over the source of his nails and as such abusively exploit him' (para. 75). As a result of these practices Hilti was fined €6 million and ordered to bring the practices to an end.

Similar considerations were to the fore in *Tetra Pak II* (92/163 (1992) OJ L72/1). Tetra Pak's standard supply contracts imposed two obligations: that only Tetra Pak cartons be used on Tetra Pak machines, and that certain supplies be obtained exclusively from Tetra Pak. These clauses would 'make the system airtight: not only is it not possible for the purchaser of a machine to use packaging other than that bearing the Tetra Pak mark, but moreover he may not obtain supplies of packaging from any source other than Tetra Pak' (para. 116). The company's defence was that it was not possible to drive a wedge between the two markets (machines and packaging) and that it was the supplier of a totally integrated system, of which many elements were integral components. As might be expected, the practice was roundly condemned. In addition to being abusive, the clauses placed competitors 'who cannot... subsidise possible losses on a given product through profits made on another product, in an extremely uncomfortable position' (para. 117). The approach of the Court and the Commission was criticized by Lord Fraser of Carmyllie in the Lords debate on the CA 98. He expressed concern at a line of jurisprudence that seems to suggest that dominance in one market creates duties in another (Hansard (HL) 13 November 1997, col. 307).

Bundling of a sort was addressed in the very long decision taken in respect of Microsoft issued by the Commission in March 2004 (2007/53/EC (2007) OJ L32/23). In this case, Microsoft was attacked for bundling its Windows Media Player software with its PC operating systems, including Windows 98 and Windows XP. The issue of technological bundling is a sensitive one; it is often pointed out that when the US authorities brought an action against IBM in the 1970s one of their complaints was that the company was bundling hard disc drives with its mainframe computers—a charge that would now seem absurd. In addition to the large fine imposed on Microsoft the Commission required the company to,

within 90 days of the date of notification of this Decision, offer a full-functioning version of the [Windows operating systems] which does not incorporate Windows Media Player; Microsoft Corporation retains the right to offer a bundle of the [Windows operating systems] and Windows Media Player. (art. 6 of the decision)

Microsoft appealed, and final judgment was given by the GC on 17 September 2007. The GC held that there were four conditions to be met for an allegation of unlawful bundling to be sustained: (1) the tying and the tied products should be separate; (2) the undertaking imposing the tie was dominant in the market for the tying product (in this case the Windows operating system); (3) customers were denied the chance to obtain the tying product without the tied product; and (4) competition was foreclosed (paras 842 and 850–69). The Court found in this case that all four conditions were met, such that the bundling of Media Player with the Windows operating system was in breach of art. 102 (the case is dealt with at Key case 22.2).

Monopolies established by law (i.e., by state action) are, unless art. 106(2) applies, subject to the same obligations under 102 as privately run enterprises. In *Télémarketing (Centre Belge d'Études de Marché-Télémarketing SA v Compagnie Luxembourgeoise de Télédiffusion SA* case 311/84 [1986] 2 CMLR 558—an art. 267 reference from the national court) the Luxembourg TV Broadcaster (CLT) operated under a licence issued by the government, and required the plaintiff telemarketing company to have calls placed in response to advertisements screened on the channel routed through an associated company, IPB. CLT argued that this was a matter of pragmatism, as IPB had good notice of changes to schedules and therefore would better be able to anticipate and respond to customers than the complainant's own company. Further, the television channel took the view that customers believed that they were dealing with it, and that it therefore had an obligation to ensure an appropriate level of service. However, for the first year in which it placed advertisements with the broadcaster the complainant had not been required to use IPB and had been able to advertise its own telephone response number. The national court asked the Court of Justice whether this extension of power over the television broadcasts into an ancillary market, telephone response numbers for advertising, was an abuse of art. 102. The Court was of the view that the action was in breach both of art. 102(a) and of art. 102(d). In insisting that any advertiser buying telephone time did not use its own agency, but instead use that allied to the company, it had imposed conditions on all other companies that it did not impose on itself. Further, the tie carried supplementary obligations with no connection with the true subject matter of the contract.

This area is further discussed by DG Comp in its *Discussion paper on the application of Article 82 of the Treaty to exclusionary abuses* (December 2005) at paras 177–206, as well as in the *Guidance on the enforcement of Art. 82 in relation to exclusionary conduct* (December 2008) at paras 33–6 and 47–62.

14.5.1.2 Abusive discounts and rebates

The use of discounts and rebates in order to facilitate tie-in sales and exclusive purchasing has been considered above. However, there are other cases in which discounts have been used abusively. Some examples are analysed in this section.

When it began to face emerging competition from France and Spain, British Gypsum, a subsidiary of British Plasterboard Industries, sought ways in which to 'reward the loyalty of merchants who remained exclusively' with them (*BPB Industries plc* 89/22 (1989) OJ L10/50, para. 58). A scheme was subsequently put in place whereby payments were to be made to selected merchants in the form of contributions to promotional and advertising expenses, and this was later extended to provide added bonuses to those entering exclusive contracts. All these rebates were condemned. The issue was revisited in 1992 when British Gypsum was encouraged to modify other rebate schemes introduced following the earlier decision. As amended, the rebate schemes, which then related to objectively identifiable savings and could be made available to all customers satisfying the appropriate criteria, were accepted by the Commission (*22nd Report on Competition Policy* (1992), p. 422).

It is now well established that rebate or discount schemes will be acceptable only where they are non-discriminatory and therefore do not fall within art. 102(c). Further illustrations may be found in *Brussels National Airport* 95/364 (1995) OJ L216/8 and in *Irish Sugar* 97/624 (1997) OJ L258/1 (on appeal *Irish Sugar plc v Commission* case T–228/97 [1999] 5 CMLR 1300). In the former case British Midland complained that a system of discounts established by Royal Decree in 1989 was such that only Sabena, its main competitor, could benefit from them. The Commission requested the Belgian authorities to end the system. In *Irish Sugar* the company was fined €8.8 million after being found to have abused its dominant position on the Irish sugar market. The company had responded to the threat of imports from France by, *inter alia*, offering various rebate schemes. These were condemned as being ad hoc and without any consistent relationship to objectively identifiable criteria. The effect of the abuse was to maintain prices for sugar in Ireland that were significantly higher than in other Member States.

The core allegation made against British Airways, substantiated by the Commission in *Virgin/British Airways* 2000/74 (2000) OJ L30/1 related to the use by BA of commission schemes, in effect discounts, to boost sales of its flights through travel agents at the expense of those of its rivals. The marginal effect of the commission scheme is clearly explained in paras 29–30 of the decision. In effect, to combat the offer by BA of a standard commission rate of 7 per cent, coupled to a 'performance reward' of 0.5 per cent, at the margin a competing airline would have to offer a commission of 17.4 per cent. It was accepted that BA would have to offer a marginal rate as high as this to *increase* sales of its own tickets, but the Commission noted that 'it is at an advantage over the new entrant who must offer this high rate of commission on all its sales'. Such a scheme was both discriminatory (the discounts bore no relation to objectively justifiable factors) and exclusionary at a time when, according to the Commission, BA should have been facing competition in a newly deregulated market.

The Commission's findings were upheld by the GC in *British Airways plc* v *Commission* case T–219/99 [2004] 4 CMLR 19. In particular, the Court dismissed arguments made by BA to the effect that the discount scheme was not discriminatory. At paras 239–40 it held that

BA's arguments based on the importance of the size of the travel agents established in the United Kingdom are irrelevant. The performance reward schemes in dispute were, in themselves, based on a parameter unrelated to the criterion of the size of the undertakings, since they were based on the extent to which travel agents increased their sales of BA tickets in relation to the threshold constituted by the number of BA tickets sold during the previous reference period.

In those circumstances, the Commission was right to hold that BA's performance reward schemes constituted an abuse of BA's dominant position on the United Kingdom market for air travel agency services, in that they produced discriminatory effects within the network of travel agents established in the United Kingdom, thereby inflicting on some of them a competitive disadvantage within the meaning of subparagraph (c) of the second paragraph of Article [102 TFEU].

On a subsequent appeal the Court of Justice supported the findings of the GC and rejected BA's appeal (*British Airways plc* v *Commission* case C–95/04 [2007] 4 CMLR 22).

In its discussion paper on exclusionary abuses, the Commission stresses that a foreclosure effect is likely to be found in situations in which conditional rebates are awarded on incremental purchases. It also notes that where rebates are granted only once a certain threshold is met, an abusive loyalty enhancing effect may be found to exist (see paras 142–76). The discussion of the effect of rebates in this document is substantial, and should be referred to for a full understanding of the relevant issues. Paragraphs 37–45 of the Guidance on exclusionary conduct are also of relevance, since they shed light on kinds of rebates prone to be more harmful. Scenarios in which 'competitors are not able to compete on equal terms for the entire demand of each individual customer' are cause for concern. Likewise, foreclosure is more likely with retroactive rebates (granted on all purchases provided that the orders exceed the minimum threshold established) than with incremental ones, and that individualized rebates may be more detrimental than those that are standardized.

Key case 14.3 *Intel* COMP/C-3/37.990 [2009] OJ C227/13—Commission decision (art. 102)

Facts

Acting on a complaint filed by Advanced Micro Devices (AMD) in 2000, the EU Commission opened an investigation into Intel—the world's largest microprocessor manufacturer and AMD's competitor—for potential exclusionary practices. The alleged breaches related to central processing units, the 'brains' of computers, 'of the x86 architecture' (hereinafter CPU x86). The Commission examined Intel's sales of this product to original equipment manufacturers (OEMs) on the one hand (such as Dell, HP, and NEC), and retailers on the other (particularly Media-Saturn-Holding GmbH, based in Germany).

Intel offered OEM discounts from its general 'Customer Authorized Price'. These rebates were mainly of two types: contra revenue discounts (direct reduction in the price paid for the CPU x86) and marketing programme discounts (which include the reimbursement of promotion expenses). With regard to the retailer based in Germany, Intel paid it considerable amounts of money for stocking only Intel's CPU x86; it also benefited from marketing contributions for advertising campaigns. The complex investigations (there were two) into the potential abusive rebates went on for almost nine years, during which the Commission gathered evidence by interviewing Intel's clients, conducting inspections, and requesting information.

Findings

In its 542-page decision, the Commission found that, in the worldwide market for CPU x86 (considered to be the relevant market in this case), Intel had a dominant position from October 2002 to December 2007. This is justified with reference to Intel's market share in the relevant market, which was 'in excess of or around 70 per cent', as well as the existence of barriers to entry and expansion in the market.

It further estimated that two of Intel's practices were abusive: the discounts offered to OEMs and the retailer in Germany for purchasing most or all of their CPU x86 from Intel on the one hand (which are conditional and amount to fidelity rebates similar to those in the *Hoffmann-La Roche* case above) and the payments made by Intel to its customers for not launching or postponing the launch of products that contained CPUs manufactured by its competitor, AMD (rather innovatively referred to as 'naked restrictions' in the decision).

As a consequence, Intel was fined a record €1.06 billion—4.15 per cent of the firm's turnover in 2008. This is, to date, the biggest fine ever imposed on a single company. In addition, the Commission ordered Intel to cease the illegal practices with immediate effect.

Comment

This is one of the few occasions in which a major investigation has been conducted under art. 102 TFEU. The tough stance taken in this decision seems to fit into what has been described as an 'unofficial policy of reserving the use of Article [102] for "big fish" in "high profile" markets' ('The European Commission's Intel Decision' (December 2009) *Greenberg Traurig Maher*). The outcome is somewhat surprising in the light of the recent review of art. 102, which advocates for a more effects-based approach to abuse of dominance. However, as the Commission has insisted, the recent guidance is not applicable given that proceedings initiated long before it was adopted.

These and other aspects are criticized by Geradin in 'The Decision of the Commission of 13 of May 2009 in the Intel Case: Where is the Foreclosure and the Consumer Harm?', (2010) *TILEC Discussion Paper Series* 2010–022). He identifies six strands of criticism:

First, the Commission decision could be read as endorsing the formalistic, quasi-*per se* case-law of the [Union] courts on rebates. This approach is based on the (fundamentally unsound) proposition that it is not necessary for the Commission to demonstrate the presence of foreclosure effects to find that rebates granted by a dominant firm constitute an abuse incompatible with Article [102 TFEU].

Second, the Commission's argument that it does not have to conduct an effects-based analysis...is again formalistic and wrong.

Third, the Commission theory of harm whereby the harm to competition would arise from the OEM's understanding that the rebates they receive from Intel would be disproportionately reduced should they decide to purchase AMD CPUs, and the impact of this understanding on their actual purchasing strategy, is highly speculative and not a sound basis for an antitrust investigation.

Fourth, some aspects of the way the Commission is assessing the evidence at its disposal are troubling and might create the impression that the Commission's analysis may have been biased. Every doubtful question is resolved against Intel; every inference goes against Intel;...This also raises questions about who bears the burden of proof. While the Commission bears that burden, some passages of the decision seem to suggest the opposite.

Fifth, while it is impossible for an outside observer to determine whether the Commission's "as effective competitor" analysis is adequate, the Commission's determination of the "contestable share" of the respective demands of the OEMs is flawed. Moreover, this test is insufficient to form the basis of a decision to condemn a given rebates regime....

Finally, the Commission's analysis of the "harm to competition and consumers" is entirely theoretical. The concrete effects of Intel's rebates on competition and consumers are not demonstrated, and yet it is clear based on price and performance trends over the last decade that the microprocessor market is very healthy....

FURTHER READING

Articles

BANASEVIC, N., AND HELLSTRÖM, P., 'When the Chips are Down: Some Reflections on the European Commission's Intel Decision', (2010) 1 *Journal of European Competition Law and Practice* 301–10

GERADIN, D., 'The Decision of the Commission of 13 May 2009 in the Intel Case: Where is the Foreclosure and the Consumer Harm?', (2010) *TILEC Discussion Paper Series* 2010–022

14.5.1.3 The abusive use of intellectual property

The application of art. 102 TFEU to intellectual property rights is considered below at 22.3.

14.5.2 **Defences**

The question of what constitutes a defence to an alleged infringement of art. 102 TFEU (or the UK Chapter II Prohibition) is answered in part by reading any of the cases referred to above or in Chapter 15. In essence, wherever conduct can be 'objectively justified' it will be found not to be abusive. In this context, it might be possible to draw a distinction between conduct which is targeted at the elimination of a competitor, and conduct which is designed to further the efficiency or profitability of the dominant undertaking which has as its (unintended, but perhaps inevitable) consequence the elimination of a competitor. Economic analysis would tend to favour the latter, but not the former. However, in practice this is often a moot distinction, being difficult to maintain.

For most of the period of its operation the question of defences under the application of art. 102 TFEU has been largely glossed over. However, in its *Discussion paper on the application of Article 82 of the Treaty to exclusionary abuses* (December 2005), as well as in the subsequent *Guidance on the enforcement of Art. 82 in relation to exclusionary conduct* (December 2008), DG Comp places great emphasis on efficiency justifications for conduct. It is argued that such a defence should be accepted when four conditions are satisfied. The first is that the efficiency is, or is likely to be, realized. The remaining three are drawn from the wording of art. 101(3) TFEU: that the conduct is indispensable to the attainment of the efficiency, that consumers benefit—a more difficult proposition in situations where there are few competitive constraints on the dominant undertaking— and that competition is not eliminated (see para. 84 of the discussion paper and para. 30 of the guidance). A justification may also be possible where the conduct is 'objectively necessary' (para. 80 of the discussion paper and 28 of the guidelines). This might apply, for example, to areas where health and safety considerations require that a dominant undertaking supplying one product obliges its customers to use a related product (e.g., a certain type of tyre with a certain type of car). However, in the relevant case law, the test of 'indispensability' is strictly applied, and where the health and safety requirement can be met by other means, an anti-competitive action to enforce it will not be permitted.

Another defensive strategy may be to argue that the conduct in question 'meets competition'. The issue is again not a straightforward one, as the 'special responsibility' that applies to dominant undertakings in the EU does not apply to their non-dominant competitors. This defence is, according to the discussion paper, 'only applicable in relation to behaviour which otherwise would constitute a pricing abuse' (para. 81), and the dominant undertaking must be able to show that the conduct is exclusively a response to low pricing by others. If, for example, the conduct required the company also to increase its capacity, the defence would not be acceptable. The Commission has also stated here that the defence is not likely to be available where the dominant undertaking is pricing below a certain cost measure and is engaged in predatory pricing (see 16.2.1).

14.6 Trade between Member States

The condemning of an abuse 'in so far as it may affect trade between Member States' is the jurisdictional test of Union involvement The same principles apply as for art. 101 (see 3.4). It is worth noting that it is the 'abuse', and not the dominant position, which must affect trade.

14.7 The relationship between arts 102 and 101

Jurisdiction under arts 102 and 101 is not mutually exclusive, and there will be situations where both apply. Such is the case for example when a dominant undertaking obliges its customers or smaller competitors to enter into restrictive agreements. This was acknowledged by the Court of Justice in *Hoffmann-La Roche* (*Hoffmann-La Roche & Co. AG v Commission* case 85/76 [1979] 3 CMLR 211). One issue considered under art. 102 related to a contract under the terms of which Merck agreed to purchase exclusively from Hoffmann a considerable quantity of vitamin B6 for a period of five years. The Court found that the purpose of the agreement was to eliminate the risk to Hoffmann of a planned increase in production, and that this constituted an abuse. The Court noted that 'the question might be asked whether the conduct in question does not fall within Article [101] of the Treaty and possibly within its paragraph (3)' (para. 116). Might the potential application of art. 101(3) therefore act as a defence to an action brought under art. 102? The answer is no. The Court went on to hold that art. 102 'is expressly aimed in fact at situations which clearly originate in contractual relations so that in such cases the Commission is entitled . . . to proceed on the basis of Article [101] or Article [102]' (para. 116).

The GC, however, has suggested that this may not be the case where an exemption has been granted on an individual basis. The presumption would be that the Commission would have considered whether art. 102 was in fact relevant, and would not have granted the exemption if that were the case. In *Tetra Pak* the Advocate General went so far as to say that a practice 'which satisfies the conditions for exception laid down in Article [101(3)] cannot at the same time be regarded as constituting an abuse' (*Tetra Pak Rausing SA v Commission* case T–51/89 [1991] 4 CMLR 334 at 350). In such a case the Commission would be expected to demonstrate either that facts had been withheld from it at the time the exemption was granted, or that there had been a material change in the circumstances in order to succeed with a new claim. Some of the block exemptions (see Chapter 10) expressly state that exemptions granted under their authority do not serve as a defence under art. 102; even where no such express provision is made, the general presumption must be that as block exemptions do not require the specific assessment that is needed in the case of art. 101(3) exceptions, they cannot serve as a defence to an art. 102 action.

Key case 14.4 *Commercial Solvents 72/457/EEC (1972) OJ L299/51; Istituto Chemioterapico Italiano SpA and Commercial Solvents Corporation* v *Commission* cases 6 and 7/73 [1974] 1 CMLR 309—Commission decision, Court of Justice judgment (art. 102)

Facts

Commercial Solvents Corporation (CSC) was a US-based company, which in 1962 acquired a controlling stake in the Italian undertaking Istituto Chemioterapico Italiano SpA (ICI). CSC produced intermediate products used in the manufacture of ethambutol and related drugs used in the treatment of tuberculosis. Until 1970 ICI acted as a reseller of CSC's aminobutanol product. One of its customers was Laboratorio Chemico Farmaceutico Giorgio Zoja SpA (Zoja) to whom ICI began selling in 1966. In 1968 ICI started production of its own ethambutanol specialities, in competition with its customers. In 1970 CSC decided to withdraw aminobutanol from the market in the then EEC. Instead, it would supply an improved intermediate product called dextroaminobutanol (which ICI would convert into bulk ethambutol) and for the manufacture of its own specialities. SCS informed its resellers that from then on aminobutanol would be available only in such quantities as had already been committed for resale (i.e., it would honour existing orders, but no more than that).

In 1970 Zoja cancelled its order for some 20,000 kg of aminobutanol as it was able to obtain the product cheaper from third-party distributors. At the end of 1970 Zoja returned to ICI and placed a new order. CSC replied that none was available. Further attempts by Zoja to obtain supplies failed, and in April 1972 Zoja made a complaint to the Commission, alleging that in failing to supply it with the product as ordered CSC and ICI were in breach of art. 102 TFEU. A statement of objections was served by the Commission in the same month, and in December of that year the Commission made a decision ordering CSC and ICI to supply 60,000 kg of nitropropane (a substitute for aminobutanol), or 30,000 kg of aminobutanol to Zoja at a price not exceeding the maximum price charged for those products, to submit to the Commission proposals for the future supply of Zoja, and to pay a fine. CSC and ICI appealed.

Market developments in the case

1 Standard supply arrangement
2 ICI enters into competition with downstream customers
3 Product upgraded, older product withdrawn

Findings

There was little doubt that CSC held a dominant position in the relevant market. The issue to be dealt with by the Court was that of the approach to the conduct. The Court focused on the fact that CSC, through ICI, had entered into competition with its customers, and found that the reluctance of CSC to supply aminobutanol was designed 'to facilitate its own access to the market for the derivatives' (para. 25). The key part of the Court's judgment is found at para. 25, where the Court stated that

an undertaking being in a dominant position as regards the supply of raw material and therefore able to control the supply to manufacturers of derivatives, cannot, just because it decides to start manufacturing those derivatives (in competition with its former customers) act in such a way as to eliminate their competition which in the case in question, would amount to eliminating one of the principal manufacturers of ethambutol in the [Internal] Market.

The Court held that it followed from this that CSC had abused its dominant position. It did not matter that Zoja had itself cancelled its earlier purchases.

Comment

The judgment in this case is clearly wrong. CSC had produced an upgraded product, and had taken reasonable steps to make this product available. It had withdrawn an older product, had notified its customers, and had committed itself to satisfying existing orders. Zoja had walked away from its contractual arrangement with ICI as it had found an alternative source of supply from a parallel trader. The Court and Commission seem to have been unduly swayed by the change to the market structure under which CSC, through its ICI subsidiary, had entered into competition with its downstream customers in the final product market. Zoja was therefore, of its own making, not a customer of ICI/CSC at the time of its complaint. The decision and the judgment put CSC in the position of having to supply a product that it had committed to withdraw from the market following the development of a better product.

Any case in which an undertaking is ordered to supply a customer opens up complex issues relating to the terms of supply—in particular pricing, and risks dragging the Commission into further policing the market. However, whatever the rights and wrongs of this particular case it remains very important. Although the Court could not have been aware of this at the time the case opened up the route to the later development of the essential facilities doctrine, and has been often relied upon by the Commission and the Court since.

FURTHER READING

Article

SUBIOTTO, R., and O'DONOGHUE, R., 'Defining the Scope of the Duty of Dominant Firms to Deal with Existing Customers under Article 82 EC', (2003) *ECLR* 683

14.8 **Review process: art. 102 guidelines**

In October 2003 a senior Commission official announced that DG Comp was in the process of conducting a review into the application of art. 102 TFEU, and that guidelines might follow (Lowe, P., 'DG Competition's Review of the Policy on Abuse of Dominance', Speech to the Fordham Corporate Law Institute, 23 October 2003). In December 2005 the Commission published its *Discussion paper on the application of Article 82 of the Treaty to exclusionary abuses*. It is stated clearly at the outset that this document 'has no enforcement status'. However, this is a significant statement from the Commission, and represents the first comprehensive attempt to produce a coherent strategy in relation to the application of art. 102 TFEU. Following a long three years' reflection, in December 2008 *Guidance on the enforcement of Art. 82 EC in relation to exclusionary conduct* was finally published. It refers to the Commission's position on these abuses in a more general way than the detailed discussion paper.

It is to be regretted that the review does not address the more complex issues relating to exploitative abuses—such as excessive pricing—but it does deal with the areas of strategic behaviour most often subject to complaint. Thus, in addition to the establishment of dominance itself, the review deals with predatory pricing, single branding and rebates, tying and bundling, refusal to supply, and control over aftermarkets.

What is most significant is the emphasis placed on efficiency and consumer welfare, which is iterated throughout. Thus, for example, it is stated at para. 4 of the discussion paper that 'with regard to exclusionary abuses the objective of article [102] is the protection of competition on the market as a means of enhancing consumer welfare and ensuring an efficient allocation of resources'. Similarly, the guidance is said to focus on those 'types of conduct which are more harmful to consumers' (para. 5). It may reasonably be argued that this is a platitude that merely recognizes the generally accepted proposition that competition is a good thing. Of more use to undertakings and their advisers are the 'soft' safe harbour of 40 per cent, below which dominance is unlikely (para. 14 of the guidance), and the recognition that 'if the conduct of a dominant company generates efficiencies and provided that all the other conditions of article [101] (3) [see 9.6.2 above] are satisfied, such conduct should not be classed as an abuse under article 102 of the Treaty' (para. 8 of the discussion paper). This implies that the actions of a dominant undertaking which lead to the elimination of a competitor may be lawful where they can be justified with reference to an efficiency defence, as long as the dominant undertaking does not 'eliminate competition in respect of a substantial part of the products in question' (see art. 101(3)(b)).

In practice, this may not be an easy rubric to fall back upon. A clear problem lies in the fact that a dominant undertaking already operates in a market where competition has been significantly weakened, although at the lower bound of dominance some 60 per cent of the market may remain occupied by competitors. It would appear to follow from this rule that defences which might be available to some dominant firms are not available to others, dependent on the scale of the dominance. Be that as it may, the effects-based approach of the reform constitutes an important step in the modernization of the application of art. 102.

Summary map

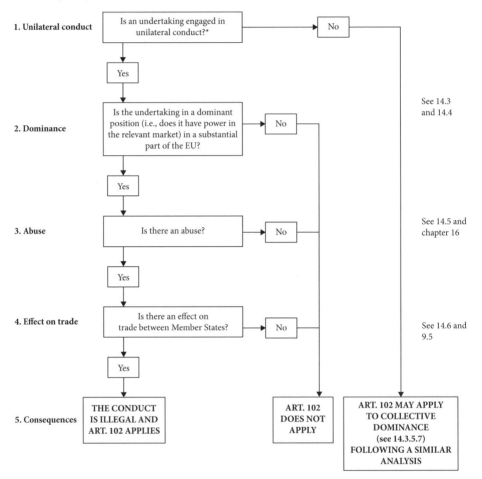

1. Unilateral conduct   Is an undertaking engaged in unilateral conduct?* → No

Yes

See 14.3 and 14.4

2. Dominance   Is the undertaking in a dominant position (i.e., does it have power in the relevant market) in a substantial part of the EU? → No

Yes

See 14.5 and chapter 16

3. Abuse   Is there an abuse? → No

Yes

See 14.6 and 9.5

4. Effect on trade   Is there an effect on trade between Member States? → No

Yes

5. Consequences   THE CONDUCT IS ILLEGAL AND ART. 102 APPLIES   ART. 102 DOES NOT APPLY   ART. 102 MAY APPLY TO COLLECTIVE DOMINANCE (see 14.3.5.7) FOLLOWING A SIMILAR ANALYSIS

* If the conduct is, at least in part, multilateral, Art. 101 may also be applicable.

FURTHER READING

Books

FAULL, J., and NIKPAY, A. (eds), *The EC Law of Competition* (2006) 2nd edn, OUP, Oxford, Chapter 3

Articles

AZEVEDO, J. P., and WALKER, M., 'Dominance: Meaning and Measurement', (2002) *European Competition Law Review* 363

EILMANSBERGER, T., 'How to Distinguish Good from Bad Competition under Article 82 EC: In Search of Clearer and More Coherent Standards for Anti-Competitive Abuses', (2005) 42 *Common Market Law Review* 129

GRAVENGAARD, M. A., and KJAERSGAARD, N., 'The EU Commission Guidance on Exclusionary Abuse of Dominance—and its Consequences in Practice', (2010) 31 *European Competition Law Review* 285

GYSELEN, L., and KYRIAKIS, N., 'Article 86 EEC: The Monopoly Power Issue Revisited', (1986) 11 *European Law Review* 134

KALLAUGHER, J., and SHER, B., 'Rebates Revisited: Anti-Competitive Effects and Exclusionary Abuse Under Article 82', (2004) 25 *European Competition Law Review* 263

LOEWENTHAL, P.-J., 'The Defence of "Objective Justification" in the Application of Article 82 EC', (2005) *World Competition Law & Economics Review* 455

MAIER-RIGAUD, F. P., 'Article 82 Rebates: Four Common Fallacies', (2006) 2 *Competition Law Journal* 85

SUBIOTTO, R., and O'DONOGHUE, R., 'Defining the Scope of the Duty of Dominant Firms to Deal with Existing Customers under Article 82 EC', (2003) 24 *European Competition Law Review* 683

WAELBROECK, D., 'Michelin II : A Per Se Rule against Rebates by Dominant Companies?', (2005) 1 *Journal of Competition Law and Economics* 149

15

Ingredients of the Chapter II Prohibition

KEY POINTS

- The Chapter II Prohibition is the domestic equivalent of art. 102 TFEU.

- It is to be applied, and its terms interpreted, in a way that is consistent with the application of art. 102 TFEU, unless there is a 'relevant difference'.

- There is, however, no requirement for an effect on trade between Member States, and the dominant position may be held only in a part of the UK.

- If art. 102 TFEU is applicable to any practice being examined under the Chapter II Prohibition, it must be applied. The Chapter II Prohibition may also be applied in conjunction with this, and although EC law permits a stricter result to be reached under national law, the terms of the UK Competition Act preclude this, unless there is a 'relevant difference'.

- A breach of the Chapter II Prohibition may incur penalties, damages, and a requirement of conduct modification.

15.1 Introduction

The Chapter II Prohibition, contained in s. 18 of the CA 98, is in the following terms:

18—(1) Subject to section 19, any conduct on the part of one or more undertakings which amounts to the abuse of a dominant position in a market is prohibited if it may affect trade within the United Kingdom.

(2) Conduct may, in particular, constitute such an abuse if it consists in—

(a) directly or indirectly imposing unfair purchase or selling prices or other unfair trading conditions;

(b) limiting production, markets or technical development to the prejudice of consumers;

(c) applying dissimilar conditions to equivalent transactions with other trading parties, thereby placing them at a competitive disadvantage;

(d) making the conclusion of contracts subject to acceptance by the other parties of supplementary obligations which, by their nature or according to commercial usage, have no connection with the subject of the contracts.

(3) In this section—

'dominant position' means a dominant position within the United Kingdom; and

'the United Kingdom' means the United Kingdom or any part of it.

The prohibition imposed by subsection (1) is referred to in this Act as 'the Chapter II prohibition'.

The similarity of this provision with art. 102 TFEU should be immediately evident, and is no coincidence: the CA was introduced by the Labour government in the late 1990s in order to bring UK competition law in line with EU antitrust rules. Further, coherence in the interpretation of s. 18 and art. 102 is guaranteed by s. 60 of the CA 98, according to which the Act is to be interpreted and applied so as to achieve results consistent with those that would be achieved under EU law (discussed in Chapter 3). Also, in its guideline *The major provisions* (OFT 400), the OFT indicates that it will follow EU Commission practice in giving opinions in novel cases. As a consequence, guidance as to the application of the Chapter II prohibition should be sought in the commentary on art. 102.

As with the Chapter I prohibition discussed in Chapter 11, the peculiarity of s. 18 is that its territorial application is constrained to the UK, and therefore it is applied to abuses of dominance that take place within its territory and that do not have an effect on trade between Member States (required for the application of TFEU provisions). Thus far, a number of decisions have been taken in respect of the Chapter II Prohibition by the OFT, concurrent regulators, and the national courts. Most of these cases are discussed in the following chapter. The aim here is to provide an outline of the operation of the Chapter II Prohibition following the relevant guidelines and decisions. As with previous chapters, a flow chart is included to clarify how the analysis is structured.

15.2 The assessment of dominance

In broad terms, the approach taken to the measurement and control of dominance in the UK will be the same as that in the EU. The two basic tests to be applied in relation to the Chapter II Prohibition are whether an undertaking is dominant, and if so, whether it is abusing the dominant position that it holds. The relevant OFT guidelines, which should be read through carefully, are *Abuse of a Dominant Position* (OFT402), *Assessment of Market Power* (OFT415). A draft guideline on *Assessment of Conduct* was published in 2004, but a final version appears never to have been adopted.

15.2.1 Defining the relevant market

In order to determine if a dominant position is held it will be necessary, like with art. 102, to define the relevant market. Unsurprisingly, the *Market Definition* guideline

([2006] UKCLR 94) 'follows a similar approach to the [EU] Commission's *Notice on Market Definition*' (para. 1.2) discussed in the previous chapter. The basic methodology of the EU Commission will be followed. However, it is worth noting that the results reached may be different, even where similar markets are being investigated, if there are divergences in the factual elements. This was made clear by the GC in *Coca-Cola v Commission* case T–125/79 [2000] All ER (EC) 460 where the Court pointed out that market definition must be sensitive to a particular time, and that at other times different conditions might prevail. In the OFT guideline on market definition, this point is dealt with at paras 5.7–5.8 in the following terms:

In many cases a market may have already been investigated and defined by the OFT or by another competition authority. Sometimes, earlier definitions can be informative when considering the appropriate product or area to use when commencing the hypothetical monopolist test. However, although previous cases can provide useful information, the market definition used may not always be the appropriate one for future cases. First, competitive conditions may change over time. In particular, innovation may make substitution between products easier, or more difficult, and therefore change the market definition. Therefore, the relevant market concerned must be identified according to the particular facts of the case in hand.

Second, a previous product market definition that concerned an area outside the United Kingdom, would not necessarily apply to an area in the United Kingdom if the purchasing behaviour of customers differed significantly between those two areas.

When defining the relevant market, an important case is *Aberdeen Journals* (analysed in relation to predation in the next chapter), in which the OFT suffered a heavy defeat when the CAT was highly critical of the approach it took to market definition. (*Predation by Aberdeen Journals Ltd* CA98/5/2001 [2001] UKCLR 856, on appeal *Aberdeen Journals Ltd v The Director General of Fair Trading* [2002] CompAR 167.) The problems related in particular to the definition of the relevant product market. The CAT set out its most trenchant criticism at paras 146–8 of its judgment:

At this stage of the analysis, we encounter the difficulty that the Decision contains hardly any factual description by the Director of the characteristics of the *Evening Express*, as compared to the *Herald & Post* and *Independent*, nor the extent to which the observable circumstances of the market show that the *Independent* competes not only with the *Herald & Post* but also with the *Evening Express*.

In order to lay the foundation for the definition of the relevant market, we would have expected the Decision to contain a brief factual description, at least in outline, of the objective characteristics of the products concerned—for example the content of each of the three newspapers in question, the kinds of advertisements carried (e.g. display advertisements, recruitment, property, motors, other trade advertisements, classified, notices, etc.), the advertising rates offered by the paid-for and free titles respectively, details of their respective circulations, target audiences and geographical distribution areas.

In our view, such a description of the objective characteristics of the products in question is almost always necessary in cases of disputed market definition, because it is on that foundation that the discussion of the relevant product market must rest.

The Tribunal remitted the contested decision to the OFT for further consideration. When it made a new decision its market definition was, in the respects cited above, much more thorough, and withstood the scrutiny of the CAT. The relevant product market was considered to be local newspaper advertising. Importantly, Aberdeen was considered to be the relevant geographic market. Thus it is clear, as with other decisions, that it does not have to extend to the UK as a whole, but could be regional or even local.

15.2.2 Establishing dominance

As with art. 102, once the market has been defined it is necessary to establish whether the undertaking whose conduct is being examined is dominant in this market. The guideline, *Assessment of Market Power* refers to the standard definition of dominant position set out by the Court of Justice in *United Brands Co.* v *Commission* case 27/76 [1978] 1 CMLR 429, discussed in the previous chapter. They indicate that it is 'unlikely that an undertaking will be individually dominant if its share of the relevant market is below 40 per cent, although dominance could be established below that if other relevant factors (such as the weak position of competitors in that market and entry barriers) provided strong evidence of dominance' (para. 2.12). This soft safe harbour is since 2008 also contained in the *Guidance on the enforcement of Art. 82 EC to exclusionary abuses*.

The broad framework for assessing market power is set out in Part 3 of the guideline, the thrust of which in essence is to consider the restraints that would prevent an alleged dominant undertaking from raising its prices. These include existing competitors, potential competitors, and buyer power. In this context, the discussion of entry barriers (paras 5.1–5.37) should be examined carefully, as they are likely to play a significant role in the analysis. As the guidelines recognize, 'assessing the effects of entry barriers and the advantages they give to incumbents can be complex' (para. 5.29). Overseas competition will be considered in this assessment as it too can provide an effective constraint on the ability of domestic undertakings to raise prices (para. 5.32). This has been a significant factor in a number of recent merger reports in which mergers have been allowed to proceed on the grounds that anti-competitive effects would be mitigated by the growth in international competition (see, e.g., *Universal Foods Corporation and Pointing Holdings Ltd* (Cm. 4544, December 1999)).

Some evidence of dominance may also be adduced from the performance of the undertaking in question, although such analysis must proceed carefully in order to distinguish an 'excessive' rate of profit (para. 6.5) from profit generated by efficient performance.

15.2.3 Collective dominance

The approach taken to collective dominance should be the same as that taken under art. 102 TFEU and is discussed at paras 4.23–4.25 of the guideline *Abuse of a Dominant Position*. However, the difficulties that are encountered in this approach are one of the major reasons underpinning the provision for market investigation references made in the Enterprise Act 2002, discussed at length in Chapter 17.

15.3 **Abusive conduct**

15.3.1 **General issues**

Much of the abusive conduct that has been considered under the Act so far is dealt with in the following chapter in relation to the various abuses, and therefore will not be covered here. The list of abuses set out in s. 18 of the Act is virtually identical to for the one contained in art. 102. One peculiarity might be noted in relation to excessive pricing, an issue in which there has been much case law at the EU level. However, it was addressed in the first infringement decision made in respect of the Chapter II Prohibition by the OFT (*Napp Pharmaceutical Holdings Ltd and Subsidiaries* CA98/2/2001 [2001] UKCLR 597, on appeal *Napp Pharmaceutical Holdings Ltd* v *The Director General of Fair Trading* [2002] CompAR 13). This and other cases relating to pricing abuses, refusals to supply, and the essential facilities doctrine are dealt with as appropriate in Chapter 16.

15.3.2 **Leveraging power from one market to another**

Oftel considered a complaint of anti-competitive leveraging made against BT in relation to the promotion of its directory enquiries service on the cover of its telephone book (*BT publishing its 118500 directory enquiries number on the front of the BT phonebook* [2004] UKCLR 850). In this case a number of providers of directory enquiry services had alleged that BT was leveraging its dominance in the market for phonebook services into the market for telephone directory enquiry services. Without feeling the need to reach a final conclusion on the matter, Oftel accepted that BT probably was dominant in the former market, and that the second market was sufficiently closely related to the first for leveraging to take place. However, examination of the effect of the promotion showed that it had no appreciable effect on competition. Survey evidence showed that in areas where the 118500 number was printed on the front of the phonebook calls to that number were only about 1 per cent higher than from other areas. There was, in addition, compelling evidence that other forms of advertising were more effective, such that competitors could match BT's promotions and were not being unfairly damaged. Of customers surveyed, 82 per cent were aware of the directory enquiries numbers from TV advertising, rather than from any other source. Research also showed that only about 40 per cent of customers kept the phonebook near the telephone, with 38 per cent keeping it out of sight and a further 10 per cent throwing it away.

15.4 **Procedural aspects and remedies**

The procedure to be followed for the application of the Chapter II provision is that examined in Chapters 5 to 7 of this book. In 2004 amendments were introduced to the provisions of the CA 98 relating to procedure, bringing them in line with the new 'modernized' EU rules that entered into force on 1 May 2004. The reform removed sections under which notifications could be made to the OFT in respect of dominant firm conduct, and like the European regime, advocated for 'a system under which businesses must self-assess compliance with both [EU] and national competition law' (OFT Press Release 215/04 (14 December 2004)). In its guidelines *The major provisions* (OFT 400), the OFT may provide confidential guidance to undertakings on the application of the Chapter II Prohibition on an ad hoc basis, although subsequently it will not be bound by such informal views.

With regard to specific remedies, Section 33 of the Competition Act 1998 provides, in part, that:

33—(1) If the OFT has made a decision that conduct infringes the Chapter II Prohibition . . . it may give to such person or persons as it considers appropriate such directions as it considers appropriate to bring the infringement to an end.

There have been relatively few cases in which infringements of the Chapter II Prohibition have been found by the OFT or other concurrent power holders. It is unusual for directions to be required, infringements normally being abandoned following the finding of an infringement, or more likely earlier on in the proceedings. However, directions have on occasion been necessary; the leading case in this respect is *Genzyme*.

The case of *Genzyme* is discussed at 16.2.4. In essence the OFT found that Genzyme Ltd had engaged in exclusionary behaviour in relation to its Cerezyme product, a medication used to treat the very rare Gaucher's Disease (*Exclusionary Behaviour by Genzyme Ltd* CA98/3/03 [2003] UKCLR 950). The decision was upheld on appeal (*Genzyme Ltd v The OFT* [2004] CAT 4), but the matter continued to exercise the competition authorities when Genzyme was slow to remedy its conduct. The case came before the CAT again in 2005 for further consideration of remedies, and the CAT at that time noted that it was 'regrettable . . . that Genzyme was able to delay matters for so long after the Tribunal's judgment' (*Genzyme Ltd v OFT* [2005] CAT 32, para. 219).

The OFT had made directions in the case in its infringement decision, but these were suspended during the appeal. It was agreed that the directions required modification. Under para. 3(2) of Sch. 8 to the Act the CAT holds the same power as does the OFT in relation to directions. Under paras (d) and (e) of that part of the Schedule the CAT may 'give such directions, or take such other steps, as the OFT could itself have given or taken'. The CAT expanded on the meaning of this power at para. 233 of its judgment:

In our judgment, the power to make a direction under s 33 of the 1998 Act includes the power to ensure that an infringement is not repeated . . . Moreover, in our view, the power 'to bring the infringement to an end' covers conduct closely linked to, or to the like effect as, the infringement found, otherwise s 33 would be ineffective. Similarly, the Tribunal's powers to give such directions or make any decision the OFT could have given or made must, it seems to us, be construed as a power to give a direction that is adapted to the developments that have taken place in the course of the proceedings, provided that the underlying problem to be addressed remains the same or similar. Otherwise, a kind of 'catch as catch can' situation could arise in which a dominant undertaking could, by constantly changing its arrangements, keep the competition authorities at bay indefinitely.

The directions attached by the CAT to its judgment required Genzyme, *inter alia*, to supply the product in question at specified price bands, to treat any trading with its former subsidiary 'at arm's length in all material respects', and to supply to the OFT any information that the OFT required in order to monitor Genzyme's compliance with the directions.

Where conduct is of minor significance, s. 40 establishes that fines under s. 36(2) may not be imposed, but other decisions may be taken by the OFT and private actions may be brought. The appropriate level of fines is set at a turnover of £50 million by the Competition Act 1998 (Small Agreements and Conduct of Minor Significance) Regulations 2000, SI 2000/262 (para. 4). This 'safe harbour' does not apply in relation to the application of art. 102 TFEU by the OFT.

Summary map

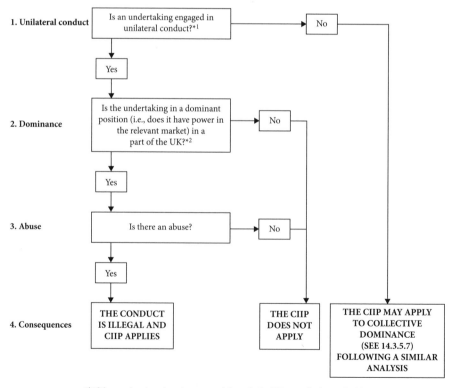

*[1] If the conduct is, at least in part, multilateral, the CIP may also be applicable.

*[2] If, in addition to these conditions, there was also an effect on trade between Member States and the dominant position was held in a substantial part of the EU, Art. 102 TFEU must be applied. The CIIP may also be simultaneously applied.

FURTHER READING

Articles

AHLBORN, C., and ALLAN, B., 'The *Napp* Case: A Study of Predation?', (2003) *World Competition Law & Economics Review* 233

CLARKE, R., 'Dominant Firms and Monopoly Policy in the UK and EU', in Clarke, R. and Morgan, E. J., *New Developments in UK and EU Competition Policy* (2006) Edward Elgar, Cheltenham, 22–50

16

An analysis of the principal abusive practices

KEY POINTS

- Predatory pricing may infringe the law when a dominant undertaking sets prices below an appropriate cost measure with the intent of eliminating competition.

- Excessive pricing could be unlawful when a dominant undertaking sets prices which bear no reasonable relation to the economic value of the product and are unfair.

- Discriminatory pricing raises issues in cases where a dominant undertaking charges different prices for similar transactions to different customers without an objective justification.

- A margin squeeze may be anti-competitive when a dominant undertaking charges a competitor a price for a product or service that does not permit an efficient competitor to compete with the dominant undertaking in a relevant linked market.

- The essential facilities doctrine requires that dominant undertakings make services or products available to competitors in order to allow them to compete.

- The EU and UK law and practice in relation to all these potential abuses is aligned.

16.1 Introduction

There are important similarities in the approaches taken by different competition authorities to the same forms of dominant-firm anti-competitive conduct, although there are notable exceptions. Even before the enactment of the Competition Act 1998 there had been an element of cross-fertilization between the EU and UK. This is more clearly noticeable in the impact EU membership has had on UK law, but domestic actions have been noted, and from time to time cited with approval, at the centre (see, e.g., *Napier Brown* v *British Sugar* 88/518 (1988) OJ L284/41, where the Commission relied in part on a MMC report).

The increasing convergence in Union and national law makes it appropriate to consider actions taken against specific forms of anti-competitive conduct in each regime alongside each other. An examination of the extensive practice in the United States and the principles of industrial economics casts further light on the approaches likely to be taken in the jurisdictions assessed here. The discussion that follows is focused on a range of pricing practices and refusals to deal, which together constitute the larger part of the anti-competitive and exploitative practices of dominant firms. It does not therefore give examples of all practices that may fall to be condemned in both jurisdictions.

16.2 Pricing policies

Price competition is one of the most visible forms of commercial rivalry and is often of short-term benefit to consumers, who are unlikely to complain about 'price wars'. It is one of the inherent contradictions of competition law that firms may be attacked for pricing too high, for pricing too low, and for setting different prices for different customers. Whether or not these actions may be of legitimate concern to competition authorities depends on the specific circumstances. In the context of art. 102 (see Chapter 14) it is clearly envisaged that the first and last of these are to fall within the meaning of abuse, as the examples set out in the article include: (a) 'directly or indirectly imposing unfair purchase or selling prices' and (b) 'applying dissimilar conditions to equivalent transactions'. Arguably predatory prices are 'unfair' and, as was the case in *ECS/AKZO—interim measures* 83/462 (1983) OJ L252/13, therefore also fall within (a); but even if they are not, their imposition may fall within the more general meaning of 'abuse'.

16.2.1 Predatory pricing

At first sight, one might think that it is unreasonable that an undertaking offering low prices for its products may incur an anti-competitive conduct. Indeed, '[l]ow prices or price reductions are normally seen as a benefit from and the successful result of the process of competition'. However, at times behind price cuts there is an intention to wipe out competitors; once they have disappeared, the dominant company can go back to its usual pricing policy. Indeed, 'predatory behaviour constitutes a class of anti-competitive behaviour where prices are *too low*, to the extent that the competitive process itself is damaged' (Myers, G., *Predatory Behaviour in UK Competition Policy*, London, OFT (1994), para. 1.1). A good working explanation of the practice of predatory pricing is given by Hay and Morris (Hay, D. A., and Morris, D. J., *Industrial Economics and Organization Theory and Evidence*, Oxford, OUP (1991), p. 580):

A dominant firm reacts to competition in one of its markets, either a geographical or a product market, by cutting price so as to drive the competitor out of business. The competitor in question may be either a new entrant or a small firm that has been a passive 'follower' of the leadership of the dominant firm but has now begun to gain market share. The purpose of the dominant firm's price-cutting is to preserve its long-run monopoly by frightening off potentially serious competition. The dominant firm is therefore quite willing to accept losses in that particular market for the time being—losses which it can absorb since it is earning high profits in other markets. The losses are the price for establishing a tough reputation, which will protect its position in all its markets in the long term.

There are three primary concerns of competition authorities with regard to predatory pricing. First, it may act either as a barrier to entry, or to drive firms out of a market. Secondly, this is achieved by making it unprofitable for entrants to compete with the incumbent, or by sending a false signal to the entrant as to the expected returns from the market. Thirdly, the intention behind such predation is to allow the incumbent to raise prices in the long term, once the short-term battle has been won. While any company could, in theory, choose to engage in predatory pricing, only a monopolist with access to significant capital reserves or to the capital market could do so with any hope of success.

Strong arguments are made, in particular by some members of the Chicago school, to the effect that predatory pricing should be of no concern to competition authorities as it can never be a successful strategy and is only ever of benefit to consumers (in particular see Bork, R. H., *The Antitrust Paradox*, New York, The Free Press (1993), pp. 144–55). A leading competition strategist, attempting to discourage firms from taking such action, argues that price competition may be 'highly unstable and quite likely to leave the entire industry worse off from the standpoint of profitability. Price cuts are quickly and easily matched by rivals, and once matched they lower revenues for all firms' (Porter, M. E., *Competitive Strategy*, New York, The Free Press (1980), p. 17).

Following more recent economic developments, and analyses based on game theory, the better view appears to be that predatory pricing can be successful where 'the potential entrant is uncertain about the post-entry [equilibrium] because it does not have precise information about the nature of the incumbent' (Hay, D. A., and Morris, D. J., above, p. 580). In such a situation the entrant is facing the situation where its knowledge does not match that of the incumbent, and it cannot determine whether the action of the price cutter is a result of superior efficiency, in which case the entrant may predict losses following even a successful entrance, or of the desire of the incumbent to gain a reputation as a tough competitor.

The first important case to consider the issue in the United States was *Standard Oil Co. of New Jersey v US* 221 US 1 (1911). It is one of the earliest cases based on s. 2 of the Sherman Act 1890 to reach the Supreme Court, and the case in which the 'rule of reason' was established (see Chapter 1). Standard Oil had been created in 1870 out of the various companies operating at different levels of the industry owned by, among others, the Rockefellers, and was one of the original 'trusts' against which the antitrust legislation had reacted. Within a period of just over 10 years the company controlled some 90 per cent of the oil industry in the United States. One reason for this spectacular growth was that the company had engaged in predatory pricing, its practice having 'necessarily involved the intent to drive others from the field and to exclude them from their right to trade and thus accomplish the mastery which was the end in view' (for a critique of this argument, see McGee, J. S., 'Predatory

Price Cutting: The Standard Oil (NJ) Case', (1958) 1 *Journal of Law and Economics*, 137–69). *Standard Oil* was followed very quickly by *US v American Tobacco Co.* 221 US 106 (1911), in which the Supreme Court similarly found that the defendant had breached the Sherman Act in fighting price wars with smaller competitors to drive them out of the market.

By the 1970s the attitude of the US antitrust authorities to allegations of predatory pricing was one of varying degrees of scepticism, and the courts too showed an increasing tendency to dismiss private claims alleging predation. In *Matsushita Electric Industrial Co. v Zenith Radio Corp.* 475 US 574 (1986), the Supreme Court rejected a complaint made against 21 Japanese manufacturers by two US producers of television sets. The latter had argued that sets sold by the defendants in the USA were deliberately sold at a low price to weaken the ability of the American firms to compete in the global market. The Court referred with approval to the arguments made by Bork:

As [Bork] shows, the success of such schemes is inherently uncertain: the short-run loss is definite, but the long-run gain depends on successfully neutralising the competition...The success of any predatory scheme depends on *maintaining* monopoly power for long enough to recoup predator's losses and to harvest some additional gain....For this reason, there is a consensus among commentators that predatory pricing schemes are rarely tried, and even more rarely successful.   (p. 589)

Four of the judges dissented from this opinion. Only nine months after *Matsushita* the Supreme Court considered an allegation of predation again in *Cargill Inc. v Montfort of Colorado Inc.* 479 US 104 (1986). Here the Court held, by a majority of six to two, that 'there is ample evidence suggesting that the practice does occur' (p. 121). The leading current position is laid down in *Brooke Group Ltd v Brown & Williamson Tobacco Corp.* 113 S. Ct. 2578 (1993). The Supreme Court took the opportunity to clarify the law, and in doing so acknowledged that predation might occur. However, the Court set a twofold test to be applied that will prove difficult for plaintiffs. For an allegation of predation to be upheld it must now be shown that the prices are below an appropriate measure of cost, and that there exists the likelihood that the investment in predatory prices will be recouped in the future by the defendant.

A major contribution to the debate as to the appropriate standard (or, *per Brooke*, 'cost measure') by which to judge predation was published in 1975 when Areeda and Turner attempted to define a test that could be used by the courts (Areeda, P., and Turner, D. F., 'Predatory Pricing and Related Practices under Section 2 of the Sherman Act', (1975) 88 *Harvard Law Review* 697). Broadly, the authors argued that predation occurs when prices are set below marginal cost (see Chapter 1 for definitions of the basic economic terms); however, as marginal cost can be difficult to determine, a proxy measurement of average variable cost, which is easier to ascertain by standard cost-accounting techniques, would produce an acceptably close result. It is difficult to argue that below marginal cost pricing should be acceptable, as it is more profitable to produce nothing than it is to sell below marginal cost (see Scherer, F. M., and Ross, D., *Industrial Market Structure and Economic Performance*, Boston, MA, Houghton

Mifflin (3rd edn, 1990), pp. 472–9). Despite its shortcomings, the Areeda–Turner rule—as it is now known—has the benefit of simplicity, and found favour with the US Department of Justice and Federal Trades Commission.

16.2.1.1 Predatory pricing in the EU

An attempt was made in the leading European case of *ECS/AKZO* to persuade the EU authorities to adopt the Areeda–Turner test (85/609 (1985) OJ L374/1; on appeal *AKZO Chemie BV v Commission* case C–62/86 [1993] 5 CMLR 215). The Commission had taken swift action following a complaint by an English firm, ECS, that a larger competitor, AKZO, was price cutting predatorily in ECS's traditional market. The product in question was benzoyl peroxide, which has uses both as a bleach in the flour market and as a catalyst in plastics manufacture. ECS had concentrated on the flour additive market in the UK and Ireland, and held a market share of 35 per cent, being heavily reliant on a single customer group, Allied Mills. In 1979 ECS began to expand its sales into the larger plastics markets, dominated by AKZO, and captured one of AKZO's larger customers, BASF, having offered a price significantly lower than that of AKZO. ECS then alleged that AKZO threatened to reduce prices in the UK flour sector, thereby threatening ECS's core operations.

A memo prepared by an AKZO executive noted that it had been confirmed to ECS's managing director that 'aggressive commercial action would be taken on the milling side unless he refrained from selling his products to the plastics industry'. The Commission reacted to the complaint initially by ordering interim measures under which AKZO's UK arm was to stay within the profit levels that existed before ECS's competitive move (*ECS/AKZO—interim measures* 83/462 (1983) OJ L252/13). In its final decision in the matter (85/609 (1985) OJ L374/1) the Commission had to consider carefully the argument made by AKZO that its prices 'were not abusive since they always included an element of profit', by which, the Commission notes, AKZO was arguing that they covered average variable costs, and therefore would not fall foul of the Areeda–Turner test (para. 42). Apart from disputing the basis of the accounts on which these figures were derived, the Commission also turned to other evidence, such as the intent underpinning AKZO's conduct. It refused to apply a pure cost-accounting approach to the problem, pointing out that

Article [102] does not prescribe any cost-based legal rule to define the precise stage at which price-cutting by a dominant firm may become abusive and indeed *the broad application of the concept of abuse to different forms of exclusionary behaviour would argue against such a narrow test.* (para. 75, emphasis added)

When the Court of Justice considered the appeal it appeared to be slightly less sceptical as to the basis of the figures on which AKZO made its arguments, but supported the EU Commission in rejecting the resolution of the issue by the exclusive application of any formal test. The Court did suggest, however, that prices below average variable costs would be considered abusive, and that prices set at higher levels than this, but below average total costs, could also breach art. 102 if other factors suggested a predatory intent.

In the more recent case of *Tetra Pak* v *Commission (No. 2)* case C–333/94P [1997] 4 CMLR 662, the Court indicated that prices set below average variable cost would be automatically held to be abusive, without the need to establish intent. However, it is likely that in such cases the undertaking pricing below average variable cost would be able to rebut the presumption of an abuse in some circumstances, such as where there is obvious over-capacity or over-supply in the market.

Where it can be established that a company is selling at a loss, an allegation of predatory conduct will in most cases be sustained. Nevertheless, exceptions might be made where, for example, there has recently been a change in the market structure and the company is still adjusting to this. In *Napier Brown/British Sugar* 88/518 (1988) OJ L284/41, the Commission found that British Sugar was selling retail sugar at a price which did not reflect its own 'transformation costs'. It was making a loss on the retail sales, which it was able to subsidize by profits from its industrial sales. The effect of this, if sustained, would be that any company which could package and market sugar as efficiently as British Sugar, but which did not have its own source of industrial sugar, would leave the market. That being so, the allegation of predatory pricing made by Napier Brown was upheld by the Commission (see para. 66). This conduct would now be characterized as a 'margin squeeze' (see 16.2.4).

In 1997 the Commission considered allegations of predation in *Irish Sugar* 97/624 (1997) OJ L258/1, on appeal *Irish Sugar plc* v *Commission* case T–228/97 [1999] 5 CMLR 1300; subsequently upheld by the Court of Justice, *Irish Sugar plc* v *Commission* case C–497/99 R [2001] 5 CMLR 29. In this case the undertaking targeted price cuts and discounts selectively so as to undermine imports. The case deals with both discriminatory pricing (see below and 16.2.3) and exclusionary pricing, the effect of which may be indistinguishable from predation. In the case itself there is a muddying of the waters between predation and exclusion. The Commission, in condemning prices that lay above average variable cost, indicated that selective reductions would be regarded as strong evidence of intent to predate. The question arose as to the extent to which a company could cut prices in order to meet competition, a matter to which critics of competition policy often point as a failing of the system. The Commission's response was that '[t]here is no doubt that a firm in a dominant position is entitled to defend that position by competing with other firms in its market. However, the dominant firm must not deliberately attempt to effectively shut out competitors' (para. 134). The 2005 discussion paper on exclusionary abuses notes that in most cases it would not sustain a finding of predation where prices are above ATC, but it does recognize that 'exceptional circumstances' might exist where such price cuts could lead to substantial harm to consumers.

Where a smaller competitor would be shut out simply by the fact that the dominant firm is more efficient and has lower costs, it would not be abusive to rely on these advantages as long as the conduct was not introduced so as clearly to target a particular competitor, or was introduced as a specific response to a short-term competitive situation. It would not, for example, be abusive for a company enjoying substantial economies of scale to price consistently, and in a non-discriminatory manner, at a level lower than could be achieved by new entrants into the market.

These arguments, among others, were considered in the Decision *Wanadoo Interactive* (16 July 2003, [2005] 5 CMLR 5, on appeal before the GC *France Télécom* v *Commission* Case T–340/03 [2007] 4 CMLR 21, and on appeal before the Court of Justice *France Télécom* v *Commission* Case C–202/07 [2009] nyr). It is the key case of this chapter.

In essence, the position taken by the European Courts under art. 102 in relation to predation may be summarized as follows:

Price below average variable costs	Predation can be assumed
Price above average variable costs, but below average total costs	Evidence on costs may indicate predation, but the Director General would need to establish evidence that the dominant undertaking intended to eliminate a competitor before predation could be found
Price above average total costs	Evidence does not indicate predation

Thus, for example, at para. 256 of *Wanadoo Interactive* (16 July 2003, [2005] 5 CMLR 5) the Commission stated that:

the existence of predatory prices is established in the following situations:

— the non-recovery of average variable costs per unit, the establishment of which in itself justifies a finding of abuse;

— the non-recovery of average full costs where this is accompanied by a plan indicative of an intention to eliminate competitors.

Even where prices are below average variable costs, evidence to justify this may be considered. Such justifications might include: short-run promotions; inefficient entry (a situation where a company mistakenly enters a market in which there is no excess capacity, forcing all firms to cut prices); mistakes; and, the fact that the undertaking is nevertheless making an incremental profit. In the UK case of *First Edinburgh/Lothian* CA98/05/2004 [2004] UKCLR 1554, for example, prices set below average variable costs did not lead to a finding of predation (see below).

Key case 16.1 *Wanadoo Interactive* (16 July 2003, [2005] 5 CMLR 5, on appeal *France Télécom* v *Commission* Case T–340/03 [2007] 4 *CMLR* 2, on appeal *France Télécom* v *Commission* Case C–202/07 [2009]—Commission decision, Court of Justice judgment (art. 102)

Facts

The case related to the market for high-speed residential Internet access, where the Commission found evidence of below cost pricing by Wanadoo Interactive, a 72 per cent owned subsidiary of France Télécom. The argument was made that this pricing was an attempt to stifle nascent competition in the relevant market. For its part Wanadoo claimed that its conduct did not constitute predation. It argued that there had been no dramatic falls in prices, that no specific groups of consumers had been targeted, and that no threats had been made against competitors to dissuade them from operating in the market. In imposing a fine of €10.35 million the Commission made it clear that it did not accept this view.

It was noted in the opening chapter of this book that competition law is an area with few sharp rules. Although the list below suggests it is possible to be reasonably specific about the approach taken to predation, in *Wanadoo* the Commission held that 'legal precedents do not cover every possible predation scenario' (para. 266). It went on to say that 'generally, predation may simply consist in dictating or inhibiting the competitive behaviour of an existing or potential rival', and need not take the form of 'the radical elimination and wholesale ousting of competitors from the market' (para. 266). The precedents Wanadoo was relying on were those in which a limited number of large customers were supplied, such that a selective policy could effectively target rivals' sales. However, as the Commission pointed out, in the present case, which related to a mass consumer market, such an analysis would be pointless, and '[e]conomic doctrine in no way limits predatory behaviour to selective strategies aimed at winning back a specific customer' (para. 268). In condemning Wanadoo's conduct the Commission was able to rely in part on several internal documents which established a link between the level of prices and a growth strategy. Further damage to Wanadoo's cause came from the fact that it had apparently adopted a deliberate strategy, set out as such in internal documents, to pre-empt competition in the relevant market. The Commission considered in para. 273 that

in the context of a new market which has entered a period of dynamic growth, and in view of the advantages derived by Wanadoo from its membership of the France Télécom group, this pre-emption must itself be treated as an intention to drive out competition.

Findings

On appeal, the GC upheld the Commission decision, and in so doing emphasized that it was not necessary, under the test for predation in EU law, to establish that recoupment of losses was likely. When the case reached the Court of Justice, Advocate General Mazák supported France Télécom's claims and recommended overturning the judgment of the GC. He argued forcefully by saying that the GC had 'completely failed' to analyse whether Wanadoo had indeed aligned its prices in an anti-competitive manner (para. 44). The GC was also criticized for not applying the law to the particular facts of the case (para. 43). In April 2009, the Court of Justice disregarded his opinion and dismissed France Télécom's appeal as partially inadmissible and partially unfounded.

Comment

The judgment of the Court of Justice confirms the divergence between the EU and US case law on predation, by arguing that an undertaking does not need to have a reasonable prospect of recovering its losses for predatory pricing to exist. Further, even if a dominant firm proves that it was merely aligning its prices with its rivals, there may be a finding of predation.

> The message this case sends to companies contemplating entry into new sectors of the economy is a difficult one, particularly where the company is dominant, or has market power, in a related 'old' sector. At the very least any undertaking in such a position would have to be extremely careful to justify the strategies it adopted in pursuing a policy of market development.

FURTHER READING

Article

Subiotto, R., and O'Donoghue, R., 'Defining the Scope of the Duty of Dominant Firms to Deal with Existing Customers under Article 82 EC', (2003) *ECLR* 683

16.2.1.2 Predation in the UK

In its first two adverse decisions under the Competition Act in relation to the Chapter II Prohibition, the OFT condemned predation. In *Napp* the core conduct attacked related to price discrimination, but the undertaking offered prices to one sector of the market place which were substantially below those offered to another sector. Furthermore, according to the decision, where it faced competition in the market for its product—sustained release morphine, or MST—Napp's 'prices to hospitals are below direct costs, where direct costs are defined, consistently with Napp's accounting system, as materials and direct labour' (*Napp Pharmaceutical Holdings Ltd and Subsidiaries* CA98/2/2001 [2001] UKCLR 597, para. 189). Napp argued that its low prices were justified as sales to hospitals of the drug guaranteed that follow-on sales would be made through prescriptions continued by GPs. In addition it was pricing across the entire usage of the drug, and therefore increasing its net revenue by pricing below cost in one sector.

On appeal the CAT rejected these arguments, and was scathing of the net revenue argument (*Napp Pharmaceutical Holdings Ltd and Subsidiaries* v *The Director General of Fair Trading* [2002] CompAR 13, paras 231–66). At para. 225 the CAT held that 'on the uncontested facts the situation that presents itself in this case is therefore that of a virtual monopolist that has been selling at prices well below direct cost'. Following *AKZO* the CAT found that this behaviour would, absent an objective justification, constitute predation. As for the net revenue argument, which had been advanced by the undertaking's economic consultants, the CAT held that it

provides no yardstick for distinguishing between what is legitimate, and what is abusive, behaviour on the part of a dominant undertaking. For instance, a monopolist driving away new entrants by predatory pricing is likely to maximise his net revenue by so doing, for example by avoiding the loss of market share and erosion of prices in the profitable market where he holds a monopoly. Yet plainly such behaviour does not cease to be abusive merely because it is profitable for the monopolist to engage in it.   (para. 259)

In *Predation by Aberdeen Journals Ltd* CA98/5/2001 [2001] UKCLR 856 (discussed in Chapter 15 in relation to the definition of the relevant market) predation was, as the title of the decision indicates, very much to the fore. The company had been selling advertising space in its journal at a loss in the hope of driving its competition out of the market. In the decision the Director concluded that 'Aberdeen Journals failed to price above average variable costs regarding the *Herald & Post* in March, May and June of 2000' (para. 87). As well as conducting an analysis of the cost structure facing the undertaking and its revenues, the OFT also relied on significant documentary evidence of intent. The undertaking argued that it was merely meeting competition, and that pricing levels were broadly equivalent between its title and that of the entrant. The OFT, however, found that the only reason for the similarity was that the competitor was being forced to meet the prices set by Aberdeen Journals, which had 'initiated and sustained price cuts, and increased pagination and circulation, rather than simply responded to competition' (para. 79). The undertaking argued that the length of time over which the OFT was analysing the conduct was insufficient to fully take into account the dynamics of the market place. The OFT accepted that there might well be circumstances in which undertakings 'might inadvertently price below average variable cost for a short period' (para. 109) but it did not accept that this was the situation in the present case. In para. 115 of the decision the Director held that

Even if there were convincing evidence that Aberdeen Journals no longer intended to predate in March 2000 (which the Director is satisfied there is not), Aberdeen Journals' conduct from 1 March to 29 March 2000 would be predatory. These pricing levels were not inadvertent or caused by any external factor. They resulted directly from the sustained predatory campaign pursued by Aberdeen Journals against the *Independent* over the preceding four years, before the Act came into force. Aberdeen Journals' failure to take effective action to cease predating (even though it was subject to investigation by the Office) by reducing its costs or increasing its revenues was, at best, negligent, and continued to have the anticompetitive effect of potentially expelling its only rival from the relevant market. Consequently Aberdeen Journals' failure to cover its average variable costs until 29 March 2000 was not legitimate competitive conduct.

In *Aberdeen Journals Ltd* v *The Director General of Fair Trading* ([2002] CompAR 167) the CAT set this decision aside, remitting it to the Director for reassessment, as it found defects in the analysis of the relevant market (see Chapter 15). The OFT made a new decision, essentially reaching the same conclusions, but supported by much more thorough market analysis (*Predation by Aberdeen Journals Ltd* CA98/14/2002 [2002] UKCLR 740). The assessment of predation is set out at paras 150–212. This was again appealed to the CAT (*Aberdeen Journals Ltd* v *Office of Fair Trading supported by Aberdeen Independent Ltd* [2003] CompAR 67). This time the Tribunal upheld the OFT's decision in relation to market definition and dominance, and agreed that the OFT had established that abusive predatory conduct had taken place.

The CAT took the view, consistent with EU case law, that 'pricing below average variable cost is not a normal business practice in normal competitive conditions' (para. 424), and that doing so 'suffices to establish the abuse alleged without it being necessary to examine the question of intention' (ibid.). The evidence brought forward by the OFT was enough to establish on the facts that the undertaking *had* priced below average variable cost, and that over the period in question—albeit a short one—Aberdeen Journals had not attempted to bring the price above variable cost.

Another case of alleged predation to emerge in Scotland was that of *First Edinburgh/ Lothian* CA98/05/2004 [2004] UKCLR 1554. Here the OFT rejected a complaint of predation made by the local authority bus service to the effect that a competitor was engaged in predation. The OFT found that there was no intent to drive out the incumbent, notwithstanding the fact that there was evidence of prices being set below average variable costs. Internal documents showed that First Edinburgh's strategy was to expand the bus network and wished to entice greater numbers of passengers on to the services offered. It appeared to be the case that the company did not believe that it could have forced Lothian out of the market even if it had wanted to do so.

In the *Discussion paper on the application of Article 82 of the Treaty to exclusionary abuses* (December 2005) predation is dealt with at some length, at paras 93–133. When discussing the relevant cost benchmarks that might be applicable the Commission places emphasis on 'average avoidable costs' (AAC), a concept not previously discussed in this book. Paragraph 106 states that 'if avoidable losses are incurred, the pricing can be presumed to be predatory'. The Commission recognizes that AVC is a suitable proxy for AAC in most cases, but not where the undertaking in question expands its production, in which case AAC will be *higher* than AVC. In such a case setting a standard based around AVC might permit an undertaking to avoid a finding of predation when it would be found to be predating were the AAC threshold to be applied.

Measuring costs themselves may not be an easy task. It is one thing to determine the appropriate benchmark—AVC, AAC—but another to calculate what that cost is. The CAT has found that the OFT failed to assess costs properly in *Claymore Dairies*, in which a complaint alleging that Robert Wiseman Dairies plc had abused a dominant position in the market for milk in Scotland had been rejected (*Claymore Dairies Ltd and Arla Foods UK plc v Office of Fair Trading supported by Robert Wiseman Dairies plc* [2005] CAT 30, [2006] CompAR 1). The CAT, in setting aside the OFT decision, stated that

[i]n any investigation of alleged predatory pricing, one of the first tasks for a competition authority is to obtain detailed and reliable evidence of the prices and costs involved. (para. 208)

The Tribunal recognized that 'determining "the costs" may not be a straightforward exercise' (para. 210), and held that in making a decision relating to an allegation of predatory pricing it was 'generally necessary' to hold 'a reasonably detailed understanding of the nature of the business and how costs arise' (para. 211). Noting that in *AKZO* the Court of Justice 'took a rigorous approach to costs issues' (para. 216) the CAT held that it was important that investigations were 'grounded on a firm and reliable assessment of what the total costs are, cross-checked as far as possible against the dominant undertaking's statutory and management accounts' (ibid.). Competition authorities will have access to accountancy expertise in making these difficult assessments, and, of course, may require information from those subject to investigation in a format specified by the authority, but it is clear that problems may still arise in practice.

The topic of predation is covered at some length in the fall 2003 issue of *Antitrust* (vol. 18, no. 1).

16.2.2 **Excessive pricing**

The popular, and not entirely accurate, view of monopoly behaviour is that it leads to 'rip-offs' and excessively high prices. As was demonstrated formally in Chapter 13, a monopolist is likely to price higher than a firm in a competitive market. While such situations can be of concern to competition authorities, there is again no standard formula by which excessive pricing may be identified. Excessive pricing occurs when a price 'is above that which would exist in a competitive market and where it is clear that high profits will not stimulate successful new entry within a reasonable period' (*Napp Pharmaceutical Holdings Ltd* CA98/2/2001 [2001] UKCLR 597, para. 203). It is a dangerous strategy as the supernormal profits of which it is indicative are an invitation to other firms to enter the market (see, e.g., the comments made by the MMC in *Cross Solent Ferries*, Cm. 1825, 1992, at para. 7.71). Such a strategy is therefore one that can be pursued successfully in the medium to long term only where there exist strong barriers to entry. These barriers might include a reputation for predation on behalf of the incumbent, so the situation can arise where, in a short space of time, a company prices first predatorily and then excessively.

A further problem in the analysis is to distinguish between excessive prices which lead to supernormal profits, and excessive prices which are the result of X-inefficiency, which might be the case where an incumbent is both inefficient and protected by high barriers to entry. In the latter case there would be no excessive, or supernormal, profits, and any decision condemning high prices would in effect be one condemning poor management and inefficiency. It is difficult to contemplate a competition authority taking such a decision, which among other things would lead to extremely complex enforcement issues.

16.2.2.1 Excessive pricing in the EU

Where the EU Commission has acted against excessive pricing, it often appears to have been on the basis of limited analysis and to have been inspired by concerns about divisions in the internal market. There has not been much EU case law in this area and it is not dealt with in the recent review of art. 102 as excessive pricing is clearly *not* exclusionary. In fact, many competition lawyers would argue that competition law should not concern itself with issues of excessive pricing in any market.

The first decision to deal with the issue in detail in the EU was that of *General Motors Continental* 75/75 (1975) OJ L29/14. At the time the decision was taken cars sold in or imported into Belgium for use were required to satisfy technical standards laid down in law, and to carry an approval '*plaque d'identification*'. Either the manufacturer or a sole agent had to issue the certificate and confirm that the vehicle met the legal requirements. General Motors Continental was the sole authorized agent for the manufacturers belonging to the General Motors Group (GM). Where the approval certificate was being issued in respect of a car manufactured and sold by a member of GM in Europe, a fee of BF1,250 was charged. However, for private customers or dealers who brought cars into Belgium other than through the standard GM distribution channels ('parallel importers') the price for the certificate rose to between BF5,300 and BF30,000, the aim presumably being to encourage such customers to purchase only through approved GM distributors. It appeared to be the case that BF2,500 would be the maximum charged for such certificates by agents authorized in respect of other makes of vehicle. Pointing to the 'extraordinary disparity between actual costs incurred and prices actually charged' the Commission found that GM had 'abused its dominant position within the meaning of [art. 102] and applied unfair prices within the meaning of heading (a)'.

Very similar facts arose in the case of *British Leyland* (BL) (84/379 (1984) OJ L207/11) where customers were buying BL-manufactured left-hand drive vehicles in continental Europe at prices substantially lower than the equivalent right-hand drive vehicle in the United Kingdom. BL's UK dealers responded to this situation by putting pressure on BL to curb the trade, and BL at first decided to refuse to grant the necessary 'national type-approval' certificates for the imported vehicles. Then, following public pressure and intervention in the House of Commons, it changed its policy, granting such certificates but at a price of £150. A Commission investigation found that BL was at the same time charging only £25 for the certificate in respect of imported right-hand drive vehicles. Whether a vehicle was right- or left-hand drive made no difference to the legal status of the certificates. BL was then condemned for charging a fee that 'was both excessive and discriminatory' (para. 26).

An interesting variant on high pricing was considered in *Sabena* (*London European— Sabena* 88/589 (1988) OJ L317/47). Following a complaint made by London European (LE), a small company operating a twice-daily air service on the Luton–Brussels and Luton–Amsterdam routes, the Commission found that Sabena, by refusing to grant LE access to its ticket reservation system, had the intention 'of placing indirect pressure on [LE] to fix a higher level of fares than, as an independent air carrier, it had planned . . . an artificial increase in fares [is] totally incompatible with a system of free competition' (para. 29).

In *United Brands* (*United Brands Co. v Commission* case 27/76 [1978] 1 CMLR 429, paras 235–68) the Court of Justice dealt with the Commission arguments to the effect that UB had charged 'unfair' prices 'excessive in relation to the economic value of the product supplied'. The Commission had argued, taking prices charged in Ireland as a base, that a price reduction of some 15 per cent would be appropriate. The Court agreed that 'charging a price which is excessive because it has no reasonable relation to the economic value of the product supplied' is an abuse. It held that the question is one of whether 'the difference between the costs actually incurred and the price actually charged is excessive and, if the answer to this question is in the affirmative, to consider whether a price has been imposed which is either unfair in itself or when compared to competing products'. Unfortunately the Commission had failed to conduct any examination of the cost structures facing UB, and had based its claim of excessive pricing on a superficial comparison of prices based on a single exception to a trend, and on a solitary letter written by UB which was subsequently withdrawn by the undertaking. In respect of this claim, therefore, the Commission decision was in part struck down. Some care must be taken in applying this analysis elsewhere—the concept of 'economic value' is an interesting but highly subjective one.

In *Duales System Deutschland AG* 2001/463 (2001) OJ L166/1 the Commission condemned what it termed 'unreasonable prices', which it said existed in cases in which 'the price charged for a service is clearly disproportionate to the cost of supplying it' (para. 111). In the case in question the undertaking, DSD, licensed the use of the Green Dot trade mark on packaging, and would in return look after the collection and recycling of such packaging. The Commission first announced that it was inclined to take a favourable view of the arrangement, but then received a number of complaints to the effect that DSD was abusing a dominant position on the German market: not all packaging bearing the mark would be dealt with by DSD, even though a licence fee would still be required for this. The Commission found that in these circumstances the fee was 'unfair' (para. 112). It argued that 'as long as DSD makes the licence fee dependent solely on the use of the mark, it is imposing unfair prices and commercial terms on undertakings which do not use the exemption service' (para. 113). The decision was upheld on appeal (*Duales System Deutschland GmbH* v *Commission* case Tribunal–151/01 [2007] 5 CMLR 1).

Again in Germany, in *Deutsche Post AG* 2001/892 (2001) OJ L331/40, the Commission dealt with a complaint from the British Post Office relating to various practices of its German counterpart. The practices complained of related to DPAG's approach to direct mail sent from the UK to addresses in Germany, but where the originating undertaking (the 'sender') had a connection in Germany. Such mail was on occasion delayed by DPAG, and a higher price was charged to the British Post Office for the onward transmission of this mail, than for deliveries that were entirely domestic in character. At paras 155–67 the Commission dealt with the arguments relating to excessive pricing, concluding that

the tariff charged by DPAG has no sufficient or reasonable relationship to real costs or to the real value of the service provided. Consequently DPAG's pricing exploits customers excessively and should therefore be regarded as an unfair selling price within the meaning of art. [102]. In conclusion, the Commission finds that DPAG has abused its dominant position in the German market.

The Commission looked at the issue of excessive pricing again in *Port of Helsingborg* (Cases COMP/A.36.570/D3 [2006] 4 CMLR 22, and COMP/A.36.568/D3 [2006] 4 CMLR 23, 23 July 2004). Helsingborg is on the south-west coast of Sweden, facing Elsinore (the home of Hamlet) in Denmark, and the port is busy with both commercial and passenger traffic. Complaints were made to the effect that the port's owner, Helsingborgs Hamm AB (HHAB), was charging the complainants excessive fees for the use of the port (fees for example appeared to be in some cases over three times higher than those charged in Elsinore). The complainants alleged, *inter alia*, that charges were excessive because they exceeded the costs incurred by HHAB, and were higher than those charged in comparable ports.

The Commission relied on the *United Brands* judgment, cited above, and paid particular attention to the distinction drawn by the Court between whether the profit margin was 'excessive', and whether the price was 'unfair'. In doing so it commented extensively on the meaning of the term 'economic value'. In relation to this latter term the Commission held that 'economic value' 'cannot simply be determined by adding to the costs incurred in the provision of [the product or service] a profit margin which would be a predetermined percentage of the production costs' (para. 199). In the present case—parts of which are highly technical—the Commission struggled to ascertain what precisely the costs were, and considered costs on an 'approximate' basis having made 'assumptions'. The Commission then noted that 'economic value must be determined with regards to the particular circumstances of the case and take into account also non-cost related factors such as the demand for the product/service' (para. 208).

This emphasis on demand—restated by the Commission at para. 214 ('economic value' must 'also reflect the demand side features...i.e. the valuation by the customers and consumers of the product/service') is interesting, as it suggests that where supply is low, and consumer demand high, high prices may not be synonymous with illegal excessive/unfair prices. The Commission pointed to the fact that its finding of excessive pricing in *United Brands* had been rejected by the Court of Justice, and appears now to have set a high threshold for establishing the existence of an abuse of excessive pricing. In *Port of Helsingborg* the Commission concluded in part that 'despite an extensive analysis including an approximate calculation and allocation of HHAB's costs based on the available information...there is not sufficient evidence to establish that HHAB charges unfair/excessive prices that would constitute an abuse' (para. 219).

16.2.2.2 Excessive pricing in the UK

Excessive pricing, which has been linked by the OFT with discriminatory pricing (see below), was attacked in *Napp Pharmaceutical Holdings Ltd* CA98/2/2001 [2001] UKCLR 597, on appeal *Napp Pharmaceuticals Holdings Ltd v The Director General of Fair Trading* [2002] CompAR 16. Price comparisons showed that Napp's prices were, to the relevant sector of the market, between 33 per cent and 67 per cent higher than those of the next nearest competitor (table 6). Napp argued that it was justified in charging higher prices because it was the innovator in the industry, and its product had a brand value. The Director however took the view that the product had lost its brand value (para. 211), and that Napp had been rewarded for its invention of the product during the period in which the patent for the product was in existence (para. 209).

The Director found that it was inconsistent with normal market processes for Napp to maintain a market share of some 96 per cent at the same time as it charged prices that were so much higher than those of competing products. An analysis of the undertaking's profit margins was also carried out, but this raised problems as the situation in the industry was not symmetrical. Although Napp made a higher margin on sales than its competitors it was also the only undertaking that manufactured the product itself (para. 225). The Director therefore compared the average selling price of Napp's product, which was £15.47, with the average cost of the goods sold by its next most profitable competitor—which it should be emphasized was thought might be *higher* than the cost of production by Napp—which was £3.01. This would lead to a gross margin of 80.5 per cent, and for the next most profitable competitor the margin was less than 70 per cent (para. 228).

On appeal the CAT upheld the findings of the Director, and held that the fact that it is difficult to calculate whether a price is higher than that which would exist in a competitive market does not mean that the exercise should not be undertaken (para. 392). The comparisons that could be made in the case all suggested that the Director was correct to find that prices were excessive, and it did not matter that the Director had not specified by exactly how much the prices were excessive (paras 393–405).

16.2.3 Discriminatory pricing

Price discrimination may be defined as the supply of goods or services of the same contract description at different prices, where the difference in price does not reflect cost differences (e.g., in transport or bulk supply). Whereas in a competitive market a producer is able usually to charge only one price for its product, in a monopolistic market the producer may be able to increase income and profits by charging a range of prices. In the extreme case of perfect differentiation the monopolist can charge each customer the maximum the customer is prepared to pay; more likely is the situation where various groups of customers are identified and prices set in relation to each group.

The welfare effects of this practice depend on all the circumstances, and in some cases it can be clearly demonstrated that there is greater output as more customers are being satisfied than is the case where a single price maintains. Where there are objections to price discrimination, it may be because the one certainty is that it results in a transfer of income from consumers to the monopolist. In the case of perfect differentiation the consumer surplus is transferred completely to the monopolist. Price discrimination can be successful only where the monopolist is able to control resale of the product, otherwise those who could purchase at low prices would resell to those who would be paying the monopolist higher prices; thus the discrimination itself is sometimes taken as evidence of a degree of market power. It may also play a part in predatory conduct: where a monopolist funds predatory prices by profits earned elsewhere an element of price discrimination is inevitable, unless the monopolist operates in more than one product or geographic market.

In the United States, the Robinson–Patman Act of 1936—'the misshapen progeny of intolerable draftsmanship coupled to wholly mistaken economic theory' (Bork, R. H., *The Antitrust Paradox*, New York, The Free Press (1993), p. 382)—was drafted expressly to deal with the 'problem' of price discrimination. Bork aside, there has been much criticism both of the theory underlying the Act and of its application in practice, and even a report prepared for the US Department of Justice has recommended its repeal.

16.2.3.1 Discriminatory pricing in the EU

In the EU, the overriding objective of creating the single market (see Chapter 2) has resulted in greater focus being placed upon price discrimination than would be likely to be the case in purely national jurisdictions. If a monopolist is going to set different prices for groups of consumers an obvious division might be between the Member States.

This was the situation in *United Brands* (*United Brands Co.* v *Commission* case 27/76 [1978] 1 CMLR 429). The Commission had attacked United Brands for charging variations in prices for bananas to its customers which were 'not attributable to any differences in customs duties or transport costs, since these [were] borne by the distributor/ripeners'. At one point, Danish customers were paying 2.38 times the price charged to Irish customers. United Brands was able to achieve this in part by introducing contractual terms that prevented its customers from reselling green bananas to other retailers; once the bananas had ripened their perishability would mean that resale other than to the end consumer was not a practical possibility. The essence of the undertaking's defence was that the price differentials in the final markets were not of its making, being the result of historical factors.

Whether United Brands charged these higher prices to some retailers would make little difference to the end consumer, for if United Brands did not take the monopoly profit the retailer would. One of the stronger points made tirelessly by Bork is that a monopoly price can be imposed only once—if there are monopolies at every step of a vertically integrated chain the price does not go on rising indefinitely as at some point the consumer's demand curve must still be faced. After conducting some particularly unconvincing economic analysis the Court of Justice found in the Commission's favour, in effect holding that United Brands had to bear some of the cost of the creation of the single market. It is unlikely that consumers benefited from the judgment, for if they were able to bear the higher prices these would be imposed by the retailers in place of United Brands.

Recital (c) of art. 102—'applying dissimilar conditions to equivalent transactions with other trading parties, thereby placing them at a competitive disadvantage'— suggests strongly that discriminatory pricing is to be considered an 'abuse', but the Commission does not generally wish to involve itself in pricing decisions. Consider, for instance, its approach in *HOV SVZ/MCN* 94/210 (1994) OJ L104/34. Here the Commission was reacting to a complaint about practices relating to the carriage by rail of sea-borne containers between Belgium, Germany, and the Netherlands, and held that

it is not part of the Commission's duties to assess as such the level of prices charged by an undertaking or to decide which criteria should govern the setting of such prices. On the other hand, where different prices are charged for equivalent transactions, *it is appropriate to assess whether such differences are justified by objective factors.* (paras 158–9, emphasis added)

As a result, the general position under EU law is that where a supplier can demonstrate that there are 'objective factors' that lead to the price differences, an allegation of abusive behaviour will not be sustained. Accordingly it will be a defence to an action if the supplier can demonstrate that discounts are given for bulk sales because it is cheaper for it to supply in bulk. Thus, for example, in *Tetra Pak II* 92/163 (1992) OJ L72/1—in which the undertaking's position in relation to packaging machines and the packaging used by the machines was under scrutiny—the Commission addressed Tetra Pak's 'selling prices for its cartons which vary considerably from one Member State to another', holding this practice to be 'discriminatory and constitut[ing] an abuse' (para. 154). It was of the view that, particularly as raw materials (the prices of which were determined on the world market and did not therefore vary from Member State to Member State) accounted for 70 per cent of the cost of the cartons, and that given the relevant geographic market for the cartons had been found to be that of the Union as a whole, the 'price differences observed [could not] be explained in economic terms'. The price differences were found to be the result of the 'compartmentalisation policy which Tetra Pak managed artificially to maintain' (para. 154).

In relation to the supply of the packaging machines themselves the Commission was even more emphatic, pointing out that 'the transport costs of machines are quite negligible in relation to the market value of the product' (para. 160). One of the requirements imposed on Tetra Pak was that it would 'ensure that any differences between the prices charged for its products in the various Member States result solely from specific market conditions... and shall not grant to any customer any form of discount on its products or more favourable payment terms not justified by an objective consideration' (arts 1, 2). Tetra Pak was fined €75 million in respect of the infringements.

A difficulty may arise in determining the extent to which transactions are 'equivalent'. In 2001 the Commission refused an exemption requested under art. 101(3) by Glaxo Wellcome in relation to its General Sales Conditions which were sent to 89 Spanish wholesalers (*Glaxo Wellcome* 2001/791 (2001) OJ L302/1). It was accepted by all parties that Glaxo sought to charge different prices for its products in different Member States. It was also common ground that each of the Member States constituted a distinct market, and that having regard to relevant regulatory frameworks, which differed, prices too differed. The Commission found an infringement of art. 101(1), and Glaxo appealed. The GC held that 'the finding of a difference in price is not sufficient to support the conclusion that there is discrimination' (*GlaxoSmithKline Services Unlimited* v *Commission* case T–168/01 [2006] 5 CMLR 29, at para. 179; see also Korah, V., 'Judgment of the Court of First Instance in *GlaxoSmithKline*', [2007] Comp Law 101). The Court further held that although the present case related to art. 101, it was proper to read across from the relevant law relating to discrimination under art. 102. The GC summed up the position arising under art. 102(c) as the following:

Art [102] does not preclude an undertaking in a dominant position from setting different prices in the various member states, in particular where the price differences are justified by variations in the conditions of marketing and the intensity of competition, but prohibits it from applying artificial price differences... (para. 177)

It is clear, then, that art. 102(c) does not force an undertaking in a dominant position to set uniform prices across the EU. Transactions will not be equivalent where the markets are not equivalent. This common sense approach however has its limits. For example, in *Irish Sugar* (see 16.2.1) an undertaking may not set different prices to consumers in different parts *within* a geographic market. This, however, raises questions as to the legitimacy of determining a single geographic market in a situation in which patterns of supply and demand are not consistent. Economists continue to struggle with this principle, and might argue that in *Irish Sugar* the areas in Dublin and on the UK/Irish border constituted different markets, which were not equivalent to the rest of Ireland.

A number of cases in recent years have dealt with the issue of landing fees at airports. Although these have been based on both art. 102 and art. 106, the issues are the same in either case. A typical case is that of *Portuguese airports* 1999/199 (1999) OJ L69/31, on appeal *Landing fees at Portuguese Airports* v *Commission* case C–163/99 [2002] 4 CMLR 31. Here the Commission ruled that differences in landing fees charged, dependent on where the flight originated, were discriminatory and unjustified. It relied on the fact that the services being purchased were the same, wherever the landing plane took off from. The Court of Justice upheld the Decision, and dismissed the appeal. In *Aéroports de Paris* v *Commission* case C–82/01 [2003] 4 CMLR 609 the Court affirmed an earlier judgment of the GC (case T–128/98 [2001] 4 CMLR 38) upholding an EU Commission decision (*Aéroports de Paris* 98/513 (1998) OJ L230/10) in which it had been established that Aéroports de Paris had imposed discriminatory rates for licence fees in relation to ground-handling services.

The second part of art. 102(c)—'thereby placing them at a competitive disadvantage'—is easily dealt with. In part, the use of 'thereby' suggests that it is presumed that a competitive disadvantage flows from the maintenance of 'dissimilar conditions'. On top of this, the Court of Justice held in *United Brands* that a competitive disadvantage existed 'since compared with what it should have been competition had thereby been distorted' (para. 233). It should be recognized that drawing a comparison with what competition 'should have been' may not be a straightforward matter. It is not necessary therefore to show that any one customer of the discriminating supplier is placed at a competitive disadvantage vis-à-vis another.

16.2.3.2 Price discrimination in the UK

In the United Kingdom the issue of price discrimination has not been subject to the same scrutiny as it has in the EU, as the quest for market integration is not present in this jurisdiction. It is also the case that discrimination will be harder to maintain in a smaller market where customers can more easily respond. Nevertheless, the issue was dealt with in *Napp* (*Napp Pharmaceutical Holdings Ltd* CA98/2/2001 [2001] UKCLR 597, on appeal *Napp Pharmaceuticals Holdings Ltd* v *The Director General of Fair Trading* [2002] CompAR 13), at paras 144–87. Paragraph 144 states that 'discounts will be an abuse if they serve to strengthen a dominant position in such a way that the degree of dominance reached substantially fetters competition'. Napp produced sustained release morphine tablets (MST), which were distributed to two sectors of the market, hospitals and the community. Hospital usage, which accounted for a relatively small share of the overall market, was a trigger for prescription by general practitioners in the community sector. Napp supplied MST to hospitals at a discount of over 90 per cent off the NHS list prices, and the OFT took the view that these discounts were targeted 'specifically at new competitors and hindered competition in the hospital segment of the market' (para. 145). The highest level of discounts was only offered on strengths of its own product line where it faced a direct rival (para. 182). Higher discounts were also offered to hospitals where Napp expected to be awarded a sole contract for a particular region (para. 183). The finding was upheld by the CAT.

It is necessary to consider allegations of price discrimination carefully, as there is not necessarily an abuse attached to such a practice. For example, the Association of British Travel Agents (ABTA) complained to the OFT that British Airways was abusing its dominant position by offering flights over the Internet more cheaply than if they were booked through travel agents. The OFT found that it was reasonable to do so, on the grounds that it was cheaper to sell flights this way (*The Association of British Travel Agents and British Airways plc* CA98/19/2002 [2003] UKCLR 136).

An allegation of price discrimination made against London Electricity plc (LE) was rejected by Ofgem in September 2003. LE had made an offer to customers who had switched to another supplier to encourage them to return to LE that was greater than that which could be matched by their existing suppliers in order to retain them, and which was out of line with the prices charged to existing LE customers. The authority held that 'price discrimination is only an abuse under the Act if it has an anti-competitive effect' (para. 34). Because there was only 'a severely limited take up of the offer' there was no such effect (*The Gas and Electricity Market Authority's Decision under the Competition Act 1998 that London Electricity plc has not infringed the Prohibition imposed under s. 18(1) of the Act with regard to a 'win back' offer* [2004] UKCLR 239).

16.2.4 Margin squeezes

In *Napier Brown/British Sugar* 88/518 (1988) OJ L288/41 (discussed at 16.2.1) a producer operated in the markets for both industrial and retail sugar. In essence the former is a repackaged version of the latter, and British Sugar was the dominant supplier of industrial sugar in the UK. If another undertaking wished to compete in the market for retail sugar it had first to purchase industrial sugar from British Sugar, and then compete with it in the downstream market. British Sugar was selling this industrial sugar at prices that did not allow a downstream competitor that was equally efficient to it in the retail market to make a sufficient margin on sales to be able to compete effectively. This practice is now known as a 'margin squeeze', and has been identified in a number of industries in which an undertaking operates at different levels of the market, and in the downstream level competes with others to whom it supplies an input at the upstream level.

The principles underlying this difficult area can be clearly explained by reference to a hypothetical supplier of a telephone network (A) where the owner of the network also sells telephony services to retail customers. Another undertaking (B) also sells services to retail customers, but is required to do so over the network provided by A. If A charges B a price higher for the network than it charges itself, or charges the same price but in effect operates its own retail services at a paper loss, subsidizing this loss by revenues earned from the network operation, B will not be able to compete even if it is as efficient in relation to retail services as A.

16.2.4.1 Margin squeezes in the EU

The first formal Commission decision in relation to margin squeeze is that of *Deutsche Telekom AG (Re Access to Local Loop)* 2003/707/EC, (2003) OJ L263/9. Unfortunately the figures relied on in finding an abuse are excised from the published decision, but in essence the Commission found that Deutsche Telekom had set prices for access to local loops (the physical circuit connecting a telephone network at a subscriber's premises to the main telephone network) that did not allow its competitors to compete with it in the provision of services to end users. Such an abuse was classed as 'very serious' for the purpose of calculating fines, but the penalty was reduced to €12.6 million in acknowledgement of the novelty of the decision. The Commission did however point out that the approach taken was part of a well-established practice by the institution. Deutsche Telekom subsequently gave the Commission a commitment to reduce significantly the fee charged to third parties for access to its local loops (Commission press release IP (04) 281, 1 March 2004). The decision was subsequently confirmed by the GC (*Deutsche Telekom AG* v *Commission* case T–271/03 [2008] ECR II–00477 (an appeal before the Court of Justice is pending).

16.2.4.2 Margin squeezes in the UK

The OFT and Oftel have considered this area on a number of occasions, but have usually dismissed the complaints. For example, in two decisions the OFT rejected complaints to the effect that British Sky Broadcasting (BSkyB) had engaged in a margin squeeze in relation to the wholesale pay-TV market in the UK (*BSkyB Investigation: Alleged infringement of the Chapter II Prohibition* CA98/20/2002 [2003] UKCLR 240; *Decision of the OFT under s. 47 relating to Decision CA98/20/2002: Alleged infringement of the Chapter II Prohibition by BSkyB* [2003] UKCLR 1075). Complaints were made alleging that the charges BSkyB made to distributors, and the charges BSkyB made to its own subscribers, did not allow distributors to compete with BSkyB in the downstream market. On a first inspection the OFT was concerned, and issued a notice to BSkyB to that effect. Subsequent analysis persuaded it that there was no breach, and when the complainants asked the OFT to vary the decision it stood by its original conclusions. Its approach was to consider whether BSkyB's distribution arm (DisCo) was profitable:

if DisCo is profitable, then distribution rivals as (or more) efficient that DisCo would also be profitable, while less efficient rivals might not be. If DisCo were not profitable then, to remain in business, it must be subsidized by other parts of BSkyB (and any other equally efficient business would also require subsidies.

Whether or not there is an anti-competitive margin squeeze therefore depends on whether or not DisCo is profitable. Since the focus is on DisCo it is not necessary to examine the performance of third parties, which is likely to be affected by various factors. It is also unnecessary to compare the performance of DisCo or third parties to some benchmark of maximum efficiency which would be very difficult. (paras 157–8 of the second decision)

The leading case in the UK is *Genzyme*. The OFT found that Genzyme Ltd had engaged in exclusionary behaviour in the market for the drug Cerezyme used to treat the rare and debilitating Gaucher disease from which about 180 people suffered in the UK at the time of the decision (*Exclusionary behaviour by Genzyme Ltd* CA98/3/03 [2003] UKCLR 950). Genzyme provided both the drug and the care system (including nursing staff) to support those taking the medication. The company supplied the drug to another health care provider, but charged the same price as it did under a previous agreement when it had also supplied the care services. The customer however did not receive any of the ancillary services. Thus in order to compete with Genzyme it had to incur those additional expenses. The OFT set out the basic principle in relation to margin squeeze at para. 364 of its decision:

A pricing policy operated by a vertically integrated dominant undertaking may infringe section 18 of the Act. This might occur where a vertically integrated undertaking which is dominant in the upstream market operates a pricing policy which does not allow reasonably efficient competitors in the downstream market a margin sufficient to enable them to survive in the long term. This pricing behaviour is known as 'margin squeeze'.

The effect of the pricing strategy adopted by Genzyme was that its homecare services arm was paying the same price for the entire package that the competitor was paying just for the drug. The OFT found that if Genzyme Homecare was required to pay that price itself it would make no margin on the drug and would make a loss on the homecare services. The conclusion that flowed from this was that 'regardless of how efficient Genzyme Healthcare might be, it is clear that it could not trade profitably on these terms' (para. 375). It was argued that there was no justification for this pricing policy, which was required to be amended, and a penalty of £6.8 million was imposed. Genzyme appealed. On 11 March 2004 the CAT upheld the OFT's decision (*Genzyme Ltd v The OFT* [2004] CAT 4), dealing with the issue of margin squeeze at paras 549–75. It found, *inter alia*, that Genzyme's pricing policy was 'intended to achieve the result of monopolising the supply of homecare services to Gaucher patients in favour of Genzyme Homecare' and that it 'must have appreciated that the inevitable result of its pricing policy would be to force Healthcare [its competitor] to exit the market' (para. 555).

In response to arguments made by Genzyme about the 'objective justifications' advanced for the conduct in question the CAT held first that the concept 'does not fall to be applied in terms of benefits which accrue to the dominant undertaking, but in terms of the general interest' (para. 583), and then proceeded to reject all of the arguments that Genzyme made in support of its practice. However, the penalty was reduced to £3 million, since the OFT had overstated the length of the infringement (*Genzyme Ltd v OFT* [2004] CAT 4, [2004] CompAR 358).

There have been a relatively large number of cases in the UK in which allegations of margin squeeze have been rejected. Examples include: a complaint against Companies House that it cross-subsidized its commercial activities to the detriment of competitors from the sales of raw bulk data to those competitors (*Companies House, the Registrar of Companies for England and Wales* [2003] UKCLR 24); an investigation relating to the prices charged by BT for residential line rental (*Investigation against BT about potential anti-competitive exclusionary behaviour* [2004] UKCLR 1695); and a complaint by fixed-line telecommunications operators relating to the pricing practices of mobile operators (*Suspected margin squeeze by Vodafone, O₂, Orange and T-Mobile* [2004] UKCLR 1639). For a discussion of relevant cases see Ridyard, D., and Chrysanthou, Y., 'Recent Margin Squeeze Cases under Chapter II and Article 82—An Economic Critique', (2003) *Lawyer's Europe*, autumn, pp. 12–15), and see also 'The Genzyme Case and the OFT's Margin Squeeze Muddle', (2003) RBB Brief 10, July.

16.3 Refusal to deal or supply, and the essential facilities doctrine

16.3.1 Refusal to supply—general aspects

A general presumption in the commercial world is that companies are free to choose with whom to have dealings. However, there are situations in which a positive obligation is placed on them to supply specific parties. In particular this is likely to be the case where refusals are: imposed to punish a customer who may have traded in more competitive fashion than the retailer wished; the result of the monopolist wishing to exclude others from directly competing with the monopolist in secondary markets; and an attempt to maintain high prices by dampening downstream competition (for example, cases in which monopolists have refused to supply discount chains). A problem in requiring supplies to be made is that the competition authorities may also have to address issues such as the terms and conditions of supply and be prepared to be involved in an element of ongoing regulation.

16.3.1.1 Refusal to supply in the EU

In 1984 the Commission stated that '[a]s a general principle an objectively unjustifiable refusal to supply by an undertaking holding a dominant position on a market constitutes an infringement of Article [102]' (*Thirteenth Report on Competition Policy* (1984), point 157). The first case to deal substantially with the issue, *Commercial Solvents*, is one of the least satisfactory of all EC cases (*Istituto Chemioterapico Italiano SpA and Commercial Solvents Corp.* v *Commission* cases 6–7/73 [1974] CMLR 309). Here Commercial Solvents (CSC), which manufactured aminobutanol, a raw material used in drugs to combat tuberculosis, was required to resume supplies to the complainant Zoja. This followed the decision of CSC to expand into production of the final product itself and to cease providing potential competitors. Even before that decision had been made Zoja had stopped taking supplies from CSC and had made unsuccessful attempts to find the product elsewhere.

Supporting the EU Commission, the Court of Justice held that 'an undertaking in a dominant position as regards the production of raw material...cannot, just because it decides to start manufacturing [the derivative product] (in competition with its former customers) act in such a way as to eliminate their competition' (para. 25). The analysis of the welfare effects in this case is unsatisfactory. It is, for instance, likely that the vertically integrated CSC would be able to produce the end drug more efficiently than would be achieved by a combination of the two undertakings each engaged in one part of the manufacturing process only.

Similarly, EU law provides that a manufacturer is not allowed to foreclose competition in the market for the repair or service of its product by unreasonably denying spare parts to independent service companies (e.g., *Hugin Kassaregister AB and Hugin Cash Registers Ltd* v *Commission* case 22/78 [1979] 3 CMLR 345, and *Volvo AB* v *Erik Veng* case 238/87 [1989] 4 CMLR 122). In *United Brands (United Brands Co.* v *Commission* case 27/76 [1978] 1 CMLR 429) retailers that participated in advertising campaigns promoting rival products, or who resupplied green bananas, were threatened with having supplies cut off. Both actions were condemned by the Commission.

In *Boosey and Hawkes (BBI/Boosey & Hawkes: Interim measures* 87/500 (1987) OJ L286/36) the products in question were musical instruments for brass bands. BBI was established by two companies, GHH, a retailer of brass band instruments, and RCN, a repairer of the instruments, with the intention of manufacturing instruments in competition to Boosey, which was the only British manufacturer of brass instruments. Boosey responded to this move by, *inter alia*, withdrawing supplies of its instruments and spare parts from GHH and RCN. The Commission supported the claimants, holding (at para. 19) that

A dominant undertaking may always take reasonable steps to protect its commercial interests, but such measures must be fair and proportional to the threat. The fact that a customer of a dominant producer becomes associated with a competitor of that manufacturer does not normally entitle the dominant producer to withdraw all supplies immediately or to take reprisals against that customer.

Under the decision adopted Boosey was 'required to meet within seven days of receipt any reasonable order...for musical instruments or spare parts' (art. 1).

Refusals to supply may be justified where, for instance, there is a general shortage and the supplier declines new customers in favour of existing arrangements (*ABG Oil companies operating in the Netherlands* 77/327 (1977) OJ L117/1). A justification may also be available where requiring that a supply take place undermined the incentives that led to the creation of the input sought by the complainant company. This line of reasoning is strongly linked to that in relation to the essential facilities doctrine (see 16.3.2 below). The case is clearly made by the Commission in its discussion paper on exclusionary abuses at para. 235:

the indispensable input...often is the result of substantial investments entailing significant risks...[T]he dominant firm must not be unduly restricted in the exploitation of valuable results of the investment. For these reasons the dominant firm should normally be free to seek compensation for successful projects that is sufficient to maintain investment incentives, taking the risk of failed projects into account... [I]t may be necessary for the dominant firm to exclude others from access to the input for a certain period of time. The risks facing the parties and the sunk investment that must be committed may thus mean that a dominant firm should be allowed to exclude others for a certain period of time to ensure an adequate return on such investment, even when this entails eliminating effective competition during this period.

In the cases referred to above, which relate largely to standard 'fungible' products, it is unlikely that such an argument could be sustained. Where, however, the input is protected by, for example, intellectual property, or is a raw ingredient developed at considerable expense, it may be justifiable to argue that requiring its supply reduces the incentive for further developments.

16.3.1.2 Refusal to supply in the UK

There has been little case law in this area under the CA 98 at the public level. The OFT considered a complaint of refusal to supply relating to a film used in the production of holographic images in *du Pont* but concluded that although the undertaking was dominant it had acted with objective justification. The OFT recognized that 'it is only in exceptional circumstances that competition law should deprive an undertaking of the freedom to determine its trading partners' (para. 28). In the case the company had moved to a policy of supplying the film only for use in applications relating to security and authentication, and that it would not be able to provide security guarantees to those customers if it was also supplying the film to customers for use in graphic arts applications (*Refusal to supply unprocessed holographic photopolymer film: E I du Pont de Nemours & Co. and Op Graphics (Holography) Ltd* CA98/07/2003 [2004] UKCLR 253).

Oftel has dismissed a number of complaints made against telephone network operators by third parties providing access on to the network via the Internet, or via GSM gateways (banks of SIM cards mounted into a device that provides connectivity between a fixed telephone line and a mobile network), in each case holding that the provider of the network was entitled to do so under the terms of the relevant telecommunications legislation. This was the case, for example, in *Disconnection of Floe Telecom Ltd's Services by Vodafone Ltd* [2004] UKCLR 313. It was the first of a chain of cases relating to this action, during which Ofcom (as Oftel became) lost an appeal (*Floe Telecom Ltd v Ofcom* [2004] CAT 18, [2005] CompAR 290), and was required to take a new decision, reaching the same conclusion but on a different formulation (*Re-investigation of a complaint from Floe Telecom Ltd against Vodafone Ltd* [2005] UKCLR 914).

16.3.2 The essential facilities doctrine

An 'essential facility' is a facility or infrastructure without access to which competitors cannot provide services to their customers. 'The owner of an essential facility which uses its power in one market in order to protect or strengthen its position in another related market…imposing a competitive disadvantage on its competitor, infringes Article [102]' (*Sea Containers* v *Stena Sealink* 94/19 (1994) OJ L15/8, at para. 66). To date, in both the EU and the UK, the doctrine has been most prominent in decisions concerned with the operation of transport networks, although it is likely to have an increasing impact on the utilities and telecommunications sectors, especially in the context of deregulation.

Like many aspects of competition law the doctrine has its origins in US practice, and is traced to the case of *United States* v *Terminal Railroad Association* 224 US 383 (1912); USSCR 56 L. Ed. 810. The 38 defendants, owners of a vital network of St Louis transport connections, denied non-owner railroads access to the facilities. Delivering the judgment of the court, Lurton MJ offered the defendants the option either of restructuring their mutual contracts so as to allow the admission of new firms into the network, or of dissolving the combination. While the court did not make explicit the creation of an essential facilities doctrine, it recognized the threat to competition posed by 'a unified system…unless it is the impartial agent of all who [are compelled] to use its facilities' (at 405).

The operation of the doctrine was clarified by the court in *MCI Communications Corp. and MCI Telecommunications Corp.* v *American Telephone and Telegraph Co.* 708 F.2d 1081 (1983). Here AT&T, a dominant telecommunications company, refused to interconnect MCI with the local distribution facilities of Bell operating companies, thus limiting the range of services that MCI could offer its customers. The court held that

[a] monopolist's refusal to deal under these circumstances is governed by the so-called essential facilities doctrine. Such a refusal may be unlawful because a monopolist's control of an essential facility (sometimes called a 'bottleneck') can extend monopoly power from one stage of production to another, and from one market into another. Thus the antitrust laws have imposed on firms controlling an essential facility the obligation to make the facility available on non-discriminatory terms.   (para. 31)

A fourfold test was put forward for the doctrine: '(1) control of the essential facility by a monopolist; (2) a competitor's inability practically or reasonably to duplicate the essential facility; (3) the denial of the use of the facility to a competitor; and (4) the feasibility of providing the facility' (para. 32). The focus on the denial of use means that the doctrine is better considered as a specific example of the wider category of cases in which there is a unilateral refusal to supply or deal.

16.3.2.1 The essential facilities doctrine in the EU

The EU Commission has been keen to embrace the doctrine, which may be applicable under both arts 101 and 102 but is more likely to be of relevance to art. 102 cases as the holding of an essential facility is strong evidence of dominance.

In *British Midland/Aer Lingus* 92/213 (1992) OJ L96/34, the Commission found that those holding dominant positions should not 'withhold facilities which the industry traditionally provides to all other airlines'. Aer Lingus, the dominant undertaking in the market for the London–Dublin air route, was ordered to resume its interline facility with British Midland, having previously withdrawn it. Interlining is based on an agreement under which most of the world's airlines have authorized the others to sell their services, as a result of which travel agents can offer passengers a single ticket providing for transportation by different carriers. The Commission appeared to accept that such a facility could be withdrawn where the dominant airline could give an objective reason for its refusal to continue, such as, *inter alia*, concerns about creditworthiness (para. 26 of the decision), but in the present case no such reason could be advanced. At para. 30 of the decision the argument is crystallized:

Aer Lingus has not been able to point to efficiencies created by a refusal to interline nor to advance any other persuasive and legitimate business justification for its conduct. Its desire to avoid loss of market share, the circumstance that this is a route of vital importance to the company and that its operating margin is under pressure do not make this a legitimate response to new entry.

Similarities in approach to the US analysis are clear in this decision, as can be seen from a comparative examination of the case of *Otter Tail Power Co.* v *United States* 410 US 366 (1973); USSCR 35 L. Ed. 2d 359.

In its *22nd Annual Report on Competition Policy* ((1992), points 216–18) the Commission made it clear that the decision was taken with specific reference to a time period in which air transport was being liberalized, and argued that airlines making use of the new opportunities for competition should be given a fair chance to develop and sustain their challenge to established carriers. However, the duty on Aer Lingus was to be of a finite duration only, as new entrants should not be able to rely indefinitely on frequencies and services provided by their competitors.

A similar decision was taken by the Commission in *Port of Roscoff* (Commission press release IP (95) 492 of 16 May, [1995] 4 CMLR 677). Here the Morlaix Chamber of Commerce, in its capacity as port authority for Roscoff, denied Irish Continental Group (ICG) access to the port. The Commission required the authority to 'take the necessary steps to allow ICG access to the port'. In fact the parties had already reached an agreement subject to the resolution of certain technical requirements, governing access to the port, but the Commission clearly wished to establish strong precedents and guidelines in this area.

A step vital for the development of the essential facilities doctrine was made explicit in *B&I/Sealink, Holyhead* (*22nd Annual Report on Competition Policy* (1992), point 219). It will be recalled that for art. 102 to apply the allegedly dominant position must lie within 'a substantial part' of the EU. Some initial doubts were raised in relation to the doctrine on the grounds that a 'facility' could not constitute the requisite substantial part In *British Midland* the point was skirted, the Commission asserting merely that '[b]oth the UK and Ireland are substantial parts of the [internal] market' (at para. 17). In *B&I* Sealink acted as port authority at Holyhead (the essential facility) in north Wales. The company instituted timetable changes which operated to the detriment of B&I and in favour of Sealink's own services. In particular, the loading and unloading of B&I services had to be interrupted to accommodate Sealink sailings. Indubitably

Holyhead is *not* a substantial part of the internal market. The Commission, recognizing that this was indeed the case, made clear that (emphasis added) 'it is important to stress that a port, an airport *or any other facility*, even if it is not itself a substantial part of the [internal] market, may be considered as such in so far as reasonable access to the facility is indispensable for the exploitation of a transport route which is substantial'. Recognizing that this argument can extend to any infrastructure, and not merely to transport routes, it stated that '[t]his consequence of Article [102] is of essential importance in the context of deregulation'.

It is important too that in both the US cases and *British Midland* it was considered significant that the offender's primary motivation for the exclusionary practice was the long-term detriment of the competitor. In *B&I* it would appear that while such a detriment was a *consequence* of Sealink's action there was little evidence that this was the primary *intention* of Sealink, which was rather to make the best use of its own resources. The requirement imposed that 'a company which both owns and uses an essential facility...should not grant its competitors access on terms less favourable than those which it gives its own services' (*22nd Annual Report on Competition Policy* (1992), point 219), is a stricter test both than that used in the US cases and that suggested in *British Midland*.

Sealink also came to an arrangement with Sea Containers regarding access to Holyhead following Commission intervention. Subsequently the Commission instituted a formal proceeding, finding in favour of Sea Containers (*Sea Containers/Stena Sealink* 94/19 (1994) OJ L15/8). The Commission expanded the doctrine further, suggesting that when a company 'is in a position such as that of Sealink in this case, it cannot normally expect to fulfil satisfactorily its duty to provide non-discriminatory access and to resolve its conflicts of interest unless it takes steps to separate its management of the essential facility from its use of it'. The point was not made as strongly as that in *Flughafen Frankfurt/Main AG* 98/190 (1998) OJ L72/31 although the Commission held that an undertaking that owned Frankfurt Airport could not use its property right in that airport and its physical infrastructure to exclude competitors in ancillary services such as baggage loading and cabin cleaning. In *Port of Rødby* 94/119 (1994) OJ L55/52 the principle was applied also to art. 106 TFEU.

Many of these Union cases could have been dealt with under the more general principles set out in other refusal to deal cases, and it thus appears, particularly in the light of comments in the annual competition reports, that the Commission took a conscious decision, in the face of moves towards deregulation, to introduce the essential facilities doctrine into EU law.

The leading case on the operation of the essential facilities doctrine is now *Oscar Bronner GmbH & Co. KG v Mediaprint Zeitungs-und-Zeitschriftenverlag GmbH & Co. KG* (case C–7/97 [1999] 4 CMLR 112). Advocate General Jacobs sounded a warning note about the expansion of the doctrine. In this case Bronner was the publisher in Austria of a daily newspaper, *der Standard*, with a market share of 3.6 per cent of circulation. Mediaprint was the publisher of papers with a combined market share of 46.8 per cent. Bronner argued that it could not feasibly develop its own home delivery service in view of its small market share, and that only such a delivery service would allow it to survive. It claimed, in effect, that Mediaprint's delivery service constituted an 'essential facility' to which it should have access. Starting from the position that 'the right to choose one's trading partners and freely to dispose of one's property are generally recognised principles in the laws of the Member States' and that 'incursions on those rights require careful justification' (para. 56) the Advocate General posited that 'intervention [under] an application of the essential facilities doctrine...can be justified in terms of competition policy only in cases in which the dominant undertaking has a genuine stranglehold on the related market' (para. 65). His view was that Bronner had numerous, albeit less convenient, options open to it, and that to allow it to succeed in this case

would be to lead the [Union] and national authorities and courts into detailed regulation of the [Union] markets, entailing the fixing of prices and conditions for supply in large sections of the economy. Intervention on that scale would not only be unworkable but...also be anti-competitive in the longer term and indeed would scarcely be compatible with a free market economy. (para. 69)

The Court followed this opinion, holding in particular that 'it does not appear that there are any technical, legal or even economic obstacles capable of making it impossible, or even unreasonably difficult, for any other publishers of daily newspapers to establish, alone or in cooperation with other publishers, its own nationwide home delivery system' (para. 44).

The test that flows from the application of *Oscar Bronner* is in effect that set out by the Advocate General, commenting on a situation where a dominant company has a stranglehold on a related market. Such a situation, he suggested:

might be the case for example where duplication of the facility is impossible or extremely difficult owing to physical, geographical or legal constraints or is highly undesirable for reasons of public policy. It is not sufficient that the undertaking's control over a facility should give it a competitive advantage.

...the test in my view must be an objective one: in other words, in order for refusal of access to amount to an abuse, it must be extremely difficult not merely for the undertaking demanding access but for any other undertaking to compete. Thus if the cost of duplicating the facility alone is the barrier to entry, it must be such as to deter any prudent undertaking from entering the market. In that regard it seems to me that it will be necessary to consider all the circumstances, including the extent to which the dominant undertaking, having regard to the degree of amortisation of its investment and the cost of the upkeep must pass on investment or maintenance costs in the prices charged on the relevant market. (paras 65–6)

The key elements then are that: (a) access to the facility must be genuinely indispensable; (b) it is not possible practically to replicate the facility; (c) even by an undertaking of the same size and resources as the holder of the facility. It is not enough that without the facility the putative competitor would find it *difficult* to compete.

In *European Night Services* v *Commission* joined cases T–374/94 etc. [1998] ECR II–3141 the Court ruled that the Commission had taken too restrictive an approach in requiring that parties to a joint venture to 'supply services on their networks on the same technical and financial terms as they allow to [the joint venture]' (see *Night Services* 94/663 (1994) OJ L259/20). In particular the Court took the view that train crews could not constitute an essential facility. One of the more recent cases in which the Commission has been called upon to consider this area arose in 1999 in *Info-Lab/ Ricoh* (*Competition Policy Newsletter* (1999) 1:35). Referring to the 'restrictive approach of the [Court of Justice] to the doctrine of essential facilities in [*Oscar Bronner*]', it rejected a complaint by a provider of toner which had wanted to oblige Ricoh to supply it with new empty toner cartridges which it could then fill in order to compete with Ricoh in the market for filled cartridges.

One recent case to deal with the essential facilities doctrine is *GVG/FS* 2004/33 (2004) OJ L11/17. Here the German railway company Georg Verkehrsoganisation GmbH (GVG) complained that Ferrovie dello Stato SpA (FS), the Italian national railway operator, had refused to grant it access to certain facilities. This prevented GVG from providing an international rail service from various points in Germany to Milan. Although the Commission found that FS was abusing its dominant position FS gave undertakings to the Commission that the abuse would be terminated and not repeated.

16.3.2.2 The essential facilities doctrine in the UK

There have been few complaints under the CA 98 which have relied on the essential facilities doctrine. The OFT did agree to reopen an investigation (in the process withdrawing an earlier decision) in relation to a crematorium which denied access to its facilities to an independent undertaker (*Harwood Park Crematorium Ltd* CA98/05/03 [2003] UKCLR 772). A new decision was taken in June 2004, and the OFT found that there was no abuse as there was no strong evidence that the refusal by W. Austin & Sons (Stevenage) Ltd to allow J. J. Burgess & Sons Ltd to have access to Harwood Park Crematorium would eliminate or cause substantial harm to competition (*Refusal to Supply J. J. Burgess & Sons Limited with access to Harwood Park Crematorium* CA98/06/2004 [2004] UKCLR 1586).

The matter was then appealed to the CAT, which was trenchant in its criticism of the OFT's analysis, and which, for the first time, substituted its own decision for that of the OFT's rather than remitting the matter back for further consideration (*ME Burgess, J. J. Burgess and S. J. Burgess (trading as J. J. Burgess & Sons)* v *Office of Fair Trading* [2005] CAT 25, [2005] CompAR 1151). The Tribunal held that the facts in this case were not complex, and concerned a business dealing with a particularly vulnerable class of customers who would obviously have a strong preference for a local service. The incumbent had a market share of some 90 per cent and had refused to deal with a customer that it dealt with in other territories it served. The CAT found that the facts in this case were precisely in the class that Advocate General Jacobs had been referring to in *Oscar Bronner* as being situations in which the essential facilities doctrine could reasonably be applied.

FURTHER READING

Articles

AHLBORN, C., and ALLAN, B., 'The *Napp* Case: A Study of Predation?', (2003) *World Competition Law & Economics Review* 233

CAPOBIANCO, A., 'The Essential Facility Doctrine: Similarities and Differences between the American and European Approaches', (2001) 26 *European Law Review* 548

CROCIONI, P., and VELJANOVSKI, C., 'Price Squeezes, Foreclosure and Competition Law—Principles and Guidelines', (2003) 4 *Journal of Network Industries*, 28–60

FOX, E. M., 'Price Predation—US and EEC: Economics and Values', (1989) *Fordham Corporate Law Institute* 687

GRAVENGAARD, M.A., 'The Meeting Competition Defence Principle—A Defence for Price Discrimination and Predatory Pricing?', (2006) *European Competition Law Review* 658

KALLAUGHER, J., and SHER, B., 'Rebates Revisited: Anti-Competitive Effects and Exclusionary Abuse under Article 82 EC', (2004) *European Competition Law Review* 263

PARDOLESI, R., and RENDA, A., 'The European Commission's Case against Microsoft: Kill Bill?', (2004) *World Competition Law & Economics Review* 513

RIDYARD, D., 'Exclusionary Pricing and Price Discrimination Abuses under Article 82 EC—An Economic Analysis', (2002) *European Competition Law Review* 286

SHER, B., 'Price Discounts and *Michelin II*: What Goes Around, Comes Around', (2002) *European Competition Law Review* 482

SWIFT, J., 'Selective Price Cuts, Discounts and Rebates: EU Competition Law at a Crossroads—Form or Effects', [2005] *Competition Law Journal* 197

TEMPLE LANG, J., 'Defining Legitimate Competition: Companies' Duties to Supply Essential Facilities', (1994) 18 *Fordham International Law Journal* 437

17

UK market investigation references

KEY POINTS

- A market investigation reference is a feature of UK law by virtue of which a market 'failing' to operate competitively as a whole may be investigated by the OFT.

- A reference may be made by the OFT to the UK Competition Commission.

- The UK Competition Commission has very wide powers to order changes to the way the market operates, or to accept undertakings to remedy defects.

- No penalties may be imposed for past behaviour, and no rights arise for third parties in relation to conduct found to be in need of change.

17.1 Introduction

Market investigations, for which provision is made in Part 4 of the Enterprise Act 2002 (EA 02), are distinctive to the UK, and are one of the strengths of the domestic competition law regime. They sit outside the prohibition framework established in arts 101 and 102 TFEU and the Chapter I and Chapter II equivalents, and replace provisions in the Fair Trading Act 1973 (FTA 1973) relating to scale and complex monopoly investigation references (see in particular FTA 1973, s. 6). Market investigations are 'not fundamentally different from the 1973 Act, many of the provisions of which are drawn on and modernised in the [Act]' (Mr Alexander, *Hansard*, Standing Committee B, col. 442). However, the discussion of the law of market investigations will be treated here as being entirely new, although reports produced under the earlier regime will be referred to where these shed light on the types of considerations and remedies that may be relevant to market investigations.

The distinctive nature of this part of the domestic regime is clearly set out in the *Explanatory Notes: Enterprise Act 2002* (TSO, 2002). At para. 292 the following introduction to market investigations is given:

The purpose of these investigations is to inquire into markets where it appears that competition has been prevented, restricted or distorted by the structure of a market (or any aspect of its structure), the conduct of persons supplying or acquiring goods or services who operate within it, or the conduct of such persons' customers, but where there has been no obvious breach of the prohibitions on anti-competitive agreements or arrangements or abuse of a dominant position under CA 1998 or Articles [101] or [102] of the [TFEU]. An example of the sort of circumstances in which these provisions might be used would be a situation where a few large firms supplied almost the whole of the market and, without there being any agreement between them (ie a non-collusive oligopoly), they all tended to follow parallel courses of conduct (eg in relation to pricing), while new competitors faced significant barriers to entry into the market, and there was little or no evidence of vigorous competition between the existing players.

In other words, the most important feature of a market investigation is that it focuses, as the name suggests, on the operation of the market as a whole, rather than on the way in which a single firm, or agreement, operates. There is no 'blame' attached to those undertakings which are subject to market investigations. It would be entirely possible for a market investigation to proceed to conclusion, for adverse effects to be identified, and for remedies to be put in place, with no individual firm being condemned. Indeed, there is no procedure for such a condemnation, and firms may only be penalized where they do not confirm to procedural requirements in relation to market investigations, or where they subsequently breach obligations either entered into voluntarily, or imposed upon them, under this Part of the Act.

An OFT guideline, *Market Investigation References*, was published in March 2003 (hereinafter 'the Guideline'), and the CC too has published guidance in this area. It is anticipated that there will be approximately two or three market investigations a year, a figure in line with the number of complex monopoly references under the FTA 1973, although the OFT has no target figure towards which it works.

17.2 Relationship of market investigations to the Competition Act 1998 and EU law

It surprised a number of commentators that the Government left in place the monopoly provisions of the FTA 1973 at the time when the Chapter II Prohibition of the Competition Act 1998 (CA 98) was introduced into domestic law. In practice, however, the scale monopoly provisions of the FTA 1973, which applied to single firm conduct, were never used after the entry into force of the Chapter II Prohibition, although the complex monopoly provisions were. During the committee discussions about the Enterprise Bill the Government indicated that

In general we would expect the OFT to use the Competition Act in cases in which it suspects that the Act's prohibitions on anti-competitive agreements or abuse of dominance are being infringed, and market investigation powers in cases in which the Act is not applicable. Whenever the choice is less straightforward, the decision about which powers to use will be at the OFT's discretion, on examination of all the facts of the case in question. (Hansard, Standing Committee B, 1 May 2002, col. 427)

The OFT has made the position more emphatic in its Guideline, stating that it will only proceed to a market investigation where either: (1) there are reasonable grounds to suspect that market features prevent, restrict, or distort competition, but are not actionable under the CA 98; or (2) action is possible under the CA 98 but it is likely to be ineffective in dealing with the adverse effects on competition (para. 2.3). The circumstances in which this might be the case are broadly considered in para. 2.8 where it is argued that there may be situations in which anti-competitive conduct by a single firm is 'associated with structural features of the market, for example by barriers to entry or regulation'.

In such a situation, it is suggested that a market investigation may be a more appropriate solution than a CA 98 action. However, in this respect it should be noted also that the market investigation provisions were brought forward before the final shape of Regulation 1/2003 became clear. Under the older Regulation 17 structural remedies were not available to the competition authorities to resolve breaches of arts 101 and 102 TFEU (and by implication via s. 60, CA 98 breaches of the Chapter I Prohibition and the Chapter II Prohibition) save in the most exceptional circumstances. However, under Regulation 1/2003 structural remedies are expressly provided for at art. 7 (see Chapter 6).

While these are only to be employed in restricted circumstances, it is likely that these would encompass precisely the concerns mooted by the OFT at para. 2.8. In other words, the presence of structural remedies under the CA 98 eliminate the need for market investigations in respect of single firm conduct falling within the Chapter II Prohibition. Thus situations such as the one examined in relation to the supply of raw unprocessed milk in 2000, in which the CC, using its FTA 1973 powers, recommended the break-up of Milk Marque, the dominant undertaking in this market, might not proceed to a market investigation reference in future (*Milk: A report on the supply in Great Britain of raw cows' milk*, Cm. 4286, 2000).

Most market investigations are likely therefore to relate to situations of non-collusive oligopoly, typically markets with a relatively small number of participants (although this has not always been the case in the past), recognizing a degree of interdependence, but nevertheless taking decisions unilaterally, and tending to act in the same, or similar, way. Such situations are not caught by art. 101 TFEU unless there is at least a 'concerted practice' (see Chapter 9), as the essential requirement of art. 101 is that there be some coordination between the undertakings in question. However, the concept of dominance may, as we have seen in Chapter 14, be applicable to situations of 'collective dominance', in which more than one undertaking enjoys a dominant position by virtue of the structure of the market, or links between the undertakings falling short of collusion (see in particular *Airtours plc* v *Commission* case T–342/99 [2002] 5 CMLR 7 at para. 62—discussed at 19.2.2.4.1). It will be remembered that it is a requirement of Regulation 1/2003 that Member States applying their own competition law to situations falling within arts 101 and 102 must first apply the relevant EU article, and may not subsequently in the application of their domestic law reach a situation which is in conflict with the result obtained under EU law (Regulation 1/2003, art. 3(1)—see generally Chapter 3). At the same time art. 3(2) expressly provides that 'Member States shall not under this Regulation be precluded from adopting and applying on their territory stricter national laws which prohibit or sanction unilateral conduct engaged in by undertakings'.

In the OFT Guidelines it is recognized that the relevant law in respect of collective dominance is 'underdeveloped' (para. 2.5), and it is likely that in the vast majority of situations in which market investigations will be carried out a collective dominant position subject to the application of art. 102 TFEU would not be found to exist. It is possible that anti-competitive agreements, and in particular vertical agreements, might be identified to exist in the course of a market investigation, in which case these would need to be dealt with by way of the application of art. 101 TFEU.

17.3 The making of market investigation references

Section 131(1) of the EA 02 is in the following terms:

The OFT may, subject to subsection (4), make a reference to the Commission if the OFT has reasonable grounds for suspecting that any feature, or combination of features, of a market in the United Kingdom for goods or services prevents, restricts or distorts competition in connection with the supply or acquisition of any goods or services in the United Kingdom or a part of the United Kingdom.

In addition to the OFT the relevant sector regulators (see Chapter 2), as a consequence of amendments to the relevant pieces of legislation, also have the power to make references in respect of the industries for which they are responsible, as does the Minister in limited circumstances (s. 132(3)). The reference to the 'Commission' here is to the CC. Section 131(2) goes on further to state that

For the purposes of this Part any reference to a feature of a market in the United Kingdom for goods or services shall be construed as a reference to—

(a) the structure of the market concerned or any aspect of that structure;

(b) any conduct (whether or not in the market concerned) of one or more than one person who supplies or acquires goods or services in the market concerned; or

(c) any conduct relating to the market concerned of customers of any person who supplies or acquires goods or services.

For the purposes of these provisions 'conduct' includes not only positive actions, but also failures to act, and any unintentional conduct (s. 131(3)). Thus, for example, conduct could include a failure to supply certain categories of customers, or a failure to compete on price where price competition might be expected and/or desirable.

In the Guideline the OFT has set out its basic position in relation to the making of references at para. 2.1:

The OFT will only make references to the CC when the reference test set out in section 131 and, in its view, each of the following criteria have been met:

– it would not be more appropriate to deal with the competition issues identified by applying CA98 or using other powers available to the OFT or, where appropriate, to sectoral regulators

– it would not be more appropriate to address the problem identified by means of undertakings in lieu of a reference

– the scale of the suspected problem, in terms of its adverse effect on competition, is such
   that a reference would be an appropriate response to it

– there is a reasonable chance that the appropriate remedies will be available.

It appears therefore to be the case that a market investigation is seen as a measure of
last resort, to be employed only when other powers are not suitable to the task.

Before making a reference the OFT is obliged to consult any person on whom the
decision is 'likely to have a substantial impact' (s. 169(1)), and when it gives its decisions is required to state the reason for the making of the reference (see the discussion
of the store cards reference at 17.7 below). Persons who are aggrieved by a decision
to make a reference may apply to the CAT for a review of that decision (s. 179(1)).
Any such application must be brought within three months of the date of the making of the contested decision. The standard of review in this respect is that of judicial
review, i.e., *Wednesbury* unreasonableness (*Associated Provincial Picture Houses Ltd* v
Wednesbury Corpn [1948] 1 KB 223), and it is hard to envisage the circumstances in
which the OFT would leave itself open to a successful application. A further appeal, on
matters of law only, may be made against decisions of the CAT to the Court of Appeal
or in Scotland, the Court of Session (s. 179(6)). The OFT has been given the power to
conduct necessary investigations in s. 174. The powers in this respect are not as strong
as those available under the CA 98, and do not confer on the OFT the ability to conduct 'dawn raids' or searches of company premises. It can compel the attendance of
witnesses and the presentation of documents.

Once a reference has been made, it may be varied subsequently although there is
a duty to consult the CC before this is done. In some cases the CC itself might ask
that a reference be varied. Such a scenario is discussed in para. 3.13 of the Guideline,
where the OFT raises the possibility that the CC might identify markets affected by
the reference which differ from those identified by the OFT (e.g., the CC might find
that a market not recognized as being affected in fact is, or it might conclude that a
market considered by the OFT to be a single market is in fact two or more separate
markets). Where the CC asks the OFT to vary the reference so as to permit the CC to
carry out further investigations the OFT has indicated that 'it is very likely that [it]
would respond positively'.

17.3.1 Undertakings in lieu of references

Section 154 permits the OFT to accept undertakings in lieu of making a reference, and
s. 154(2) is in the following terms:

The OFT may, instead of making such a reference and for the purpose of remedying, mitigating or preventing—

(a) the adverse effect on competition concerned; or

(b) any detrimental effect on customers so far as it has resulted from, or may be expected
     to result from, the adverse effect on competition;

accept, from such persons as it considers appropriate, undertakings to take such action as it considers appropriate.

It is not likely that such undertakings will be commonly made. First, the OFT may not be convinced, in the light of its own analysis of the situation, which would be less rigorous than that of the CC following a reference, that any undertakings offered would properly remedy the situation. Secondly,

trying to negotiate undertakings with several parties, in circumstances in which possible adverse effects on competition have not been comprehensively analysed, is likely to pose serious practical difficulties. By contrast, where an adverse effect on competition arises from the conduct of a very few firms there may be more scope for accepting undertakings in lieu, provided that the OFT is confident that they will achieve a comprehensive solution. (Guideline, para. 2.21)

17.4 Market investigations and the CC

Any reference made by the OFT, other regulator, or Minister, is made to the CC. Once a reference is made the CC has up to two years in which to make its report on the matters referred (s. 137(1)), although it is hoped that the majority of investigations will be completed in a shorter period than this. In its *Annual Report and Accounts* 2008/09, the CC expressed its intention to complete investigations in 18 months, and perhaps even a year for smaller markets. The first reference made under these provisions, in relation to store cards, is discussed at 17.7 below.

Section 134 of the EA 02 states that the primary role of the CC is to determine whether there is an adverse effect on competition in relation to the referred matter. Section 134(2) provides that

For the purposes of this Part, in relation to a market investigation reference, there is an adverse effect on competition if any feature, or combination of features, of a market in the United Kingdom for relevant goods or services prevents, restricts or distorts competition in connection with the supply or acquisition of any goods or services in the United Kingdom or a part of the United Kingdom.

The reference here to 'features' of a market is deliberately broad, and relates to both the structure of a market, and the behaviour of firms on that market. It could also encompass matters such as the flow of information, or government regulation. For the purposes of carrying out a market investigation the CC has been given the necessary investigative powers (s. 176—under which powers from other parts of the Act are brought into play to govern the conduct of market investigation references). The CC may compel the attendance of witnesses and the production of documents and other necessary information, and penalties may be imposed if obligations imposed under these powers are not met.

Where the CC finds that there is an adverse effect on competition, or 'any detrimental effect on customers' (s. 134(4)(a)), it is required to determine what action should be taken, either by it or by other relevant parties, to remedy this effect. The meaning of the term 'detrimental effect on customers' is further clarified in s. 134(5) as being:

(a) higher prices, lower quality or less choice of goods or services in any market in the United Kingdom (whether or not the market to which the feature or features concerned relate); or

(b) less innovation in relation to goods or services.

At this point the CC may balance the harms that arise from the conduct or structure with any claimed countervailing benefits. This is not a 'legal exception' and it does not mirror art. 101 TFEU, but in practice the same considerations are likely to be considered. In essence the countervailing consumer benefits are those to customers which are the mirror of the detriments referred to in s. 134(5) (s. 134(7)).

In undertaking its analysis the CC is free to set its own methodology. In its own guidelines published in relation to market investigations (*Market Investigation References: Competition Commission Guidelines*, CC3), the CC breaks the process of evaluation into two key areas: market definition; and the assessment of competition.

17.4.1 The market

Following on from the equivalent provision in the FTA 1973 the 'relevant goods or services' referred to in s. 134(1) and (2) EA 02 means 'goods or services of a description to be specified in the reference'. It is possible therefore, but unlikely, that the OFT could make a reference based on an erroneous understanding of the relevant market. In such a case it would be open to the CC to request that the reference be appropriately varied following its initial examination of the facts. The CC Guidelines, *inter alia*, set out the now standard approach to market definition of the SSNIP test when determining the relevant product and geographic market. The discussion in this section of the document is particularly sensitive to the problems of obtaining necessary information, and the 'cellophane fallacy' (see 1.4.4.3).

17.4.2 The assessment of competition

The assessment of conditions of competition on the market will include a large number of factors. At para. 3.3 of its Guidelines the CC indicates that its analysis in the first instance 'will typically include a consideration of rivalry from other firms within the market, the threat of entry and/or countervailing power of customers, but need not be restricted to these'. Inter-firm rivalry may be conditioned by factors such as market shares and concentrations. Where the potential for competition within the market is not strong, other factors need to be considered, in particular barriers to entry, expansion, and exit. Other factors influencing competition within a market where the structure is not conducive to competition might include countervailing buyer power, supplier power, the extent of vertical integration, switching costs facing customers who wish to change their supplier (i.e., the expense of actually moving from one supplier to another), and information problems.

The primary distinguishing feature of market investigations, noted above, is the ability of the OFT and CC to deal with non-collusive coordinated conduct. This cannot be tackled via a prohibition on illegal agreements or other forms of active coordination, as there is no active behaviour to condemn. Neither can it be dealt with on the basis of the application of art. 102 TFEU or the Chapter II Prohibition, unless the relevant markets are characterized by at most three firms (although not impossible it is highly unlikely that the law of 'collective dominance' could be applied to four or more firms; the EU Commission indicated as much in the case of *Price Waterhouse/Coopers and Lybrand* 1999/152 (1999) OJ L50/27, when it held that collective dominance involving more than three or four suppliers would be unlikely because of the complexity of the interrelationships involved, and the consequent temptation to deviate (see paras 94–119). The basic dynamics of such a situation are explained at para. 3.58 of the CC Guidelines:

Where markets are sufficiently concentrated, the actions of individual firms can have identifiable effects on their competitors, such that firms recognise their interdependence. The interdependence of oligopolistic firms may lead them to anticipate competitors' responses to their own actions and take this into account in their own decisions. If, as will often be the case, this interdependence persists through time in such markets, the repeated nature of such decisions can have significant effects on business strategies and on competition. In particular, under certain conditions discussed below, it can become rational to refrain from initiating price cuts which would be unavoidable in more competitive circumstances.

A further possible outcome in such markets is that 'price increases by one firm to levels that might otherwise have been uncompetitive may well prove profitable' (para. 3.60). Markets with these features were regularly investigated under the complex monopoly provisions of the FTA 1973. The problem of coordinated effects, as the CC refers to this position, may also be dealt with under the EU merger regulation (see Chapter 19), but the law in this respect has yet to develop to maturity. The CC Guidelines provide a clear discussion of the factors which may underpin such markets, and a large part of this section is reproduced here:

3.62 A number of conditions are necessary for such behaviour to occur and be sustainable through time. First, the market has to be sufficiently concentrated for firms to be aware of the behaviour of their competitors, and for any significant deviation from the prevailing behaviour by a firm to be observed by other firms in the market. Where prices are transparent any deviation from the prevailing behaviour will be clear. However, even where they are not transparent, as is often the case in intermediate markets, any deviation from the prevailing behaviour by a competitor may nonetheless be readily apparent, because the essence of interdependence is that price cuts by one firm will have a significant impact on others' volumes.

3.63 Secondly, it must be clear that it will be costly for firms to deviate from the prevailing behaviour; so costly that it will be in a firm's interests to go along with the prevailing behaviour rather than seek to deviate from it. In many cases, the mere fact of the interdependence and hence the strong likelihood of a matching price cut may be enough to create such a disincentive. Timing will, however, be significant here. If prices can be adjusted quickly then such a response is very likely, but in markets where prices can only be set infrequently, the short-term gains from lower prices until a response is possible could outweigh the long-term gains of higher oligopolistic prices. If price setting is very infrequent then the basic perception of interdependence may cease to hold at all.

3.64 Thirdly, this type of parallelism can only be sustained in markets where there are relatively weak competitive constraints. If barriers to entry are low, then the threat of entry will tend to undermine such conduct. Alternatively, if there is a fringe of other firms in a market outside the core oligopolists, and if the competitive fringe firms have both the incentive to undercut and scope to attract significant volume away from the core oligopolists, then an uncompetitive price level is unlikely to be sustainable.

A number of factors are set out which might tend to reinforce the tendency of a market towards the production of coordinated effects. These include most obviously the degree of concentration in the market, and the presence of entry barriers protecting the incumbent firms from the disruption new entrants would bring with them. Other factors include the degree of transparency in the market (the more information that flows the more likely it is that firms will tend to move towards a common position), and the homogeneity of the product(s) in question.

It will not always be the case that a simple examination of the conditions of competition will produce a clear picture of the actual way in which competition is working in practice, and in particular whether there are the adverse effects the CC is directed to consider. The outcomes of competition can be as important in this respect as the conditions of competition, and the CC will examine evidence in this respect as part of its overall investigation. The most obvious factor to consider in this respect is that of prices. While a straightforward assessment of whether prices are 'high' or 'low' may appear superficially attractive, any such consideration would be subject to value judgements as to what constitutes a high or low price. More useful is consideration of the movements of prices over time. Typically price fluctuations between firms may be indicative of price competition, as firms vie with each other to win customers, whereas price stability might be indicative of a coordinated effect (see para. 3.79 of the Guidelines). Another indication of the state of competition might be the amount of profits being made by participants in that market. However, this analysis can be fraught with difficulty. The essence of the position taken by the CC is explained in the Guidelines in the following terms:

3.81 Profitability is the crucial incentive and signal in a market economy and high profits by individual companies at various times are fully consistent with competitive markets. More generally, a competitive market is likely to generate significant variations in profit levels between firms as supply and demand conditions change, but with an overall tendency towards levels commensurate with the cost of capital of the firms involved. At points in time, the profits of some firms may exceed what might be termed the 'normal' level. Reasons for this could include, for instance, cyclical factors, transitory price or other initiatives, the fact that some firms may be more efficient than others and, the fact that some firms may be earning profits gained as a result of past innovation. However, in nearly all cases competition should result in pressure on profit levels towards the cost of capital in the medium to long run.

3.82 However, a situation where, persistently, profits are substantially in excess of the cost of capital for firms that represent a substantial part of the market could be an indication of limitations in the competitive process. For instance, in some cases a high level of profitability could be indicative of significantly coordinated behaviour.

It must also be recognized that low profits may also be indicative of ineffective competition, if they are suggestive of inefficiencies that can be maintained because firms lack the discipline imposed by effective competition.

International price comparisons may also be invoked, although the CC is aware that the scope to use them as an indication of a lack of competition is limited, and that a number of factors need to be considered in order to be able to make a useful comparison.

17.5 **Remedies**

Where the CC identifies adverse effects s. 138 of the EA 02 creates an obligation on it to

take such action under section 159 or 160 as it considers to be reasonable and practicable—

  (a) to remedy, mitigate or prevent the adverse effect on competition concerned; and

  (b) to remedy, mitigate or prevent any detrimental effects on customers so far as they have resulted from, or may be expected to result from, the adverse effect on competition.

Section 134(6) further requires the CC

in particular to have regard to the need to achieve as comprehensive a solution as is reasonable and practicable to the adverse effect on competition and any detrimental effects on customers so far as resulting from the adverse effect on competition.

Part 4 of the CC Guidelines deals with the remedying of the adverse effects. The general position is that it is unlikely that the CC would identify an adverse effect and not at the same time impose a remedy for this. However, there could be some circumstances where no remedies will be put forward. This could include situations where any remedy would be ineffective due to international factors (remedies cannot be imposed outside the UK). Apart from some statutory limits there are virtually no restrictions on the remedies which the CC may seek to impose in market investigation reference cases. Remedies set out in the Guidelines include: divestment; the reduction of barriers to entry; behavioural orders; price caps; and monitoring remedies (which might include, e.g., the imposition of a requirement to report regularly to the OFT with certain information).

Under investigations carried out under the FTA 1973 a great many different remedies have at different times been set, although the procedure for their implementation was very different. Price controls were, for example, imposed on British Telecommunications plc in respect of its advertising rates for its *Yellow Pages* publications in July 1996 following the publication of the MMC report, *Classified Directory Advertising Services* (Cm. 3171, March 1996). In 2001 the operation of the undertaking given by BT in relation to prices was reviewed by the OFT (*Classified Directory Advertising Services; Review of undertakings given by BT to the Secretary of State in July 1996*, OFT 332, May 2001, [2001] UKCLR 1140). At this time the OFT recommended that the price cap be tightened, BT's profits from publishing the *Yellow Pages* directories having remained exceptionally high, but along with this greater restriction it also recommended that a number of other undertakings be relaxed.

17.5.1 Undertakings and orders

There are two main mechanisms by which remedies required under this Part of the Act may be created. These are by way of undertakings, and by orders. Undertakings are entered into voluntarily by the parties, and orders are imposed upon them. However, once undertakings are entered into they become binding and are enforceable before the courts.

The possibility for the OFT to accept undertakings in lieu of making a market investigation reference to the CC has already been noted above at 17.3.1. Interim and final undertakings may be sought by the CC or, in the case where a public interest consideration is invoked (see below), by the Secretary of State. In all cases the party requiring the undertaking may subsequently release the parties from it if it is appropriate to do so. Orders may be made at both the interim and final stage in the proceedings, and may contain anything set out in Schedule 8 to the Act. The list here is very wide indeed. Where orders and undertakings are not complied with they may be enforced by way of civil proceedings brought against the wrongdoers by the OFT for an injunction, interdict, or any other appropriate remedy or relief (s. 167(6)). Third parties who are harmed by non-compliance are also able to take action, and can seek damages or other relief as appropriate (s. 167(4)).

17.6 Public interest cases

In exceptional cases the Secretary of State for Trade and Industry can become involved in market investigations. This situation can arise only where a public interest issue, as provided for in s. 152, has been raised. At the time of Royal Assent the only such interest was specified to be that of public security, although the power was left open to add to this list. Where a public interest issue arises the Secretary of State may issue an intervention notice (s. 140). Where any such notice is in force the CC is required to determine, in addition to the competition questions, whether further action is required in light of the public interest consideration. It is then up to the Secretary of State, within 90 days of the delivery of the report, to publish a decision as to the matters raised.

17.7 **Reference reports**

Several market investigation references have been completed by the Competition Commission, and others are currently under way. The number of references made in any one year is unlikely to exceed five. In 2008/2009 the CC published three completed reports: Groceries, Payment Protection Insurance, and BAA (Competition Commission, *Annual Report and Accounts 2008/2009*).

The first market investigation reference made by the OFT to the CC was on 18 March 2004 and related to the supply of store card services. This followed a study undertaken by the OFT in response to concerns raised by the Treasury Select Committee (OFT 706, *Store Cards*, March 2004). The OFT was concerned that the market was insufficiently transparent in relation to the offering and use of store cards. The CC found that the average rate of interest was too high, at 10–20 per cent, and that there was a consumer detriment of in excess of £50 million a year as a result of this (*Store Cards Market Investigation*, 7 March 2006). A number of remedies were put in place most of which involved giving consumers more information and options relating to the methods of payment. A formal order to this effect came into force in May 2007.

In 2006–7, reports on the supply of bulk liquefied petroleum gas for domestic use and the home credit market responded to concern that in the relevant market only four suppliers accounted for about 90 per cent of the supply, and that contracts made it difficult for customers to switch suppliers (thus creating barriers to entry). The CC required that a package of remedies be imposed, all of which were designed to make it easier for customers to switch suppliers. In these two cases remedies were to be imposed by way of orders. In another 2007 study relating to classified directory advertising services, market remedies were effected by undertakings given by Yell Group plc (the publisher of the Yellow Pages directory). In this investigation the central concerns were that Yell was able to charge advertising rates which were largely unconstrained by competition, based on the very high brand recognition of the Yellow Pages directories. Although the growth in Internet advertising might alter the dynamics of competition in the future the evidence that this was the case at the time of the inquiry was limited. Under the undertakings given by Yell its prices were to continue being pegged at RPI-6 per cent until March 2008, and after that time to the level of the RPI. Some limitations were imposed on the publication of second-tier directories.

In 2008/2009, three major investigations were completed: Groceries, Payment Protection Insurance, and BAA. Importantly in the groceries market, after a two-year study the CC was concerned about the weak competition in some local markets, where barriers to entry were present as a result of the strong position of certain retailers. Furthermore, often excessive risk and other costs were transferred to suppliers, with an adverse impact on innovation in the supply chain (CC, *Annual Report and Accounts 2008/2009*). Among the remedies suggested were to force retailers to give up control over landsites in areas where entry for competitors is difficult, and a recommendation that 'a competition test be applied, as part of the planning process, to proposed new stores' favouring new entrants over long established ones. Tesco, fearing that it would be prevented from opening new stores or expanding existing ones', challenged this particular remedy, and the CAT upheld its complaint on the grounds that the Commission 'had not properly evaluated whether the costs of introducing the competition test would outweigh any benefits it might bring' (See King, I., 'Tesco Wins Fight Over Store Competition Test' (4 March 2009) *The Guardian*). The CC was thus forced to consider its proposition. For further details, see Davis, P., and Riley, A., 'The UK Competition Commission's Groceries Market Investigation: Market Power, Market Outcomes and Remedies', (2009) *International Association of Agricultural Economists Conference*, Beijing).

17.8 Conclusion

While market investigation references have not received the attention that has fallen on the cartel offence—for perhaps understandable reasons—the weapon is potentially very useful indeed. There are likely to be two or three such references a year, and these are most likely to be focused on oligopolistic markets. These markets defy analysis under either the 'agreements' route, or the 'dominance' route, and the power to impose remedies under the Act is virtually unfettered. Under the Fair Trading Act 1973 a similar procedure led to sometimes impressive results (as we have seen above). It remains to be seen how effective market investigation references will be in the future.

FURTHER READING

Articles

Davis, P., and Riley, A., 'The UK Competition Commission's Groceries Market Investigation: Market Power, Market Outcomes and Remedies', (2009) *International Association of Agricultural Economists Conference, Beijing*

Pickering, J., 'UK Market Investigations: An Economic Perspective', (2006) *Competition Law* 206

Sufrin, B., and Furse, M., 'Market Investigations', [2002] *Competition Law* 244

18

An introduction to the economics of merger control

KEY POINTS

- Mergers may create monopolies, or may increase market power of the merged entity (unilateral effects).

- By reducing the number of competitors in a market a merger may increase the likelihood of a cooperative solution to competition being adopted by the remaining firms in the market (cooperative effects).

- Horizontal mergers are more likely to raise competitive concerns than are vertical mergers; the latter may raise concerns where the effect is to gain control of an input or distribution source which is necessary for competitors.

- Where a firm is failing, a merger that would otherwise be anti-competitive might be efficient and welfare enhancing.

18.1 Introduction

Even those commentators and analysts who would argue that competition law should be greatly curtailed on the grounds that its application causes more harm than good would in most cases support the existence of some form of merger control. However the economics of merger control is not a matter that has been subject to a great deal of scrutiny until recently. For a fuller discussion of the issues dealt with here, see Bishop, S., and Walker, M., *The Economics of EC Competition Law*, London, Sweet & Maxwell (3rd edn, 2010).

In this brief chapter we will deal with the key arguments that underpin the policy goals behind merger control. In essence these relate to two factors: first, the creation or extension of monopoly power, including the raising of barriers to entry for potential competitors; and secondly, increasing the scope for collusion in a market which, post-merger, will be more oligopolistic and less competitive than was the market pre-merger. It will be noted that the first of these two factors is related to the control of dominant firm conduct, and that, as we have already seen, dominance itself is not condemned in either the EU or the UK. Nevertheless in merger control we find a situation where the attainment or extension of dominance may be condemned.

The greatest procedural difference between merger control and the control of dominance post-merger is that any analysis of a merger will usually be undertaken *ex ante*, and any assessment of dominant firm behaviour will always be made *ex post*. The assessment of individual mergers may therefore be particularly contentious as the undertakings concerned and the authorities are arguing on the basis of *anticipated*, rather than *actual*, results, and the scope of the transactions concerned is sometimes very substantial.

For the present purposes the term 'merger' will be taken to refer to any situation in which the ownership of two or more undertakings is joined together. In the world of business the process that may lead to this joining of ownership may take many different forms, and may be either amicable and consensual, or unwelcome and hostile. In Community law the term used in preference to 'merger' is 'concentration' and a concentration is deemed to arise where there is a merger of 'two or more previously independent undertakings or parts of undertakings' (Regulation 139/2004, art. 3(1)(a)), or where an undertaking or person controlling an undertaking acquires control of another undertaking (art. 3(1)(b)). The law relating to these tests is dealt with in Chapter 19.

Mergers may take place either vertically or horizontally. The latter case, which will typically be of more concern to the competition authorities, arises where firms in the same industry, dealing in the same goods or services in the same geographic market, merge. A third type of merger, a conglomerate merger, may also be identified. A conglomerate merger is one in which firms produce products which are not in the same market, but which may to a greater or lesser extent be substitutes for each other. Although merger activity tends to fluctuate depending on the state of the economy and of the structure of particular industries the statistics show that the majority of mergers are horizontal ones, although in the 1960s there was in the United States a wave of conglomerate mergers in response to the harsh line being taken towards horizontal mergers by the antitrust authorities.

Mergers take place, like most business moves, primarily in order to increase profits. This may come about either because the effect of the merger is to reduce competition between the participants to the merger, or where the merger leads to cost savings through the gaining of efficiencies as a result of the joining of assets and fixed factors of production, allowing prices to be reduced and market shares to be increased. Increased concentration however will not inevitably lead to increased profits, and in some situations it may be demonstrated that the combined profits of a merged entity might be lower than the profits of the two independent undertakings were pre-merger. The argument whereby this result is achieved is a technical one.

A merger might have advantages over other forms of expansion (internal growth is an alternative to a merger). If an undertaking is seeking to increase its market share, the alternative to a merger is to expand production unilaterally. The result of this will be to lead to lower prices across the industry, and lower profit margins, and the ultimate impact on market shares will be uncertain *ex ante*. A merger may have particular advantages when an undertaking wishes to diversify into a market in which it is not presently based, overcoming barriers to entry, and again avoiding intense competition should the incumbent choose to defend its territory. Mergers also allow a much quicker, and a more certain response than does a strategy of internal growth. It might take only three months for a significant merger to yield results, but several years for the same results to be achieved by way of a 'competitive' process.

Mergers may also be undertaken for other reasons than merely to increase profits. In uncertain markets a merger may reflect differing views on future market performance among differing entrepreneurs. One owner may take a dim view of long-term market prospects, and another may anticipate brighter prospects. This might lead the former to be susceptible to offers from the latter. In some cases mergers might be driven by the desire of business leaders to manage a larger entity, and perhaps to operate at a global, rather than local, level. Even in this case however the rational entrepreneur would be presumed still to be making profit-maximizing decisions.

The fact that mergers take place for diverse reasons, and that the outcomes cannot be certain, suggests that a *per se* rule prohibiting mergers should be rejected, and that mergers should be assessed on a case-by-case basis. This is the process that exists in the EU and the UK, as well as the USA, although in the case of horizontal mergers there are some presumptions relating to the size of market shares pre- and post-merger which may come into play.

18.2 Horizontal mergers

Horizontal mergers may be substitutable for cartels, and Neumann points to the fact that 'in the US, after cartels were declared illegal by the Sherman Act, they were replaced by mergers which could more effectively be defended by invoking the rule of reason' (Neumann, M., *Competition Policy: History, Theory and Practice*, Cheltenham, Edward Elgar (2001), p. 113). The very fact that this is true suggests that horizontal mergers should be treated with some suspicion. However, the position is not a straightforward one. Cartels may self-destruct, but will in most cases be less efficient than mergers. Mergers are likely to be more efficient than cartels as they may generate economies of scale and of scope, but they are structurally embedded in a way that cartels are not. The key issue with horizontal mergers is that they may allow market power to be wielded, either by single-firm monopolists, or by collusive oligopolies. The EU Commission has produced a *Notice on the appraisal of horizontal mergers* (2004) OJ C31/5, which should be referred to for further discussion.

18.2.1 The creation of a monopoly

The situation in which a merger creates a single-firm monopoly, or adds to the power of a single-firm monopoly, is relatively straightforward, and follows the relevant economic processes concerning monopoly conduct. Where the effect of a merger is to substantially lessen competition, or to create or strengthen a dominant position as a result of which competition will be impaired, the merger is likely to be blocked. As we have seen in relation to monopolies, harm may be presumed to flow from the mere fact of the existence of a monopoly. However, as there are substantial harms in misapplying regulation or competition-law solutions to what may be later shown to have been efficient conduct, and as most monopolies will over time be eroded, the existence of monopoly itself is not condemned. Nevertheless, in the case where it can be clearly demonstrated that a single, preventable, transaction will lead to the creation of a monopoly there are strong policy reasons why that transaction should be prevented. Of course the analysis needed to demonstrate that a monopoly will be created is not always straightforward, and the concept of market definition was first developed by the competition authorities to deal with the issue of whether a 'relevant market' was being monopolized as a result of a merger. These issues are best left to economics, and while the role of a legal team is likely to be of paramount importance in the process of any substantial merger, the role in relation to the substantive test of the merger's effect is likely to be less so.

18.2.2 Oligopolies and oligopolistic coordination

The Commission, in its *Notice on the appraisal of horizontal mergers*, identifies two aspects in which concerns may be raised in respect of oligopoly markets. The first of these relates to competitive oligopolies in which competitive constraints may be weakened by the fact of the merger. In these situations the Commission will pay strong attention to measures of market concentration, and will be concerned about the ability and the incentive of the merging firms to increase prices (a unilateral effect independent of any collusion).

The second area of concern, that a merger will lead to a more concentrated market in which oligopolistic collusion will be facilitated, is both theoretically and practically a difficult one. The basic danger is noted in the US DOJ *Horizontal Merger Guidelines* of 1992, s. 2.1:

A merger may diminish competition by enabling firms in the relevant market more likely, more successfully, or more completely to engage in coordinated interaction that harms consumers. Coordinated interaction is comprised of actions by a group of firms that are profitable for each of them only as a result of the accommodating reactions of the others. This behaviour includes tacit or express collusion, and may or may not be lawful in and of itself.

The Commission approach is similar, emphasizing that a change in the market structure may be such that firms would consider it possible, rational, and therefore preferable, to coordinate activity on the market such that prices would be set above competitive levels, but without any agreement to this effect being necessary.

The economic issues that arise in these cases have been examined in a number of decisions taken in the EU. These are considered in the section on 'joint dominance' at 19.2.2.4.1. The EU Commission has developed a 'checklist' of factors that it considers to be relevant to a finding of a situation in which an oligopoly can successfully coordinate action. In these cases, if the factors arise only following a merger, that merger is likely to be blocked. The factors highlighted are: concentration (probably up to a maximum of three firms), product homogeneity, symmetry of market shares and costs, transparency in pricing, the ease with which a firm may retaliate to another's competitive action, barriers to entry, inelastic demand, and absence of buyer power. It is also important that the market be relatively stable and mature. However, each of these factors should be considered carefully, as any industry is likely to show some of these features, and even if the majority of these factors are present an analysis sensitive to the particular conditions of the relevant market is necessary to determine if collusive conduct is likely to follow.

The collusion itself may take various forms. Most typically it would take the form of increasing prices, as was feared would be the case in the *Gencor/Lonhro* merger (97/26 (1997) OJ L11/30). Alternatively, as in *Airtours/First Choice* 2000/276 (2000) OJ L93/1 it may take the form of reducing capacity, or production, with the end result of increasing prices albeit in a competitive structure where price competition still existed; or it may take the form of market sharing. In each case different conditions must exist in order for such collusion to be effective. When analysing the possibility for collusion it is necessary to consider the problem in four stages. First, a plausible mechanism whereby collusion can take place must be identified. Secondly, the market must be analysed to determine whether it has within it characteristics or features which would support the suggested collusive mechanism. The third step is to identify whether those particular features exist in the particular case under consideration. The fourth step is to consider whether evidence of past conduct is suggestive that a collusive outcome might emerge in the new market situation. For example, in *Gencor/Lonhro* the Commission was concerned that there was evidence of previous collusive activity in the South African mining industry.

18.2.3 The failing-firm defence

An argument is sometimes made that a merger which 'saves' a failing firm should not be blocked, on the grounds that were it not for the merger the market would also be more concentrated following the exit of the failing firm, and there would be social costs to this failure. Thus in the US DOJ *Horizontal Merger Guidelines* of 1992, s. 5.0 we find:

A merger is not likely to create or enhance market power or to facilitate its exercise, if imminent failure . . . of one of the merging firms would cause the assets of that firm to exit the relevant market. In such circumstances, post-merger performance in the relevant market may be no worse than market performance had the merger been blocked and the assets left the market.

This argument underlay the Competition Commission inquiry into the Air Canada and Canadian Airlines Corporation merger (Cm. 4838, August 2000). Here the Canadian Airlines Corporation would 'sooner or later run out of money' (report, para. 2.13) were it not saved by the merger. Although the Competition Commission was concerned about the reduction in competition on transatlantic routes from the UK to Canada following the merger it accepted that these were the result not directly of the merger, but of the fact that one of the parties was going out of business.

The failing-firm defence was dismissed in the CC report into the Safeway merger (*Safeway plc and Asda Group Ltd (owned by Wal-Mart Stores Inc.); Wm Morrison Supermarkets plc; J. Sainsbury plc; and Tesco plc: A report on the mergers in contemplation*, Commission, 5950, September 2003)) in which the CC considered a number of prospective mergers in what was viewed as a socially sensitive market. The CC here noted that in order to 'conclude that Safeway was failing, we would need to be satisfied that it was unable to meet its financial obligations in the near future and that in this respect it was unable to restructure itself successfully' (para 2.182). In fact, in this case, Safeway was still competing effectively, albeit not on the basis of the scale economics achieved by its larger rivals.

In the *Notice on the appraisal of horizontal mergers* the Commission stressed that it would be for the notifying parties to demonstrate that there was indeed a failing-firm defence, and indicated that three criteria were relevant:

First, the allegedly failing firm would in the near future be forced out of the market because of financial difficulties if not taken over by another undertaking. Second, there is no less anti-competitive alternative purchase than the notified merger. Third, in the absence of a merger the assets of the failing firm would inevitably exit the market.

18.3 Vertical mergers

Vertical mergers generally give rise to less economic concern than do horizontal mergers, although

[v]ertical mergers can make entry more difficult by foreclosing rivals from previously independent firms at either the vertical level, by increasing capital requirements associated with entry and by promoting product differentiation. A vertically integrated oligopoly is insulated from competitive pressures that come from vertically related, competitive levels. This makes oligopolistic output coordination easier.   (Martin, S., *Industrial Economics*, New York, Macmillan (2nd edn, 1994), p. 309)

Vertical mergers will not further concentrate a market, and the danger most often identified is that, as Martin suggests, they might foreclose a market to competition. For example, if a television broadcast network were to merge with a film production studio competing networks might find it more difficult to obtain products to transmit, and might therefore find it harder to compete for viewers. Where both of the relevant vertical markets are competitive there is likely to be no competitive harm from a vertical merger, and the presumption should instead be that the firms are merging as they have identified efficiencies of doing so that competition will force them to pass on to the consumer.

The process whereby oligopolistic collusion might be facilitated by vertical mergers is not immediately intuitive. However, the problem may be explained clearly by way of an example. Consider the situation where a four-firm oligopoly packages 85 per cent of the budget short-haul foreign package holidays sold to holidaymakers in a particular territory, but that these holidays are marketed by 20 independent chains of retailers, some of which have very large customer bases. Competition between these chains for custom, and the buying power that some of them are able to exercise, should compel the four firms producing the product to compete for their patronage, and should therefore dampen the adverse effects of there being a narrow oligopoly. If on the other hand each of the four firms bought four retail chains the position would be somewhat different, and it is likely that the oligopoly would be able more effectively to coordinate at all levels of the chain, raising prices to end consumers. Vertical integration may therefore be an essential condition for an oligopoly successfully to exploit its market power. However, such concerns will normally arise only where both markets, upstream and downstream, are concentrated, and where entry barriers are significant. The fact remains that the great majority of vertical mergers are not seriously challenged by the application of merger control procedures.

FURTHER READING

Books

SCHWALBE, U., and ZIMMER, D., *Law and Economics in European Merger Control* (2009) Oxford University Press, Oxford

ILZKOVITZ, F. and MEIKLEJOHN, R., *European Merger Control: Do We Need an Efficiency Defence?* (2006) Edward Elgar, Cheltenham

Articles

LYONS, B., 'An Economic Assessment of EC Merger Control: 1957–2007' (2008) *CCP Working Paper* No. 08–17, University of East Anglia, Norwich.

19

The EU merger control regime and the treatment of joint ventures

KEY POINTS

- Where a merger ('concentration') meets the relevant thresholds it falls, within the EU, within the exclusive competence of the EU Commission to examine the merger.

- Undertakings contemplating such a merger are required compulsorily to notify the Commission of that merger.

- The test of a merger's acceptance is that of whether it substantially impedes effective competition in the internal market, in particular, but not exclusively, by creating or strengthening a dominant position.

- Using the powers set out in the Merger Regulation the Commission may authorize, or block, the merger over a two-stage process. Tight time limits apply.

- Although Member States are largely excluded from the process, they may, in certain defined circumstances, take control over aspects of, or the whole of, the merger.

- Appeals against Commission decisions are to the General Court.

19.1 Introduction

This is the first of two chapters providing an outline of the application of competition law to mergers—the UK law is dealt with in the following chapter. They aim to provide the basis for further study of this complex area; the subject is too vast to be dealt with completely in an introductory textbook. The majority of competition law regimes give a prominent place to the control of mergers, which cannot be treated in the same way as other anti-competitive practices. Anti-competitive agreements, and dominant firm conduct, are in most cases, although not exclusively, investigated and analysed after the event (although of course the parties to an agreement or conduct may themselves evaluate this prior to going ahead, and in some circumstances notifications may be made to the relevant authority). Mergers are better dealt with prior to their being implemented—or 'consummated'—as it can be both very difficult and exceptionally costly to disentangle a merger which has already taken place. This prior assessment is necessarily undertaken without the benefit of hindsight. In the case of the EU regime only the very largest mergers fall to be reviewed. This means inevitably that the stakes are high, both for the EU Commission, which, subject to certain express provisions, has exclusive competence to rule on mergers falling within its jurisdiction, and for the merging undertakings, who may have invested heavily in the merger process, and for whom much may ride on a successful outcome.

Certain key questions may be asked of any merger regime. Over what mergers is jurisdiction to be asserted? Is notification compulsory or voluntary? What is the subjective test by which mergers are evaluated? What procedures are in place to ensure the efficacy of the merger regime? In the case of the EU merger control regime, the answers to these questions are found primarily in Council Regulation (EC) 139/2004 on the control of concentrations between undertakings (the EU Merger Regulation) (2004) OJ L24/1. Hereinafter this regulation will be referred to as the EUMR (pre-Lisbon literature will refer to the regulation as ECMR). As is the case with the application of arts 101 and 102 TFEU the approach taken to merger control in the EU has changed to some extent over time. The single market considerations that were so important in determining some of the key principles of the application of art. 101 have also played a role in the shaping of the merger regime, and the response taken to the assessment of mergers, as has the need of industry to adapt to this change in market conditions. Thus in the EUMR at recitals (3) to (5) it is provided that:

(3) The completion of the internal market and of economic and monetary union, the enlargement of the European Union and the lowering of international barriers to trade and investment will continue to result in major corporate reorganisations, particularly in the form of concentrations.

(4) Such reorganisations are to be welcomed to the extent that they are in line with the requirements of dynamic competition and capable of increasing the competitiveness of European industry, improving the conditions of growth and raising the standard of living in the [Union].

(5) However, it should be ensured that the process of reorganisation does not result in lasting damage to competition; [Union] law must therefore include provisions governing those concentrations which may significantly impede effective competition in the [internal] market or in a substantial part of it.

Changing responses to the role and importance of merger control, and to the assertion of jurisdiction by the EU at the expense of the Member States, has been reflected too in the development of the EUMR itself. The EUMR was first enacted as Regulation 4064/89 (consolidated version with corrections published at (1990) OJ L257/13), and this in turn was amended by Regulation 1310/97 (1997) OJ L180/1. The 2004 version of the EUMR represents a significant development, although not as significant as some would have hoped, of the EU merger regime, the examination of which will occupy most of the remainder of this chapter.

Joint ventures will also be considered in this chapter. A joint venture is a form of arrangement between undertakings which is usually designed to facilitate long-term cooperation (although some joint ventures may be of deliberately short duration). At EU level, they are closely related to merger control: a distinction is drawn between joint ventures which are 'concentrative', and which fall to be dealt with under the EUMR, and those which fall within the direct framework of art. 101 TFEU. This symmetry does not exist in the case of the UK, where there is no specific legal entity recognized as a joint venture, although various vehicles are available to companies seeking to implement such an arrangement.

19.2 Merger control in the European Union

19.2.1 The application of arts 101 and 102 and the development of the Merger Regulation

Articles 101 and 102 do not, explicitly, provide for the control of mergers, and for some time the general consensus was that they could not be applied to merger situations. This view was given added support by the fact that the older European Coal and Steel Community (ECSC) Treaty expressly dealt with merger control at art. 66. The fact that such an express provision had been omitted from the then EEC Treaty suggested that the control of mergers was not to be encompassed within the competition law regime. However, the application by the Commission of first art. 102 and then art. 101 to merger situations, and the approval of this action by the Court of Justice, confirmed that Union competition law could be applied to mergers in certain circumstances.

The first such action, taken under art. 102, was in the *Continental Can* case (*Europemballage Corp. and Continental Can Co.* v *Commission* case 6/72 [1973] CMLR 199. By way of a decision taken in 1972 (*Re Continental Can Co. Inc.* 72/71 (1972) OJ L7/25) the EU Commission had found a breach of art. 102 in a situation in which a takeover bid was made by a dominant undertaking for a smaller competitor. The Commission first intervened in the deal, which took the form of a takeover bid made for Thomassen & Drijver Verblifa (TDV) by Europemballage, itself a subsidiary of a much larger American company, Continental Can, with large interests in Europe. The Commission indicated that such an arrangement might be an abuse of art. 102 (see Chapter 14) in that it would adversely affect the structure of competition in a situation where competition was already weakened by the presence of the allegedly dominant undertaking. The takeover nevertheless went ahead, whereupon the Commission found that an abuse had indeed occurred, and ordered that steps be taken to bring the infringement to an end.

On appeal the case was rejected by the Court of Justice on the grounds, largely, that the Commission had failed adequately to identify the relevant market, and had therefore not established that Continental Can was dominant within the meaning of art. 102. However, the Court did confirm that the article could be applied to situations in which a dominant undertaking sought to reduce further competition by the takeover of another undertaking, even in situations in which the transaction was in no way coerced. In particular the Court was not persuaded that the inclusion of a merger control provision in the ECSC Treaty meant that no such powers were to be available under the EEC Treaty.

By expressly considering not only the wording of arts 101 and 102, but also the more expansive wording of art. 3(g) EC (removed from the TFEU by the Lisbon Treaty reform), to the effect that competition in the internal market should not be distorted, the Court adopted a wide interpretation of the relevant provisions. Given that the Commission had been given the power by the Court, although again not expressly in the relevant legislation, to adopt interim measures (*Camera Care Ltd v Commission* case 792/79R [1980] 1 CMLR 334), the spectre was raised of the Commission using its authority to order that contemplated mergers not be consummated where they involved an undertaking in a dominant position. Such uncertainty could be damaging to merger plans, which are often highly sensitive, and in the course of which terms may be inserted to the effect that any regulatory intervention will see the abandonment of the plans.

In *BAT Ltd and R. J. Reynolds Industries Inc.* v *Commission* cases 142 and 156/84 [1988] 4 CMLR 24, the Commission considered the application of art. 101 to an agreement between cigarette manufacturers including Rembrandt Group, which had a controlling interest in Rothmans, and Philip Morris which would have given Philip Morris a strong degree of control over the Rembrandt tobacco division. The two parties notified their agreement to the Commission, and, following negotiations between the parties, the agreement was given the approval of the Commission. However, the very fact that the parties had chosen to notify the agreement, and the fact that the Commission chose to consider it, was evidence of the possibility of the application of art. 101 to agreements leading to mergers. BAT and Reynolds, two large undertakings competing with the notifying parties, brought an action before the Court of Justice on the basis of art. 267 TFEU to challenge the clearance decision of the Commission. The Court rejected the applicants' argument holding that it could not be demonstrated that the notified agreements actually had the object or effect of preventing, restricting, or distorting competition. At the same time the Court, supporting the stance taken by the Commission, held that agreements which lead to concentrations in the market could be reviewed in the light of art. 101 and could fall within the prohibition of art. 101(1).

These two strands of administrative and judicial development led to a degree of uncertainty for mergers taking place within the Union, and raised the prospect that a clearance by a national authority examining the transaction on the basis of an application of a domestic merger regime could subsequently be followed by a condemnation under EU competition law. The spectre was also raised of third parties, or, for example, aggrieved shareholders, bringing actions on the basis of the application of either art. 101 or art. 102 in national courts. In particular it was recognized that the application of art. 101(2) to a fully consummated merger could have disastrous and unpredictable consequences. Further, the application of art. 101 or 102 would depend on their individual jurisdictional bases, and might fail to catch other mergers which were equally harmful. This is recognized in recital (7) of the EUMR:

Articles [101] and [102], while applicable, according to the case-law of the Court of Justice, to certain concentrations, are not sufficient to control all operations which may prove to be incompatible with the system of undistorted competition envisaged in the Treaty.

Accordingly the EU Commission brought forward proposals to introduce a measure to clarify the position, on the basis not only of art. 103, but also of art. 352 TFEU, under which the Union may give itself powers to perform tasks necessary for the attainment of the objectives of the EU, in situations where an express power has not been made available. This proposal resulted, after intense negotiations with the Member States, in the enactment of Regulation 4064/89 on the Control of Concentrations Between Undertakings (1989) OJ L395/1—as a result of a substantial number of textual errors in the first publication this was republished at (1990) OJ L257/13). This regulation entered into force on 21 September 1990.

Fundamental to the new regime was the fact that, save with certain defined exceptions, the EU would have exclusive competence in relation to mergers falling within the thresholds set out. In 1997 the regulation was subject to some significant amendment by the introduction of Regulation 1310/97 (1997) OJ L180/1. The amendments, which particularly affected the thresholds at which the EU merger regime would apply, were not as substantial as had been hoped for by the EU Commission, and at the end of 2001 the Commission launched a major review of the mergers regime (*Green Paper on the Review of Council Regulation (EEC) No. 4064/89* COM(2001) 745/6 final, 11 December 2001). This was designed in part to open up a discussion as to the extent to which the regime should align itself more closely with that of the USA in an effort to avoid conflict (in this respect see also Chapter 4). As discussed below, the test of a merger's acceptance under Regulation 4064/89 was strongly linked to the concept of dominance set out in art. 102 TFEU. The USA, on the other hand—along with a number of other jurisdictions, including the UK—employs a different test, that of whether the merger under examination would tend to 'substantially lessen competition' (hereinafter the SLC test). As the Green Paper recognized, this would

Facilitate merger parties' global assessment of possible competition issues arising from contemplated transactions, by obviating the need to argue their case according to differently formulated tests. This would in turn provide competition agencies with a better basis on which to build effective cooperation in cases that are notified in several jurisdictions. (para. 160)

The response to this argument, and the nature of the evaluative test embedded in the EUMR are discussed below in some detail.

At the same time as raising discussion about the test itself, the Commission sought to reduce the very high threshold at which Regulation 4064/89 applied. This the Commission had also attempted at the time of the 1997 revisions, in an effort to allow more mergers to be considered under a single 'one-stop shop' procedure. This is an issue that, with the enlargement of the EU in May 2004 and January 2007, has become more important over time. In essence the mergers considered at the Union level are only the very largest ones, and at this level of transaction undertakings face the risk of having their mergers considered by the authorities of a number of jurisdictions, both inside and outside the EU, with the financial and legal risks to which that gives rise. From the outset of the regime the thresholds have been higher than the Commission would have liked, and there has been constant pressure placed on the Member States to revise these in a downward direction. The Commission was not successful in this regard; in its recent *Report on the functioning of Regulation No 139/2004* (2009), published on 18 June 2009, the Commission confirmed that the regime was generally working adequately, and did not suggest any proposals in this regard (see 19.3).

19.2.2 The application of the EUMR

The EUMR applies only where two conditions are fulfilled: first, there must be a 'concentration' of two or more undertakings (within the specific meanings given to these terms in the legislation), and second, the turnover of the undertakings concerned must meet the thresholds set out in the legislation. In July 2007 the Commission published a *Consolidated jurisdictional notice* (2006) OJ L272/3, which provides guidance in relation to key matters arising under the EUMR, such as the concept of concentration, and the assessment of whether there is a Union dimension. This notice replaces a number of separate older notices. The text of this notice is not considered in detail in this chapter, but it should be referred to in studying the law of EU merger control.

19.2.2.1 The meaning of 'concentration'

Although the EUMR is subtitled 'the EU Merger Regulation', the control extends to 'concentrations', which may take many forms. The definition of 'concentration' for the purposes of the EUMR is given in art. 3 of the regulation. In essence the test is one of whether there is a 'change of control on a lasting basis' (art. 3(1)). This follows recital (20) which makes reference to a definition applying to a situation in which there is 'a lasting change in control of the undertakings concerned and therefore in the structure of the market'. Article 3(1) provides that such a change of control may result from:

    (a) the merger of two or more previously independent undertakings or parts of undertakings, or

    (b) the acquisition, by one or more persons already controlling at least one undertaking, by one or more undertakings, whether by purchase or securities or assets, by contract or by any other means, of direct or indirect control of the whole or parts of one or more other undertakings.

'Acquisition' is given a wide meaning, to include a direct financial purchase by contract, a purchase of shares or securities, or any other means. Control may be direct or indirect, and shall be constituted by rights, contracts or any other means which, either separately or in combination and having regard to the considerations of fact or of law involved, confer the possibility of exercising decisive influence on an undertaking.   (art. 3(2))

Control is defined in art. 3(2) EUMR as relating to the *possibility* of exercising decisive influence on an undertaking. In other words, the Commission does not have to demonstrate that this influence will be, or has been, exercised. Both ownership and rights may give rise to control. For example, a minority shareholder may exercise rights on the basis of particular rights attached to their shares, effectively giving them a 'decisive influence' over the affairs of the undertaking in question. The question of whether control exists is to be determined pragmatically, the essential ingredient being that of an influence over the business strategy of the undertaking(s) concerned. For example, the right of a minority shareholder to veto certain decisions might not be found to constitute control for the purposes of the EUMR.

The term 'decisive influence' is not defined in the EUMR, and it is not entirely clear where the boundaries of this concept lie. Only in the most exceptional circumstances has the Commission found that a decisive influence existed where less than 25 per cent of the share capital of an undertaking has been held by a single person. However, in the case of *CCIE/GTE* (1992) OJ C225/14 a share of 19 per cent was found to trigger control. In this instance all remaining shares were held by an investment bank, whose approval was not necessary for significant decisions. In essence, whether there is a 'decisive influence' is a fact to be determined in the light of all the relevant circumstances (see, for example, *Gencor Ltd* v *Commission* case T–102/96 [1999] 4 CMLR 971, paras 167–94).

For the purposes of the EUMR concentrations must take place between undertakings (the meaning of which term has been dealt with above (see Chapter 2), and the regulation refers also to 'persons'. Where an individual acquires an undertaking they may, by virtue of other commercial interests, be considered to be an undertaking for the purposes of the regulation. This was the case, for example, in *Asko/Jacobs/Adia* (1993) in which a private investor, holding interests in a number of undertakings, was himself considered to be an undertaking. Member States, even though they are not for the purposes of competition law considered to be undertakings, may be 'persons' for the purposes of the regulation, and public bodies are certainly encompassed within the terms of the EUMR. In *Air France/Sabena* [1994] 5 CMLR M1, the Commission noted that their finding that the Regulation applied 'cannot be called into question by the fact that the Belgian state is not an undertaking' (para. 11). The fact that state involvement in industry and potentially in mergers is intended to be caught by the EUMR is further evidenced in recital (22) which makes reference to a general 'principle of non-discrimination between the public and the private sectors'. There is also specific reference, here, to the calculation of the turnover of an undertaking operating in the public sector. This rule does not apply, however, where the state is exercising its role as a public authority, rather than as a commercial actor.

19.2.2.2 'Union dimension'

Where a concentration has a Union dimension (referred to as 'Community dimension' in the Regulation as it dates from before the entry into force of the Lisbon Treaty) the EU Commission has, subject to specific exceptions set out on the face of the EUMR, exclusive jurisdiction within the EU to review that concentration. Article 21(3) provides therefore that 'no Member State shall apply its national legislation on competition to any concentration that has a [Union] dimension'. This provision therefore encapsulates the 'one-stop shop' underpinning EU merger control. For the purposes of the EUMR mergers have a Union dimension where:

(a) the combined aggregate worldwide turnover of all the undertakings concerned is more than EUR 5,000 million; and

(b) the aggregate Union-wide turnover of each of at least two of the undertakings concerned is more than EUR 250 million, unless each of the undertakings concerned achieves more than two-thirds of its aggregate [Union]-wide turnover within one and the same member state. (art. 1(2))

This basic threshold criterion is significantly higher than that which was sought by the Commission, both at the time of the introduction of the regime in 1989, and at the time of the 1997 revisions. In 1996 the Commission produced a Green Paper proposing that the thresholds be reduced to a worldwide turnover of €2 billion, and a Union level of €100 million. This proposal was rebuffed in 1997, when the Council adopted a compromise, leaving the basic requirement of art. 1(2) intact, but adding to it a new layer of jurisdiction now set out in art. 1(3). This is in the following terms:

A concentration that does not meet the thresholds laid down in paragraph 2 has a [Union] dimension where:

(a) the combined aggregate worldwide turnover of all the undertakings concerned is more than EUR 2,500 million;

(b) in each of at least three Member States, the combined aggregate turnover of all the undertakings concerned is more than EUR 100 million;

(c) in each of at least three Member States included for the purpose of point (b), the aggregate turnover of each of at least two of the undertakings concerned is more than EUR 25 million; and

(d) the aggregate [Union]-wide turnover of each of at least two of the undertakings concerned is more than EUR 100 million,

unless each of the undertakings concerned achieves more than two-thirds of its aggregate [Union]-wide turnover within one and the same Member State.

This test, while not going as far as the Commission sought, was designed to bring within its ambit mergers that would have faced multiple notifications in the individual Member States, although the Commission's own research indicated that only around 10 extra mergers would be caught a year under this rubric. As indicated above, the Commission is required to report on the operation of these criteria by the end of 1 July 2009. Article 5 of the EUMR sets out more detailed rules relating to the way in which the turnover of the relevant parties is to be calculated, and this is supported by further clarification published by the Commission.

Although it does not form part of the definition of a concentration having a Union dimension, a further jurisdictional test may be mentioned here. This is provided for in art. 4(5) which relates to situations in which a concentration 'is capable of being reviewed under the laws of at least three Member States'. In such a case the parties may notify the concentration to the Commission, indicating that they would prefer it to exercise exclusive jurisdiction. This is not an obligation on the parties, but is subject to their own assessment as to which route is preferable. In these circumstances the Commission is then required to transmit this submission to the Member States, and will assert jurisdiction unless any of the states express their disagreement within 15 working days.

Because the formula set out in art. 1 is not an obviously easy one to apply, a simple example of its application is given here (Figure 19.1). Many other permutations are of course possible, and the most effective way to understand the operation of this

Turnover (€ m)	A	B
Worldwide	3,500	2,000
Community-wide	1,500	200
Germany	75	100
France	110	15
Italy	100	30
United Kingdom	1,200	30
Netherlands	15	25
Two-thirds earned in one MS	Yes, UK	No

The acquisition of undertaking B by undertaking A (the two undertakings concerned) would not fall within the original jurisdiction of the Commission because B does not earn 250 million euro turnover in the [Union]. The acquisition would, however, be caught by the additional thresholds since:

(a) A and B each earns more than 100 million euro from sales in the Union (art. 1(3)(d) is satisfied);

(b) the combined aggregate turnover of A and B exceeds 100 million euro in four Member States (France, Germany, Italy, and the United Kingdom (art. 1(3)(c) is satisfied));

(c) the aggregate turnover of each of A and B is more than 25 million euro in Germany, Italy, and the United Kingdom (art. 1(3)(c) is satisfied); and

(d) the two-thirds proviso does not apply since B does not earn more than two-thirds of the [Union] turnover in the United Kingdom (or, indeed, any Member State) even though the acquirer A does.

Source: Cook, C. J., and Kerse, C. S., *EC Merger Control*, London, Sweet & Maxwell (3rd edn, 2000), p. 63. Reproduced with permission.

Figure 19.1 Application of operation of Regulation 4064/89, as amended

article is to work through some of these. The example given is taken, with kind permission, from Cook, C. J., and Kerse, C. S., *EC Merger Control*, London, Sweet & Maxwell (3rd edn, 2000), p. 63.

The two-thirds rule set out at the end of both art. 1(2) and art. 1(3) is designed to leave to Member States control over those mergers in which the effects will be very substantially felt within that state, even though these may also be situations in which the Union as a whole is affected. This test can produce unwelcome results. For example, in 1992 two undertakings, Lloyds and the Hong Kong and Shanghai Banking Corporation (HSBC), were bidding for Midland Bank in the UK. The proposed takeover between Lloyds and Midland fell outside the terms of the regulation as both companies had more than two-thirds of their turnover in the UK. HSBC, on the other hand, did not have two-thirds of its turnover in the UK, and accordingly its bid fell to be considered by the EU Commission. When the Lloyds bid was referred to the UK regulator (the Monopolies and Mergers Commission, now the CC) it collapsed. In effect the Union consideration of the HSBC bid gave it a substantial advantage; having satisfied the Commission as to the nature of the concentration, and its effects, this bid was successful.

There is no explicit territorial limit placed on the application of the criteria set out in relation to the Union dimension of a concentration. In recital (9) it is recognized that

The scope of application of this Regulation should be defined according to the geographical area of activity of the undertakings concerned and be limited by quantitative thresholds in order to cover those concentrations which have a [Union] dimension.

In recital (10) there is an express recognition of the fact that this should apply 'irrespective of whether or not the undertakings effecting the concentration have their seat or their principal fields of activity in the [Union]'. The effect of this is that a merger between two undertakings based outside the EU will fall within the terms of the EUMR as long as the relevant thresholds are met. This was the case, for example, in respect of the merger between Boeing and McDonnell Douglas in the USA (97/816 (1997) OJ L336/16), and between Gencor and Lonhro in South Africa (see *Gencor/Lonhro* 97/26 (1997) OJ L11/30; see also Chapter 4). In *General Electric/Honeywell* (Decision of 3 July 2001), the Commission blocked a merger between two American undertakings that had been approved by the relevant authorities in the USA. Article 7 of the Decision published on the Commission website makes clear the rigidity that follows the application of these straightforward turnover criteria:

The undertakings concerned have a combined aggregate worldwide turnover of more than EUR 5,000 million...Both GE and Honeywell have a [Union]-wide turnover in excess of EUR 250 million...but they do not achieve more than two-thirds of their aggregate [Union]-wide turnover within one and the same Member State. The notified operation therefore has a [Union] dimension.

The decision was upheld by the GC in December 2005 (*Honeywell International Inc.* v *Commission* case T–209/01, judgment of 14 December 2005).

While the assertion of jurisdiction over 'foreign' mergers is sometimes treated with hostility by the home states of the merging undertakings it is not unusual for extra-territorial jurisdiction to be asserted in the case of large mergers. The USA in particular has reviewed a number of mergers entered into by parties based primarily in the EU.

19.2.2.3 Notification

Although this section is concerned with the notification of mergers, it should be noted that it is in practice common for there to be contact between representatives of the merging parties and the Commission prior to formal notification. Any contacts of this nature are entirely voluntary, but the Commission itself stresses the usefulness that such contacts may have. In its *Best Practice* guidance, available on the DG Comp website, the Commission points out that in its experience 'in cases in which notifications have been declared incomplete, usually there were no or very limited pre-notification contacts' (at para. 7). The Commission is prepared to give informal guidance to merging parties where there is 'an actual, planned transaction', and if it is given sufficient information to permit it to properly assess the issue (*Best Practice*, para. 25).

Undertakings engaged in a merger with a Union dimension are required to pre-notify that merger to the Commission. This obligation, according to recital (34) arises 'following the conclusion of the agreement, the announcement of the public bid or the acquisition of a controlling interest'. No concentration with a Union dimension may lawfully be consummated until the Commission has taken a final decision as to the compatibility of that concentration with the EUMR. Notifications are dealt with in the EUMR, art. 4.

Along with the obligation to notify in the circumstances specified in recital (34), notifications may also be made in situations in which parties are contemplating a merger and seek the security of regulatory clearance prior to going ahead. Not all regimes require compulsory pre-notification: the US does, but the UK does not, for example. In recital (34) it is stated that notification is necessary in order 'to ensure effective control'. Article 4(1) states baldly that concentrations with a Union dimension '*shall* be notified to the Commission prior to their implementation and following the conclusion of the agreement the announcement of the bid, or the acquisition of a controlling interest'. However, the Commission will only accept such notifications where the parties demonstrate 'a good faith intention to conclude the agreement' or where they have announced their intention to make a public bid. This is to prevent the Commission having to consider numbers of speculative applications that would clog up its already overstretched resources. Notifications are to be made either by the parties jointly, or by the party acquiring control (art. 4(2)). Once a notification of a merger with a [Union] dimension is made the Commission is required to publish the fact of the notification, although in doing so it must 'take account of the legitimate interests of undertakings in the protection of their business secrets' (art. 4(3)).

Further provisions relate to instances in which the parties notifying the concentration consider that it may, in parts, fall within the jurisdiction of a Member State on the grounds considered below at 19.2.2.6. In addition, where the concentration does not fall within the EUMR thresholds, but where the merger would fall to be considered by at least three Member States, the parties may make a 'reasoned submission' to the Commission, informing it that the concentration should be examined by it (art. 4(5)). In these circumstances the Commission is required to liaise with the relevant Member States in accordance with the rules set out in art. 4.

Where a notification is made to the Commission under the terms of the EUMR, a standstill provision may be applied under which concentrations shall not be put into effect while they are assessed by the Commission. Provision for this is made in art. 7 EUMR. Any concentration 'which is to be examined by the Commission pursuant to art. 4(5) [EUMR], shall not be implemented either before its notification or until it has been declared compatible with the [internal] market' (art. 7(1)). On request the Commission may grant a derogation from this provision, permitting a merger to go forward, and may impose conditions or obligations if such requests are granted. As always the concern of the Commission will be the problems that may arise should a later decision be taken to the effect that the concentration falls foul of the substantive test. In practice it is rare for this part of art. 7 to be invoked, and is more likely to be employed in situations in which the undertaking that is being acquired is facing substantial difficulties such that its very survival is threatened. This was the case, for example, in *ING/Barings* (case IV/M.573 (1995)).

In the event that a transaction is carried out in contravention of art. 7(1) EUMR its validity is dependent on a relevant decision being taken by the Commission, and if no such decision is made, the undertakings may face a penalty of up to 10 per cent of their aggregate turnover under art. 14(1)(c) EUMR.

19.2.2.4 The substantive test

The most important difference between the current EUMR and the earlier version lies in the substantive test under which the concentration in question is to be evaluated. The test set out in Regulation 4064/89 was one exclusively related to dominance (discussed further below). As noted in 19.2.1 the EU Commission mooted, in the Green Paper, a move to the SLC test. The position in the EUMR is now a hybrid of the two tests. The central difficulty with the operation of the dominance test, as it stood, disregarding international convergence, lay in the application of the EUMR to situations in which mergers were taking place in oligopolistic markets, where single-firm dominance was not being created, but where the argument was made that a position of collective dominance (also known as 'joint dominance' and 'oligopolistic dominance') was being created. The difficulties of analysing such situations, and applying the law of dominance to them, are considered further below.

In recitals (25) and (26) of the EUMR the rationale for expanding the evaluative test, and the links between this and the dominance test, is made clearly, in the following terms:

(25) In view of the consequences that concentrations in oligopolistic market structures may have, it is all the more necessary to maintain effective competition in such markets. Many oligopolistic markets exhibit a healthy degree of competition. However, under certain circumstances, concentrations involving the elimination of important competitive constraints that the merging parties had exerted upon each other, as well as a reduction of competitive pressure on the remaining competitors, may, even in the absence of a likelihood of coordination between the members of the oligopoly, result in a significant impediment to effective competition. The [Union] courts have, however, not to date expressly interpreted Regulation (EEC) No 4064/89 as requiring concentrations giving rise to such non-coordinated effects to be declared incompatible with the [internal] market. Therefore, in the interests of legal certainty, it should be made clear that this Regulation permits effective control of all such concentrations by providing that any concentration which would significantly impede effective competition, in the [internal] market or in a substantial part of it, should be declared incompatible with the [internal] market. The notion of 'significant impediment to effective competition' in Article 2(2) and (3) should be interpreted as extending, beyond the concept of dominance, only to the anti-competitive effects of a concentration resulting from the non-coordinated behaviour of undertakings which would not have a dominant position on the market concerned.

(26) A significant impediment to effective competition generally results from the creation or strengthening of a dominant position. With a view to preserving the guidance that may be drawn from past judgments of the European courts and Commission decisions pursuant to Regulation (EEC) No 4064/89, while at the same time maintaining consistency with the standards of competitive harm which have been applied by the Commission and the [Union] courts regarding the compatibility of a concentration with the [internal] market, this Regulation should accordingly establish the principle that a concentration with a [Union] dimension which would significantly impede effective competition, in the [internal] market, or in a substantial part thereof, in particular as a result of the creation or strengthening of a dominant position, is to be declared incompatible with the [Union] market.

The test of significantly impeding effective competition will hereinafter be abbreviated as 'SIEC'. To encapsulate the principle underlying the new test more succinctly

[it] is intended to deal with situations of non-collusive oligopoly [i.e., situations lying outside the application of art. 101(1)] where the effect of the merger may still impede competition, although the merged entity's market share falls below the traditional dominance threshold. The new SIEC formula is likely to enhance the Commission's power to block transactions particularly in cases of 'unilateral effects' where a merger may reduce competition even though it does not lead to joint or single firm dominance. (Clifford Chance, 'The New EC Merger Regulation: What Has Changed?' Client Briefing, December 2003)

The legal test to be applied to any concentration with a Union dimension is set out at art. 2 of the EUMR. Article 2(2) provides that

A concentration which would not significantly impede effective competition in the [internal] market or in a substantial part of it, in particular as a result of the creation or strengthening of a dominant position, shall be declared compatible with the [internal] market.

The reverse of this is that a concentration which does significantly impede effective competition to the extent set out here, shall be declared to be incompatible with the internal market (EUMR, art. 2(3)).

19.2.2.4.1 Collective dominance under the EUMR

It has been noted above that the test of a concentration's acceptance is a hybrid of that of whether the merger tended to create or strengthen a dominant position, and SIEC. Until the revision of the EUMR the sole test lay in the first plank of this rubric. There was a clear linkage between the wording adopted in Regulation 4064/89, and art. 102, which makes explicit reference to a dominant position held by 'one or more undertakings'. The EU Commission, supported to varying degrees by the Court, has developed the law of 'joint' dominance, in the context of both art. 102 and the EUMR, to deal with situations in which dominance could be considered to be held by more than one party (in the context of merger control the economics of this situation is considered briefly at 18.2.2).

While the relevant law in this respect developed in tandem under art. 102 and Regulation 4064/89, from the operation of the current EUMR it is anticipated that there will be a separation between arguments made under art. 102 and those made under the EUMR. As critics of the Commission's approach have pointed out, this has in fact always partly been the case. An analysis that is taken prospectively anticipating future conduct is to some extent necessarily sundered from an analysis taking place with full knowledge (if not always with full understanding) of an observable market situation.

The starting point for the collective dominance case law was *Kali und Salz* case IV/M080 (1994) OJ L186/38 (on appeal *France v Commission* case C–68/94 and *Société Commercial des Potasses et de L'Azote (SCPA) and Entreprise Miniére et Chimique (EMC) v Commission* case C–30/95 [1998] 4 CMLR 829) in which a proposed joint venture was blocked on the grounds that it 'would lead to a situation of oligopolistic dominance'. This decision was affected by the fact that the products concerned—potash and rock salt—were homogenous (i.e., not subject to consumer differentiation), and that the joint venture would be matched by only one other Union producer in the geographic market. There were already close links between the undertakings concerned. The decision was overturned by the GC, but the Court accepted the basic argument that Regulation 4064/89 could be applied to positions of collective dominance. This case left some difficulties in its wake. In the course of the decision the Commission had made reference to 'economic links' between the undertakings, and it was unclear whether these links were an essential ingredient of collective dominance.

Collective dominance is also sometimes referred to as 'oligopolistic dominance', and although this term is not preferred it gives some indication of the problems that may be encountered in markets in which there are few players, and which tend towards parallel conduct, even if this falls short of a concerted practice (it will be remembered that undertakings are permitted to align their conduct to other undertakings if this is a truly independent action—see 'Concerted practices' at 9.2.3). If the number of undertakings in a concentrated market is reduced by a merger between two or more of them, a possible effect is that such parallel action is more likely. This will be the case in particular where the product is homogenous, the market is highly concentrated, the market is transparent in the sense that there is a strong flow of information, and the market is relatively stable.

The problems left by *Kali und Salz* were tackled further by the EU Commission in *Gencor/Lonhro* 97/26 (1997) OJ L11/30 (on appeal *Gencor Ltd* v *Commission* case T–102/96 [1999] 4 CMLR 971). Here the Commission made clearer its view of collective dominance, holding that

[it] can occur where a mere adaptation by members of the oligopoly to market conditions causes anti-competitive parallel behaviour whereby the oligopoly becomes dominant. Active collusion would therefore not be required for members of the oligopoly to become dominant and to behave to an appreciable extent independently of their remaining competitors, their customers and, ultimately, their consumers.   (para 140)

In *Gencor* the relevant market was that for precious metals, platinum and rhodium, worldwide, and there were only three significant competitors, all based in South Africa. The merger would reduce the number of competitors to two, and there was also a history of parallel behaviour in the South African market. The GC agreed with the Commission that the concept of economic links could be drawn widely to include economic interdependence, irrespective of the mechanisms by which this situation came about. Thus the GC held that

there is no reason whatsoever in legal or economic terms to exclude from the notion of economic links the relationship of interdependence existing between the parties to a tight oligopoly within which, in a market with the appropriate characteristics in particular in terms of market concentration, transparency and product homogeneity, those parties are in a strong position to anticipate one another's behaviour and are therefore strongly encouraged to align their conduct in the market, in particular in such a way as to maximise their joint profits by restricting production with a view to increasing prices. In such a context each trader is aware that highly competitive action on its part designed to increase its market share (for example, a price cut) would provoke identical action by the others, so that it would derive no benefit from its initiative.   (paras 104–5)

In another mergers decision, *Price Waterhouse/Coopers and Lybrand* 1999/152 (1999) OJ L50/27, the Commission recognized that some of the elements that had been mentioned in *Gencor* were also factors in the accountancy market. However, after the merger there were to be five competitors in the market and here the Commission held that 'collective dominance involving more than three or four suppliers is unlikely because of the complexity of the interrelationships involved, and the consequent temptation to deviate' (see paras 94–119).

The clearest statement of these principles to date, and in light of the amended test in the EUMR perhaps the final statement, is that in *Airtours/First Choice* 2000/276 (2000) OJ L93/1 in which the Commission blocked a merger between two companies in the UK market for short-haul foreign package holidays, travel agency services, and the supply to tour operators of seats on charter flights to short-haul destinations. At para. 87 of its decision the Commission set out the conditions that it felt needed to be in place for a finding of collective dominance to be sustained. These included: product homogeneity; low demand growth; low price sensitivity of demand; similar cost structure of the main suppliers; substantial entry barriers; and insignificant countervailing buyer power. The Commission expressly held that collective dominance did not require that there be any collusion between the parties, stating in response to concerns raised by Airtours that 'active collusive conduct of any kind is not a prerequisite for collective dominance to occur. It is sufficient that adaptation to market conditions causes an anti-competitive outcome' (para. 53). The decision came as a surprise to many, given that the market would appear to be very dynamic. The economic consultancy NERA argued, in its regular newsletter, that 'package holidays are differentiated, branded consumer products' and that the market was one in which 'there has been a huge variability in supplier shares and profitability and in which high profile exits…have been counterbalanced by instances of equally dramatic entry and growth'. On appeal to the GC the Commission decision was overturned (*Airtours plc v Commission* case T–342/99 [2002] 5 CMLR 7). At para. 62 of its judgment the GC stated that three conditions were necessary for a finding of collective dominance. This part of the judgment is of such importance that it is worth quoting at length:

— first, each member of the dominant oligopoly must have the ability to know how the other members are behaving in order to monitor whether or not they are adopting the common policy. As the Commission specifically acknowledges, it is not enough for each member of the dominant oligopoly to be aware that interdependent market conduct is profitable for all of them but each member must also have a means of knowing whether the other operators are adopting the same strategy and whether they are maintaining it. There must, therefore, be sufficient market transparency for all members of the dominant oligopoly to be aware, sufficiently precisely and quickly, of the way in which the other Members' market conduct is evolving;

— secondly, the situation of tacit co-ordination must be sustainable over time, that is to say, there must be an incentive not to depart from the common policy on the market.

As the Commission observes, it is only if all the members of the dominant oligopoly maintain the parallel conduct that all can benefit. The notion of retaliation in respect of conduct deviating from the common policy is thus inherent in this condition. In this instance, the parties concur that, for a situation of collective dominance to be viable, there must be adequate deterrents to ensure that there is a long-term incentive in not departing from the common policy, which means that each member of the dominant oligopoly must be aware that highly competitive action on its part designed to increase its market share would provoke identical action by the others, so that it would derive no benefit from its initiative...

— thirdly, to prove the existence of a collective dominant position to the requisite legal standard, the Commission must also establish that the foreseeable reaction of current and future competitors, as well as of consumers, would not jeopardise the results expected from the common policy.

In the present case the GC found that the Commission had made 'a series of errors of assessment as to factors fundamental to any assessment of whether a collective dominant position might be created' (para. 294). The decision was annulled.

In July 2006 the GC discussed the approach to collective dominance in the merger case *Impala (Independent Music Publishers and Labels Association (Impala, international association) v Commission* case T–464/04 [2006] 5 CMLR 19). This important and complex merger constitutes our key case of this chapter.

Key case 19.1 *Independent Music Publishers and Labels Association (Impala, international association)* v *Commission* case T–464/04 [2006] 5 CMLR 19—GC judgment (merger control); *Bertelsmann AG and Sony Corporation of America* v *Independent Music Publishers and Labels (Impala, international association)* case C-413/06 [2008] ECR I–0000—Court of Justice judgment (merger control)

Facts

A concentration was notified to the Commission on 9 January 2004 to be effected between Bertelsmann AG and Sony Corporation of America. It would involve a merger of the respective parties' global recorded music businesses (artists affected included Bob Dylan, Pink, the Foo Fighters, and Kasabian, among many others). On 12 February 2004 the Commission made a decision under art. 6(1)(c) EUMR, and on 24 May 2004 the Commission sent a statement of objection (SO) to the parties, indicating that it believed the concentration to be incompatible with the internal market in that it would strengthen a collective dominant position in the recorded music market, and in the wholesale market for licences for online music. However, the parties submitted substantial further economic evidence to the Commission which on 19 July 2004 made its art. 8(2) clearance decision, although the case was one of only 22 per cent cleared without any commitments being made. The applicants—who were not parties to the merger—lodged an appeal, and the GC agreed to the use of the fast track procedure.

The applicants relied on five grounds, all of which went to the substance of the decision, in that they argued that the Commission had erred in finding that the concentration, as amended by the parties, would not create or strengthen either individual or coordinated dominant positions.

Findings

The GC accepted that, under art. 263 TFEU, Impala had standing to bring a challenge to the decision taken by the Commission. The leading case in relation to collective dominance (coordinated effects) was *Airtours* (see 19.2.2.4.1), and the GC substantially followed the approach set out therein. It argued that although the conditions set out in *Airtours* were 'necessary' they could be established 'indirectly on the basis of what may be a very mixed series of indicia and items of evidence relating to the signs, manifestations, and phenomena inherent in the presence of a collective dominant position' (para. 251). In the present case prices had been aligned over the previous six years, even though the products were differentiated (as each CD album is different), and prices were held at a stable level even though demand had fallen. The GC held that in the absence of evidence to the contrary this would indicate the existence of a collective dominant position when combined with an oligopolistic market and stable market shares (para. 253). It was unusual for the Commission to have taken one position in its SO and then to make a volte-face in its clearance of the merger. Although the GC stressed that the Commission was not obliged to explain its decision 'by comparison with the [SO]' (para. 284) it did state that the 'fundamental U-turn in the Commission's position may indeed appear surprising, particularly in view of the late stage at which it was made' (para. 283). The relevant question, however, was not of the extent to which the final decision differed from the SO, but that of whether the final decision was sufficiently reasoned. The GC found that the part of the decision dealing with transparency in the market (a requirement for a finding of collective dominance) was 'insufficient' (para. 325), and that there was inconsistency between the arguments relied on in court and those advanced in the decision itself. The GC further pointed to 'numerous sources of transparency on the market', although the Commission had not found that the market was sufficiently transparent to permit a collective dominant position to exist (para. 364). In this respect, 'the evidence, as mentioned in the decision, does not support the conclusions drawn from it' (para. 377). The GC annulled the Decision.

It was not until 3 October 2007, some three years and ten months after the merger was first notified to the Commission that final clearance was given in a second decision (see IP/07/1437). This second decision was also challenged by Impala before the GC (it is worth noting that in 2008 the Commission adopted a third decision approving Sony Corporation of America's acquisition of Bertelsmann's 50 per cent holding in the capital of Sony BMG, which has not been challenged).

In 2008, the GC set aside the ruling of the GC annulling the first decision. The principal argument the GC relied on was that there was deficient reasoning. However, in analysing the approach of the GC, the Court of Justice found that it had in fact erred in law (paras 180–1). The GC had also pointed to the concerns raised in relation to collective dominance that were contained in the Statement of Objections (SO) and criticized the Commission for a lack of reasoning in abandoning these concerns. The Court of Justice found that complex assessments were involved and as such, the conclusions in the SO, the Court reasoned, must be considered provisional only. It is 'inherent in the nature of the SO that it is provisional and subject to amendments to be made by the Commission in its further assessment on the basis of the observations submitted to it by the parties and subsequent findings of fact' (para. 63).

The position that the application of the three-step Airtours test could be relaxed in the event that there is indirect evidence of oligopolistic conduct—for instance, when parallel prices occur—was not contested; however, the Court disagreed with the GC's assessment of the Commission's conclusions. It estimated that the GC had applied an unduly 'mechanical' approach (para. 125) and had misinterpreted the principles concerning market transparency (para. 126). Importantly, the Court of Justice found that the GC had relied on Impala's unsubstantiated allegations and documents which were classified as confidential (paras 97 and 107). Thus the GC committed an error of law in relying as a basis for annulling the decision on these documents which the Commission could not have employed as a basis for reaching its own decision (para. 102).

The case was referred back to the GC for reconsideration. On 30 June 2009 the GC declared Impala's appeal 'devoid of purpose', since Impala would have to challenge the third Commission decision in order to undo the merger, and the GC would have to adjudicate on the two previous challenges before coming to a decision on the third (para. 30). Given the length of such a process, even if Impala was to succeed it would be very difficult to dismantle the merger by the time the GC had adjudicated, and therefore a judgment on the challenged merger no longer has any practical interest (para. 29). As a consequence, the GC considered that there was no need to adjudicate on the matter (para. 32).

Comment

When the GC annulled the Commission decision, concerns were raised about the risk that clearance decisions could be overturned on appeal, as it could go some way to undermining a system based on compulsory pre-merger notification and review. The fact that a merger could be legal at the time of its consummation, based on a full review by the Commission, and then subsequently be deemed to be illegal on the grounds that its review was defective raised, to say the least, problems. The *Financial Times* reported that the case 'present[ed] a real challenge for the EU Commission', and 'shattered' the confidence of officials (Buck, T., 'Watchdog Reels at Sony/BMG Ruling', *Financial Times*, 13 July 2006). In the light of *Schneider Electric SA* v *Commission* case T–351/03, judgment of 11 July 2007 (see 19.2.5.1) it was feared that the Commission may be required to pay damages to parties whose mergers have been incorrectly blocked. More worrying were the problems that could arise were a consummated merger to be unravelled following a failure of the Commission to block a merger that has been cleared in error.

Although the ruling of the Court of Justice does not answer the questions above, it appears to have restored commercial certainty. Furthermore, the Court did make some important clarifications. It shed light on the legal nature of the SO, which is to be considered provisional and non-binding. This, it argued, is the only interpretation that ensures an equal standard of proof for the evidence presented by the parties after the SO has been drafted. Despite annulling the judgment of the GC, the Court of Justice did not accept the argument put forward by the parties that a notified concentration ought to be presumed to be compatible with the internal market. In addition, it is clear that mechanical application of tests to determine the likelihood of tacit collusion is unacceptable; the authority applying these needs to take into consideration the specific circumstances of the particular case. Following this decision, it is to be hoped that in future arguments as to the existence or otherwise of a collective dominant position can be avoided by reference instead to the SIEC part of the test of art. 2 EUMR, rather than by shoehorning such cases into a dominance analysis.

Van Rompuy has argued that the question that remains unanswered is whether the Commission possesses the means and the expertise to meet the standard of proof imposed by the European Courts (see 'further reading' below).

FURTHER READING

Articles

Hirsbrunner, S., and Köckritz, C., 'Rebalancing EC Merger Control: The ECJ's Judgment in Case C–413/06 P (Bertelsmann and Sony)', (2008) *Global Competition Policy*, July 08(2)

Van Rompuy, B., 'The Standard of Proof in EC Merger Control: Conclusions from the Sony BMG Saga', (2008) *IES Working Paper* 4/2008

19.2.2.4.2 The consideration of countervailing efficiencies

As with art. 102 TFEU, the EUMR is a unitary instrument—and any balancing of the good arising out of a concentration, with the harm that is anticipated to flow, is to be undertaken by the Commission. This is recognized in recital (29), as is the obligation of the Commission to publish guidance in this respect:

(29) In order to determine the impact of a concentration on competition in the [internal] market, it is appropriate to take account of any substantiated and likely efficiencies put forward by the undertakings concerned. It is possible that the efficiencies brought about by the concentration counteract the potential harm to consumers, that it might otherwise have and that, as a consequence, the concentration would not significantly impede effective competition, in the [internal] market or in a substantial part of it...

Article 2(1)(b) reflects this, as it makes reference to the Commission's ability to take into account, *inter alia*, 'the development of technical and economic progress provided that it is to consumers' advantage and does not form an obstacle to competition' (the same wording as in Regulation 4064/89).

The position as set out in recital (29) is somewhat different from that of Regulation 4064/89, under which it was argued that the Commission was not in a position explicitly to consider efficiency claims, an early provision to this effect having been removed from the draft of that regulation. (This subject is well dealt with in Lindsay, A., *The EC Merger Regulation: Substantive Issues*, London, Sweet & Maxwell (2003), at heading 8.2.) The Commission argued that the regulation did not permit such claims to be taken into account, either because such arguments were not well made, or because art. 2(1)(b) of Regulation 4064/89 did not allow them to be. There are, however, a number of cases in which it has been argued that such efficiencies have played a role in allowing the Commission to clear mergers that might otherwise have been problematic (see Camesasca, P. D., 'The Explicit Efficiency Defence in Merger Control: Does it Make the Difference?', [1999] ECLR 14). Camesasca accepts that 'the wording of the [regulation] legally does not leave scope for taking dynamic efficiencies into account once dominance is concluded upon' (at pp. 24–5). However, in *Aerospatiale-Alenia/de Havilland* (91/619 (1991) OJ L334/42), the first merger to be blocked under Regulation 4064/89, the Commission addressed the argument that the merger would reduce costs of production. The Commission, at para. 64, argued that any such savings would be 'negligible' and could, in any event, be achieved by other means. The mere fact, however, that such arguments were debated by the Commission, in the terms which were adopted, suggested that, in the words of Camesasca, 'the Commission requires efficiencies to be substantial and merger specific' (at p. 25). This position is reflected in the 2004 guidelines prepared by the Commission, which require any such efficiencies now claimed to be substantial, verifiable, timely, and of direct benefit to consumers.

Even allowing for the consideration of countervailing efficiencies it would appear that not all matters claimed as countervailing benefits will be accepted by the Commission. For example, in an appeal against the *Nestlé/Perrier* decision (92/553 (1992) OJ L356/1), in which the merger was cleared, trade unions argued that as a result of the concentration employment interests would be damaged. The Commission argued before the GC that it did not have any positive obligation to take such considerations into account, although the GC appeared to suggest that the Commission was, to a limited extent, required to consider the general aims and objectives of the EU as set out in, for example, former art. 2 EC. The GC rejected the unions' argument on the grounds that the workers' rights were protected under other EU instruments, and were not directly harmed by the Commission decision to permit the merger (*Comité Central d'Entreprise de la Société Anonyme Vittel* v *Commission* case T–12/93 [1995] ECR II–1247).

19.2.2.4.3 The economic assessment of concentrations
DG Comp used to have a Merger Task Force which operated alongside the other enforcement activities of the Directorate, with its own staff and procedures. In the run-up to 2004 and the 'modernization' of competition law, DG Comp saw some important restructuring, as a consequence of which officials of the Merger Task Force were gradually incorporated into other Directorates. The Commission has also appointed a Chief Economist to oversee the Commission's work generally in this area, and has set up an internal panel to assess the conclusions of the investigating team with a 'pair of fresh eyes'. It has been noted by commentators that the quality of analysis undertaken

in merger cases is more sophisticated than in standard art. 101 and art. 102 cases, and is having the effect of improving the standard of economic analysis overall. Initiatives such as the notice on market definition (see Chapter 14) have emerged in response to the experience gained in merger cases. In that notice it was recognized not only that the approach overall could be made more transparent, but that mergers and joint ventures required special consideration.

The Commission has published guidelines relating to horizontal mergers (February 2004) and non-horizontal mergers (October 2008), the latter covering also conglomerate mergers (defined in Chapter 18).

19.2.2.5 Procedures under the EUMR

19.2.2.5.1 Phase I proceedings

One of the defining characteristics of the EUMR, in contrast to arts 101 and 102, is that its operation imposes strict timetables on all the relevant parties, including the EU Commission, at all stages of the proceedings. Proceedings under the EUMR may be broken down into two main stages: Phase I and Phase II. Phase I applies to the procedures leading to a first decision, and Phase II to the procedures which apply when a more substantial review of the notified concentration is necessary.

Article 6 provides that the Commission is obliged to 'examine the notification as soon as it is received' (art. 6(1)), and the Commission has 25 working days to take a decision under art. 6(1) (art. 10(1)—although this time period may be extended where a request from a Member State is received under art. 9(2) (see below)). Three decisions are possible at this stage. The first is that the concentration does not have a Union dimension. In this case the procedures are terminated at this stage, the Commission recording that fact by a decision. The second scenario is that the concentration does have a Union dimension, but 'does not raise serious doubts as to its compatibility with the [internal] market' (art. 6(1)(b)). In this case the Commission shall declare that the concentration is compatible with the internal market. Any decision taken in this respect is also deemed to cover 'restrictions directly related and necessary to the concentration'. This is to say that any terms of the transaction which might fall within either art. 101, or national competition law, are cleared at the same time as long as they bear a sufficiently close relation to the concentration itself.

At this stage the undertakings also have the opportunity to offer 'modifications' to the transaction, which might include, for example, divestitures of certain elements of the package, or conduct remedies, designed to allay the serious doubts. Where such commitments are offered the strict time limit of 25 days for the making of a decision can be increased by 10 days to allow the Commission time to review these commitments. The GC has indicated that a different approach should be taken to accepting commitments at Phase I and at Phase II (see below). In *Royal Philips Electronics* v *Commission* case T–119/02 [2003] ECR II–1433 the GC stated that

the specific purpose of the commitments entered into during the Phase I procedure, which, contrary to the commitments entered into during the Phase II procedure, are not intended to prevent the creation or strengthening of a dominant position but, rather to dispel any serious doubts in that regard. It follows that commitments entered into during the Phase I procedure must constitute a direct and sufficient response capable of clearly excluding the serious doubts experienced. (para. 79)

The Commission may also, when making such a decision, attach to it conditions and obligations necessary to ensure that any commitments entered into by the undertakings are adhered to. Where any decision made under art. 6(1)(a) or (b) is based on incorrect information provided by the undertakings concerned, or where it has been made as a result of deceit by those undertakings, the decision may subsequently be revoked. Decisions may also be revoked if the parties breach any obligation attached to such a decision (art. 6(3)).

The third possibility is that the concentration both has a Union dimension, and 'raises serious doubts as to its compatibility with the [single] market' (art. 6(1)(c)). In this case the Commission will initiate proceedings under Phase II.

Where a concentration is notified to the EU Commission in accordance with art. 4, and indeed even where a concentration with a [Union] dimension has not been notified, 'it shall not be implemented either before its notification or until it has been declared compatible with the [internal] market' (EUMR, art. 7(1)). A derogation from these suspensory, or standstill, provisions may be granted by the Commission on receipt of a reasoned request (art. 7(3)).

19.2.2.5.2 Phase II proceedings

The central substantive powers of the Commission under the EUMR are set out in art. 8, which makes provision for the key decisions that the EU Commission can take. Article 8(1) provides for the making of a decision to the effect that the notified concentration is compatible with the internal market. Under para. 2 of the article the Commission may find that a concentration is compatible following the offer of modifications by the undertakings making the notification. It may also 'attach to its decision conditions and obligations intended to ensure that the undertakings concerned comply with the commitments they have entered into'.

Decisions taken pursuant to art. 8(1) or (2) 'shall be taken as soon as it appears that the serious doubts referred to in art. 6(1)(c) have been removed', and at the latest within 90 working days from the date at which the Phase II proceedings are initiated (art. 10(2)).

In July 2006, for the first time, the Commission originally lost an appeal against a clearance decision taken under art. 8(2) EUMR (*Independent Music Publishers and Labels Association (Impala, international association)* v *Commission* case T–464/04 [2006] 5 CMLR 19; an appeal against case COMP/M.3333 *Sony/BMG* (2004)—see also 19.2.2.4.1)). This was the first time *any* clearance decision taken by the Commission had been annulled, and the judgment caused a great shock. However, the decision of the GC was overturned by the Court of Justice. The complex Impala saga is discussed as Key case 19.1.

Paragraphs 3 and 4 of art. 8 relate to decisions made to the effect that concentrations are incompatible with the internal market. Here it is provided in particular at art. 8(3) that

> Where the Commission finds that a concentration fulfils the criterion defined in Article 2(3) or, in the cases referred to in Article 2(4), does not fulfil the criteria laid down in Article 101(3) of the Treaty, it shall issue a decision declaring that the concentration is incompatible with the [internal] market.

Decisions taken in respect of art. 8(3) shall be made within 90 working days from the date on which the Phase II proceedings are opened, although this period may be increased to 105 working days where the undertakings offer commitments, unless these are offered within the first 55 days, or where the notifying parties ask for an extension (art. 10(3)). All timetable conditions set out in art. 10(1)–(3) may be extended where the Commission, as a result of action by one or more of the notifying parties, needs to resort to the information-gathering powers set out in the EUMR.

Where a concentration has been wrongly implemented the Commission has substantial powers to require that the situation be remedied. Article 8(4) therefore provides that

> Where the Commission finds that a concentration:
>
> (a) has already been implemented and that concentration has been declared incompatible with the [internal] market, or
>
> (b) has been implemented in contravention of a condition attached to a decision taken under paragraph 2, which has found that, in the absence of the condition, the concentration would fulfil the criterion laid down in Article 2(3) or, in the cases referred to in Article 2(4), would not fulfil the criteria laid down in Article 101(3) of the Treaty,
>
> the Commission may:
>
> — require the undertakings concerned to dissolve the concentration, in particular through the dissolution of the merger or the disposal of all the shares or assets acquired, so as to restore the situation prevailing prior to the implementation of the concentration; in circumstances where restoration of the situation prevailing before the implementation of the concentration is not possible through dissolution of the concentration, the Commission may take any other measure appropriate to achieve such restoration as far as possible,
>
> — order any other appropriate measure to ensure that the undertakings concerned dissolve the concentration or take other restorative measures as required in its decision.

The Commission may also take interim measures where a concentration has been implemented, and no final decision has yet been taken, or a condition of implementation has been disregarded, or where a merger declared incompatible with the internal market has been implemented (art. 8(5)). While the Commission may at Phase II make a simple decision to the effect that a merger is to be blocked (art. 8(3) EUMR) it may also permit a merger to be consummated if suitable remedies are offered. At 19.2.2.7 several decisions in which the Commission has blocked mergers are considered in further detail. It will be noted that the effect of art. 8(4) (set out above) is that the Commission may impose remedies when it finds that mergers are incompatible with the internal market and have already been implemented. In both cases its approach to remedies will be broadly the same as regards their efficacy, although for the merging parties there will be advantages in discussing and implementing remedies prior to the consummation of a merger rather than following a finding that a merger has proceeded unlawfully.

In 2001 the Commission published its *Mergers Remedies Guidelines* (2001) OJ C68/3, which set out its basic approach to the imposition of remedies in such cases, and in 2005 it published a study analysing the design, implementation, and effectiveness of some 96 remedies imposed in 40 cases under the EUMR from 1996–2000 (*Merger Remedy Study*, available on the DG Comp website) (see also Went, D., 'The Acceptability of Remedies Under the EC Merger Regulation: Structural Versus Behavioural', (2006) ECLR 455). Revised *Mergers Remedies Guidelines* (2008) OJ 267/01 were recently adopted in an attempt to bring the regime in line with the 2004 EUMR, placing emphasis on the importance of structural remedies. Important changes include clarifications on aspects as divestiture, access remedies, and the role of the trustee. In addition, a new form (RM Form) is introduced which the parties have to use for the submission of specified information.

Former Commissioner Kroes stated in October 2005 that the Commission should accept remedies only when they 'clearly and unambiguously eliminate the identified threats to competition' (Press Release IP/05/1327). The most commonly imposed remedy is divestiture. As explained in the new *Mergers Remedies Guidelines*, structural remedies are preferable to behavioural remedies. The advantages of the latter over the former include that they do not require ongoing monitoring, or the establishment of complex supervisory mechanisms. The principle is set out at para. 22 of the *Guidelines* that the most effective way to restore competition is to create the conditions for either the emergence of new competition or the strengthening of an existing competitor. At Phase II divestiture remedies are far more common than behavioural remedies. The leading statement from the GC on the approach to be taken to remedies is found in the case of *Gencor*, at para. 316, where the Court stated that:

Since the purpose of the [EUMR] is to prevent the creation or strengthening of market structures which are liable to impede significantly effective competition in the [internal] market, situations of that kind cannot be allowed to come about on the basis that the undertakings concerned entered into a commitment not to abuse their dominant position, even where it is easy to check whether those commitments have been complied with.

This is, it may be argued, an overly conservative approach which creates a strong bias against the acceptance or imposition of conduct (behavioural) remedies, in favour of the imposition of one-off structural remedies.

Divestment remedies usually involve the undertaking concerned agreeing to sell a part of the relevant undertaking within an agreed period. Where divestment is required the Commission will insist that the divested entity is viable, and will impose a time limit within which the divestiture must be made. It may also require that it has approval over the transaction, to ensure that it is divested to a party or parties able to offer effective competition to the merged entity. In a few cases, in which divestiture appears to be difficult, the parties may agree to suspend a merger until a suitable purchaser is found (see for example *Bosch/Rexroth* case COMP/M.2060 (2000)).

The Commission remains open to the possibility that behavioural remedies will sometimes be more suitable than divestiture remedies, and there are cases in which such remedies have been accepted. These remain in a minority.

19.2.2.5.3 Investigation and enforcement
Regulation 1/2003 (see Chapters 5 and 6) sets out rules on investigations and procedures in respect of the application of arts 101 and 102 TFEU and not in respect of concentrations with a Union dimension. Instead the EUMR sets out its own rules relating to investigation and enforcement in this respect. The powers in the EUMR are stronger than those set out in Regulation 4064/89, and are substantially in line with those of Regulation 1/2003. Article 11 makes provision for requests for information. Article 11(2) allows the Commission to send a 'simple request for information' to a person or undertaking, and art. 11(3) allows the Commission to proceed by way of a formal decision. In both instances penalties are available if information provided is incorrect or misleading, or in the case of art. 11(3) is not supplied within the appropriate time limit. The Commission may also interview any natural or legal person, but only with their consent (art. 11(7)). Governments and competent authorities of the Member States are required to supply all necessary information to the Commission to allow it to carry out its duties (art. 11(6)). The Commission also has the power to conduct 'all necessary inspections of undertakings and associations of undertakings' (art. 13), and may ask Member States to carry out inspections on its behalf (art. 12). Under art. 13 the powers of the Commission are comparable to those of Regulation 1/2003, giving it the power to enter premises, examine books and records, take copies or extracts of these, seal business premises for the period of the inspection, and to ask any representative or member of staff of the undertaking for explanations (art. 13(2)).

Under art. 14 the Commission may impose financial penalties in a number of situations. Fines of 1 per cent of turnover of the undertaking or undertakings may be imposed in relation to procedural breaches, and fines of 10 per cent of turnover may be imposed in situations in which substantive breaches of the EUMR occur. As with Regulation 1/2003, 'in fixing the amount of the fine, regard shall be had to the nature, gravity and duration of the infringement' (art. 14(4)). There are no guidelines specifically relating to the imposition of penalties under the EUMR. Article 15 provides for the imposition of periodic penalty payments of up to 5 per cent of the average daily aggregate turnover of the undertaking concerned for each working day of delay from the deadline given in a decision to compel an undertaking to supply information, comply with an investigation, or comply with any decision imposing an obligation in relation to a concentration's consummation. As with all matters over which the Commission exercises jurisdiction, the Court of Justice has the power to review decisions taken by the Commission imposing a fine or periodic penalty (art. 16).

Before taking the decisions specified in art. 6(3) (revocation of a decision not to proceed to Phase II), art. 8(2)–(6) (Phase II decisions), and arts 14 and 15 the Commission must give the undertakings the opportunity to make their views known (art. 18). Decisions of the Commission are to be published (art. 20), but in doing so the Commission is to have regard to the obligation not to disclose 'information they have acquired through the application [of the EUMR] of the kind covered by the obligation of professional secrecy' (art. 17).

19.2.2.6 The role of Member States

Subject to certain specified situations the EUMR gives the Commission exclusive competence over concentrations with a Union dimension. There is a general obligation on the Commission to 'act in close and constant liaison with the competent authorities of the Member States' (recital (13)). The principle of subsidiarity underpins the EUMR. The operation of this principle in the context of merger review is set out in recital (8) which indicates that mergers 'the impact of which on the market goes beyond the national borders of any one Member State' should be reviewed at Union level. In fact this is not the case as is clear from the definition of Union dimension. Many mergers not falling within this threshold of jurisdiction will still have effects beyond the borders of a single Member State. At the same time some mergers having a Union dimension will have effects which are particularly pronounced in a single Member State, or in more than one Member State. In the appropriate circumstances, defined in the EUMR, such mergers may be referred back to the Member States, either in whole or in part. Equally, a Member State may request that the EU Commission take over jurisdiction in the case of a concentration which does *not* have a Union dimension, but which falls within the jurisdiction of the requesting Member State.

In the EUMR itself are to be found two exceptions to the principle of exclusive Commission competence. Article 9 makes provision for the referral of concentrations to the competent authorities of the Member States. Article 9(2) (sometimes called 'the German clause') provides that any Member State, either on its own initiative, or at the suggestion of the Commission, may inform the Commission that the Member State should be granted the right to assert jurisdiction where:

(a) a concentration threatens to affect significantly competition in a market within that Member State, which presents all the characteristics of a distinct market, or

(b) a concentration affects competition in a market within that Member State, which presents all the characteristics of a distinct market and which does not constitute a substantial part of the internal market.

Once these criteria are met, the Commission may, under art. 9(3), either deal with the case itself taking into account the concerns of the Member State, or refer all or part of the case back to the relevant national authority. A number of requests have been made on the basis of art. 9(3) of the EUMR. One such request was made by the UK authorities in the case of *Exxon Corpn/Mobil Corpn* (EC Case No IV/M. 1383; DTI press release P/99/780, 29 September 1999). Here the DTI welcomed the EU Commission's 'resolution of competition detriments in the North West of Scotland, following which the Commission did not need to refer the case to the UK authorities as had been requested'. In 2000 the EU Commission referred back to the UK authorities several proposed mergers, including Anglo American plc/Tarmac plc (DTI press release P/2000/19, 13 January 2000), Hanson plc/Pioneer International Ltd (DTI press release P/2000/212, 18 April 2000), Nabisco Group Holdings Corp./United Biscuits (Holdings) plc/The Horizon Biscuit Co. (DTI press release P/2000/280, 18 April 2000), Interbrew SA/Bass Holdings Ltd (DTI press release P/2000/585, 22 August 2000), and Go-Ahead Group plc/Caisse des Dépôts Développement SA (C3D)/Rhône Capital LLC (DTI press release P/2000/695, 20 October 2000). In 2003 however, only one such referral was reported, Arla/Express Dairies (OFT press release PN 74/03, 11 June 2003). In this latter case the UK argued that the market for the supply of fresh processed milk fell under art. 9(2)(b), and that the market for the supply of fresh non-bulk cream (cream for retail supply in small pots, or to caterers in larger pots) fell within art. 9(2)(a). This merger was subsequently approved by the UK authorities on 15 October 2003. This was the fifteenth such request made to the EU Commission under art. 9 by the UK authorities.

Article 4(4) of the EUMR provides that the Commission may itself initiate the process set out in art. 9, and parties engaged in concentrations with a Union dimension may alert the Commission to the fact that the whole or parts of the concentration should be referred to a relevant Member State.

Article 21(4) of the EUMR allows for referral of a concentration with a Union dimension back to a Member State in the event of there being the need to 'take appropriate measures to protect legitimate interests other than those taken into account by [the EUMR]'. These legitimate interests expressly include 'public security, plurality of the media and prudential rules'. These provisions are rarely invoked, but in June 2000, for example, the UK authorities asserted jurisdiction over the public security aspects of Thomson CSF's proposed acquisition of Racal Electronics plc (DTI press release P/2000/401, 12 June 2000). This provision was also invoked in November 2002, in the case of BAE System/Astrim/EADS (DTI press release P/2002/732, 22 November 2002).

Under the terms of art. 22 ('the Dutch clause'), Member States may refer a concentration to the Commission where it does not have a Union dimension, but 'affects trade between Member States and threatens to significantly affect competition within the territory of the Member State or States making the request' (art. 22(1)). This provision is rarely used, although in 2002 the DTI asked the Commission to consider the competition aspects of the proposed merger between GE Engine Services and Unison Industries (DTI press release P/2002/134, 28 February 2002). Once art. 22 is invoked the national authorities referring the matter to the Commission lose control over the process, and cannot determine the scope of the Commission's review (*Endemol Entertainment Holding NV v Commission* case T–221/95 [1999] 5 CMLR 611, paras 37–47).

In the rewriting of the EUMR in 2004 the Commission had hoped to extend its jurisdiction to mergers falling under the control of three or more Member States. This power was not formally granted, but art. 4(5) EUMR permits parties to a merger that would be subject to the possibility of review in at least three Member States to request that the Commission take exclusive jurisdiction. However, this process is not obligatory for the Commission, and may be frustrated by the objection of any relevant Member State.

A final exception to the principle of subsidiarity is found in the Treaty itself, at art. 346(1). This is in the following terms:

1. The provisions of the Treaties shall not preclude the application of the following rules:

 (a) no Member State shall be obliged to supply information the disclosure of which it considers contrary to the essential interests of its security;

 (b) any Member State may take such measures as it considers necessary for the protection of the essential interests of its security which are connected with the production of or trade in arms, munitions and war material; such measures shall not adversely affect the conditions of competition in the internal market regarding products which are not intended for specifically military purposes.

19.2.2.7 Mergers blocked

Over the years, the Commission has blocked a number of mergers falling within its jurisdiction under art. 8(3) of Regulation 4064/89. The most recent example was the prohibition of the merger between Ryanair and Aer Lingus (27 June 2007), a decision subsequently backed by the GC in June 2010. The courts have not always agreed with the Commission, and have sometimes given the green light to mergers originally struck down (such as in *Tetra Laval/Sidel* analysed below).

Three illustrative blocked mergers are analysed in this section.

19.2.2.7.1 *Tetra Laval/Sidel*

In *Tetra Laval/Sidel* the undertakings had already put into effect a concentration at the time at which it was blocked by the Commission. The notification was received on 18 May 2001, and the Commission found that there were three main horizontal overlaps in the relevant markets which lay in packaging systems for various foodstuffs and liquids. The undertakings offered commitments to the Commission to alleviate the concerns raised, but the Commission rejected these as being insufficient. At the time at which the Commission made its decision pursuant to art. 8(3) of Regulation 4064/89 (30 October 2001) Tetra Laval had acquired just over 95 per cent of Sidel's shares by virtue of a public bid. By virtue of art. 8(4) of the regulation the Commission presented to the parties proposals to remedy the harm, which required the divestiture of the two undertakings in a very short space of time. Tetra did not object to the divestiture, but did argue that there was no necessity to do this as a matter of urgency, and argued that there was 'virtually no competition at present between the two businesses'. The Commission did not agree, and expressed strongly its concerns about the effect of current investment and product development decisions on future competition between the parties. The Commission insisted that

An effective and final divestiture should consist of the sale of Sidel as a going concern without any change in its status, or in the scope or current range of its activities, which might weaken its viability and effectiveness as a competitor on the markets in question.   (para. 22 of the Decision of 30 January 2002, DG Comp website)

Tetra Laval would have the choice of the method of divestiture as long as this basic objective was met, and the Commission made an order to that effect. Tetra Laval was also banned from maintaining any minority shareholding or other financial interest in Sidel which might have the effect of impeding the restoration of competition.

The undertakings appealed both decisions to the GC, which annulled the art. 8(3) decision and found as a consequence that the divestiture decision was also invalid (*Tetra Laval BV* v *Commission (I)* case T–5/02 [2002] 5 CMLR 28; *Tetra Laval BV* v *Commission (II)* case T–80/02 [2002] 5 CMLR 29). The GC rejected arguments to the effect that the Commission had breached procedural requirements, but did find that the Commission had 'committed manifest errors of assessment in relying on the horizontal and vertical effects of the modified merger to support its analysis of the creation of a dominant position' (para. 141). Further, the Commission had overstated the conglomerate effects of the merger, and had wrongly disregarded the commitments offered by Tetra Laval. On 13 January 2003 the Commission lodged its appeal against the GC judgments, but it was dismissed by the Court of Justice (*Commission* v *Tetra Laval BV* cases C–12 and 13/03 P [2005] 4 CMLR 8).

19.2.2.7.2 Schneider/Legrand

In this case the Commission blocked a merger between two French electrical equipment manufacturers who were both active worldwide, holding that the merger would create or strengthen a dominant position in various sectors of the market, and that commitments proposed by Schneider were not sufficient (Commission decision of 10 October 2001). A number of relevant product markets were identified in the general area of individual components, or of particular types of switchboard, and other built products, and the Commission found that the geographic markets were national in scope. Brand loyalty was a strong feature of the market, with some electricians working with the same brands for their entire careers, with the effect that branding was very important, and that manufacturers sought to develop as wide a range of products as possible. This in turn raised a substantial barrier to entry, as any new entrant would have to build a brand from scratch. Further, there was a lack of price sensitivity. Prior to the merger both parties had very wide ranges of products and following the merger there would be only two countries in the EEA in which the combined entity would not occupy a leading position. The Commission also found that there was little countervailing buyer power, as given the fragmented nature of the market at the purchaser level, and the nature of brand loyalty, no buyers would be in a position to exercise a significant competitive constraint on the producer. In conclusion the Commission found that the merged entity would be able to raise the price of its products for its own benefit, and declared the merger to be incompatible with the internal market.

Schneider launched a successful appeal against the decision (*Schneider Electric SA* v *Commission* case T–310/01 [2003] 4 CMLR 17). The GC found that the Commission had failed properly to evaluate the geographic market, noting that there were different national geographic markets, but referring to the Europe-wide coverage of the merged entity to show that a dominant position would be created (paras 176–7). While the Court did not rule that the Commission could not undertake such an exercise it did require that were the Commission to do so it was obliged to demonstrate clearly the link between the two different geographic situations, and had failed in this case to do so. The Court further found that the Commission had failed to consider adequately the role of wholesalers, and had not demonstrated that they would be unable to exercise a restraint on the merged entity. The decision was annulled.

19.2.2.7.3 *General Electric/Honeywell*

The blocking of the GE–Honeywell merger was particularly contentious, given that the US authorities had expressly consented to the same merger proceeding (see above, at 4.1 and 4.2.2). The relevant parties entered into an agreement on 22 October 2000 under which Honeywell would become a wholly owned subsidiary of GE. The primary markets affected were parts of the aerospace and power systems industries, and the Commission found that 'in these sectors the transaction brings about significant horizontal, vertical and conglomerate effects' (art. 8—in all cases here references are to the version of the Decision published on the DG Comp website). In the market for the supply of jet engines for large commercial aircraft the Commission found that GE enjoyed several of the features of a dominant undertaking, and that the effect of the transaction would be to transmute this position of dominance into one of monopoly (para. 86). In the market for large regional jet engines there existed various factors which contributed to GE's dominance, including its considerable financial strength, and its ability to buy large quantities of aircraft and to offer comprehensive packaged solutions to airlines (para. 163). In particular, 'no other engine competitor has the size, financial strength or vertical integration to replicate such offers' (para. 173). In the market for avionics (products relating to the range of equipment used for the control of the aircraft and for navigation, communication, and the assessment of flying conditions) and for some non-avionics products Honeywell was found to be the leading supplier, and no competitor was able independently to replicate its range of products (para. 330). In the case of engine controls the merger would have led to vertical foreclosure effects, eliminating Honeywell as an independent supplier of engine controls to jet engine manufacturers competing with GE (para. 340).

Finding that the proposed merger would bring about anti-competitive effects, and that suggested solutions advanced by the parties would not be sufficient to remedy these, the Commission blocked the merger. Its decision was upheld by the GC.

19.2.2.7.4 *Airtours/First Choice and Gencor/Lonhro*

The approach of both the EU Commission and the GC to these mergers has already been discussed above at 19.2.2.4.1.

19.2.3 **Joint ventures and the EUMR**

Joint ventures (JVs) are expressly encompassed within the definition of 'concentration' at art. 3(4) of the EUMR. This provides that 'the creation of a joint venture performing on a lasting basis all the functions of an autonomous economic entity shall constitute a concentration'. The two key elements here are those of the JV being 'lasting' and 'autonomous'. In 1998 the Commission published its *Notice on the concept of full-function joint ventures under Council Regulation (EEC) No. 4064/89 on the control of concentrations between undertakings* (1998) OJ C66/1. Recognizing that JVs cover a wide range of activities, 'from merger-like operations to cooperation for particular functions such as R&D, production or distribution' (para. 3) the purpose of the notice is to draw a distinction between those JVs to which the EUMR applies, and those which fall to be analysed under art. 101.

The essential characteristic of a full-function (or 'concentrative') JV is that

[it] must operate on a market, performing the functions normally carried out by undertakings operating on the same market. In order to do so the joint venture must have a management dedicated to its day-to-day operations and access to sufficient resources including finance, staff, and assets (tangible and intangible) in order to conduct on a lasting basis its business activities within the area provided for in the joint-venture agreement.   (para. 12)

A JV will not therefore fall within the terms of the EUMR if it performs only a single limited function on behalf of its parents. This would include, for example, a JV limited to fulfilling a R&D activity, or producing goods on behalf of the parents, or principally acting as a sales agency merely distributing the goods of its parents.

Where a JV is found to be full function, and therefore subject to the EUMR (assuming the relevant thresholds are met) it may also serve as a means of coordinating the activity of the parent companies. If this is the case any such coordination is to be considered at the same time as the evaluation of the JV under the terms of the EUMR, although this analysis will be carried out through the application of art. 101.

19.2.4 Joint ventures and article 101 TFEU

Cooperative joint ventures are horizontal agreements which fall to be considered within the terms of art. 101(3) where they do not have the concentrative aspects that bring them within the terms of the EUMR. The EU Commission *Guidelines on the Applicability of Article 101 to Horizontal Cooperation Agreements* are the most complete statement on the position. There is a welcome recognition in the new guidelines, that it is the fact of horizontal cooperation, and not its form, that should form the basis of analysis within the competition rules. Thus the guidelines recognize, at para. 7, that there is a 'potentially large number of types and combinations of horizontal cooperation and market circumstances in which they operate'. In effect, therefore, the separate treatment accorded to horizontal joint ventures under the old Notice has been replaced by a more economically driven and less formalistic approach. Research and development agreements, and specialization agreements which take the form of cooperative joint ventures, are to be analysed in accordance with the terms of the block exemptions discussed above where the market thresholds are below the levels required of the regulations. Other cooperative joint ventures should be analysed in accordance with the principles set out in Chapter 9, and the guidelines are discussed there in relation to horizontal cooperation.

19.2.5 **Appeals**

As with other areas of the Commission's jurisdiction, appeals against decisions taken may be made before the GC. These may be made by either the addressees of the decision, or third parties with the appropriate *locus standi*, which may include those who have participated in the proceedings before the Commission, and might include, for example, competitors or others opposed to the merger. From 1 February 2001 a 'fast track' (or expedited) appeals procedure was introduced into the GC. The procedure may be made available where an urgency test is met, as will likely be the case in relation to a merger that has not been abandoned notwithstanding a decision by the Commission blocking the merger. The fast track procedure was used in *Schneider/Legrand*, and the case took only ten months to be completed. However, a consequence of the availability of this procedure appears to be that undertakings are more likely to appeal decisions against mergers. It has been noted elsewhere that prior to the availability of this process any victory by the would-be merging parties on appeal would likely be pyrrhic (see Nucara, A., '*Schneider/Legrand* and *Tetra Laval/Sidel*: Fast Track Towards Merger Reform?', (2003) *European Business Law Review* 193).

Appeals do not have the effect of suspending the decision taken by the Commission (see art. 278 TFEU), but art. 279 TFEU gives the GC and Court of Justice the power to order interim measures where it is appropriate to do so. This may be particularly important in cases where the Commission has ordered that partly or fully consummated transactions be broken up.

19.2.5.1 Article 340 TFEU

In July 2007 the GC handed down its judgment in the case of *Schneider Electric SA v Commission* (case T–351/03, judgment of 11 July 2007—at the time of writing the report was available only in French). The facts of the case are set out above at 19.2.2.7.2. The applicant then sought damages on the basis of art. 340 TFEU (see 2.3.4.4.1) which provides for the non-contractual liability of the Commission. The GC found that Schneider was entitled to compensation following the failure of the Commission to make the correct decision when it blocked the merger, although the Court did not determine the amount of damages owed. It required Schneider and the Commission to propose an expert or list of experts to the Court, with a chosen expert then being required to present to the Court a report assessing the damages that would be due to Schneider (see also Bailey, D., 'Damages Actions under the EC Merger Regulation', (2007) 44 *Common Market Law Review* 101, but note that this article was written before the final judgment in *Schneider*). Other cases have been brought on the same basis, but it is too early to determine the effects of the judgment. There has been speculation as to the effect on the Commission of having to pay what may be very substantial damages in the event that it is found to have acted incorrectly when blocking a merger, or when requiring, for example, divestiture, with some commentators suggesting that this may lead to the Commission being reluctant to condemn mergers.

19.2.6 Third-party rights

Third parties have only limited rights in relation to merger control. This should be the case. Mergers, particularly those which fall under the very high jurisdictional thresholds set within the EUMR, are complex and very expensive transactions, and the parties are entitled to enter into the transaction in an environment which produces legal certainty. It is also the case that the most likely complaint of a third party will be that they face increased competition from the merger, and it is not the purpose of merger control to protect undertakings from better competition. At the same time there may be some cases where third-party rights are genuinely threatened. It is only decisions of the Commission that may be challenged, under the rules set out in art. 263 TFEU, and only those with the appropriate *locus standi* may bring a challenge forward. In the case of *Zunis* v *Commission* case C–480/93P [1996] ECR I–1, an action was brought by certain shareholders who objected to the Commission decision taken in respect of the *Mediobanca/Generali* merger (case IV/M.159 (1991)). The Advocate General argued that while the shareholders were undoubtedly *directly* affected by the decision they were not *individually* affected on the grounds that there were some 140,000 of them.

Competitors may have the right to challenge decisions. This was recognized by the GC in *Air France* v *Commission* case T–3/93 [1994] ECR II–121 when it held that the decision was 'of direct concern to the undertakings engaged in the international civil aviation market or markets who could, on the date of the [decision] be certain of immediate or imminent change in the market'. In *BaByliss SA and DeLonghi SpA* v *Commission* case T–114/02 [2003] ECR II–1279 the GC permitted a challenge from a competitor which had participated in Phase I proceedings and which was active in the general markets affected by the merger, although the Commission had argued that BaByliss was not a direct competitor of the merging parties. The position of employees and workers' representatives is referred to in the legislation itself, with art. 18 EUMR providing that they 'shall be entitled, upon application, to be heard'. In *Comité Central d'Entreprise de la Société Générale de Grandes Sources* v *Commission* case T–12/93 [1995] ECR II–1247, however, the GC held that employees' representatives and trade unions seeking to challenge the decision to clear a merger did not have the right to challenge the decision on the grounds that it was not inevitable that any detrimental effects would flow to them from the merger. However, the GC did hold that employees' representatives had the right to protect their rights in relation to the EUMR procedures, which might include the right to challenge a decision where these rights were not observed.

19.3 The review of the Merger Regulation

The EUMR required the Commission to put together a report on its first five years of application by 1 July 2009 (arts 1(4) and (5)). As a result, on 18 June 2009 a *Report to the*

Council on the functioning of Regulation No. 139/2004 was published. On the whole, the Commission considers that the current merger regime is working adequately:

> the jurisdictional thresholds and the set of corrective mechanisms provided for by the [EU] Merger Regulation have provided an appropriate legal framework for allocating cases between the [Union] level and the Member States. This framework has in most cases been effective in distinguishing cases that have a Community relevance from those with a primarily national nexus, in pursuit of the objectives of "one-stop-shop" and the principle of the "more appropriate authority"... (para. 23)

Some room for improvement is nevertheless possible, in particular, in relation to the system of case allocation. It appears that a number of transactions with important cross-border effects still remain outside the scope of the EUMR. As a consequence, there is a recommendation that an effort is made to ensure 'further convergence of the various national rules governing merger control and their relation to [Union]' (para. 15).

Summary map

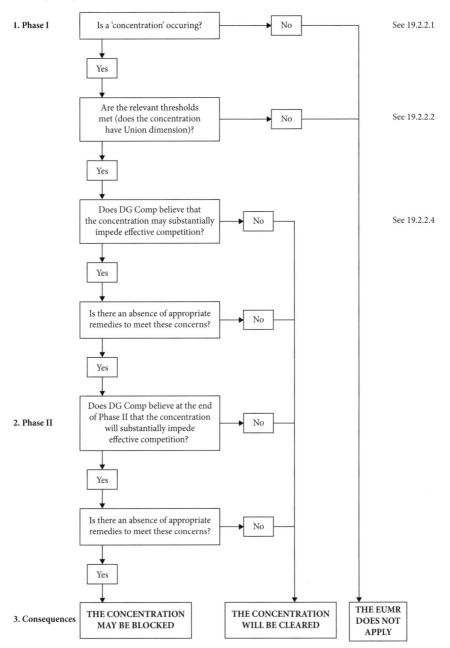

This schema presumes that there is no involvement of Member States in the process at any point.

FURTHER READING

Books

BROBERG, M., *The European Commission's Jurisdiction to Scrutinize Mergers* (2007) 3rd edn, Kluwer Law International, The Hague

FURSE, M., *The Law of Merger Control in the EC and UK* (2007) Hart Publishing, Oxford

NAVARRO, E., *et al.*, *Merger Control in the EU* (2005) 2nd edn, OUP, Oxford

Articles

BAILEY, D., 'Standard of Proof in EC Merger Proceedings: A Common Law Perspective', (2003) *Common Market Law Review* 845

BAY, M. F., and CALZADO, J. R., '*Tetra Laval II*: The Coming of Age of the Judicial Review of Merger Decisions', (2005) *World Competition Law & Economics Review* 433

KOCMUT, M., 'Efficiency Considerations and Merger Control—Quo Vadis, Commission?', (2006) *European Competition Law Review* 19

LUESCHER, C., 'Efficiency Considerations in European Merger Control—Just Another Battle Ground for the European

Commission, Economics and Competition Lawyers?', (2004) *European Competition Law Review* 72

MOTTA, M., 'EC Merger Policy and the Airtours Case', (2000) *European Competition Law Review* 199

PAAS, K., 'Non-Structural Remedies in EU Merger Control', (2006) *European Competition Law Review* 209

SCHMIDT, J., 'The New ECMR: "Significant Impediment" or "Significant Improvement"?', (2004) 41 *Common Market Law Review* 1555

TODOROV, F. and VALCKE, A., 'Judicial Review of Merger Control Decisions in the European Union', (2006) 51 *Antitrust Bulletin*, p. 339

VOIGT, S., and SCHMIDT, A., 'The Commission's Guidelines on Horizontal Mergers: Improvement or Deterioration?', (2004) 41 *Common Market Law Review* 1583

VOLCKER, S. B., and O'DALY, C., 'The Court of First Instance's Impala Judgment: A Judicial Counter-reformation in EU Merger Control?', (2006) *European Competition Law Review* 589

20

The UK merger control regime and the treatment of joint ventures

KEY POINTS

- Where a relevant merger situation is created, the Office of Fair Trading has the power to review the merger.
- Notification is, unlike in the EU, not compulsory.
- The OFT may clear the merger, clear it subject to conditions, or refer it for further consideration to the Competition Commission.
- The CC may clear the merger, clear it subject to conditions, or block it.
- The test of a merger's acceptance is that of whether it substantially lessens competition.
- Decisions of the OFT or the CC may be appealed to the CAT.

20.1 Introduction

The operation of the EU merger control regime was dealt with in the preceding chapter, where it was seen that, subject to only a small number of exceptions, where EU law applies to a merger it does so to the exclusion of relevant Member State law. The merger control regime of any Member State therefore remains very much a matter of national law, and jurisdiction may be asserted over any merger that is not reserved to the EU. The UK merger regime is set out in the Enterprise Act 2002, which replaced in this respect the regime of the Fair Trading Act 1973. The discussion here relates to mainstream merger control and does not include, for example, discussion of mergers in the newspaper industry, which have their own special regime. At the time of writing there have been few reviews of mergers under these provisions, so most of the discussion here is necessarily based on the words of the legislation and the relevant guidance.

Part 3 of the Enterprise Act 2002 made several key reforms to the merger control process in the UK. It was the shift towards an economic approach that drew most comment. In fact, however, this merely reflected a policy change that had already taken place in practice. A new test for a merger's acceptance, the 'substantial lessening of competition' (SLC) test was adopted, which is therefore not the same as the test in

392 Competition Law of the EU and UK

the EU regime, although again differences may be less noticed than the similarities in practice. Perhaps the most important change, however, lay in the redefining of the roles of the OFT and the Competition Commission (CC), with merger control now being largely a two-stage process—as is the case in the EU. In the UK the first hurdle the merger has to clear is that of the OFT, which may decide to refer a merger to the CC, or to try and negotiate a solution where it considers that there may be an SLC (the 'stage one procedure'). The CC has the role of evaluating a merger more fully following a reference by the OFT, and where it finds that the merger is to be blocked or condemned is responsible for imposing its own remedies (the 'stage two procedure'). In some special public interest cases, for example mergers in the media sector, the relevant Secretary of State may become involved. Both the OFT and the CC have published guidance in relation to merger control. On 8 September 2010, the first ever joint OFT/CC *Merger Assessment Guidelines* were published. While no major changes have been introduced, the new Guidelines introduce a consistent, updated approach and provide a comprehensive overview of the intricacies of the system. It is hopefully a sign of closer cooperation between the OFT and the CC.

20.2 **Stage one**

20.2.1 Notifications and references

Like the EU Commission, the OFT may be receptive to some pre-notification contacts and may offer informal advice to merging parties. However, it has withdrawn from a system under which there was a semi-formalized mechanism for this following a number of cases in which its informal guidance was later found to be inconsistent with the approach taken by the CC. The OFT recently reviewed the procedure for applications for informal advice in its publication *Mergers: Procedural Guidance* (June 2009), at ss. 4.28–41. If the parties choose to use this process, the OFT will provide them with non-binding information on the likelihood of the notified merger to be referred to the CC for review. In order to avoid an excessive reliance of this procedure, the parties are only able to seek informal advice when there is a 'good faith' intention to proceed with the merger (s. 4.30) and the merger raises genuine competition concerns (s. 4.31).

Unlike the position under the EU merger regime (EUMR) there is no requirement in the UK to notify mergers to the OFT. At the same time the OFT has a legal duty to refer certain completed mergers to the CC. This is the case where a relevant merger situation has been created which has resulted, or may be expected to result, in an SLC (s. 21(1)). While notification is, therefore, voluntary, there exists arrangements under which formal pre-merger notifications may be made to the OFT (Enterprise Act 2002 (Merger Prenotification) Regulations 2003, SI 2003/1369). These regulations are based on ss. 96–102 of the Enterprise Act. The procedures may be invoked only in respect of anticipated mergers which have been made public. Where a merger notice under the

Regulations is made the OFT has 20 days within which to make a decision whether to make a reference, although this period may be extended by 10 days if necessary. The merger notice requires the supply of a large amount of information, including, for example,

copies of analyses, reports, studies and surveys submitted to or prepared for any member(s) of the board of directors, the supervisory board, or the shareholders' meeting, for the purpose of assessing or analysing the proposed transaction with respect to competitive conditions, competitors (actual and potential), and market conditions…   (OFT, *Merger notice under section 96 of the Enterprise Act 2002*, June 2003, point 14)

The OFT publication, *Mergers: Substantive Assessment Guidance*, gives indications as to the situations in which the OFT is likely, or not likely, to refer mergers to the CC.

There are two major qualifications to the general rule set out in s. 21(1). The first is that where the merger does not affect a sufficiently important market no reference is necessary. In the view of the OFT this is likely to be the case only rarely. Section 22(2) provides that a reference need not be made where

any relevant customer benefits in relation to the creation of the relevant merger situation concerned outweigh the substantial lessening of competition concerned and any adverse effects of the substantial lessening of competition concerned.

The concept of relevant customer benefit is set out at length in s. 30 of the Act. Section 30 provides that a relevant customer benefit exists if it provides customers with 'lower prices, higher quality or greater choice', or 'greater innovation'. The benefit must accrue within a reasonable period of time, and must be unlikely to accrue without the creation of the merger situation, and the SLC.

The Enterprise Act 2002 gives the OFT the power it needs to obtain information relating to mergers that it is evaluating. Where notifications are made we have already seen that there are significant burdens placed on the parties, and s. 117 of the Enterprise Act provides that parties must neither knowingly, nor recklessly, provide false or misleading information. The OFT may request additional information, and time limits may be suspended when this is not forthcoming in a timely manner. In the case of mergers that have been completed s. 31 of the Act sets out the powers of the OFT to obtain information.

20.2.2 Merger situations falling within the Act

In order to qualify as a merger falling within the terms of the Act the requirements are that

- two or more enterprises (defined in s. 129) cease to be distinct; *and*
- the value of the turnover in the UK of the enterprise being taken over exceeds £70m; *or*
- in relation to the supply of goods or services of any description, at least one-quarter of all the goods or services of that description which are supplied in the UK are supplied by or to one and the same person (s. 23(1), (2), (3), and (4)).

These criteria, while being substantial, nevertheless caught a merger early in 2004 between Tesco plc and a Co-op store in Uxbridge Road, Slough (OFT press release 14/04, 2 February 2004).

20.2.2.1 Cease to be distinct

Enterprises 'cease to be distinct' where 'they are brought under common ownership or common control' (s. 26(1)). Three levels of control may be discerned: material influence over policy; control over policy; and a controlling interest in the relevant enterprise. Section 26(4)(a), for example, would cover the situation in which there was a change from 'material influence' to 'control'. Section 29 provides that in situations where control is obtained by 'a series of transactions', these may be treated as having occurred simultaneously on the date on which the last of them occurred, thus obviating the need to examine the transactions individually, consolidating the examination of all into a single reference. This applies only over any two-year period. Section 27 deals with the time when enterprises cease to become distinct. The effect of the section is to allow the authorities to treat any incremental changes in control achieved through a series of transactions ('successive events') as having all taken effect on the date of the last transaction, and there is no need to determine which precise transaction led to the increase in control necessary to qualify as a merger situation. The difference between this section and s. 29 is that s. 27 applies to what might be deemed a single transaction, whereas s. 29 applies to a series of discrete transactions.

There are various ways in which 'common control' may be found to exist. Section 26(2) provides that enterprises may be treated as being under common control if they are:

(a) enterprises of interconnected bodies corporate;

(b) enterprises carried on by two or more bodies corporate, of which one and the same person has control; and

(c) an enterprise carried on by a body corporate and an enterprise carried on by a person or group of persons having control of that body corporate.

There are three ways in which 'control' may be established: there exists an ability by the acquirer to influence the target's policy materially; the acquirer may have the ability to control the policy of the target ('*de facto* control'); and the acquirer may have a controlling interest in the target ('*de jure* control'). Whether there exists the ability materially to influence policy is a matter of judgement from case to case, and no precise rules can be drawn to determine this. Before 2009, it was already accepted that a shareholding of 25 per cent would be sufficient to meet this threshold. In *Stora Kopparbergs Bergslags AB/Swedish Match NV/The Gillette Company* (Cm. 1473, 1991) the MMC concluded that a shareholding of 22 per cent was, on the facts, sufficient to confer the ability materially to influence policy. The *Procedural Guidance* (June 2009) lowered this soft threshold even further, and establishes that 'the OFT may examine any case where there is a shareholding of 15 per cent or more in order to see whether the holder might be able materially to influence the company's policy' (s. 3.20). Furthermore, in some exceptional circumstances, even a shareholding of less than 15 per cent can be monitored 'where other factors indicating the ability to exercise material influence over policy are present' (s. 3.20). It is likely, however, that the OFT will need to consider aspects such as the distribution of the remaining shares, and the practice of voting at general meetings, where the percentages are low.

The OFT will thus take a case-by-case approach to the determination of whether *de facto* control exists, but it is clear that where a shareholding exceeds 50 per cent it will be presumed that *de facto* control exists. *De facto* control may also exist where the advice of the acquirer is followed in most cases, and in *Lonhro plc and the House of Fraser plc* (Cmnd. 9458, 1985) a reference was made when Lonhro proposed making changes to the way in which the House of Fraser was managed, and nominated 12 new board members. *De jure* control will normally exist whenever a holding in the target exceeds 50 per cent.

20.2.2.2 Turnover exceeds £70 million

The turnover test, set out in s. 23(1)(b), and expanded on in s. 28, represents a compromise between the Government, which had insisted on a figure of £45 million up to Third Reading, and the House of Lords, which was insisting on a figure of £100 million. The effect of the move from £45 million to £70 million is estimated to be that 50 per cent fewer mergers would be caught by the provisions. The value of the turnover, which must be turnover in the UK, of the enterprise being taken over is to be determined in accordance with rules made by the Secretary of State. The OFT has published guidance on turnover and its calculation.

20.2.2.3 Twenty-five per cent of relevant goods or services

A relevant merger situation is created where the merger creates or enhances a share of the market, however defined, of 25 per cent or above. Section 23 allows the person making the reference to determine what the reference framework in terms of the relevant goods or services is, as well as the appropriate benchmark by which the 25 per cent figure is determined. The OFT has indicated, in its guideline *Mergers: Procedural Guidance*, that

[it] will have regard to any reasonable description of a set of goods or services to determine whether the share of supply test is met. This will often mean that the share of supply used corresponds with a standard recognised by the industry in question, although this need not necessarily be the case. In applying the share of supply test, the OFT may under s 23(5) of the Act have regard to the value, cost, price, quantity, capacity, number of workers employed or any other criterion in determining whether the 25 per cent threshold is met. (para 3.55)

The reference to 'any other criterion' can make it difficult for companies to determine whether or not they are caught by the provisions of the Act. It may be the case that the 25 per cent market share arises in a part of the UK, and need not be in the UK as a whole. This 'part' must be substantial. For example, in a merger investigation in 2004 Hertfordshire was considered substantial, having a population of 1,034,000, an area constituting 0.7 per cent of the UK land area, and 'a number of important towns' (*Arriva plc and Sovereign Bus & Coach Company Ltd*, January 2005).

20.2.2.4 Territorial jurisdiction

The Enterprise Act does not set express rules relating to territorial jurisdiction, but the OFT has indicated that 'at least one of the enterprises must be active within the UK' (OFT, *Mergers: procedural guidance*, June 2009, para. 3.4). There have been a number of cases in which mergers entered into by 'foreign' companies have been subject to the UK regime.

20.2.3 Time limits

References must be made to the CC within four months of the completion of the relevant merger, or within four months of the notice of material facts being made public or given to the OFT, where this is later (s. 24). There has been no reported case in which the issue of 'being made public' was a key factor, and it has been suggested that 'the filing of documents at Companies House should be sufficient to place the information in the public domain and make it readily ascertainable' (Livingston, D., *Competition Law and Practice*, London, FT Law and Tax (1995), para. 33.52). Section 31 gives the OFT the power to request information in relation to mergers from any person carrying on an enterprise which has ceased to be distinct. The time limits provided for may be extended by a further 20 days by agreement between the OFT and the relevant parties, or by notice by the OFT where it has not been given requested information, where undertakings are being sought, or where the UK has made a request to the EU Commission under art. 22(3) of the EU Merger Regulation (see 19.2.2.6).

The 2009 *Procedural Guidance* introduced a fast-track reference procedure to the CC for mergers that clearly pose competition concerns (ss. 4.71–75). Those operations falling within the terms of the EA 02 may be referred to the CC within 10 working days of notification. The procedure can only be used if the parties have given their consent, and when competition concerns 'would impact on the whole or substantially all of the transaction' (s. 4.73).

20.2.4 Anticipated mergers

In addition to being able to make references in cases where a relevant merger situation has arisen, the OFT may also make references in respect of anticipated mergers (s. 33). In recent years, the majority of references have been in relation to anticipated mergers. Exactly the same provisions are made in respect of such references as apply to consummated mergers, save that in the case of anticipated mergers these operate prospectively rather than reactively.

20.2.5 The substantial lessening of competition test

Both the OFT and the CC must carry out SLC analysis. For the OFT the question is whether, in light of potential or actual SLC, the merger should be referred to the CC. For the CC the analysis is that of whether the merger should be blocked, or condoned, or if some remedy may be imposed that will render the merger acceptable. The broad approach to the SLC test is set out at para. 133 of the DTI *Explanatory Notes to the Enterprise Act 2002* in the following terms:

The concept of a substantial lessening of competition and its application to the context of a reference inquiry will be for the CC to explain in detail in its guidance. Similar language is used in the legislation controlling mergers in a number of other major jurisdictions, including the US, Canada, Australia, and New Zealand. The concept is an economic one, best understood by reference to the question of whether a merger will increase or facilitate the exercise of market power (whether unilateral, or through coordinated behaviour), leading to reduced output, higher prices, less innovation or lower quality of choice. A number of matters may be potentially relevant to the assessment of whether a merger will result in a substantial lessening of competition. The matters may include, but are not limited to:

- market shares and concentration;
- extent of effective competition before and after the merger;
- efficiency and financial performance of firms in the market;
- barriers to entry and expansion in the relevant market;
- availability of substitute products and the scope for supply- or demand-side substitution;
- extent of change and innovation in a market;
- whether in the absence of the merger one of the firms would fail and, if so, whether its failure would cause the assets of that firm to exit the market;
- the conduct of customers or of suppliers to those in the market.

Although the SLC test is not the same test as that adopted in the EC, it must be stressed that the SLC test replaces the test of the Fair Trading Act 1973 which was that of whether a merger might operate, or be expected to operate, against the public interest. In this context the SLC test is to be greatly preferred for its economic coherence, although an argument can be made that it would be preferable were the UK regime to adopt a test aligned to that of the EC. There is, however, no requirement that it do so at present, and in practice many parts of the analysis are substantially the same. The general concerns raised about mergers have been discussed in Chapter 18.

For the OFT to make a reference to the CC on the basis of an actual or anticipated SLC it is required that it 'has a reasonably held belief that, on the basis of the evidence available to it, there is at least a significant prospect that a merger may be expected to lessen competition substantially' (*Mergers: Substantive Assessment Guidance*, para. 3.2). The broad approach that the OFT will take to the SLC test is set out at paras 3.5–3.24 of the guidance. For the CC the approach is set out, in more detail, at Part 3 of its guideline, *Merger References: Competition Commission Guidelines*, June 2003.

One useful indicator of competition in the market place may be found in a concentration ratio, of which the most commonly used is the Herfindahl–Hirschman Index (HHI) (see 9.3.2.2). The OFT places some weight on this measure, and it has indicated that it

is likely to regard any market with a post-merger HHI in excess of 1,800 as highly concentrated, and any market with a post-merger HHI in excess of 1,000 as concentrated. In a highly concentrated market, a merger with a delta ['Delta' is the change in the HHI achieved by subtracting the pre-merger HHI from the post-merger HHI] in excess of 50 may give rise to potential competition concerns. In a concentrated market, a merger with a delta in excess of 100 may give rise to potential competition concerns.   (OFT guideline, para. 4.3)

For the CC, on the other hand, less weight is likely to be placed on these measures. It is not involved in the process of determining whether to refer a merger, and is more sensitive to a wider range of factors. Thus the CC notes that reference to concentration thresholds will be used 'only as one factor in its wider assessment of competition' (para. 3.10). Broadly the approach to HHI changes before the OFT and CC is as follows:

	HHI	Δ leading to concern
Highly concentrated	>1800	>50
Concentrated	>1000	>100

Where efficiencies are claimed for any mergers the OFT requires these to be demonstrable, merger specific, and likely to be passed on to consumers (para. 4.34). This follows the approach taken to consumer benefit in s. 30 of the Act, although efficiencies and consumer benefits are not exactly the same thing. This follows the response of the Irish Delegation to the EC Commission's suggestion that an efficiency defence be explicitly recognized in EC merger control:

The Green Paper seems to us to be inherently correct in expressing scepticism about efficiencies arising from mergers.

- Empirical studies indicate that, on aggregate, the *ex post* performance of merged companies is, at best, mixed, suggesting that efficiencies may systematically fall below the parties' genuine expectations.

- From an economic theory perspective, there is a fundamental doubt about efficiencies in mergers where market power increases. If we believe that competition is fundamental to driving cost reductions, then efficiencies are less likely to be attained precisely in the case where a merger creates market power...

- It is not always obvious that a merger (involving market power) is necessary to achieve many efficiency benefits.

- If an efficiency defence is allowed, then firms will have a strong incentive to exaggerate the efficiencies and it can be extremely difficult for a competition authority to verify them in advance. For this reason, the burden should likely lie on the parties to show the efficiencies, and a high standard of proof should be required.

20.2.6 **IBA Health Limited v The OFT**

At the end of 2003 a decision by the OFT not to refer a merger to the CC was appealed by a competitor of the merged entity to the CAT (see 20.5 for appeals). The case led to a substantial amount of litigation and clarified the criteria to be taken into account by the OFT when deciding whether or not to refer a merger. By an application dated 21 November 2003 IBA Health Ltd (IBA), an Australian public company and a global supplier of IT solutions to the healthcare industry, applied pursuant to s. 120 of the Enterprise Act 2002 (EA 02) to a review of the decision of the OFT not to make a merger reference to the CC on an anticipated acquisition by iSOFT Group plc of Torex plc, both providers of IT applications to the health sector.

The OFT found that by any measure the market shares of the parties post-merger would be substantial, being either 39 per cent of contracts awarded over the past five years, or 44 per cent of the installed base of systems on a historic basis. However, the OFT was swayed by the fact that a new procurement system for healthcare IT in the public sector in England was being launched, and the OFT took the view that this would alter the pattern of future purchases such that past market shares were no indication of likely success in the future. It was primarily on this basis that the decision was taken not to refer the merger. IBA argued, *inter alia*, that it would take many years for the new system to come fully on line, and that in the interim period the installed base would continue to be significant, particularly as regards contracting activity at lower levels in the health service.

The CAT held that the first question to be considered was whether the OFT was confronted with a real question as to whether or not it was, or might have been, the case that the iSOFT/Torex merger might be expected to lead to a substantial lessening of competition (*IBA Health Ltd* v *The OFT* [2003] CAT 27). The CAT suggested that in 'grey area' cases where real issues as to the substantial lessening of competition potentially arise, there was a two-part test. The OFT must satisfy itself that (1) there is no significant prospect of a substantial lessening of competition; and (2) there is no significant prospect of an alternative view being taken in the context of a fuller investigation by the CC (para. 197). The CAT held that where there is a real issue as to whether there is an SLC it is only in the exceptional case that the OFT should seek to resolve the matter itself rather than make a reference to the CC (para. 199). In 'grey area' cases it is inherently difficult for the OFT to explore the matter in sufficient depth to be able to decide *not* to make a reference with the necessary degree of certainty.

The broad question the CAT had to ask itself in the course of such a proceeding as in the present case was whether it was satisfied that the OFT's decision was not erroneous in law, and was one which it was reasonably open to the OFT to take, giving the word 'reasonably' its ordinary and natural meaning (para. 225). The Tribunal was unable, on the basis of the evidence before it, to be satisfied that the OFT had asked itself the right question, namely whether the OFT was satisfied *not only* that there was no significant prospect of an SLC *but also* that there was no significant prospect of the CC reaching an alternative view after a fuller investigation (para. 232). The CAT quashed the decision, and the OFT appealed to the Court of Appeal (*OFT and others* v *IBA Health Ltd* [2004] EWCA Civ 142).

The Court of Appeal held that the two-part test formulated by the CAT was not the right test to apply, and that the right test was that stated in s. 33(1). It was necessary for the OFT to form the relevant belief which must be reasonable and objectively justified by the relevant facts. The test for the OFT was whether the anticipated merger 'may result in a relevant merger situation or not'. The CAT did, however, apply the proper standards for judicial review. It did not reverse the burden of proof on the applicant, but was entitled and bound to examine with care why adverse hypotheses were rejected by the OFT in so short a time, and whether that rejection was justified, particularly in view of the statutory requirement on the OFT to give reasons (para. 57). The Court held that the OFT applied too high a test of likelihood when forming their belief, or failed to adequately justify the belief that they formed in accordance with the proper test. Notwithstanding the fact that the CAT adopted a wrong test as to likelihood, their ultimate conclusion was right and should be upheld (para. 75).

20.2.7 Initial and interim measures, and undertakings in lieu of references

Where the OFT is considering whether to make a reference under s. 22, it may, for the purpose of preventing pre-emptive action, that is to say action taken by the companies which might thwart the OFT or the CC, accept undertakings from the relevant parties to take such action(s) as it considers to be appropriate (s. 71). The OFT's *Mergers: Substantive Assessment Guidance* (May 2003) points to the sorts of situations in which such undertakings may be appropriate:

undertakings in lieu have typically been used in merger cases in the past where a substantial lessening of competition arises from an overlap that is relatively small in the context of the merger (e.g. a few local markets affected by a national merger.   (para. 8.3)

The OFT has stated that it will consider any initiatives taken by the merging parties to propose undertakings in lieu of a reference, and may itself invite undertakings to be made. There have been a number of cases already in which the OFT has sought undertakings in lieu of references. These are always notified on the OFT website. For example, in relation to the acquisition of the Wales and Borders rail franchise by Arriva plc the latter company indicated that it would be willing to offer an undertaking opening up integrated ticketing arrangements to bus companies. This dealt with the OFT concern that competition from rival bus companies could be harmed if Arriva introduced integrated ticketing only in relation to its own services (OFT press release 44/04, 16 March 2004). Undertakings were also accepted from Tesco plc in relation to its purchase of the Slough Co-op store, which it agreed to sell (OFT press release 14/04, 2 February 2004). The CAT considered the effect of undertakings in lieu of a reference in the case of *Co-operative Group (CWS) Ltd* v *OFT* [2007] CAT 24. In that case the OFT had accepted undertakings relating to a divestiture of part of the merged enterprise, but had then refused its permission for the sale to be made to a particular purchaser. The CAT gave the OFT a considerable margin of appreciation, holding that where undertakings were accepted in lieu of a reference this pre-empted a detailed investigation into the full competitive scenario, which would take place only in the event that a reference was made to the CC. The merging parties could refuse to offer such an undertaking and could instead take their chances with the CC. If undertakings were offered this was because the parties decided that it was preferable to do so, and they would, unless there were manifest errors, be held to them.

As an alternative to accepting undertakings under s. 71, the OFT may make initial enforcement orders under s. 72. For such an order to be made, the OFT has to believe not only that a relevant merger situation has been created, but also that pre-emptive action is either in progress or in contemplation. Since the concern raised by mergers is a structural one, the OFT has indicated that it is more likely to accept structural than behavioural undertakings (*Mergers: Substantive Assessment Guidance* (May 2003) paras 8.6–8.9). Once an undertaking has been accepted, the OFT is prevented from making a reference in relation to the merger situation, unless material facts have not been notified to the OFT or made public before the undertaking concerned was accepted (s. 73(2)).

Where an undertaking made under s. 73 is not being fulfilled, or where information given to the OFT or made public, which informed the undertaking, was false or misleading, the OFT may make an order compelling performance, or anything permitted by Sch. 8 (s. 75—see 20.3.5 below).

Standstill provisions are enshrined in ss. 77 and 78. In the first case, once a completed merger has been referred to the CC, the parties are prevented from completing any arrangements which have resulted in the merger, or making further arrangements in consequence of that result, or transferring the ownership or control of any enterprises to which the reference relates (s. 77(2)). The consent of the CC may be given to such transactions, however. These provisions apply also to a person's conduct outside the UK, but only if he is: (a) a UK national; or (b) a body incorporated under the law of the UK, or any part of the UK; or (c) a person carrying on business in the UK. Section 78 operates in relation to anticipated mergers, and imposes a prohibition on the acquisition or transfer of shares (directly or indirectly) in a company in any enterprise to which the merger reference relates during the relevant period.

Section 80 gives the CC the power to accept interim undertakings once a reference has been made to it. These undertakings may be, in addition to any initial undertakings, accepted by the OFT, or may be a re-adoption of OFT undertakings in the appropriate circumstances.

According to the 2009 *Procedural Guidance*, the OFT may accept binding undertakings in lieu of reference to the CC, if and when those undertakings are enough to remedy the competition concerns. Until now, the parties only had one opportunity to make an offer and avoid a review. The new Guidance establishes an exception in 'near miss' cases when the undertakings almost solved the competition concerns, provided that the offers were in good faith and credible (s. 8.21). In such circumstances, the OFT will give the parties a second opportunity to clarify their initial undertakings (s. 8.19). As regards hold-separate undertakings—those initial undertakings to suspend integration if a problem is identified in a completed merger that was not originally notified—the Guidance clarifies that the OFT may request them where it suspects that the completed merger may raise competition concerns and undertakings are appropriate to prevent integration.

20.3 **Stage two**

20.3.1 **Questions to be decided by the CC**

In addition to determining whether there is a relevant merger, and whether it may result in an SLC, the CC is required to consider what actions it should take in order to prevent, mitigate, or remedy the SLC. It is required in this respect

to have regard to the need to achieve as comprehensive a solution as is reasonable and practicable to the substantial lessening of competition and any adverse effects arising from it. (s. 35(4))

This provision is elaborated on in the *Explanatory Notes* at para. 134:

The reference to a 'comprehensive solution' will require the CC to consider remedies that address the substantial lessening of competition itself (e.g. the features arising from the merger that give rise to the creation of market power) because it is generally more effective to tackle the cause of any problems at their source rather than by tackling the symptoms or adverse effects.

This appears to be suggesting that structural remedies—either blocking an anticipated merger, or requiring divestiture post-merger—are to be generally preferred to conduct remedies where the CC has found that there is SLC flowing from the merger. The application of remedies by the CC is considered in Part 4 of its merger guidelines.

The CC is also required to take into account any relevant customer benefits that flow from the merger, and to balance these against the SLC. Where the CC identifies that a merger has an anti-competitive outcome, it is under a duty, imposed on it by s. 41, so far as it is practicable and reasonable to do so, to remedy, mitigate, or prevent the adverse effects in relation both to the SLC itself and from any effects of the SLC. In doing so, it is given the discretion to take into account any relevant customer benefits, and has scope

if it considers that customer benefits are of sufficient importance, to impose a lesser competition remedy or no remedy at all if the only steps that the CC could take to remedy the competition problem are steps that would mean that the customer benefits could not be realised. (*Explanatory Notes*, para. 149)

The CC itself has indicated that it would be likely that remedial action would be required in situations in which it determined that a merger would be likely to result in an SLC, unless it did identify the existence of customer benefits. There might also be some other rare cases, such as where any remedial action lay outside the jurisdiction of the UK, where it would be outside the power of the CC to impose a remedy.

The CC will also consider the cost of any remedy when considering whether to impose it. However, the CC has indicated that in the case of completed mergers, it will not consider the costs of divestment to the parties, as the parties would have had the opportunity to seek a clearance of the merger prior to its consummation. Nor will the CC consider costs outside the competitive structure, such as environmental costs, or the social costs of unemployment, unless it is required to do so by the Secretary of State through the imposition of a specified public interest consideration (see below).

Remedies should also be proportional to the harm identified as arising out of the merger. This means that where two remedies are being considered, each of which is equally effective, the cheaper should be the one chosen.

The types of remedies that are available to the CC are set out at para. 4.17 of its guidelines as follows:

The CC will consider any of the following types of remedies:

(a) remedies that are intended to restore all or part of the status quo ante market structure, for example:
  - prohibition of a proposed merger;
  - divestment of a completed acquisition;
  - partial prohibition or divestment;

(b) remedies that are intended to increase the competition that will be faced by the merged firm (whether from existing competitors or new entrants), for example
  - requiring access to essential inputs/facilities;
  - licensing know-how or IPRs;
  - dismantling exclusive distribution arrangements;
  - removing no-competition clauses in customer contracts;

(c) remedies aimed at excluding or limiting the possibility that the merged firm will take advantage of the increased market power resulting from the merger to behave anti-competitively or to exploit its customers or suppliers, for example:
  - a price cap or other restraint on prices;
  - a commitment to non-discriminatory behaviour;
  - an obligation to increase the transparency of prices;
  - an obligation to refrain from conduct, the main purpose of which is to inhibit entry.

The starting point for the CC when considering its approach to the remedy, if one is considered necessary, will be to choose the action that is most likely to restore the competition that has been damaged by the merger (para. 4.23). This is to say that, like the OFT, it is more likely to favour structural remedies than behavioural remedies. An additional factor in favour of structural remedies is that they do not require ongoing policing. The CC may also recommend that action be taken by others, for example, by way of legislation, where regulations exist that limit entry, or to amend licence conditions in the case of regulated undertakings.

20.3.2 Merger reports

The CC is required to publish a report on a merger reference within a period of 24 weeks from the date of the reference concerned (ss. 38(1) and 39(1)), although, in exceptional circumstances, this period may be extended by up to a further eight weeks (s. 39(3)). The period may also be extended where a relevant person has failed to comply with the requirements of s. 109, which relates to the attendance of witnesses and the production of documents. This report is to contain its decision, the reasons for its decision, and any information necessary to understand the decision. It has the power to carry out necessary investigations in order to prepare the report (s. 38(2)).

20.3.4 **Powers of investigation**

Sections 109–17 deal with the power of the CC to require the presentation of evidence and documents needed for the purposes of a merger inquiry. Section 109 confers on the CC the power to compel the attendance of witnesses and the production of documents. A notice may be given to any person requiring them to attend a specified hearing, and to give evidence to the CC or a person nominated by the CC (s. 109(1)). A similar power exists in relation to the presentation of documents. The CC may also require the supply of 'estimates, forecasts returns or other information' (s. 109(3)). The CC may take evidence on oath (s. 109(5)). No material may be required where the production of such could not be compelled in civil proceedings before a court. This preserves the right against self-incrimination, and a protection in respect of legally privileged material. In the context of a wide-ranging mergers investigation, it is unlikely that these limitations would be often invoked.

Where the CC finds that a person has, without reasonable cause, failed to comply with an obligation imposed by way of s. 109, it may directly impose a penalty on that person, subject to an appeal to the CAT (s. 110(1)). Any penalty imposed under this section 'shall be of such an amount as the Commission considers appropriate' (s. 111(1)). The amount may be fixed, or may be calculated on a daily rate until such time as compliance is ensured. An offence is committed if any person intentionally alters, suppresses, or destroys any document which he has been required to produce, and, on conviction, he may face a fine not exceeding the statutory maximum, or a term of imprisonment not exceeding two years, or a combination of the two. However, no offence may be deemed to have been committed if the CC has acted under s. 110(1) and imposed its own penalty. The maximum penalty that may be imposed in the case of a fixed amount is £30,000, and, in the case of a daily penalty, the maximum amount per day is £15,000 (s. 111(7)). Where it imposes a penalty, the CC is required, as soon as is practicable, to give a notice relating to the penalty. The person to whom the notice is addressed may, within 14 days, apply to the CC for it to specify a different rate, or different dates for payment of the penalty. The CC has published its *Statement of Policy on Penalties* (June 2003) which deals in particular with the assessment of situations in which there has been a failure to comply with the requirement to supply information, and the imposition of penalties in relation to this. In relation to the failure to supply information, the CC will consider 'whether there is any reasonable excuse for the failure to comply, and, in particular, 'the extent to which the failure arose from circumstances outside the control of the person who has failed to comply' (para. 12). Five factors are set out as being likely to increase the prospect of a penalty being imposed (para. 13):

(i)   the failure affected the efficient carrying out of the CC's functions;

(ii) other persons were adversely affected;

(iii) deterrence of future non-compliance;

(iv) the absence of good reason; and

(v) whether the person failing to comply sought to gain, or did gain, by so doing.

Appeals against penalties may be made to the CAT. Appeals may be made against the imposition or nature of the penalty, the amount of the penalty, and the date on which the penalty is to be paid (s. 114). The CAT may not substitute its own assessment of the penalty unless the substituted figure is lower than the figure that would be required by the CC. A further appeal may be made to the Court of Appeal against the judgment of the CAT (s. 114(10)).

An offence is committed in any case if a person supplies the OFT or the CC or the Secretary of State with information that is false or misleading in a material respect, knowing that to be the case, or recklessly to that effect (s. 117).

20.3.5 **Final powers of the CC**

The CC has the power to accept final undertakings from parties in order to remedy concerns raised in its reports (s. 82). It also has the power to make orders where any such final undertakings are not fulfilled, or where information which was false or misleading in a material respect was given to it or to the OFT. If an order is made under this section, it may not be varied or revoked unless the OFT advises that such a change is appropriate in the light of changed circumstances. Final orders may also be made by the CC, in accordance with s. 41 (s. 84). Any order made under this section may contain anything permitted by Sch. 8. No order shall be made under this section if an undertaking has been accepted and is being complied with under s. 82. An undertaking made under s. 82 may contain matters *not* set out in Sch. 8 (s. 89).

Schedule 8 contains the list of matters that may be imposed in orders for the purpose of remedying any adverse effects of mergers identified by the CC in its report. Most of the items set out in the Schedule are self-explanatory. The most significant of the new items included on the list is that at para. 10, under which an order may require any relevant person to supply goods or services 'to a particular standard or in a particular manner'. An example of the way in which this provision might be applied is given in the *Explanatory Notes* and relates to the fact that it would be possible to tell a bus company to maintain a certain frequency of service (para. 238).

Key discussion 20.1 Weakening the authority of competition law at a time of crisis? A reflection on the Lloyds–HBOS merger

In a time of great instability in the world's financial markets, and following a steep drop in the value of Halifax/Bank of Scotland (HBOS) shares, the Lloyds TSB Group plc announced in September 2008 that it intended to acquire HBOS. The merger was to bring together Britain's fourth and fifth largest banks. The resulting entity would enjoy almost 30 per cent of the markets for both retail banking and mortgages, and 18 per cent of the life insurance market. As such, it was to become the biggest operator in all three markets. Moreover, in Scotland the deal was to give the new super bank between 40 and 50 per cent of small-business services. It is clear that the planned merger raises serious competition concerns. Indeed, such an operation would be simply inconceivable under normal circumstances, as evidenced by the fact that in 2001 Lloyds TSB sought to purchase the Abbey National in similar conditions, yet the merger plan was rejected due to fear of a substantial lessening of competition. Such worries appear to have been downplayed in the current exceptional economic circumstances.

In the months following the announcement of the proposal, shareholders and politicians voiced their concerns. Importantly, the OFT issued a report in October 2008 (OFT, *Anticipated Acquisition by Lloyds TSB plc of HBOS plc: Report to the Secretary of State for Business Enterprise and Regulatory Reform*) where it concluded that it is likely that there will be a substantial lessening of competition 'in relation to personal current accounts (PCAs), banking services for small and medium sized enterprises (SMEs) and mortgages' (para. 2). As a consequence, it recommended referring the matter to the Competition Commission (CC) under s. 33 of the EA 02. The conclusion of the report is moreover coherent with the OFT's earlier study in July 2008 of PCAs in the UK (OFT, *Personal Current Accounts in the UK: An OFT Market Study*), where it found that the market was relatively concentrated, barriers to entry existed, and demand elasticity was low as consumers were slow to switch providers (p. 4). In spite of these findings, the OFT report does reflect the leading position of a raft of stakeholders that 'in light of the extraordinary conditions in the financial markets, the merger would support financial stability, and was therefore in the public interest' (para. 19). The OFT received submissions from both HBOS and Lloyds TSB, the Financial Services Authority, the Treasury, the Bank of England, the First Minister of Scotland, third parties active in the financial services sector, consumer interest groups, one newspaper, and several individuals (see para. 18). The then Business Secretary Lord Peter Mandelson cleared the merger, rejecting the OFT recommendation that the matter should be referred to the CC, on the ground that competition issues were outweighed by public interest considerations. The Court of Session in Edinburgh gave the merger the final green light in January 2009.

FURTHER READING

Articles

BBC News, 'Lloyds HBOS Merger Gets the Go-Ahead', 12 January 2009

The Economist, 'Monster Mash', 25 September 2008

20.4 **Public interest cases**

20.4.1 **Intervention by the Secretary of State**

The OFT has a duty to notify the Secretary of State in any case where it is considering making a reference under ss. 22 or 33 of any matter which it believes to relate to public interest considerations (s. 57(1)). The CC has a duty to bring to the attention of the Secretary of State any representations made about the exercise of his powers under s. 57(2). Section 44 gives the Secretary of State the power to intervene in cases where a relevant merger situation raises public interest issues which are specified in s. 58. This is to say that

the Secretary of State should have the power to refer a case that qualifies for investigation if he or she believes that the merger may operate against the public interest. The result will be that the Secretary of State will refer cases to the Competition Commission. The public interest test that the Secretary of State will apply under the new regime will be more limited than that in the [FTA 1973]. The Secretary of State will be limited to taking account of the relevant public interest considerations and any substantial lessening of competition.   (Hansard, Standing Committee B, col. 347)

At the time of writing the only such consideration is that of national security, although the power exists for the Secretary of State to add to this list.

Intervention notices may be issued by the Secretary of State only where the OFT has not yet made a decision in respect of a merger situation. However, a notice may be issued where the OFT has made a decision to accept undertakings under s. 71 as an alternative to making a reference (see below). The details that must be included in intervention notices are set out in s. 43. They come into force when they are given, and cease to be in force at the point when the matter is finally determined. Where an intervention notice has been given, the OFT is required to give to the Secretary of State a report containing its advice on the considerations relevant to the making of a standard reference under ss. 22 or 33. In essence, the report is to be the summary of the position that the OFT would take in relation to the making of a merger reference, and may also 'include advice and recommendations on any public interest consideration mentioned in the intervention notice concerned' (s. 44(6)).

Following the receipt of the OFT's report, it is for the Secretary of State to refer the matter to the Commission if he or she is minded to do so. References may be made in two circumstances, either where the Secretary of State believes at the time of the receipt of the OFT report that there is, or there is not, SLC as a result of the merger, as long as he or she believes that 'the situation operates or may be expected to operate against the public interest' or where the Secretary of State decides, having received the report of the OFT, that there is no public interest consideration to which he or she is able to have regard. In the former situation, the Secretary of State is bound by the views of the OFT as regards the competition matters, but not as regards matters relating to the public interest consideration. Section 45(6) therefore provides that *any* anti-competitive outcome identified by the OFT shall be treated as being against the public interest, unless it is outweighed by the relevant public interest consideration. Some qualifications on the power to refer are set out in s. 46. These mirror those which limit the OFT's power to make references set out in ss. 22 and 33. In the second situation, the Secretary of State does not make a reference, and therefore the matter is to be remitted to the OFT for it to deal with as it considers appropriate under the normal merger rules (s. 56(1)).

The requirements of reports made by the CC in response to a reference made by the Secretary of State are at first the same as for those in the case of references made by the OFT. However, the CC must also consider

whether, taking account only of any substantial lessening of competition and the admissible public interest consideration or considerations concerned, the creation of that situation operates or may be expected to operate against the public interest.   (s. 47(2)(b))

As with references made by the OFT, the CC also has a duty to determine what action should be taken to remedy the situation, the difference being that in this case, the recommendation will be for action to be taken by the Secretary of State under s. 55. Where the relevant intervention notice has ceased to be in force, the CC will revert to an analysis of the merger as if the reference had been made under ss. 22 or 33, as appropriate. In this case, it will have an extra 20 days in which to produce its report from the date set by the Secretary of State (s. 56(3)–(5)).

20.4.2 **Decisions of the Secretary of State**

Where the Secretary of State has received a report from the CC, he or she 'shall decide whether to make an adverse public interest finding in relation to a relevant merger situation or whether to make no finding in the matter at all' (s. 54(2)). No finding shall be made in situations in which the Secretary of State decides that there is no public interest consideration which is relevant to the consideration of the merger situation (s. 54(4)). An adverse decision may be made in any case in which the Secretary of State, taking into account the public interest consideration, finds that the merger may be expected to operate against the public interest. The Secretary of State is bound by any decision taken by the CC in relation to the competitive effects of the merger. Any decision shall be made within 30 days of the receipt of the CC's report (s. 54(5)). Where the Secretary of State makes an adverse finding, he or she may take such action under Sch. 7, para. 9 or para. 11 as he or she considers reasonable in order to remedy, mitigate, or prevent any of the adverse effects of the merger on the public interest.

20.5 **Appeals**

Any decision of the OFT or the Secretary of State in connection with a merger reference may be appealed to the CAT within three months (s. 120). The standard for appeals is that of judicial review, meaning that the focus will be on the procedures adopted rather than the substance of the decision taken. As noted in the *Explanatory Notes*:

Case law suggests such grounds could include: (i) that an error of law was made; (ii) that there was a material procedural error; such as a material failure of an inquiry panel to comply with the Chairman's procedural rules; (iii) that a material error as to the facts has been made; and (iv) that there was some other material illegality (such as unreasonableness or lack of proportionality). Judicial review evolves over time and the approach in subsection (6) has been taken to ensure the grounds of review continue to mirror any such developments.   (para. 284)

When it reviews any decision, the CAT may quash the whole decision, or only a part of that decision. Further appeals on points of law only may be made to the Court of Appeal or the Court of Session, with the leave of the CAT. This right to appeal is available to third parties (for an example, see 20.2.6), as well as to those subject to the reference. Schedule 3 provides for tribunal rules that may, *inter alia*, permit the CAT to reject proceedings if it appears to it that the persons bringing them do not have sufficient interest in a decision, or where it believes that the appeal is vexatious.

The CAT has now heard a number of appeals relating to the exercise of the powers of the OFT and the CC in the domestic merger control regime (see also 20.2.6). In *Somerfield plc v Competition Commission* [2006] CAT 4, [2006] CompAR 390 the CAT upheld the CC's findings. The CC had found that Somerfield's acquisition of 115 stores and other assets from Wm Morrison Supermarkets plc could, in twelve local markets, give rise to an SLC, and had ordered Somerfield to divest itself of stores in seven of those areas (*A Report on the acquisition by Somerfield plc of 115 stores and other assets from Wm Morrison Supermarkets plc*, 2 September 2005). The CAT found that the CC was entitled to order the divestiture of the stores, had followed its own guidelines, and had acted entirely reasonably. The CAT found that the starting point of the CC in relation to remedies—to restore the pre-merger status quo where possible—was reasonable, and that for reasons of practicality the onus would fall on the merging parties to satisfy the CC that it should take a different approach. In the case of *Stericycle International LLC v Competition Commission* [2006] CAT 21, [2007] CompAR 281 the CAT held that the CC had acted correctly when it required Stericycle to put in place very specific arrangements, including the appointment of a 'hold-separate' manager during the merger inquiry.

As noted below third parties may in appropriate cases have the standing to appeal. This was the case in *Celesio AG v OFT* [2006] CAT 9, [2006] CompAR 515, in which a pharmaceutical distribution company was given the right to appeal against a decision of the OFT not to refer to the CC a merger between Alliance UniChem plc and Boots Group plc if suitable undertakings were offered. Celesio argued that the effect of permitting the merger would be to create a gulf between the merged entity and smaller competitors, to the detriment of the market. On the facts the CAT rejected the appellant's arguments as to the competitive assessment.

20.6 **Third-party rights**

Apart from the third-party rights to appeal decisions made in relation to merger references, ss. 94 and 95 ensure that those injured by the breach of enforcement undertakings, orders, and statutory restrictions may bring actions before the courts. A duty is
owed 'to any person who may be affected by a contravention of the undertaking or (as
the case may be) order' (s. 94(3)). Any breach which results in loss or damage is actionable. It is a defence, however, for the defendant 'to show that he took all reasonable
steps and exercised all due diligence to avoid contravening the undertaking or order'
(s. 94(5)).

20.7 **Joint ventures in the UK**

There is no specific recognition in UK domestic law of the concept of a 'joint venture'.
Instead there is a variety of ways by which companies can put into place mechanisms
to facilitate long-term cooperation. These can include the creation of a third company,
legally separate, in which the two partners play a joint role in terms of management
and ownership, and putting into place contractual arrangements. The consideration
of any such scheme will fall to be considered under the general competition law applicable in the UK.

FURTHER READING

Books

SCOTT, A., HVIID, M., and LYONS, B., *Merger
Control in the United Kingdom* (2006)
OUP, Oxford

Articles

BROWN, C., 'IBA Health: The First Challenge
under the New UK Merger Regime', [2003]
Competition Law Journal 347

GOODMAN, S., 'Steady as She Goes: The
Enterprise Act 2002 Charts a Familiar
Course for UK Merger Control', (2003)
European Competition Law Review 331

LAWRENCE, J., and MOFFAT, J., 'A Dangerous
New World—Practical Implications of
the Enterprise Act 2002', (2004) *European
Competition Law Review* 1

LESTER, M., 'Unichem Limited v Office of
Fair Trading', [2005] *Competition Law
Journal* 99

Summary map

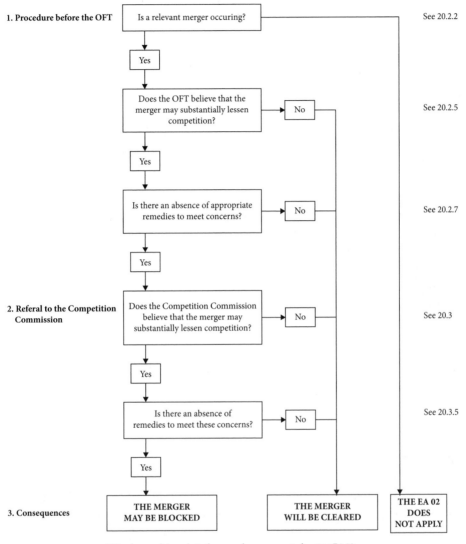

1. Procedure before the OFT | Is a relevant merger occuring? | See 20.2.2

Yes

Does the OFT believe that the merger may substantially lessen competition? → No | See 20.2.5

Yes

Is there an absence of appropriate remedies to meet concerns? → No | See 20.2.7

Yes

2. Referal to the Competition Commission | Does the Competition Commission believe that the merger may substantially lessen competition? → No | See 20.3

Yes

Is there an absence of remedies to meet these concerns? → No | See 20.3.5

Yes

3. Consequences | **THE MERGER MAY BE BLOCKED** | **THE MERGER WILL BE CLEARED** | **THE EA 02 DOES NOT APPLY**

This schema relates only to the general mergers control regime EA 02.
It presumes no EU engagement.

21

State aid

KEY POINTS

• State aid might create an advantage for some competitors and thus lead to a distortion of competition.

• Over the years, the European Courts have aimed to establish solid criteria for differentiating between subsidies that may invigorate the competitive process and those which may pose a considerable threat.

• As with arts 101 and 102 TFEU, economic analysis plays an increasingly important role in the assessment of the legality of State aid under art. 107 TFEU.

• Since the 2005 State Aid Action Plan, attempts have been made to simplify the rules applicable to State aid, which were previously dispersed in multiple block exemptions, frameworks, guidelines, and notices.

• Temporary (more tolerant) measures have had to be introduced for the approval of State aid in the context of the current economic crisis.

21.1 Introduction

Until now, this book has focused on the rules that control anti-competitive practices of undertakings. Competition law however is not limited to controlling the conduct of businesses. States often rush to the rescue of national industries when they are in trouble, or may decide to provide financial aid to certain sectors of the economy which may also have the capacity to harm the competitive process. It is reasonably frequent for governments to intervene to avoid certain national businesses from collapsing. The reasons for State involvement are obvious: there are clear social problems derived from the collapse of industries—such as increased unemployment—and there may be consequences for competition if one or more competitors stop operating in the market. Some activities may be invigorated through the financial support, and at times the aid is the only way to effectively bring forward crucial structural reforms.

Such subsidies may of course be acceptable under EU competition law. The Union itself is no stranger to providing financial help. For instance, through the Common Agricultural Policy (CAP), direct subsidies are provided to farmers across rural areas of Europe. However, State aid may have harmful effects on the competitive process.

On the one hand, the financial support could give recipients an unfair advantage over competitors. As a result, EU competition law aims at ensuring a level playing field to prevent this. On the other hand, artificially protecting unproductive firms could imply that economic efficiency, one of the main goals of competition policy, is squandered. In previous chapters, it has been clarified that it is widely recognized that the aim of competition law is to protect competition, not individual competitors. Inevitably, State aid needs to be closely monitored to ensure that the potential harmful effects are controlled. In the context of the European Union, additional concerns arise given the potential to give an advantage to national (subsidized) goods over imported products, which could have detrimental consequences for the proper functioning of the internal market—particularly on the free movement of goods and services.

Naturally, demands for State aid rocket at times of crisis. A look at the last 10 years serves to reflect this tendency. By way of example, in 2001—shortly after the 9/11 attacks—European airlines called on their governments for financial help to face the steep drop in demand for flights. More recently, the current economic crisis has placed State aid at the core of the discussions on competition law. Across various sectors of the economy, calls have been made for government intervention, and States find it difficult to resist the temptation to rush to the rescue of troubled industries. As former Commissioner Kroes put it, protectionism can be like 'a raging wildfire…almost impossible to control' (speech 'Antitrust and State Aid Control—the Lessons Learned' (24 September 2009) New York). A clear example is that of the European car industry, which experienced enormous decreases in sales in 2008 and 2009 and led to manufacturers turning to their governments for help to overcome the crisis. The British Government, for instance, recently agreed to invest £70 million in their domestic car industry. The European Commission has warned of the dangers of this strategy, and has carefully scrutinized governments' policies. Indeed, a plan to invest €4.5 billion on the part of the German Government to enable the purchase of Opel had to be aborted in 2009 after meeting strong opposition in some Member States, which led to the intervention of the EU Commission (see 21.7). Kroes insisted that a subsidy race be avoided at all costs. Despite these concerns, recent figures show that nearly €100 billion a year is granted in different forms of State aid. These vast figures reflect the importance of ensuring that any financial support is granted in a way that is not detrimental to the competitive process.

21.2 Article 107(1) TFEU: the prohibition

The general principle governing State aid is contained in art. 107(1) TFEU, which establishes a general prohibition for State aid:

Save as otherwise provided in this Treaty, any aid granted by a Member State or through State resources in any form whatsoever which distorts or threatens to distort competition by favouring certain undertakings or the production of certain goods shall, insofar as it affects trade between Member States, be incompatible with the internal market.

The prohibition is not absolute, and the very text of art. 107(1) TFEU acknowledges that it will apply '[s]ave as otherwise provided in this Treaty'. There is a raft of mandatory and discretionary exemptions in art. 107(2) and (3), along with additional specific exemptions in other parts of the Treaty. In order to fully grasp the *modus operandi* of the prohibition, it is necessary to first examine all the elements required for its application. As explained in *Altmark* (Case C–280/00, *Altmark Trans GmbH* v *Regierungspräsidium Magdeburg* [2003] ECR I–7747, para. 75), there are four conditions that must be met for art. 107(1) to enter into play:

First, there must be an intervention by the State or through State resources. Second, the intervention must be liable to affect trade between Member States. Third, it must confer an advantage on the recipient. Fourth, it must distort or threaten to distort competition.

Importantly, in addition to these conditions it is essential to define State aid. The definition is not exempt from controversy, as seen below.

21.2.1 Definition of aid

The Treaty does not contain a definition of aid. Rather, art. 107(1) TFEU is broadly construed and refers to 'any aid [...] in any form whatsoever'. In practice, the ample scope of this wording has led to disagreements as to what constitutes State aid. Indeed, in the aftermath of 9/11, Richard Plender, QC remarked that '[s]eldom had the definition of State aid presented more difficulties' ('Definition of Aid', in Biondi, A., Eekhout, P., and Flynn, J. (eds), *The Law of State Aid in the European Union*, Oxford, OUP, (2004), pp. 3–40). In the light of the current economic crisis and the growing demands for financial support, it seems more important than ever to specify the kind of aid that may be caught by this prohibition.

On its website, the Commission currently gives a rather imprecise definition of State aid as 'a form of state intervention used to promote a certain economic activity'. The European Courts have attempted to clarify the ambiguous concept. The first time the Courts referred to 'aid' was in the context of the interpretation of art. 4 of the now defunct Treaty establishing a Coal and Steel Community (ECSC), which referred to 'subsidies or aids granted by States'. In the case *De Gezamenlijke Steenkolenmijnen in Limburg* v *High Authority* (case 30/59 [1961] ECR 1 at 19), the Court of Justice focused precisely on the distinction between 'aid' and 'subsidies':

A subsidy is normally defined as a payment in cash or kind made in support of an undertaking other than the payment by the purchaser or consumer for the goods or services which it produces. An aid is a very similar concept, which, however, places emphasis on its purpose and seems especially devised for a particular objective which cannot normally be achieved without outside help. The concept of aid is nevertheless wider than that of a subsidy because it embraces not only positive benefits, such as subsidies themselves, but also interventions which, in various forms, mitigate the charges which are normally included in the budget of an undertaking and which, without, therefore, being subsidies in the strict meaning of the word, are similar in character and have the same effect.

The Court of Justice opted for a wide definition of aid which in an attempt to be able to control any kind of benefit that may grant a competitive advantage to recipients. Usually, the aid will be either a direct payment or a tax reduction—both of which clearly have an impact on public funds. It is considered that an advantage is gained not only when the beneficiary's net position improves, but also when the aid precludes what would otherwise have been an unavoidable decline in the recipient's situation (Quigley, *European State Aid Law and Policy,* Portland, Hart, 2nd edn (2009), p. 3). Importantly however, this case already establishes an essential condition: the aid must be granted in order to achieve an objective. This limit has been reiterated by the Commission (Notice on Cooperation between National Courts and the Commission in the State Aid Field OJ 1995 C312/8 para. 7), and confirmed by European Courts in subsequent cases. In *Kirshamer-Hack* v *Sidal* (C–189/91 [1993] ECR I–6185) it was held that exempting small firms from a legal requirement to pay compensation for unjustified dismissals would not constitute aid in the meaning of art. 107(1) TFEU, since according to the Court it would only intend to

provide a specific legislative framework for working relationships between employers and employees and to avoid imposing on those businesses financial constraints which might hinder their development.

The consideration of the objective of the aid differentiates the application of the Treaty's State aid rules from that of the antitrust provisions of arts 101 and 102 TFEU. As Morgan de Rivery and Le Berret-Dodet ('Controlling State Aids' (12 July 2005) *Competition Law Insight* 8–9) explain:

Indeed, the analysis conducted under articles [107 and 108 TFEU], which aims to assess the compatibility of an aid with the [internal] market, is not based solely on a market appreciation that is limited to verifying whether normal market conditions are maintained. Broader and more diverse considerations are taken into account, such as the possibility of an aid achieving objectives other than free and undistorted competition (eg economic growth, improved levels of employment, social cohesion and environmental protection), which are also recognised as contributing to a balanced and liveable [Union].

21.2.2 'Granted by a Member State or through State resources': the market economy investor principle and its limits

Since the prohibition of art. 107(1) TFEU applies to State aid, it seems logical that the Treaty requires that the aid be granted 'by a Member state or through state resources'. Therefore, the financial burden of the advantage gained ought to lie with the State. The General Court has explained that the notion of 'State resources' goes beyond the transfer of public funds to an undertaking, and also includes 'waiv[ing] revenue which would otherwise have been paid to the Treasury' (Case T–67/94, *Ladbroke Racing* v *Commission* [2008] ECR II–1 para. 109). However, in May 2010 the judgment of the Court of Justice in *French Republic and France Télécom* v *Commission* case C–81/10 P (nyr) established that statements made by the government assuring France Télécom of its support through a crisis, do not fall within the scope of art. 107(1) TFEU as there is no transfer of State resources.

In order to determine whether or not the actions of a Member State represent State aid in the sense of art. 107(1) TFEU, the market economy investor principle (MEIP) or market investor test has been crucial since the 1980s when it was originally formulated. This principle implies that an investment will not be considered State aid when its conditions would also be acceptable to a private investor under normal market economy conditions. One of the first references to the MEIP can be found in the Commission's 1984 *Communication to the Member States on the Application of Articles [107] and [108] of the [TFEU] to Public Authorities' Holdings* (Bulletin EC 91984).

[I]t is apparent that a public authority which injects capital by acquiring a holding in a company is not merely providing equity capital under normal market economy conditions, the case has to be assessed in the light of Article [107] of the Treaty [...] [T]here is State aid where fresh capital is contributed in circumstances that would not be acceptable to a private investor operating under normal market economy conditions. This is the case where the financial position of the company, and particularly the structure and volume of its debt, is such that a normal return (in dividends or capital gains) cannot be expected within reasonable time from the capital invested.

The Commission's interpretation of the requirement that the support must not be acceptable to a private investor to constitute State aid has been criticized for being excessively broad. By way of example, in 2004 the Commission estimated the low-cost airline Ryanair had been receiving unlawful State aid from the Belgian airport of Charleroi and the Walloon Region of Belgium (Commission Decision 2004/393/EC, (2004) OJ L137/1). The advantages granted by this publicly owned airport were similar to those granted by other private airports, which would lead to the conclusion that private investors would invest in similar conditions. However, the Commission distinguished between the benefits granted by the airport and those awarded by the Walloon Region for the application of the MEIP (airport management services and infrastructure). It insisted that, on the one hand, the Walloon Region's fixing of landing charges was not an economic activity that ought to be assessed under the MEIP. On the other hand, the advantages granted by Charleroi airport itself were considered unacceptable for a private investor, given that the latter would not take into account economic development or the creation of jobs for investing.

In 2008, the General Court overturned the Commission decision forcing Ryanair to pay back the advantages received (Case T–196/04 *Ryanair v Commission* [2008] ECR II–03643). The Commission, it estimated, had erred in treating the Walloon region and Charleroi airport as separate for the purposes of applying the MEIP. Furthermore, the MEIP should also have been applied to the Walloon Region, since the economic nature of the benefits granted to Ryanair remains unaltered even when it is granted by a public authority with regulatory powers.

The European Courts have provided additional clarifications as to the scope of the MEIP. The *PreussenElektra* v *Schleswag* case (C–379/98 [2001] ECR I–2099) is of particular importance in this context. Through a preliminary ruling, a German court of first instance raised the question as to whether a legal obligation imposed by the State which would bear benefits for private parties would amount to State aid within the meaning of art. 107(1) TFEU. More specifically, the case analysed the obligation imposed on private electricity suppliers to purchase electricity generated exclusively from local renewable sources at a minimum (excessive) price. In its written submissions, the Commission argued that the effectiveness of this provision would be put at risk should the term 'State aid' not be extended to catch measures financed through private undertakings. The Court however reiterated its long-established principle that art. 107(1) TFEU only applies to advantages granted directly or indirectly through State resources. Furthermore, the Court took the opportunity to explain the distinction between two non-cumulative conditions of the provision, namely 'aid granted by a Member State' and aid granted 'through State resources', saying that it

does not signify that all advantages granted by a State, whether financed through State resources or not, constitute aid but is intended merely to bring within that definition both advantages which are granted directly by the State and those granted by a public or private body designated or established by the State.

Only a year after *PreussenElektra*, the Court established a further delimitation to the scope of art. 107(1) TFEU in the case *France* v *Commission* (better known as the *Stardust Marine* case, C–482/99 [2002] ECR I–4397). According to this case, the provision only applies to State measures that are 'imputable to the State'. The Court annulled a Commission decision prohibiting the financial support granted to Stardust Marine by two French banks on the grounds that public authorities' involvement 'in one way or another' had not been proved. This involvement, the Court went on to explain, could be inferred by the circumstances of a case—such as the nature of the activities of the entity or the degree of effective control by public authorities—and therefore it does not impose an obligation to show that the public authority specifically instructed an entity to adopt a measure.

Finally, the decision to grant aid must be unilateral and autonomous. This implies that art. 107(1) TFEU will not apply when the State is merely complying with 'obligations stemming from the Treaty' unless some discretionary power is retained (Case T–351/02, *Deutsche Bahn* v *Commission* [2006] II–01047).

21.2.3 'Which distorts or threatens to distort competition' by conferring an advantage to the recipient

An additional requirement for the application of art. 107(1) TFEU is that competition is or may be distorted in some way. The wording of the prohibition contained in the Treaty makes clear that potential threats to the competitive process will also be caught. As a result, it is not necessary to demonstrate actual detrimental effects for the rule to come into play.

In his opinion in the landmark *Altmark* case (Case C–280/00, *Altmark Trans GmbH* v *Regierungspräsidium Magdeburg* [2003] ECR I–7747) Advocate General

Léger posited that '[a]s a general rule, it may be assumed that all public aid distorts or threatens to distort competition'. The Court of Justice was more specific, and clarified that the recipient of the aid must obtain an 'economic advantage' for a potential or actual distortion to exist. Paragraph 84 held that

Measures which, whatever their form, are likely directly or indirectly to favour certain undertakings [...] or are to be regarded as an economic advantage which the recipient undertaking would not have obtained under normal market conditions [...] are regarded as aid.

The key issue therefore is to consider whether the aid puts the undertaking in a position that it would not had achieved without it—'under normal market conditions'. Furthermore, for such an economic advantage to constitute State aid, it must display some degree of selectivity. According to the Commission, this means that 'certain economic sectors or activities are treated more favourably than others', which leads to a *de facto* discrimination between those who benefit from the aid and those who do not—hence the distortion of competition. As a result, in order to escape the prohibition of art. 107(1) TFEU aid would have to be granted to the economy in general and not to specific undertakings or sectors.

It is, however, frequent that general measures that apply indiscriminately to all sectors of the economy may include provisions for specific companies or sectors. This is common in tax and social security: imagine, for instance, a rule within the tax system of a Member State granting relief for undertakings located in rural areas. Such specific rules within the general measures may fall within the definition of State aid if they are selectively imposed. This is not to say that every measure that will lead to a benefit of a specific sector will be considered unlawful. As the Commission explains in its Notice on the application of the State aid rules to measures relating to direct business taxation:

[t]he fact that some firms or some sectors benefit more than others...does not necessarily mean that they are caught by the competition rules governing State aid. Thus, measures designed to reduce the taxation of labour for all firms have a relatively greater effect on labour-intensive industries than on capital-intensive industries, without necessarily constituting State aid. Similarly, tax incentives for environmental, R&D or training investment favour only the firms which undertake such investment, but again do not necessarily constitute State aid.   (para. 14)

In this context, the case law has elaborated on the concept of selectivity. Measures will be considered selective if, like in the example above, they benefit regions within a national territory. This is known as geographic selectivity. The exception to this rule relates to countries with autonomous regions; differentiated measures in this context will not be unlawful if the areas are institutionally, procedurally, and economically autonomous from the central government of the country (Advocate General Geelhoed in *Portugal* v *Commission* case C–88/03 [2006] 3 CMLR 45).

Selectivity also occurs, as shown in *France* v *Commission* case C–241/94 [1997] 1 CMLR 983, when general rules can be applied with discretion by public authorities. The case law seems to point towards the need of establishing objective criteria, so that when these are met the rules automatically apply. This was the logic behind finding that a company placed by a public authority under an expedited insolvency procedure had been unduly advantaged (*Ecotrade Slr* v *Altiforni & Ferriere di Sevola* case C–200/97 [1999] 2 CMLR 825).

Some measures that may seem *a priori* selective may however escape the prohibition by virtue of art. 106(2) TFEU, which provides a general exception from the application of competition law provisions to 'undertakings entrusted with the operation of services of general economic interest' when it may 'obstruct the performance, in law or in fact, of the particular tasks assigned to them'. The exception is only applicable if '[t]he development of trade [is] not…affected to such an extent as would be contrary to the interests of the Union'. The recent *BUPA* case provides a good illustration (*BUPA* v *Commission* case T–289/03 [2008] 2 CMLR 41). Here, the Irish authorities ran a scheme in the private medical insurance sector that compensated companies that took on 'above average' risk work (i.e. the elderly or chronically sick) by imposing a levy on those who worked 'below average' risk. BUPA, one such company, refused to pay the levy on the grounds that it amounted to State aid and was therefore prohibited by art. 107(1).

The Commission, and subsequently the GC in what was a very detailed judgment, found that this scheme was meant as a compensation for a service of general economic interest, as it met four criteria established in the *Altmark* ruling. First of all, there was a clearly defined public service obligation to be carried out. Against BUPA's argument that the service was not universal, the GC held that it is not required that the service must be essential to the entire population or the totality of the territory. Secondly, the parameters for compensation were objectively and transparently established in advance, and it was irrelevant that the level of payment was not specified or that the Irish authorities had discretion when setting the parameters. It will be recalled that what is crucial is that the parameters are not *applied* with discretion (see above). Thirdly, the compensation was proportionate, as it was calculated taking into consideration the actual risk profile of an insurer and the average market risk profile. Fourthly, the level of compensation was determined following an analysis of the expenses of an average well-run undertaking. Indeed, insurers had an incentive to behave efficiently as their average claim costs were considered for calculating the compensations.

The European Council has raised concerns about the excessively broad interpretation given to the 'economic advantage' requirement by the Commission and the European Courts. This led the Commission to declare that it would aim for 'a more transparent evaluation of distortions' using elaborate economic analysis in its 2005 State Aid Action Plan (analysed below). Subsequently, the Commission adopted a *De Minimis* Regulation (Commission Regulation No. 1998/2006 [2006] OJ L/379) establishing the minimum economic value an investment needs to have to constitute State aid.

21.2.4 Effect on trade between Member States

As with arts 101 and 102 TFEU, the application of art. 107 requires the existence of an effect on trade between Member States. This jurisdictional requirement operates in a similar way to that of the antitrust provisions. In the sphere of State aid, the essential issue to consider is whether the support strengthens the position of an undertaking in respect to competitors in intra-EU trade (established, *inter alia*, in T–298/97, *Alzetta Mauro and others* v *Commission* [2000] ECR II–2319). Potential effects also suffice for this requirement to be satisfied, as the *Altmark* case specified that it 'does not [...] depend on the local or regional character of the [...] services supplied or on the scale of the field of activity concerned' (C–280/00, *Altmark Trans GmbH* v *Regierungspräsidium Magdeburg* [2003] ECR I–7747). It comes as no surprise that Advocate General Léger remarked that this condition is 'easily satisfied', insisting that it was not necessary for the beneficiaries to be involved in exporting goods or services. Nonetheless, it should be borne in mind that currently the thresholds of the 2006 *De Minimis* Notice must be exceeded for art. 107(1) TFEU to apply.

21.3 The mandatory exemptions of art. 107(2) TFEU

The prohibition of State aid established in the Treaty is subject to a wide range of exemptions. These are granted to aid which would normally be forbidden as it meets all the requirements of art. 107(1), but which nonetheless can be considered lawful. The second paragraph of art. 107 contains a first list of exceptions to the general rule:

The following shall be compatible with the internal market:

   (a) aid having a social character, granted to individual consumers, provided that such aid is granted without discrimination related to the origin of the products concerned;

   (b) aid to make good the damage caused by natural disasters or exceptional occurrences;

   (c) aid granted to the economy of certain areas of the Federal Republic of Germany affected by the division of Germany, insofar as such aid is required in order to compensate for the economic disadvantages caused by that division. Five years after the entry into force of the Treaty of Lisbon, the Council, acting on a proposal from the Commission, may adopt a decision repealing this point.

In the above circumstances, granting aid will be lawful. Since the support is *a priori* contrary to art. 107(1) TFEU, it will still have to be notified to the Commission in order to be exempted. Once the notification requirement has been met, the aid is automatically lawful and the Commission has to declare it compatible with art. 107 TFEU. This list of derogations is exhaustive, and therefore no other measures may be invoked which would make the aid mandatorily valid.

21.3.1 Social aid

The first of the three exemptions refers to 'aid having a social character, granted to individual consumers'. As such, it applies to aid that is not granted to specific undertakings directly, although it is provided with the intention that it will indirectly help specific sectors.

By way of example, the recent decline of the car industry in Europe has led to the emergence of government incentive schemes to encourage consumers to purchase new motor vehicles. For instance, in 2009 the British Government operated a scrappage campaign which awarded £2,000 to owners of motor vehicles over 10 years old for trading their old car for a new one. Such a measure is not directed to specific manufacturers but ought to increase car sales in general, allowing the consumer to ultimately decide which firm offers a more appealing vehicle. The encouragement to purchase cars should indirectly increase sales and provide a boost to the industry. It is therefore understandable that such a measure would be likely to qualify for a mandatory exemption on the basis of art. 107(2)(a) TFEU.

21.3.2. Natural disasters and other exceptional circumstances

The second mandatory exemption prevents the application of the prohibition to 'aid to make good the damage caused by natural disasters or exceptional occurrences'. Under 'natural disasters' aid to repair damages consequential to, *inter alia*, flooding or an earthquake would be exempted. However, normal risks to agriculture are not considered to be covered. 'Exceptional occurrences' generally refers to uninsurable calamities such as war or water pollution. By way of example, these would include the funds granted to airlines in the aftermath of 9/11 to be able to cope with the endless compensation claims for flight cancellations and delays. Such aid however is subject to some limits in order to qualify for an exemption under this provision. The Commission and the European Courts have specified that it must comply with the principle of proportionality and thus not go beyond what is necessary to repair the damage caused by the adverse event. Moreover, it should only aim at heeding direct damage and not the promotion of industrial development of areas affected by a natural disaster or an exceptional occurrence (*Italy* v *Commission*, case C–364/90 [1993] I–2097).

21.3.3 Specific exemption for Germany

The third and final mandatory exemption can only be understood in the context prior to the reunification of Germany. It is for that 'aid granted to the economy of certain areas of the Federal Republic of Germany affected by the division of Germany, insofar as such aid is required in order to compensate for the economic disadvantages caused by that division'. Germany has insisted that it is important to maintain this exemption even today to cover the aid granted to the former German Democratic Republic (East Germany) after reunification. The Court of Justice however has insisted that nowadays this exemption should be interpreted narrowly (*Freistaat Sachsen, Volkswagen AG and Volkswagen Sachsen GmbH* v *Commission*, joined cases T–132/96 and T–143/96 [1999] ECR II–03663). The recent Treaty of Lisbon seemed like a unique opportunity to finally remove this anachronism. However, the pressure exerted by Germany led to the compromise decision of keeping it in the Treaty but with the addition of a new sentence allowing the Council to repeal this point in five years.

21.4 **Article 107(3) TFEU: discretionary exemptions**

In addition to the mandatory exemptions, art. 107(3) TFEU contains a list of circumstances under which State aid that falls within the prohibition of art. 107(1) TFEU may be lawful:

The following may be considered to be compatible with the internal market:

(a) aid to promote the economic development of areas where the standard of living is abnormally low or where there is serious underemployment, and of the regions referred to in Article 349, in view of their structural, economic and social situation;

(b) aid to promote the execution of an important project of common European interest or to remedy a serious disturbance in the economy of a Member State;

(c) aid to facilitate the development of certain economic activities or of certain economic areas, where such aid does not adversely affect trading conditions to an extent contrary to the internal market;

(d) aid to promote culture and heritage conservation where such aid does not affect trading conditions and competition in the Union to an extent that is contrary to the common interest;

(e) such other categories of aid as may be specified by decision of the Council on a proposal from the Commission.

This pivotal provision enables a detailed analysis of the aid granted in order to determine if the possible risks for competition could be compensated by, for instance, potential benefits to employment or the environment or regional development. As with the mandatory exemptions, when these conditions are invoked, art. 108(3) TFEU requires that the Commission be notified in order to grant its approval so that the measure may escape the prohibition. As a consequence of the very general wording of the discretionary exemptions, the notification system gives the Commission remarkable control over the legality of the financial support granted by the Member States, which in turn implies noticeable legal uncertainty for governments granting aid. Indeed, Sánchez Rydelski (*The EC State Aid Regime: Distorting Effects of State Aid on Competition and Trade* (2006) Cameron May Ltd, London) explains that

A compatibility assessment is a careful and complex balancing act, where free competition is weighted against other laudable objectives, such as, for example, regional development, employment and environmental protection. The Commission realised at an early stage that the wording in Article [107](3) [TFEU] was insufficient to provide for the necessary transparency and legal certainty in its compatibility assessments.

Aware of this problem, the Commission has attempted to heed concerns by issuing a wide range of Frameworks, Guidelines, Notices, and Communications providing details as to how it will deal with specific types of aid. The aim of this soft legislation is to establish general rules for the application of art. 107(3) to specific types of aid, explaining the quantity of aid that would be lawful and the conditions under which it should be granted. Specific block exemptions were also adopted for particular sectors using art. 109 TFEU (the legal base for EU legislation on State aid). Over the years, this resulted in a complex legal framework with rules scattered around the raft of legislation adopted. In order to heed concerns over the lack of coherence of the rules, the 2005 State Action Plan was set out to provide a coherent set of rules for State aid and the possible exemptions to the prohibition.

21.4.1 Regional aid

Paragraphs (a) and (c) refer to the development of certain disadvantaged regions. It should be noted that regional aid has been referred to as the 'backbone' of State aid measures considered compatible with the Treaty (Sánchez Rydelski, ibid. p. 15), hence the importance of these exceptions. The former is designed to exempt measures to promote economic development of areas where the standard of living is 'abnormally low' or where there is serious 'underemployment'. Importantly, in the Guidelines for National Regional Aid for 2007–13 ([2006] OJ C54/13) the criteria for determining which regions may benefit from the support can be found. It is required, *inter alia*, that they have less than 75 per cent of the average GDP of the Union. With regard to the latter—which exempts aid to promote 'development of certain economic activities or of certain economic areas'—one of the following three criteria must be met: the standard of living must be lower than the national average, the density of population has to be low, or the region in question must be eligible for structural funds. For the application of this exemption, the Guidelines for National Regional Aid specify that regions in which GDP per capita was less than the percentage of the average of EU-15 in 1998, but currently do not meet the condition may also be included here. As a result, it is an exemption riddled with exceptions, and will only be applicable if the aid contributes to regional development and has a local impact.

The initial approach to the application of the exemption contained in art. 107(3)(c) involved a three-stage test which carried out a balancing of common interest on the one hand and the effects on trade and competition on the other: first of all, the objective of the aid was required to be of interest to the Union. Secondly, the aid in question had to be necessary to achieve that objective (the necessity requirement). Thirdly, the duration, intensity, and scope of the support must be proportional to the intended result (again, bringing the proportionality principle into play). This was established in the *Philip Morris* case (Case 730/79 *Philip Morris Holland BV v Commission* [1980] ECR 2671, para. 26). This initial balancing test has somewhat been redefined following the 2005 State Action Plan analysed below. It should further be noted that paras (c) and (d) establish a limit to the application of the exemption, as the aid may only be lawful 'where such aid does not adversely affect trading conditions to an extent contrary to the internal market'.

21.4.2 Projects of common European interest or serious disturbance in the economy of a Member State

Paragraph (b) provides an exemption for 'aid to promote the execution of an important project of common European interest or to remedy to a serious disturbance in the economy of a Member State'. The Commission has somewhat tried to clarify what should be 'projects of common European interest'. For instance, in a decision on German tax depreciation (Commission Decision 96/369/EC [1996] OJ L146), the Commission confirmed that this requirement is met when the project is 'of benefit to the whole of the [Union]'. In the specific case, this requirement was not met because the aid was granted only to air carriers registered in Germany and to aircraft that were used for international flights—which appears to be contrary to the 'growing importance of trade by air transport in the liberalized common market for civil aviation'. Despite similarly shy attempts to specify the concept of common European interest, as Cremona argues, it still remains greatly undefined ('State Aid Control: Substance and Procedure in the Europe Agreements and the Stabilisation and Association Agreements' (2003) 9 *European Law Journal* 265–87). Until recently, this exemption was rarely invoked. For some years, it played a crucial role for upholding the legality of State aid in the field of research and development. Nonetheless, in the context of the current economic crisis, this exemption has played a crucial role in the quick approval of a wide range of emergency aids, as seen in 21.7. Regarding the interpretation of 'serious disturbance', in a scenario involving the support granted by the Greek Government to national undertakings for financial reconstitution (Commission Decision 88/167/EEC [1988] OJ L/76), the Commission established that this requirement was met since

[t]he economic situation in Greece had been constantly deteriorating up to October 1985. Both internal and external imbalances had created a difficult situation which demanded firm policy measures. In particular the Greek authorities were confronted with very serious external payments and pressures on the exchange rate in September 1985.

However, the aid granted was still considered to be subject to some constraints. In particular, it

must not result in [the recipients] being left in a stronger competitive position vis-à-vis industries in other Member States than would otherwise occur had those difficulties not arisen in the first place. Accordingly the aid must not promote expansion of production capacity nor must it merely shift the problem without finding a genuine solution to the social and industrial problems facing the [Union] as a whole or even aggravate the situation still further in the medium or long-term future. Moreover, the effect should not be to obstruct or even compromise the specific aid policies already in existence and applied in certain sensitive sectors.

21.4.3 The promotion of culture and heritage conservation

In 1992, the Treaty of Maastricht introduced the exception currently contained in art. 107(3) para. (d), which may serve to justify aid 'to promote culture and heritage conservation'. This provision complements art. 167 TFEU, which places a duty on the European Union to contribute to the promotion and blossoming of the cultures of the Member States respecting the existing diversity. The Treaty contains no definition of what should be understood as 'culture', and it appears that anything that may be considered culture for a Member State would fit within this concept. As a result, it emphasizes diversity rather than common cultural heritage (Woods, 'The Application of Competition Rules to State Aids for Culture', (2005) 6 *ERA Forum* 1, 37–45). In accordance with the general position of the Commission and the European Courts for exempting State aid, it seems imperative that the underlying national cultural interests outweigh the common interests of the EU in the necessary balancing test (Castendyk *et al.*, *European Media Law*, the Netherlands, Kluwer Law International, (2008)). Although the Commission has insisted that this exemption may only be used restrictively, it has been invoked to exempt aid granted to film production, theatre, public broadcasting, and books.

21.4.4 The residual clause

The last of the discretionary exemption is a residual clause which may be used to uphold any other types of aid, provided the specific measures are approved by a decision of the Council. This last paragraph implies that the list of exemptions of art. 107(3) is non-exhaustive, as virtually any aid may be lawful as long as it meets the requirements laid down in para. (e). Despite its seemingly broad scope, in practice it has not been frequently used as it should only be invoked in exceptional circumstances. It served as a legal basis to adopt a Regulation for State aid to the coal industry (Council Regulation 1407/2002 [2002] OJ L/205), where it was argued that financial support was essential given the major restructuring of the Union's industry necessary to overcome the EU's dependence on external sources of energy.

21.5 Exempting State aid from the prohibition of art. 107(1): procedural issues

In the enforcement of the Treaty's State aid provisions, the Commission retains a crucial role. As established in art. 108 TFEU, it alone may grant exemptions—and the Council in a few exceptional circumstances—and no aid may be settled until it has been notified to and approved by the Commission. Enforcement rules differ from those of arts 101 and 102 TFEU, and are laid down in Council Regulation 659/99/EC laying down detailed rules for the application of art. [108] of the Treaty ([1999] OJ L83/1). This Regulation was introduced in 1999 in an attempt to codify the previously dispersed procedural rules for greater coherence and control over State aid.

21.5.1 The notification process

State aid which falls within the prohibition established in art. 107(1) but which may nonetheless be exempted by either art. 107(2) or 107(3) needs to be notified to the Commission in order to qualify for an exemption according to art. 108(3) TFEU:

The Commission shall be informed, in sufficient time to enable it to submit its comments, of any plans to grant or alter aid. If it considers that any such plan is not compatible with the internal market having regard to Article 107, it shall without delay initiate the procedure provided for in paragraph 2. The Member State concerned shall not put its proposed meas-ures into effect until this procedure has resulted in a final decision.

The notification system is comparable to that established by Regulation 17/62 for exemptions granted under art. 101(3) TFEU for agreements between undertakings (abolished in 2004 by Regulation 1/2003). After notification, the Commission has to determine whether or not the aid qualifies for an exemption, and in the case of art. 107(3), it also has the power to decide whether or not the specific circumstances justify allowing the financial support to go ahead. As a result, the Commission has a greater deal of control over discretionary exemptions.

  Either way, no aid can be paid until it has been notified and subsequently approved. The only exceptions to the obligation of notification are when the aid is below the thresholds of the *De Minimis* Regulation (analysed in 21.6.1) or when it is existing aid and not exceeded by 20 per cent. If this requirement is breached the support will be unlawful, in which case the Commission may 'issue an interim decision requiring [the State] to suspend immediately the payment of such aid' (Case C–301/87 *France* v *Commission* ECR I–307, para. 18). Chapter III of Regulation 659/99 provides further details with regard to the consequences of aid being granted without being notified or before it is approved, and the procedure to follow. Importantly, if the aid is deemed illegal the Commission may, by virtue of art. 14, oblige the Member State 'to take all necessary measures to recover the aid from the beneficiary' for a period of ten years since the aid was awarded (art. 15). Furthermore, the Court of Justice has rec-ognized the possibility to seek damages from the State who awarded unnotified or unapproved aid for those competitors of the recipient who may have been affected by the money that was unlawfully provided (Case C–39/94 *Syndicat Français de l'Express International* v *La Poste* [1996] ECR I–3547).

21.5.2 Exceptional exemptions granted by the Council by virtue of art. 108(2) TFEU

The second paragraph of art. 108 contains details regarding the procedure to fol-low when the Commission does not consider that the aid notified to it merits an exemption:

If, after giving notice to the parties concerned to submit their comments, the Commission finds that aid granted by a State or through State resources is not compatible with the inter-nal market having regard to Article 107, or that such aid is being misused, it shall decide that the State concerned shall abolish or alter such aid within a period of time to be determined by the Commission.

  If the State concerned does not comply with this decision within the prescribed time, the Commission or any other interested State may, in derogation from the provisions of Articles 258 and 259, refer the matter to the Court of Justice of the European Union direct.

  On application by a Member State, the Council may, acting unanimously, decide that aid which that State is granting or intends to grant shall be considered to be compatible with the internal market, in derogation from the provisions of Article 107 or from the regulations provided for in Article 109, if such a decision is justified by exceptional circumstances. If, as regards the aid in question, the Commission has already initiated the procedure provided for in the first subparagraph of this paragraph, the fact that the State concerned has made its application to the Council shall have the effect of suspending that procedure until the Council has made its attitude known.

If, however, the Council has not made its attitude known within three months of the said application being made, the Commission shall give its decision on the case.

From the wording of this provision, it is clear that the Commission's powers in the context of State aid are more extensive than in other areas of competition law. It can order the abolition or alteration of any aid it considers incompatible with the internal market. Despite this broad authority, in exceptional circumstances it is the Council—by unanimity—that may declare certain aids exemptible, provided the Commission has not yet reached a final decision on those same investments. In practice, the use of this provision has been mainly limited to agriculture and fisheries.

21.6 **State aid reform: the 2005 State Aid Action Plan and its aftermath**

In 2005 the Commission launched a comprehensive review of procedures and rules in relation to State aid. It followed the reforms of antitrust rules and merger control that had taken place in previous years, and constituted an attempt to bring State aid rules in line with those developments. Generally speaking, the reform intended to reduce the overall amount of State aid granted, and at the same time to ensure that a coherent set of rules replaced the previous fragmented, scattered legal regime. Eventually, this review led to the adoption in 2008 of the General Block Exemption Regulation (GBER) which consolidated the previous raft of legislation into one instrument covering block-exempted types of horizontal agreements. A *De Minimis* Regulation was also adopted in 2006 in an attempt to improve economic analysis when deciding on the legality of investments.

The Action Plan has four principal goals (para. 18): fewer and better-targeted state aids; a more refined economic approach; more efficient procedures, better enforcement, higher predictability, and enhanced transparency; and a shared responsibility between the Commission and Member States. What each of these targets implies and what has been done in order to work towards achieving these objectives is the focus of this section.

21.6.1 **Fewer and better-targeted state aids: focus on horizontal objectives**

The intention behind the new rules is to reduce the enormous amounts of State aid granted in the Member States. This goal has been somewhat undermined by the recent economic crisis, which has led to an overall increase in the total financial support for companies. Besides a reduction in quantity, the aid ought to be 'better targeted', which would imply giving up aid for specific sectors or companies in favour of the support granted for so-called horizontal objectives. These merely address the removal of a market failure regardless of regional or sectoral considerations, and are therefore less harmful for competition. Traditionally, horizontal aid would be directed to goals such as environmental protection, SMEs, research and development, employment. The General Block Exemption Regulation introduced in 2008 (Commission Regulation (EC) 800/2008, [2008] OJ L214/3) exempts certain kinds of horizontal aid, and attempts to harmonize horizontal aspects to all the areas concerned. It will be analysed in 21.6.3.

21.6.2 A refined economic approach: the *De Minimis* Regulation

At the outset of this chapter, we saw how State aid may have beneficial effects for the economy. It may serve to finance essential structural reforms, or to invigorate activities that need to be encouraged. The State Aid Action Plan acknowledges these advantages and insists that it is crucial to engage in a careful balancing test, which ought to be substantiated by economic analysis. This comes as no surprise after the reforms carried out in antitrust rules in the decade prior to the Action Plan, which refer to the importance of economics as the pillar to distinguish between lawful and unlawful restrictions of competition.

The acknowledgement of the vital role of economic analysis is a welcome recognition that was virtually unavoidable at a time when leading scholars around the world had insisted upon its importance for years. However, the Action Plan is silent as to how this economic analysis is to be enhanced. Some authors have emphasized that, to be beneficial, State aid has to be 'granted disgressively and limited in time' (Sánchez Rydelski, ibid. p. 13). This position has had noticeable consequences in the current rules for State aid. In particular, the *De Minimis* Regulation (Commission Regulation No. 1998/2006 [2006] OJ L/379), automatically exempts subsidies of less than €200,000 granted over no more than three years. The exemption however does not apply to aid granted to firms in difficulty even when they are below the threshold, and it is necessary to be able to calculate the precise amount of the aid in advance for the Regulation to apply.

21.6.3 More efficient procedures, better enforcement, higher predictability, and enhanced transparency: the General Block Exemption Regulation

The uncertainty resulting from the complex and disperse legal framework that existed until 2005 is acknowledged by the Commission in the State Aid Action Plan. The accretion of block exemptions, Frameworks, Guidelines, Notices, and Communications had led to complex exemption procedures and needed to be thoroughly transformed. It took another three years for this goal to materialize into regulatory reforms. It was in 2008 that the GBER (Commission Regulation (EC) 800/2008, [2008] OJ L214/3) was finally adopted to replace the specific block exemptions.

In the new Regulation, there is a clear intention to increase the possibilities of granting aid without the obligation to notify the Commission for prior approval. In the context of the broadly construed concept of State aid, and the rise in financial support consequential to the financial crisis, such a measure seems wise. It consolidates those areas in which aid was already liberated from the notification procedure by the previous five block exemptions, but also extends this benefit to other kinds of horizontal aid which will now also qualify for an exemption. The GBER refers to aid granted to SMEs, research and innovation, training, employment, risk capital, and regional development. As a novelty, it also covers environmental aid and that given to innovative new businesses. The rules for exempting all these varieties of aid are all now contained in the one block exemption, which will expire in 2013.

21.6.4 Shared responsibility between the Commission and Member States

The plans for reform also refer to the importance of extending current decentralized enforcement trends to the competition law provisions that regulate State aid, in the conviction that it should result in greater efficiency. As a result, the Commission considers it crucial to ensure that national authorities are more closely involved in the control of the financial support granted, and proposes a series of desirable measures. For instance, it recommends better cooperation between the Member States and the Commission, the implementation of EU State aid rules by national judges (who however tend to be reluctant to tamper with the aid granted by their governments) and even perhaps introducing independent authorities to facilitate the detection and recovery of illegal State aid. This is the aspect of the reform that currently remains more underdeveloped, possibly as a consequence of the imminent priorities that emerged with the economic crisis.

21.7 The future of State aid: reactions to the economic crisis

The Commission's insistence to reduce the amount of State aid has recently been put into question by the current economic crisis and the increase in demands for financial support. The difficult situation has forced the Commission to assess the compatibility of the need to help struggling businesses with the pursuit of the objective of having 'less, better targeted aids'. Has this principle had to be relaxed in order to overcome the delicate economic situation? The Commission claims it has not, and that any measures to defeat the crisis must fully respect this general objective of State aid policy reform. However, some flexibility has been virtually unavoidable, leading to the difficult task of ensuring consistency in enforcement. An analysis of recent communications and decisions reveal at least some transitory exceptions.

Overall, as Gerard ('EC Competition Law Enforcement at Grips with the Financial Crisis: Flexibility on the Means, Consistency in the Principles', (2009) 1

Concurrences 46–62) argues, the Commission ought to ensure consistency in the principles used to analyse competition law issues related to the financial crisis, while at the same time allowing a certain degree of flexibility when applying those principles. The Commission focuses on the 'better targeted' aid aspect—rather than the 'fewer' aid element—to justify how the current rules are compatible with the general trends of reform. In its Communication *The application of State Aid Rules to Measures taken in Relation to Financial Institutions in the Context of the Current Global Financial Crisis* ([2008] OJ C/270/8) there is a recognition that it is 'necessary to adopt appropriate measures to safeguard the stability of the financial system'. However, the communication acknowledges a wide range of exceptions to the illegality of State aid, and in an attempt to emphasize that the measures are compatible with the general aims of competition policy, the Commission explains (para. 5) that

[w]hile the exceptional circumstances prevailing at the moment have to be duly taken into account when applying the State aid rules to measures addressing the crisis in the financial markets the Commission has to ensure that such measures do not generate unnecessary distortions of competitions between financial institutions operating in the market or negative spillover effects on other Member States.

But the institution has had to go further than merely tolerating the rise in State aids. The approval system—subject to notification—was also exceptionally accelerated through the introduction of a temporary procedure for 'emergency rescue measures' established in October 2008 for only three months. This practice implied that decisions could be taken by the Competition Commissioner, the President of the Commission, the Commissioner for Economic and Monetary Affairs and the Commissioner for the Internal Market (rather than by the entire College of Commissioners). Although it could only be used in exceptional circumstances, more than 20 decisions were adopted in only eight weeks. The most significant example was the approval in October 2008 of aid to be granted by the British Government to the bank Bradford & Bingley after only 24 hours of being notified (Commission Decision NN 41/2008, OJ C–2008/290), and on the very day the procedure was agreed.

Importantly, while until October 2008 measures in support of financial institutions were analysed and approved using art. 107(3)(c) TFEU, the unprecedented number of notifications and the urge to act fast in the light of the extreme circumstances eventually made the Commission turn to the 'serious disturbance' exemption of art. 107(3)(b) TFEU. This exemption had barely been used until then, but the lack of liquidity consequential to the freeze in inter-bank lending required the imminent approval of State aid measures. As a result, the Communication *The application of State Aid Rules to Measures taken in Relation to Financial Institutions in the Context of the Current Global Financial Crisis* ([2008] OJ C/270/8) admits that 'Article 107(3)(b) is, in the present circumstances, available as a legal basis for aid measures undertaken to address this systemic crisis' (para. 9).

Further measures were adopted before the end of 2008. In December, a new Temporary Framework was introduced (Communication of 17 December 2008 and amended on 25 February 2009, [2009] OJ C83/01). The Framework, based on the European Recovery Plan approved only a month earlier, introduced important temporary measures to combat the crisis. The most notable novelty is that it removes the notification requirement for subsidized loans, loan guarantees at a reduced premium, risk capital for SMEs, and direct aids of up to €500,000 (considerably above the threshold of the *De Minimis* Regulation). The legality of the unnotified aid is limited to two years (until the end of 2010) and is subject to two conditions: it must be granted within the context of aid schemes and the beneficiaries must not be in difficulty as of 1 July 2008.

The first measures approved under the Temporary Framework were a €15 billion German loan programme to provide liquidity for undertakings in trouble (Commission Decision N 661/2008 OJ C/29/2009) and a Federal framework scheme to allow economic policy actors to grant aid of up to €500,000 to firms who need it (Commission Decision N 668/2008 OJ C/152/2009). Nevertheless, when the German Government announced in 2009 its intention to offer €4.5 billion to a bidder for purchasing Opel, the plan was immediately met with strong opposition (Weiland, S., 'The Opel Magna Debacle: A Disgrace for the Populists', (11 April 2004) *Der Spiegel*). It was perhaps no coincidence that the deal, which would help prevent the collapse of one of the country's most important manufacturers, was announced in the run-up to the 2009 general election. The aid was offered on the specific condition that Magna, an Austro-Canadian manufacturer of car parts, would be pre-selected to acquire the majority of Opel's shares (ignoring other bidders, such as financial investor RHJ International). The UK, Spain, and Belgium—all of which have Opel production sites—raised concerns to the EU Commission that the German Government was in fact 'bribing Magna to ensure that most of the pain of restructuring the perennially lossmaking car firm is borne by non-Germans' (*The Economist*, 'A Deal That Stinks' (24 September 2009)). The EU Commission was quick to remind the German Government that it would not accept

that State aid granted under the Temporary Framework is conditional upon the implementation of a specific business plan, previously discussed and/or negotiated with Member States, which defines the geographic distribution of restructuring measures, without leaving to the beneficiary undertakings the possibility to revise their plans if necessary.

State funding under the Temporary Framework is meant to tackle the financing problems due to the credit crunch, and cannot be used to impose political constraints concerning the location of production activities within the internal market. The beneficiary undertakings must therefore retain full freedom to develop their economic activities in the internal market.   (Press Release 'State Aid: Commission Statement for Aid on Opel Europe (23 September 2009) MEMO/09/411)

In the end, General Motors decided against selling Opel, and in June 2009 the German Government rejected a request from Opel for State aid (BBC News, 'General Motors: Germany Rejects Request for Opel Aid' (9 June 2009)).

The political sensitivity is obvious. The area is likely to remain controversial in the light of the economic crisis, with a large number of companies on the brink of collapse calling for help. Former Commissioner Kroes' words with regard to the Commission's line of action have been sharp and to the point:

We cannot accept one government bribing companies in order to steal or end the jobs of another. We cannot accept companies becoming addicted to aid. Such behaviours are a recipe for a trade war and poverty—not a way out of this recession.

FURTHER READING

Books

BIONDI, A., EEKHOUT, P., and FLYNN, J. (eds), *The Law of State Aid in the European Union* (2004) OUP, Oxford

QUIGLEY, C., *European State Aid Law and Policy*, 2nd edn (2009) Hart, Portland

SÁNCHEZ RYDELSKI, M. (ed.), *The EC State Aid Regime: Distorting Effects of State Aid on Competition and Trade* (2006) Cameron May Ltd, London

Articles

BAUDENBACHER, C., AND BREMER, F., 'European State Aid and Merger Control in the Financial Crisis—From Negative to Positive Integration', (2010) *Journal of European Competition Law and Practice* 267–85

DA CRUZ VILAÇA, J. L., 'Material and Geographic Selectivity in State Aid—Recent Developments', (2009) 4 *European State Aid Law Quarterly* 443

GYSELEN, L., 'Services of Economic Interest and Competition under European Law—A Delicate Balance', (2010) *Journal of European Competition Law and Practice*

22

Competition law and intellectual property

KEY POINTS

- Competition law may limit the ability to exercise intellectual property rights.
- Article 101 TFEU and the Chapter I Prohibition may apply to agreements to license intellectual property, while Article 102 TFEU and the Chapter II Prohibition may apply to the use of intellectual property rights by a dominant undertaking.
- The existence of intellectual property rights does not automatically confer a dominant position—the product or service may still face competition.
- In the EU the Treaty provisions relating to the free movement of goods may limit the ability to use intellectual property rights to divide the internal market.

22.1 Introduction

Whether there is a tension between the existence and exercise of intellectual property rights, and the application of competition law, is a matter of debate. The traditional view has been to suggest that intellectual property—the grant of a monopoly by the state as a reward for innovation—was inconsistent with a body of law which existed to attack the exploitation of monopoly power. However, it is not the role of competition law to attack the very existence of monopoly, and in practice it will be rare that the grant of intellectual property creates a 'monopoly' as defined in competition law and economics (see 22.3). In April 2007 the US Department of Justice and the Federal Trade Commission published a major report examining the link between antitrust and intellectual property (*US Dept of Justice & Fed Trade Comm'n, Antitrust Enforcement and Intellectual Property Rights: Promoting Innovation and Competition* (2007), available from the DOJ website). The first paragraph of the report notes the change in approach in recent times:

Over the past several decades, antitrust enforcers and the courts have come to recognize that intellectual property laws and antitrust laws share the same fundamental goals of enhancing consumer welfare and promoting innovation. This recognition signalled a significant shift from the view that prevailed earlier in the twentieth century, when the goals of antitrust and intellectual property law were viewed as incompatible: intellectual property law's grant of exclusivity was seen as creating monopolies that were in tension with antitrust law's attack on monopoly power. Such generalizations are relegated to the past. Modern understanding of these two disciplines is that intellectual property and antitrust laws work in tandem to bring new and better technologies, products, and services to consumers at lower prices.

The position in the US and the EU is, however, somewhat different: in the US it is generally accepted that antitrust law has a very specific function of supporting efficiency; in the EU the role of competition policy is a little more diverse. Further for the purposes of intellectual property law the US constitutes a single jurisdiction, whereas in the EU each Member State may constitute a separate jurisdiction, giving rise to tensions between national protection, and single market considerations.

Clearly an IP right is a form of property right, and art. 345 TFEU provides that 'The Treaties shall in no way prejudice the rules in Member States governing the system of property ownership'. We have also seen that while competition law does not generally seek to condemn the existence of a monopoly (or dominant position), it does seek to impose some constraint on the way in which a monopoly can be exploited or defended. In order to exploit IP it may be necessary to license it to parties better placed to produce, market, and distribute the end products. Thus, both arts 101 and 102 TFEU may be applied to the exercise of IP rights in the EU. IP rights may also be exploited so as to divide the 'internal market'. For example, a holder of patents in respect of a given technology in France, the UK, and Germany may attempt to exercise their patent right in each Member State independently of each other state, and may seek to exclude products from one state being traded in the other. Such a 'right' was for many years a traditional and accepted feature flowing from the possession of IP, but is clearly not consonant with the creation of a single market among 27 Member States. In the discussion earlier on in this book it was seen that the case of *Consten and Grundig v Commission* (*Établissements Consten Sarl* v *Commission* cases 56, 58/64 [1966] 1 CMLR 418) was of seminal importance in relation to the application of art. 101 TFEU to vertical agreements (see 9.3.1.1). It is worth noting at this stage that an important feature of that case lay in the assignation of a trade mark by a German producer to a French distributor, as a result of which the French distributor attempted to rely upon the trade mark in a French court to prevent imports of the products in question from Germany. Other provisions of EU law, in particular those relating to the free movement of goods, may also be invoked to frustrate the use of IP rights in this way, and there is a sufficiently close nexus between the operation of this law, and the operation of competition law, to merit treatment in this book.

In essence, then, there are three core ways in which the use of IP rights may be subject to restrictions arising under EU law. Article 101 TFEU may be applicable to agreements relating to the assignation or exploitation of intellectual property; art. 102 TFEU may control the use of IP by a dominant undertaking (this is particularly the case where the subject matter of the IP right represents to a third party an essential input); and the provisions of the Treaty relating to the free movement of goods may limit the extent to which IP rights can be asserted so as to fragment the common market.

In this chapter the term IP is used to encompass: patents, trade marks, copyright (including computer software), know-how, designs, plant breeders' rights, databases, and semi-conductor topographies unless a specific IP right is referred to.

22.2 IP and the application of art. 101 TFEU and the Chapter I Prohibition

22.2.1 The general application of art. 101 TFEU

Article 101 (and the Chapter I Prohibition) may be applicable to situations in which IP is assigned, or licensed. For the purposes of EU competition law the two are treated in the same way, although the effect may be different: an assignment is, in effect, a complete transfer of the IP in question, as a result of which the assignor ceases to be able to exploit the right; a licence permits the licensee to exploit the IP which remains owned by the licensor. IP licences may be exclusive, or non-exclusive, and may be restricted by territory or by use. Thus, for example, a licence may be granted in respect of a patented process exclusively to A, in territory B, covering all uses. At the other extreme a number of licences may be granted in territory B, to a number of parties, with restrictions on the use to which they can put the process. Any licence is likely to include conditions relating to the payment to be made to the licensor, the use to which the IP can be put, the territory within which it can be exploited, and requirements on the licensee to maintain the integrity of the IP.

The Commission took the view early on that IP licensing would fall within art. 101(1) TFEU unless the licence merely confirmed the existence of the property right in question. The most important case in this respect is that of *LC Nungesser KG and Kurt Eisele* v *Commission* case 258/78 [1983] 1 CMLR 278 ('the *maize seed* case'). This dealt with the commercial exploitation of a modified type of maize seed, where the right owner, an agency of the French Government, INRA, granted an exclusive licence to a German resident, Eisele. An agreement was concluded in 1965 under which Eisele was granted territorial protection in relation to the seed variety in Germany. When Eisele sought to enforce his rights in the German courts to prevent parallel imports, following which a settlement was reached, a complaint was subsequently made to the EU Commission, which found that both the grant of the right and the settlement of the case were in contravention of art. 101(1). An application for an exemption under art. 101(3) was rejected. An appeal was made to the Court of Justice which ruled that although the grant of the exclusive licence itself did not violate art. 101(1), a 'closed licence' may contravene art. 101(1). In this context a 'closed licence' is one which not only confirms an exclusive licence in a given territory on the licensee, but further affects the position of third parties, i.e. by restricting their ability to distribute the product in that territory. The Court of Justice preferred a model of an 'open licence' which merely confirmed the grant of the licence, and an obligation on the licensor itself not to compete with the licensee. At the same time the Court linked the benefits of the open licence with the need to disseminate *new* technology, and suggested that if the technology licensed was not sufficiently new, then even an open licence might contravene art. 101(1). This approach has been followed by the EU Commission on a number of occasions since, and in particular the Commission has stressed that while restrictions might be permissible in the early years of a development of new technology, they cannot be permitted to continue indefinitely. While this case dealt with 'plant-breeder's rights' the Court indicated that the same approach could be applied to other types of intellectual property, including, presumably, patents and know-how.

The case of *Windsurfing* dealt with non-territorial restraints in a licence (*Windsurfing International* v *Commission* case 193/83 [1986] 3 CMLR 489). Here a US company engaged in developing windsurfing equipment had granted a number of licences in relation to patents it held in Germany. There was a dispute as to whether the patents in question related just to the rig, or to the board as well, and the Commission took the view that they related only to the rig. The Commission found that a number of terms of the licences infringed art. 101(1). These included clauses which required the licensee to: fit the rigs only to boards approved by the licensor; not supply the rigs individually, but sell them only as part of an entire piece of windsurfing equipment; pay royalties based on that entire piece of equipment, and not just of the rig itself; not challenge the validity of the IP license; and to only manufacture the rigs at a specified fabrication plant. The Commission rejected most of the arguments made by Windsurfing to the effect that the clauses were a necessary element of its product quality system. On appeal the Court upheld most of the Commission's findings, although on narrow grounds it rejected the finding that an infringement had occurred in relation to the requirement to pay royalties on the price of the entire equipment, holding that this did not restrict competition in relation to rigs—the subject matter of the decision—although it did in relation to boards. Although *Windsurfing* is cited with approval by the Commission in its technology transfer guidelines, some of the conclusions reached in the case would appear, in the light of the terms of Regulation 772/2004, to be questionable.

Where Regulation 772/2004 (discussed below) does not apply, art. 101 may remain applicable, as is made clear in the guidelines (paras 131–235). Thus the analysis should proceed within the general framework established within art. 101(1) and art. 101(3). The Commission considers that art. 101 is not likely to be infringed where there is significant competition in relation to the processes covered by the IP. Thus it states that where, apart from the subject matter of the licence itself, there are four independent technologies that may be substituted 'at a comparable cost to the user' (para. 131) there is unlikely to be an infringement. This does not apply where hard-core restrictions are present. Whereas the block exemption regulation relates only to agreements limited to two parties, even patent pools may be justified under a direct application of art. 101—indeed in some markets (e.g., integrated circuits) it may be impossible to develop a product without a patent pool being in place given the large range of technologies involved (paras 210–35). For a clear analysis of the approach to be taken to various terms in licences not falling within the block exemption regulation the guidelines should be referred to.

The block exemption regulation does not apply to the licensing of trade marks, which remain subject to the general principles of art. 101 TFEU, and the principles set out in the guidelines should *not* be treated as if they apply equally to trade mark licences (see para. 53 of the guidelines). Here the Commission states that trade mark licensing is 'more akin to distribution agreements than technology licensing', and indeed, where a trade mark licence is ancillary to a distribution agreement it falls to be considered under Regulation 330/2010 (see 10.3.1). A good illustration of the approach taken to trade marks may be found in the *Campari* Decision (*Agreements of Davide Campari-Milano SpA* 78/253/EEC (1978) OJ L70/69). Although there were several factors at play in the Decision, to a substantial degree it related to the use of the trade mark 'Campari'. The Commission held that a number of restrictions did not fall within art. 101(1): a ban on exports outside the EU (as there could be no effect on trade between Member States); manufacturing only at approved sites which could guarantee the required quality; the purchase and subsequent use of 'secret' ingredients from Campari itself; and the protection of the know-how involved in the manufacture of the product. A ban on active sales outside the assigned territory was found to fall within art. 101(1), but benefited from an art. 101(3) exemption. The Commission found that clauses requiring the licensee not to deal in competing products did not fall within art. 101(1), and in doing so illustrated a difference in approach between trade mark and technology licences, as this

prevents the licensees from neglecting Campari in the event of conflict between the promotion of Campari sales and possible interest in another product. Although a non-competition clause in a licensing agreement concerning industrial property rights based on the result of a creative activity, such as a patent, would constitute a barrier to technical and economic progress by preventing the licensees from taking an interest in other techniques and products, this is not the case with the licensing arrangements under consideration here...The prohibition on dealing in competing products, therefore, makes for improved distribution of the relevant product in the same way as do exclusive dealing agreements containing a similar clause. (paras 71–2)

The licensing of *performances* which are subject to copyright (including, e.g., the broadcast of films) raises particular problems given the nature of the product in question. In these cases, uniquely, the Commission takes the view that absolute territorial protection does not infringe art. 101(1). This flows from the fact that the specific subject matter of a performance right is the right to profit from the performance each time it is shown (see *Compagnie Générale pour la Diffusion de la Télévision, Coditel* v *Ciné Vog Films (Coditel I)* [1981] 2 CMLR 362). In the second *Coditel* case, relating to a right granted to a Belgian broadcaster to transmit Claude Chabrol's excellent film, *Le Boucher*, the Court of Justice held that

the mere fact that the owner of the copyright in a film has granted to a sole licensee the exclusive right to exhibit that film in the territory of a Member State and, consequently, to prohibit, during a specified period, its showing by others, is not sufficient to justify the finding that such a contract must be regarded as the purpose, the means or the result of an agreement, decision or concerted practice prohibited by the Treaty. (*Coditel* v *SA Ciné Vog Films (Coditel II)* [1983] 1 CMLR 49, at para. 15)

The fact that copyright performances merit distinctive treatment is reaffirmed in the guidelines at para. 52.

22.2.2 **Regulation 772/2004**

Block exemption regulations generally have been dealt with in Chapter 10.

Regulation 772/2004 is the third piece of legislation to deal with the application of art. 101(3) TFEU to vertical agreements under which technology is transferred from one party to another. It entered into force on 1 May 2004, although in respect of earlier agreements falling within the terms of Regulation 240/96 (on the application of art. [101(3)] of the Treaty to certain categories of technology transfer agreements (1996) OJ L31/2) which was repealed by Regulation 772/2004 there is a transitional period extending up to 31 March 2006 (art. 10). Regulation 240/96 itself replaced and consolidated the law found in two earlier regulations, but was criticized for its rigid approach, and in 2000 the Commission published an *Evaluation Report on the Transfer of Technology Block Exemption Regulation No 240/96*. The response to suggestions for reform was generally favourable, and the new regulation reflects a greatly simplified approach. A Commission notice providing *Guidelines on the application of art. 81 of the EC Treaty to technology transfer agreements* has been published at (2004) OJ C101/2 and this sheds further light on the operation of the regulation. The regulation is due to expire on 30 April 2014.

It is a matter of common commercial practice that the originators of intellectual property or new technologies are often not those who themselves are best in a position to directly exploit them, and will instead license this task to a second party or parties. As recognized in recital (5) to the regulation:

Technology transfer agreements concern the licensing of technology. Such agreements will usually improve economic efficiency and be pro-competitive as they can reduce duplication of research and development, strengthen the incentive for the initial research and development, spur incremental innovation, facilitate diffusion and generate product market competition.

As with the other block exemption regulations the position of the parties to the agreement on the relevant market is considered to be important:

The likelihood that such efficiency enhancing and pro-competitive effects will outweigh any anti-competitive effects due to restrictions contained in technology transfer agreements depends on the degree of market power of the undertakings concerned and, therefore, on the extent to which those undertakings face competition from undertakings owning substitute technologies or undertakings producing substitute products.   (recital (6))

Article 1 of the regulation provides the basic definitions necessary to understanding the later terms of the regulation. Most important of these is the definition of a technology transfer agreement. This is

a patent licensing agreement, a know-how licensing agreement, a software copyright licensing agreement or a mixed patent, know-how or software copyright licensing agreement, including any such agreement containing provisions which relate to the sale and purchase of products or which relate to the licensing of other intellectual property rights or the assignment of intellectual property rights, provided that those provisions do not constitute the primary object of the agreement and are directly related to the production of the contract products; assignments of patents, know-how, software copyright or a combination thereof where part of the risk associated with the exploitation of the technology remains with the assignor, in particular where the sum payable in consideration of the assignment is dependent on the turnover obtained by the assignee in respect of products produced with the assigned technology, the quantity of such products produced or the number of operations carried out employing the technology, shall also be deemed to be technology transfer agreements.   (art. 1(b))

'Intellectual property rights' are further defined in art. 1(g) to include 'industrial property rights, know-how, copyright and neighbouring rights'. Know-how, which is not generally defined in the law of intellectual property, is defined in art. 1(i) as being 'a package of non-patented practical information' which meets three further criteria. It should be (1) secret; (2) substantial; and (3) identified. It might be asked why such a definition is actually necessary as it would be unlikely that anyone would pay for a right to the use of know-how that was neither secret, nor substantial, nor capable of being clearly identified and explained.

The basic exemption from the application of art. 101(1) provided by the regulation is set out in art. 2, and the time period of the exemption in any particular case is the period of the existence of the intellectual property right in question, which may vary depending on the type of intellectual property, and by which body or bodies the right has been recognized. In the case of know-how the time period extends for as long as the know-how remains secret. The relevant market share thresholds are set out in art. 3. These are 20 per cent in the case of competing undertakings, and 30 per cent in the case of non-competing undertakings. The calculation and application of these thresholds is further expanded on in art. 8. In particular a 'safe harbour' is provided whereby the exemption shall continue for a period of two years following an increase of the market share above the levels specified in art. 3.

Prohibited hard-core restrictions are set out in art. 4. The standard prohibition on restricting the ability of a party to determine its selling price, and limitations on output (in this case subject to certain conditions), and the allocation of customers or markets are all found here. The licensor may impose restrictions on the *type* of use to which the technology is put, i.e. the licence may be for a particular purpose only (art. 4(1)(c)(i)). What is perhaps worthy of particular note is that some territorial restrictions may be imposed which go further than are permitted under any of the other block exemption regulations, and which go further than would be suggested by the general application of art. 101(1). Thus art. 4(1)(c)(iv) *permits* 'the restriction, in a non-reciprocal agreement, of active and/or *passive sales* by the licensee and/or the licensor into the exclusive territory or to the exclusive customer group reserved for the other party' (emphasis added). Similarly, in the case of licences between undertakings which are not competing with each other passive sales may be restricted into an exclusive territory or to an exclusive customer group (art. 4(2)(b)(i)) or to the customers of another licensee during the first two years that the licensee is selling that product (art. 4(2)(b)(ii)). It is to be presumed that the licensee may *not* refuse to supply, within its own territory, a known parallel exporter, although this is much harder to monitor, and the effect of these terms of the regulation is to allow for much greater market division than is the case elsewhere in the application of EU competition law.

Article 5 sets out certain excluded restrictions, the presence of which does not serve to invalidate the agreement as a whole, but which individually will not benefit from the exemption provided for in art. 2. These include: an obligation on a licensee to compulsory license back, or to assign to the licensor or a nominated third party 'severable improvements' that it creates in relation to the new technology, and any direct or indirect obligation not to challenge the validity of the intellectual property which forms the subject matter of the agreement.

The Commission may withdraw the benefit of the block exemption in individual cases in accordance with art. 6. The list of circumstances in which this may happen is not a closed one, but includes situations where the parties, 'without any objectively valid reason' do not exploit the technology (art. 6(1)(c)), or where parallel networks of similar agreements restrict competition (art. 6(1)(a) and (b)).

22.3 IP and the application of art. 102 TFEU and the Chapter II Prohibition

It was made clear as early as 1968 that art. 102 could be applied to the use of IP rights, as long as the relevant conditions relating to the operation of the article were in place—the fact that an undertaking holds an IP right does not necessarily mean it is dominant. In *Parke, Davis & Co.* v *Probel, Reese, Beintema-Interpharm and Centrapharm* case 24/67 [1968] CMLR 47 the Court of Justice held that the fact that a patent was being exploited was not by itself sufficient to incur the application of art. 102 TFEU, but that the provision could be applied 'if the utilisation of the patent could degenerate into an improper exploitation of the protection'. In this case the Court held that to charge a higher price for a patented item than a non-patented item was not an abuse of a dominant position, but in confirming that art. 102 could be applied to the exploitation of IP rights it opened the door to a chain of cases that has its most recent manifestation in the action taken against Microsoft Corporation by the EU Commission in 2004 (see below).

The holding of intellectual property does not necessarily confer a dominant position (*Sirena* v *Eda* case 40/70 [1971] ECR 69, para. 16) as it may be the case that the relevant market encompasses products, services, or processes other than the one for which the right is held. There are, however, a number of cases in which it has been found that an intellectual property right acts as a barrier to entry, consolidating the strength of a dominant position (see 14.2.5.5). In *Tetra Pak I* 88/501 (1988) OJ L272/27 the EU Commission condemned the acquisition of a licence to intellectual property in an area where the undertaking in question was already dominant.

The leading case, although one that is peculiar on its facts, relating to the abusive use of intellectual property is that of *Magill* (*RTÉ and Independent Television Productions* v *Commission* cases C 241 and 242/91P [1995] 4 CMLR 418; this case is also dealt with as Key case 22.1). Here the Commission found that broadcasters in Ireland had abused their dominant position by exploiting the copyright they held in television programme listings to prevent the publication of those listings by third parties. They published their own television guides and were able to prevent competition in what was viewed as a separate market from that of the television broadcasting itself. The Court noted, at paras 53–4, that

The appellants—who were, by force of circumstances, the only sources of the basic information on program scheduling which is the indispensable raw material for compiling a weekly television guide—gave viewers wishing to obtain information on the choice of programs for the week ahead no choice but to buy the weekly guides for each station and draw from each of them the information they needed to make comparisons.

The appellants' refusal to provide basic information by relying on national copyright provisions thus prevented the appearance of a new product, a comprehensive weekly guide to television programs, which the appellants did not offer and for which there was a potential consumer demand. Such refusal constitutes an abuse under heading (b) of the second paragraph of art. 102 of the Treaty.

The conclusion of the Court was that the Commission was in a position to remedy an abuse by ordering the compulsory licence of the intellectual property held by the appellants:

In the present case, after finding that the refusal to provide undertakings such as Magill with the basic information contained in television program listings was an abuse of a dominant position, the Commission was entitled under [Regulation 17], in order to ensure that its decision was effective, to require the appellants to provide that information. As the Court of First Instance rightly found, the imposition of that obligation—with the possibility of making authorisation of publication dependent on certain conditions, including payment of royalties—was the only way of bringing the infringement to an end.   (para. 91)

Key case 22.1 *Magill TV Guide/ITV, BBC and RTE* 89205 [1989] OJ L78/43; *RTÉ* v *Commission* case T-69/89 [1991] 4 CMLR 586; case T–76/89 *ITP Ltd* v *Commission* [1991] 4 CMLR 745; *Radio Telefis Eireann and Independent Television Publications Ltd* v *Commission (Magill)* cases C 241–242/91P [1995] 4 CMLR 718—Commission decision, GC judgments, Court of Justice judgment (art. 102 and access to intellectual property)

Facts

Television broadcasting companies operating in the UK and Ireland produced listings magazines setting out a full schedule of programmes, with supplementary information, for the week ahead. Each listings magazine contained only the programme information relating to the broadcasting network publishing the magazine. *TV Times* was published by the ITV network in the UK, *Radio Times* by the BBC, and *RTÉ Guide* by RTÉ in Ireland. There was no single guide that covered all the channels broadcast by the three networks, a position different to that which arose in other Member States. The programme listings were protected by copyright protection by virtue of the UK Copyright Act 1956 and the Irish Copyright Act 1963. The listings were treated as literary works and compilations. The broadcasters would license the information contained in the listings to daily and weekly newspapers, and in some cases to magazines, but the licences contained conditions under which the publishers could only provide listings for, at most, two days ahead, along with selected weekly highlights. In 1985 an Irish publisher, *Magill* began to publish a weekly paper in Ireland and Northern Ireland containing full weekly listings which could be obtained in the two countries. RTÉ, BBC, and ITV obtained an interim injunction restraining the publication. Magill had already lodged a complaint with the Commission under the terms of Regulation 17/62. The Commission took a decision finding that the refusal of the three broadcasting companies to license the information so as to permit the emergence of weekly comprehensive listings guides was an abuse under art. 102 TFEU. The Commission required the parties to bring the infringement to an end 'by supplying each other and third parties on request and on a non-discriminatory basis with their individual advance weekly programme listings and by permitting reproduction of those listings by such parties...any royalties...should be reasonable (art. 2). The three broadcasters appealed to the GC, which upheld the Commission decision, and a further appeal was made to the Court of Justice.

Findings

The key part of the judgment of the Court of Justice is very short (paras 46–58). The Court first confirmed that the mere holding of an intellectual property right does not, axiomatically, create a dominant position (para. 46) but that in the present case 'the basic information as to the channel, day, time and title of programmes is the necessary result of programming by television stations, which are thus the only source of such information...By force of circumstances, RTÉ and [ITV] enjoy, along with the BBC, a *de facto* monopoly' (para. 47). While refusal to grant a copyright licence could not, in itself, constitute an abuse 'the exercise of an exclusive right by the proprietor may, in exceptional circumstances, involve abusive conduct' (para. 51). A number of factors in the present case supported the findings of the EU Commission and the GC that an abuse had taken place. First, there was no actual or potential substitute for a weekly television guide offering information on the programmes of the week ahead, and there was 'a specific, constant and regular potential demand on the part of consumers' (para. 52). Second, there was no justification for the refusal of the appellants to supply the information requested, and third 'the appellants, by their conduct, reserved to themselves the secondary market of weekly television guides by excluding all competition on that market' (para. 56). RTÉ had sought to rely on the Berne Convention for the Protection of Literary and Artistic Works (as revised in 1971), which permitted signatory states to require compulsory licensing of copyright as long as reproduction did not conflict with the normal exploitation of the work and did not unreasonably prejudice the legitimate interests of the author (art. 9(2)). The GC and the Court of Justice held that the Union was not a signatory to the Convention, and was not therefore bound by its provisions.

Comment

The chain of cases relating to abusive refusals to supply began with *Commercial Solvents* (Key case 14.4) and *United Brands* (Key case 14.2). The first principle established was that an abuse could be found where a dominant undertaking refused to supply an existing customer without objective justification. The essential facilities doctrine then provided that the refusal to supply a new customer might be an abuse where the product or service being sought was truly essential, and could not be replicated by a supplier of the same size and resources as the incumbent (see *Oscar Bronner*). *Magill* extended this principle to intellectual property, and was followed and refined in *IMS* which was in turn followed in *Microsoft* (Key case 22.2). The conditions for supply to be required become progressively stricter from the standard doctrine, to the essential facilities doctrine, to cases where what is sought is protected by intellectual property. Intellectual property lawyers have criticized the application of this principle as stifling innovation by reducing the incentive to invest in intellectual property. *Magill*, *IMS*, and *Microsoft*, have all dealt with what might be called 'soft' intellectual property—TV listing information; a 'brick structure' collating postcodes for marketing and distribution purposes; and computer software protocols (not source code). There has not yet been a case where the principles of *Magill* have been applied to material benefiting from patent protection, although there appears to be nothing in the three judgments cited here which would preclude such an application. A broad schema of the increase in the strictness of the test to be applied in relation to refusals to supply might be illustrated as follows:

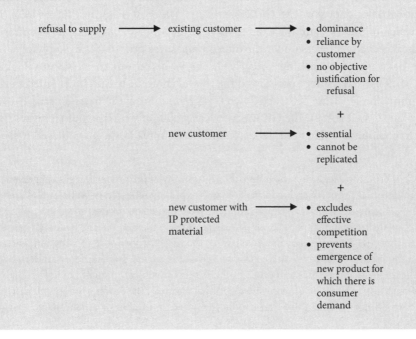

FURTHER READING

Article

GREAVES, R., 'Magill est arrivé . . . *RTE and ITP* v *Commission of the European Communities*', (1995) *ECLR* 244

The *Magill* judgment was heavily criticized by a number of intellectual property and competition lawyers, and it is generally considered to be 'exceptional', although it is not doubted that it remains good law. However, the Commission resorted to a similar approach in the case of *IMS*. It took an interim measures decision in relation to the use of intellectual property recognized under German law. This related to pharmaceutical sales data services, which sprang from a database built around a '1,860 brick structure', in which the country was divided into 'bricks', with each brick containing relevant data about pharmacies, and drug prescription levels. IMS Health Inc held the copyright in this system, and refused to grant a licence to the complainant, National Data Corporation Health Information Services (NDC), an American company expanding sales into Europe. NDC argued that the brick structure was an essential facility, without which it could not compete in providing a rival regional sales service. The Commission agreed, relying on the chain of cases beginning with *Istituto Chemioterapico Italiano and Commercial Solvents* v *Commission* cases 6–7/73 [1974] 1 CMLR 309, including *Magill* (see also the discussion of the essential facilities doctrine in Chapter 16), and held that the 'exceptional circumstances' referred to at para. 50 of the *Magill* judgment were present in this case. IMS was required to grant a licence 'without delay to all undertakings currently present on the market for German regional sales data services' (*IMS Health Inc. (Interim measures)* (2002/165)). IMS appealed to the GC, and the Court first held, in August 2001, that the Commission had exceeded its powers under the interim measures procedures by applying a remedy that was so 'far-reaching' (*IMS Health Inc.* v *Commission* case T–184/01 R I [2002] 4 CMLR 1). Later, after considering the matter more fully the Court ruled that the Commission Decision be struck down (*IMS Health Inc.* v *Commission* case T–184/01 R II [2002] 4 CMLR 2). The GC was very clear that only rarely would it be appropriate to compulsorily licence intellectual property in response to an alleged breach of art. 102:

It is important to recall that the public interest in respect for property rights in general and for intellectual property rights in particular is expressly reflected in Articles [36] and [345 TFEU]. The mere fact that the applicant has invoked and sought to enforce its copyright in the 1,860 brick structure for economic reasons does not lessen its entitlement to rely upon the exclusive right granted by national law for the very purpose of rewarding innovation.

In the present case, where there is, on the face of it, a clear public interest underlying the applicant's effort to enforce and profit from the specific subject-matter of its copyright in the 1,860 brick structure, the inherently exceptional nature of the power to adopt interim measures would normally require that conduct whose termination or amendment is targeted by such measures fall clearly within the scope of the Treaty competition rules. However, the characterisation of the refusal to licence at issue in the present proceedings as abusive turns, prima facie, on the correctness of the Commission's interpretation of the case law concerning the scope of 'exceptional circumstances'. It is this case law which explains the clearly special situations in which the objective pursued by art. [102 TFEU] may prevail over that underlying the grant of intellectual property rights. In this context, where the abusive nature of the appellant's conduct is not unambiguous having regard to the relevant case law and where there is a tangible risk that it will suffer serious and irreparable harm if forced, in the meantime, to licence its competitors, the balance of interests favours the unimpaired preservation of its copyright until the judgment of the main action.   (paras 143–4)

An appeal to the Court of Justice by NDC and the Commission was dismissed (*NDC Health Corporation* v *IMS Health Inc. and Commission* case C–481/01 P(R) [2002] 5 CMLR 1). A separate proceeding into other aspects of IMS's conduct was closed late in 2002 when the Commission found that the company had, in the face of its investigation, amended its conduct (Commission press release IP (02) 1430, 4 October 2002). By a decision in 2003 (*IMS Health* 2003/74 (2003) OJ L268/69) the Commission withdrew decision 2002/165.

In a separate development following proceedings in Germany the Court of Justice was asked, via the art. 267 TFEU referral route, whether it might be an abuse within the meaning of art. 102 were a dominant undertaking to refuse to grant a licence to copyright material in situations in which the claimant company had rejected alternative products not making use of that material because their set-up relied upon it. The Court reiterated the position that, save in exceptional circumstances, the refusal to grant copyright by a dominant undertaking cannot, in itself, be an abuse. Three cumulative conditions had to be met for an abuse to occur: (1) the refusal prevented the emergence of a new product for which there was demand; (2) refusal was unjustified; and (3) refusal would exclude competition on a secondary market. It was the third condition that was most contested in the present case, and the Court referred to its judgment in *Oscar Bronner GmbH & Co. KG* v *Mediaprint Zeitungs-und Zeitschriftenverlag GmbH & Co. KG* case C–7/97 [1999] 4 CMLR 112. Following the latter it was necessary to determine whether the 1,860 brick structure constituted an essential upstream factor in the downstream supply of sales data for pharmaceutical products. Whether this was the case was a fact that only the national court could determine (*IMS Health GmbH & Co. OHG* v *NDC Health GmbH & Co. KG* case C–418/02 [2004] 4 CMLR 28).

A recent case to deal substantively with the issue of compulsory licensing of intellectual property is that of *Microsoft* (2007/53/EC (2007) OJ L32/23). The Commission required Microsoft to supply its competitors in the market for group server operating systems with certain 'interoperability information' relating to its Windows suite of operating systems. In essence the argument was that without access to code in Windows, developers of server systems were unable to construct such systems to work effectively with Windows, and were therefore at a disadvantage in this related market to Microsoft. The company appealed to the GC seeking interim relief from the effect of the decision until such time as the substantive appeal was heard. The President of the Court referred back to the *IMS* case, and noted that although it was a 'substantial breach of the exclusive prerogatives' flowing from intellectual property rights to require an undertaking to grant licences affecting its copyright (para. 248):

the fact remains that that breach is the necessary consequence of the principle established in *IMS Health*, since the examination carried out by the Community judicature consists specifically in weighing up, on the one hand, the protection conferred by an intellectual property right on its holder and, on the other, the requirements for free competition laid down in the [TFEU].   (para. 249)

The President was not convinced that the damage that Microsoft alleged would flow if it complied with the requirements of the decision would be irreparable, as required for interim relief to be granted. Microsoft had made a 'vague allegation' (para. 256) that it would cost it 'tens of millions of dollars' to comply with the ruling. The President found these arguments insubstantial, and further argued that even if Microsoft were to suffer financial loss this could not 'be regarded as serious, owing to the financial power of Microsoft' (para. 257) (*Microsoft Corp.* v *Commission* case T–201/04 R (II) [2005] 4 CMLR 5). The GC upheld the Commission decision in September 2007 (*Microsoft Corp.* v *Commission* case T–201/04, judgment of 17 September 2007). As in *Magill* the Court appears to have drawn a distinction between different qualities of intellectual property, noting that in this case the Commission was not forcing Microsoft to disclose 'certain protocols and not the source code' (see, e.g., para. 203). It is unclear however whether the position of the Court, which was based on the application of the principles enunciated in *IMS* (above), would have been different had the Commission ordered that disclosure (see also Key case 22.2).

Key case 22.2 *Microsoft Corporation* (2007/53/EC, (2007) OJ L32/23); *Microsoft Corporation* v *Commission* case T–201/04 R [2005] 4 CMLR 18 (interveners); [2005] 4 CMLR 5 (interim measures); T–201/04, judgment of 17 September 2007—Commission decision (art. 102); GC preliminary measures and final judgment

Facts

Microsoft is the most prominent provider of operating systems for desktop and laptop computers in the world. Its Windows operating system (OS) is found on over 90 per cent of computers. In December 1998 DG Comp received a complaint from Sun Microsystems Inc. stating that Microsoft was abusing its dominant position on the OS market by refusing to supply interoperability information relevant to software products necessary for network computing (work group server systems) and that without such information competitors in this market could not develop products that were fully compatible with the dominant Windows OS. In February 2000 the Commission opened a case in relation to the supply by Microsoft of Windows Media Player which was being incorporated into its Windows 2000 OS. In August 2001 a statement of objections (SO) was sent to Microsoft relating to the Media Player development, and the Commission incorporated into this an earlier SO relating to the interoperability issue. On 24 March 2004 the Commission took a decision finding that both practices were in breach of art. 102 TFEU, and imposed a penalty on Microsoft of €497,196,304. The Commission required Microsoft: (1) to make the interoperability information available to any relevant undertaking on reasonable and non-discriminatory terms; (2) to keep this information up to date in a timely manner; (3) to create an evaluation mechanism to support this system; (4) to notify the Commission of the measures it was taking; and (5) to offer a full functioning version of its OS which did not incorporate Media Player (significant fines were subsequently imposed for breaches of the first set of conditions relating to interoperability). Microsoft appealed, and at an interim stage asked the President of the GC to suspend the effect of the Commission decision by way of interim relief. This request was denied. Various third parties sought to take part in the proceedings, and a number of requests to intervene were granted.

Findings

Microsoft did not argue before the Court that it was not in a dominant position in the market for PC operating systems. What it said was that the Court should annul the decision, or in the alternative should reduce the amount of the penalty and award it costs. The Court held first that while the Commission had a margin of appreciation in economic and technical matters, the Court was required to review the Commission's interpretation of economic and technical data, and determine whether evidence relied on was factually accurate, reliable, and consistent, and that no relevant material was ignored (para. 89). Microsoft argued that the requirement to disclose interoperability information as determined by the Commission would amount to a restriction on the free exercise of its intellectual property rights, and argued that criteria established in *Magill* and *IMS* (see this chapter) were not met. The Commission had adopted its decision on the basis that it was indeed dealing with IP rights and chose the strictest legal test (para. 284). In certain circumstances, the GC stated, an undertaking's refusal to supply IP protected material could constitute an abuse of a dominant position (paras 319–31), but these circumstances must be exceptional (para. 332). In the present case the information required was indeed indispensable, competition would have been eliminated were the information not supplied, and the emergence of a new product for which there was demand was being frustrated (art. 102(b) TFEU makes reference to 'limiting production, markets or technical developments'). Finally there was no objective justification for Microsoft's refusal to supply the data required. In relation to the issue of the bundling, or tying, of Media Player with the Windows OS the GC held that there existed two separate products, with independent demand for applications software with streaming capabilities. Following from *Tetra Pak* and *Hilti* the Court found that an abuse had also taken place in this practice. On one ground only did the Commission incur a significant loss. It had appointed an independent monitoring trustee to supervise the interoperability disclosure process, and the GC held that the trustee had been given powers which were not legally the Commission's to provide.

Comment

Microsoft Corporation has had extensive engagement with, and impact on, competition law in a number of jurisdictions, and serves as the exemplar of a multinational corporation subject to the strictures of disparate national competition laws. It operates at the time of writing under the restrictions of a consent decree in the US (with reporting requirements imposed—see the DOJ website), and has negotiated with the EU Commission in relation to the development of its Vista platform. There has been significant comment as to the extent to which competition law may be appropriately applied to the 'new technologies', which are information dependent, which move quickly, and where competition is sometimes described as being *for* the market, rather than *in* the market. In the present case the analysis of the issue of tying/bundling follows that applied in relation to food packaging systems and to fixing materials in the construction industry. The present case was launched by DG Comp in February 2000, and the judgment of the GC in the appeal was given in September 2007, seven years and seven months after the proceedings opened. Two issues dominate the case: the first is that of the extent to which the standards imposed under EU law stifle development in integrated high-tech products (should, for example, spelling checkers not be supplied with word processing software?), or enhance competition; the second that of whether by requiring the disclosure of intellectual property the EU is reducing the incentive to invest in product development. Comment from the US following the judgment was strident and critical, although a more measured debate among US antitrust lawyers following the decision was more supportive of the approach of DG Comp. The EU approach has been followed elsewhere—in Korea, for example. It was hoped that the GC judgment might address some of these fundamental issues head on, and might provide a robust and critical underpinning for the development of competition law into the twenty-first century, but in fact the judgment avoids larger statements, and deals rather with both aspects of the case on a fairly traditional and uncritical basis.

FURTHER READING

AHLBORN, C., and EVANS, D. S., 'The Microsoft Judgment and Its Implications for Competition Policy Towards Dominant Firms in Europe', (2009) 75 *Antitrust Law Journal* 3

While the cases discussed above relate to the extreme position in which the issue of compulsory licensing has been raised, the situation more normally encountered continues to be that in which it is the exercise of IP rights that is curtailed by the application of competition law, although there have been rare cases relating to the process of applying for IP rights and the management of IP systems. Thus the use of patents and related IP rights to partition the market was condemned by the EU Commission in *AstraZeneca plc* (2005/1757/EC, decision of 15 June 2005), with the AstraZeneca group being fined €60 million in respect of various infringements relating to the marketing of an anti-ulcer medicine, Losec. Following the end of patent protection pharmaceutical companies may, in appropriate circumstances, apply for 'supplementary protection certificates' (SPCs), which, in effect, extend the period of patent protection. Generic medicine manufacturers complained to the Commission alleging that two abuses had taken place. First, AstraZeneca was alleged to have made misleading representations in making its SPC applications, and in particular that it had provided misleading information relating to relevant dates, so as to extend the protections given. Second, AstraZeneca changed the format in which drugs were made available, and 'deregistered' in some markets the earlier format. The effect of this practice was to prevent, or delay, generic entry into the market, and to restrict parallel trade. The Commission decision is a very long one, but in summary the Commission found that both alleged abuses had taken place. It rejected arguments made by the defendant to the effect that the grant of the SPCs could not be challenged, as this would constitute an attack on the *existence* of an IP right (paras 741–4). In this respect the Commission held that 'the laws of the Member States are not affected by qualifying as abusive misleading representations made in the context of applications for [IP] right, in the absence of which the right or rights in question would not normally be granted' (para. 741).

22.4 IP and the free movement of goods in the EU

22.4.1 Introduction

The provisions in the TFEU directly relating to the free movement of goods are among the most important, being fundamental in the creation of the internal, previously 'common', market. They have led to a significant amount of case law, and have had a major impact on the freedom within which goods can be distributed throughout the EU. The treatment here is necessarily brief, and is directed exclusively to issues relating to the exploitation of IP rights. For a more detailed treatment reference should be made to one of the specialist texts dealing with the free movement of goods or intellectual property.

Article 34 TFEU provides that

Quantitative restrictions on imports and all measures having equivalent effect shall be prohibited between Member States.

It should be immediately obvious that national-based IP rights have the ability to frustrate the application of this article. If a German manufacturer of hi-fi equipment can assign exclusive trade marks in different Member States such that the holder of an assigned trade mark in one Member State may lawfully prevent the import of the same good bearing the same trade mark assigned to someone in another Member State there would appear to be a fundamental breach of art. 34. However, art. 36 provides some exceptions to this general principle. It states:

The provisions of Articles 34…shall not preclude prohibitions or restrictions on imports, exports or goods in transit justified on grounds of…the protection of industrial and commercial property. Such prohibition or restrictions shall not, however, constitute a means of arbitrary discrimination or a disguised restriction on trade between Member States.

The Court of Justice has held that the term 'industrial and commercial property', which is not defined in the Treaty, extends, *inter alia*, to copyright, and the term is now taken to be synonymous with 'intellectual property' (see *Deutsche Grammophon Gesellschaft v Metro-SB-Grossmarkte GmbH* [1971] CMLR 631). It would appear therefore that art. 36 expressly allows restrictions based on the assertion of IP rights, as long as such restrictions do not amount to 'arbitrary discrimination or a disguised restriction on trade between Member States'. It is this final caveat which has permitted the Court of Justice to develop a line of jurisprudence which significantly restricts the ability of holders of IP rights to exercise those rights in a way which divides the internal market. In doing so the Court has drawn an uneasy distinction between the 'existence' of an IP right, and the 'exercise' of that right. Many would question the validity of such a distinction, and it may be reasonably argued that the existence of a right is determined precisely by the ways in which it can be exercised. However, notwithstanding these intellectual objections, the Court introduced this principle in the case of *Consten and Grundig* v *Commission* (*Établissements Consten Sarl* v *Commission*) cases 56 and 58/64 [1966] 1 CMLR 418, discussed in detail at 9.3.1.1). Here the Court held that

Article [36]…cannot limit the field of application of Article [101]. Article [345] confines itself to stating that the 'Treat[ies] shall in no way prejudice the rules in Member States governing the system of property ownership'. The injunction contained in…the contested decision to refrain from using rights under national trade-mark law in order to set an obstacle in the way of parallel imports does not affect the grant of those rights but only limits their exercise to the extent necessary to give effect to the prohibition under Article [101(1)].   (para. 50)

22.4.2 The doctrine of exhaustion

This distinction between the existence and the exercise of an IP right was more fully developed in the case of *Deutsche Grammophon* v *Metro* (above), in which the competition provisions of the Treaty were not applicable, such that the case relied on the application of arts 34 and 36. In this case Deutsche Grammophon (DG), the holder of copyright in recordings pressed some records in Germany which were transferred to its subsidiary, Polydor, in France. These were in turn sold to a third party and eventually marketed in Germany at a price lower than that charged by DG. DG sought to rely on its copyright to prevent the resale, and following an art. 267 reference the matter came before the Court of Justice. At para. 13 of its judgment the Court summed up the principle that has become known as the exhaustion doctrine:

it would be in conflict with the provisions prescribing the free movement of products within the common market for a manufacturer of sound recordings to exercise the exclusive right to distribute the protected articles, conferred upon him by the legislation of a Member State, in such a way as to prohibit the sale in that State of products placed on the market by him or with his consent in another Member State solely because such distribution did not occur within the territory of the first Member State.

Although the exhaustion doctrine was not expressly defined in this case, it has become clear that the principle is that the exclusive rights conferred by the holding of IP are exhausted once the goods have been placed on the market in the EU. It is this right of first marking, and presumably of making a 'monopoly' profit at that time, which is regarded as the fundamental attribute of IP in the Union. Thus, in the case of *Centrafarm BV and Adriaan de Peijper* v *Sterling Drug Inc.* case 16/74 [1974] 2 CMLR 480 the Court held that the 'specific subject matter' of the patent right in question was

the guarantee that the patentee, to reward the creative effort of the inventor, has the exclusive right to use an invention with a view to manufacturing industrial products and putting them into circulation for the first time, either directly or by the grant of licences to third parties, as well as the right to oppose infringements.

Although the application of this doctrine in EU law has given rise to some controversy, the Union was not the first jurisdiction to apply an 'exhaustion' principle to the exploitation of IP rights. What makes the case particularly distinctive, however, is the fact that the principle was applied so vigorously across state boundaries.

One implication of this is that a rational holder of an IP right will market the resulting product first in the Member State where it can command the highest price. Were the first marketing to take place in the Member State with the lowest price, parallel importers could legally purchase the product in that state and resell it in states with higher prices taking the profit for themselves. This is one reason why manufacturers of some products limit the quantities they will supply to Member States where prices are cheaper. An illustration of the application of such a parallel import practice may be seen in the case of *Centrafarm BV and Adriaan de Peijper* v *Sterling Drug Inc.* case 16/74 [1974] 2 CMLR 480. Here Sterling Drug held patents in respect of a drug in both the Netherlands and the UK, and marketed the product in both states. The price was far higher in the Netherlands and parallel importers purchased substantial quantities in the UK for resale in the Netherlands. Sterling Drug was unable to rely on its patent in the Netherlands to prevent the import of the drugs from the UK on the grounds that it had consented to the marketing in the UK. This case also made it clear that in order for rights to have been exhausted they must have first been exploited by the holder of the right, and the patent holder must have consented to the first marketing of the product in question. This was not the case in *Parke, Davis & Co.* v *Probel and Centrafarm* case 24/67 [1969] CMLR 47 where drugs made without authorization in Italy were imported into the Netherlands. In this case the Court of Justice held that the patent owner in the Netherlands could rely on the exclusive right allowed within the patent to prevent the parallel imports. The doctrine does not frustrate the ability of the owner of the IP right to prevent imports which flow from third states which are neither in the EU nor the EEA (see, e.g., *Polydor Ltd and RSO Records Inc.* v *Harlequin Record Shops and Simons Records* [1982] 1 CMLR 677).

22.4.3 **The doctrine of common origin**

In the case of *Van Zuylen Freres* v *Hag AG* case 192/73 [1974] 2 CMLR 127 the Court of Justice dealt with an exceptional set of circumstances in which a trade mark, Hag, was owned by different persons, but had a common origin (as a result of wartime sequestration of assets). There was no legal link between the two owners, and no agreements had been entered into by the first common owner relating to the distribution of the trade mark to its present owners. The Court held that neither owner could rely on their rights against the other. This principle was subject to severe criticism at the time of the judgment, in part because it appeared to contradict the principle that the owner of IP was entitled to put the products into circulation for the first time. Fortunately the principle has since been abandoned, and may now, apart from this historical nicety, be regarded as of no value (see *SA CNL-Sucal NV* v *Hag GF AG* case C–10/89 [1990] 3 CMLR 571).

FURTHER READING

Books

ANDERMAN, S. D., and KALLAUGHER, J., *Technology Transfer and the New EU Competition Rules: Intellectual Property Licensing after Modernisation* (2006) OUP, Oxford

BENTLEY, L., and SHERMAN, B., *Intellectual Property Law* (2004) 2nd edn, OUP, Oxford

Articles

DERCLAYE, E., 'The IMS Health Decision: A Triple Victory', (2004) *World Competition Law & Economics Review* 397

DOLMANS, M., and PIILOLA, A., 'The New Technology Transfer Block Exemption', (2004) *World Competition Law & Economics Review* 351

GARROD, D., and ROSEN, A., 'The New Safe Harbour for Technology Transfer Agreements', [2004] *Competition Law Journal* 31

KANTER, D., 'IP and Compulsory Licensing on Both Sides of the Atlantic—An Appropriate Antitrust Remedy or a Cutback on Innovation?', (2006) *European Competition Law Review* 351

KORAH, V., 'The Interface between Intellectual Property and Antitrust: The European Experience', (2002) 69 *Antitrust Law Journal* 801 (and see also, Fine, F., 'NDC/IMS: In Response to Professor Korah', (2002) 70 *Antitrust Law Journal* 247)

PEEPERKORN, L., 'IP Licenses and Competition Rules: Striking the Right Balance', (2003) *World Competition Law & Economics Review* 527

23

The common law and competition

> ## KEY POINTS
>
> - Certain doctrines of common law may be applied to situations in which competition is being restrained, or to competitive conduct.
> - These are becoming less important following the growth of modern competition law.
> - The restraint of trade doctrine remains vibrant, and is often relied on in certain professional disputes.
> - Restraint of trade is a doctrine of contract law, under which certain contracts are unenforceable if they unreasonably restrain the activity of a party after the termination of the main contract.
> - A number of rarely used torts may also be relevant to certain competitive situations.

23.1 Introduction

While there is not a common law of competition as such, there are areas in which the operation of the common law impacts upon issues that are closely related to the public regulation of competition. As was seen in Chapter 1, the common law was originally important in this area, and at the time of its enactment the Sherman Act was viewed within the United States largely as a codification of existing common-law principles. The fact that common law now occupies only a residual role in relation to competition law generally may be attributed to several factors. One may be the apparent success of forms of public regulation, which have reduced the need for reliance on a common law. Another lies in the reluctance of the judiciary to venture into what is seen as a difficult and technical area; it was Fry LJ who commented in *Mogul Steamship* v *McGregor* (1889) 28 QBD 598, at 625, that 'to draw a line between fair and unfair competition ... passes the power of the courts'. A related reason may be found in the reluctance of the judiciary to distinguish economic interests from those of personal liberty. The comment of Lord Atkinson in *H. Morris Ltd* v *Saxelby* [1916] 1 AC 688, at 700, HL is typical: 'no person has an abstract right to be protected against competition *per se* in his trade or business'. The most important area in which the common law continues to have relevance is the contract-based restraint of trade doctrine. Other areas where the common law may play a role are in the statutory tort lying in relation to breaches of arts [101] and [102], conspiracy, and a bundle of related 'economic torts'.

23.2 The restraint of trade doctrine

23.2.1 The development of the doctrine
The roots of the doctrine of restraint of trade are obscure. In *Chitty on Contracts* it is stated that 'cases go back to the second half of the sixteenth century' (Guest, A. G. (ed.), *Chitty on Contracts*, London, Sweet & Maxwell (27th edn, 1994), para. 16–066), although the first reported case appears to be *John Dyer's* case (1414) YB 2 Hen 5, fo. 5, pl. 26. In this case, the defendant, a dyer, had given a bond to the plaintiff not to exercise his trade in the same town for six months. The bond was declared void by Hull J in no uncertain terms (technically the case was not one of 'restraint of trade', which was unknown then as a cause of action, but the case may be appropriately categorized as such at this distance).

The essence of the restraint of trade doctrine is that it is contrary to public policy to enforce contracts that are in unreasonable restraint of trade. It is generally considered to be the case that a contract in restraint of trade is void, unless that restraint can be shown to be a reasonable one. However, in *A. Schroeder Music Publishing Co. Ltd* v *Macaulay* [1974] 3 All ER 617, HL, Lord Reid suggested that the contract in this case was 'unenforceable' (at 623), i.e., voidable, and whether such contracts are in fact void or voidable remains unclear. Whether a restraint is 'reasonable' is to be considered both in relation to the parties themselves, and in relation to the public interest.

Restraint of trade thus relates primarily to situations in which 'a party (the covenantor) agrees with any other party (the covenantee) to restrict his liberty in the future to carry on trade with other persons not parties to the contract in such manner as he chooses' (*Petrofina (Great Britain) Ltd* v *Martin* [1966] Ch 146, *per* Diplock LJ at 180).

All contracts restrain trade: if A agrees with B to sell B a car, then A cannot, without breaking that contract, sell that car to C. Clearly restraints of this nature are the essence of contractual relationships and will not, save in exceptional circumstances, be struck down. The difficulty with restraint of trade is to identify those situations in which the doctrine will apply, which is to say those in which the restraint is both unreasonable between the parties and against the public interest.

As is the case today, the doctrine, even in its earliest development, was determined by reference to the 'public interest', and public policy will also have an impact on the way in which the private interests of the parties are to be determined. This flexible criterion has meant that 'the law as to contracts in restraint of trade had, more than any other class of contracts, been moulded by changing ideas of public policy' (Holdsworth, W., *A History of English Law*, London, Methuen (1937), vol. 7, p. 6). The development of the doctrine became for a time inextricably linked with the resistance to the grants of monopoly by the Crown (see 1.2.1 above). In the reign of Elizabeth I, for example, all restraints were likely to be condemned as being contrary to public policy

(*Colgate* v *Bacheler* (1602) Cro Eliz 872). By 1711, in the case of *Mitchell* v *Reynolds* (1711) 1 P. Wms 181, the courts had begun to distinguish between restraints which operated at the local level and those which purported to be countrywide. In *Mitchell* a countrywide restraint was criticized in the following terms: 'what does it signify to a tradesman in London what another does in Newcastle?' Even in the twentieth century *Mitchell* was referred to as 'among all the decisions, the most outstanding and helpful authority' (*H. Morris Ltd* v *Saxelby* [1916] 1 AC 688, HL, *per* Lord Shaw at 717). Public policy now recognizes that there is a broad interest in encouraging the sale and transfer of businesses, and mobility of employment. If an employer could not to a certain extent restrain the activities of an employee once he or she leaves the employment there might be less incentive to employ the worker in the first place. The same may be true of someone buying a business, who would be less attracted were the vendor immediately able to set up in competition to the new purchaser (see, e.g., Lord Watson in *Nordenfelt* v *Maxim Nordenfelt Guns and Ammunition Co. Ltd* [1984] AC 535, at 552).

The concept of 'reasonableness' appears to have entered into the application of the doctrine in the seventeenth century, and is usually traced to *Rogers* v *Parrey* (1613) 80 ER 1012. Here the judges, including Coke CJ, were called upon to determine the validity of a restraint under which the defendant had promised not to exercise his trade as a joiner 'in a shop, parcel of a house, to him demised in London, for 21 years'. Croke J expressed his concern as to the effect of the restraint: 'The doubt which at first troubled me, was, for the binding of one, that he should not use and exercise his trade, being his livelihood'. However, the fact that this was not the case here swayed the court, which unanimously agreed with Coke CJ that 'as this case here is, for a time certain, and in a place certain, a man may be well bound, and restrained from using his trade'. In *Broad* v *Jolyffe* (1620) Cro Jac 596, the court considered a case in which a trader selling his old stock to another had promised as part of the bargain that he would not trade in competition with the purchaser by keeping a shop in a particular place. When the plaintiff brought an action to enforce this term, the court was of the view that this was sustainable:

upon a valuable consideration one may restrain himself that he shall not use his trade in such a particular place; for he who gives that consideration expects the benefit of his customers; and it is usual here in London for one to let his shop and wares to his servant when he is out of his apprenticeship; as also to covenant that he shall not use his trade in such a shop or in such a street; so for a valuable consideration and voluntarily one may agree that he will not use his trade.

The extent to which the test of reasonableness could be reduced to clear criteria continued to exercise the courts through the eighteenth and nineteenth centuries. A problem facing the courts during this period was the rapid development in the patterns of commerce, and in particular the growth in transport and communications that would quickly render obsolete restrictive interpretations of the doctrine. In *Horner* v *Graves* (1831) 131 ER 284, the court refused to adopt a strict definition, holding instead (at 743) that

we do not see how a better test can be applied to the question whether reasonable or not, than by considering whether the restraint is such only as to afford a fair protection to the interests of the party in favour of whom it is given, and not so large as to interfere with the interests of the public. Whatever restraint is larger than the necessary protection of the party, can be of no benefit to either, it can only be oppressive; and if oppressive, it is, in the eyes of the law, unreasonable. Whatever is injurious to the interests of the public is void, on the grounds of public policy.

The test of reasonableness became the overriding consideration in *Nordenfelt* v *Maxim Nordenfelt Guns and Ammunition Co. Ltd* [1894] AC 535, and it was here that the modern test for determining the validity of any restraining contract was formulated by Lord Macnaghten, where he held (at 565):

The true view at the present time I think, is this: The public have an interest in every person's carrying on his trade freely: so has the individual. All interference with individual liberty of action in trading, and all restraints of trade of themselves, if there is nothing more, are contrary to public policy, and therefore void. That is the general rule. But there are exceptions: restraints of trade and interference with individual liberty of action may be justified by the special circumstances of a particular case. It is a sufficient justification, and indeed it is the only justification, if the restriction is reasonable—reasonable, that is, in reference to the interests of the parties concerned and reasonable in reference to the interests of the public, so framed and so guarded as to afford adequate protection to the party in whose favour it is imposed, while at the same time it is in no way injurious to the public.

In this case the flexibility of approach that Lord Macnaghten's summary of the position called for meant that a restriction unlimited geographically, and lasting for 25 years, was upheld. The restriction had been accepted by a manufacturer of guns who had sold his business and all the patents associated with it, and who had accepted a worldwide restriction on setting up a competing business. Given the nature of the arms trade, the court found that such a worldwide restriction served to protect the genuine commercial interest of the purchaser of the business and did not contain unreasonable restrictions. *Nordenfelt* may be contrasted with *Mason v Provident Clothing and Supply Co. Ltd* [1913] AC 724, in which a restriction on a salesman working for a cloth company, to the effect that he could not work within 25 miles of London for three years after leaving his job, was held to be too restrictive in relation to the interest being protected and the relevant circumstances. While it appears that the extent to which restraints are 'purchased' may be persuasive, the general principle is that the courts will not allow a party to 'buy' a restraint, and will not, in assessing whether a restraint is reasonable, consider the 'reward' given to the plaintiff in return for the acceptance of the restraint. To do so would raise the spectre of the courts assessing the adequacy of consideration, in this case for a single term in the contract, which is a matter that the courts generally avoid.

It has been suggested by Lever that

Any idea that courts are inherently ill equipped to apply *any* sort of economic regulatory rules is readily dispelled when it is recalled that it was the English courts themselves that developed, without legislative assistance, the doctrine. (Lever, J., 'UK Economic Regulation: Use and Abuse of the Law', [1992] *ECLR* 55)

However, the interpretation given to 'reasonable', and in particular the restricted role assigned to the 'public interest', means that the doctrine serves a limited function, and the courts have very obviously rejected any scope for extending it so as to provide a more general protection to the competitive process itself.

23.2.2 The current operation of the doctrine

Restraint of trade concerns will not, save in exceptional circumstances, be raised in standard commercial contracts. There are two situations where the doctrine remains vibrant, both of which have obvious implications for the competitive market. The first concerns post-contract employment considerations, where an employee accepts restrictions on future conduct if he or she leaves that employment. Typically such restrictions might include a limitation on the time that must elapse before the employee works for a competing company, or sets up in direct competition himself. It is also common for a geographical area to be identified, within which the employee is, for a set period, not permitted to compete. The second common situation relates to the sale of businesses and the goodwill attached thereto, where the seller will agree to restrictions on its liberty to maintain a similar business. This was the position in *Broad* v *Jolyffe* (above), where the court recognized that there were often benefits accruing to the seller in accepting such a restriction, if, by doing so, the value of the business it is selling increases: a business is worth less if purchasers know that they are shortly going to be facing competition from the very person selling them that business. Both of these situations have important consequences for competition. For example, if a pop star covenants with his recording label not to record for another label for a certain period after the termination of his contract, that may reduce the ability of labels to compete with each other. If a business owner covenants not to set up in competition to the purchaser of his business, that may reduce the consumer choice in that area.

The position remains that there are three requirements for the operation of the doctrine:

(a) the restraint must protect a legitimate interest of the party in whose favour it operates;

(b) the restraint must be no wider than is necessary to protect this interest; and

(c) the restraint must be reasonable in relation to the public interest.

These last two requirements appear to be often conflated into an overall balancing act undertaken by the courts. Whether a restraint is reasonable or not is to be considered in the light of the circumstances at the time when the restraint was imposed (see, e.g., *Watson* v *Prager* [1991] 3 All ER 487).

It is for the party claiming the benefit of the restraint to show that it is reasonable and that there is a legitimate interest to protect. This was made clear in *H. Morris Ltd* v *Saxelby* [1916] 1 AC 688, HL, where Lord Atkinson held (at 700) that

the onus of establishing to the satisfaction of the judge who tries the case facts and circumstances which show that the restraint is of the reasonable character [between the parties] [rests] upon the person alleging that it is of that character, and the onus of showing that, notwithstanding that it is of that character, it is nevertheless injurious to the public and therefore void, [rests], in like manner, on the party alleging the latter.

This *dictum* has been used in support of the contention that the test of whether a restraint is reasonable between the parties is a private matter between them, and that only if the restriction is found to be reasonable should the public interest then be considered. However, such a clear division between the two factors is difficult to sustain. The point was made by Lord Pearce in *Esso Petroleum Co. Ltd* v *Harper's Garage (Stourport) Ltd* ([1968] AC 269 at 324:

There is not, as some cases seem to suggest, a separation between what is reasonable on grounds of public policy and what is reasonable as between the parties. There is one broad question: is it in the interests of the community that this restraint should, as between the parties, be held to be reasonable and enforceable?

In the same case Lord Hodson gave further credence to the notion that the two factors tend to become conflated, when he noted (at 319) that 'the interests of the individual are much discussed in the cases on restraint of trade which seldom, if ever, have been expressly decided on public grounds'.

If the case does revolve around the public interest consideration, it is for the party claiming that the restriction is unreasonable to demonstrate that it is against the public interest (*Morris* v *Saxelby*, above). However, although this places a significant burden on the party challenging the restraint, the court is entitled to consider all surrounding aspects, and will be expected to achieve a balance between the private and public interest. There may be situations in which the defendant is expected to explain why a particular restraint is justifiable when, on the face of it, the restraint appears to be contrary to the public or private interest.

The consideration of public interest has caused some problems for the judiciary. The application of the doctrine to the economically important area of exclusive distribution contracts (or 'solus agreements' as they are sometimes referred to in the English cases) shows both the problems with applying a public interest test, and the application of the doctrine to areas central to competition law.

Esso Petroleum (above) was the first important case to consider this issue, and the case remains of fundamental importance to this area. This concerned a vertical distribution agreement under which the respondents agreed to buy petrol only from the appellant. The respondents owned two garages. In relation to the first the exclusive agreement was to last four years and five months, in return for which commitment the respondents were to be entitled to a discount on the petrol they obtained from the wholesaler. In relation to the second garage the respondents had accepted a £7,000 loan from the appellant, which was to be repaid as a mortgage over 21 years. The obligation to obtain petrol exclusively from the appellant was to continue for as long as the loan continued to be owed. Having decided that such a tie could fall to be considered within the restraint of trade doctrine, the court proceeded to consider whether either tie was in unreasonable restraint of trade. The first tie was considered to be in the interests of both the parties and was not found to be against the public interest. The longer tie was considered to be excessive in relation to the interest being protected, and was thus rendered unenforceable. The factors that were considered to be legitimate interests of the parties included the maintenance of the distribution system and the benefit of a stable flow of petrol to the market.

Their Lordships gave different reasons for the application of the doctrine to this situation, but the majority agreed on the formulation of what has been labelled the 'opening the door' test. Lord Reid set this out (at 298):

Restraint of trade appears to me to imply that a man contracts to give up some freedom which otherwise he would have had. A person buying or leasing land had no previous right to be there at all, let alone to trade there, and when he takes possession of that land subject to a negative restrictive covenant he gives up no right or freedom which he previously had.

Rightly, this formulation has come in for some criticism, notably, but not exclusively, by Valentine Korah ('Solus Agreements and Restraint of Trade', (1969) 32 *MLR* 323). While the approach has formal attractions, carrying as it does a degree of certainty, it takes little account of the realities of situations. The application of the test presumes that the surrendering of an existing freedom is somehow worse than entering a market for a first time carrying a restriction on freedom. In practice there may be little distinction between the two, particularly if it becomes apparent that the restricted entrant could have found much better terms and conditions elsewhere which would equally have facilitated entrance. Although the House devoted a lot of discussion to the concept of the public interest in the case, there is no point at which the public interest in the particular facts of the case itself are adequately resolved or discussed. It was also not made clear to what types of vertical restraints the doctrine would be applied. It was suggested, for example, that the traditional ties between landlords and breweries would not fall within the application of the doctrine as these were so much a part of accepted commercial practice (see too the comments of Lord Denning in *Petrofina (Great Britain) Ltd* v *Martin* [1966] Ch 146). If this is indeed the case, then it may be that over time the acceptance of solus ties will see a reduction in the scope of the application of the doctrine to these.

An example following *Esso* is *Texaco Ltd* v *Mulberry Filling Station Ltd* [1972] 1 All ER 513. The defendant, owner of a petrol filling station, had borrowed £36,000 from the plaintiff's agent, and accepted an obligation to buy petrol only from that supplier for a period of four years and seven months. The defendant subsequently broke this tie, and when he was sued under the contract sought to avoid the obligations on the basis of the restraint of trade doctrine. Ungoed-Thomas J accepted Lord Macnaghten's formulation of the doctrine from *Nordenfelt* (above), but was concerned that 'the doctrine has been much considered since, and has been the subject of observations which are by no means easy to reconcile' (at 521). In an effort to reconcile the authorities the judge took a very restricted view of the meaning of public interest, so as to exclude 'the interests of the public at large'. The judge's view (at 526) was that restraint of trade

is part of the doctrine of the common law and not of economics... if it refers to interests of the public at large, it might... involve balancing a mass of conflicting economic, social and other interests which a court of law might be ill-adapted to achieve; but, more important, interests of the public at large would lack sufficiently specific formulation to be capable of judicial as contrasted with unregulated personal decision and application—a decision varying, as Lord Eldon LC put it, like the length of the chancellor's foot.

Such a restrictive approach has not been taken since, but it is established law that the interests of the competitive economy are not part of the doctrine.

A final limitation of the doctrine arises from its place in contract law: the doctrine of privity means that only parties to the contract may invoke the doctrine, and third parties may not recover damages under it. There has, however, been a sprinkling of cases in which a more flexible approach has been taken, the most significant of which is *Eastham* v *Newcastle United Football Club Ltd* [1964] Ch 413. George Eastham was a distinguished inside forward for Newcastle United, but wished to transfer to another club. He was prevented from doing so by the rules of the Football Association (FA) and the League. These were binding on all the 92 league clubs. Under these rules a player could be retained by a club for the following season by the offer of a minimum wage acceptable to the League, which in this case was £418. Until the offer was accepted the player would not actually be under contract to the club and would not be playing. Only if players were able to persuade the FA that there were special grounds for allowing them to change their clubs could they move; and without such approval it would be virtually impossible to play professional football anywhere in the world, with the notable exception of Australia. That the agreement between the clubs and the FA operated in restraint of trade was evidently clear, and the justifications advanced for its continuance were rejected by the court. The fact that Eastham was not himself a party to the agreements was not held to be a bar to his action, given that his interests were so immediately affected by the agreement (see also *Greig* v *Insole* [1978] 1 WLR 302, relating to Test- and county-match bans on cricketers who had played for Kerry Packer, and *Watson* v *Prager* [1993] EMLR 275, relating to contracts between professional boxers and their managers). A similar approach was taken in *Pharmaceutical Society of Great Britain* v *Dickson* [1970] AC 403, where an individual chemist outlet was able to challenge a rule of the Pharmaceutical Society restricting the types of goods in which their members might deal; and in *Nagle* v *Fielden* [1966] 2 QB 633, the court held invalid a rule of the Jockey Club that prevented a woman from holding a trainer's licence. The issue of the 'right to work' considered in both this latter case and others raises further complexities that lie beyond the scope of this text.

The restraint of trade doctrine, for all its longevity, continues to play a vibrant part in domestic contract law, and to impact on competitive situations. For example, in *Hollis & Co.* v *Mark Richard Stocks* [2000] UKCLR 658, the appellant was a solicitor employed by the respondent. A restraint in his contract of employment restricting him from working within a 10-mile radius of the respondent's office from the termination of his employment was found to be a reasonable one when it was challenged as being in restraint of trade. In *Lapthorne* v *Eurofi Ltd* [2001] UKCLR 996, on the other hand, the respondent was successful in challenging a post-termination clause in his contract which restricted his future employment. The relevant clause was too widely drawn, and hence fell within the restraint of trade doctrine and was unenforceable. Restraint of trade was a central argument in the case of *WWF—World Wide Fund for Nature (formerly World Wildlife Fund) and World Wildlife Fund Inc.* v *World Wrestling Federation* ([2002] UKCLR 388) which related to the use of the initials 'WWF' by the defendant. In 1994 after a number of disputes the parties had entered into a contract under which the defendant would limit its use of the initials. In 1997 the Wrestling Federation set up a website making extensive use of the initials, and in 1998 it altered its logo so as to make it more obviously constitute the letters WWF. The fund objected, relying on the contract, and the defendant argued this was in restraint of trade. The court found that the federation 'gains no assistance... from the doctrine of restraint of trade' (para. 66), holding that where parties enter into a contract to avoid litigation and settle a dispute 'the presumption is that the restraints, having been agreed between the two parties most involved, represent a reasonable division of their interests' (para. 48).

23.2.3 The restraint of trade doctrine and EU law

In a recent case the restraint of trade doctrine was pleaded alongside the operation of art. 101 by a defendant seeking to avoid contractual obligations entered into in relation to a vertical distribution system for scooters for the mobility challenged manufactured by the defendant (*Days Medical Aids Ltd* v *Pihsiang Machinery Manufacturing Co Ltd* [2004] EWHC 44 (Comm), [2004] UKCLR 384). Following a disagreement with the distributor, a company based in Wales, the defendant, based in Taiwan, had repudiated the contract, and then faced an action for damages, which were eventually awarded in substantial amounts. At paras 265–6 of the judgment Langley MJ, referring to cases such as *WWF* (above) held that the restraint of trade doctrine did not 'predominantly pursue an objective different from articles [101] and [102]', and therefore held that he was precluded from applying the doctrine in situations in which art. 101 was applicable by virtue of the operation of Regulation 1/2003, art. 3, and the general principles governing the relationship between national and EU competition law. If this is held to be the case in future, and it is by no means certain that this judgment will be followed, this is a remarkable recognition of the extent to which the doctrine has moved from being a matter of individual liberty, and become one of economic regulation.

23.2.4 Conclusion

The fact that restraint of trade can be applied to vertical commercial arrangements, and to the rules of professional associations, as well as to the classic sale of business or employee/employer relationships means that it continues to be relevant to competition law. In some situations the doctrine has been able to fill in gaps left by the statutory regulation. It is also becoming increasingly important in relation to ties between recording artists and their record companies, and to those between sportsmen and sportswomen and their managers or teams (see, e.g., Greenfield, S., and Osborn, G., *Contract and Control in the Entertainment Industry*, Dartmouth, Ashgate (1998)). The doctrine may also be examined as part of the wider class of illegal or unenforceable contracts, and may in particular be relevant to situations in which there are inequalities of bargaining power. Those interested in these aspects of restraint of trade should refer to a more detailed contract law text.

23.3 **Economic torts**

As early as 1410 it was clear that the mere act of competition could not be classed as tortious, even though the competition might have harmful effects for some parties (*The Schoolmasters of Gloucester Case* (1410) YB 11 Hen IV, fo. 47, pl. 21). While the view persisted through the nineteenth century that it might be unlawful in some circumstances to deliberately act in such a way as to harm another's economic interests, judicial acceptance of this principle diminished, and the general position in English law was summed up by Bowen LJ in *Mogul Steamship* v *McGregor* (1889) 23 QBD 598, CA:

The substance of my view is this: that competition, however severe and egotistical, if unattended by circumstances of dishonesty, intimidation, molestation [or other illegalities] gives rise to no cause of action at common law. I myself should deem it to be a misfortune, if we were to attempt to prescribe to the business world how honest and peaceable trade was to be carried on in a case where no such illegal elements as I have mentioned exist, or were to adopt some standard of judicial 'reasonableness' or of 'normal' prices or 'fair freights' to which commercial adventurers, otherwise innocent, were bound to conform.

This view informs the various torts which relate to matters of competition. In each case, whether it be conspiracy, or inducement to break a contract, or interference with economic interests, the general rule is that an action which by itself is lawful does not become actionable if it results in adverse consequences for any particular trader. The courts are not well equipped to regulate competition, and in recognition of this fact will generally intervene only following an act that is itself recognized as unlawful. For a thorough discussion of the following torts, see Carty, H., *An Analysis of the Economic Torts*, Oxford, OUP (2001).

23.3.1 **Conspiracy**

If there is an exception to the general principle set out above, and it has been recognized that 'the tensions in this history have, however, left their mark...there remains a penumbra of doubt' (Brazier, M. (ed.), *Clerk & Lindsell on Torts*, London, Sweet & Maxwell (17th edn, 1995), para. 23–04), it lies in the tort of 'conspiracy to injure'. Conspiracy in relation to economic torts has two arms, and a tort may also lie in situations in which there is a conspiracy to use unlawful means, which is related to the crime of conspiracy, although the unlawful means need not be criminal ones. The tort of conspiracy to injure may exist in situations in which there is a combination to harm another for no legitimate reason (see *Crofter Hand Woven Harris Tweed* v *Veitch* [1942] AC 435, HL).

The general proposition may be expressed thus:

(1) A combination of two or more persons wilfully to injure a man in his trade is unlawful and, if it results in damage to him is actionable. (2) If the real purpose of the combination is not to injure another, but to forward or defend the trade of those who enter into it, then no wrong is committed and no action will lie, (although damage to another ensues).   (*Sorrell* v *Smith* [1925] AC 700, *per* Lord Cave CJ)

Mogul Steamship v *McGregor* (1889) 23 QBD 598, CA, [1892] AC 25, HL, is further authority for the proposition that it is quite legitimate, at common law, to conspire with others to improve a business position, even if harm to another is a direct consequence of this. In this case a group of shipowners formed an association to restrict access to routes, to raise prices, and thence to increase the profits made. When the plaintiff company attempted to enter the market by undercutting the group's prices, the group acted in concert and reduced prices so as to drive out the entrant. The action was brought on the basis of both restraint of trade and conspiracy. Even had it been established that there was a restraint of trade issue, privity of contract would have prevented the plaintiff from recovering under this head.

There have been cases where the plaintiff has been successful in an action for damages following conspiracy. One such is *Quinn* v *Leathem* [1901] AC 495, in which a butcher employing a non-unionized workforce lost custom when the union persuaded one of those being supplied meat by Leathem to cease to do business with him. Here there was no legitimate benefit to the union or to the customer in agreeing that the customer should cease to trade with Leathem, and the real object of the 'conspiracy' was to injure the plaintiff. In this, and other similar cases, it is necessary to establish, on the facts, that it is the intention to injure which is paramount. The House of Lords has labelled this tort 'anomalous' as A is able to recover following B's otherwise lawful act that is made tortious only because it is committed as part of an agreement with C. However, the tort is 'too well established to be discarded, however anomalous it may seem' (*Lonhro Ltd* v *Shell Petroleum Co. (No. 2)* [1982] AC 173, at 189).

Although these principles remain good law, they have largely fallen into disuse, and it is unlikely that competition practitioners will have much recourse to the conspiracy doctrine now that art. 101 TFEU and the Chapter I Prohibition of the Competition Act 1998 are better able to provide a remedy in similar situations.

Where a conspiracy employs unlawful means and causes injury to a party a claim may also be upheld. This principle may extend to situations where the act complained of is not a criminal one, and in one case conspiracy was raised successfully when it was argued that the arrangement would, under the terms of the Restrictive Trade Practices Act 1956, be against the public interest (*Daily Mirror Newspapers Ltd* v *Gardner* [1968] 2 QB 762). It appeared briefly to be the case that intention to injure was also to be a determining factor in cases based on conspiracy using unlawful means, at which point the distinction between the two heads of conspiracy would be eroded. This was suggested in *Lonhro Ltd* v *Shell Petroleum Co. (No. 2)* [1982] AC 173, HL. In *Lonhro plc* v *Fayed* [1992] 1 AC 448, HL, the House of Lords retreated from this position, holding that it was necessary only to show that there had been an intent to injure, and not that this was to be the purpose of the conspiracy.

23.3.2 Unlawful interference with economic interests

Unlawful interference with economic interests will arise in situations in which a defendant commits an actionable wrong with the intention of harming the plaintiff. The tort is an independent one that is not dependent on conspiracy (see above), or inducement to breach a contract (see below).

In *Lonhro plc* v *Fayed* [1990] 2 QB 479, the plaintiff alleged that it had been tortiously deprived of the chance to bid for the share capital in the House of Fraser, which among other things owned Harrods, by virtue of the defendants misrepresenting their financial status. The plaintiff relied, in part, on the speech of Lord Watson in *Allen* v *Flood* [1898] AC 1, in which may be found the basis of a tort of *unlawful* interference with economic interests. This tort may apply where A intends damage to B, and achieves this by wrongful behaviour towards C (in *Lonhro*, a deceit), so that C's behaviour will damage B. A may then be liable to B. The Court accepted that such a tort existed, but, Dillon LJ argued, 'the detailed limits of [the tort] have yet to be refined' (at 489). It may be the case that there is little to distinguish *Allen* v *Flood* from *Mogul Steamship*, with the difference being that *Allen* v *Flood* relates to the actions of a single person and *Mogul Steamship* to conspiracy. Dillon LJ suggested, however, that it need not necessarily be the case that it was the predominant purpose of the tortfeasor to injure the victim rather than to pursue their own benefit (at 488–9), and that an action might lie on the basis merely that there had been wrongful conduct with respect to a third party, such as wrongful interference with a third-party's contract, which caused harm to the plaintiff. The action complained of *must* be unlawful, and it was stressed in *Allen* v *Flood* that a lawfully exercised right cannot, in this context, become unlawful whatever the motive of the party.

23.3.3 Unlawful interference with contractual relations and inducing a breach of contract

It is a tort for C to induce B to breach a contract with A, to the detriment of A, without there being a reasonable justification. For example, in *Greig* v *Insole* [1978] 1 WLR 302 promoters of a cricket tournament brought an action against the English cricket authorities when the latter induced players contracted with the promoter to break those contracts. The application of this doctrine may be particularly pertinent to competitive situations, as it means that it may be tortious for one party to acquire another's customers by unlawfully inducing those customers to break contracts, or where existing contractual relationships are otherwise unlawfully interfered with (*D. C. Thomson and Co. Ltd* v *Deakin* [1952] Ch 646). It will not apply to situations in which A merely tries to persuade B's customers that A offers a better deal; B must show that A both knew of the existing contract and intended to interfere with it.

Although there have been some suggestions to the effect that a simple interference with a contract will lie within the tort (see, e.g., Lord Denning in *Torquay Hotel Co. Ltd* v *Cousins* [1969] 2 Ch 106), the better view remains that no action lies unless a full breach is induced.

23.3.4 **The tort of unfair competition**

The Paris Convention for the Protection of Industrial Property, art. 10*bis* requires that:

(1) The countries of the Union are bound to assure to nationals of such countries effective protection against unfair competition.

(2) Any act of competition contrary to honest practices in industrial or commercial matters constitutes an act of unfair competition.

The United Kingdom has not introduced specific instruments to ensure compliance with this principle, which relates primarily to intellectual property, and it is generally accepted that the obligations imposed by this article are met by the torts of passing off and injurious falsehood, and by the Trade Descriptions Act 1968. While these laws may indeed be invoked to protect economic interests 'it may be safely asserted that there is no tort of unfair competition in this country' (Adams, J., 'Is there a Tort of Unfair Competition?', [1985] *Journal of Business Law* 26, at p. 32). Because of its close relationship with intellectual property law, consideration of these issues belongs more properly to a text on intellectual property law. For a clear summary of the present position the reader is referred to Robertson, A., and Horton, A., 'Does the United Kingdom or the European Community Need an Unfair Competition Law?', [1995] *EIPR* 568.

23.3.5 **Statutory torts**

Because of the close relationship between the statutory torts based on breaches of arts 101 and 102, and those to be based on the Chapter I and II Prohibitions of the Competition Act 1998, and the public regulation of competition, the doctrine of statutory torts is dealt with in Chapter 7.

FURTHER READING

Books

CARTY, H., *An Analysis of Economic Torts* (2001) OUP, Oxford

HEYDON, D. J., *Restraint of Trade Doctrine* (1972) Butterworths, London

TREBILCOCK, M. J., *The Common Law Restraint of Trade: A Legal and Economic Analysis* (1987) The Carswell Company, London

Index